Also by Peter Ustinov

DEAR ME

DEAR ME

by Peter Ustinov

An Atlantic Monthly Press Book

LITTLE, BROWN AND COMPANY · BOSTON · TORONTO

LIBRARY OF CONGRESS CATALOGING IN PUBLICATION DATA

Ustinov, Peter.
  Dear me.

  Autobiographical.
  "An Atlantic Monthly Press book."
  Includes index.
    1. Ustinov, Peter—Biography.   2. Authors, English—
  20th century—Biography.   3. Actors—Great Britain—
  Biography.   I. Title.
  PR6041.S73Z514   791′.092′4 [B]   77-9021
  ISBN 0-316-89057-0

FIRST EDITION

T 9/77

An excerpt from this book appeared
in *The Atlantic*.

ATLANTIC-LITTLE, BROWN BOOKS
ARE PUBLISHED BY
LITTLE, BROWN AND COMPANY
IN ASSOCIATION WITH
THE ATLANTIC MONTHLY PRESS

*Published simultaneously in Canada
by Little, Brown & Company (Canada) Limited*

PRINTED IN THE UNITED STATES OF AMERICA

DEDICATION

To all those who,
by accident or design,
have not been included
in this book

DEAR ME

1

D<small>EAR ME,</small>

I have always thought that most of the anomalies which afflict mankind are merely fragments of nature blown up out of recognizable proportion. In other words, split personality — schizophrenia — is an exaggeration of a natural state at a point where the whole of a person's character is colored by its overweening contradictions. And yet, the personality of any normally constituted person must be capable of at least a certain flexibility, otherwise the machinery for doubt would be absent, and what is a more irrefutable proof of madness than an inability to have a doubt?

No, no, to ensure sanity, there must be at least the elements of an internal disagreement ever present in a personality, and it is for that reason, in the dearest hope that you exist, that I address this attempt at an autobiography to you, Dear Me.

We were born in the normal manner in a London nursing home, and here I must already give up the collective pronoun in case it be mistaken for *folie de grandeur* on my part, speaking for both of us. Grandeur there always has been, in a purely physical sense, although I hope not *folie*. I weighed nearly twelve pounds as a consequence of a reluctant and tardy birth. I have always been loath to acknowledge the applause of an audience unless its volume more than justified such an initiative and I must have started the habit very early on, at my first public appearance in fact.

Of the actual events surrounding my birth I remember very little, and must therefore base my report on data from other sources. What I do know for certain is that whereas I was born in London (in a section ominously called Swiss Cottage), I was in fact conceived in Petrograd, in a tall, draughty and shell-pocked house to which I made a pilgrimage of thanksgiving relatively late in life. It stands to reason that I traveled a great deal during the more than nine months that separated my conception in the shadow of revolution and political slogan and my birth in the cold embrace of industrial smog and respectability; but once again, my memory of the great social upheavals through which I passed disguised as a piece of overweight luggage can only be described as hazy, and therefore unreliable.

My mother, whose recollection of these events was curiously enough more acute than mine, in spite of her advanced age, wrote a book called *Klop* about her married life — a book I found charming and fascinating when it dealt with the period before my birth and intensely embarrassing thereafter, which, I suppose, is human. "Klop," as I discovered later, was the name by which my father was known, a name denoting "bedbug," somewhat unflattering perhaps, but preferred by him to his only Christian name of Jona. There is no accounting for taste, as those who believe they are blessed with it never cease to say.

At the time of my birth, Klop was the London representative of the German news agency, at that time called the Wolff-Büro. He was selected for this job not only because of his natural talent, which was considerable, but because Ustinov is a name that sounded — and was — non-German. Only a little while before many minds had been eased in their wartime tasks by the pleasant prospect of hanging the Kaiser, and it stood to reason that after four years of exhaustion, deprivation, and tragedy, the Germans had exacerbated British phlegm. This the Germans themselves shrewdly guessed, and so my father with his Russian surname, his Russian wife, and his urbane manner was sent in as a pioneer to pave the way for a later normalization of relations.

It was, I gather, no easy task, although I must say that in the nursing home any hint of prejudice was in my favor. Once I had actually been cajoled to enter this world, I apparently behaved as though I had never hesitated, and held up my head to look around, even when suspended by my feet like a bat. In case of general incredulity, I must say that I have always benefited from an unusually powerful neck, a fact which an Italian singing professor discovered to his cost many years later when he tried to strangle me. I recovered almost immediately, whereas he has been prone to depressions ever since, which is understandable since he is only five feet seven inches high. He was foolhardy to give in to temptation.

My initiative in the nursing home provoked cries of admiration from the matron, who said to my mother, "He's a very strong little chap, aren't you, precious? Yes, you are, my Little Blessing."

It was as well to know. My mother's reaction to me was of a less factual nature. In spite of my exploit she found me helpless and vulnerable, which is of course the prerogative of all mothers, and at the same time curiously wise and reminiscent of certain rotund statuettes of Buddha. However, she told me at a time when her opinion was less prone to the exigencies of literary style, in reality I was spherical in form, and everyone heaved a sigh of relief whenever I performed the exploit with my neck, since at those moments it was possible to see whether I was the right way up or not.

I gather that I was not very talkative, which is rather understandable under the circumstances; that I very rarely cried; and that I smiled almost constantly, from which I deduce that my indigestion was usually bad enough to produce the kind of writhing grin which mothers confuse with contentment, but that it rarely became unbearable enough to reduce me to tears.

So much for me and my limited means of expression at the time.

It might be well to pause at this early juncture and try to make some order out of the arbitrary events that led me to my appointment with the gynecologist in Swiss Cottage at eleven o'clock on April 16, 1921. I was, of course, accompanied by my mother, since I was too young to go alone.

I remember, with pleasure and a shudder, a reflection of that great advocate Clarence Darrow in his memoirs. He always regarded the chapter of accidents that led back from his birth into pre-history as utterly extraordinary, and therefore had the same feelings about his presence in the world as about winning a lottery against staggering odds; moreover, he added, not without an element of self-pity, if any one of thousands of people had been late for an appointment with destiny, he would not have been born at all. I have at least as much cause as Clarence Darrow to entertain such a thought, without having had the originality to conceive of such a terrifying speculation.

Consider the facts. One great-great-grandfather born in 1730, living the life of a pious county squire in Saratov on the lower reaches of the Volga; another great-great-grandfather born in 1775 in Venice, winning the competition for the post of organist at St. Mark's; a third great-great-grandfather a village schoolmaster a hundred kilometers southeast of Paris; a fourth no doubt a strict Protestant living in Rheinfelden, near Basel, while a fifth survived the endless struggle for power in Addis Ababa. One does not need to know the activities of the other eleven great-great-grandparents to understand that likelihood of all these people joining forces to produce me was extremely slim. By the time the situation had whittled itself down to the level of grandfathers, the odds against my birth had hardly improved. Admittedly my paternal grandfather had been exiled to the West, but meanwhile my mother's family had immigrated to the East, a lack of coordination remarkable to the point of perversity. My father's father had acquired German nationality; and after a period of living in Italy — a singular choice for a Protestant convert — he settled in Jaffa of all places, and married, *en seconde noce,* the daughter of a Swiss missionary and an Ethiopian lady.

They had nothing but miscarriages for seven years, my father, their firstborn, making his appearance when his father was fifty-seven years of age. Imbued with none of my reticence, Klop displayed an extraordinary eagerness to be born and rushed into life, allowing his mother a pregnancy of something under seven months and weighing only just over two pounds. He was kept alive by the extraordinary patience and application of my grandfather, who fed him his milk, drop by drop, from the container of a Waterman fountain pen. This is no place for commercials, but I do wish to take this opportunity to thank publicly a company to whom I feel I owe so much.

My mother, on the other hand, was the youngest of the large family of Louis Benois, architect, in St. Petersburg. She skated on the frozen Neva while my father galloped his Arab steed alongside trains in Palestine, frightening the passengers by racing them to the level crossings. It needed the precipitate action of a Serbian student in Sarajevo, the saber-rattling of the Austro-Hungarian war party, the limitless ambitions of the Kaiser, the French desire for revenge, the immense speed of the Russian mobilization, the war at sea, in the air, on land, gas, revolution, humiliation, and conquest to bring them together. I can never hope to repay the huge war debt which I personally owe to millions of people, whose concerted egotism, self-sacrifice, stupidity, wisdom, bravery, cowardice, honor, and dishonor made it possible for my parents to meet under the least likely of circumstances and with the most farfetched of pretexts. There is no alternative but humility for me.

It is not without reason that Russia and the United States have drifted into a sort of collusion after their years of bitter opposition to one another, for the fact of the matter is that they have a great deal in common, and not the least of these shared characteristics is size. Britain, France, and others have hacked empires out of the available corners of the earth, and the sun set over seascapes while rising over other seascapes, but neither Britain nor France has ever had to come to terms with the endless horizon, mile after mile in all directions, leading to an infinity of miles, and then a few more for good measure. In America the wild men, the lawless, those with a golden glimmer in the drink-sodden eye, opened up the West just as before them the shaggy cowboys called Cossacks, fugitives from justice all, opened up the East in Siberia, hotly pursued by the soldiers of the central government. There it was not yet the Gold Rush, merely the Fur Rush. As long ago as 1689 the Cossacks reached the Pacific, founding the town of Okhotsk, and were rewarded with freedom from pursuit for their pains. At first tentatively, the Russian antennae (so far from their head in St. Petersburg) felt their cautious way over to the American mainland, and Alaska became the eastern outpost of the Russian Empire, enabling her merchants to trade with China, exchanging pelts, European glass, and strangest of all exports, dogs, for silks and tea.

Whereas the younger sons of socially accepted families in the West went to the colonies to make good — to India or Canada in the case of England, to Africa or Indochina in the case of France, to Sumatra, or Angola, or the Congo for the others, or wherever Europe had cast an avid eye and a possessive net — it was quite in order for young Russians to scour Siberia in search of possibilities. This huge land was not merely a system of penal colonies as it appears in the Western imagination, but a place of untold wealth, a place where fortunes could be made. The rigors of its climate have given it the kind of reputation which even as rapidly evolving a country as Australia has only recently shaken off. In a sense, Siberia was Russia's Australia, at once a punishment and a new life, an arena for worldly redemption.

As long ago as the last year or two of the seventeenth century, Adrian Mikhailovitch Ustinov returned from his stint in Siberia a wealthy man. He had made his money in salt.

Russia had acquired all the trappings of conventional European heraldry late in her history, and consequently took them with the seriousness accorded by American tourists to researches into the origin of coronet and kilt. Already, in order to guarantee the Pharisaic isolation of the nobility from the low practices of the merchants, an Imperial decree had compelled those of high birth to relinquish their titles should they stoop to commercial activity. Later this somewhat draconian measure was amended, but made even more humiliating for those who take such symbols seriously, by the order that the nature of a family's business be placed on the crest for all to see. As always, such decrees change their character with the passage of the years. What constituted a humiliation then is by now a proof of relative antiquity, to be displayed with pride. In the case of the Ustinovs, it is a primitive salt press which occupies its quartering alongside an eagle's wing, a star, and a bee buzzing away over two crossed blades of wheat.

Adrian Mikhailovitch's son, Mikhail Adrianovitch, was the great-great-grandfather born in 1730, and he benefited from a law decreeing that two and a half hectares of land (just over six acres) at any one time could be purchased at a price reduced in proportion to every lamb raised on it. He settled in Saratov, where he must have raised an inordinate number of lambs, because at his death in 1838, at the age of 108, he left his children two hundred and forty thousand hectares of land, spread over various districts, and six thousand serfs to work it, as well as sixteen brand-new churches for prayer and contemplation. The biography of the Chevalier Guards Regiment states specifically that estimations of the old man's age at death range between 108 and 113, and that 108 must be taken as a conservative estimate. So here again we have, if not a cattle baron, at least a baron of lamb in the fine young tradition of the Wild West. Even the name of his country mansion, Almazovo, is redolent of the New World rather than the Old, *almiaz* meaning diamond, the name of a ranch rather than that of a country seat.

The portrait of this exceptional man suggests that he was stout, his bald head the shape of a rugby football, set on his body so that the ears would be near the pointed ends, and garnished with wisps of white hair. His mouth was small and puckered in mischief, while his eyes display a healthy playfulness. That he was overweight is certain, but evidently he owed his unusual longevity to the fact that in those days there were no doctors competent to warn him of the dangers of obesity. He married twice, at first to Varvara Guerassimovna Ossorgina, who died when he was 78, and then to a Marfa Andreievna Vechniakova for the remaining thirty years of his life. Among the other acquisitions of his fruitful life were five sons, who settled in their various country houses with the exception of the third one, Mikhail Mikhailovitch, who became Russian ambassador to Constantinople, and who was to be of enormous help to my grandfather later on. The youngest of the five boys, Grigori Mikhailovitch, was evidently a poor specimen of mankind, living only fifty-four years of rare dissipation and libertinage.

Owning two lavish town houses in St. Petersburg as well as inheriting Almazovo, Grigori Mikhailovitch married a woman of exceptional beauty, Maria Ivanovna Panshina, who brought the village of Troitskoïe, near Moscow, as part of her dowry. By all accounts he behaved disgracefully, setting her up in one of the town houses while he caroused in the other with teenage peasant girls from his estate, only emerging occasionally from his bedroom to pick at a table covered with *zakouski*, pickled herrings, salted cucumbers, and the like, in order to renew his failing powers for further onslaughts on his victims, whom he preferred to enjoy two or three at a time. It was small wonder that his three sons grew up with a deep feeling of revulsion for their father, and in the case of my grandfather it inspired an introspection about the state of Russia and the corruptibility of the Orthodox Church.

As a young subaltern in the Chevalier Guards Regiment, my grandfather fell off his horse during maneuvers, damaging his back. Because of this accident, he was bedridden for more than a year, which caused him to read a great deal and to think even more. Over the Volga was a settlement of German Protestants, and before long my grandfather made the acquaintance of a pastor eager to add to his score of conversions, and of his pretty daughter. As all too often in this life, the affairs of the heart and the affairs of the mind were soon hopelessly entangled, and he embraced both the Lutheran faith and Fräulein Metzler.

At this time, the Imperial Army compelled all officers to take an oath of allegiance once a year to both the Czar and the true faith, which meant, of course, the Russian Orthodox Church. You could evidently be a Protestant if you were a Balt, or be a Catholic if you were Polish, or be a Moslem if you came from Azerbaidzhan, but you couldn't become anything as exotic if you had the misfortune to be Russian. That year, in the so-called House of the Nobility at Saratov, my grandfather took his yearly oath to the Little Father of all the Russias, but refused to take it to the God of the Eastern rite. A scandal ensued, which resulted in my grandfather's exile to Siberia. His uncle, the aforementioned ambassador, heard about this family disgrace and, galloping north from the Golden Horn, engaged the Czar in a game of cards interspersed with bouts of drinking, the outcome of which was a commutation of the sentence to an exile of forty years abroad, a penalty which bears a strange similarity to a more recent example of Enforced Estrangement under the Communists, that between Solzhenitsyn and the source of his inspiration.

This exile was a severe punishment; and yet, from the point of view of my grandfather's personal safety it was probably just as well, for he was defiant enough and courageous enough to have decided to liberate his serfs, and this only eight months before their ultimate liberation by decree. And here once again we encounter a similarity between the histories of Russia and America. The liberation of the serfs was almost coeval with the American Civil War and the freeing of the slaves. Emancipation of a sort was in the air.

My grandfather was allowed to sell his vast estates for a handsome sum, and left for the West a rich man, a condition which suited his life-style but ran counter to his convictions. The logical place for a Russian exile to head in those days was the kingdom of Württemberg. Bismarck had not yet decreed the Union of Germany — that was to come ten years later in the Palace of Versailles — and Stuttgart was the pleasant capital of a small and civilized monarchy. More important still, its queen, a daughter of the Czar, was contaminated by liberal practice, and she extended a hand both welcoming and generous to any victim of her father's severity. My grandfather's titles of nobility were restored — titles seem to have had considerable value in those days — and so, in his Germanized form, he became the Baron Plato von Ustinow. His repayment of all this hospitality was hardly exemplary, however, since he decided to settle down in Italy, and built himself a villa at Nervi, near Genoa.

Altogether, he must have been an extremely difficult man to live with, especially for the pretty Fräulein Metzler, who had meanwhile become his wife. According to legend, or perhaps his own account, which is worse, he discovered on their wedding night that she was no longer a virgin, and consequently declined to have anything more to do with her. It is hard to conceive of a more monstrous excuse for a withdrawal of marriage vows, and yet to the austere Protestant convert of a century ago it seemed reason enough. He had other peculiarities besides his irrevocable decision about his wife. Money was a thing almost unbearably vulgar to him, a carrier of disease. As a result of his abhorrence, he never invested any of it in a bank, but carried his fortune around with him in satchels, trunks, and suitcases, spilling coins into a sink in order to wash them in carbolic before going shopping and, as an added precaution, never handling the degrading stuff without gloves. Christ's scourging of the moneylenders in the temple probably supplied the mental block for this extraordinarily convenient view of money as a source of physical and moral contagion, without any reference whatever to its undoubted value as a means for survival.

Whatever the quirks of his character, it was hardly they which rapidly drove his wife to other sources of comfort, a fact that he seemed to ignore, as well he might, for he regarded divorce as even more unthinkable than adultery. His wife did not share his prejudices and eventually ran away with a sea captain, which was about the best solution for all concerned. After the Second World War, I received a charming letter from an Australian aviator who turned out to be her grandson, whose existence supplied the proof that her escapade was not merely another deception and also gave a pretty clear indication of the direction in which her ship had sailed. Before this happy ending she had apparently attempted to dispose of my grandfather, aided by a gardener with whom she was carrying on, *à la* Chatterley. The conspirators knew my grandfather to be a man of powerful temper, and so plugged the muzzle of his pistol with lead, and then attempted to incite him to use it on them, the idea being that he would blow himself up in the process. Unfortunately for them, my grandfather was meticulous as well as emotional and noticed that someone had been tampering with his firearm. I believe he dismissed the gardener.

Divorce turned Platon Grigorievitch's thoughts to introspection, and eventually he gave up Italy for the Holy Land, building a large house in Jaffa which became the Park Hotel, and is, at the time of writing, the residence of an English vicar and his small family. It was here that my father, his three brothers, and his sister were born, to a mother whose origins have remained stubbornly mysterious to this day.

As I have said before, her father was a Swiss pastor from Rheinfelden near Basel, who was also (and here the evidence is an ancient photograph) a missionary in Ethiopia. Being Swiss, he was apparently something of an engineer, and among his other religious duties, he built a cannon for the mad Emperor Theodore, who had him chained to his own invention so that he couldn't get away and build a cannon for anyone else; this strategy confirms the Emperor's lunacy to many, whereas to me it seems primitive perhaps, yet certainly effective. The result was that my grandmother, whose Christian name was Magdalena, was born in a tent during the battle of Magdala, which opposed Ethiopian forces to British ones under Lord Napier, while the expectant father was being shaken to pieces by his own invention on another part of the battlefield.

There was also some connection with Portugal through my grandmother's mother, who had lived for a time in Goa. My grandmother's youngest sister was still, until recently, a lady-in-waiting at the court of Haile Selassie, when she was granted quarters in the governor's palace in Asmara, where the altitude was less detrimental to her aged heart. This suggests that, whatever their origins, they were personae gratae with the Lion of Judah.

I remember my grandmother quite well as one of the simplest and most sentimental of souls, and with the readiest of tears. The story of the Crucifixion was enough to set her off, as though it were not so much a monumental tragedy as a personal misfortune. When it came to the two robbers, the sobbing began. It was her habit to capture me and place me on her knee for the evening recital, pressing me to her ample bosom, and I still remember my striped flannel pajama tops dampened by tears which soon grew chill against the skin. At times I asked for some more conventional story at bedtime, but even if it began with wolves and piglets and fairies, gingerbread street quickly changed to Calvary, and I was left with the mystery of the Passion to fret over in my sleep.

No doubt my father was subject to the same treatment, perhaps to an even more passionate degree, for his mother was younger then, with a more objective and even colder tear, which may explain the fact that he was the most irreligious man I ever knew — not in the sense of blasphemy or of agnosticism; he merely completely ignored the whole business and never seemed to feel the need to accept it or reject it, or even fear it as a superstition. It didn't exist.

By his own admission, he was extremely spoiled, which is the normal outcome for a heavenly gift after seven years of fruitless attempts to have issue. There were to be four subsequent children, but all the fervor of thanksgiving was invested in my father. He could do no wrong. And yet all was not perfect. My grandfather was frequently a source of embarrassment to those close to him. He was antisocial to the extent of retiring to his room if his guests bored him; and yet he frequently appeared on the beach naked, since it never occurred to him that there was a difference between being dressed and undressed, an ideal absence of complex perhaps, and yet hardly considerate toward those less endowed with indifference. He also found it impossible to understand why eating in public should have social connotations, and thought that if people defecated together instead, the hated social contacts might be that much briefer. In other words, he was what is known as an eccentric, and eccentrics have the gift of making their children ill at ease.

The world was changing rapidly around the quiet, inefficient, and on the whole curiously benevolent Turkish Palestine, which knew an unparalleled epoch of religious tolerance at the time. The kingdom of Württemberg existed only as a junior partner in the German Federation. The Kaiser visited Jerusalem, and his statue, in the absurd guise of a Siegfried, still stands within the enclave of the Lutheran Hospital, staring disease unflinchingly in the eye. Without really realizing it, my grandfather was now German, and 1914 was rapidly approaching.

At the outbreak of hostilities, my father and his brother Peter found themselves in Düsseldorf and entered the German Army as a matter of course. In a regiment of Grenadiers, my father's company commander was the future General Speidel, of Wehrmacht and ultimately NATO fame, and his orderly was Erwin Piscator, the celebrated theater director of the pre-Hitler Communist avant-garde. As the war dragged on, both brothers transferred to the Air Force, and Peter, after whom I am named, was shot down and killed on Friday the 13th, in July 1917, near Ypres. He had white streamers on his wing tips, and was delivering mail from British prisoners of war over the Allied lines. Blinded by the sun, the British antiaircraft batteries failed to see the streamers and shot the aircraft down over no-man's-land. They apologized for their mistake.

Meanwhile, in Jerusalem, Platon Grigorievitch, now eighty years old, his exile up nearly fifteen years previously, suddenly remembered that, Martin Luther or no Martin Luther, he was a reserve officer of the Chevalier Guards Regiment. He had spent his fortune, and there was precious little left, so the prospect of negotiating the eye of the needle was no longer as formidable as it had seemed when he was younger. But now his country was in danger and there had to be a riderless horse just waiting to convey his valor to within striking distance of the enemy. He presented himself to the Russian Consul-General in Jerusalem, standing rigidly to attention so that his five foot four would look its impressive best in the white alpaca he always wore, even during winter visits to the north, and placed his sword at the disposal of the authorities. He was told very gently that his services were not urgently required, an allegation he refused to accept. Selling his properties (the one in Jerusalem to Haile Selassie), he packed his belongings, including his enviable collection of Greek, Roman, and Egyptian antiquities and the last remaining suitcases full of money, and set off with his family on the long sea road to Russia. He paused in London long enough to put his two younger sons into a school at Denmark Hill, where they suffered like martyrs under the stinging tongue of a sadistic headmaster, who goaded them about the German prefix "von" and never ceased mentioning their nationality in class, blaming them for every local success of Hindenburg and Ludendorff, and rejoicing with indecent glee at every counterblow of Foch or Haig.

The penultimate step on my grandfather's odyssey was Oslo, where he sold his collection for a derisory price to a Norwegian shipping magnate, and then sailed on, with his wife and his daughter Tabitha, to be swallowed by darkness and confusion.

The war ended with revolution, not only in Russia, as everyone knows, but also in Germany, which most people have forgotten. My father's epaulets were ripped off his shoulders in a Hamburg tram. People took their pleasures where and how they could. He realized it was time to return to civilian life, and he managed to become the representative of the German press agency in Amsterdam. From here he took some leave almost before he had begun his work and set off in the direction of the Soviet Union in order to trace the whereabouts of his parents and his sister. Since it was difficult to travel to Russia at a time when so many people were bent on getting out of it, he managed to integrate himself into a large group of prisoners of war being repatriated. They knew about the Revolution, of course, and they also knew that it was they who were the starvelings so recently awakened from their slumbers, to which "The Internationale" alludes. Their enthusiasm overflowed into song and simple rapture as the day of their return to the paradise of the workers approached. Many of them had bicycles which they had acquired at the end of their captivity, and these undreamed-of vehicles became the status symbols of the new dawn, grasped possessively by those about to cross the threshold of Utopia. As soon as the ship steamed into Narva harbor, at the frontier between the Soviet Union and Estonia, the bicycles were confiscated for the urgent needs of the war against the Poles, and the returned prisoners, including my father, were locked into cattle trucks to be shunted to recruiting centers farther in the hinterland for induction into the Red Army.

As the train crept through the night with its embittered complement of silent men cringing amid the dung and straw, my father planned his escape. Stops were frequent, and at one of them, he forced open the door. The first traces of dawn were visible, flecks in the icy sky, and in the distance the unseen evidence of a city: a glint, a certain unmistakable heaviness about the horizon, the roar of silence, as in a seashell. He dropped off the train with his suitcase full of chocolate, rashers of bacon, lumps of sugar — the backlash of troubled times. An hour or two later, he was in the heart of Petrograd. He spoke very little Russian, which did not seem much of a hindrance when the Herculean nature of his labor was taken into consideration; he had quite simply to find an old man and his wife and daughter in a country which covers one-sixth of the earth's surface. He began by meeting my mother socially, and that seemed to be a step in the right direction. At least I think so.

2

How my mother kept her rendezvous with my father is a story no less dramatic or curious. Denis Benois, or Bénois, was a laborer in the village of St. Denis-les-Sejanne, which seems to have disappeared off the map. His wife came from the town of Coulommiers, a place of wonderful cheeses, southeast of Paris. He died in 1702, and his wife, a laundress by profession, moved to the village of St. Ouen-en-Brie, between Melun and Nangis. It is, today, a depressing village, or perhaps it just succeeds in concealing the richness of the surrounding soil in the same way a peasant will hide his fortune in a miserable mattress. Many of the windows of the church are broken, and it is one of eight tiny parishes which are the responsibility of a single ambulant priest. I never saw him, but I presumed that at least one of the many bicycle-tire tracks crisscrossing the muddy pathways must have been his. The clock on the town hall has been broken for more years than the villagers can remember, so it is only accurate for two minutes every twenty-four hours. At the time of my pilgrimage, the town hall was only open when other town halls are shut, and this for the reason that the mayor was the schoolmistress, who could only attend to civic business during the luncheon break, and who sat in her dark office, a pen in one hand and a sandwich in the other.

The scattered houses, with their peeling walls, stand shrouded in mists which settle for no apparent meteorological reason and remain, drifting aimlessly over the cowpats and the acrid puddles long after other parts of the plain are softly bathed in sunlight. If it is a morose place today, it cannot always have been so. At least, at the time the newly widowed laundress settled there, some of the houses must have been new. She was evidently a resourceful and wise woman, because her only son was not only literate but became the village schoolmaster, a vocation shared by his son later on. By the time the third generation had appeared, however, in the shape of a boisterous fellow called Jules-César, a certain restlessness had manifested itself, an eagerness to carry the advances of the family fortune a step further. He decided not to become a schoolmaster, and moved a little closer to *le beau monde* by becoming an apprentice pastrycook. He was evidently very successful at this, since before long he was the pastrycook to the duc de Montmorency. The relationship of master and servant must have been rather like that between Don Giovanni and Leporello, for when the Revolution struck France, they were compelled to immigrate to Holland, where the Duke was quickly out of funds. They stayed together as accomplices and eventually as friends, seeking to rectify the decline in their fortunes in St. Petersburg. It was here they eventually split up, the Duke going back to France now the excesses of revolution were over and Jules-César becoming *Chef de Cuisine* to the Dutch legation. Evidently by now his authority had extended from mere *entremets* to the whole gamut of culinary arts and crafts. So celebrated did he become that it was not long before he deserted the legation and was appointed *maître de bouche* to the Emperor Paul I.

In case it be thought that he was extremely fortunate to find such exalted employment so soon, it is only fair to point out that to be *maître de bouche* to Paul I was a little like being accredited foodtaster to Nero. Both emperors spent their lives hovering on the edge of lunacy, yet were sane enough to be in constant fear of assassination, a fate which attended them both. A magnificent statue of Paul stands in the courtyard of Peterhof palace, his minute nose perched like a comma on his face, rendering his expression both proud and petulant. It is one of those rare works of official art, like the royal portraits of Goya, which seem so packed with accurate subversion that one wonders how the victims ever accepted them, let alone allowed them to be accorded pride of place.

Paul liked to play with toy soldiers in bed. It must have come as a surprise to the Queen that among her wifely duties was to be a natural feature for the toy artillery to cross as they bombarded the enemy on the eiderdown, and it was a still uglier awakening for the real troops lined up for his inspection that he belabored them with a stick for the slightest real or imagined misdemeanor as though they had no greater sensitivity than their tin reproductions.

Any native Russian would probably rather have walked to Vladivostok on foot than accept the job of teasing the palate of such a degenerate monarch, and it took an able and resourceful immigrant with no prior knowledge of the problems to make a success of such employment. And make a success of it Jules-César did, to the extent of marrying the royal midwife, a woman of a surprisingly fragile beauty for such a massive job, if the miniatures of the period are to be believed. Fräulein Concordia Groppe and Jules-César not only survived, but virtually ran the imperial household between them, as well as finding time to produce seventeen children of their own. Jules-César gradually began to fancy the spelling Jules-Césard, perhaps because a French condiment in the spelling gave the diner confidence, but more probably because spelling was not his strong point. And, after all, he was in good company, since as great a writer as Shakespeare could never decide exactly how his own name should be spelled. The insistence on accurate spelling at modern schools is an effort to invest a living language with rigor mortis, and to prepare a rhapsodic means of self-expression for the glacial corridors of computerdom.

Be that as it may, Jules-Césard left a book of memoirs in which the orthography is as erratic as the thoughts are sunlit and serene.

This work is still in manuscript, in the safekeeping of another great-great-grandson, Professor Fyodor Franzovitch Benois, an expert on underwater soldering, whatever that may be. It describes with a wonderful ingenuousness what life must have been like at the time. I was only able to read the beginning, where he talks about his own life as though he were a casual bystander.

"Le 20 Janvier 1770 à neuf heures du matin ma bonne merre [sic] après avoir souffert quatre grandes joures [!] des douleurs extraordinaires quoque très ordinaries en pareille circonstance — fit un grand effort de courage, et, étant couchée sur le dos, s'apuyant des deux extremitté [!!] du corps qui sont la tête et les pieds essaya de relever le centre et, par cet heureux mouvement, me fit prendre la porte par où j'étais entré." ("On the 20th of January, 1770, at nine o'clock in the morning, my good mother, after having suffered four days of the most extraordinary pains, albeit quite ordinary under such circumstances — made a great and courageous effort. Lying on her back, and anchoring the two extremities of her body, by which I mean head and feet, raised what lay between, and by this happy initiative caused me to take the portal by which I entered the world.")

A few pages later, he describes how, at the age of four and a half, he was whipped by his father. They were receiving company, which included an extremely corpulent and self-important aunt who attempted sportingly to lower herself onto a three-legged stool, there being far more guests than chairs. Her initiative failed, and she rolled onto the floor, her legs in the air. Jules-Césard, or César, as he still was then, had learned none of the finesse which was to stand him in good stead later on. All he could think to do was to announce in a piercing voice to the crowded room that he was able to see his aunt's thing (*"je pouvais voir sa chose"*). An audible whipping was the only possible penance in those days, even for a four-year-old.

Still further into this strange little book, which would at times have brought a blush to the cheek of Restif de La Bretonne, he confesses his remorse at having raped a few girls. In fairness to him rape seems to have been a pastoral activity, a sudden impulse and a tumble in the high grass such as can be seen in the background of many Dutch, Flemish, and indeed French pictures, rather than the sordid premeditated action of today. Admittedly the results are identical, but there was certainly a degree of complicity in rural sports which is quite lacking in the urban variety, hovering as they do around parked cars and lonely bus stops. Nevertheless, whatever his motives and whatever degree of collaboration he inspired, his remorse was real enough to drive him into the confessional. He cut short his story halfway, however, when he noticed that the interest of the Father Confessor in certain details of the transaction was excessive, an impression which even the presence of a grille failed to conceal.

In an effort to purify himself without the help of the local church, he sought out his first love, hoping to turn the clock back and erase his feelings of moral confusion. The young lady in question had moved to Paris, and invited him to join her there. When he arrived, he discovered what she had neglected to tell him in her letter — that, in the interim, she had become a prostitute. She had no further interest in him apart from an evident affection, which took the form of inviting him to observe her activities with clients through a keyhole. He acceded, one gathers, out of pure politeness and watched six or seven performances of this kind, eventually declining to continue "for fear this might become a habit." He still had seventeen children to sire, and simply could not afford to be old before his time.

He also left a rather less controversial and generally more useful volume, all the recipes of his cuisine, which was destroyed in manuscript during the German bombardment of Leningrad. The damage which the Nazis caused to the art of living will never be finally assessed.

The one of his sons who is of most immediate concern to me was an architect, Nicholas, who married Camilla, the daughter of the Italian immigrant composer Catterino Cavos. This new addition to the family brought with it the theatrical strain that enriched with an Italianate sense of drama the already present character of mischief, humility, and meticulous application to the job at hand, be it procreation or pastry.

Catterino Cavos was the son of the Primo Ballerino Assuluto of the Fenice Theater and of the diva of the same celebrated opera house in Venice, a distinguished lady from Perugia, Camilla Baglioni. They possessed a smallish palazzo on the Grand Canal which is today a far from smallish hotel. At the age of eighteen, young Catterino (did his parents hope for a daughter?) won the post of organist to the Cathedral of St. Mark's in a competition. On learning that his leading competitor was a man in his sixties, in poor health and with a large family to support, he resigned in favor of the older man. Later on, after he had become Director of the Imperial Theater at St. Petersburg, he received the manuscript of Glinka's first opera, *Ivan Susanin*, sometimes also called *A Life for a Tsar*. Acknowledging that Glinka's opera was superior to his own on the same subject, he voluntarily removed his own from the repertoire on condition he be accorded the honor of conducting Glinka's premiere. Writing to a friend, he expressed the opinion that "it is the duty of the old to make way for the young." He was by all accounts one of nature's rare natural gentlemen, and one of the few artists on record who assess their own talents accurately, which is an advantage in some circumstances and a drawback in others. At all events, he was the last in a long line of foreign composers to hold the post of Director of the Imperial Theater, beginning with Manfredini in 1759 through Galuppi, Traetta, Paisiello, Sarti, the wonderful Cimarosa, and Martín y Soler, composer of one of the tunes played by the onstage orchestra in the last act of Mozart's *Don Giovanni*, to my great-great-grandfather, who took over in 1797.

In 1798, the same crazy Paul I suddenly banned Italian opera, with the result that Cavos began writing works on Russian subjects like Ilya the Hero, in 1807, and Ivan Susanin, a patriotic epos which must have fitted the emotional climate of 1815. When Glinka's work arrived on his desk in 1836, he explained his gesture further in a note to a friend, as perspicacious as it was disinterested, written carefully in Italian, about the Russian Glinka: "*E poi — la*

sua musica è effettivamente meglio della mia, e tanto piu che dimos-
tra un caractero veramente nazionale" ("And then — his music is in
fact better than mine, the more so since it displays a truly national
character").

And yet, his music cannot have been as undistinguished as he
sometimes made it out to be. In 1867, Borodin's only stage work
apart from the celebrated *Prince Igor* was performed. Entitled *Boga-
tyri,* it was a hodgepodge of melodies, according to Alfred Loewen-
berg's admirable *Annals of Opera,* some composed by Borodin himself, others borrowed from Meyerbeer, Rossini, Offenbach, Cavos,
Verdi, Serov, and so on. Pretty good company. The work was revived in 1936, and after a few performances was banned by the Soviet censor, which suggests that it must have had some merit.

On a visit to Leningrad I discovered Cavos' tomb in the Lavra, an
open-air cemetery which is the Russian equivalent of Poets' Corner.
No member of my family had ever realized it was there, demure
and undemonstrative among the tombstones of his peers, Tchaikovsky, Glinka, Borodin, Moussorgsky, to say nothing of the great
writers and artists. There are quite a few weeping angels about, and
weather-beaten busts, and other outbursts of petrified grief. In this
quiet and damp place, Cavos is remembered by a simple black marble stone, setting off the restrained flamboyance of golden letters.
Of all the epitaphs in this Slavonic Valhalla of the arts, that on
Cavos' tomb is the only one defiantly written in the Roman alpha-
bet; the language, Latin.

One of his sons, my great-grandmother's brother Albert, an architect, acquired fame at least as great as his father's by building the
Maryinsky Theater (now the Kirov) in Leningrad, as well as rebuild-
ing the Bolshoi in Moscow after it was entirely destroyed by fire in
the 1860s.

By now, practically every member of the Benois and Cavos families was expected to make a career in the arts. Both families supplied a constant stream of young people who only rarely wished to
enter other fields than those traditionally theirs.

My grandfather was an architect as his father and grandfather and great-uncle had been. I do not pretend he was a great architect, but he was a fine, ordered, patient, and tasteful man with at least a hankering for new materials and new techniques which would have enabled him to be more daring. Above all, as Principal of the Academy of Arts he was a much admired teacher, remembered with affection by the older generation of Russian architects to this day. When he died, in 1928, he was given a state funeral by the Soviet government, the Mozart Requiem was sung as he lay in state, and his students stood vigil in the Conference Hall of the Academy and carried his body to the place of burial, the Novodievichy Cemetery.

His brother Albert, a strikingly handsome man with a knack for seducing the ladies while playing the violin, one of the minor art forms which has entirely disappeared from the libertine's repertoire, was a leading member of the Russian watercolor school, with a special predilection for melancholy sunsets, of which he produced an inordinate quantity. As with so many casually talented people, he was accused of an overriding facility, but critics often fail to recognize that no amount of fretful application would have improved those particular sunsets. To heed criticism to the extent of refraining from painting sunsets when sunsets are your particular forte is to go the way of many facile people who scandalously betray their facility in order to work hard and masochistically at things they are no good at; while the critic who is not much good at anything himself breathes down their necks with the sterile satisfaction of a sadistic schoolmaster. Albert had too light a touch to fall into such a trap. Others might have done more convincingly with seascapes and mountain idylls, but in sunsets he led the field. His house was so well known as a salon that he often had to ask in undertones who his guests were, while his venerable housekeeper Masha kept her eye riveted on the silver. Even as an old man, when bothered by mosquitoes (who, as is well known, like sunsets as much as anyone) he had no compunction in asking passersby to fan him with fir branches while he captured the elusive moments in paint. Legend has it, however, that he preferred the mosquitoes to male passersby. He only asked for help from very young and pretty girls, of whom, according to my aged aunts, there were many before the Bolsheviks spoiled it all.

The youngest brother, Alexander, was the animator of the celebrated magazine *Mir Iskustva* (the Life of Art), designer for the Ballet Russe, art critic, historian, and onetime curator of the Hermitage. He was the most internationally known of the brothers, perhaps not entirely due to his intrinsic qualities, but also because he was by far the youngest, and therefore escaped from the fallout of mutual admiration which is an inevitable adjunct to large families all engaged in the same type of work. Also he left Russia as his fame was beginning to spread, and designed up to the moment of his death in 1960. I knew him well, and therefore only pass him by swiftly here in order to reintroduce him on a later page as the man I loved and respected.

There were two other brothers of this brood, who were not artists, and who paid the penalty. One of them, Mikhail, was a businessman who had something to do with the river steamers which plied up and down the Volga, and was described as a silent and gloomy man. I do not know to what extent his morose nature was inspired by the monotony of his employment, but the fact is that one of his daughters married an architect, and his two grandsons are both architects in Argentina. Perhaps he should have been one too.

Nicholas was a soldier, with a rough vocational manner and an unhappy marriage. He and his wife used to throw plates at each other in public places, with a shameful lack of accuracy for military people. He was the Commanding General of the Akhtirsky Hussar Regiment, and I learned all I really know about him from a taxi driver in Paris who turned out to have been his aide-de-camp in the First World War.

"Ah, I remember," said the old driver, "I remember a reception in the officers' mess. There was a minstrels' gallery, with a Cossack orchestra playing light music. After he had drunk copiously, General Benois mounted the stairs and attempted to conduct the orchestra. When he had had enough, he made signs to another subaltern and myself, which we failed to understand since they were not explicit, you see. Then he leaped into space. I thought Lieutenant Gromov was going to catch him, and apparently Gromov thought I was going to. In short, neither of us did."

"What happened?" I asked in trepidation.

The effort of memory had been too much for the driver. The taxi slowed to a crawl in deference to his exhaustion, and his lined face became expressionless as the immediacy of his recollection faded into oblivion. There was a long pause.

"He hurt himself, I believe," said the driver flatly. He seemed irritated, although whether it was with that young idiot Gromov I had no means of knowing.

When my father reached Petrograd in the spring of 1920, with his suitcase full of bacon and chocolate, most of these people were still alive, although hardly active. My mother, like her uncle Alexander, by far the youngest of a large family, was therefore addicted to rebellion. She was already a little more than an art student, and spent much of her time at Uncle Alexander's home, soaking up the lively debates animated by forward-looking young people like the composer Sergei Prokofiev, her cousin the composer Alexander Tcherepnin, and her uncle's son, Nicholas, until recently the head of the design department (*Capo dell'Allestimento*) of La Scala, Milan. Prokofiev used to try out some of his early works on my great-uncle's piano, which had survived the Revolution in a better state than many of its fellows. They were a boisterous and flirtatious lot, these young people, eager to react against the existing order, endlessly jocular in manner and explosive in matter, and yet curiously respectful towards the achievements of the past.

I have always been vaguely frightened of Russian academicians, because when Russians dedicate themselves to the path of artistic righteousness, there are no people more tenacious in the pursuit of the absolute than they. Compared to the Russians, the Germans are lighthearted children, romantic and capricious where the Russians are rigorous and single-minded to a point of absurdity. The composer Taneyev struggled endlessly with fugues for string quartet, of monumental boredom and the most laudable thoroughness. The baffled and bearded Rimsky-Korsakov, who was never short of a neo-oriental melody, devoted a part of his early life, when appointed director of naval music, to a painstaking and ultimately painful research into the possibilities of brass instrumemts, which neither enriched the repertoire nor gave its composer any satisfaction. Even Balakirev, the doyen of the so-called mighty handful of nationalistic composers, amateurs all, revolted against the existing order only to become intolerably overbearing and dogmatic in his demands upon his followers. His revolution against the academic quickly hardened into an academicism of his own, with new rules to replace the old, applied with identical vigor and inflexibility. It must therefore be a quirk of national character to subject oneself to impossible strictures until the spirit is almost broken. Then comes the time of liberating revolution, with its slogans of goodwill to all — a long weekend of intoxicating folly as a presage to the application of new strictures as impossible as those that have been replaced.

God was discredited with the same religious fervor with which he had been praised before. Out in the playground, there was a brief flowering of national genius in disorganized abandon. One thinks of Mayakovsky, Esenin, Alexander Blok, the Constructivists, Malevich, and of course, the young Prokofiev. Then the schoolbell rang, and the refreshed schoolchildren filed back into the classroom to find the icon replaced by a red star, the benign picture of the Little Father, Nicholas II, by the portrait of V. I. Lenin, and the lessons started afresh with the same hermetic sealing against the intrusion of doubt. Everything had changed but the manner, yet the manner was all important. Even the spirit of the confessional, of *mea culpa, mea maxima culpa* was deflected from the ornate robe of the priest to the frostbitten ear of the commissar, but the spirit reigned on unchanged. We heard it with painful regularity as the brilliant composers and the magnificent writers confessed their errors of judgment to lamentable hicks like Andrei Zhdanov, and the inquisition of the people, with its condemnation of bourgeois values, continued round the clock among the potted palms and table-runners of the most bourgeois of proletarian societies, stinking of pious hypocrisy and self-righteous indignation, of ignorance and vodka.

Nineteen twenty was still a year of grace. The excesses which accompany all revolutions were over — the vengeful arrests and the denunciations — and the rot had not yet set in under Stalin, who was well fitted for his role of dictator, having been brought up in a seminary. My father met a girl in the course of his quest for his parents, who invited him to a party that evening, where he set eyes on my mother for the first time.

It was an eventful two weeks for both of them, at the end of which they were married, but that was not all which occupied their minds. My father discovered somehow that my resolute old grandfather, disdaining many admonitions to enjoy what retirement he had left, had charged off in the general direction of the fighting to offer his services to his old regiment. It was at Pskov that he had been overtaken by the Revolution, and succumbed to famine. His half-Ethiopian wife and her daughter, my aunt Tabitha, languished in a local prison, presumably because they were unable to make themselves understood. Had they spoken Russian, they would doubtless have been either freed or shot. The problem was to secure their release, but in the country which, in more affluent times, had invented the internal passport, and which had managed miraculously to combine extreme red tape with a chronic shortage of paper, this was understandably difficult.

My father was reduced to corruption — oh, not on the scale of modern industry, not in our understanding of the inflated word; a few slices of Dutch bacon and half a bar of good neutral milk chocolate. The commissar at whom these tidbits were aimed was none other than Ivan Maisky, later a most civilized Soviet ambassador in London, and he gracefully declined the delicatessen, producing a few herrings and some dry lentil soup wrapped in a week-old copy of *Izvestia* for my father's delectation, as well as the necessary travel document. Before shaking hands and wishing my father Godspeed to Pskov, Maisky sprinkled some eau de cologne on himself. My father used to describe the odor of cheap perfume mixed with herring oil as one of the most ingeniously awful smells in creation and shuddered visibly at the recollection half a century later.

He managed to secure the release of his mother and sister, dispatching them to Cairo via Istanbul and the Crimea, and at the end of that week, married my mother in church. He was dressed in long white tennis trousers and a blazer of sorts, whereas my mother wore her grandmother's nightdress, a magnificent mass of fidgeting lace and frayed ribbons, which lent both weight and dignity to the occasion.

Once again through the intervention of Mr. Maisky, my father managed to procure false documents describing him as a German prisoner of war ready for repatriation with his new Russian wife, and the couple set sail for Amsterdam aboard a Swedish steamer.

Quite recently, some fifty-three years later, I made a pilgrimage to the house from which my parents set out on their odyssey, the building in which I was conceived. It stands in a stately yet disheveled row of elegant town houses on the Vassilievsky Ostrov, the Basil Island, amid the Leningrad lagoons. The façades are pockmarked with rifle and machine-gun bullets, and occasionally it seems as though a cornice or an ornament has been carried away by some larger projectile, or else just fallen off in despair. A feeling of awe came over me as I stared at the dusty ocher colonnades and realized that a moment of abstract passion somewhere among the icy corridors had set in motion a process culminating in the corpulent bearded figure who now stood meditating on its porch.

I entered, since I had heard that my aunt still lived there in one shared room. The pervading odor was that of cabbage soup, not today's, not yesterday's, but the day before's, and of all the days before it, through regimes and revolt and Imperial decrees. I recognized it as a hallmark of Russianness. Another aunt lived in Berlin between the wars, in an agglomeration of emigrés clustered around an Orthodox church. Here too the smell of cabbage soup lingered over the staircase, but mingled with incense. In spite of the intensity of the holy vapors, secular cabbage soup emerged the victor by a soupçon. Nothing links the generations more poignantly than aroma. The sweet smell of an old book is far more eloquent than the ancient words and eroded sentiments printed on its worm-eaten pages; the hint of airless moisture in a dungeon or a cloister brings by way of the nostril a pang of fear or devotion as it came to people now long dead, with other criteria for fervor, different portals of pain.

Here, in the cold mist of cabbage soup, I fancied my mother was still waiting to be born, as I had waited. The architecture seemed uninspired and even illogical, as it often does when a great house has changed its character to accommodate changing times. Outside it was spring, inside winter. It was a day with a light and frivolous breeze. You would never have known it from the gales that howled under arthritic doors and through the cracks in the glass. A clearing of the throat sounded like the rumble of a distant avalanche, a cough like a congregation taking to its knees. It was too dark to read the names typed on an irregular piece of paper by a series of bells, names in a frame of orange dampness. At last, a strange shuffling, the noise of an ancient Russia to go with the cabbage soup, the sound of slippers pushed along the floor like skis by legs used to immense distances. A moment after it had grown to an unnatural intensity, as though aided electronically, an old woman appeared, thin, bursting with questions and expressing in advance her misgivings at the replies.

"Who are you?"

"The son of Nadezhda Leontievna."

"Ah, the foreigner. The actor and playwright. Have I got it right?" This without warmth, and certainly without enthusiasm.

"Yes."

"You are no doubt looking for your aunt, Ekaterina Leontievna?"

"Indeed, yes."

And then, on a note of triumph. "She's not here."

"Oh."

"I suppose you now wish to be taken to where she is?"

Extraordinary intuition.

"Have you a motor vehicle?" She went on, and then answered the question herself. "Obviously. You're a foreigner, with rubles. And now I suppose you want me to take you there?"

"If you have nothing better to do."

"Better to do?" she snapped, and waited a second for the echo to evaporate. "What on earth could I have to do that would be better?"

I could make no contribution to the conversation.

"Wait for me, I'm going to change."

The sound of slippers receded; then, before it had really died away, it began to grow in volume again. Eventually she reappeared, wearing a threadbare coat, carrying a plastic handbag, but still wearing the slippers. She was ready for the April showers.

My taxi was an aged Zis from the time of the great purges, a monumental imitation of a vintage Packard with cut glass receptacles inside for a couple of dying flowers and with a mass-produced Caucasian carpet on the floor. I encouraged her to occupy the back by herself while I sat next to the expressionless driver. Once the car was in motion, I turned to look at her. To judge by her expression, the backseat might as well have been a throne. There was no trace of surprise in her face, and in fact, she sat in the center as though emphasizing her birthright.

"You must have had a terrible time here during the war," I said, by way of conversation.

The chauffeur nodded in a patient, heroic, understated way. The old lady went further. She seemed to shrug it off as negligible.

"What leads you to say that?" she asked, "A knowledge of history?"

"Not only," I replied. "I noticed that the building was raked by machine-gun fire . . . German bullets."

"German bullets?" the old lady spat out. "The Bolsheviks . . . during the Revolution . . . the bastards never repaired the damage they did!"

I glanced in alarm at the driver, caught his eye in the driving mirror, set far forward in the huge driving compartment. He smiled slightly in a way which suggested that one must be patient with the old, more especially since they have a virtual monopoly on the truth.

I felt I had a finger on the pulse of my origins.

A few minutes later and we were in other, lighter, corridors, of more recent and more miserable construction. We even went up in an elevator decorated with lewd Cyrillic graffiti by those who had spent hours incarcerated there while waiting for it to be repaired. I was encouraged to ring a bell next to an unvarnished wooden door, and once again, through it, I heard the noise of slippers gliding on linoleum. The door opened a crack, and what looked like a caricature of my mother peered up at me with amber eyes.

"Yes? What is it?"

Feeling unaccountably like a secret policeman, I prepared to reveal my true identity, but the lady who had accompanied me forestalled all my tactful preparations with a maelstrom of truncated words, explaining in detail everything that had happened up to that moment. It was clear both that the two old people were bound in inseparable friendship and that they couldn't stand each other, a phenomenon that is possible anywhere but that reaches heights of subtle paradox more outrageously in Russia than anywhere else. My aunt Katya, whom I had never seen before, regarded me with a quiet hostility, not because she held anything against me but because I was responsible for bringing her best friend along to plague her. Seated in the kitchen, drinking tea with jam in it, conversation was difficult. I never expected it to be easy, but what was nevertheless disconcerting was the formality of the occasion, which made me feel almost like a prisoner who had refused to reveal more than his name and number. Curiously enough, it was only when the conversation descended to the conventional level of claims and counterclaims about the Germans' bomb damage to London, to Coventry, to Leningrad, and to Stalingrad that it lost its imperious reserve and acquired true, if silly, animation. The best friend watched the exchanges with an excitable eye, as though following the ball in a game of tennis.

"I don't know about England. About England I don't know," she screeched at length, "but over here, the Bolsheviks did most of the damage themselves, and don't try to tell me otherwise." My aunt Katya relapsed into a patriotic sulk, while the best friend added fuel to the embers by declaring that she would stay behind to keep my aunt company after I had gone; and "Thank you for the lift," she muttered grudgingly, like a child who has been forced publicly to express gratitude for something he neither wishes nor enjoys.

I took the hint and left, kissing my aunt in a clumsy manner. The two ladies let me go, now united in a sudden complicity of silence.

On reflection, I feel that my aunt Katya resented the fact that her younger sister had left Russia, and with a "German" at that. Her feelings were latent, but the sudden appearance of the offspring of a half-forgotten union — in the shape of a middle-aged man with only a few words of Russian at his disposal and hardly any syntax at all — stirred up the old sediment.

I reached the street, and found the driver seated at the wheel, neither asleep nor entirely awake. He expressed as little as the two old ladies, and yet seemed in some mysterious way to realize what I had been through. Here was the patience, the sense of timelessness, which had kept people standing in line for vegetables, for meat, or for a glimpse of Lenin in his mausoleum. "Yes . . ." he said, ". . . the old . . ." And allowed me to fill in the blanks.

We traveled from the past back into the present, and found the two in many ways identical. An old foolishness is not improved with age, nor are ancient hostilities dignified by the fact that they happened long ago. Don't you agree, Dear Me?

Ah, I was wondering when — and if — you were ever going to consult me. After all your fine intentions at the beginning of your book —

Our book! Our book.

We'll see about that — thank you all the same — I was beginning to fear that you had forgotten all your ambitious schemes and were going to embark on just another autobiography, with all its self-justifications, its sensitivities (which, I may add, you don't manifest in life) and its exploitations of one aspect of the truth at the expense of others —

May I interrupt?

Must you? You have held the floor for an inordinately long time all by yourself, and now you wish to interrupt me after only a single sentence.

I have my reasons. There has been very little need to consult you up to now. Our story has been largely factual, and prenatal, an area in which there is hardly any opportunity for opinion. That was true, certainly, up to the introduction of our aunt Katya. Is your impression of meeting Aunt Katya any different from mine?

Of course not. It's the same impression. My interpretation may be different.

In what way?

She may have been tired or exasperated by some other, extraneous element. What do you know of her state of health at the time? You had never even seen her before and were never destined to see her again. Was that her normal method of conducting a conversation? You noticed her arthritis. She may have been in agony.

Now you are just being unreasonable. In order to tell a story, there must be some elbowroom, some breathing space, some license — otherwise you become as squeamish as a vegetarian. The truth is often painful.

And often untrue. It is only your *truth, remember.*

It is my pain too, as often as not. And my pleasure. It is not *the* story I am telling, it is *my* story. *My* story. *My* story. Not even *our* story.

I will sit back and listen.

Then take that smile off my face.

On to Chapter Three, and co-existence!

3

As I have said before, I was born on April 16, 1921, at around eleven o'clock in the morning. The event took place at a nursing home in Adelaide Road, Swiss Cottage, London. Since my parents had left Petrograd on the Swedish freighter nine months previously, I had traveled extensively in embryonic form, spending some time in Holland while preparing to make my entrance. A chance decision of a Herr Von Maltzahn at the German Foreign Office apparently changed my destiny. It was he who decreed that my father be sent to London as representative of the Wolff-Büro, the German news agency of the time.

My mother arrived at the port of Harwich sometime in February 1921, and was immediately apprehended by the British authorities for having filled up her landing form with undue accuracy. To the question "Where born?" she had answered St. Petersburg. To the question "Where educated?" she had answered Petrograd. To the question "What was the point of departure from country of origin?" she had answered Petrograd. The immigration authorities were convinced that she was making light of the questionnaire, and I feel bound to add with a certain pride that it was only my presence that saved her from further unpleasantness. This tendency to answer official questions too literally seems to run in the family, perhaps owing to the many frontiers we all have crossed since such encumbrances were invented.

I got into similar trouble myself on my first application to enter the United States when I described my color as pink. I was told sternly that I was white, a fact that I denied, relying upon an Embassy mirror for evidence. A great deal of time was wasted, more especially since I failed to realize the subliminal implication of the word "pink" in those days. It speaks highly for the equitable spirit of American officials that I was accorded a visa, even if their sense of color was somewhat slapdash.

Once she was released by the equally persnickety British authorities, my mother traveled to London by train through a thick industrial murk, which culminated in a swirling yellow fog: impenetrable, choking, and claustrophobic. She records that she had never seen or smelled such unadulterated filth in her life. Before the names of the stations were entirely obliterated toward the end of the journey, the impression of Kafkaesque horror was increased by the fact that every station seemed to be called Bovril. It is necessary to explain to the uninitiated that Bovril was, and is, a most excellent beef tea. Being the fruit of private enterprise in a highly competitive capitalist society, it had bright and brilliant advertisements, unlike the names of stations which, although privately owned, were without direct competition and so tended to conceal their identities behind layers of grit and grime.

The train finally pulled in to the greatest Bovril of them all, and my mother was taken by her old governess to a boarding home run by an elderly Puritan couple, where nothing was allowed except total silence. She knew, as she conversed in surreptitious whispers with Miss Rowe, who had taught her in St. Petersburg, that she had made the mistake of her life in coming to this nightmare of a country with her unborn child. And yet, such is the power of acquired tastes in those of sensibility that this is the self-same country she was to die in fifty-four years later, refusing for the last ten years of her life to leave even for a brief vacation, wrapping up against the pervasive damp, making casual excuses for every discomfort, deeply involved in village life, warmed by soulless electric stoves and the great hearts of her neighbors.

The reason she was left alone to face the initial rigors of her new island home was that my father had preceded her and was already deeply involved in his new job. She even had to be rushed alone to the nursing home when her time came, since my father was busy hollering the contents of a speech by Lloyd George through a defective line to Berlin.

I was a precocious reader, being able to master one word at the extremely early age of nine months. The second word was to follow some time later. It was, however, in the choice of word that I displayed a certain gift for diplomacy which has caused me more trouble than it is worth all through my life. The word, which I called out on top of a double-deck bus to the consternation of the passengers, while pointing a diminutive finger at a huge advertisement near Victoria Station, was Oxo. Once again, I must explain — Oxo was, and once again, is, as far as I know, a valid and determined rival to Bovril in the world of beef tea. It was a kind of tactful revenge for all my mother's early misgivings on the train that I now drew the attention of a busload of passengers to the virtues of a rival reducer of cattle to size.

It is difficult to know what one remembers in truth, and what one has reconstructed from photographs and anecdotes of loving relatives. For instance, there is one event of which I have absolutely no recollection but which I see in the mind's eye as clearly as though I had been an active rather than a passive participant, and that is my baptism.

My gently lachrymose grandmother, with her extraordinary capacity for reliving the events of the Bible as though they were headline news in the paper, wrote from Cairo, insisting that I be baptized in the waters of the Jordan, for old time's sake. My father, now enjoying himself in his new peacetime job, was properly impatient with such jaded symbolism and said he couldn't possibly take leave of absence for such a specious reason. Anyway, he couldn't afford the fare. Backward and forward flowed the correspondence, until a compromise was reached. It was decided that the interested parties meet halfway between London and Cairo. Since my grandmother's knowledge of geography was hazy, apart from Ethiopia, which she knew like the back of her hand, it was easy to convince her that the halfway mark between the capitals lay in Stuttgart, or, more accurately, in Schwäbisch Gmünd, a town a few kilometers away. I traveled there in a basket kindly lent by the White Heather Laundry of London, and I wish to take this belated opportunity to thank that excellent organization for the comfort and aeration of their larger baskets, although I must add that I have never found that part of *The Importance of Being Earnest* in which Mr. Worthing was alleged to have been discovered in a handbag remotely amusing, possibly because it was too close to the truth in my case.

My grandmother advanced on Schwäbisch Gmünd from the south, clutching a stoneware hot-water bottle filled to the brim with muddy Jordan water which she had procured, after a special journey, by wading in the shallows, holding up her skirts with one hand and immersing the hot-water bottle with the other.

All went well until the actual christening, when the aged clergyman, who suffered from the shakes, let slip the hot-water bottle at the climactic moment of the ceremony; it broke neatly in two on the Victorian mosaic, sending rivulets of yellowish water, alive with the agitation of primitive and almost invisible river life, exploding among the cracks and crevices of the neo-Gothic Bible scenes depicted on the floor. Without so much as a flicker of anguish, the clergyman promptly substituted some sterile sanctified water for the Old Testament impurities, and named me Petrus Alexandrus to lend a classical tone to the proceedings which was now lacking.

I am grateful not to have been born into a backward tribe where such an event might have been interpreted as the displeasure of some god or other, for I might easily have been sacrificed in a cowardly act of appeasement. As it was, my grandmother's eyes began to water whenever she clapped them on me. In less atavistic surroundings, back in London, I prospered despite this early brush with Fata Morgana.

The first nurse I remember was black, but instead of the full-bosomed, contralto, crooning warmth associated with black mammies in antebellum surroundings, this lady came from the Cameroons, a part of Africa formerly under German hegemony, and she possessed the febrile eye and the rasping voice of a Prussian drill sergeant. Her name, if you please, was Fräulein Bertha, which sounds like some kinky creation of Strindberg's fevered imagination. I spent most of my time standing in the corner with a wet diaper on my head while she screamed and ranted in barrack-square German. She was caught beating me mercilessly by my father, who fired her on the spot, which caused her to feel great bitterness about white overlordship. Where she went, I do not know. Her country was now a French mandate. The hated enemy was there, as in Alsace-Lorraine. She was a misfit in a world that had changed, and like most misfits she was a splendid potential recruit for the Nazi party. She had risen to a tiny, meaningless authority through the ranks of servility, and now she was in temperament more European than the most rabid Junker. All that stood in her way was her appearance. I often think of her, with pity.

Her successor was Irish, a girl in her twenties who dressed like a woman in her fifties, in grim gray flannels, with a black hat through which a hat pin cut, seeming to pass through her head. Her hair was plaited, and she wore a rimless pince-nez which wobbled on the bridge of her nose as she spoke. She was all mildness of manner and hypocritical whispers and nursery jingles. She had a saying or a saw for every situation, but in spite of the prissy piety of her comportment, a habit she must have picked up in some convent, I spent just as much time in the corner as under Fräulein Bertha, and even more time with soggy underwear on my head. Whereas Fräulein Bertha didn't give a damn who knew of her educational methods, since she had suffered just such an upbringing and came out of it with head high and vocal chords higher, Miss O'R. was full of murmured threats about what would happen to me if I ever complained to my parents about what went on. Among those specified occurrences was her habit of wheeling me into the park, ostensibly to take a breath of air in my pram, a practice encouraged by my mother. We never went far, however, although we stayed out a long time. My daily constitutional took us two streets away, to a relatively low neighborhood. Here I would be parked next to a railing, and be left to my own devices while Miss O'R. disappeared down some steps into a basement, where a door opened mysteriously to let her in.

Presumably in order to keep me quiet, a man in shirt-sleeves would emerge and place a bird cage on the steps, exciting a large green parrot inside to converse with me. There are, of course, limits to the conversation one can have with a parrot, especially when one's own vocabulary is not yet much more extensive than the bird's. It imitated me and I imitated it, but since our relationship could hardly move much further without a slightly greater experience of life, and since the fixed and surprised expression of its eye gave me hardly any intellectual satisfaction, I soon tired of its intrusion into my privacy and ended by ignoring it. This ritual was repeated day after day, until I began to loathe the sight of the bird, and it took scant pleasure in seeing me, remaining as silent as a Trappist.

Eventually Miss O'R. would emerge, all flushed, having taken much more color on our excursion than I did, her eye rejuvenated and flashing behind her pince-nez. She whispered her usual threat about all the horrid things I could expect if I breathed so much as a single word to my parents, and wheeled me back home.

For a while all went well for her, until I began to imitate the parrot at home. At first my parents were delighted with my performance, until it occurred to them that I could scarcely have encountered a parrot in Green Park. "Where," they asked me, "did you see a parrot?" I grew red with embarrassment and said that I had sworn not to tell. In such a manner are children prepared for the ethics of adult life, for Watergate and all the rest. My mother mentioned it no more, although she did tell my father that she had noticed that my clothes were covered with particles of soot every time I went to the park. The tentacles of justice were beginning to close on poor flushed Miss O'R.

The next day, we went around the corner as usual. Miss O'R. clattered down the steps, the man in shirt-sleeves put in a brief appearance as he placed the bird in position as though it were an early morning cup of tea in a guest house. What had started excitingly as a conspiracy had now become a routine rite. I sought to break the monotony that day by shouting at the bird. The bird looked surprised as usual, as though finding these new sounds difficult to assess. We were interrupted by a presence. It was my mother, who had followed the pram like a detective. That was the end of the road for Miss O'R., whose tears welled out of downcast eyes, making her look for once younger than her years. She packed her bags and went, giving me a twisted little kiss on the way. She undoubtedly set the seeds in my mind for a conviction that there is nothing more boring in this world than someone else's love story, especially if you are told it by a parrot.

A procession of temporary nurses was halted by the arrival of Frieda from Hamburg. Here was a true eccentric, and she and my parents deserved each other. My mother had been an art student in Russia, and now attempted to become a full-fledged painter. She sketched a great deal, and had acquired a very personal, rather fey, pale, stylized technique in oils. In the full flush of young achievement, she submitted one or two of her works to the New English Art Club. My father did a floral piece of his own as a joke and submitted it also. His was accepted, hers were refused. Then Frieda arrived as a cook, and as a counterweight. She was a woman of unprepossessing appearance, one of the tragic generation engaged to a man who was killed in the war, or worse, "missing," a word which invariably introduced an element of hope into a hopeless situation. She was barely literate, and yet her instincts were individual and sure, as though her schooling had failed to replace her native wit with a social efficiency less personal.

First she was a good cook, then a great cook, eventually a celebrated cook. Not content with this, she looked after me between courses, and as if that weren't enough of a handful, she began to paint in a manner somewhere between Le Douanier Rousseau and Grandma Moses, and to pose for my mother in the nude when in need of rest. She entered into the stormy life we shared and was, in fact, responsible for at least some squalls.

It is perhaps necessary to give a brief description of my parents at this juncture, simply because nothing can be understood from now on without at least an appreciation of my prejudices in their regard. I do not pretend to tell the truth about them, simply because I am probably the last person in the world qualified to do so. After all, I lived with them, in the most oppressive proximity. In any case, I believe they were utterly different when they were alone, without my presence.

My father, Klop, was short, all of five foot two, and had been slight. Early photographs show him as dapper, affecting pomaded hair, cut very short, and often a monocle. I always felt he was somewhat of a ham. One can tell by the way a man will look at himself in the glass, and by the expression he adopts when posing for photographs. He never smiled on those occasions unless shamed into it by the photographer, and even then he injected a quizzical look as a condiment to his bonhomie. Usually he assumed a rather dictatorial look or else one of disconcerting scepticism, hypnotizing the onlooker with an eye either all-seeing or indomitable. In short, he seemed to fancy himself as something he was really not — a man of mystery — at least not in the way he understood it.

There is a cliché which maintains that traits of character tend to jump one generation, and if such is in fact the case, it is probably due to a tendency of children to react against their parents in their formative years rather than to any purely genetic reason. Klop's father became what he was as a reaction against that wicked father of his, who had made of his bed a track meet rather than a place of rest, and whose unshaven jowls could be seen at intervals chewing on a pickle in the hallway while his wife wept, consoled by her three sons, in the town house down the street. Such scandalous comportment in a father is liable to engender introspection in a son.

Whatever Klop's father was really like, it is obvious that he was more of an age to be a grandfather to the lad, since he was turning seventy when Klop was thirteen. Klop never denied being spoiled, although he didn't care to dwell on it, making out instead that his father was a terrifying martinet, probably in order to impress me with his own relative leniency. Klop never tired of telling me, as I crept home with one of those ambiguous report cards English schoolmasters have specialized in ever since they read their Dickens, that he had been so brilliant a pupil that when he left school in Jaffa, his name had been inscribed in letters of gold on a marble slab for all to know that Jona von Ustinov had been a scholastic *Wunderkind*.

I was less impressed than I should have been, since having my name inscribed on a marble slab has always been a fear rather than an ambition, and because other sources had told me that Klop had had help with his homework from none other than his father, eager for his progeny to shine. On the one occasion I had any help from Klop, I got lower marks than usual, and that's saying something. In case it can be thought that I blame my father for failing with my homework after all this time, I hasten to state that I do.

All this is not to say that he was in any way stingy with his exceptional intelligence, but this intelligence was strictly post-scholastic in character and, as he would himself have insisted, superficial. His most profound visible quality was his utter belief in life as an artful exercise, as an expanse of thin ice to be skated on, for the execution of arabesques and figures of fun. He lived for the day, and was, as I have stressed before, totally irreligious, perhaps as a reaction against his father's Calvinist austerity and the tasteless ecumenical excesses of the Holy Land.

It was natural for such a temperament to find real joy in the quicksilver world of journalism, which gave him every opportunity to exercise the kind of talent he possessed and also to spend a little more than his salary on entertaining. I am convinced that I am one of the few people he knew who will remember him as a highly paradoxical person rather than as an admirable host, and I say this without the remotest implication of criticism, in the added conviction that he would far rather have been remembered as an admirable host than as a person of any kind. It was all part of his hedonistic message to mankind.

He had large and expressive eyes, the precise color of white grapes, which were often trained on the passing forms of women, seeming to assess them with the shameless detachment of a trainer observing the finer points of racehorses. On those rare occasions when I found myself alone with him as a child, he would offer me an ice cream or a lemonade in a café, as an exercise in public relations or child psychology. I used to dread these moments even more than I dreaded his temper, because he would use them to scan the passing crowd and consult me as an adult accomplice on the physical qualities and shortcomings of the females present. Quite often he would become riveted on to some potential victim and would indulge in that suggestive ocular flicker which used to be described as a "glad eye." The victim would then either blush and appear scandalized or else wait for the next move with a suppressed confusion, as though impaled on Klop's liquid gaze. Small wonder that I became a kind of pocket Puritan, devoting the same massive attention to my ice cream that Klop was exerting on his mesmerism, refusing to look, refusing to answer, and bursting with a sense of outrage.

At home, while entertaining, he was a master of the risqué, of the double entendre, always galloping like a daring scout in the no-man's-land between wit and lapse of taste. Oh, his thousand and one nights would seem innocuous enough today, and he would have been as depressed by the brave show of pornography as any self-respecting rake, but in those times of nuance and pastel shades it was infinitely depressing to me to see my mother enter into the gales of laughter which greeted remarks of his, qualified gratefully as outrageous by his guests, in a pure spirit of sportsmanship.

Not that she was in the least narrow-minded. On the contrary, she was far more intrinsically unshockable than he, but her conduct

was always impeccable, while his seemed juvenile even to the child
that I then was.

I have always doubted that he was really the womanizer he would
have liked to be. First of all, he lacked the quality of secrecy necessary for those who lead double lives. His whole quality was public,
and he shared his predilections and temptations with my mother,
or, on rare occasions, over an ice cream, with me. He needed an
ear, be it friendly or merely infantile. Like Casanova, he was a flitter
from flower to flower, a grazer of bottoms rather than a pincher, a
catcher of glimpses rather than a patient voyeur, a man in a hurry
with an avid taste for the unpredictable, the unaccountable, the sudden. At the same time, he was a real danger to no one. He had a
distaste for the brutal and the cruel which was innate, and a moral
courage which was at times surprising in a man so devoted to the
good life. Toward the end of his life he was as surrounded by young
girls as a guru, so that even then he offered a consistent amusement,
an elegance of spirit, a sense of joyous irresponsibility to say the
least. It was perhaps only as a father that he was sometimes difficult
to stomach, and, by the same token, as a husband.

My mother was a large woman — in comparison with him, that
is. She had a fine face, with the kind of natural warmth and simplicity that attracted everybody, from my father's girl friends to homo-
sexuals, who found in her an uncomplicated friend and mentor. She
grafted her personality on to the kind of life she was asked to lead,
and never showed any of the humiliation and degradation she must
have felt. Basically she was a much stronger and more stable person
than my father, which caused her to emerge from her turbulent existence with an illusory sense of impervious independence. When
asked to paint some transitory flame of my father's, she did so with
grace, and often became a friend and confidante of the young person
while my father was directing his electric gaze on to some newer fly
entangled in his social web.

There was never a trace of self-pity about her, nor did she ever
give the impression that her life with this strange fellow was anything but normal, a fact I found bewildering and disturbing from an

early age. She was expected to go on an endless round of parties, to entertain at home, and still to paint, living what was left of her time as a Bohemian in a single room. But even here her life was invaded by Klop, who had acquired very dogmatic ideas about the arts and who invariably stood behind her easel telling her what was wrong with her latest canvas in terms both categorical and irrefutable. She listened, often remonstrated, but on the whole acceded to his demands. This is not to say that she didn't stick up for herself, but since he had a mercurial temper and, at times, a wicked and hurtful tongue, much of her energy was devoted to keeping a fragile peace in the household. The family rows were far too frequent, and were obviously exacerbated as I grew older and developed a mind of my own, and a kind of recklessness in expressing it.

On one occasion, I left for school after catching a glimpse of a picture my mother had painted. It was a very fine paraphrase of a painting by El Greco, and it struck me as a work of surpassing beauty. On returning home, I found that my mother had destroyed it, and was in fact already at work on the same canvas, painting a dish of apples. My fury knew no bounds. I surprised both my parents by the violence of my sentiments, and for the only time in my life had them both shouting at me. I banged the door of my room and locked myself in, refusing to emerge or answer for hours. Once inside, I felt a new strength I had never experienced before. It was the premature rage of an adult. There was no trace of a tear in my eye. For the first time, or so it seemed to me, I had spoken from a platform of my own, and not merely made excuses or reacted against some other initiative. From then on, I became calculatedly cold, deliberately impervious to my father's sarcasms and even to my mother's appeals for good sense. The atmosphere at home was no longer changeable, but glowering and intense.

I do not know in retrospect whether I would have the same high opinion of my mother's El Greco variant today, although in honesty, as I remember it, I think I would. As for the apples, they were reminiscent of Renoir, much beloved by my father at the time, but Renoir did his apples well enough not to need emulation. In any case, even he painted far too many apples. That awful day was a date in my calendar. I had become myself, to myself.

Before this, I had been used by my father as a cabaret, which was my first introduction to show business. My ability to imitate had manifested itself very early on, as well as my instinctively unconventional way of going about it. After all, I had started this tendency by imitating a parrot, which is unusual in that a parrot is supposed to imitate you. By taking the initiative, you allow the parrot no alternative but to be itself, which proves once again that attack is often the best defense. At the age of two, I apparently did a passable imitation of Lloyd George and later on I added Hitler, Mussolini, and Aristide Briand to my gallery as these gentlemen became available in the public domain. I also did a complete voyage around Europe by radio while hidden behind a curtain, which was remarkable by virtue of the fact that we possessed no radio in the house until 1936.

Fourteen years previously, during the great exhibition at Wembley, Haile Selassie had come to London to buy a few machine guns for the Ethiopian army. My father, making use of his Ethiopian connections, invited the Lion of Judah to dinner. Frieda cooked a great dinner for four. At the appointed time, Haile Selassie arrived at our small apartment accompanied not only by the Empress but by Ras Imru, Ras Kassa, the chief of general staff, six aides-de-camp, and a few princesses. Nobody in my family had sufficient faith to trust in miracles, so the German Embassy was apprised of the situation and prepared dinner for twenty, which was driven over in a fleet of Mercedeses. All this took time, however, even for the chef of the German Embassy, so in desperation I was woken up, and prevailed upon to do my entire repertoire, as well as to draw out the encores, if any. I have no recollection whatever of the occasion, but many years later, at the Ethiopian pavilion at the Osaka World's Fair, I was encouraged to go and talk to Haile Selassie by his grandson, Alexander Desta, then head of the Ethiopian navy. I sat by the aged monarch and reminded him of the evening. Before I had finished my very brief résumé of the event, he had fallen into a fitful sleep at the recollection, which leads me to believe that my performance in 1924 had not been a success.

In one sense, I was eager to be called on to perform. There was probably in me a premature professional sense, a feeling I remember quite well to this day, since it has been with me for a long time now. I can best refer to it as a kind of purification of the senses, a cutting-down of nonessentials, the emotion which finds its most faithful physical expression on the face of a high jumper about to take a stab at a record. And yet, in another sense, I dreaded these moments, because despite the laughter of my father's guests, I could discern in their appreciation a tinge of awe at the little monster I would become if encouraged to continue in this way. There was only one saving grace, and that was that I was irrevocably betrothed to laughter, the sound of which has always seemed to me the most civilized music in the universe.

At all events, these early flirtations with satire were infinitely more pleasant than another of my father's initiatives, which was to bring all his guests to see me in my bath. These guided tours used to burst in on me unheralded, and my father, who always considered himself a connoisseur of the arts, would compare me to this or that unfinished study by Donatello or a young Bacchus of the Etruscan school, often carrying a thick tome with him in order to prove his point.

My mother knew that I hated these intrusions, but didn't really understand why, believing it a small enough sacrifice to keep Klop sweet. Inevitably I tended to gravitate toward Frieda, who had a peppery nature of her own when my rights or hers were violated, and who never spared my father's complicated feelings. I think she must have given notice at least twice a month for the ten or more years she was with us. Notice was always given with extraordinary finality but somehow she never got around to packing her bags. She amused Klop, even, or perhaps especially, in the higher flights of anger, and his own heightened emotions were expressed with a malicious twinkle, laced with irony.

It was when she had finally left (at the time my father lost his job), this time of course without a scene, and in an aura of melancholy — her departure was dictated by economic considerations — that I realized how valuable a domestic equilibrium she had provided. When there were only three of us again, my father's attitude toward me became more virulently critical, and his humor grew more tetchy, only really coming in to his own when there was entertaining to be done. He was, I am told, jealous of my mother's attentions toward me — she herself supported this theory, which I can neither confirm nor deny, as I have absolutely no natural feeling for or recognition of jealousy. This does not mean that I am entirely incapable of being jealous myself — that would be too beautiful to be true — but I have always regarded it as a base and fundamentally stupid vice, and I would rather be caught dead than express it. Othello, clutching his handkerchief and rolling his eyes, has always struck me as a bit of an ass, and I only began to lose my lofty sense of ignorance in the face of jealousy when I became the father of more than a single child myself and could watch human relations in their most unsophisticated form, in the nursery.

It may be true that an only child is spoiled, not so much with gifts as with the time allotted to his problems, but believe me, there are occasions on which he wishes there was a brother or a sister to share the brunt. What is certainly true is that he tends to become self-centered, which is the outward form of self-sufficiency. He spends more time alone, and in the company of adults. He learns less about human nature faster, but I was staggered how much my own children revealed to me about the human condition, relatively obvious things that had just never occurred to me.

There were breaks in the monotonous pattern, little fragments of memory which I still possess. My parents dancing to the tune of "Valencia" and "Tea for Two" and "I Miss My Swiss Miss, My Swiss Miss Misses Me" while I was allowed to wind the portable gramophone. It was the only time I ever saw them dance together, and curiously enough for once there were no guests in the house. Then Klop bought a very early record of the Lener Quartet playing one of

Beethoven's last works. I noticed that there was a tendency for the listeners to close their eyes when savoring Beethoven, so I followed suit. It seemed to me strange later on, at school, that during lessons of so-called musical appreciation, it was quite in order to shut your eyes. In fact, by this simple strategy, you quickly acquired a reputation of possessing an intensely musical nature, and yet, if you shut your eyes during Latin or mathematics, it was generally supposed that you were asleep.

Then there were the holidays, the first conscious introductions to other lands and other cultures. My mother's brother Nicholas, who had been a regular officer with the Preobrazhensky Regiment, then transferred to Imperial Russia's first and only armored-car unit because of "bad feet," now followed in the great tradition of emigré officers by driving a taxi in Paris. He used to fetch us at the Gare du Nord and transport us to the Gare de Lyon free of charge. It was a relief to be comfortably seated on the cloth upholstery of his maroon Delage after having spent some hours on the wood-slatted seats of a third-class compartment, even if the excesses of the Paris traffic were even wilder than they are today. The air was charged with the trumpeting of bulb-horns, forbidden today, and the torrents of abuse from driver to driver, also discouraged but perforce tolerated as social intercourse between consenting adults.

My mother used to go to the south of France in order to paint. Her style had deepened into something altogether richer than before, a sternly unaffected impressionism. The strength of her pictures was also, to my mind, their limitation, which is another way of saying that she had personality. Everything she painted had behind it a very acute temperament, both serene and warm. Much more heart and instinct than thought had gone into her work. To paint what she saw was enough for her. What she felt would inevitably follow.

She strode across the paintable landscape wearing espadrilles, an old straw hat on her head, sniffing out the best angles and compositions, while Frieda and I followed like native porters in an African movie, carrying canvases and easels and boxes of paints. It was a curious way of spending vacations, since there was nothing else to do but to paint as well, although for me to paint what I saw was never satisfying. I could not bring myself to aim for a more faithful reproduction, nor did any work without comment, without an edge, interest me for long. I remember the astonishment of both my mother and Frieda once when, at the end of a smouldering day in the hills behind Tourettes-sur-Loup, I showed them my painting, the subject of which was a post-Christmas sale at Harrod's.

This event became the pretext for a family joke, which was brought out on every and any occasion, and I hope I laughed with good grace every time I heard it. The fact was that I did not consider it much of a pastime for a boy away from school to be sitting before a landscape nature has put together with great competence, and to seek to reproduce it on a small piece of paper. It was more of a school punishment than a relaxation, and it was useless to tell me that Cézanne had attempted to fracture light or that Seurat had reduced the universe to dots. These were men who had chosen their professions, and who had applied the alchemy of thought and vision to their paintbrushes in necessary loneliness, and who did with a discreet conviction that which I was doing only because I had no one with whom to play. In case it be thought that a note of self-pity has crept in to this account of my apparent boredom, I must say that the intention was never to complain about my fate, but merely to explain the form of my protest. A Christmas sale in a department store should have been enough to convince anybody that I had no ambitions to be a landscape painter, but no, it was taken, told and retold, as evidence of youthful high spirits in someone who would no doubt settle down later on; and I, social animal that I already was, laughed with the others and gave credence to the myth.

If the sacrifice I felt I was making had been of some use to my mother's career, there would have been a point to all the discomfort. But once back home, there was always the terrifying day when all these canvases passed in review before my father, and he decreed which should be exhibited and which should not. It was worse than being stopped at customs with contraband. He was by now not the only arbiter. There were the people from the galleries as well, and it is very probable that between the lot of them they made the right choice, but I felt then as I feel now that the one great joy of leaving school is that you no longer have the impression of sitting for exams, and there is no excuse on God's earth for giving a grown person this lamentable impression.

I had cooled toward the visual arts, and it took a long time for my instinctive love of them to reassert itself.

Now, Dear Me, I suppose that you will tell me I have been too harsh on my father.

Not at all. I realize that you are making every effort to recapture the emotions of a child faced by the problems of growing in the shadow of a man at once dogmatic and capricious, and that your criticism is at no time the criticism of one adult by another.

I wouldn't know how to criticize him in that way. I had known him too long and too well. I feel now that he hadn't the remotest idea of how to deal with children. To him they were just inadequate adults.

Oh, that's not true. He could be perfectly adorable and show incredible patience with other people's children.

Toward the end of his life that was so, but I wonder if that isn't so toward the end of most people's lives. There is a natural complicity between the very old and the very young. Children tend to enjoy the company of their grandparents, which often leads their parents into little tantrums of jealousy (ah, I recognize it here!), complaining that their children are being spoiled. But is there not a precise biological reason for this? There is a tendency for the old to begin to remember their youth with extraordinary clarity, as though there were some metaphysical connection between the mysteries of birth and death, whereas those in the flower of life are the farthest away from those distant frontiers we all pass. They are at their most intelligent, at their most active, at their least instinctive. They brush away the reflective, the poetic, the opaque as wastes of valuable time. They read the papers with a sense of personal involvement, they fret and fume, make and lose their fortunes, carve what they imagine to be their futures out of the present which seems so permanent, and leave the foolishness to the very old and the very young.

Yes, of course I agree, even though I might criticize your language as being a little high-flown. Your own son, remember, made a most astute observation the other day. When you confided in him that you felt it was a little early in life to be writing your memoirs, he replied that later on you would begin to remember everything and would run the risk of being a crashing bore because of a dotard's inability to be selective. The time to write memoirs is when total recall has not yet invaded the cavities of the mind left empty by the inaction of retirement.

I remember that observation with great pleasure, although since I have not yet revealed the existence of my son, I feel I should be a little careful about running ahead of myself. I have not yet gone to school myself, in fact.

You are lucky to have me by your side to remind you where you are in the narrative. Very well, we will forget your son for the time being, and concentrate on your father. I do not think you were too tough on him. I do not think you were tough enough.

Oh, come on. Have you any idea how difficult it is to be a father? Children seem to regard them as infallible authorities at one time of life, and when the disillusionment comes, it is invariably painful, leading to an absurd and unhappy bitterness. Children forget that although they have no previous experience of being children, their fathers have no previous experience of being fathers. And, in any case, no one on this earth is infallible. There are no heroes, and nobody is worth the worship due to heroes.

There you are, talking about your son again, in spite of your good intentions.

I am talking about myself, and about my father, which comes to the same thing as talking about my son. You are right, there's no getting away from it. We all make mistakes, but at least, if we are intelligent, we make other mistakes than those which were made on us. Only if we are unintelligent do we make the same mistakes. But whether we are intelligent or unintelligent, we make mistakes, and often intelligent mistakes are the worst, since so much careful thought has gone into them.

How about your mother?

A remarkable woman — a sister, an aunt, sometimes a daughter, always a mother, and yet without a trace of that saccharine possessiveness which traditionally marks a certain aspect of maternity. She never made me feel that the pain attending my birth was a moral debit account which could never be entirely honored, and she taught me that independence is the rarest of life's commodities by making the fullest use of the ration she was accorded. She was always blissfully uninquisitive, which was an important aspect of her independence. She was also entirely faithful, simply because she could not conceive of not being so. My father was the one and only man in her life. She had given her word that this should be so, and the idea never occurred to her, even under the most blatant provocation, that she could go against her word. Sometimes this extraordinary uprightness was a source of irritation, simply because the insults poured on her dignity were so scandalous that decency itself called for a reaction of some kind, and yet there was no trace of self-righteousness, of holier-than-thou about her attitude. Her eyes merely became sightless, her ears deaf, her mind absent, and she concentrated with relaxed application on the highlight on this apple or the shadow in the armpit of that nude. And yet, it is humanly impossible that she did not suffer a great deal, but she probably reflected, as people of such temperament invariably do, that she was made to suffer because she had the moral capacity to bear suffering with a shrug, in silence.

I asked you about your mother, and now, inadvertently, you have been as tough on your father as I wished you to have been from the beginning.

She was, curiously enough, even tougher than I could possibly be. For years after his death she struggled with a book entitled *Klop*, which was to be an eulogy and a memoir of a man she considered remarkable, the only man she had ever known. A year before her death it appeared, and it was greeted by many readers as a tribute to a remarkable man, and yet there were those even among the critics who discerned a darker side to the jocular narrative, and who came to the conclusion that my father was a bigot, a snob, and an unrepentant egotist.

How is it possible to read such different conclusions from one and the same book?

First of all because many remarkable men are bigots, snobs, and unrepentant egotists, and second because the book was delightfully free from recrimination. And yet, it possessed another characteristic that was its key to those willing to look beneath the surface. It told the truth, simply and unaffectedly, because my mother was incapable of not telling the truth simply and unaffectedly. And so what was sincerely intended by her as an amusing epitaph to her man became a much sadder little volume to those willing to treat it as other than pure entertainment, as an account of events that actually occurred, recollected in cheerfulness. My mother stuck her press cuttings into a book, including the one with the headline "Ustinov's Father Was a Bigot and a Snob." She made no reference to it, but did not attempt to hide it. I dare say it was probably the only act of revenge she was capable of, the only one which was not an offense to her pride.

How touching. I know this is not really the place for such a question, and yet in the interests of equity there is no alternative to my asking it now. They were quite close at the end, were they not?

It was during the war, Dear Me, that my father suddenly declared, quite out of the blue, that he refused to live over seventy years. His categorical announcement took everyone by surprise, particularly because there was nothing in the conversation to warrant it.

Why do you think he made it?

I believe he felt his powers waning — not only physical powers, but his credibility as a seducer — and he refused a life of mere observation, with the promise of nothing but senility.

You said he was totally irreligious.

To the extent of fearing nothing more than eternal life. He infinitely preferred oblivion, and he prepared for it with the grace of an ancient Roman. It was sheer willpower on his part that made him die four hours before his seventieth birthday.

Incredible. It sounds as though he didn't merely die, he gave up the ghost.

Asking nothing in return. Toward the end of his life he sulked like a child who had been denied eternal youth. This attitude, utterly bereft of volition, irritated my mother, who tried unsuccessfully to instill a little zest into him. But he knew what he wanted. And he left instructions that he was to be cremated. He wished to disappear. My mother cringed at the idea of cremation, but we obeyed his wishes. Then, once he had gone, my mother gradually wilted into the same baleful inactivity she had found so annoying in him, as though in obedience to some signal from beyond the grave. She faded away exactly as he had done, only coming to life momentarily on the publication of her book. At her death, she left instructions to be cremated, an idea which had always horrified her. I placed their ashes together in the same village graveyard in Gloucestershire.

They were reunited.

They had never really been separated. That is to say there was a difficult period just after the war in which they lived apart, he in a bachelor flat in London where he cooked his rich but succulent dishes for the delight of his guests, or guest. Later they were re-united, first of all in London, later in the country.

Was the breach between them a real one?

I don't know. It wasn't a breach, you know, it was an absence, a physical absence. After my mother's death, I found huge piles of letters from one to the other, all graded by vintage and held together by rubber bands. At a glance, they were talkative, informative, benign, and confidential. But there were those among them which made me feel like an eavesdropper, since they seemed to go beyond privacy into what was practically a private language. In this way, they are certainly love letters pure and simple, and I have no desire or inclination as yet to penetrate their secrets. I have merely kept them in neat piles, as she left them.

And the letters are from the period during which your parents were not living together?

Many of them, yes.

Has it occurred to you that perhaps it was you who injected an element into their relationship which they had never foreseen?

At the time they were not living together, I had long before left home. I hope what you suggest is not true.

I am not blaming you, merely the fact of your existence.

The fact of my existence?

How could Tristan and Isolde have survived if there had been a child; or Romeo and Juliet? All the poetry would have been lost in irritation at feeding time.

I do not think my parents were lovers in that sense. What they created was something far less ambitious and far more profound. And Wagner would have been the last one to set their story to music. Offenbach perhaps, or Mozart. Nor would Shakespeare have been right as an author. Feydeau on good days, Chekhov for the rest, with a little help from Tolstoi and Michael Arlen; but most of all, themselves.

Well, whatever blame we must take for our existence, Dear Me, I think it time we accorded them a little privacy. It is time for us to go to school.

4

M R. Gibbs' Preparatory School for Boys occupied a house in
Sloane Street in London, 134 to be precise. Whereas other British
schoolboys wore caps that fitted fairly tightly on the head and that
boasted a multiplicity of colors, with coats of arms or monograms in
evidence, the boys of Mr. Gibbs' wore caps curiously like those
favored by Lenin, and what is more, cherry red without any heraldic symbol. Mr. Gibbs himself was a fairly burly old gentleman,
who was extremely cordial and also extremely absentminded. He
seemed to have some difficulty shaving, apart from his immaculate
white military moustache, since his jaw was often decorated with
tufts of bloody cotton wool. He also sang a great deal, as though the
cherished privacy of his bathroom traveled with him. What he sang
were not so much recognizable tunes, as a kind of personal parlando
set to melodies very much his own, reminiscent of Schönberg by
negligence rather than design, for he was not very musical. He imparted news in this manner, both pleasant and unpleasant, rather
like the town crier in his own little city.

"Oh, Oosty-Boosty," he would chant as he saw me, "can't tie his
shoe laces . . . Come over here . . . Mr. Gibbs will help him,

won't he . . . sit down, fatty," all this in a high tenor, like an evangelist. A far lower register was used for news unfavorable, although the quality was as doggedly in advance of its time.

"Thompson minor deserves to do a hundred lines . . . come and see me after school."

I learned at Mr. Gibbs' how to survive by emphasizing the clumsy and comic aspects of my character, and to hide my secret ambitions for fear of challenging too openly those better equipped by nature. For instance, I was often encouraged to play in goal during football matches, partly because I was not the fastest of runners with the ball, and partly because I was large and therefore occupied more of the goal mouth than a slender boy, the theory being that there would be a greater chance for me to deflect the ball unwittingly simply by being hit by it.

During the summer I was introduced to the game of cricket, and felt my inherent foreignness for the first time. The ball is far too hard for my taste, a lethal projectile left over from some long-forgotten battle. (I have always imagined cricket as a game invented by roughnecks in a moment of idleness by casually throwing an unexploded bomb at one another. This game was observed by some officer with a twisted and ingenious mind who devoted his life to inventing impossible rules for it.) The genius of the British lends itself not so much to the winning of games as to their invention. An astonishing number of international games were invented by the British, who, whenever they are surpassed by other nations, coolly invent another one which they can dominate for a while by being the only ones to know the rules. Whoever thought up cricket deserves a special commendation, since it is a game so doggedly peculiar and dangerous that no foreign nations, apart from those of relatively recent independence subjected to an English type of education, have even adopted it. The Americans, as a reaction against the indignities of the redcoats, grew tired of the sight of stumps on their village green and took up baseball, which is more adapted to a country of vast spaces with fewer architectural features to damage; whereas the French and Rumanians, who think nothing of flinging themselves at each other in the wild excesses of rugby football, would be bored stiff on the cricket pitch, faced by hours of langor punctuated by the mean crack of ball on bat and a bit of choreography.

It is against this background that children in British schools are taught to lose gracefully, often at the expense of winning. The real encounter is won in the dressing room after the event, in which the extraordinary grace of the loser makes the victory seem hollow and even vaguely indecent to the winner.

No wonder that old colonels have been heard to bark, "Play the game, sir," or "Gad, sir, it isn't cricket," referring to events far from the playing grounds; nor is it surprising that such an authority on aggrandizement and gamesmanship as Cecil Rhodes once gave the following advice to a nervous young officer about to police a bit of Empire, "Remember that you are an Englishman, and have consequently won first prize in the lottery of life."

Well, it was at Mr. Gibbs' school that boys were issued their tickets for this lottery, and although I was still technically von Ustinov, I was given the benefit of the doubt and slipped my ticket when not too many people were looking.

There were occasions on which Mr. Gibbs must have wondered if he had not been too free with his tickets, as when an Argentine boy and I were caught picking flowers instead of fielding during an important cricket match against another school, thus allowing the opponents no less than seven runs, simply because neither of us could find the ball. We were violently upbraided by a master, our bunches of wilting daisies still in our hands.

I redeemed myself later, however, when it had been admitted that cricket was hardly my forte, and perhaps for that very reason I was made the scorer for another vital match. The rival school also had a scorer, a small, anemic, and impressionable lad who looked hard done by. I was very agreeable with him, and he became almost pathetically grateful for a conversation absolutely devoid of threats or taunting, eventually being so immersed in it that he quite neglected to fill up his scorecard. As a result of this extremely relaxing afternoon, my school won the match by the smallest of margins in spite of having far fewer runs, a victory greeted with disbelief by our opponents, who only had to check the figures of their scorer, gratefully copied off my scorecard in the last moment, to see that it was unwise during matches against Mr. Gibbs' school to judge by appearances, above all if I was the scorer.

Mr. Gibbs hugged me with exceptional warmth after this most unexpected win, and it seemed to me that in his heart he knew that, thanks to him, I had at long last learned to play the game.

Among the other teachers, there was Mlle Chaussat, a slightly deformed spinster in her fifties, small and frankly frightening to look at. Her malformed back made her walk half-crabwise, and her broad-brimmed felt hat, which she never took off, gave her the aspect of a Hieronymus Bosch creation, a hat with legs. To add to the sense of menace exuded by poor Mlle Caussat were a mouth which never stopped moving, as though endlessly assessing and reassessing some outrage, a sallow face from which her defiant brown eyes shifted angrily above a spatulate nose and an explosion of moles, and a pair of open scissors which dangled from a satin cord down to where her knees must have been.

Bless her heart, she was the one subversive element admitted into a classroom which was dominated by a large print entitled "The Boy Scout's Oath." In it an evidently bewildered Boy Scout was led by the hand by Jesus, who, with his other hand, indicated a map of the world on which the Empire was lit by a strange, unearthly radiance. She often glanced with sheer hatred at this work of art, and shook her head at the gratuitous expropriation of Jesus by the Protestants. Whenever the national anthem was played, Mlle Chaussat remained seated, her twitching increasing, and her gaze showering the assembly like water from a hose. Her actions were never questioned, and she never amended them. She did, however, invite me to tea, which was the first gesture of friendship she had been known to make to anyone.

Our tea took place at M. Debry's Confiserie in Knightsbridge. I was plied with the most delicious chocolate cakes and a host of other goodies. At M. Derby's, Mlle Chaussat's entire character changed. She became playful and even ribald, passing remarks both salty and Gallic. I hardly recognized her as the grim French mistress who wore her scissors as a sword.

Then followed the reason for the tea, which was a temptation rather than a treat. With a surreptitious step, heeding the traffic with more than usual attention, she led me across the road to a French convent, which turned out to be her lair. Here, there was another Christ, as biased as the one showing such an unnatural interest in a Boy Scout and the British Empire; this one was on his cross, but with a painful smile reserved for the French. The advantages of Catholicism were shamelessly exposed.

"*Le protestantisme, ce n'est pas une réligion,*" Mlle Chaussat spat out with contempt, to the embarrassment of a group of nuns with gold teeth and suspect skins. I smiled at them. "*Ce n'est que dans le catholicisme qu'on trouve la vraie foi!*" On and on it went. Only a layman could afford to be as categorical or as wild. The nuns offered me more tea, a mournful lot of plain buns with the same scrubbed look as they had, after the sensuous opulence of M. Debry's éclairs. I declined as politely as I could.

"*Le petit a déjà managé,*" snapped Mlle Chaussat, suggesting that a glimpse of Satan was intended to make the cold clutch of Mother Church more desirable. I hid my thoughts in the guise of deep spiritual reflection, much as I had suggested my love of music by shutting my eyes during Beethoven. To this day I have never been subjected to so shameless a barrage of religious propaganda as on that sunny London afternoon, when Mlle Chaussat attempted to force her way into heaven, using me as a battering ram. The only moment of my life commensurate with this one occurred many years later, when a Russian Orthodox bishop told me, with the relish of the trainer of a sporting team, "Yes, we are making headway everywhere, mostly at the expense of Catholics."

Events like these make me wonder if there isn't something in the attitude of crusty British colonels — if it isn't a game after all, and may the best church win. I avoided giving Mlle Chaussat any hope whatsoever, but from that day on, she searched my face for signs. Every smile on my part was regarded as an indication that grace was beginning to seep into my soul through cracks in my defenses, whereas every negligence on my part was sensed as a local reverse for the truth at the hands of the infidel. Relations with Mlle Chaussat could no longer be normal, since we were never alone. There was always Jesus or Martin Luther or both to complicate the issue.

At the beginning of my scholastic life, the mothers were expected to attend school in order to help their fledglings with the written part of a history exam. The history we learned was, at that time, entirely English, as though children of very tender years were too fragile to be exposed to the existence of foreigners and their past, except when they appeared briefly as enemies for the English to defeat. The standard text was a fat book, printed in large type as though children are half blind, and about as silly an introduction to reality as one can imagine. Alfred and the cakes was a shining example of its probings into the past, presumably to explain the English indifference to the culinary arts. I remember a colored illustration of a Pre-Raphaelite Boadicea gazing into the distance with determination, while the flaxen-haired warriors around her seem distinctly worried. My poor mother, who had mastered everyday English by now but who had had little cause to probe into the Arthurian twilight, was compelled to take down my dictation, as I attempted to make sense of the comings and goings of Uther Pendragon, of Hengist and of Horsa, and of King Canute, who told the sea to back up but had the good sense not to be surprised when he got his feet wet. It became clear before my essay on ancient Britain was half over that my mother didn't know what I was talking about and was beginning to entertain doubts about the standards of education in England. Since they could hardly punish me for my mother's spelling errors, I came out of the exam relatively well, but it was the last personal appearance my mother made at school except for an eventful day at the school sports, held on the eve of the long summer holidays.

Not only my mother but — exceptionally — my father turned up at one of these, wearing his monocle. Among the events was a so-called Fathers' Race, in which the fathers of boys were supposed to demonstrate their spirit of sportsmanship by lending themselves to a curious flashback to their own school days over 100 yards. I asked my father to uphold my honor by running. He declined my offer with the usual mixture of humor and blarney. He was bound, he affirmed, to be in the lead, since he had been inordinately fast at school. At that point, he would also be bound to lose his monocle, without which he could not see the course, and naturally the monocle would be bound to be destroyed by the stampede of other fathers battling for second place. Since monocles were expensive and necessary items, he preferred not to take the risk of running.

My mother understood my evident disappointment, since we both knew that my father could see rather better without a monocle. He had them for both eyes, incidentally, and wore them when the spirit moved him. She now made the great sacrifice of entering the mothers' race, and I wish to this day she hadn't. My father was outraged by her initiative, but she could be very stubborn at times, especially when it had nothing to do with her painting. For the first yard or two I thought she had a chance, but then she began falling back, handicapped by her own explosion of laughter at the absurdity of the situation. It must have been one of the slowest 100 yards sprints on record, with my mother entirely alone at the tail end of the copious field of cantering maternity. She must have come in over five minutes after her departure; in other words she would have been wiser to walk. The actual time is, thank heavens, not on record, but I do remember that she was still running when the next race began, and, despite her enormous lead, she didn't even win that one, which was for the under-sixes.

The humiliations of the day were not over yet, however, since the final event of this joyous festival in an era of snobbery and privilege was a chauffeurs' race. It was impossible for me to redeem my misfortunes, since we had no car; and even I recognized that it would have been an absurd luxury to maintain a chauffeur specially for the yearly race without having anything for him to do the rest of the year. My best friend at school was the son of a celebrated banker, and with the instinct born of comradeship he read the distress on my face. Taking me aside, he informed me in a whisper that his father had two chauffeurs, and felt sure he could prevail on Daddy to lend me the slower one of his stable. My pride had been sufficiently wounded for me to decline his generous offer. It would have been hard to stomach a third setback, with borrowed personnel to boot.

My first attempts at acting occurred at Mr. Gibbs', but I was averred by the mistress in charge of dramatics to have but little talent. As a consequence I was compelled to make my debut masked, playing the role of a pig in some dramatized nursery rhyme, which I did adequately according to the school reports. I have had many bad notices since, but I do not think one can argue that one started one's career from the bottom with any more eloquent proof than to produce a document stating that one was adequate in the part of a pig.

When finally unmasked, I was typecast in the part of Friar Tuck, and my first apotheosis, or perhaps farewell performance, was as one of three nymphs tempting Ulysses from an Aegean beach. I was the one with blond tresses, stage left, who sang flat. Ulysses wisely passed us by.

On the whole, my stay at Mr. Gibbs' was a happy time for me. During the day, at all events, I was away from the pressures and problems of home, and although I still made my scheduled appearances in pajamas at dinner parties to give my imitations, the intrusions into the privacy of the bathtub were now few and far between. Contact with other boys of my age gave me a release from my introversion, although a certain timidity has stayed with me to this day. I was, I believe, fairly popular with both the masters and boys, and even if certain subjects like mathematics, algebra, and up to a point, Latin, gave me great difficulties, I was always top in ge-

ography, and near the top in French, history, and English. Mr.
Gibbs was a charming old gentleman, in spite of his belief in corporal punishment and the sanctity of the Boy Scout movement. He
used to invite the senior boys to camp on the grounds of his house at
Goring-on-Thames and drove us down there in his copious Austin
tourer. His absentmindedness made him a very dangerous, very
slow driver, and since I was often seated next to him, he was known
to change gears with my kneecap, then fail to understand why the
engine raced or stalled. We would stop by the roadside while he examined the carburetor, attributing to it the fault which was his
own — and mine, I suppose, for having kneecaps that resembled
the gearshift of an Austin Heavy Twelve.

Everything within this academy was safe and sunlit. The values
were as certain as they had been for years, and even if they seemed
vaguely ridiculous, they had longevity and usage to speak for them.
Nobody questioned the rectitude of King or Country, and both
Jesus and the Boy Scout seemed in place, as indeed did those por-
tions of the map colored red. The only questioning gaze (it was not
even a voice) was that of Mlle Chaussat, and what she had to offer
as an alternative was merely the same thing again in another guise,
the map painted green, a president with a tricolor sash, Marianne in
a Phrygian cap, a Jesus with drops of blood where the crown of
thorns had bitten into the skin, the bees and eagles of L'Empereur.

Because of that "von" before my name, I was often taunted about
the defeat of Germany in what was then the Great War, but when
my colleagues felt they had gone too far, they flattered me about the
cleanliness of the German trenches as compared with the unmitigated filth of the French ones, which seemed the only message their
fathers had learned from the holocaust. Once again, when Caracciola
won a race in his supercharged white Mercedes-Benz, I was con-
gratulated as though I had been at the wheel, whereas when the
team of green Bentleys won, I received formal condolences. "Hard
cheese, von Ustinov" from my acquaintances; "Better luck next
time, Oosti" from my friends.

I was, for some reason, the acknowledged expert on motorcars, being able to tell many makes by their sounds alone. In fact, in my younger years I *was* a motorcar, to the dismay of my parents. Psychiatry was in its infancy then, both expensive and centered in Vienna. There was no one yet qualified to exorcise an internal combustion engine from a small boy. I know to this day precisely what make of car I was: an Amilcar. Why I chose this spindly little vehicle, with its look of an angry insect, I do not know, but I suspect it was a dream-wish for a tubby little fellow constantly teased about his nascent corpulence to transmogrify himself into a svelte and insubstantial *"bolide."*

At one period of my life, I switched on in the morning and only stopped being a car at night when I reversed into bed and cut the ignition. It was an admirable escape. I avoided answering questions, and every other contact, rational or unreasonable. It was a luxury I could afford in a safe and immobile world.

It was only during the holidays that the anxieties began, with evidence of another, unhappy, part of existence, away from the handclasp of an Anglo-Saxon Jesus, the lime-flavored water-ices, the smell of new-mown grass on the cricket patch, and the reassurance of Mr. Gibbs' uncertain bel canto.

When I was seven years old, we went to Estonia for our summer holiday, my mother and I. No paints were taken. Estonia was then, briefly, an independent republic on the Baltic. Its capital, Tallinn, better known under the Russians and the Teutonic Knights as Revel, was and is a lovely city, compact and crenellated, redolent of the commercial acumen of medieval and pre-medieval northern traders. The country people came to town and walked about barefoot, carrying their shoes in their hands to show they were the proud possessors of such marks of civilization, while, in the neighboring countryside, horses would still bolt at the sight of motorcars.

Our purpose in coming to this attractive little country was that my mother's father, Professor Louis Benois, principal of the Academy of Arts in Leningrad, was allowed by the Soviet government to leave the national territory as far as Estonia for a period of one month because of his advanced age and contribution to the Soviet arts. We stayed in a dacha in the middle of a forest and lived a pre-revolutionary Russian life for a while. The raised wooden veranda with its peeling paint and splintering steps, which groaned and creaked at every footfall, was straight out of some Chekhov stage set. The forest whispered, sighed, and sometimes roared. It was infested with adders and mushrooms, both poisonous and edible. To be lost in it was to be lost in a fairy tale, an impenetrable continent of unidentified noises and lingering menace, a taunting, chattering, cajoling prison which seemed to move with you and trick all sense of orientation. Through it, with luck, one could find the sea, a gray primeval shore of clay and boulders washed by fussy waters. It was possible to sculpt with the clay of the beach. Most people bathed and sculpted naked, only dressing again to meet the hazards of the forest and the journey home.

The pervading odors of the dacha were those of mushrooms and of apples drying in the barn, a sweet and pungent mixture which I can recall instantly to this day.

My grandfather made a great impression on me, since he exuded severity and balance despite his age and ill health. I saw him feebly swatting some flies which circled in great number over our bowls of milk, some left to turn to yogurt. He explained to me that flies were the harbingers of disease and that it was man's duty to protect himself against these harmless-looking annoyances. I took the fly-swatter from him and began laying about me with all the vigor of my young years. After a short while he indicated it was time to stop the chase. Disappointed, I asked him why.

"Because now you are beginning to take pleasure in what you are doing and killing can never be allowed to become a pleasure."

"How about the disease?" I asked hopefully.

"Better we should become ill than that we should take pleasure in the death of living things," he replied quietly, and that was that.

My mother had a toothache one day, an abscess I believe, whereas the engine of my Amilcar was in particularly fine fettle. I changed gear on every conceivable occasion, revving up as I came to every bend in the road and hooting with my simulated Klaxon to warn oncoming traffic of my presence. Suddenly my mother could bear it no more.

"For God's sake, shut up for a moment!" she cried from the depths of a yellow cloche hat.

Her father, who was walking slowly with us, held up an admonishing hand.

"Never shout at him!" he instructed his daughter quietly. "I know it is irritating, even without a toothache, dear child. But don't think of it as the sound of an automobile; think of it rather as the sound of his imagination developing and then, you will see, it will become bearable."

I understand now why he was known as a great teacher, and I felt even then an immense empathy for him and his undemonstrative wisdom.

Back in London, I agitated for a tie other than the cherry-red school one which I had to wear on every occasion. I longed for a multicolored striped or polka-dot one like my father's. Eventually my mother surrendered and gave me a little money. I went to Harrod's department store with Frieda and unaccountably returned wearing a black tie. I found my mother in tears, having received a cable ten minutes before my return that her father had died peaceably in Leningrad.

On later holidays, we were compelled to go to Germany so that my father could report to his directors, a Herr Dietz who lived in Cologne, and a Herr Heller who lived in Berlin. I remember little about those people except the rasping sound of German when it is spoken in the intolerant, dogmatic voice of officialdom, and the querulous diapason of the ladies when they add what they imagine to be a human or sentimental note to the necessary noisiness of the men. I do recollect having to go to the toilet at the house of Herr Heller, who had a reputation for stinginess. This was confirmed when I discovered that the toilet paper was composed of quartered sheets of typing paper with holes in one corner, through which a piece of string attached them to a nail arbitrarily driven into the bathroom wall. These pieces of paper were covered in messages printed in violet ink, many of them marked "Secret" and some of them "Most Secret." How much simpler a method of disposal than all the latter-day complications thought up by those involved in the activities of the CIA and FBI! And they say we have advanced in technology!

On that same day, there was a ticker-tape parade in Berlin for a fearless aviatrix of the period called, if I remember rightly, Elly Beinhorn, who had flown from somewhere to somewhere else without incident, thereby advancing the cause of German technology. I watched the parade from Herr Heller's window and saw Hindenburg himself, yellow and immobile in his car, looking as though he had been inflated like a mattress.

On my grandfather's death, his widow received permission from the Soviet government to emigrate to Berlin, where her daughter, my aunt Olga, lived as a hospital X-ray technician. My mother and I visited them in 1933, when I was twelve. Germany was already in a turmoil. Truckloads of horrid-looking men, packed like sardines in a complicity which had something obscene about it, drove through the streets shouting *"Deutschland, erwache!"* ("Germany, awake!"). If groups of grown men could find no better pastime than that, it boded ill for the rest of us. Jewish shops had already had their windows smashed by the more ardent of these idiots, and the public was weary of the complications of an increasingly impotent democracy. Everything was ugly and ill-natured.

Naturally my aunt went out of her way to find friends of my own age for me, but unfortunately it is no easier to impose friends on children than it is on adults. She found me the son of a neighbor, a brawny little fellow with his hair cut in a *"Berliner Schnitt,"* rather long on top and shaved to above the ears, the most unaesthetic of all coiffures. He introduced me to his best friend, who was Jewish. It was a few days before the Reichstag fire.

We went into the Grünewald to play, at what I had no idea. As we strolled among the trees, we talked politics. The young neighbor was a convinced Nazi, and spoke highly of the new Germany that would rise from the shameful embers of Versailles. What he said and also the way he said it seemed imitated from a source both authoritative and obtuse, probably his father. He also made some long-winded declarations about the purity of the race and explained how from time immemorial the Jews had infiltrated into the lifeblood of the German people like amoebas, and that the time had come to remove this foreign body. Surprisingly enough, the Jewish boy agreed with him, nodding the while and assuring me it was all true.

The wood seemed full of young people training German shepherds, throwing sticks, shouting, making signs. In flurries of leaves these bounding dogs would appear, almost fall over in their dripping eagerness to obey, and leap out of sight again, gripping some object in their fangs. Far from being a place of sylvan repose, the Grüne-wald was a training ground for some of the wild excesses yet to come. The shepherds were immense, of heroic mold, and bent to the will of the sheep who exercised them. A group of youths stamped by, singing an old folk song, now syncopated in the rhythm of a march. Not boy scouts, I was told, but *Wandervögel,* and their kindly light was beginning to glow from a thousand braziers in Nuremberg.

My two imposed chums lit cigarettes stolen from home, and they told me they did it deliberately to excite the attention of the forest-watcher, who was a pervert seeking any excuse to tie small boys over an ironing board he kept in his forest hut and belabor their buttocks with a rattan cane. While he flagellated them, he would lecture them on the evils of smoking, or masturbation, or whatever else he had caught them at. After this explanation, the boys offered me a cigarette they had kindly stolen for me, an offer I gratefully declined. I nevertheless kept my eyes open for the forest-watcher, since I was rather less enthusiastic about his hobbies than the two boys who explained the delights of being flogged with many lurid details, although they admitted they had never been caught nor did they even know what the evil forest-watcher looked like. It was all part of the underground folklore which fitted all too well with the regimented hounds and the militarized Schubert in the innocent frame of the German forest.

What happened next was to sicken me for good and all. Laying the ranting and the erotica aside, they passed from the theoretical to the practical. They realized they would have to part, like star-crossed lovers, since the weight of race and geopolitics lay too heavy in the balance; mere personal affection had to make way for great historical realities. They had come to a secluded spot for their pale variation on the *Liebestod*, inventing a ritual both repugnant by its ambition and risible by its inadequacy. After they had sworn eternal brotherhood, whatever destiny held in store for them, they proceeded to cut their veins with a rusty kitchen knife in order to allow their bloods to mingle in an irrefutable gesture of union. Since I had no reason to suppose they knew the difference between veins and arteries, and more importantly since I felt I was going to vomit, I ran all the way home, defying the angry perplexity of the dogs, who were excited by rapid motion.

"Butterfingers" cried the angry spectators as I dropped the ball for perhaps the thousandth time during one of my last games of cricket at Mr. Gibbs'. I could smile. Everyone knew in their hearts now that I was going to drop the ball anyway, and nobody expected me to be able to play the game. Foreign origin, you know. They also failed to realize for far too long that, away from the whimsicality and absurd charm of Mr. Gibbs' playing fields, others of foreign origin were beginning to invent other games played to other rules, and eventually, to no rules whatsoever.

5

I HAD the choice, said my parents, who couldn't afford either, between St. Paul's and Westminster School. Students at the former
wore straw hats, like Harold Lloyd; the latter, top hats like Fred Astaire. I thought that once I was to look ridiculous, I might as well
look utterly ridiculous, and opted for Westminster. Officially I was
not yet quite of a height to warrant a tailcoat, but since I was
believed to be still growing, I was spared the ignominious bum-
freezer reserved for smaller lads, a kind of black bolero with a collar
spilling over the top like froth from a Guinness. As the greater of
minute mercies I was given the clothes of an undertaker, together
with a furled umbrella, in order, so the school brochure explained,
to distinguish the boys from City of London Bank messengers. The
final mockery on the head of a fourteen-year-old boy was a top hat,
a crown of thorns if not a calvary, especially if your daily way to school
took you through a virtual slum.

But there, for a year and a half, my parents wanted me both at
home and away, the clearest indication of a love-hate relationship;
and so I was sent away to school, not where my lungs might fill with
ozone or my skin might burn in the wind, but a tuppenny bus ride

from home. Of all possible compromises this was the most ludicrous and, for me, the most onerous. Far away I might have become used to new surroundings much more quickly, and reveled in a relative independence, become what they like to call a man, but this was frankly impossible in the shadow of Big Ben, with a bus stop just underneath the window of my dormitory, and my bus stopping there every five minutes.

Westminster is an exclusive school that has advanced rather happily with the times. It comprises both day boys and boarders and nestles in secrecy amid the ecclesiastical surroundings of what might be called the Kremlin of Westminster Abbey. There are arches galore on which to hit your head, steps of time-worn irregularity on which to break your neck, portraits of dead clerics before which to lose your faith. Owing to the proximity of Church House, the quiet bit of greenery known as Little Dean's Yard was invariably the striding ground of deans and bishops in couples, discussing some new posting or administrative detail in terms of opulent secrecy. And there was endless choir practice to rend the air, some of the most appalling sharps and flats ever emanating from the unbroken voices of unhappy cherubim behind stained glass, evilly lit.

When all the boys were awaiting the daily morning prayers in the abbey, we looked like a migration of crows which had made a haphazard landing in a field. The pervading atmosphere was doggedly morose and gothic and our faces began to show the premature signs of that nervous affectation which passes for breeding. This impression was enhanced by the fact that many sons of Members of Parliament were sent to Westminster, so that, whereas their fathers were gripping their lapels in portentous and jowly gravity a stone's throw away in the House of Commons, the offspring were busy imitating their fathers in school debates, waving notes instead of order papers and bending their treble voices into all the respectable mannerisms of British oratory.

"Indiah — " some piping voice would declare, and pause, while its owner, stooped with a premature bookishness, would scan the listeners for signs of inattention — "Indiah" it would repeat, to drive home a point which needed no driving — "Indiah cannot be accorded home rule at this — ah — time." And a groan of "Hear, hears" would rise from the audience, punctuated by solitary bleats of "Shame" from enlightened boy sopranos. I understood very quickly the purpose of education such as this when I was called aside by a master to tell me that I would be involved in a debate, in order to second the motion that "The Death Sentence Should Be Retained as a Deterrent." I informed the master in charge of debates that I was categorically opposed to the death sentence in all its forms, on moral grounds.

"That may be," said the master in a silky voice, "but you are still seconding the motion in favor of retention."

"I don't understand, sir — "

"You will," he chanted quietly and left.

I realized then that this was a school in which lawyers, diplomats, and businessmen were formed and there was no room here for the sloppy thinking of those who wished to change society.

I made what I deemed was an excellent speech against the death sentence, but such was the bloodthirsty temper of the times that there was an overwhelming vote in favor of retention, and my reputation as a debater rose in spite of what I had said. My eyes met those of the master. He was smiling slightly and nodded his congratulation at the victory of my side. I was being prepared for life, in more ways than one.

When new boys arrived, they were entertained at tea by the headmaster, who was at that time a clergyman of advanced age with a permanent grin of considerable intensity on his face. I have no doubt that the Very Reverend Dr. Costley-White was a good man, but he was also a big man, who walked quickly, so that the wind would make his black gown billow behind him, while the tassel on his mortarboard spread over his face like a claw. He frankly terrified new boys. When, during that initial tea party, he called out "Will no boy select the chocolate éclair?" there was no response, because no boy dared. "Oh very well," cried Dr. Costley-White and ate it himself.

After that benign and warmhearted introduction to my new school, my hopes rose, in spite of being what was known as a "fag" (not to be confused with the modern American usage of the word as a camp description of a homosexual; a fag in England was either a cigarette or else the nearest thing to a slave since William Wilberforce — a small boy at the beck and call of a big one). I was serving some kippers to the prefects in the medieval dining hall, which was one of the functions of fagging, when Dr. Costley-White swept into the room, his landing flaps down and his hat at a jaunty angle. His smile was spread from ear to ear as usual.

A pinup photo had been discovered, he bellowed, a pinup of a woman in a bathing costume, clutching a beach ball. He wished the perpetrator of this filth to own up at once. There was, of course, silence.

"Very well," he declared, as his smile attained even more extraordinary proportions, "When the culprit is found — and found, he will be — I shall beat him!" And then, very gently, as a summer breeze after a squall, "I am in the need of exercise."

As he turned to go, his gathering speed caused his gown to billow once again. I had the feeling he would take off as soon as he was out of sight.

Of course, what constitutes filth and the mysteries of sex have always been a cause of contention in British schools. An old friend and mentor, Sir Clifford Norton, told me about sex education in Rugby before the First World War. The headmaster, who must have been an enlightened man, summoned all the boys who had reached the age of puberty to his study and, after reassuring himself that the door was firmly secured, made the following brief announcement: "If you touch it, it will fall off."

The boys were then invited to file back into their classes, now equipped to face adult life.

Many years later, Britain was still irked by this elusive yet fascinating subject. Arriving at a theater for a performance of a play of mine, I ran into a fellow actor of our troupe, Cyril Luckham, a true friend and magnificent performer who happens also to have very fair skin and hair. He gave every evidence of having wept. It is always disturbing when grown men are reduced to tears, so I took him aside and asked him tactfully what was the matter. He replied that nothing was the matter apart from laughter which had been racking him intermittently for the past couple of hours; and of course laughter and tears leave very similar aftereffects, especially in those of fair pigmentation.

He let me in on the cause of his joy. It was, apparently, the first day of a new term at his son's school. The headmaster, obeying the instructions of a government by now aware of the dangers of ignorance, was compelled to explain the facts of life to those of a certain age group. The poor man had been rehearsing his speech all through the summer recess, and eventually, in a panic of prudery, unable to bear the sniggers he could already hear in his head, he was reduced to composing a pamphlet, published at his own expense, which every boy found lying on his desk as the new term began.

This pamphlet began with the following seven words: "You may have noticed, between your legs . . ."

This unreal atmosphere pervaded Westminster School, but the sheltered charm which had characterized Mr. Gibbs' had gone forever. Von Ribbentrop was the new German Ambassador in London, and as a good Nazi, hoped to send his son to Eton, perhaps in order to take photographs of the playing fields and find out exactly what Wellington had meant when he had alleged that Waterloo had been won there. Eton, jealous of its secrets, refused young Rudolf. The Ambassador, in a rage, demanded that the youth be taken at Westminster. Perhaps he had already bought his top hat, since these were worn in both places. At all events, the British government, in its habitual dither of appeasement, exerted pressure on Westminster to accept the lad, and lo, a hugh white Mercedes with external exhaust pipes panted its way into Little Dean's Yard every morning, picking its gargantuan way among the parked minicars of visiting bishops, and disgorged Rudolf, dressed like the rest of us, but with the Nazi party youth badge — swastika, eagle, and all — prominently and incongruously displayed in his lapel. For a moment he and the Embassy chauffeur would engage in hushed conversation, and then both would leap to attention, lift their right arms as though a military marriage were being celebrated beneath them, and shout "Heil Hitler!"; Rudolf would hurry in to morning prayers, while the chauffeur picked his way meticulously into the open traffic once again.

He was an overgrown and shy fellow with glasses, reddish hair, and freckles, who kept very much to himself, and yet it was impossible not to notice a smirk on his face as he walked past on the one day in the week devoted to the parade of the O.T.C., the Officer's Training Corps. Britain's well-bred youth were in training then, but if you were to ask what we were training for, I would be compelled to answer that it was for Dunkirk and a series of military disasters in the best tradition.

I stood stiffly to attention in my 1914 military uniform, my puttees either working loose, which occasioned a sense of relief, or else so tightly tied that all feeling had long since departed from my legs. My cap was pulled very low over my eyes, which is in the tradition of the Brigade of Guards and is supposed to give soldiers a correct military stance, although I privately believe it is to make the men share the blindness of their leaders. In my hand I carried a rattle, like those used by spectators at football matches. The reason for this was twofold; not only were there insufficient rifles to go around, but I represented an entire machine-gun company by myself.

Once a week I lay in the wet bracken in Richmond Park, swinging my rattle and killing thousands and thousands of adversaries — and occasionally, owing to my bulk, which was difficult to camouflage, being killed myself. In this way we were preparing for the next War to End Wars, alive to the most modern battle techniques and ready to "hit the Hun for six."

It was almost a relief to get back into the absurd costume of every day after these military masquerades. At least I could look Von Ribbentrop in the eye. Not far away, at the German Embassy, my father was in trouble with his father. By now promoted to the rank of press attaché, Klop was more and more frequently reprimanded for not distorting the news at source, but giving the editors in Berlin all the trouble. He was reaching the end of the line. With the help of Sir Robert Vansittart, he applied for British nationality secretly, printing his mandatory intention of doing so in a Welsh-language newspaper which defied the expertise of German Intelligence. One morning he walked out of the Embassy, never to return.

At precisely that time, young Von Ribbentrop entered the school art competition with an atrocious triptych depicting ancient Germans encamped before a blazing dawn, their horned helmets silhouetted against the red and mauve of the empyrean, while the breastplates of the flaxen-haired women were aglint with hateful optimism. This huge work was entitled "Armed Strength," and was, of course, totally devoid of mystery.

I earned my first money thanks to Von Rippentrop, which was perhaps justice, although hardly poetic. I wrote a piece about his artistic effort, an original manner for a young party-member to emulate his Führer, and sent it to the *Evening Standard*. They printed it, having altered it somewhat, I thought for the worse, and they sent me a letter asking if 7 shillings and sixpence would be adequate remuneration. I forgot to answer their letter, and they sent me £ 1, thereby rewarding both my malice and my procrastination.

There was an immediate upheaval at school. The German Embassy was, apparently, absolutely furious. The housemaster, a retired opera singer by name Mr. Bonhote, called me into his study. The school, as usual, was thoroughly ill-informed about the most recent events, and believed my father still to be an employee of the German Foreign Office. Mr. Bonhote asked me, in confidence, to bring the matter to my father's attention, in order to trace the identity of the culprit. The *Evening Standard* had evidently already refused to cast any light on the origin of the leak.

I didn't think the matter was of sufficient urgency to warrant my disturbing my father's peace of mind, and so I merely allowed a couple of weeks to elapse before returning to Mr. Bonhote in order to tell him that the most thorough investigation had failed to reveal the name of the villain. All I was able to confirm was that the German Embassy was, indeed, furious.

Mr. Bonhote grunted. "I can't help feeling that whoever is responsible will go far in life. Damned clever."

"Yes," I agreed gravely. "Still, one doesn't want to encourage that kind of thing, does one sir?"

"No," he replied; and then added with a twinkle, "Of course, some people don't need encouragement."

In a short while Von Ribbentrop returned to Germany and became foreign minister, and Rudolf departed with his father to complete his preparations for the conquest of the world.

My father had, meanwhile, fallen on evil days. I was withdrawn from the boarding section of the school to become a day boy because it was cheaper, and even then I had the uncomfortable feeling that my school bills had remained unpaid. The school behaved with exemplary elegance, however, never making me feel that the penury mattered or making my parents feel that their plight was in any way out of the ordinary.

Jobs were offered my father, but he couldn't hold them down. At one point he became art critic for the *News Chronicle,* and I knew perfectly well from his ranting behind my mother's easel and his inflexibly epicurean opinions that this could never last. At the end of his first week he poured scorn on a sculpture of Henry Moore's in his jocular and punning fashion, and was amazed at the uproar which ensued. That was that. He was then employed as an accountant at the Vaudeville Theatre. From his inability to help me with my homework, I could hold out no greater hope for this venture, and indeed, it too lasted a week.

I felt immensely sorry for him, since he was humiliated by his inactivity, which took the form of fits of anger interspersed with periods of sullenness. He considered my reports from school a disgrace, he continued to harp on his own prowess as a scholar, and he called me lazy, which was undeniably true. I had foolishly gone on the modern side as opposed to the classical side in school, simply because two or three of my friends had taken that course, and now I was faced by mathematics, physics, and science on an unprecedented scale.

Of physics I could understand nothing at all. Why imaginary wheels should gather speed running down hypothetical slopes and create friction, I could neither understand in the terms in which it was taught, nor care about. As for chemistry, the acrid smell of the lab made me queasy to start with and I was always distinctly nervous of spilling any substance smelling stronger than water on my fingers.

The master in charge of science was named F. O. M. Earp, from which his nickname of Fome, or Foam. He was a man so utterly dedicated to the abstractions of science that he would often point a finger between two boys and tell "that boy" to see him afterward. Since he never managed to aim at anyone in particular, nobody ever came to see him. By then he had forgotten the incident anyway. Once he mixed a couple of liquids in a test tube. There was a most resounding explosion, breaking several panes of glass in the lab. When the smoke cleared, there was no sign of Fome. He had disappeared, as in a fairy tale. There was an audible gasp from the boys, caught between shock and laughter. Then, slowly, he emerged from behind his desk, black, singed, and disheveled. "What did I do wrong, you!" he said in unemotional tones, pointing between me and my neighbor.

The whole classroom broke into a roar of relieved laughter.

Fome did not even smile.

"Come and see me afterwards, the boy responsible for the laughter."

Needless to say, I didn't, nor did my neighbor.

Owing to the shortage of teachers even then, Fome was supposed to teach not only chemistry but also divinity, of which he knew very little. He got around this difficulty, which might have daunted many less inventive spirits, especially in such unrelievedly ecclesiastical surroundings, by proceeding to explain most of Christ's miracles scientifically. It was clear from his attitude that even if he had mustered a little faith in Christ, he had absolutely none in the miracles. I do not remember in detail every one of his explanations, but do recollect him attributing the illusion of water turning into wine to the surreptitious addition of permanganate of potash, which could quite easily have bamboozled a crowd of simpletons.

In the field of sports, I had put my name down for tennis, the only sport for which I felt any real affinity, but my request was refused owing to a limited number of courts available, and I was made to row. This seemed to me a monotonous and draughty pursuit, and somehow wasteful to make all that effort in order to be going in the wrong direction. It is, in any case, never very reassuring for a young person of my weight to be seated in a boat seemingly made of cigar wrappers, and to be overlapping its sides.

I eventually took an inadvertent revenge on my tormentors during a "friendly" encounter with the second or third eight of another school. The old boy who had presented the school with the boat I was rowing in was bicycling along the riverside pathway bellowing incomprehensible instructions to us through a megaphone. He was in his sixties and affected the dress of a schoolboy in order to give us the garbled weight of his experience. Meanwhile the other school slipped gradually from view. At first I could see nine men out of the corner of my eye, then eight, then seven, then eventually nothing but a little disturbed water.

Then came an end to my misery. The fragile little seat beneath me was derailed and fell sideways. I immediately "caught a crab," and in attempting to resist the pressure of the water on my oar, I pushed the wheel of my seat through the hull. We began sinking, and there is no sight more ludicrous than eight men, with a small ninth the size of a jockey facing them, settling gracefully into the water in Indian file. The veteran on the shore, who had spent a lot of money on the boat, moaned, but since the sound of his distress was distorted by the megaphone, he became as grotesque as everything else. We drifted helplessly into the side of a Dutch ship moored in the Thames, whose crew, far from helping us, bent over the rail and laid bets as to which of them could hit us squarely with gobs of spit. After that, miraculously, room was found for me on the tennis court. I learned yet another lesson.

I could at times beat members of the school tennis team in unofficial games, but I was only once on the team myself, and that was as a reserve. I came to the conclusion that there was something disconcerting about my personality as far as games masters were concerned, and that the undefinable quality which consistently got me out of trouble also kept me from being taken seriously as an athlete. Although I had inherited my mother's gifts as a sprinter, and had insufficient breath for the mile, and though my elevation and projection were entirely inadequate for jumps high or long, I was and — dare I say it? — even am surprisingly quick around the tennis court. In other words, when I see the point in moving quickly, I am capable of doing so.

In order to restore my morale, which was rather low at this time, I entered a tournament at a wonderfully nostalgic organization called the "Anglo-Russian Sports Club," where septuagenarian Czarist officers would lob each other to a standstill in immaculate whites. There was an aged Sergeant-Major in charge of the dressing room, bald as an egg, with a pointed white beard and a fixed pair of blue eyes, who would click his heels at the end of every curt sentence. He would take orders for kasha, blinis, and pickled herring in the canteen as well as leap at you with hot towels as you emerged from the tepid shower. Life was good on the *Potemkin* before the mutiny, at least for the officers. I won my little tournament, and a pile of ashtrays in various colors which I still guard jealously as though they were *objets* by Fabergé.

The reason my morale was low was not only due to frustrations, both at home and at school, but also to the ominous hurdle of examinations, called "O" levels today but called the School Certificate then, which plague youths in all countries and at all times. Rumors abounded then as they abound today. You couldn't even get a job as a dustman without one. In case of war, failure meant permanent relegation to the ranks. The majority of suicides in Japan were occasioned by a failure in exams. And so on and so forth.

There was little or no possibility of my passing them, at least on the modern side. Despite my prowess in certain subjects, I was absolutely without a vestige of hope in the general field of science and mathematics, and that was going to ruin my chances of advancement. At home, I hardly received any encouragement, although, to be fair, I doubt whether encouragement would have done much good.

My father's temper had become a little more equitable as he became used to the new situation. His counterattack against misfortune expressed itself in different ways. Once every few months he would declare that he was writing a novel. There was to be no noise in the flat. He settled in the living room while we tiptoed around the small space left over. At the end of the day he would emerge with a single page of foolscap, as full of corrections, scratchings, and emendations as a manuscript of Beethoven. He would then read the first page to us. When we had laughed — the style was unrelievedly epigrammatic — he would then read this page to visitors and guests over the next six weeks or so, until the novelty had worn off, when all would be quiet until the start of the next novel, and history repeated itself. It is not so much a matter of literary record as of interest to the *Guinness Book of Records* that my father wrote six or seven of the shortest novels ever.

When inspiration flagged, he involved himself in art-dealing, an area in which he was at first more enthusiastic than knowledgeable, but he quickly revealed something perhaps even more important than mere knowledge, which was flair. Although he made many minor errors of judgment, he would, on big occasions, take an atlas of the British Isles and a pin, and sit there like a medium awaiting a call. When he heard it he stabbed the atlas, put on his hat, took his walking stick, and left the flat in silence.

As a result of these mysterious celestial communications, he returned from Tewkesbury, of all places, with a Rubens study for the Farnese bull in sanguine, which he then sold to the Rijksmuseum in Amsterdam for £1,000, a very modest figure even for those days, but a magnificent windfall for him. He would then remain inactive, apart from perhaps a novel or two, until the money ran out, when he would once again reach for the atlas and the pin. Other jaunts into the English countryside produced several little oil sketches by Hogarth for Butler's "Hudibras," long lost, to say nothing of a Bonnington or two, a few Constantine Guys, a Daumier, and eventually a collection of Renaissance bronzes.

My mother seemed less affected by the events of the day than either of us, since it was she who kept our ship on a relatively even keel. Her reputation as a painter was established, and she was even represented in such reputable galleries as the Tate and the Carnegie Institute. Apart from her sale of pictures, she was known as a designer, especially for the ballet. Her work for the Ballet Rambert included *The Descent of Hebe, Bonnet over the Windmill, Lady into Fox,* and *Dark Elegies* for Anthony Tudor. When this last work was produced in America, under the extraordinary system then prevailing her designs and costumes were attributed to the distinguished American designer Raymond Sovey. I have never understood how a professional union could have so little respect for its own dignity or integrity to make rules like that. Are stage designers so much lower a species than painters pure and simple? If not, then why do the same ridiculous rules not apply to painters? Why are the Michelangelos in the National Gallery in Washington not attributed to Ben Shahn, or the Velázquezes to Jackson Pollack?

In any case, these are reflections out of context, based on a very ancient sense of outrage. At the time, I was merely shocked by the fact that my mother's work could not be appreciated as hers in the United States. She spent more and more time in the theater, doing many sketches in the wings of the Compagnie de Quinze, the French avant-garde troupe run by Michel Saint-Denis. He had just immigrated to England in order to open a drama school. My mother, who after all came from the Benois family as I have said, a clan that would have flinched had they thought for a moment that one of their scions was destined for the Stock Exchange, and would have suggested sculpture as a safer profession, now looked the facts squarely in the face. She recognized with a greater sense of reality that either Klop or I that I was not going to pass the School Certificate, and that it would cause the most terrible commotions in the household when the news of my failure was known. Why should I be put through this moral mangle, she argued, when I had no intention of being a chemist or a doctor or even a chartered accountant? Had I not held the attention of small audiences with my imitations? And what is the difference between small audiences and large ones except their size?

My father raised objections, of course, for the sake of form, but his energies were more and more taken with the inevitability of war. Distinguished Germans came to the flat to listen to Hitler's latest speeches and lament at the blindness of the Western democracies. Even at school, the ominous atmosphere made itself felt as the Spanish Civil War was going badly for the legitimate government of Spain, while the German and Italian dictatorships were being encouraged by our benign negligence to go from excess to excess.

Before I left Westminster, there were mock elections in my house, encouraged by the headmaster under the guise of citizenship. We all made speeches and campaigned; and whereas it was natural in such a school that the Conservatives would win, there was a feeling of shock and even of dismay at the showing of the Liberals and Socialists, especially when we united in a kind of Front Populaire to form what was called the United Front of Progressive Forces, or Uffpuff. The headmaster met our delegation to reassure himself that we were neither subversive nor undemocratic in spirit, and when he found we were merely exasperated with the smugness of the Conservative majority, he blessed us with one of his more extravagant smiles.

I mention this with absolutely no wish to attribute any importance to our activities, but it is rather remarkable in retrospect that feelings ran high in one of the nobler seats of learning as early as 1937, and that the young were almost equally divided between unflinching support for the appeasement of Mr. Chamberlain and a desire to resist aggression before it was too late. There were those, young and inexperienced and foolish in many other ways, who were wise before the event.

I did not participate in many of the subsequent arguments, because I took an audition at Michel Saint-Denis's academy at Islington. Typically, I failed to understand the terms of the audition. One of the stipulations was to choose a page of any celebrated drama and learn it by heart. It did not occur to me that I was supposed to learn a single part, and that the other parts would be read by senior students, so I just took an arbitrary page of Shaw's *Saint Joan* and learned all the parts. My procedure seemed to amuse Michel Saint-Denis and George Devine, who was one of the other professors, and I was accepted even though they considered me, at sixteen, to be on the young side.

My mother begged them to take me, adding that, in her opinion, I had eyes very like M. Saint-Denis.

The great man studied me shamelessly through the swirling smoke of his pipe, and agreed.

"He has good eyes," he said in his French accent, and then added, with a sense of drama — "But, you realize, Nadia, that there will be divorce, there will be unpleasantness, there will be scandal, but *it must be like that!*"

His eyes lifted heavenward to await confirmation of his mystique, and I was launched into the world of adults, even if I was a little on the young side.

You have been quiet for a long while now.

I have been reflecting on various aspects of your story, and reflecting mainly on the kind of tricks which memory plays — not memory perhaps as much as time.

Have you spotted any inaccuracies?

Oh, inaccuracies there are bound to be in the story of one man, because after all, most things in life are matters of opinion. No, it is not that which disturbs me. Take Westminster School, for instance, and Mr. Gibbs' Preparatory School for Boys. Did we hate them or love them? Or perhaps, were we indifferent in the main?

There were days on which we loved them, Gibbs more than Westminster perhaps, and days we hated them, Westminster perhaps more than Gibbs, and yet on the whole they were ways of life, inevitable, boring, routine, which we had no strong feelings about.

Indifference then?

Not indifference exactly; you can't live in the shadow of punishment or indeed reward and be indifferent.

D'you remember that horrid boy who used to stick a rusty hypodermic needle into his victims?

Indeed I do. Lived in Markham Square.

Absolutely correct. Name of —

Quiet! He's probably a high court judge by now, and utterly respectable. That dangerous needle may have been his first and only, and perhaps even necessary, contact with crime.

You never can tell. Remember that timid boy, Wakeford, with an inability to pronounce his r's? Victoria Cross. Heroism in battle.

Exactly. And that joyous little gnome, Wedgwood Benn? And Michael Flanders, agile and slim in pre-polio days? Only Donald Swann hasn't changed at all.

Well, there you are. We know what we feel about these colleagues now. What did we feel about them then?

Much the same as we feel today. Remember that fellow, such a great buddy of yours at school, who burst into your dressing room in Boston, and turned out to have become saturated in alcohol?

Yes, of course I remember, since he didn't confine himself to Boston. He burst into your dressing room in Toronto and London as well, lamenting that he'd just lost his job with the airlines.

What was he?

A pilot, I believe.

Yes, well, there you are. Among my matters of reflection while you have been busy with your narrative are friends. Contrary to general belief, I do not believe that friends are necessarily the people you like best, they are merely the people who got there first. Most of my friends have faults which are all the more blatant because of their proximity, and yet they are people you are never out for if they ring. Even with your drunk, you let him into your dressing room on three different occasions because you were animated by ancient and guilty feelings of friendship. And yet there are many people you meet casually with whom you could be the best of friends if only you had met them sooner. All in all, I don't believe you choose your friends any more than you choose your parents. After all, if you were able to choose your friends with the same application and caution with which you choose your wife, you'd have antagonized most of them years ago, and lost them. No, no, you drift into friendships and there is no divorce. You are stuck with most of them for life. And friendship revives quickly even after a long absence, often with people who are entirely reprehensible, unreliable, and even spiteful.

Does that mean you are opposed to friendship?

On the contrary, I wouldn't know what to do without it. Sometimes a friend will ask — usually after making a normal gesture to which he wishes to attribute abnormal or even charitable characteristics — "After all, what are friends for?" I'll tell him what friends are for. They are there to remind each and every one of us of the imperfections which surround us, of the vagaries of human nature, the unpleasantness of which man is capable, the meanness, the narrowness, the hypocrisy of society; and they also teach us to forgive, but never to forget. We would all be lost without friendship.

How about pets, what are they for? Our *dumb* friends?

They remind us that whereas man, alas, is an animal, animals, thank God, are not men.

With all that liveliness in you, how can you even discuss indifference?

You cannot have opinions about everything under the sun. You cannot be interested in everything. There just isn't the energy. And one aspect about living which psychologists too often ignore is stamina. Why is only the object you are looking at in focus? It would be too exhausting to have everything in your field of vision in focus all the time. Why do you daydream? To recover your strength—permanent attention is impossible. Even the eyelid blinks. And so it is with our emotions. There may be a time to love and time to hate, but most of the time is spent doing neither. Indifference is restful when it is negative, insulting when it is positive. It can be cultivated. Voltaire could have said, *"Il faut cultiver son désert."* I would be willing to swear that more tragedies are due to human indifference than to human engagement, and yet, it is the guardian of our balance, the bandage around our ills, the refuge in the maelstrom.

Are you indifferent then?

I can be passionate now about that which I treated with indifference then.

Why?

Perhaps because had I spent my passion on such people, places, or events long ago, I might have been left with only indifference today. It's all a question of stamina.

Stamina?

6

IT was a new and invigorating experience to go to school dressed as I wished. Since I had only one suit, however, bought from an organization of lunatic optimism called the Fifty Shilling Tailors, this solitary mark of independence constituted a uniform of a kind. It was not until I had scraped together enough to purchase some gray flannel trousers and a tawdry blazer that I felt the full flush of liberty. I, who was unused to the problems of choice, was often minutes late for class, largely because I couldn't decide which of my two outfits to wear.

Money was, of course, yet another problem. Earlier, in an unaccustomed fit of paternal munificence, my father had solemnly proclaimed that the time had come for me to receive pocket money. He then produced a shilling out of his pocket, and told me that this would be my weekly salary. I was, not unnaturally, as delighted by the gesture as I was disappointed by the amount. As an avid listener to my father's novels, I could have spared myself my emotions, however, since this shilling was the first and last pocket money I ever received. Whenever I reminded Klop of it, he either denied that a week had yet elapsed since my last payment ("What payment?

Don't be impertinent!") or else told me in no uncertain terms that I was a spendthrift and a wastrel, which was a little like telling Gandhi he was overweight.

It was not that he was in any sense stingy, it was just that the possession of money did not seem to him an important step on the way to civilized living. And once he did not admit the perils of poverty to his own well-being, there was no reason why he should admit them for those less gifted than he in the refusal of reality. It was for that reason that I sometimes wished he would realize that he was poor instead of being that most nerve-racking of phenomena, a rich man without money. And yet, one could hardly blame him for looking facts in the face and seeing nothing. Even if it gave me moments of anxiety, there was always the consolation that he was affected not at all by penury. Humiliations, real or imagined slights, indignities, offenses, all took their toll of him, but when short of cash he merely slapped his pockets as though trying to trace elusive assets which had never been there, and expressed irritation that other people had no sense of order. Then, his wallet empty, he went shopping and invited people to dinner.

Naturally, anybody with any financial sense at all will realize that I couldn't have survived on no money whatsoever, especially as my drama school was at the other end of London. It was, of course, my mother who gave me what she could from secret funds — the sale of a picture, housekeeping money, dribs and drabs. God only knows how she made sense of it all, puffing at her easel with incredible serenity, cigarette smoke coiling up to the ceiling, closed by now even to my father's counsels. Perhaps it was the Revolution that had taught her to live for the moment, without ever succumbing to the temptation of living in moments past as did so many other emigrés.

My requests for money were never exorbitant. I had too much respect for the difficulties of living for that, but of course, quite apart from my newfound freedom of dress, I was for the first time plunged into the world of girls.

I had been to dances, where I had been an active and determined wallflower, believing that the bodily contacts of waltz and tango went for naught once the mind was fully occupied in chopping out a complicated rhythm. In other words, I was not a natural dancer, by shape or inclination. To me, it was more mathematics than choreography, and the penalty for an error was more palpable and eloquent than it had been at school — a tearing of delicate material or a howl of agony. I even found the courage, at a later date, to decline a charming invitation (or should it be a command?) to dance with the Queen by warning her of the physical dangers attendant on such an initiative. British democracy having matured over the centuries, my distress was greeted with a gracious smile by Elizabeth II, whereas under Elizabeth I it would no doubt have cost me my head, although, to be fair, I would have had less compunction in trotting out a gay galliard with Elizabeth I, since the volume of her clothes would have made it an act of positive malevolence instead of one of mere incompetence to have flattened her royal toes.

I had even, on holiday, bathed naked in mountain pools with girls and women, under the aegis of a nature-loving godmother, whose hiking habits invariably ended in some glacial mountain torrent as an act of communion with the earth; but again, the numbing temperature of the water took the same precedence as had the rhythm in the dance, to the exclusion of all other possible emotions.

Here, at drama school, I was for the first time exposed to the permanent presence of a veritable battalion of girls, all dressed on the first day of term in black bathing costumes — all that is, except one, a Canadian girl called Betty; I will refrain from identifying her further — whose black costume had not yet arrived and who crouched among us in salmon-pink bloomers and a bra, looking like a Rubens nymph who had wandered into a sinister witches' coven by mistake.

Real life had begun, very late in life; and in the happy absence of my father, my eye could wander over the graceful features unguided and free from extraneous comment. I needed pocket money as never before.

I was not irresistibly drawn to the drama. It was an escape road from the dismal rat race of school, but I never understood how actors learn all those lines, and, I must admit, I do not understand it to this day, any more than I understand how a pianist remembers all those notes. I had, however, started writing plays at school. The first one, I remember, was a comedy-farce-melodrama-tragedy involving Chicago gangsters in the English countryside. It was fifteen pages long, and designed as a full-length play. There were four or five deaths per page, which meant that it had a huge, expendable cast. I was caught writing it during a mathematics lesson at Westminster, and punished by being forced to stay late. Since I was the only boy so punished on that particular day, the master in charge of the punishment class felt himself victimized and left me to my own devices, which merely meant that for once I could continue writing under virtually ideal circumstances. The school had the last laugh, however, since the play was lousy.

After that, I had written others: a play called "Jackson," a somewhat Priestleyish affair about an average man, but as I knew nothing about average men, it turned out rather peculiar; a Pirandello-like drama entitled "Uneasy Lies the Head," in which the characters created by a reprehensible dramatist come to life and badger him into an introspective suicide; a drama in verse about Maximilian of Mexico called, unavoidably, "La Paloma"; and the most indicative if not the best of a particularly poor lot, the only autobiographical work I have ever written in the guise of fiction, a play called "Trio" about a father, a mother, and a son, in which there was more bickering and more mental and physical disorder than in *Look Back in Anger*, and, of course, far less dramatic discipline as well.

If it did nothing else for me, my work on this play, which was never finished, convinced me that my one aim in life was to leave home. I did not for a moment wish to run away. I am not the type, and in any case, it was too late for gestures. I wished to continue the contact with my parents, who fascinated me, from a position of dignity and independence. I also felt, rightly or wrongly, that my absence would enable my parents to rediscover what they had first seen in each other during the brief nine months before I arrived to complicate things.

I had been treated as a childlike adult for so long that I had an enormous impatience to be responsible for myself, and to be professional. I admired my mother's application, her staying power, the ability to outlast a problem — the heritage of centuries of artisans, from architects to pastrycooks, from court musicians to makers of cheese for family consumption, each function as important as the other; a balance to be found between logic and inspiration in infinite patience and infinite pains; the state of grace which comes with utter concentration.

At the same time, I mistrusted my father's facility, his mercurial and whimsical changes of direction as his mind was blown weightlessly hither and thither during the social banter in which he so excelled. He was a delight to his friends; perhaps even more so to his acquaintances. It was only in company that he flourished, with an impermanent radiance peculiar to him, merely to relapse into an illtempered, querulous gloom when the last guest had departed.

I knew that I had both these elements within myself, the dogged and tenacious as well as the urbane, and with the earnestness of youth I set about consciously making the best of the turmoil of my natural inheritance. Already at Mr. Gibbs' school I had become sickened by my own cowardice, my squeamishness in the face of pain, my panic when confronted by strange dogs or flying cricket balls, and I had deliberately — to my watching mother's horror — entered the school diving competition without knowing the first thing about it. I had climbed up to the highest diving board, and with all the school and all the parents watching, there was no way back. From up there I saw the green water below, which looked much like a stamp on an envelope, and I wondered what guarantee there was that I would not miss the water altogether and end up a red smudge on the gleaming tiles. Taking myself by surprise — it was the only way to do it — I made a graceful gesture in the air, rather like the Rolls-Royce mascot, and fell, a tangled ball of flesh, until I heard a tremendous explosion and fingers of chlorine bored their way brutally into my nostrils. My stomach felt as though it had been unzipped. "You must remember to keep your feet together," called out the expert, but I could hardly hear him over the wailing sirens in my ears.

Nobody was to know, in spite of their amused smiles, that what had really occurred in that swimming pool was a victory that I had won over myself, even if I brought myself and my house no glory. Now I had another kind of timidity to conquer: the absurd and the unnecessary one in the face of girls. I felt for the wretched Betty, crouching like Susannah in her salmon-pink lingerie on the first day of a new life for us all. It could not have happened to a less fortunate victim.

Whenever we had to read from classical texts, she was invariably selected for the interpretation of amorous or, what was worse, suggestive poetry by the saucy giants of the past, and even discreet references like "the sweet disorder of her dress" caused the unhappy Betty to stammer and to giggle, turning a deep accusing red, and casting a veil of embarrassment about her. Her calvary came in a play of Beaumont and Fletcher, when her partner in a dramatic text was supposed to say "Then will I pay a visit to the Low Countries," a thinly disguised reference not to the Netherlands so much as to the nether reaches of the human body. This was too much for poor Betty, whose convulsive giggles eventually turned to bitter tears. I hope she is happily married, far from the coaxing reach of libertine poets, for she helped me to realize that my problems were negligible compared with some.

Michel Saint-Denis, a tweedy Frenchman with a short Roman nose, nostrils flared like a nervous horse, teeth gripping a dribbling pipe, short yellow hair covering his huge head and lapping over his neck like little waves, was a formidable figure, dedicated to the theater as a priest is dedicated to his God. There was permanent amusement in his eye, a lip twisted to accommodate the pipe, and the dangerous look of a minotaur assessing the quality of the human sacrifices offered up for his gratification.

For one whole term, we were asked to be an animal of our choice, in order to "broaden our imaginations." The more ambitious and energetic pupils selected wild predators or gossamer victims, according to their temperaments. Poor Betty trotted around as an elk from her native plains, entangling her antlers with imaginary thickets and being hunted by erotic braves, while a South African girl with acne outran Betty in both speed and archness as an okapi. She ended the term pounds lighter and in a depressed frame of mind.

Gifted with my habitual foresight in the face of the unusual, I decided to be a salamander, and just dozed comfortably in the sun for three whole months, occasionally tilting a quizzical eye at the members of the faculty, and darting out my tongue to ensnare an unwary fly. This exercise certainly revealed more about my character than it did about what goes on in the heads of lizards.

There was, at the beginning, a great and salutary emphasis on physical suppleness, an art in which we were instructred by a little lady called Gerda Rink, who worked on my discordant limbs as though I had the makings of a Nijinsky. Her patience and kindness were rewarded as far as I was able, which was not much, although I did become aware of the possibilities of physical coordination, and recognize its importance for an actor.

A Mr. Scott and Miss Iris Warren worked hard on our breathing and our voices, my own gradually increasing in power from the inaudible mumbling which my natural shyness had imposed upon me. I made slow yet perceptible progress in the purely physical branches of my chosen art, but the reports were perhaps more penetrating and unkind than any I had yet received at Westminster or Mr. Gibbs'.

"Has a long way to go." "He is still lamentably stiff." "He seems to find great difficulty in walking, or running, or jumping." "His mind wanders easily during gymnastics." "His voice is unresonant and very monotonous." There was no end to the well-meaning but stern prognostications about the dimness of my prospects, and my father, who had by now abandoned his monocle for glasses for fear of appearing Prussian, read these remarks with growing alarm.

"At your age," he would say, "I was supple as a willow, I jumped, ran, and walked most outstandingly, my mind never wandered whatever the subject, my voice was powerful and sparkling with color. Nothing will come of you. Nothing."

He had gained in assurance since he had now found employment, the nature of which was so secret that it was obvious. There were often strange visitors in our flat, English colonels with so little to say that their very appearance seemed like an uncrackable code, foreign gentlemen who darted meaning looks at each other then quickly pretended they hadn't. An aura of the unspoken and the unspeakable hung over our home, and I was exhorted to ask no questions, ever, which, of course, automatically gave me half the answers.

When my father had left the German Foreign Office, several important Englishmen, including Sir Roderick Jones, the head of Reuter's, had declined to sponsor my father's application for British nationality, on the grounds that such an initiative on their part might have "offended the German government." Sir Robert Vansittart had no such scruples in the face of Nazi sensibilities. Consequently when Klop left the German Embassy for the last time, he did so with a British passport already in his pocket. The immediate reaction of the Bendlerstrasse was to order him to return at once to Berlin in order to "report." This cable from the Foreign Office was followed within half an hour by another one from the German General Staff, telling my father that, as an ex-officer and holder of the Iron Cross, he should on no account return to Germany. This fact is an interesting reminder of the temper of the times.

One day, in 1938, when I returned home from the drama school, I found Klop in an unusual state of agitation. There were glasses on the table, a bottle of champagne on ice, an open box of cigars.

"You're late," he snapped.

I began to think of an excuse.

"No time for that," my father barked. "You are to go to the cinema."

"What do you want me to see?" I asked. Sometimes, when I was younger, we had gone as a family to see a film deemed suitable, usually something like *Tabu* or *Trader Horn*, which gave me nightmares for weeks afterwards, but never had my father sent me to the cinema.

"What do I care what you see?"

"Well, I need some money."

"Again!" (The last time had been in 1934.)

Irritated, he rummaged in his trouser pocket and came up grudgingly with sixpence.

"It costs more than that."

"There's no need to take an expensive seat, you know."

"The cheapest one costs more than that," I murmured.

"Since when?" he cried, as though I had announced the outbreak of hostilities.

"About two years," I said.

"What is it now?"

"Ninepence."

"*Ninepence!*" he shouted.

My mother came to the rescue with threepence, and I was sent on my mysterious mission.

It was evidently too late. We lived on the fourth floor of a Victorian building without a lift. As I reached the second floor, I was forced to flatten myself against the wall to make way for a procession of elderly gentlemen who were climbing the stairs laboriously, some with bowler hats, some with green trilbies, grunting and wheezing like a group of mature elephants on the way to a watering hole. They seemed oblivious of my presence as they concentrated on the business at hand, looking upward every now and then to see if there was still a long way to go. At last the rearguard passed me, and I was free to leave.

I no longer remember what film I saw at the local, but when I returned it was dark. I climbed the three flights of stairs and was greeted by a blue haze of cigar smoke. A thin bar of light from under the living room door and a murmur of hushed conversation suggested that it would be imprudent to enter. I brushed my teeth and went to bed. Next morning, neither of my parents was awake. I made myself some tea and went to the drama school, quickly forgetting the whole incident.

It was several years later, during the war, that it suddenly came back to mind for some reason, and I asked Klop about it. He was in an expansive mood. Apparently the German military attaché, Major General Geyr von Schweppenburg had telephoned him from a public phone box, complaining that Von Ribbentrop, during his tenure at the embassy, had so alienated British opinion that now all contact was lost with people of influence.

"My dear von Ustinov," the General had said, "you are the only one who can still help us, and whatever your feelings toward us, you cannot deny us this request. We simply must convince the British to stand firm at Munich. If they give in to Hitler now, there will be no holding him. Now is the moment, more especially since we are far from ready for war. Even a relatively simple operation like the annexation of Austria showed us the tremendous gaps in our equipment and our capacity for staff work on a large scale."

"What do you want me to do?" Klop asked.

"If you can organize a meeting between the British and German General Staffs, our people will all take leave on different days, and make their way independently yet indirectly to London on private airlines," the General had replied.

For the historically minded, the meeting in question took place on the fourth floor of number 134 Redcliffe Gardens, London SW 11, while I was at the movies. And the outcome?

"The British declined to cooperate, believing there to be a risk that the whole thing was an elaborate German trap," said Klop, and the facts are confirmed by General Geyr von Schweppenburg's memoirs, published in Germany after the war.

A while later, when war had already broken out, I identified one of the silent British officers at the flat as Major Stevens, one of the shrewdest of the shrewd. A couple of days after I had seen him, he appeared at a secret rendezvous at the Dutch-German border in order to take possession of a top German defector. The British General Staff did not believe *this* to be an elaborate German trap, but this time it was one. Instead of taking possession of the top defector, who turned out to be nonexistent, Major Stevens was himself spirited away into Germany, and spent four long and undoubtedly heroic years being as silent there as he had been here.

After these debacles, I was no longer encouraged to go to the cinema. I was merely asked to tell no one about the comings and goings at the flat. What was curious, however, was to watch how Klop, who once had fancied himself as the dapper German officer, now shed these mannerisms to become more and more British. He even began to stammer on certain words, and indulge in a host of oratorical mannerisms that were the hallmark of Conservative politicians. Klop even referred to the British fleet as though he had a vested interest in it; and eventually, when exhorted to write a book of memoirs, he declined to do so because he did not wish to mention any of his more interesting activities for fear of, to use his own words, "letting the side down" — and this after every general with half a star the world over had revealed all, and after Philby, Burgess, and MacLean had "let the side down" irrevocably and thoroughly. In his gratitude for his acceptance by the British, he became loyal to a point of touching absurdity, believing that any scrap of ancient information could still bring comfort to an enemy utterly discredited, destroyed, and scattered to the Bolivian and Paraguayan winds.

While odd occurrences continued at home — I never knew whom or what I would encounter on the staircase — at drama school things were mercifully less dramatic. I began to find some little favor among one or two of the teachers: John Burrell, and in particular George Devine, who was in charge of improvisations. Whenever forced to concentrate on pure gymnastics or vocal exercises, I still lagged behind the others, but when I applied what I had learned to a dramatic, or more especially, a comic text, I showed great improvement. At all events, I became at last deeply concerned with the job in hand, and work, for the first time in my life, became a pleasure. Even if the theater had not been a vocation, at least it was becoming a profession.

I was greatly helped in finding a kind of personal focus by the fact that for the first time I felt an attraction for a girl. At last, painfully late, instead of being compelled to confirm or deny my father's impressions of a passing female, I was doing the staring and the maneuvering all on my own, instinctively and evidently not too badly. I noticed her on the very first day. She wasn't obviously pretty or beautiful. She belonged to no particular type. She held mystery for me, and that was enough to cause indescribable confusion in my thoughts and feelings. I found myself planning to sit close to her, or in her sight line, or behind her. Eventually we just drifted into one another's company.

She was Isolde, the daughter of a playwright, Reginald Denham, an amusing and eternally youthful man. He was no longer married to Isolde's mother, a delightfully vague and splendidly proportioned lady who had formed an attachment with a Scottish military gentleman and shared his house in Highgate. The atmosphere in this house was somewhat strained, since the Scottish officer kept his tin hat from the Great War and a loaded revolver from the same conflict suspended from a hook on the bedroom door, threatening to use the gun on himself if ever his mistress should leave him. The expression in his bloodshot eye when aroused tended to confirm his sincerity.

The mixture was further enriched by the presence of two large boys from his former marriage, one of whom had formed an unhealthy passion for electric guitars, with the result that the langourous music of Hawaii caressed the ear, interspersed with howling atmospherics.

And if this disparate and ill-matched household needed a symbol to crystallize its discordancy, it received it in the shape of a bloodhound puppy, which had acquired the attractive habit of placing its paws on your shoulders while it peed on your legs.

"He's not yet fully grown," barked the Scottish officer in evident satisfaction.

It was clear that poor Isolde had even more reason to leave home than I, and with the discovery of our mutual secrets and penury, a solid and comforting bond was formed between us.

I have never derived much satisfaction from working for myself. There must be some deeply patriarchal side to my character, an atavistic need to be responsible for a clan or family, which sometimes contrasts with my desire, my habit, of being alone. Whatever the truth of this, it is undeniable that my work improved owing to my attachment to a single person. I was now working for a purpose, building something, showing off discreetly to my chosen partner, a champion in a mental joust.

Our relationship had its ups and downs, but in spite of depressions I clung to it as though my life depended on it. We both still lived at home and were as chaste as Puritans. During the summer holidays, I appeared before the public for the first time at a small theater in Surrey called the Barn Theatre, Shere. Probably in imitation of Michel Saint-Denis and George Devine, who both smoked pipes as though they were badges of rank among the high priests of the theater, I bought myself a pipe, hailed a taxi for the first time in my life, and drove to Victoria Station in order to take the train for my first engagement. Inside the taxi, I lit the pipe and said to myself that I was now an actor, on his way to work. I sat back and ruminated magnificently until my head began to swim and I managed to suppress an urgent desire to throw up. My forehead was covered in an icy sweat as I paid the cab. The pipe was evidently not my mark of masculinity.

My first appearance on any stage before a paying and anonymous audience was in the role of "Waffles" in *The Wood Demon*, the first version of *Uncle Vanya*, by Chekhov. I was on stage as the curtain rose, seated in my grandfather's smoking jacket and pretending to eat ham. The overture was the Polonaise from Tchaikovsky's *Eugene Onegin*, and I can still remember my feelings of controlled panic as the record neared its end — the hiss of the rising curtain, the sudden blinding light isolating us on the stage, and the vague outline of heads, like cobblestones on a wet night.

My role was not an easy one, since I spoke roughly once in every twenty speeches and experience tells you that it is easier to play someone who speaks frequently than to maintain an intense concentration "counting bars." I came through my baptism of fire not too badly, however, and by the second night I felt I had done it most of my life.

In the next play, the first performance in England of *Mariana Pineda* by Federico García Lorca, translated by Charles David Ley and directed by John Burrell, I played a very different role, that of a lecherous Spanish chief of police offering the heroine the kind of crooked deal Scarpia offers Tosca. In the Chekhov it had been all twilit impressionism; here it was Andalusian symbolism, blinding white and rhythmic as the grumbling of a guitar, all of which was far outside my experience, or, for that matter, outside the experience of anyone connected with the production. John Burrell brought us some books to look at, with pictures of rows of sullen gypsies sitting before their caves in Granada, and of crowds of functionaries, a priest and a surgeon or two, all jockeying for position in the photograph of a newly expired torero. Everybody was smiling for the photo with the exception of the dead man and the Virgin Mary on the wall, both of whom seemed rather less enthusiastic. Far from opening any doors for us, these bits of evidence only served to make Spanish folklore even more hermetic, and I launched myself into a text of which I understood not a single motivation, not a single image. It was difficult to comprehend why lust should be so talkative, although it is undeniably a tremendously valuable adjunct to an actor to be able to cope with a text in which he simply doesn't know what the hell he's talking about, while his expression must imply that he has a vital message to impart.

The *Times* was, as ever, cautious in its assessment, and small wonder: Lorca had a great reputation, augmented by the tragic circumstances of his death. He appeared as a lyrical variation on the Ché Guevara theme, and yet the translation of his burning mysteries into marbled words of English was bound to be difficult, especially in the hands of drama students. The first press notice I ever received from a national newspaper said that "Peter Ustinov gave the part of Pedrosa a sinister restraint which was acceptable." It was a great moment for me; in retrospect even greater than I could imagine at the time. Never since have I been called either sinister or restrained.

During the course of the two-week run we received the visits of Charles Laughton and Elsa Lanchester. He always blossomed when surrounded by youth, since he had something of the major prophet in him. At that time, he had a strange tree house not far away and we were all invited there for tea. I picked up a pinecone that had fallen on to the front steps, packed it in a parcel, and sent it to Isolde, who was holidaying on an Irish island. I hoped it would bring us both luck.

Not long afterward I went to see *The Sign of the Cross* in London, in which Laughton was playing the part of Nero and in which Claudette Colbert took her famous bath in asses' milk. I sat through the film and came out into the early afternoon, worn out by the fustian and blinded by daylight. I walked across Green Park, ruminating on ancient Rome and its influence on the architecture of the Empire State Building, of which I had seen photographs, when I suddenly found myself face to face with Laughton again. To my amazement, he recognized me and asked me to walk with him. I was too overwhelmed to refuse. He talked a great deal in his meticulously authoritative way, flooding his eyes with acute expression, then letting them flicker away to a pained docility, while his mouth expressed a voluptuous pleasure in its own disgust. What he said was invariably intelligent and precious, bearing platitudes to you as though they had been announced to him by a passing archangel, and as though you were the only person privileged to share such knowledge. He then wearily announced that he was going to give me a treat. I thought this might take the form of a drink, or at least a cup of tea. Too late I realized that we were heading back to *The Sign of the Cross*. Before I could react, Charles had called out the manager, asked him to look after me, and left with the airy wave of someone who is sure of himself and pleasantly warmed by his own generosity.

I didn't dare tell the manager I had seen it a couple of hours ago, more especially since he gave me a seat I couldn't possibly have afforded. Every time I looked around for a chance to escape, I found him still standing there.

"There's nothing like spectacle, is there?" he said.

"No," I agreed.

"What a lovely man Mr. Laughton is."

"Yes," I agreed.

"I mean, the very idea of going out of his way to bring a young student here — it's an education, you know — and you're never going to forget this!" he almost threatened.

I saw Nero scowling at me from the screen, and believed the manager to be telling the truth.

At the London Theatre Studio, we began preparing for the end of term. Michel Saint-Denis directed us in the *Alcestis* by Euripides. I, wearing nothing but a tiger skin conceived by the Motleys, made a lot of noise in the part of Herakles, or Hercules. I suppose you might refer to the reasons for the noise as labor pains. At all events, M. Saint-Denis treated the drama as a bold, imperishable monolith until, shortly before we were to open, he called us together, telling us he had made a vital error, since he had treated the play as though Sophocles had written it, whereas it should be full of Euripidean ironies. We all said we understood, then performed it exactly as we had previously; he said how much better it was played that way, and what luck he had discovered his mistake in time.

Since there was a great shortage of men, as always at drama schools, all the lads had parts in several plays. I was cast in the role of Branwell Brontë in that archest of plays, *Wild Decembers*, by Clemence Dane, a lady who entered rooms like a yacht in full sail, her mouth forever puckered as though savoring some inspirational ambrosia. She gave me one of the choicest fruits of her meditation when the wretched Branwell, exhausted by the incessant comings and goings of his bluestocking sisters Charlotte and Emily across the blasted heath, to say nothing of the inane complaints of his father, the reverend, suddenly rushed to the door, announcing to his family that he too was going for a prowl on the moor now that the weather was bad enough, and, as an afterthought, delivered himself of the following piece of beastliness: "But you needn't try to stop me — nothing can. Not the grave itself nor the devils who sit on the tombstones on the other side of the wall and grin at us on winter nights."

With that, I rushed into the gale, thankful to be out of the cottage. Unfortunately I never once got that line right at the time, and now, nearly forty years later, I can't forget it.

I was, of course, utterly unsuited to either part; Herakles, eager to clean out Augean stables, and Branwell, eager to be listened to but with nothing much to say, were both beyond my reach. The third part I played, Sir John Moneytrap in *The Plain Dealer* by William Wycherley, was one of those Restoration bundles of gripe and style which submerge any but the finest actors in a haze of filigree. Altogether, as I often suspected, the parts selected for students at such academies are never designed to procure them work in the commercial theater, but rather to drive them, out of desperation, into tiny temples of true art, making their own masks and coffee in chipped mugs, in the belief that, because money corrupts, poverty must therefore be equated with integrity.

I once said to a Belgian dramatist, Herman Closson, who had started with the Compagnie de Quinze, playing in villages, that I believed its motto to be: "*Nous vaincrons parce que nous sommes les plus faibles.*"

He corrected my impression by saying, "*Cher ami, c'est pire que ça; nous vaincrons parce que nous sommes les plus pauvres.*" The whole quasi-religious aspect of our activities became clear. If we were very good we would be elevated to the position of apostles; if not we would be thrown out into the impure world of scribes, Pharisees, and Philistines, and the eye of the needle would shrink to nothing from the triumphal arch it was for those willing to follow glowing ideals in mute subservience.

Michel Saint-Denis was a man of great and persuasive charm, with the finely honed cruelty of a minotaur. Once, during the rehearsals of a French play, he told me that the way to express fear was to contract the buttocks. I didn't understand how such a muscular change could be conveyed to the public, especially to those seated far away. A little later he stopped the rehearsal to ask me why I was waddling instead of walking. I explained that, according to the text, I was still very frightened, but that it was extremely difficult for someone with my lack of experience to walk while contracting his buttocks. He nodded dangerously, savoring my semiconscious sarcasm as though it were a qualified declaration of independence and for a little while longer I was allowed to express fear by more personal methods.

At the end of the second year, he sent for me. The interview was an awkward one, he maintaining that I was not yet ready at the age of eighteen to face the rude, unscrupulous world of moneylenders — "I don't know what kind of parts you can play," he said coolly; "Shakespearean clowns *à la rigueur*, and then . . . Shakespearean clowns are not wanted every day . . . there are others, with experience. Take my advice and stay here another year."

My yearning for freedom was too great. I told him, as steadily as possible, that I wished to try my chance.

He attempted to outstare Judas.

"The decision is yours," he said, disguising his disappointment with difficulty, and added, somewhat sourly, "You will — if by some chance you succeed — fall into the world of tricks, like Charles Laughton."

For a moment, I had the illusion that I was being taken to see *The Sign of the Cross* for a third time, but this time by Jesus Christ himself.

I didn't answer. I rose to go and said goodbye with some emotion.

It was a school which had taught me a great deal, especially about voice and movement. Aesthetically I quarreled with much it had to offer, but this was even better for me, since I had to work out in my own mind reasons with which to back up my instinct. Deriving from Stanislavski, it was much given to analysis, making the smallest gesture the pretext for lengthy discussions. My instinctive quarrel with the so-called Method, valid to this day, is that so much of what is said, done, and more importantly, thought, during rehearsal is untranslatable into dramatic terms. This leads to the all-too-frequent phenomenon of actors who have reached devious and impractical conclusions about their roles doing incomprehensible things with an aura of self-satisfaction and even authority, which not unnaturally tends to alienate an audience.

As with every artistic movement, it is necessary to examine the style against which it rebelled in order fully to understand it. Stanislavski and Chekhov cannot be entirely appreciated without being at least conscious of the melodramatic style of acting against which they reacted. The husband, finding love letters from another man to his wife would stagger back a couple of paces unsteadily and raise his hand to his forehead as though warding off one of destiny's blows. "Life," affirmed Chekhov, "is not like that," a sentiment faithfully echoed by Stanislavski. A man finding such letters usually does not react at all, at least visibly. His immediate concern is to try to capture a kind of diabolical initiative by leaving the letters exactly as he found them so that he has all the time in the world to study his quarry and to decide on his reaction. After all, he doesn't wish an accusation of snooping to lessen his moral ascendancy.

Naturally each man would have his own reaction to such a situation, as would each theatrical character, but what both Chekhov and Stanislavski were sure of was that only a ham actor, obeying the instructions of a conventional dramatist and a workaday director, could totter back the two statutory steps and bring his left hand up to his brow. Chekhov thereupon set about showing up the false by a poetic mobilization of all that is inconsequential and wayward in human intercourse, with the result that his plays are not so much dialogues as many intertwined monologues, plays in which people talk far more than they listen — a technique which illuminated all the bittersweet selfishness and egotism in the human heart and made people recognize, if not themselves, at least each other.

Not without reason, the new introspection of the Stanislavski method coincided admirably with the new introspection of Chekhov. Actors were encouraged to work by themselves with a growing disregard for external problems and consequently they were invited to be as egotistical as the characters they so brilliantly played. The fame of the Moscow Art Theater was built on Chekhov, and it is indicative that its forays into Molière, Goldoni, and even Maeterlinck made much less of an international mark. It is therefore to be suspected (and indeed, has been confirmed by my great-uncle, Alexander Benois) that this modern and revolutionary technique did not lend itself all that happily to the interpretation of the classics.

It is not difficult to understand why this was so. Since Chekhov, the journeys into the depths of realism and beyond have been accomplished more thoroughly if not more profoundly by the cinema. Now the theater has once more sought to break out of the frame to which it had been consigned by naturalism and gentility. It is the one dramatic art form left that exploits a living audience, as does a sport — a living audience, for which the canned laughter of television is but a corrupt and artificial substitute.

As a consequence of this reversion to its fullest potential, I submit today, as I have always submitted, that the theater is basically a sport, based on integrated team play, with, as in all sports, room for improvisation and the opportunities of the moment, and very much dependent on physical and vocal condition. Whereas the so-called Method tends to slow down reactions by giving precedence to the intelligence at the expense of instinct, I believe that the duty of the intelligence is merely to correct the instinct in cases of emergency, and that speed of reaction is all-important.

The driver of a racing car maintains a loose grip on the steering wheel and uses it merely to correct the car when an emergency looms. The rest of the time, he "feels" his car around the course. So it is with acting. The mental processes are too fast to intellectualize at every curve in the road and to grip the steering wheel as though your life depended on it.

Once again, one has seen actors of a certain school seeming to take themselves by surprise by strange and sudden inflections, by hesitations so exaggerated and external that they appear to be a caricature of naturalistic behavior. Once again one must invoke the sport. I am not, to quote Ken Tynan, smitten by Bull Fever. There is nothing in this world uglier than a bad corrida, and I have insufficient intellectual power to enter into the realm of Mediterranean tragedy or Minoan antiquity and be totally indifferent to the unpleasantness which accompanies the thrills. Nevertheless, there are aspects to bullfighting which have a direct bearing on the art and craft of the actor.

The great torero minimizes his movements to the utmost. Why? To give a scale to the map of our vision, without which nothing can be clearly understood. The bull is a clumsy and unconcentrated animal. A fly, entering the field of its vision even at the height of its agony, is liable to deflect its attention from its tormentor. The loss of tension is immediately felt by the public. To regain the attention of the bull, the torero makes a brief, curt, studied movement. He has to compete with the wayward fly. His movement must have some meaning to the bull. How can he ensure this? By being as still as possible the rest of the time. Stillness is one of the prime adjuncts of the actor; to be able to maintain tension by total immobility.

Even the game of cricket, which I have spoken of without love, has revealed sufficient of its mysteries to me for me to understand that it is also one of the "restrained" sports in which much of the excitement is produced by anticipation and a stillness on the field, which gives importance to the sudden outbursts of activity. It is this stillness which furnishes the scale of the map and enables us to calculate the exact meaning of the outbursts of hitting and running. The stillness is, once again, all-important. As it is in conversation — and since dialogue is but organized conversation, the same rules apply to both. People have been heard to remark time and again that the art of conversation is dead. Pessimists with a profound if erroneous historical sense will maintain that there has been a gradual decline since Dr. Johnson.

To believe this is to misunderstand one of the most important prerequisites of conversation, which is the ability to listen. Whenever Dr. Johnson bellowed an irrefutable "Sir!" all conversation stopped at once while the great man pontificated. He did not need to listen all that closely. After all, he had Boswell to do that. And Chekhov's characters did not need to listen either. They had Chekhov to do it for them. But actors simply must not only listen but show that they are listening. As in a sport, you cannot score every time. There are moments, and many of them, when it is important to pass the ball so that a colleague may eventually score. To be aware, and convincing, it is absolutely essential to listen to everything, with the sensitivity and sensibility of an insect, and not just confine yourself to inner voices. It has, of course, taken a long time and much experience to arrive at such conclusions with any degree of lucidity, but they are merely formulations of a direction which my instinct had been urging on me from the very beginning, from my drama school in fact.

I left M. Saint-Denis's office and prepared to face the world. I had written a few letters to agents and had had no replies. All doors seemed to be closed. I had blotted my copybook as a potential apostle and now discovered there was no room even for a Judas. The cock crowed twice and I was given another chance. Saint-Denis was about to do an all-star production of *The Cherry Orchard*, with Edith Evans as Mme Ranevska. He had previously done a memorable *Three Sisters*, and it was the kind of play he did best, one in which there were no great claims on visual imagination or decorative taste. Now I was offered the understudy of George Devine who was going to play Lopakhim, which was not bad going for a Shakespearean clown in retirement before the start of his career. I accepted and made plans to leave home at the first payday. Unfortunately that master of the dramatic, Adolf Hitler, opened before we even had a chance to go into rehearsal. With him as impresario I slowly prepared to play a part I was totally unsuited to, for the worst pay, in a run lasting over four years. Fortunately for me, I was allowed a brief whiff of freedom before going back to school in the Army as what is so ironically, so inhumanly, so inaccurately called a Private.

7

LOOKING back from this nuclear age, our preparations for survival in 1939 seem both charming and pathetic. My mother and I pasted strips of adhesive paper over the windows in a Union Jack pattern to prevent them from shattering. We had blankets in readiness to be laid at the foot of the living room door in case of a mustard gas attack, and we read the pleasantly archaic instructions of what to do in the case of any particular form of German initiative. A mustard gas victim, according to the handbook, was to be taken to a zone outside the contaminated area, wrapped in blankets, and administered hot, sweet tea. Nice clear thinking to thwart the holocaust.

War was declared at eleven o'clock on a particularly fine Sunday, and within half an hour the sirens wailed, announcing the first air attack on London. Far from running for our shelter, we opened the window wide and clambered out on to our tiny, sooty balcony to see the dogfights. Every balcony in the street was similarly occupied. So much for government handbooks and their instructions.

Within a few minutes the enemy raiders had been identified as a flock of gannets with no recognizable markings on their wings. It was a fine start to the Phony War.

I was still at home with no immediate prospects. I had outgrown the room which had housed me for seven or eight years, and I tried hard and miserably to stay out of the way of the mysterious people who still clogged the stairs. My father was in a far better frame of mind, since there was to him more than a trace of the adventurer, and he really seemed to come to life now that the boil had been lanced and the war was definitely upon us. He was as bitterly opposed to Hitler and all that constipated stridency as anyone in the world. Once, on returning home from Westminster, I had found my father in tears, a rare and embarrassing occurrence. It was the day of Mussolini's attack on Ethiopia, and Klop was weeping on behalf of his Ethiopian antecedents. He had never told me about them, in his determination to be as English as possible, carrying the touching charade so far as to believe that I would be adversely affected by the knowledge of "a touch of the tarbrush." Even my mother, in her book, did not reveal this guilty secret. She must have also believed that it would be "letting the side down."

At all events, now that Mr. Chamberlain was discountenanced and the war was irrevocably under way, Klop was cheerful enough even within the immediate circle of the family to suggest that instead of waiting around idly to be called up, I might join Military Intelligence. He went so far as to arrange an interview for me, which was to take place outside Sloane Square Underground Station. I could scarcely believe my ears that fact should follow fiction quite so slavishly. I was to go up to a man who would be reading the *News Chronicle* and ask him the way to Eaton Square. He would ask me what number I wanted. I was to reply number nine, after which we would go for a walk together.

I arrived at Sloane Square Underground Station at the appointed hour, and saw a man holding a copy of the *News Chronicle* in such a way that it was evident that he was not actively reading, but merely waiting. I could just see the top of his homburg hat over the top of it. "Could you please direct me to Eaton Square?" I asked. He lowered the paper and studied me as no man ever studies another unless recruiting him for the secret service. "What number was it you were wanting?" he inquired. He was obviously a man of few words.

"Number nine."

"Very good," he snapped, forcing the paper into his mackintosh pocket. "I will indicate the general direction for you to follow. If you will kindly walk with me . . ."

As we walked, he never looked at me and I consequently didn't trust myself to look at him.

"I know your particulars from your proud parent," he said. "Education, hobbies, and the like. I will therefore just ask you what makes you think yourself to be suited to this work?"

"I don't really know," I replied, "Good memory. Language."

"*Sprecken see Dutch?*" he inquired.

"*Ja,*" I replied, and he seemed extremely impressed, even out of the corner of my eye.

"*Parlez-vous les français?*"

"*Oui, monsieur.*"

"Good man . . ."

After a while, he looked at his watch and remembered an urgent appointment. He left, and I took care not to follow him. I don't know why, but I had an idea people like that simply hated being followed.

The result was a disappointment for my ambitions as a budding undercover man. I was told I was unsuitable since I did not possess a face that could be lost easily in a crowd. Yet, on reflection, the very element that made me inadequate as a spy gave me a curious confidence as an out-of-work actor. Klop, on the other hand, was somewhat saddened by my latest failure, as though I had in some way declined to take over the family business.

Among those who had for years been assailed with my party performances was a Miss Babs Ortweiler, by that time Mrs. Hilton, a friend of my parents who arranged an audition for me with Leonard Sachs, a South African actor who ran, and still runs, a Victorian cabaret called "The Players' Theatre."

I did a monologue for him based on a real visit to Westminster of a decrepit colonial bishop, who delivered himself of a sermon in the Abbey demonstrating the onward march of Christian Soldiers in the heart of darkest Africa, the climax of every moral example being rendered in Swahili. The old cleric either forgot, or else did not think it necessary, to translate his words of wisdom into English for the betterment of English boys. I rather cruelly adapted this octogenarian's sermon for my own nefarious purposes. I passed my audition and began to appear at the Players' in company with Alec Clunes, Bernard Miles, and others of great achievement.

Klop, far from being entranced, sighed a deep and fatalistic sigh, and uttered the words "Not even drama . . . vaudeville!"

This crushing verdict was quite inadequate to detract from my joy at earning my own money, even if it only amounted to £5 a week, and then only intermittently, since I was only engaged every now and then. I was told that I should work on another monologue, which is how I came upon the idea of Mme Liselotte Beethoven-Fink, an aging Austro-German lieder singer, who sang bits of unknown Schubert — that is, unknown even to Schubert — such as "*Der Musenvater.*" She was a sort of blowsy Malaprop — in order to clarify Schubert's tangled family relationships, she cannily half-closed her mascaraed lids and cattily proclaimed there must be "a little bit of insect in that family."

She became a veritable triumph, attracting the kind of critical acclaim reserved for the newcomer. James Agate and Ivor Brown, the two leading critics, were full of the most elaborate praise, although neither went as far as Herbert Farjeon, the genial writer of revue material, who was at the time the critic of the *Tatler.* He wrote, quite baldly, that Liselotte might have been the work of Edmund Kean in a lighter moment entertaining friends.

I enjoyed my success to the fullest, especially since I had made a small breakthrough without the overwhelming assistance of Shakespeare and one of his incomprehensible clowns, and without ever having had to understudy or to carry a spear in Laurence Olivier's *Macbeth,* which some of my chosen contemporaries had had the privilege of doing. My pleasure was increased when I observed my father and friends tiptoeing into the back of the auditorium just as my act was starting, and leaving again before I reemerged into the auditorium as myself. Agate, Brown, and Farjeon had given me my only unmitigatedly good reports since I had first gone to school at the age of six, and now Klop was evidently becoming resigned to Vaudeville once it attracted critical acclaim worthy of Drama.

Once again, my engagements were intermittent, and I earned pocket money rather than a wage that allowed me to go my own way. In the interests of experience, I accepted an engagement at the Aylesbury Repertory Theatre at £2.10 a week. There was just enough for my digs and a single chocolate-covered peppermint cream bar per week. I played a French professor in Terence Rattigan's *French Without Tears*, a German seal-trainer in Robert Morley's *Goodness How Sad*, Colonel Higgins in *Pygmalion*, the Robertson Hare part in *Rookery Nook*, and the depressing doctor in that superb piece of far-flung Empire kitsch, *White Cargo*.

In this latter play, I had to make an appeal for medical magazines from Blighty so that I might keep up with the latest trends in Vienna, Harley Street, and the Mayo Clinic in spite of the sweat, heat, and filth of tropical existence. A copy of *Lancet* arrived at the stage door, with a letter from the editor, saying that he had been so moved by my appeal that he had dispatched the latest copy forthwith. Not another notice from Herbert Farjeon, perhaps, but as heartwarming in its own way. I still have the copy, which is by now as out of date as the play was then.

Londoners were recovering from the first impact of war, and although the bombing had begun, this had only strengthened their resolve instead of breaking their spirit. Norman Marshall, who had successfully run the little Gate Theatre, which performed plays by Steinbeck and Maxwell Anderson for the first time in England, now conceived a revue starring, among others, Hermione Gingold and Robert Helpmann. I was summoned for an interview and engaged to appear in the West End of London for the first time in my life. My salary was considerably augmented, and flushed with this success, I went flat-hunting. Characteristically I found a tiny penthouse

in Dover Street, one of the centers of traditional British hypocrisy — high-class commercial addresses by day, low-class commercial addresses by night. Normally such a little apartment would have
cost the earth to rent, despite the fact (or perhaps because of the
fact) that my next-door neighbor was a distinguished prostitute. Now
it cost very little, and I grabbed it as though it were a rare bargain.
It never occurred to me that with its large expanse of glass roof it afforded very little protection from the German bombers and
required a very thorough and meticulous system of blackout curtains.

The decor was nothing short of awful, with a false Venetian Negro
youth holding a trayful of dusty glass grapes at the entrance, and
other bits of camp and chichi cast like confetti over the blood-red interior. The flat had belonged to a high-strung homosexual who had
committed suicide very recently when crossed in love; and his
mother, a plaintive, tear-stained lady, insisted on looking after me
with all the care she had lavished on her son. I am afraid I was a
considerable disappointment to her, for although I listened to her
woes with patience, I was hardly mercurial enough to replace, even
for a few minutes every day, the comfort she had lost.

My appearance in the revue was not at first the success I had
hoped for, since I wrote new material that tried to widen the scope
of what I had developed and in doing so lost the esoteric audience I
had acquired. A lesson learned, which I have had to learn over and
over again. My original text I can no longer remember, nor can I
even recollect the nature of the character I conceived. All I do know
is that I almost immediately replaced it with a Russian professor who
was jealous of Chekhov's success, and this creature had sufficient
contradictions in him to be interesting. He was both pathetic and
basically frightfully unpleasant, which set my mind exploring along
the lines of dramatic paradox. It must be understood that the British
theater of the period was sweetened with distinguished elderly
actors and actresses who were determined to be liked by the public
even if they were playing totally unsympathetic characters. The

stage was cluttered with semi-sympathetic performances of disreputable people, and the audience was beset by little signals from such performers, signifying that although they had just killed their wives or husbands on the stage owing to the exigencies of a particularly silly script which only the difficulties of the times had made them accept, they were not really like that in life at all.

I suspected then, as I believe now, that the most interesting parts to play are those in which there is wide span of often divergent characteristics, so that the reactions are unpredictable and only consistent at the end. After all, the stage can hardly hold a mirror up to the nature of all theatrical characters, because these must expose their complexities within two and a half hours, and have therefore to be simplified to fit within the rigors of convention. Chekhov solved the problem by suggesting a constellation of unsaid things; Pirandello spelled out the paradoxes with glacial precision; Shakespeare gave his actors more elbow room than they really needed. What is known in technical terms as a well-rounded character really means one with insufficient mystery, one with theatrical life at the expense of human credibility.

The Russian professor was so academic that the need for mystery totally escaped him. His quarrel with Chekhov was based on such alleged absurdities as Irina's phrase "I want to be a seagull!" He shrugged his shoulders in denigration.

"For me . . . physical impossibility," he said.

It was during the run of *Swinging the Gate* that I was married to Isolde Denham at the Marloes Road Registry Office. She was nineteen years old, and so was I. My father expressed no opinion about the advisability of such a marriage, nor did my mother. They were probably both too shocked by my precipitate departure from home to have fully recovered yet. Through the good offices of a remarkable woman, Lady Norton, who was my de facto godmother, Isolde's mother was able to leave for America in charge of a group of evacuee children, which included her own offspring. By this well-timed action she deflected the reprobation — or indeed the bullet — of the Scottish military gentleman, whose passion was easily melted by patriotism.

Isolde knew a little about the realities of adult existence; I absolutely nothing. Had I realized for a moment how little I knew, I would doubtless have been more cautious about plunging into marriage. It is not my intention at this late stage to level any accusations or attribute any blame for this curious situation, which astonished my mother many years later when I dropped a hint about its existence. The fact is that an entire dimension of my life had been lacking ever since my precocious introduction to the dance and counterdance of adult seduction. The antics of men assessing women I found annoying, whereas the response of women went so far as to sicken me. It is even extremely difficult for me to write about this today, two marriages and four children later, since it requires a real effort of honesty and the most intense recollection to place myself once again in the sterile prison from which I escaped so long ago.

I developed such a streak of puritanical frigidity that whereas love and affection were at no time excluded, the idea of their physical expression just did not exist for me; or at least I imagined that a remote instinct, which had not manifested itself to any great or puzzling extent, would, at the required moment, take over everything — initiative, aggression, know-how's. I could even, like so many others, exchange lascivious jokes with a splendidly relaxed air and yet I knew nothing other than that which others told me with the same easy assurance.

There is in existence a photograph of me at the age of one year holding a Russian toy comprising ten wooden women, one within the other, from a great bulbous earth mother to a woman the size of a pea. I am brandishing two halves of this educational toy with evident pleasure. It apparently occurred to me at an early age that a pregnant woman had another pregnant woman inside her, and then another one right down to the smallest. I don't think I ever really suspected that this smallest might be a baby. I like to believe I did, simply because I like to believe I was what the Americans so depressingly call "bright," but in my heart I consider it more likely that I believed the embryo to be a very small woman indeed — dressed, of course, in peasant costume.

The truth of this probability is given further credence by the fact that when my mother informed me of the facts of life at an embarrassingly late stage of my youth (my father being too shy to talk about men, although more than willing to banter about women), I underwent a long moment of utter incredulity. My first reaction was one of horrified claustrophobia. I didn't understand how I had survived nine months of incarceration in a belly, without a breath of fresh air. Then I got used to the idea and quickly accepted such a process as being distinctly odd, but no odder than some of the other phenomena which had been brought to my attention.

It seems to me that I was always half a step behind the others, having no brothers or sisters and being brought up in an atmosphere of rare sophistication without any of the basic hurdles so essential to mental and physical balance. It was as though my cerebral diet were composed entirely of delicatessen and vintage formula.

I was, if anything, overprepared for a life of inconsequential refinement within extremely narrow horizons and absolutely unprepared for choppier seas and fresher winds. I did, however, recognize from the beginning the nature of my shortcomings, but it was only when I had children of my own to appreciate and to study that I finally realized the full extent of the distance I had traveled.

However people may carp or cavil about what has become known as the Permissive Age, I believe that free communication, even if pushed to excess, is infinitely preferable to the murk of ignorance. Better a generation that has come to terms with its physical existence than one in which a lack of knowledge is veiled by social propriety and the hypocritical grace notes of piety and breeding. Even pornography, which is the antithesis of the erotic and which has now settled on us as a garish consumer-oriented commodity, is, in its early stages, a liberator from the greater evil of social censorship.

It may seem strange that I can write with evident feeling about a battle which today is won. I do so only to remind the incredulous that it was not always so; that whereas men and women have always found a way, up to the relatively recent past, there were prejudices, both parental and institutional, which made subjects of vital interest to human happiness taboo.

Thrift was the first necessity brought home to me, and we moved out of the penthouse into a basement flat in Redcliffe Road, a fall from mincing grace to workaday gloom which had about it a symbolism worthy of a medieval morality. Virtually our only possession was a small spaniel dog we had acquired, which soon began having epileptic fits in the cavernous darkness of our new abode. The gas fire was supplied by a meter into which shillings could be fed, or, in moments of penury, pennies. The pervading odors were those of damp and cats. The one advantage of these sordid lodgings was a garden, a somber Victorian-looking patch of balding grass, in which all the greens seemed a couple of shades darker than natural and the broken trellises appeared to sag under several coats of immovable dust. There was a shattered and unvarnished table with a hole in the middle, which had accommodated a parasol in happier days, and a couple of white wicker chairs on legs of different lengths which were unwinding themselves suicidally. It was not the ideal place for a honeymoon. But then, it wasn't the ideal time for a honeymoon either.

The great daylight raids had begun. The sky was filled with hundreds of planes. The climax came on one glorious summer day when the Italians, in wooden aircraft, joined the Germans in their effort to annihilate the RAF. We sat in the garden and drank tea, feeling like privileged VIPs and watching the immense drama enacted above our heads with the remote fascination of royalty. There were flames, trails of black smoke, metal glinting in the sun, the noise of a thousand dental drills, even parachutes drifting sideways in the wind; and yet, try as we might, we could not associate these conventional scenes of war with the many human tragedies enacted within our field of vision. Thanks to the movies, gunfire has always sounded unreal to me, even when I was being fired at.

Swinging the Gate was now off, and my father began a series of dangerous trips abroad. My mother moved to the country, to the Cotswolds, where she was to spend the rest of her life, with one brief interlude in London. I began to be solicited by the films. It all started with a semidocumentary called *Mein Kampf — My Crimes* in which I played Van Der Lubbe, the half-witted Dutchman blamed for the burning of the Reichstag. I had a wax nose to give me the syphilitic look, and a boil on my cheek only added to my appearance of listless guilt. My next effort was a preposterous short film called *Hello, Fame!* in which I performed a monologue I had written, and then climbed one of a series of star-spangled rope-ladders and waved at Jean Kent, who was rather nimbler than I on another one. We were supposed to be a lot of young people on our way to the top of the ladder, you understand.

The third was a really serious film called *One of Our Aircraft Is Missing,* directed by Michael Powell and boasting some of the most distinguished British actors, such as Godfrey Tearle and Eric Portman. I was selected, probably because of my un-English look, to play a Dutch priest. The fact that I also looked un-Dutch didn't seem to matter a great deal, especially in time of war. Much of the little I had to say was in Latin, a little less in Dutch, and there were a few words in English.

I had so often been warned by well-meaning elderly actors of the dangers of overacting, most especially on the screen, that I approached this important first serious venture into film acting with enormous circumspection. Britain had already supplied Hollywood with a whole battalion of elegant understaters, immaculate actors of the Du Maurier school, who, as I have intimated, were able to play anything from cuckolded husbands to dainty blackmailers, and from chiefs of Scotland Yard to masterminds of underworld gangs without their assumed characters in any way being allowed to affect their performances. One such paragon was the late Hugh Williams, at once heroic yet vulnerable, but at all events perfectly groomed and impeccably mannered. He watched me rehearse my Dutch priest

with an acuity that made me singularly uncomfortable. Eventually
he came up to me and asked, with commendable politeness, "Excuse
me, young man, what exactly are you going to do in this scene?"

I struggled to find words to express adequately my devotion to
this school of acting.

"I don't really know, Mr. Williams," I replied, and added, hopefully, "I thought I'd do nothing."

A trace of hardness entered his eyes and voice. "Oh no you
don't," he said, "*I'm* doing nothing."

I reminded him of this incident many years later and he laughed
in merry disbelief. We had all changed with the times.

Still, that did not solve my problem then. Discovered in my evil
act of poaching nothing, I had to find something to do. In desperation I clung to the one element that separated me from the others
and became almost unbearably Dutch, seeming to understand little
that was said to me yet attempting to exude a vocational glow of
compassion which the lower orders of the priesthood are encouraged to wear as an integral part of the uniform. The film company had in addition engaged two technical advisers, both priests
and both Dutch, who happened to be in temporary exile in London.
Both of these fathers were no doubt excellent, as two fine Swiss
wristwatches may be excellent, even if to consult them both may be
unwise. Since the two fathers outshone me in radiance, it was quite
a relief that they had not much time for each other, never being
present on the set at the same moment. When one was there, the
other was in the canteen, and vice versa. They were in utter disagreement about whether I should wear a cross or not, although the
conflict never came into the open but was conducted in ferocious
whispers with the director. The result of this painful schism was that
every scene involving me was shot both ways, with cross and without. Thanks to them I worked twice as many days as I had been
engaged for, with the consequent economic advantage. Amen.

I next put in an appearance as a dialogue director in a very broad
adaptation of one of J. B. Priestley's most accessible books, *Let the
People Sing*, in which I also played an elderly Czechoslovak profes-

sor, and finally I played a brilliant pupil in a Nazi school for spies in the farce *The Goose Steps Out*, starring the celebrated comic Will Hay. For the first and practically only time in my career I played a man younger than myself. Before this sudden involvement with the cinema, however, I had undergone a fallow period, which corresponded with the height of the Blitz. All the theaters were shut, with the exception of the famous Windmill, inventor of the immovable nude to thwart the censorship of the times. Its proud boast, only understandable in the context of the air raids, was "We Never Closed," and evidently no nude so much as flexed a muscle even under the most intensive bombardment. At that time, fear of the censor far exceeded fear of the Germans.

Herbert Farjeon, once again my benefactor, saved my bacon by inviting me to participate in a daytime revue called *Diversion*, which was to include Edith Evans, Dorothy Dickson, and Bernard Miles, and was to do for the dressed what the Windmill was doing for the undressed. I performed Liselotte Beethoven-Fink, and also gave impressions of three different directors to whom I had been exposed, the Continental with a sense of mission, the Communist doctrinaire of the time, and the Semi-Precious. I also appeared in supporting parts in other scenes, notably an Edwardian bathing party in which two mashers attempted to seduce a couple of beauties by discreetly splashing them. The other mustachioed gallant was a young fellow called Dirk Bogarde, with whom I shared a dressing room.

Sir Bronson Albery was the owner of the lovely Wyndham's Theatre in which this daily matinee performance took place. He was a rubicund gentleman who had been old for so long there were rumors that he was immortal, and other rumors which claimed that when the pipes in the theater burst in midsummer, it was his cold feet that were to blame. Actually, he was not so famous for his reticences as for his uncertainties and for his extraordinary capacity for talking to himself at full volume — contradicting himself, scolding himself, agreeing with himself, and in general coming out of such arguments moderately well. I can't imagine that he ever felt a pang of solitude, or that he ever needed an assistant.

Trying to cast a play of mine later on he decided after a lengthy conversation with himself, in which of course there was absolutely no room for any contribution that I might make, that a certain elderly actor would be ideal for a role, especially since he had, with commendable prudence, never asked for more than £20 a week. He ascertained the name of the actor in question and lifted the receiver of the telephone. At this juncture, he had a moment of reflection and replaced the receiver with the simple reminder to himself, "Of course, he's dead."

I was not dead, and whereas Bronny Albery was willing to offer a dead man £20 a week in the knowledge that certain obstacles would stand in the way of his generosity, there was no such guarantee in the case of the living, and he consequently offered me £5 a week to appear in the West End with two solo acts for which I had also written the material, with, as an added temptation, half of one percent of everything over £2,000, which came to just over £1 during one bumper week. I was so astonished by this magnanimity that I accepted. I had no choice.

The week previously, squatting in the basement during an air raid, we had fed our last penny into the gas meter and watched it flicker to nothingness. I announced my intention of swallowing my pride and running around the corner to borrow a few pennies from my parents.

"Do be careful," said Isolde, as the bombers droned overhead. The British had built street shelters, looking like modern sculpture, which were not designed to withstand a direct hit but which afforded protection against that greater danger, bits of our own shrapnel which flew around. I set off at a steady canter. Our antiaircraft guns were firing away and the sky was lit with searchlights, as at a Hollywood premiere. Suddenly there was a formidable crackle of gunfire and I sprinted to a street shelter, just having had time to notice another dark figure running and entering the shelter from the other side. We met in the pitch darkness somewhere near the center of the edifice. It was my father who was short of cash and who had swallowed his pride to come and borrow some from me.

We laughed until our eyes were full of tears and the bombers had gone home.

In January 1942, I received my call-up papers. I had made inquiries earlier about the submarine service, since I had once read a book by Lowell Thomas which had fascinated me, but I had been told I was of more value where I was, in the only entertainment running in London apart from the static nudes. Why on earth I should have been attracted to submarines I cannot now understand at all. After all, a small boy who had felt an acute pang of claustrophobia when told the facts of childbirth would not seem drawn to the selection of a steel womb for military service. I am very glad they turned me down.

At my selection board interview, I was asked if I had any preference as to the arm I wished to serve in. I told the officer I was interested in tanks (once again, the lure of the airless womb!). His eyes blazed with enthusiasm.

"Why tanks?" he asked keenly.

I replied that I preferred to go into battle sitting down. His sparkle faded abruptly, and I shortly afterward received a letter ordering me to report to an infantry regiment. I arrived in Canterbury on January 16, 1942, and was allowed to keep my own clothes a day or two in the absence of anything to fit me. For me, if not for the Allies, this date marked a turning point in the war.

8

BEFORE we hear once again the cannon's belch and the bugle's sour note, perhaps you'd care to say a word.

Had I wished to say a word, I would most probably have said it. Would you?

You're right, probably not. As we are about to embark on our military career, we must take care not to talk. Words are always misunderstood in the Army, at least intelligible ones. They get you into trouble. They commit you.

Not really. Hardly anybody ever understands them. I got the impression that most of the noncommissioned officers had a vocabulary of ten words, used in an infinity of different ungrammatical patterns.

And the officers?

Somewhat fewer, but they had a vast selection of distinguished grunts to fall back on.

You are talking of the regulars, of course.

Of course. The conscripts came armed with words and even sentences, but they had nowhere to put them, nowhere to practice them, so they gradually surrendered them, and as they ate the food they were given, they likewise used the words they were given. Only the thoughts they were given they rejected solemnly, in the silence of the night.

Remember Sergeant C.?

Is it out of forgetfulness you don't call him by his name?

Out of disdain. He was only twenty-eight years old and had lost all his teeth — not fighting, you can be sure of that, but out of ignorance. He munched on gums, like an old man, and had a predilection for cake, soft crumbly cake he could assimilate. He would watch parcels arrive and make a mental note as to who were their recipients. It was about as complicated a mental note as he was capable of. Then he would prowl around, asking in a thin, sinister voice: "Any cake?" At first, the timid would give in and share their cake with this monstrous young fellow. Then they got wise to the fact that surrender only led to obligation, not to consideration, and whatever the parcels contained we would inform him that we had some excellent toffee to offer him. His cratered face would twitch with irritation. "Fuckin' date," he would rasp, "you fuckin' well knows I can't fuckin' eat fuckin' toffee," and he would slink away. The monotony of his conversation was remarkable even by the standards set by his colleagues.

I recognize the first word, of course, as well as the fourth, the ninth, and the eleventh, but what is a "date"?

I never found out. It is, I suspect, an Edwardian term of derision, perhaps deriving from the conquest of the Sudan or some other place with oases. Do you further remember that extraordinary parade conducted by Sergeant C., during the course of which he made a graceless and terrible exit from our life? False teeth had been ordered from the Army Dental Corps around 1936, but with the usual administrative complications, they did not arrive at the right mouth until the late spring of 1942. His gums were suddenly separated by two sets of gleaming white castellated fortifications, while his cheeks were stretched unnaturally, so that his murderously pale eyes reposed on wet, red carpets, like a bloodhound. He croaked and barked his incomprehensible orders as usual but with a hideous assurance. Suddenly, a particularly grating yell turned into an unearthly wail. We all dared to look, and saw him stagger. After a moment blood streamed from his mouth. Unused to his new em-

bellishments, he had bitten right through his tongue, and now was near to fainting with pain and panic. A corporal rushed to the rescue, and we saw Sergeant C. leave the parade ground, not to return during our time.

Will I ever forget him? His greatest love was soldiering, his greatest fear, active service. In retrospect, his bite really was worse than his bark. And do you remember Company Sergeant Major R.?

Anonymous for similar reasons?

What other? Charity, perhaps. He had been a boxer and was now what is called punch-drunk. He was incapable of looking you in the eye without dancing on toes deadened by stamping, ducking his head, bobbing and weaving to avoid your imaginary blows. Among his multitude of nervous tics was his repeated litany of "Stand Up Then," even if people were lying patiently by their machine guns. This maniac had a seven-day leave due and we all counted the hours. The morning of his presumed departure, he was still there. He was still there in the afternoon and evening and the next day. He utilized his leave to spy on us and put us on charges without the restriction of other duties. On the seventh day, I had the courage to ask him why he had not gone home. He feinted, blinked, and steadied himself on the bar where his tenth beer stood half finished.

"I'm a Comp'ny Sar'nt Major, i'n I?" he asked, and when no answer was forthcoming to this question, which I presumed to be rhetorical, he wheezed dangerously, "I'n I?"

"Yes, you are," I acknowledged.

"My dad, 'e's all I go' left, i'n'e?"

"Yes," I agreed.

"An' I'm all 'e's go' left, i'n I?"

"Yes."

"Yes what then?"

"Yes, sir."

"That's fuckin' be'er. Well, my dad, 'e's a Regimental Sar'nt Major, and I ain't never goin' 'ome on leave till I can talk to the old bastard as an heequal, go' it?"

"Yes, sir."

"I got my rights, i'n I?"

"Yes, sir. Indeed you have, sir."

"Right then. Fuck off then, a'fore I lose me temper."

"Yes, sir."

A fiendish grin lit his face.

"Tell you what you can do a'fore you go. Buy me hanother beer." Not even Dickens could have invented such a lyrical flow of rustic awfulness.

We had been moved from a dramatically overcrowded billet into a new and better one. Shortly afterward, I met him in the street.

"Stand up then," he said, and added: "Ow's the new billet, U'nov?" (The last word is my name.)

"Oh, much better, sir, thank you," I replied, "It's much less congested."

"I know," he snarled, as though I had uttered an unworthy imbecility, and then, on reflection, he added, "More room too, i'n there?"

Yet another time, he held aloft a plastic grenade, the latest fruit of British ingenuity, a weapon which did no great damage but which made a most deafening noise. "I want you to look at this 'ighly careful," he said mysteriously, holding it aloft. "This grenade I got 'ere is 'ighly detrimental to henemy morals."

When his remark was greeted with a titter of laughter, he bobbed and weaved as never before, pointing a tremulous finger at the esplanade of the seaside town we were stationed in, which was visible through the window, and yelled: "Laugh, will you? I'll 'ave you all runnin' hup an' down the hescapade with full packs on till tomorrow mornin'. I don't care, I got time, i'n I?"

"Yes, sir," we all chanted.

Many years later, the odious fellow was admitted to a lunatic asylum. His unquiet spirit had led him into the habit of beating up new recruits in camera, and he chanced on a better boxer than himself. The shock was too great, and he lost all coordination.

Tell the story we first heard on entering the service, and after that, you're on your own. I haven't thought of all this for so long it fills me with a sense of awe that it should have happened at all, to us of all people, in this lifetime.

How well I understand you. The story we first heard on going in? Ah yes, an illustration of the sensitive ironic soul's existence beneath the veneer of incomprehensible shouting and stamping which constitutes the outward show of military efficiency.

It happened at St. Margaret's Bay, in Kent, a resort a few miles east of Dover, where a pebble beach nestling at the foot of the famous white cliffs is the target for innumerable Channel swimmers in times of peace, it being the closest landing place to France, a fraction under twenty miles away.

In time of war, it was melancholy indeed. The bungalows on the beach were deserted, and had been used as part of a street-fighting course by the military. Complicated barbed-wire constructions to a height of over ten feet added to its desolate hostility. Up on the cliffs was the village itself and countless holiday homes, now largely taken over by the Army. Dominant among these was the Granville Hotel, a white building with slatted verandas, redolent of distant summers and sweet idleness.

Here I stood in my civilian clothes, together with a few other depressed recruits, staring into a roaring fire, under the penetrating scrutiny of an old sweat who had remained a Private soldier for nigh on forty years. He had lived totally without ambition, with a clear, precise concept of his position in society. The coming of war had prevented his retirement, and now he studied us and our civilian sadness with eyes both critical and kind.

"I'd 'ave to cast me mind back forty years and more to put myself in your shoes, an' yet I remembers it as though it was yesterday," he mused; and then, with a sudden buoyancy, he added, "There was an old sweat like myself to greet me the day I said good-bye to civvie street, and I'll tell you the story he told me to cheer me up, see. The story went as follows. Once upon a time there was two Private soldiers engaged in latrine fatigues. It was autumn, and they was sweepin' the bits o' soiled toilet paper into piles for incineration, see, when a gust o' autumn wind come along, and sent one of these bits o' bumph up in the air like a leaf, just out o' reach o' the two men, and before they could do anything about it, it 'ad gone in the Colonel's window. Now one of the men says to the other, 'Listen, you go on sweepin' up. If there's any questions asked, I've been taken short. It's only 'uman, isn't it? Meanwhile, I'll go in there and try to get that bit of soiled bumph back. The old man's quite deaf, short-sighted an' all, 'e may not notice me.' After a couple o' minutes, 'e's back, see, and the other Private, still sweepin' away, says, 'Well?'

"The first Private shakes 'is 'ead, gloomy-like. 'I was too late,' 'e said. "E'd already signed it.' "

The comfort which this piece of folklore imparted was inestimable at that moment. It suddenly humanized the conspiracy which seemed bent on destroying the human spirit in the interests of an illusory efficiency. Amid all the hoarse yells of the morons who rushed around us like sheepdogs, nipping our ankles, shoving and threatening while our bleating mass stamped hither and thither on the parade ground, there was the solace of this ancient legend, dry as the season in which it was set. Its final wisdom lay in the fact that the man who told it was, with all his simplicity and the lowness of his rank, more literate, more poetic than any of the noncommissioned officers who identified the voice of even the most slow-witted of officers with that of God.

It is, of course, possible that I was abnormally sensitive to the brutalizing effects of military life because I already considered myself destined for better things than being a successful robot, and it is not without reason that I have entirely overlooked a date of primordial importance in my life. It was June 22, 1941, the day on which Hitler launched his fatal invasion of the Soviet Union. At that time, I was not yet in the Army.

While appearing in *Diversion* at Wyndham's Theatre, I had written a play, partly in my dressing room, partly at home during the nightly bombardments. It was written in pencil in a couple of school exercise books. When I deemed it to be finished, I rather shyly gave it to my habitual benefactor, Herbert Farjeon, who took it away to read. Four weeks passed, and I heard nothing. I began to believe that it had either displeased him or else that he had mislaid it. Although it was in manuscript — I have never learned to type, nor could I, at that time, afford to take it to a typing agency — I was not convinced that it was a very great loss. Whenever I saw him, and dropped a hint of my impatience to know his opinion, he was subtly, smilingly evasive.

Then came the weekend of Hitler's greatest initiative. I was down in Gloucestershire with my parents when the news broke. The village postmistress, Miss Pitt, rode recklessly over the somnolent Sunday-morning landscape on her ancient bicycle, shouting "Russia Invaded" as though selling newspapers in a crowded thoroughfare.

We seized the papers and began speculating about all the imponderables that an event of such magnitude automatically turns up. I even toyed with an old radio, capturing in a hail of static garbled voices which we imagined were both Russian and hysterical. It was only after lunch that I settled with the interior pages of the Sunday newspapers to find out what had been going on in calmer backwaters. In James Agate's column of the *Sunday Times* I glimpsed a headline, "A New Dramatist," and felt a pang of envy. The foremost dramatic critic of the day had seen fit to bestow his accolade on some fortunate soul; good luck to him.

Then I read the article. The new dramatist was none other than myself. I reread it several times before daring to impart my secret to my parents. Now I understood the mischievous smile on Farjeon's face, the cool, uncharacteristic evasiveness. He had had the play typed at his own expense and had given it to Agate. The article was superb. It ended with the following words: "When peace permits the English theatre to return to the art of drama as opposed to the business of war entertainment, this play will be produced. Let not the ordinary playgoer be dismayed at the prospect before him. This tragi-comedy is funny to read and will be funnier to see. Yes, a new dramatist has arrived, and his play will be seen."

I showed it shyly to my father as though it were an item which might be of vague interest to him, and I must record that he took the news remarkably well.

It is hard to accept the rigors of military life when you have been so flattered, and yet this unique happening also gave me a glow of serenity, even when the Sergeant Major was lavishing his choicest obscenities on me. There was, I remember, an odious procedure called kit inspection. All of one's kit had to be laid out in prescribed geometrical patterns, with the socks somehow arranged in square shapes, flanking the oblong greatcoat on top of the blankets. Now it is all very well for square people to have square socks, but once they have been worn by round people, they faithfully adopt the shape of the wearer. I did what I could to hammer them into the squareness demanded by military protocol, but to no avail. The moment I left them alone, the wool expanded slowly into a voluptuous rotundity, and they lay there like buns on a breakfast tray. The Sergeant Major entered my room in a fairly jovial mood, but when his eye fell on my socks, I fancied I saw smoke emerging from his flared nostrils. He just had time before the appearance of the inspecting officer to promise me the direst punishments in the nastiest of manner.

The officer entered the room. " 'Shun," screamed the Sergeant Major, his expression fixed on my socks with a kind of satanic premonition. The officer didn't even glimpse the kit. He came straight over to me and asked me if I were indeed Ustinov. I confirmed it.

"I read about you in James Agate's column," he said agreeably, and then spoke warmly about the theater for about ten minutes. He had, apparently, been assistant stage manager at the Shakespeare Festivals in Regent's Park and found military life intolerable. He was, he confided, near a nervous breakdown. I told him I understood him only too well. He agreed that it was of some consolation to him that it must be worse for me. We both laughed, and he went out. The Sergeant Major came over to me with a perplexed expression.

"What 'e say?" he inquired.

I looked at him in quiet, compassionate triumph.

"He said that he had read about me in James Agate's column —
sir!" I said.

"What the fuck's 'e talkin' about?"

And he followed the officer, murmuring about the decadence of
the modern army owing to the influx of civvies.

As one of the coldest winters on record gave way to one of the
hottest summers with hardly a hint of spring in between, life became more bearable, even under these circumstances. As a result of
one of the innumerable administrative breakdowns to which all
armies seem to be prone, we welcomed to our ranks a Polish Jew
who could neither read nor write, who spoke practically nothing
apart from Polish and Yiddish, and who stood five foot in his socks.
Even before the arrival of the computer to add chaos to society, it
was practically impossible for the Army to undo a mistake of this
order once it had been made. Consequently the powers that be
were forced to improvise, and our padre, a Welshman who looked
like Beethoven but with a predilection for dull hymns sung in unison, appealed for anyone capable of speaking Yiddish to come forward. One man stepped forward, but he was a gypsy with an earring
who thought Romany might do the trick. It didn't. Eventually I
asked to be able to try German. For the first time a tiny ember of
recognition flickered in the eye of the newcomer. It was not his favorite language, of course, but Yiddish is merely a distortion of medieval German mixed with a few onomatopoeic and exotic elements,
and a bridge of sorts was created.

With the help of the padre, I was given moments of compassionate leave in the regimental canteen, or rather my new friend
was, and I was instructed to help him decipher love letters from his
wife, who could not read or write either. These letters, written by a
neighbor I never met and was never meant to meet, were extremely
touching by virtue of their ingenuous eroticism, and my mind was
broadened considerably in struggling with the replies to his dictation.

On parade, human contact was less easy to maintain. The British
Army at the time formed threes rather than fours, so that whichever

direction a platoon turned, the central file was always somewhat hidden from view. It was therefore normal that the two of us were relegated to this central file, and I received formal instructions to translate the orders into German out of the corner of my mouth, so that seconds after the body of men accomplished their movement, we would follow suit. Since he was not sure which was left or which was right, it stood to reason that *links* and *rechts* didn't mean much to him either. He, however, was saved by his five feet, whereas I was more prominent. After a while, tired of getting the blame for his sake, I gave up my German whispers and told him to just do what I did, which he succeeded in doing with increasing artfulness, sometimes even forestalling the rest of us by guessing correctly whatever was going on in the Drill Sergeant's mind. When we eventually obeyed the order, he had already done so, and was even manifesting impatience.

At about this time, somebody decided that I was potential officer material, which meant that I was put in temporary charge of a position which dominated the western cliffs of St. Margaret's Bay. This position was an earthwork imitation of a pillbox, part of a rapidly improvised system of front-line defenses linked by a path which snaked hither and thither on the edge of a precipice, and which no self-respecting mountain goat would ever hazard, leaving such wild risks to boys of the British Army festooned with obsolete equipment. Inside the dank and perilous position, there was room for three men to squat and peer into the unpromising darkness through tiny slots. It was a place ideally suited to study the habits of seabirds but hardly adequate to stem the attack of a German division. In the center, on a small trestle table, there was a wooden box full of the phosphorous grenades which had been described as detrimental to enemy morals, presented as a huge and rather austere selection of liqueur-filled chocolates, and in one corner lay a small aerial bomb, bright yellow in color and covered in technical information in red, with, next to it, a wooden ramp. We had the orders to push the bomb manually down the ramp and over the cliff edge in case the Germans got a foothold on the beach.

The powers that be gave me two men to hold this position with, one a Berkshire farmer with a face purple as beetroot and a pair of joyous and bloodshot eyes to match. The other was the inevitable little fellow from Poland, who had nowhere else to go. We each were armed with rifles, of which mine was the most modern, dated 1912.

The beach, which we often had to patrol at night, was a sinister and even tragic place. Apart from the noise of the sea on the pebbles, there were rodents under the duckboards and bats in the eaves of the mined houses, and endless bits of flotsam landing — a burned aviator's cap; a few sodden pamphlets exhorting the French populace to fresh efforts, which had missed their mark and been blown back; crumpled and twisted pieces of metal and charred wood from sunken ships; even a shattered case full of dripping erotica, the life's savings of some solitary voluptuary, which landed at my feet on a blanket of boiling surf early one morning, and caused me to call out the guard.

Rumor had it that before our arrival a German commando had abducted the entire guard of the regiment which had preceded us, leaving no trace of their absence apart from the mugs of spilled cocoa and the vague signs of struggle. True or not, we were armed with four grenades each, which hung from our belts, as well as submachine guns, recently arrived from the United States, so that to the military this was clearly a position of some sensitivity.

It was against this background that the invasion alarm sounded one night, a wail of sirens. There had not been much sleep in any case. The RAF was bombing the French coast, and there was the crisp bark of artillery as well as the rumble of war, an indefinable noise like a magnification of silence. I struggled into my equipment and ran blindly along the clifftop path, my grenades beating a tattoo on my uniform as they danced on my belt. I had no faith in the damned things. All I saw was a child's drawing of conflict. There were fires burning near Calais, and the sky seemed to have a scarlet pulse. In the inky Channel, I noticed spasmodic lines of tracer bullets, which suggested there was some kind of engagement between motor torpedo boats. Perhaps this was it, what we had been led to expect. I plunged through the canvas curtain at the entrance of my stronghold. The farmer was already there, his goofy chuckle echoing against the dank walls. The little Pole was there too, fingering the glass grenades and shaking them in his hot little hands as though they contained cough medicine.

"Little bugger got 'ere afore I did," giggled the farmer, "an' I reckon I'se a fast dresser."

I was less concerned with the Pole's uncanny ability to forestall events than with his reckless handling of the odious little grenades, which had been known to explode when held or shaken in the hand. "*Das müssen Sie nicht anrühren!*" I cried. "*Diese Handgranaten sind mit Phosphor gefüllt! Sie können in ihren Händen explodieren!*"

In a sudden rage, I understood why we were being invaded. Hitler, of two minds about whether to try his luck, had received information from a spy that the British position nearest to the French coast contained two Private soldiers who could only communicate in German. Immediately the adrenalin began to flow. He slammed his fist on a map of the British Isles and shouted to his entourage: "*Meine Herren, Wir fahren gegen England!*"

My lightning reverie was interrupted when the Pole put the grenade back in the box and complained that he had found it difficult to sleep.

"Why?" I asked, incredulous.

'*Zu viel lärm.*" (Too much noise.)

As is often the case in the Army, before you have the time to savor one absurdity, it is already replaced by another. The Sergeant Major burst through the curtain and held it for our Company Commander to enter. In the dim light of a torch, I could see that the officer was wearing pajamas, over which he had flung his greatcoat, a map case, a revolver, and other martial accoutrements. He was a paunchy but energetic man, his hair in an iron gray crew cut, and a mustache bristling chaotically on his upper lip. At the moment, he blinked furiously. The coolness of the night notwithstanding, he was perspiring freely, and the prickly drops flowed in a continuous stream into the corner of his eyes.

Despite the agitation on his face, he spoke softly and calmly, with almost a tinge of melancholy.

"Men," he said, "I can now reveal to you that we are a suicide battalion. Inland there are massed mortar and artillery batteries trained on this beach. In the very nature of things, some of the shells are bound to fall short. Good luck. Good luck. Good luck."

He shook all three of us by the hand and bowed his head, to sweep out and carry his message of great joy to those still blissful in their ignorance. The Sergeant Major screeched again, and followed the Company Commander.

The farmer laughed serenely. "I never seen the old man in such a state," he observed, amused. "All that sweat . . ."

The Pole was less reassured. He didn't much care for handshakes under such circumstances.

"*Was sagt er?*" he asked.

I heard my own voice, as though from far away, speaking in immaculate German: "*Der Herr Major hat soeben festgestellt das wir ein Selbstmord Batallion sind.*"

Before I had time to elaborate and explain about the "*Minenwerfer*" trained on the beach, our diminutive friend had decided to carry his questions to a higher level. Sinking to his knees, his face turned to the humid walls, he began a religious chant as old and as lacerated as time itself.

Naturally, such a sound in the midst of battle had all the noncommissioned officers running hither and thither like hens on an arterial road. The quizzical whistle of shells and bombs, earthshaking explosions, the barking of incomprehensible orders — all that was natural; but the lamentation of a tiny Jeremiah whose forehead was streaked with mud where he had beaten it to claim attention — that was a disruptive influence in the midst of a grand show of sterile manliness.

I could not silence him, nor did I see much point in it. He was merely expressing what I felt, an exasperation with mortal folly, and making his point much more eloquently than I could ever have done. Two Sergeants, tugging with all their might, couldn't budge him an inch. It was only after silence had fallen over the seascape that he consented to go with his captors. It had been either a false alarm or else a sortie in strength to test our defenses. We never fired a shot. The yellow aerial bomb and the tray of phosphorous bombs lay tidily where we left them. We returned to our palliasses, removed our equipment, and set out to sleep through the little that was left of the night.

It was impossible. From far away, the guardhouse no doubt, thin and pure as a flute, the strains of an ancient Hebraic song permeated the midsummer night and gave no less peace than the sounds of war. At dawn it ended. Shortly afterward, the Pole was released from the Army, to go back to his craft of tailoring. He, with the help of a few prophets and of God, had taken matters into his own hands and had convinced the British Army that he was not for it, and therefore that it was not for him, and all this without knowing a single word of English — simply by singing songs.

Months later, on leave, I crossed Piccadilly on foot. Who should I meet on an island in the center of the thoroughfare but the hero of St. Margaret's Bay. On his arm was a dumpling of a woman, an inch or two shorter than he, a grin wrapped halfway around her head.

"Wie geht's?" I asked.

He answered in English:

"Diss my vife." I nodded. "Tings moch better. I now make ooniforms," he said gravely, in the knowledge that at last his full potential as a man was being tapped in the interests of the war effort.

I was happy for him, and yet somehow saddened that he had become so much more ordinary. The purity of his gesture could not possibly be renewed. He was interpreted into a new society, and was busy acquiring the color of his surroundings. Soon he would share its prejudices and its small-talk as well.

Not long after this incident, we were marched away from St. Margaret's to make way for elements from another regiment. We passed our successors, whistling the same silly songs of masculine loneliness as they marched toward the pretty little village we had just left. They seemed robust and jolly chaps as they chanted "She'll be coming round the mountain when she comes," and I thought to myself, "There, but for the grace of God, goes a suicide battalion."

Our next duty was to try and capture the town of Maidstone from the Home Guard, that civilian task force of veterans and the infirm who were supposed to harass the Germans in case of a landing and hold vital positions until better-armed units of the Army could be deployed.

We were, on this occasion, supposed to be German. As soon as the battle began, I detached myself from my unit and advanced alone to the center of the town by the simple expedient of knocking on people's doors. When they were opened, invariably by men in pajamas or women in nightdresses (for it was a little before six in the morning), I would explain the vital nature of the maneuver, without ever revealing which side I was on. Flushed with patriotism, the good burghers of Maidstone forgot their annoyance at being woken so early and let me through their houses and into their gardens. From there I would climb into a neighboring garden, and knock on the back door of another house. These people would then let me out of their front doors. Looking both ways, I would then race across the road and knock at another front door, and the process would repeat itself. It took me over two hours to penetrate into the center of the city at right angles, as it were, to the traffic.

There, I suddenly found myself before the Home Guard head-quarters. A choleric General emerged. I aimed my rifle at him and fired. Since the rifle was empty, it only produced a click, which neither he nor the umpire, a very stout Lieutenant, heard. I consequently shouted "Bang!" and then informed the General, politely, that he was dead.

Death was the farthest thing from the General's mind, and he spluttered, "Don't talk such tommyrot. Who are you, anyway?"

The umpire turned out to have a terrifying stammer. His face scarlet with effort and apology, he told the General that he was indeed d-d-d, but the word simply would not come.

It was the delay in the verdict which more than anything seemed to enrage the General. "Look here," he snorted, "it's not good enough. Fellow points a gun at me and says bang. May be a bad shot for all I know. Might have come out of the encounter unscathed, what?"

"Would you have preferred me to use ammunition?" I asked.

The General lost his head.

"Who asked your advice?" he blustered. "Haven't you done enough harm?"

"D-d-dead!" the umpire managed at length.

"I won't accept it. Won't accept it, d'you hear? Not from a mere Lieutenant."

It was the Lieutenant's turn to be annoyed.

"I am the acc . . . the . . . oh . . . acc . . ."

"I don't give a damn about all that," ranted the General. "I'm off to inspect the forward positions, and I'd like to see the chap who's going to stop me."

"*Sie sind tod!*" I cried.

The General spun on me, suspicious for the first time.

"What did you say?"

"*Sie sind tod, Herr General!*"

"Are you talking some foreign language, or something?" asked the General, as though he was on the trail of something big.

"*Ich bin Deutscher.*"

"German, eh?" the General asked, his eyes narrowing.

"Acc . . . redited umpire of this exc . . . exc . . . sss," the Lieutenant declared.

Just then, some other Home Guards appeared out of headquarters.

"I've caught a German prisoner," cried the General. "Put him under lock and key." And then, brushing the umpire aside, he jumped into his staff car, and told the driver to leave the scene of his humiliation as quickly as possible.

The umpire was boiling with frustration. "I'm s-s-so . . ." he hissed.

"So am I, sir," I said as I was led away.

A Home Guard Major read all my correspondence, culled from my pockets, and then began a cross-examination.

I refused to answer in any language but German.

The Major became very irritated.

"Now look here, I'm going to report you to your unit if you don't pull up your socks and answer a few questions."

"*Das ist mir ganz egal,*" I rasped.

"That's your final word?" he asked, evilly.

"*Heil Hitler!*" I shouted.

"That does it."

They chose to lock me in the armory.

I seized a Sten gun, broke open the door, upset the staff table, and smeared ink on the maps and plans of the local high command before I was overpowered by a cohort of old gentlemen, to whom I wished no harm and whom I therefore allowed to lock me into a disused scullery. They were all very angry indeed, and I felt that the frontier between fact and fiction had become unclear. One or two of them looked at me as though I were indeed a Nazi.

In the midafternoon, the Colonel of my battalion arrived. He was a man whose voice rarely rose above a whisper, and whose head emerged from the front of his uniform at such an extravagant angle that from the side one could read the name of his tailor inside his jacket. He had the curious prehistoric look of a bemused turtle, and I always felt that if we ever had to face actual warfare in the company of this gentleman, he might well, in a moment of difficulty, disappear into his uniform until the storm blew over.

"Now what is all this?" he asked me almost inaudibly.

I explained, as so often, my version of the truth.

"I see," he murmured. "But was it really necessary to confuse the issue by speaking in German?"

"It's a manner in which the Germans are likely to confuse the issue, sir, if they should ever land in Maidstone," I suggested.

"See what you mean," he said, "although that's an eventuality I consider to be most unlikely, don't you?"

I was a little surprised to be consulted, but decided to suggest that if there was no likelihood of the Germans landing in Maidstone, we were all wasting our time.

"Quite, quite," he agreed absently, then smiled briefly. "Full marks."

On his way out, he hesitated a moment.

"You are one of my men, are you?"

"I'm wearing the uniform, sir," I pointed out.

"Yes, yes. I just thought you might belong to the Home Guard. But then, of course, there'd be absolutely no point in your talking German."

Muttering confirmations of his own opinion, he left the room and secured my release by suggesting the Home Guard should all learn German in order to know how to deal with recalcitrant prisoners if, of course, the Germans ever had the bad taste to come to Maidstone.

Something happened to the British Army around this time. While it was loath to abandon the extraordinary abstract attitude of many of its officers, to which it believed it owed many of its successes in history, it was nevertheless exasperated by the endless retreats before Germans and Japanese, who seemed to have got hold of something new by way of battle procedure. The result of these meditations in high places took various forms, all of them immensely unpleasant. It was determined that a new, more aggressive fighting man would arise like a khaki phoenix from the fires of abandoned supplies and gutted citadels. We were made to rush up and down the pebbled beaches barefoot in what were called "foot-'ardenin' hexercises" by the noncommissioned officers who ran by our side, boots on their feet, encouraging us to ignore the pain of jagged stones, broken glass, and desiccated seaweed. Then there were the battle courses, usually converted golf courses, in which the conditions and some of the idiocy of battle were simulated, officers lying in ambush among the bushes with pots of animal blood with which they would try to spray you in order, so they declared, to get a man used to the sight of blood. These traps were quite easy to avoid since the officers were not very adept at concealment and had no great faith in the psychological soundness of their task. Machine guns would blast away over our heads to give us confidence in covering fire, which didn't prevent them from killing a man running near me. Those responsible had negligently mounted their guns on sand, and when they began firing, these automatically dug themselves in, with the result that instead of giving us covering fire they were merely shooting through us. This may be another reason why the officers lay low with their pots of blood.

Then there was a new secret weapon called Battle Drill, in which an infantry unit was subdivided into platoons, each man having a specific and prescribed duty during an advance on any enemy position. I have no idea what was supposed to happen during a retreat, because we never practiced those anymore. Anyway, linking the activities of this combat group was a runner, who was supposed to charge over exposed ground with vital messages. My battalion was selected to produce the demonstration squad that would inject the whole South-Eastern Command with this new formula for success. My Battalion Commander selected my Company for the honor of forming this squad. The Company Commander then picked my platoon, and I need hardly add that I found myself in the demonstration squad, not as one of the chess men but as the connecting runner! Out of the entire South-Eastern Command, they had to pick on me as a runner, with my heredity. Their horribly fallacious theory was that, being an actor, I was trained to commit long and complicated messages to memory. What they failed to realize was that, on eventual arrival at my destination, I was far too out of breath to deliver the message and that by the time I had recovered my breath, I had forgotten the message.

All over the counties of Surrey, Sussex, Middlesex, and Kent we traveled in trucks in order to demonstrate this new method of defeating the Germans. I must have run hundreds of useless miles carrying information I was unable to deliver. For many years, before the advent of new highways, I was never lost in these counties. I recognized every hedgerow as a refuge where I had panted my lungs out, with the grass going in and out of focus as I stared at it in order to avoid looking at the Corporal who cast his shadow over my wheezing form.

"Deliver the fucking message, damn you!"

I recognized every hillock as an obstacle I had had to run across, doubled up, in order to lessen the target. I recognized every ditch as a gaping mouth ready to snatch my ankle in its jaws. Dante had his inferno, I had mine.

There was still one lesson to learn.

When eventually an application arrived to join Carol Reed, in Scotland, in order to write a film about the techniques of Combined Operations, I was marched in to see the Colonel. He vaguely recognized me from somewhere, Singapore, Kuala Lumpur, Maidstone . . .

"You don't want to leave us, do you?"

"Yes, sir, I do."

"How very odd."

He informed me that I could leave the very next day after lunch, and after a morning spent in the rifle butts I was so intoxicated with relief at being able to leave this Alice-in-Wonderland unit that I shot like a sheriff in a Western, fast and furious and carefree. When they fetched my target, it was revealed that I had shot all ten bullets into the same hole. The center of the target was just demolished. The Colonel affixed the target to his notice board, my posting was canceled, and I was sent on a sniper's course. Not only did Great Britain have Battle Drill up its sleeve, it also had a Wyatt Earp. The only trouble, as they were to find out, was that however good a shot I might be, I needed the help of ten men to lift me into a position from where I could wreak havoc. A few days later I left for Scotland after all.

And here is the lesson I learned in the Army. If you want to do a thing badly, you have to work as hard at it as though you want to do it well.

9

OFFICIALLY I still belonged to my old regiment, but was seconded to the Directorate of Army Psychiatry. It would have taken a lunatic to discern any immediate change in my condition. I traveled up to Glasgow by train, and was put up for the night by an ordnance depot in a huge warehouse full almost to the ceiling with mattresses. There was, indeed, just room for a man between the top layer of mattresses and the ceiling. I dreamed of tanks and submarines all night, and had my ration of claustrophobia for life. The next morning, I left for Troon.

It was in the pleasant if rather baleful surroundings of a half-deserted seaside town, with a particularly strident colony of gulls, that I first met Carol Reed and Eric Ambler. Carol was a Captain who behaved as though the war was a superb invention of Evelyn Waugh's. He had a tendency to daydream which was most engaging and blissfully unmilitary, and his mind was tremulous with tender mischief. Eric, on the other hand, was a Gunnery Major who talked fitfully of trajectories and ballistics as though he were the young Napoleon, giving an impression of tetchiness and vanity that was quite illusory, for once circumstances divorced him from his playthings he mellowed into the most gracious and considerate of men. I was, I admit it, abnormally sensitive to the changes that uniforms seemed to impose on people, because I was privileged to have a snail's eye view of the whole giddy structure. Since I was the only member of the unit who was not an officer, I fell victim to a superannuated makeup man from a small film studio, who was now a Lieutenant and whose battle dress sported medals from the 1914 war. This man, perfectly docile in peacetime and an excellent makeup man within the limits of his epoch, insisted on commandeering a military vehicle every Friday and driving with me to a disused boardinghouse, for which he borrowed the keys. There I would wait in the entrance hall until he had set up all his paraphernalia. When he was ready, he would call, like a child during a game of hide and seek. I would knock at the door.

"Come in!" he would command.

I would open the door to see him seated majestically behind a tin box at the head of the dining table. I would then march up to him, salute, sign for my pay, gather the miserable pittance into my pocket, salute again, and march out. There I would wait once more while he collected his props, and perhaps his thoughts as well, and when he appeared at length, all chipper with a kind of postorgasmic glow, we would drive back to work in the same commandeered vehicle while he regaled me with tales of great paydays of the past, in Gallipoli and on the road to Mandalay.

Among Carol's first initiatives was to interview a Colonel who had become famous as a fearless leader on various dangerous excursions up sheer cliffs and rocky promontories.

"If I may pose a rather delicate question," said Carol, oozing tact, "what would the average casualties be on one of your commando raids?"

"On the contrary," replied the Colonel, "damn good question. Got to be asked sooner or later." And he thought for a moment, his white eyelashes like the legs of a centipede against his irises. "Of course, you have to realize that most of your casualties are not caused by the Hun at all, but by your own covering fire." The others looked at each other, but after my experiences on the assault course, I can't say this was much of a revelation. "Eighty percent," said the Colonel at length in a reasonable sort of a voice, and added, "but I don't think we ought to frighten the public. Say seventy percent."

Before we had achieved very much, the famous raid on Dieppe took place, which occasioned a fundamental revision of all landing procedures, and it was realized that whatever film we managed to produce would be out of date long before reaching the screens. We were sent home, but not before I had entered a local talent competition at the local theater in Troon. My chief rival was an eleven-year-old lad in a kilt who sang "Annie Laurie" ingeniously and consistently flat. Here was obviously a great future talent for atonal and dodecaphonic scores. His only drawback on this occasion was that he foolishly chose a melody that was known. I scraped home by improvising a Bach cantata, doing all four vocal timbres, and the instruments of the orchestra as well. The first prize was ten shillings, which I accepted gracefully, using a heavy Scottish accent in case it be suspected that my talent was not local. I have always had slight feelings of remorse at having robbed the unmusical child of his ten bob, but my excuse was that, not for the first or last time in my life, I was flat broke.

In London, seated with the military psychiatrists, we debated how we could avoid being sent back to our parent units. This threat was especially grave for Carol Reed, who had no parent unit, having been made a Captain for this specific duty, so there was no telling where he might not end up. I must say, as an officer he had perhaps even less natural aptitude than I did as a Private. He wore his clothes with exemplary elegance, but had an unfortunate tendency, perhaps as a result of having directed one or two historical films, of raising his cap to those who saluted him. I was in mortal fear of being sent back. I could already visualize my old Colonel in my mind's eye. "Ah, there you are! Now where have you come from . . . Dar es Salaam, solitary confinement . . . Maidstone?" It was desperation that made me eloquent. I suggested a film specifically for those who had just entered the Army, a film in which the bridge between civil and military life would be created by means of humor and comprehension.

Since none of the psychiatrists nor Carol Reed had ever been Private soldiers, they listened to me with an awesome respect to which I was quite unused. Eric, who had been a gunner, agreed that such a film would serve a purpose in the modern world, where patriotic duties could no longer afford to seem to be punishments.

On October 6, 1942, *House of Regrets*, the play which Agate had so praised, opened for a limited season at the Arts Theatre in London. It was beautifully directed by Alec Clunes and received a press which I have never had since and can never hope to have again. The headline of the *Daily Mail* was bold: "Best Play of the War." The press chased me into Hyde Park, and took photos of me hugging Isolde and smiling. Jonathan Cape published the play, so that I could actually see myself in print. The play was dedicated to Herbert Farjeon. I had arrived, and this event was the coup de grace which convinced the military psychiatrists that the recruiting film was worth doing.

For administrative purposes I was now attached to the Army Kinematograph Service in Wembley Park, a unit composed of filmmakers posing as soldiers. The quasi-military atmosphere was uncongenial to creativity of any sort, while the fact that we were all artists and technicians in peacetime, linked by certain shared interests and democratic habits, made us rather shabby soldiers. In spite of being allowed to sleep at home, I had to cross the whole of London before dawn every day in order to march to the Express Dairy, knife, fork, and spoon in hand, in order to eat breakfast. Then I had to march back and wash up my utensils, after which I was free to cross the whole of London again in order to settle down to work in an annex of the War Office. Once a week, I had to stand guard all night at Wembley Park in case the Germans tried to capture some of our films.

It was a great improvement on my previous existence, and yet full of administrative silliness that served no purpose other than to prevent the best work from being done. I had, however, grown in cunning. London was a nightmare for Private soldiers, for there seemed to be someone to salute every ten yards. Since the only greatcoat to fit me across the shoulders reached almost down to the ground, I wore this even when the weather hardly justified it. I puckered the cloth of my beret by means of affixing a safety pin to the inside, which sucked my regimental badge into a fold of material. I wore glasses all the time, smoked cigarettes from a long amber holder, and carried an empty briefcase. As a result of this, I no longer saluted anyone, but Poles of all ranks saluted me.

Once, while on forty-eight-hours leave, I did salute a French officer, making an exception to my rule. Since we had no obligation to salute foreign officers, my gesture took him by surprise. He stopped me and asked in halting English why I had saluted him.

Without really thinking, I replied in French: *"Parce que la France me manque, mon Commandant."* (Because I miss France.)

The officer immediately broke down in a flood of tears. I was stuck with him for practically the entire length of my leave, going from bar to bar, drinking toasts to eternal friendship. He was in no condition to reveal his identity, and if by chance he did, toward the beginning of the odyssey, mention his name, I was in no state to remember such a detail. This was the last time I voluntarily saluted an officer in the street while on leave.

Our little film, entitled *The New Lot,* seemed to go extremely well, and it was still being shown to recruits until quite recently. Many celebrated actors gave their services, including the late Robert Donat, who was very amusing as a kind of Errol Flynn hero in a film within a film, which our recruits, now trained in modern methods, laughed to scorn, to the embarrassment of the regular patrons of the cinema.

Filippo del Giudice was an extraordinary man, a kind of Diaghilev of the English cinema. He lived beyond his or most people's means in a huge house about thirty miles from London. As an Italian, he had been interned as an alien, and there had laid plans, as idealistic as they were crazy, for a golden cinematic future. On a practical level he charmed Arthur Rank, a man diametrically opposed to him in spirit and in manner, and Rank gave him the use of a palatial mansion and capital to play with.

At first all went well. Noël Coward's celebrated naval epic, *In Which We Serve*, was the result of Del's initiative, and it was splendidly successful. His secret was simply to go straight to what he called his "talents," whom he infected not only with his enthusiasm, but whose confidence he inspired by his outspoken and often bitter reflections about distributors and exhibitors, whom he saw as the moneylenders in the temple of the arts, to be scourged in moral imitation of Jesus Christ. It was so unusual to hear a producer give opulent expression to the secret misgivings of directors and writers that it truly seemed as though a renaissance were upon us, even if one at times suspected that the mantle of the fanatical reformer lay uneasily on the shoulders of this volatile hedonist, with his unending stream of pinchable starlets.

At this point, however, a series of circumstances led to a new and happy situation. First of all, the Army Council, jealous of the success of *In Which We Serve*, searched around for a propaganda film that would do some good to the Army, which traditionally enjoyed rather less prestige than the Navy, known in England as the "Senior Service." Secondly, one of the untarnishable glories of the international screen, Lieutenant Colonel David Niven, was at hand and available, by kind permission of Samuel Goldwyn and his own elevated sense of duty. Thirdly, *The New Lot* was enjoying a success with recruits.

It was decided to expand *The New Lot* into a full-length film which would accommodate David Niven as both star and symbol. It was at this point that the Army Kinematograph Service sent me to an officer selection board. I informed the Army psychiatrists to whom I was still reporting during this transitional period. They were extremely put out by my news until they heard that I had been called to an establishment at Watford. All at once their conversation became conspiratorial, and I was asked to "wander to the further end of the room." Eventually they invited me to return within earshot and gazed at me as the Puritans in that famous picture, "When Did You Last See Your Father?"

"You know our method?" asked one, with fearful intensity, the saliva in his pipe making little clicking noises as he tried to force a passage for the smoke.

"I think, so, sir."

"Oh, don't bother about the 'sir' for God's sake. Not here." He laughed, suggesting the office was a haven of superior sensibility. "At all events," he went on, seeming to find even simple expressions with some difficulty, or at least after considerable rumination, "at all events, you are no stranger to our way of thinking."

"No," I agreed. They conspired again in whispers, which enabled me to remember all the marvels they had revealed to me. One of these was the danger of showing men about to go into action films of the high seas fleet with heavy guns beginning to train on the camera. It had been observed that men who had been exposed to this kind of newsreel invariably slept the night with their tin hats over their genitalia, suggesting that a castration complex was the conditioned reflex to having a 15-inch howitzer pointed at them. I had no way of knowing whether such a phenomenon was true or not, but as with nearly every other manifestation of Freudian psychology applied to the events of every day, I found it highly improbable. In any case, it would seem to me to need a man of extraordinary sexual prowess to feel his virility threatened by a battleship. At the risk of laying myself open to suspicions of inadequacy, I would suggest that in my case a battleship would make me feel that my life was threatened rather than my potency, and that had I a nature to be impressed by newsreels, all the tin hats in the world would still fall short of assuring me of a tranquil night.

My meditations on the often unrecognizable world in which these brilliant men existed was cut short when their leader spoke again.

"Truth to tell," he said, "we are not terribly sure of one man out there. Naturally, as an applicant for a commission, you will be interviewed by him. Would it be too much to ask you to hand in a confidential and, needless to say, quite unofficial report on the kind of questions he asks you, the way he phrases them, et cetera, et cetera?"

I told him I would willingly report the facts and allow him to draw his own conclusions from them.

"Now why do you say that?" he suddenly asked.

"Because the greatest psychiatric literature was written before Freud," I suggested. "Shakespeare and Dostoevski achieved by sheer observation and instinct what no one has been able to achieve since these seas were charted. I will therefore humbly learn my lesson from these two titans, watch my quarry like a hawk, and carry my findings back to you, so that you, with your superior knowledge of navigation in the subconscious, can draw your own conclusions."

I left them arguing fiercely about Shakespeare, Dostoevski, Freud, Jung, and their man at Watford.

On arrival at the Gothic establishment in the middle of a great park, we were all given numbers, and told we had no names for the next two or three days. We were put in a classroom to await some elucidation and perhaps an address of welcome by the Commanding Officer. To while away the time, a Sergeant spoke to us. He had curly brown hair and a waxed mustache, and spoke with curious gentility, as though the effete, oblique colloquy of the officer's mess had seeped out and infected his rougher ways with its contagion. Had he not been a Sergeant, he could very well have been a butler.

"Good morning, sirs!" he said, and swung on us. "That took you by surprise, didn't it! You 'adn't thought of that, had ye-e-ew? Well, it's time. Some of ye-e-ew are going to be called "sir" and you'd better fuckin' get used to it."

All this was said in a tone of menace, as though a commission were a death sentence. Since the C.O. was a long time in coming, the Sergeant warmed to his subject, terminating by shouting: "While in this establishment, you will be treated as though you were officers and gentlemen, whether you are or not, is that clear? You'll undergo a lot of tests, sense of leadership, esprit de corps, table manners, and the like. I don't hold with these goings on, but then, who am I? A mere Sergeant. If I were you, I'd treat the whole thing as a game, and I don't know about you, I play games to *win!*"

His tirade was cut short by the entrance of the Commanding Officer.

"Now, I don't want you to consider any part of your stay here as a game . . ." he began, and behind his back, the Sergeant smiled evilly and winked.

I sat next to an officer at lunch, who told me how much he had enjoyed my play at the Arts. I was loath to answer, since I felt this might be a trap to lure me out of my anonymity and attribute to me qualities of earthly vanity incompatible with officers and gentlemen unless they happened to be called Montgomery.

I told him frankly of my quandary, and how difficult it was for 6411623 to take credit for a play written by Ustinov.

"Oh shit," said the officer, "if I'd stuck by the rules of this idiotic establishment, I'd have gone off my rocker years ago. I'm supposed to sit here and observe the manner in which you eat peas. I've given up watching men eat six months ago. I pass them all, on principle."

I was much heartened to know I had not flunked in table manners, but I did have problems with the more strenuous tests. After lunch, we were supposed to disappear into a hole in the ground at five-minute intervals, and crawl for a small eternity in pitch darkness until we found a way out. This was, without doubt, a test of a man's nerves, and most unpleasant it was. I was dispatched five minutes after the previous man, and advanced slowly on all fours. All sorts of uninvited fantasies invaded the mind — lack of air, being buried alive, what happens if I faint? At long last, I fancied I saw a glow of light in the distance. I stopped crawling for a moment, and reflected with enforced calm. It would be just like the Army to place bars across the distant opening so that a man would have to crawl backward, searching blindly for the diversion. Anything to make life difficult. Was it not better to search the sides of the tunnel now, before going any farther? In fact, my left hand met no resistance. I veered off to the left, haunted by new doubt that perhaps this extension of the tunnel, once again entirely black, was made for unobservant creatures who hadn't seen the light. However, it seemed more likely that the Army would penalize the thoughtlessly vigilant rather than the thoughtfully myopic, and I crawled on my way. All at once there was another distant radiance. It was once again just like the Army to attempt to break your spirit by making you fall into the same trap twice. This time there was no resistance to my groping hand on the right. For the second time I plunged into the darkness.

All further doubt was dispelled when my head met the earth-caked trousers of the previous aspirant, and my hands fell onto the backs of hobnailed boots. He had, of course, lost time by being lured like a moth by the light, and had had to go backwards, search-ing for a way out of the trap.

"Once, or twice?" I asked.

"Twice," he grumbled.

"What prevented you from getting out?"

"Fucking bars, thick as your wrists."

We both emerged from the final hole. The officer was smiling when he saw my precursor, but his smile faded when he noticed me.

"Who tipped you off?" he inquired.

"No one, sir," I replied.

"Now look here," he said dangerously, "someone is bound to have tipped you off. You couldn't possibly have picked up five minutes on the other man all by yourself. I'll soon find out."

It was evident that my foresight was going to count against me, and that the other man was more likely to get his commission since he had paid the Army the necessary courtesy of falling into its traps. Traps, after all, are made to be fallen into, and any avoidance of them displays an unwillingness to understand the spirit of the ser-vice, and may even be interpreted as idleness or malingering.

The climax of a series of unfortunate episodes such as the one I have described came with the visit to the psychiatrist.

Pictures of a vaguely troubled nature were flashed on to a screen, and we had to write a short story in three minutes based on what we had seen.

One of these drawings was that of a man in tatters letting himself down by rope over some crenellated battlements. It looked very much like one of Goya's "Desastres de la Guerra." I therefore wrote a piece cunningly conceived to please a knowledgeable examiner.

"This is perhaps," I wrote, "a Spanish insurgent contained in the fastness of Zaragoza during the Peninsular War making good his escape with some vital information from General Palafox to the advancing troops of Sir Arthur Wellesley."

I thought this fanciful legend to the drawing remarkably astute. Wellesley was not yet Wellington, and the British were advancing, which was calculated to please. My pains were wasted. Once again my judgment was deficient in the mysteries of things English.

I entered the room where the psychiatrist sat in wait for me, a great shaggy man with a mop of muddy white hair and the kind of lost-and-found expression of clergymen who go on peace marches. He pretended to be immersed in my writing, then bent the first page over so that it hung upside down over his hand. I recognized my favorite piece. My elegant literary beginning, "This is perhaps," had been underlined with no less than three red pencil marks, accompanied by the single word, "Indecision."

I felt the blood rush to my cheeks. He had evidently reached a decision about me without as much as raising his eyes from the page. I now repaid the compliment. He gave me a bad report. Back in London, I gave him a worse one. I failed to become an officer. I was told he was removed from his job. So ended the most fruitless of many fruitless days spent under arms.

My I break in?
You don't have to ask.
All this foolishness reminds me of your son coming home from school in tears of rage, complaining of the unfairness of some schoolmaster or other.
That was much, much later. My son hasn't been born at this juncture.
Of course not, but it was in consoling him that you realized for

the first time that the most difficult acceptance in life is the realiza-
tion that there is no arbiter and no appeal. We are condemned to
rub shoulders with injustice all our lives, and we are often judged by
our acceptance of this fact. The spirit in which we manage it can
even be said to be a measure of our maturity.

I agree, of course, but find it strange that you should bring it up
at this particular juncture. Justice had no place in the Army. I never
expected it, and therefore I was never disappointed by its absence.
As for being an officer, I frankly didn't give a damn whether I was
one or not.

I wonder how true that is. You were always fascinated by military
history and techniques. I suspect that if they had given you the re-
sponsibility you craved, you would have thrown yourself into it
wholeheartedly and would even have been extremely sensitive
about the kind of criticism you see fit to hurl at it today.

Oh, if I had been accepted as a spy that morning in front of
Sloane Square Underground Station, I would have seen to it that I
became a very good one, at least while hostilities lasted. That is
hardly the point. I am as interested in military history and the organization of armies as I am in lawn tennis or football or the processes
of justice, but the idea of gratuitous death scandalizes me. Let me
explain myself. The French are deemed an extemely intelligent —
or at the very least, an extremely intellectual — people. In Pierre
Laval they had a politician who saved millions of French lives by
processes which were judged to be below the dignity of France. As
a reward he was degradingly prevented from committing suicide,
and was led before the firing squad so weakened by stomach pumps
that he could barely stand. Such a procedure seemed more in
keeping with the dignity of France. At the same time, a romantic
little mafioso like Napoleon splashed French blood liberally all over
the European landscape; assured the unification of Germany by
compelling German to fight German, therefore being directly responsible for Prussian sentiments of revenge in 1870, 1914, and
1939; and is worshiped as *l'Empereur* by a nation of republicans who
consider that the gratification of panache, the lump in the warrior's

throat, outweighs the millions of dashed hopes, of broken lives, of annihilated talents in the balance of national history. This seems to me and will always seem to me a distortion of the values we are born with.

Were you not opposed to Laval at the time?

Exactly as I would have been opposed to Napoleon at the time. I hated the idea of striking bargains with the Fascists, especially since I had a pretty good idea of the sinister side of the Nazi adventure, to which the only answer for us was its total destruction, but on the other hand I do not think it commensurate with human dignity for us to lower ourselves to the level of an enemy as though revenge were only possible below the belt. I am not saying for a moment that Laval was right. I am merely saying that he and Pétain between them saved millions of lives, an error for which France could never forgive them.

It is perhaps a little easier to reach such conclusions in retrospect.

I thought so at the time. I even wrote a play about it in 1950. In many ways it is the best play I have written, although few people agree with me.

I remember. But why this sudden outburst? All because I invoked the name of justice?

What higher name could you invoke, especially at a moment when it was far indeed from my mind? Do you recollect the precise wording of the result of my War Office Selection Board? "On no account is this man to be put in charge of others."

That makes you smile now?

It made me smile at the time. Doesn't it remind you of something?

"He shows great originality, which must be curbed at all cost"?

Precisely. Our favorite school report. And, do you remember being asked the name of the greatest composer who ever lived?

Remind me . . .

I put down Bach, and I was told I had the wrong answer, since Beethoven was the greatest of all composers. I was heard to murmur that, to my mind, Mozart was his superior, and was made to write out one hundred times "Beethoven is the greatest composer who ever lived."

It's a wonder we can still stand fate knocking at the door after such an unpromising introduction to his genius. And wasn't there another question, in a general knowledge paper? Name one Russian composer?

Exactly. The correct answer was Tchaikovsky, wasn't it?

It was indeed.

What did you put?

I put Rimsky-Korsakov and was upbraided before the whole school for showing off.

I see your point about living with injustice.

10

I JOINED Lieutenant Colonel Niven, Captain Reed, and Major Ambler in an office at the Ritz Hotel. The film, now blessed by the Army, was to be produced by Two Cities Films (the Two Cities being, no doubt, London and Rome), of which Filippo del Giudice was the guiding light.

My status was still rather obscure. It was easy to gather a handful of officers together arbitrarily for the pursuit of a particular end. To add a Private to this assembly was virtually impossible. There had been no reason for such an anomaly at Waterloo; there was no reason for it now. Not much had changed in military thinking since then. The only conceivable reason for a Private soldier to have any prolonged contact with an officer was if he were appointed that officer's servant, or batman. I consequently became David Niven's batman, with one set of barked instructions to keep his boots and belt polished at all times, and with another set of whispered ones to help produce a film as good in its way as *The New Lot*.

Our work in a room at the Ritz Hotel had some advantages as far as I was concerned. By the intervention of David Niven, I was excused from crossing London in the dawn's early light for the purpose of marching to breakfast. Another was a pass, conceived by David, which announced to the prying eye of the Military Police that "This man may go anywhere, and do anything at his discretion in the course of his duty." (An MP who stopped me in front of the Hippodrome Theatre and demanded to see my pass, read it. His cruel mouth dropped open, and he asked me, " 'Ow d'you wangle that?" I told him that such passes were extremely rare, but that they came with "David Niven's autograph, an' all." He sent me on my way with an obscenity of such surpassing vulgarity that even the permissiveness of the day does not allow me to quote, but it did adequately dramatize the degree of his envy.)

There was, from my point of view, one drawback in working at the Ritz. All my distinguished colleagues had made a certain capital before the war, and therefore had a little to fall back on. I had had no time for this. Consequently they rang room service as we worked away at the script, and absently ordered rounds of drinks. My embarrassment increased with each glass because of my utter inability to reciprocate. I calculated that on those rare occasions when I did call the waiter and order a round with what I imagined was the same nonchalance as they, it cost me ten days' pay. Quite clearly this could not go on.

I had at home one single article of value, which I had bought in a moment of folly. It was a nude by Derain. I now solemnly took it to a dealer, who told me it wasn't a very good nude and that it wasn't a very good Derain, and who bought it for £60. With this, I reckoned to be able to keep up with my officers in hospitality for a couple of months at least.

Many years after the war, in Hollywood, David Niven invited me to dinner. There, on the wall, I was staggered to see my Derain. I asked him where he got it.

"Dear chum," he replied, "it's perhaps the best bargain of my life. D'you remember when we were all working at the Ritz?"

I felt the color drain from my cheeks.

". . . Well, I bought it from a dealer for sixty-five pounds."

Earlier, while still in the infantry, I had been commissioned by a small London gallery to write a piece for a catalogue about human physiognomy, which was to accompany an exhibition of portraits. The fee was £5. When I turned up with my article, written by the light of a failing torch on the barrack-room floor, the owner of the gallery told me he could no longer afford £5, and he was going out of business. Seeing my evident distress, he said the best he could do was to give me a picture out of stock, and call it a day. He gave me a framed picture which I didn't even deign to look at, such was my anger. It was only in 1965, when I built a chalet in Switzerland, that I looked through all my neglected belongings to take stock of what I possessed. I found this picture again, and looked at it for the first time. It is a large watercolor by Kokoschka.

As I said before, half the time injustice is on your side. My heart goes out to the two dealers, who were the ones who really suffered in both instances.

The film progressed, and we were accorded military advisers who had a high enough rank to acquire facilities for us, but who were not urgently needed in the war effort. These specifications limited us to officers temporarily in limbo because they had had rows with Montgomery. There was quite a pool of these. The first one inspired immediate confidence. He had a neat black mustache and earnest brown eyes, and carried a leather attaché case which I imagined to be full of secret documents. When eventually he opened it, it was revealed to be full to the brim of pipe tobacco. In other words, he filled his pipe directly from the attaché case. He apologized because he had been away from the day-to-day business of soldiering for quite a time.

"One officer," said Eric Ambler, referring to the script, "marches his men along a defile waiting to attack the enemy. What would he do when he comes within the sudden sound of gunfire?"

The adviser's eyes narrowed as he lit his pipe in order to concentrate better.

"What would he do . . . what would he do . . ." he kept mur-

muring. "Christ, it's so long since I . . . hm . . . officer . . . defile
. . . enemy . . . gunfire . . . what would he do . . ."

At length, when the meditation had extended itself to embarrassing lengths, I broke in nervously.

"Would he halt them?" I asked.

His face brightened. "That's it! Of course! What else could he do? Halt them," he said. While Eric and I exchanged glances, the officer, his confidence now restored, asked, "Next question?"

Eventually shooting began in Denham Studios, and with it, the exciting news that we would do our locations in North Africa. Once again, the problem arose as to what to do with me. As a Private on a troopship, I would be isolated from my collaborators, and the same might well be true in Africa. This time, the project had advanced sufficiently for me to be made a temporary civilian, so that I could at least deal with the military advisers on equal terms. The good news was charmingly broken to David Niven by a friendly general, who was also a movie buff: "Tell Ustinov he can reach for his bowler hat."

The journey to North Africa was uneventful, if one can call frequent submarine alarms and mountainous seas uneventful. We were aboard a luxury liner, *The Monarch of Bermuda*, together with Canadian, British, and New Zealand troops, and a single Italian officer, the first we had seen on our side, foolishly ostracized by many Allied officers, but befriended by an English nurse in what was to become a touching shipboard romance.

Some years after the war, during my first and only visit to a certain London restaurant, I saw them again at a distant table. Curiously enough, after all that time, I recognized them instantly. They were engaged in a somber and difficult discussion. He had been weeping. I risked going up to them. They were now married, she was pregnant, and he had been told that his permit to stay in the United Kingdom could not be renewed owing to the fact that he had no employment. I asked him what his profession had been before the war. He told me he had been an announcer on Rome radio. I called a friend in the Italian section of the BBC and discovered that they had just lost one of their announcers. The shipboard Romeo went to the BBC, and I am told eventually rose to dizzy heights within that hierarchy.

As an ancient Boy Scout, I can say that this is one of the very few neat and tidy good deeds I can come up with in my favor at the pearly gates.

Also aboard were a handful of American sportsmen, on their way to entertain American troops with illustrated films of their exploits. Among the group was Jack Sharkey, an ex-heavyweight champion of the world. He was an engaging if monosyllabic character who drank rather heavily one night when the seas were particularly high, with the result that he was obsessed with dreams of bygone glory and staggered into the large stateroom in which I was trying desperately to control my queaziness, looking for a fight. I was right on the level of his haggard eye, and tried to make myself small and insignificant.

In the bunk above me lay Bob Fellowes, an officer attached to us, who had lost a leg by standing on a land mine and who was not to survive his injury for long. He had just received the latest artificial limb from the United States, and he now began easing it out of his trouser leg. When Mr. Sharkey had already loomed into the immediate foreground, Bob held his leg above his head, and said in the voice of a strict governess, "Mr. Sharkey, if you don't leave us alone, I'm going to kick you."

Sharkey must have seen, as in a haze, a man holding his own leg above his head in a menacing gesture, without realizing that it was artificial. A khaki sock and a handmade brogue shoe were still attached to it. At all events, he let out a howl as though in the presence of the supernatural, and staggered melodramatically out into the passageway.

My only other memory of this troubled voyage was the inevitable ship's concert, in which I was constrained to do my party turns, but the star of which was undoubtedly a Maori unit who performed a war dance. At the end of the show, the entertainment officer, an elderly major with sandy hair and a monocle, proposed a vote of thanks for all those who had contributed to the gala, "Most especially," he went on, "the group of talented aboriginals."

The well of insensitivity is indeed bottomless.

In Algiers we acquired another temporarily rejected Colonel to help us, this one with a predilection for sitting on his shooting stick indoors, at the expense of carpets.

Naturally, being cooped up in England for the duration had given me a somewhat parochial viewpoint of the war. Now we began to have our vision broadened, forcibly. Shooting in Philippeville before a fine stucco house, I noticed the curtains rustling. Someone was observing us. After a while, an Arab girl dressed as a European maid, with white lace cap and apron, ran out toward us and curtsied. Her master had been watching the shooting and invited Carol Reed and myself in for a brandy after lunch. We accepted.

He was sitting at the end of a long table, eating an orange. His napkin was tucked into the top of his sports shirt. He was a man in his fifties, bald and portly, with sad, unscrupulous blue eyes. His wife sat not at the other end of the long table, but by his side.

Ah, he complained, in a flat voice, what a tiresome war it was, and what a cruel destiny to have been born on the wrong side of the Mediterranean. The Arabs, he said confidentially, were dirty and unreliable. We wandered out into the pool area, where he offered us cigars. What would we prefer — Uppmann, Hoyo de Monterey, Punch, Romeo y Julieta, Henry Clay? He had them all. And as for a brandy, did we fancy Martell, Remy Martin, Hine, Courvoisier? He had had the presence of mind to lay in a stock. He beckoned to the deck chairs while the chlorinated water sent its little shivering reflections onto the parasols. Yes, he repeated, the Arabs were dirty and unreliable, and he chose to say it as the Arab maid was serving us. We puffed our cigars and swilled our cognac around slowly in our balloon glasses.

He was, it transpired, a wholesale wood merchant. He would have given anything to transplant his house to Cannes or to San Remo — his family had come from the luxuriant region between the two, this French *pied-noir* of Italian origin — but one must be realistic; over on the other, civilized bank of the Mediterranean, there were neither the business opportunities nor the cheap labor. There were small mercies in abundance, and one must be grateful for them. More brandy? Only yesterday, for instance, he had returned from Algiers after having concluded yet another large and lucrative contract with the Allied High Command.

"A contract?" I asked. "What for?"

"Coffins," he replied.

Episodes like this help explain subsequent history. Naturally, being in the hands of the military is not the ideal way to visit foreign countries, but sometimes poetic images are enhanced by the abnormality of the situation. The casbahs of Bizerte, for instance, in which the inhabitants seemed to have been evacuated at a moment's notice. Coffee cups, some with coffee still in them, stood on the little Moorish tables, as though a latter-day Pompeii had been the victim of a false alarm. Elsewhere, we were blowing up buildings for the benefit of a film, in which I was also playing the part of an Italian innkeeper. American sappers were joyously doing the damage, and when in their cups, played practical jokes on each other with booby traps and dynamite.

Our Colonel was absolutely impervious to what his hosts were up to as he sat impassively on his shooting stick in the living room, puffing at flat Turkish cigarettes flown out specially for him by Fribourg and Treyer, London's most exclusive tobacconist. He demonstrated once again those qualities of sangfroid and steadfastness which had won him the highest medals at Salerno. A huge explosion rent the air, bringing half the ceiling down on him. He did not move an inch. He just sat there, ridges of cream-colored dust on the brim of his cap and the top of his whiskers, and carefully examined his cigarette, which he had only just lit.

"Ruined my confounded weed," he grumbled. The American engineers, sobered by the miscalculation in their practical joke, gazed at him as though he were some kind of Machiavellian spoilsport.

One day, Carol Reed was directing a scene with Stanley Holloway and some other actors playing a game of darts in my café. He asked me to bustle around in the background, talking Arabic to the extras. I told him that Arabic was one of the enormous number of languages I didn't know. He told me to make Arab noises. "It's almost out of earshot," he said. "Who's to know?"

I did as I was told, and all went well until take four, when without warning, all the extras rose and left. "Cut," said Carol. "What's wrong?"

They seemed to be on strike, although the reasons for their industrial action were, to say the least, obscure. Eventually it was explained as intermediaries argued with the extras. Apparently, in improvising my Arabic, I had appeared to refer to them as tortoise droppings. I swore to them that nothing had been further from my mind. After all, why should a restaurateur call his clients tortoise droppings while he is taking their orders?

"We thought you didn't speak our language until you called us that unmentionable name," said the henchman, his eyes flashing with fury. "Now we know you do!"

Apparently it was not the fact that I had inadvertently referred to them as droppings which was offensive — it was the size of the droppings which counted. Camel droppings, or better, lion droppings, would be deemed almost flattering, as far as insults can be flattering. Flea droppings would have occasioned assault with the cutlery. Tortoise droppings were just on the borderline between assault and strike action, and they had taken a clement view of my lapse.

Two hours later, shooting resumed. I steered clear of the tables of the troublemakers, and stuck to Italian.

All too soon, the great breath of fresh air was over, and we were back in England, our job finished. *The Way Ahead* opened the morning of the invasion and was a great success. Flushed with my contribution to this triumph, I was called back into the Army. Whereas it was admitted that the Germans now had their hands too full to bother much about Wembley, there were perhaps fears that the Japanese might parachute Kamikaze editors into the outskirts of

London in order to disrupt our training films. Whatever the truth about this, Wembley had become far more military with the passing of an overt military threat.

Now it was hard to believe that the place had anything to do with a craft, let alone an art. A new and extremely busy Sergeant Major had been installed in order to whip the establishment into shape, with the result that it was difficult for it to fulfill its primary function, the production of training films, even though, in compensation, brasses gleamed brightly and spoken instructions were now shouted.

I remember the projection of a training film about how tanks should use smoke, toward which I had made some miniscule contribution. A celebrated General came to see the result of our work, and all the officers, the ex-production managers, second-assistants, and clapper-boys jockeyed for position to receive the congratulations of the gilt-edged pundit. As the lights went up, the General patently ignored the gallant assembly, opened the door of the projection booth, and said to the Private in charge, who didn't even have time to hide his comic-book: "Damn good show. Keep up the good work," and strode away unaccompanied to his staff car.

It was not I who began to crumble in this fruitless atmosphere, but my stomach. Despite the fact that I was ostensibly doing my duty by being in uniform, I have never in my life had such feelings of being absolutely useless as I had during my four and a half years in the service. At the same time, I am by no means ungrateful, since it did enable me to work with highly disciplined and talented creators such as Carol Reed, Eric Ambler, and David Niven, and to form friendships which have lasted throughout my life. Nevertheless, the shock of being consulted by high-ranking officers and psychiatrists one moment and being berated the next for having boots in which some oafish Corporal could not see an entirely faithful reproduction of his face began to tell on my constitution. I suffered from cramps, which may well have been psychosomatic, but the word was not yet in common use. I was sent to a military hospital for observation.

My observer was a charming Singhalese (or is it now Sri Lankan) doctor with a Portuguese name, who had a greater sensibility than usual toward the vagaries of the spirit under martial law. It was established that my gallbladder was emptying too slowly, and that the origin of my complaint was surely nervous. I was consequently ordered a complete rest in a wing of the hospital which overlooked the playground of a lunatic asylum. Through the window I could see, at all hours of the day and night, elderly ladies looking distressingly like those in Thurber drawings running about, hooting like peacocks, and lifting their shifts over their heads. It was as though these delightful caricatures had suddenly broken away from their master's pen and turned sinister.

Since my complaint had been put down to nerves, I was eventually sent to see a man called a Personnel Selection Officer, who was in fact a kind of lay psychiatrist with the function of avoiding what were known as, in the jargon of the day, square pegs in round holes. All was to be done to find me employment compatible with my inclinations. That was the theory. The practice, as so often, was rather different. The man was Scottish, with the rather unusual physical features of a coal-black mustache and a snow-white crew cut. He looked like Groucho Marx in his heyday in a very bad print, but he was less engaging, less comic, and finally, far less human.

He said he had examined my case, and asked me how much I earned in civvy street.

I told him that since I was self-employed, my earnings would fluctuate.

He patiently renewed his question, as though dealing with some dim-witted colonial.

"It's not too difficult to understand," he crooned in his lilting Scots accent. "I merely wished to know your weekly income in time of peace."

I told him I had understood his question, and would make every effort to make the answer as simple.

"Since I am an actor and a writer, I have no regular employment. I very often make nothing in a week — " I attempted a laugh, in which he failed to join. "When I do make something, it is of a variable or inconsistent nature."

He closed his eyes as though summoning hidden reserves of patience, and breathed deeply.

"I don't know why you are making this so difficult," he murmured in a clenched voice. "I merely asked you the extent of your paycheck at the end of every week."

"And that is precisely the question to which I cannot give you an accurate answer," I replied between my gritted teeth. "You must have heard of an actor having a bad year. Well a bad year is made up of a preponderance of bad weeks over good weeks. By the same token, a good year is made up of a preponderance of good weeks over bad weeks. It surely stands to reason that it is impossible to give a mean ratio of good and bad weeks because I haven't been going that long."

He sighed, and looked up at the ceiling as though something of rare interest were going on up there. I declined to follow his gaze, since I knew perfectly well that nothing at all was going on up there.

"Let me phrase my question differently," he said at length. "If we were at peace this week, how much money would you have made?"

At this juncture, I had a brain storm.

"If you wish, sir, I can tell you how much money I have made this week."

He shut his eyes and broke a pencil.

"I know how much money you have made this week," he moaned, as though tears were not far off. "You are a Private soldier in His Majesty's Armed Forces. I *know* how much money you have made this week!"

"But you do not, sir," I insisted. My fourth play, *The Banbury Nose*, had opened in Edinburgh, starring Roger Livesey and Ursula Jeans. The notices were very promising, and I had just received a royalty check. I consulted a bit of paper. "Last week, I made eighty pounds seventeen shillings and fourpence, not counting my Private's pay."

He banged his fist on the table, and sprang to his feet.

"You're lying!" he yelled.

I explained the facts of the case, hoping that the mention of Edinburgh might soothe his anger. He was probably a Glaswegian, for my information did nothing but stiffen his intractability.

"Right," he said, fixing me darkly across the table, on which lay one of those simple-minded games which children of six play with ease, but over which the hesitations of grown men are supposed to betray their strengths and failings. "Right, these are my findings. You are clearly psychologically unsuited to film writing, therefore I am sending you as a clerk-storeman to the Royal Army Ordnance depot in Donington Park, where your duties will be to grade underwear in sizes — "

I neither listened nor heard any more. For once in my life, I surrendered to an outburst of temper. All my frustrations with the idiocy and the uncertainty of this cringing existence overflowed into a transcendant rage. I picked up the game, and dashed it to the ground. The Scotsman, alarmed, backed to the door and called for help. I was seized by a couple of Military Policemen, and rushed to see the resident psychiatrist, who turned out to be a female Colonel with flashes on her shoulders carrying the surprising word "Bermuda."

Asked about my reactions to the Personnel Selection Officer's decision, I pointed out that it was hardly his province to say that I was psychologically unfit for film-writing when a film I had helped to write was on general release to extravagant critical acclaim. I went on to speak sentimentally about the happy times I had spent working for the Directorate of Army Psychiatry, times that were no more, now that I was destined to grade underwear so that the Japanese could be brought to their knees more effectively.

She was sensitive to my sarcasm, and laughed merrily as though the absurdity of my situation brought her a certain relief from routine. She ordered me a cup of tea, and told me not to worry. I would be transferred in a week or so to a branch of the Army specializing in entertainment. I went back to my hospital room unaccompanied by the Military Police, and gazed at the mentally ill.

A man dressed in a morning coat was being upbraided by a gray-haired woman in a shift.

"Harold, you always come and see me in your working clothes!" she howled.

There were, as ever, far worse predicaments than mine.

With my mother.

Fred Astaire in preference to Harold Lloyd.

My father and his airplane in the Great War.

With Isolde in Green Park the day after the opening of *The House of Regrets*. London News Agency Photos Ltd.

Liselotte Beethoven-Fink.

Advice from a great actor, Sir Ralph Richardson.

Romanoff and Juliet.
President of my own country at last. Courtesy of Universal Pictures

Captain Vere in *Billy Budd*. Allied Artists.

Script conference with Kirk Douglas. Courtesy of Universal Pictures.

Beau Brummell, with Elizabeth Taylor. From the N

lease *Beau Brummell* © 1954 Metro-Goldwyn-Mayer Inc.

My parents.

Their son and grandson.

Andrea and Pavla Ustinov.
Rayner Fichael.

On the set of *The Last Remake of Beau Geste*
with Andrea and Igor. Courtesy of Universal Pictures.

Photo Finish, with Paul Rogers. Tom Hustler, Ltd.

With my wife Hélène. DPA.

11

I was still at the military hospital when *The Banbury Nose* opened in London at Wyndham's Theatre. My second play, a one-acter, the only one of the genre I have ever written, opened successfully at the Arts Theatre in 1942 on a double bill with *The Playboy of the Western World*, and my third, *Blow Your Own Trumpet*, put on by the Old Vic in 1943, was an unqualified disaster. Of rhapsodic construction, somewhat reminiscent of Saroyan, it seemed far too wayward for the very critics who had so spoiled me initially, and the play ran for thirteen performances.

Now I had written another tragicomedy, this one running backwards from the nineteen forties via the nineteen twenties to the turn of the century. The ironic content was given a sharp dramatic relief by this construction, since the characters were all old and bitter at the beginning and young and full of hope at the end.

Bill Linnit, the impresario, wished me to attend the dress rehearsal in order to effect last-minute changes should these be necessary, and rang the Commandant of the hospital. The latter, a Colonel, was quite agreeable to my going, but let drop a huge hint that he, and more especially his wife, were very keen on the theater and that their hostage would be more readily released at the price of two good box-seats. A bargain was struck, and I traveled to London.

The first night was a qualified success, and I was forced to accept several curtain calls along with the cast. This was the first of my plays to run over a hundred performances and James Agate in his notice referred to me as "the greatest master of stage-craft at present working in the British Theatre." Here was another example of injustice working in my favor. A balance was struck when, on returning to the military hospital, I found myself on a charge for having taken my curtain-calls in uniform, wearing suede shoes.

Before any penalty could be exacted for this unthinkable affront to military protocol, I was hurried out of the hospital by the psychiatrists, and sent to an Army entertainment unit. First I had to return to my parent establishment, the Army Kinematograph Service, where my reception was cool, to say the least. The new Sergeant Major made some caustic remarks about my being a "nut-case," his unblinking eyes boring into what he imagined to be my vulnerability. As he helped load a mountain of kit on to my back, tightening straps unbearably to contain me like a corset, his parting shot was, "And I can tell you, young man, that *whoever* your next Sar'nt Major turns out to be, you will remember me as *mild*, as *helpful*, and the soul of *kindness*, is that *clear?*"

These words were, by their very nature, snarled. I arrived at my new destination, an early Victorian house in Grosvenor Square, and faced my new Sergeant Major. He smiled at me and said, "Let me help you out of all this *hideous* equipment." In his way, he was quite as emphatic as his counterpart in Wembley.

He was, in normal times, a celebrated wigmaker, a career he pursues profitably and brilliantly to this day. I was sent to Salisbury, where I directed *The Rivals* by Sheridan. Dame Edith Evans, as a gesture of customary generosity toward the war effort, played Mrs. Malaprop for the first time in her long and glorious career, while I attempted the role of Sir Anthony Absolute. We had a happy mixture of civilian and military actors, and as an unexpected bonus, eight members of the Berlin Philharmonic Orchestra, under their leader, Lance Corporal Professor Doktor Reinhard Strietzel, and seven members of the Vienna Philharmonic, under their leader Private Professor Doktor Rudolf Stiasny, all now members of the Pioneer Corps, a section of the British Army organized as a reserve of foreign talents, eager to do their "bit" against Hitler.

Rehearsals had their ups and downs. The orchestra seemed divided against itself, the first violin and conductor, Professor Strietzel, seeming to be at loggerheads with the first cello, Professor Stiasny, which culminated in an ugly scene — a storm, as it were, in a schnapps glass — during which Lance Corporal Strietzel threatened to put Professor Stiasny under close arrest. He pointed to the single stripe on his arm with the tip of his bow, calling out in a thick German accent — "You know vat zis means?"

The conflict was complicated by the intervention of Edith Evans, who reminded us all that it was a play with music, not an opera with dialogue. Immediately the musical contention between Austria and the Reich was forgotten. All fifteen bickering musicians were united against the Muse of drama, or more accurately, against Edith Evans. As they filed out of the rehearsal hall to make way for the mummers, Professor Strietzel, carrying his violin case as though it contained a machine gun, looked straight at poor Edith and said with a wealth of sinister meaning, "I don't know . . . how all zis . . . shall end!"

The play, performed in garrison theaters in very flimsy yet evocative sets, assuring a rapid continuity of action, opened in Salisbury and was an instant success. One distinguished Admiral was even compelled to admit to Edith Evans, "By Jove, I'm embarrassed to say that this is the first play by Shakespeare I've seen since *Richard of Bordeaux!*"

One drawback of these garrison theaters was that there was no method of concealing the orchestra. Its members sat on the same level as the audience. It was merely the actors who were elevated. I noticed on the first night that the orchestra made use of a miniature chessboard in order to while away the time during the histrionics, and often musicians crept forward like troops in a dugout to make some snide move. As far as I could understand it was a permanent championship, Berlin versus Vienna.

I hoped and prayed that Edith Evans wouldn't notice what was going on, but on the fourth night, during a brilliant tirade, she stopped dead. One eye had alighted on the tiny chessboard just as an Austrian viola player had spotted a crack in the enemy defense and was creeping forward on all fours to deliver the coup de grace.

She faltered, fumbled, and then, with superb dramatic instinct, she looked at me and said, in a tone of pained surprise, "What did you say?"

Determined not to be placed on the defensive, I invented a little Sheridan:

"Madam, though the humors of Bath be but a diversion to our contumely, I will not presume on your generosity to the extent of belittling those very qualities which, while they do us but scant justice before the evil tongues of the town, nevertheless becalm the odious, and bring success to fools."

Neither I nor the audience knew what on earth I was talking about, but I said it, or something like it, with immense conviction, with a result that an exit was rewarded by a burst of spontaneous applause.

Poor Edith was livid, and kept referring to the chess playing as a "Gilbertian situation." After the show, I accosted Professor Strietzel. To soften the blow somewhat (for after all, he *was* a Lance Corporal, and I had seen how hostile he had become toward poor Private Stiasny) I told him he had never played better than on that night.

His face lit up.

"You are a *real* musician," he counter-flattered; "tonight, for ze *först* time, ze Boccherini was good, alzo I still have trouble mit ze Mozart und ze Dittersdorf."

"Yes," I replied reasonably, "but even there, I noticed a distinct improvement."

"Even there, even there!" he agreed.

"There's only one thing . . . one criticism."

"Ach!" His face darkened once again in anticipation of some searing words of truth.

"The game of chess," I said.

He bridled like a frisky horse.

"Are you zerious?" he asked quietly.

"I'm afraid so. There has to be an end to it. It is frightfully distracting for the actors. We can see your every move down there, and — "

"It distracts you?" he inquired, all innocence and soft surprise.

"Yes," I said.

"No!" he roared. "You are too fine an artist to be distracted. It's zis voman!"

"Now come on!" I snapped, simulating crossness. "She's a most distinguished actress and a wonderful person — "

"It's not as zough it vas a big chessboard," he shouted, and then his voice became dramatically diminutive. "It vas a little chessboard." His two index fingers reduced its imaginary size to about one-inch square.

"The smaller the chessboard the greater the distance you have to travel to make a move, and the greater the distraction for us," I declared.

He knew a checkmate when he saw it, and retired from the scene of battle.

The next night, Edith found it hard to concentrate, which was unlike her, being a creature of a ferocious inner discipline and usually impervious to external influence. As soon as I hobbled on the stage in the guise of my gouty paterfamilias, I saw what was happening.

The orchestra, deprived of its chessboard, had now arranged the lights from its music stands so that its members were lit from beneath, and they now followed Edith's every move in this ghostly light, looking for the world like war criminals following the arguments of their advocate with misgiving and resignation.

Once again, at the end of the performance, I was compelled to accost Professor Strietzel.

"Tonight," I said sternly, "it was not so good."

He was in surly temper.

"Vonce again," he grumbled, "you giff proof of your musicianship. Stiasny is like a mule zo stubborn. Ze Boccherini vas vun funeral march, not vun minuet. A disgrace. Ze Mozart vas a little better, and ze Dittersdorf superb. Ze rest — "

"I have a criticism."

"Please." He smiled like a headwaiter confronted with a fly in the mayonnaise.

"Why do you follow Edith Evans with your eyes in a manner calculated to disturb any performer, any artist?"

What was left of his smile faded, and he became controlledly rational.

"First, it vas ze chessboard. Correct me if I am wrong. Chess ve shouldn't play . . ."

"That is correct."

"So ve leave ze chessboard at home. Vot else can ve do? Ve follow ze play. Ve look at ze voman."

Suddenly the constriction of his voice and the coolness of his presentation of the facts deserted him. He shouted volcanically:

"You tink it giffs us *pleasure* to vatch zis voman? Ve, who haff seen Paula Wessely at her height!"

I tried to top him in bluster, but he lowered his voice to a kind of lugubrious mutter, at the same time looking into the distance to lend a cosmic significance to his words.

"You know, ven ve left Germany, mit conzentration camps and persecution, ve tought ve vould come to a land vere ve could breathe — "

Here he gave an ingenious impression of a plant opening its petals to the sun, but he quickly shriveled.

"But no," he said brokenly, "it's all ze same — persecution . . . prison bars . . ."

I was outraged. I told him angrily that I saw no connection between myself and a Gauleiter.

"Not you, dear friend — "

Nor did I think that any more ludicrous comparison could be made than one equating a dear, human, and profoundly religious creature like Edith Evans with Heinrich Himmler.

He nodded in a way which suggested that everyone is entitled to his own opinion, no one more so than he who has suffered a deprivation of liberty to play chess in an orchestra pit.

The next night Edith was brilliant. The only trouble was the almost total absence of laughs. I made my entrance, and, inspired by the zest and brio of Edith Evans, I acted as well as I knew how, in complete and utter silence. It was acutely depressing. Not even the presence of three Generals in the front row could justify the extraordinary dullness of the audience.

When I had a free moment, I rushed to the back of the auditorium in order to unravel the mystery. I did not have far to seek. The musicians had now reversed their positions, and sat facing the audience, their heads just visible above the rail of the orchestra pit. Lit from beneath, like mournful skittles waiting for the usual knocks of fate, they dampened the spirits of the onlookers.

Edith was very upset by the deterioration in the audience's quality, and left the stage with the unspoken conviction that she was face to face with *force majeure.* I found no words to express my horror at such diabolical ingenuity. I just shook a negative head at Professor Strietzel, who smiled imperceptibly and shrugged a fatalistic shoulder.

The rest of the run was most successful, and for the record I must add that the chess games on the miniature board were resumed and Edith never seemed to notice them any more. By the last performance, the Austrians were leading the Germans by twenty-four matches to twenty-one, with nineteen drawn matches.

I was faced by the prospect of being sent to the Far East, playing a comic bishop reduced to his underwear in a well-known farce, the rights of which were owned by an officer of the unit. This was certainly one way of increasing his pocket money, and I only mention it because when an application to join SHAEF, the Allied Supreme Headquarters, saved me from this destiny, he roundly accused me of a lack of patriotism.

Another officer of even higher rank called me to his office and told me to lock the door behind me. He talked awkwardly about the uncertainties of life now that the war was coming to an end and commended me on *The Banbury Nose,* which he said he had enjoyed. Then he tried to sell me his wristwatch.

SHAEF wished an official film to be made about the war in the West. It had assembled Carol Reed and myself representing the British side, Garson Kanin, the poet Harry Brown, and the screenwriter Guy Trosper from the United States, and Claude Dauphin from France. The music was to be written by Marc Blitzstein, then in the American Army.

The scheme of the film was ambitious, in that Harry Brown was to write lyrical bridges in blank verse for the various episodes, which were to be constructed as they came in from the material of courageous front-line cameramen. It was often my duty to go to the seat of military censorship in Davies Street, near Claridge's Hotel, and watch these films as they arrived. This work could be quite boring, more especially since a Dutch censor might ask for certain shots to be cut owing to the fact that a physical landmark might give away the Allied dispositions, or his Belgian counterpart might decide that a church steeple or belfry was easy to recognize, and that therefore it was unwise to release the film of a battle in such a locality before the place was well behind our lines. In such cases, everything stopped while the incisions were made. My work was to earmark certain highly dramatic or evocative sections for use by us.

One day of heat, without any warning whatsoever, Hermann Goering appeared on our screen. There had been no mention whatsoever of his capture, no hint even. He was, to our astonishment, surrounded by American officers who were posing with him for pictures, smiling, patting his back in friendly fashion, demanding autographs on behalf of small relatives who would live close to history from that day on, and offering to initiate him in the mysterious rites of chewing gum. Goering looked sallow and thinner than I had imagined, quite apart from being distinctly nervous. Having been informed about the Allied war aims, he certainly had every right to his nervousness. This began to wear off, however, under the relentless impact of these big puppies, leaping all over him and licking his face.

By the time the lights went up in the auditorium, he was as relaxed and playful as any of his captors, and we spectators could only look at each other in petrified amazement. Later that day, so I gathered subsequently, General Eisenhower saw the film, and in an uncharacteristic rage sent every recognizable officer home to less exacting duties. The next time we saw Goering, he was having his belt forcibly and unceremoniously removed by a United States Top Sergeant. I shall always remember the pain on his face at this brusque behavior, which so contrasted with the earlier delights of captivity. I never thought I would feel a pang of sorrow for the man.

The second document that will always live with me was of a graver and more terrible character: the entry of British troops into Belsen concentration camp. A Sergeant came out of the gates, and even on the black and white screen his face had gained an expression over which he had no control. It was of extraordinary complexity, at once earnest, furious, resolved, and glacial. His men had fallen out by the roadside. They were smoking and chatting among themselves. He shouted an order. They were not too quick in obeying him. He shouted again. Needless to say there was no sound on any of this film. It was all pantomime, which often made it seem exceptionally graphic in that the onlooker's imagination was stimulated to fill in the gaps.

The troops seemed puzzled as the Sergeant gave the order to slow march. They could hardly believe the order, because they could see no necessity for such solemnity. Once again, it was repeated.

The long line of soldiers marched slowly through the gates into the stench and came face to face with the obscene evidence of genocide — the mountains of bones, linked by a webbing of flesh; the expressionless eyes of the fittest, the survivors; the miserable human garbage scattered on the soil. One after the other, individual soldiers fell out, vomiting helplessly on all fours. The Sergeant could threaten and bluster; it made no difference. The shock had felled these men with a blow to the stomach, and there was nothing discipline could do. Suddenly one soldier went berserk. He broke ranks for no visible reason. Eyes wild, he ran, and the camera followed him.

On a step sat a derelict German soldier, an overage man in a huge greatcoat and a muffler. The flaps of his forage cap had fallen over his ears, and he looked like an exhausted gundog as he sat staring at nothing. The British soldier ran up to him, let his rifle drop to the ground, picked up his victim by the collar of his vast coat, and began kicking and hitting him without mercy. The Sergeant arrived at the double and struggled with his man. The German dropped into precisely the same position he had occupied before. On his face there was now something horribly like gratitude.

This irresistible assault on our sense of normality was, happily, matched by a counterpoint of slapstick worthy of Laurel and Hardy. The formal surrender of Field Marshal Milch to a youthful British General, in which the Field Marshal, true to protocol, saluted by bringing his baton up to his cap, and then formally handed it over. The British General took the baton, weighed it for a moment, and smacked it down hard on the Field Marshal's head, sending him down for the count. It was all so surprising, and so unexpected, that it released an explosion of laughter from the censors, quickly controlled as they realized the embarrassing consequences of such an act. Since I was more bound by the rules of comedy than by the terms of the Geneva convention, I have always marveled at the pure, untrammeled comic technique of that particular General.

Filippo del Giudice, who had always befriended me, now thought the time had come for me to write and direct a film of my own. Since I was twenty-four years of age, it struck me that the time had, indeed, come. The Air Ministry, eager to have a film of their own about the discovery of radar, had approached del Giudice, known as Del by friends and enemies alike, guaranteeing full cooperation for such a project. Del, in his turn, decided to confide in me, and asked the spokesman of the Air Ministry, an ebullient gentleman by name of Sir Robert Renwick, to apply for me to be attached to the Air Force pending demobilization.

I was flattered and delighted, and, as so often, foolishly free of qualms about the magnitude or the difficulty of the project. Sir Robert Renwick liked to do things by telephone, and went his bustling way organizing the assistance that would be given me when I visited Malvern, the semisecret government scientific research establishment.

He telephoned me, and said, more or less: "Now look here, Ustinov, I've laid everything on. You are to be treated as a VIP and nothing will be held back. Feel free to ask what questions you will, and if there's any holding back, I want to know about it. We want a good film, an informative film, a commercial film, a little laughter, a little pathos, a lot of hard facts and rip-roaring adventure. Because that's what it is, you know. Adventure. Unadulterated bloody adventure. No fiction can stand up to it. I'm sending a staff car to fetch you at O-nine-hundred hours tomorrow morning, as ever is. Look out for a mud-colored Humber, with RAF markings, and — oh, Ustinov, since this is a somewhat formal visit, I should wear a uniform."

"But sir — " I pleaded urgently.

"Call me Bob," he snapped, and hung up.

Just after nine o'clock, a mud-colored Humber limousine drove into the mews in which we lived. I stood there, once again carrying all my equipment on my back and holding a rifle.

An RAF Sergeant was at the wheel. He whistled for me to come toward him and cast a critical eye over my appearance.

"D'you know where No. 34 is then?" he asked.

"Yes," I replied, "it's my house, over there. Since you are a little late, I thought I'd save time by waiting for you in the street."

Privates can be cruel too, give half a chance.

We drove in utter silence. Two Military Policemen on motor-cycles nearly fell off their mounts when they saw us pass. They turned around, caught up with us, and gave me a cautious once-over. I nodded gracefully to them, and made a gesture with my hand, regal in its economy. They gave up the chase out of prudence, and the last I saw of them, they were discussing the matter by the roadside.

I had been told to report to the officer's mess in Malvern, where I was greeted by an elderly Squadron Leader, the soul of kindness.

"Hello, laddie," he cried, in his singsong voice, "and what can we do for you?"

"I believe there is a room booked here in my name, sir."

"Oh, I'm afraid that's impossible, son," he said, with genuine regret. "This is the Officer's Mess, savvy? Anyway, full marks for trying."

"I'm here on official business — "

"Now look here, boyo — " a sterner note could be heard under the banter — "there is a camp toward the Welsh border. It's only about twelve miles away. Why don't you hog a lift — some kind soul will be bound to take a soldier, what? Then you can conduct your official business from there. Now, hop it!"

"My business is with Bob Renwick."

The Squadron Leader fell back a pace, and paled.

"Sir Robert? Sir Robert Renwick? You've absolutely no right to call him Bob."

"He asked me to call him Bob."

"That's no reason . . ."

"And what is more," I said, "I don't need to hog a lift. If I have any reason to go to the Welsh border, I have my staff car here."

The Squadron Leader looked as though he were going to faint. Always a believer of striking while the iron's hot, I leaned out the door, and called, "Oh, Sergeant! Driver, here a moment, please."

The driver, in deepest sympathy with the Squadron Leader, told his side of the story. Together, they scanned a reservation book. At first they could not find my name, but suddenly they looked up from the pages as though some new act of God had struck. Bob Renwick had done his work so thoroughly that I had been given a suite usually reserved for Air Marshals and over.

My battle dress was pressed by female Corporals, tea was brought with embarrassing frequency, and even my rifle was dusted. My first duty was to go on a tour of inspection of the unit in the company of Air-Chief-Marshal Sir Charles Portal and Air-Vice-Marshal Sir Victor Tait, Director General of Signals. I was not introduced to the two high-ranking officers until the whole ghastly joke was over, and with true British timidity they could not bring themselves to ask the identity of the sad sack bobbing in their wake.

Whenever they stopped to ask questions, I stopped also. After all, I couldn't very well overtake them. Thus I frequently found myself standing negligently before some Colonel or Group Captain, staring at his buttons, and glancing down at his shoes. I could hardly ask him the kind of questions he would ask me under similar circumstances, so I remained silent, trying not to make the silence seem insulting. Whenever some expert explained technicalities in answer to questions from the two Air Marshals, I leaned forward and nodded sagely, and whenever the Air Marshals glanced nervously back at me, I seemed to be digesting this knowledge while making rapid mental calculations.

Eventually Bob Renwick joined us for yet another tea, and thought the whole thing an enormous joke. "Why didn't you tell me you were only a Private?" he laughed, and characteristically gave me no time to reply.

The so-called Boffins, or scientists, lent themselves to dramatic interpretation with extraordinary unconscious felicity. The first one I met had cut himself shaving at least as doggedly as old Mr. Gibbs in my youth, and most of the fly buttons of his corduroy trousers were open or missing.

"I want you to clear your mind of the old cliché about the absent-minded professor," he said, "all that is just so much . . ."

Here, for some reason, he could find no end to his sentence, so just left it in the air, and went on to speak of other things.

Another one invited me to dinner. Many of them were surprised by this invitation, since my host had a reputation for stinginess and had apparently never extended his hospitality to any of his colleagues. Accompanying the dinner was water, not of the greatest vintage. It was old lecturer's water, with tiny gondolas of dust clearly visible to the naked eye. The sight and taste of this unexpected nectar has absolutely effaced from my memory the meal itself, although I do remember that it was not even tempting by regimental standards.

After dinner, I was tactless enough to offer my host a Havana cigar. My father had brought some from Portugal, and they were a little powerful for me at the time. He regarded it with incredulity, almost as though I had stabbed him in the back. He didn't trust my offer; he made a gesture to take it, then withdrew his hand and searched my face.

"Oh, no . . . may I really . . . no, indeed I shouldn't . . . what? I can't believe it. No, it's your last. No. D'you really mean it?" His hand trembled a little as he lit it, and allowed the half-forgotten vapors of untroubled civilization to invade his oral cavities. His eyes closed in ecstasy. Then he suddenly woke from his voluptuous daydream as though some urgent social necessity were claiming his attention. He looked furtively around his room in order to find some riposte to this normal generosity which had so scurrilously invaded the stagnancy of his instincts. Suddenly he brightened.

"I tell you what . . ." he cried, and rushed to a drawer of his desk. "Barley sugar!"

He produced a paper bag in which some barley sugar had been hibernating. It had by now congealed into a tortuous mass, which clung to the interior of the paper bag and threatened to rip it to pieces if attacked in its lair.

I struggled for a while with the contents of the proffered bag, while he tried to hold it as still as possible. As the unequal struggle grew embarrassing, he was evidently suffering a frightful indecision,

as though his avarice was being put to some unusual and terrible
test. At last the bubble of his thoughts burst.

"Oh never mind," he blurted recklessly. "Take two bits."

I completed the script of *School for Secrets* while still technically
in the Army, and was not released until I was actually shooting the
film on the floor, when we had to stop production for a day, at
considerable expense, in order to allow me to be formally dis-
charged and to receive a civilian suit, the last object to be thrown at
me by a Sergeant.

May I say something?

You don't have to ask.

*You enjoy yourself a great deal at the Army's expense, and evi-
dently this exercise of yours finds some favor, since you are often
asked on the television to tell some story or other from your military
experiences.*

What are you driving at?

*No need to be irritated. I am merely suggesting that you know
perfectly well that without the Army — or rather, without armies in
general — there would have been no possibility of defeating Hitler,
and —*

I obviously know that as well as anyone else. I trust you are not
trying a thoroughly reprehensible maneuver, hoping to make me
recant like a fainthearted heretic before the true faith of regimental
tradition?

*That would be useless. You forget, I hated the Army too. I hated
the reduction of my potential to practically zero.*

Then why, for Heaven's sake . . . ?

*I want you to give the correct impression of your protest against
the great waste. It is not something frivolous or facile, but a deep-
rooted, well-argued revulsion. It is not merely lighthearted mischief,
but a scream of horror.*

There you are wrong. I have neither the temperament nor the
build for screams of horror. I am resigned to the fact that anything
profoundly felt by me takes on the mantle of lighthearted mischief

just because it emanates from the heart of a jocular rotundity. Appearances cannot alter an intrinsic content, however. To defeat Hitler, the countries of the so-called free world had to play the same time-dishonored game as he, each falling back on traditions of comportment that history had rendered solemn to some, ridiculous to others.

There is no profession in which the books are easier to cook than the military. Generals are capable of mistakes so gross that they would lose their jobs in any other walk of life, but since the losses are not so much financial as merely human, they are either given posts of more responsibility or else left where they are. There is hardly a battle in the entire history of conflict that was fairly and squarely won. They were nearly all lost, and it was invariably the loser who realized it first, retiring from the field to the intense surprise and often disbelief of the victor. Inefficiency on the scale of warfare would be impermissible in any field in which the prosperity of shareholders was involved, while the wastefulness of battle is comparable only to the arbitrary exchange of wealth in a casino.

Mark you, I am not speaking of war alone, with all its mindless horrors, but of peace. In the interests of defense, all advanced nations have the capacity of destruction out of all proportion to the requirements of legitimate self-protection. The superpowers have the privilege of being able to destroy our planet several times in rapid succession, and yet there are still those who try to score political points by declaring that one or other of them is lagging dangerously behind the other in potential for obliteration. It is not melancholy that such arguments should be advanced seriously. The world has never been short of idiots, however hard the times. What is melancholy is that such arguments should be listened to, and acted upon, as though they made the remotest sense.

The cost of this gargantuan and useless arsenal is such that thousands upon thousands die every year because there is not enough left in the physical and moral treasury to bring the most elementary succor to those in need. That is to say that if the great countries would be content with a two-fold or at most three-fold destruction of the globe as a valid deterrent, the problems of famine and disease would be easily solved; but no, there is evidently no security in logic, but only in absurdity.

Thus thousands die, not because of the cannon's roar, but because of the cannon's existence. Armaments today take their toll of life even without a shot being fired.

Yes, today, today. You are expressing your views today, now that you work intermittently for UNICEF and UNESCO, but when did you first begin to think of such monstrous paradoxes?

Oh, that's easy to answer. While standing stiffly to attention, staring at nothing with the intensity of a zombie, awaiting the next primeval howl from a Neanderthal with three stripes on his shoulder. And perhaps, partially, even earlier, while lying among the damp ferns of Richmond Park with my rattle, pretending to be a machine-gun company. I never had a greater impression of wasting my time and, indeed, my country's time than I did in the Army. As I have already said, I loathed every moment of it, and I would not have missed it for the world.

12

On July 25, 1945, our daughter Tamara was born at the Woolavington wing of the Middlesex Hospital in London. She is now a creature of grace and charm, with an expression ever youthful and delicate. Then she was entirely bald, a physical feature she retained for an alarming length of time, and her face had about it much of the secrecy and doggedness of a Soviet Field Marshal. As I looked at her, trying to kindle feelings of paternity, which are entirely intellectual with such tiny children, she stared straight back at me with surprisingly steady blue eyes as though awaiting a complete confession.

My confusion at this inquisitorial gaze was checked by the remark of a swarthy gentleman next to me, who was gazing for the first time at his daughter, in the next slot on the hors d'oeuvre tray. His girl had a full head of black hair and carried an expression of irritation on her small features, as though she couldn't get her castanets to click. "They're all much of a muchness, aren't they?" he said, heaving with fraternity.

We moved from our mews house, a small, rather ramshackle bohemian pad, into a most uncharacteristic apartment full of amenities but without any character whatever. After the long enforced absences of the war and the independent development of two creatures who had entered marriage at the age of nineteen, there was nothing more calculated to put a strain on a fragile relationship than this enormous abode, which could in fairness and without political bias be termed bourgeois.

I was kept very busy directing my first film, which did not make me the most communicative of husbands. Having been involved in forms of propaganda, and having observed Carol Reed at work, I was fairly well equipped to deal with a semidocumentary subject of this nature, and I was at home with the more or less academic camera techniques of the time. As soon as I was out of the Army, I applied for the release of my favorite Corporal, Michael Anderson, today a renowned director.

Our paths have crossed with entertaining frequency throughout our careers, and we could not have met under more fortunate circumstances than in the topsy-turvy world of the Army Kinematograph Services. As yesterday's makeup artists and assistant production managers pointed to the pips and crowns on their epaulets and sent us out on menial errands, our eyes met in constant disbelief that a change of circumstances could make men of doubtful fiber take advantage of their temporary condition of marginal superiority in such a shoddy fashion.

Now Mickey joined me as a first assistant, but from the beginning he was much more than that — a mentor, a collaborator, and a friend. We were fortunate in obtaining the services of Ralph Richardson for the lead. He was then playing Falstaff at the Old Vic, and in the finest fettle.

There is always something engagingly lunatic about Ralph, a quixotic quality, although his windmills are ditches and his faithful nag a powerful motorcycle. He is always magnificently surprised to see you, his eyes rounder than two perfect circles, his eyebrows raised to somewhere near his hairline. Then, with a little negative wobble of the head, he elocutes his delight at this perfectly foreseeable encounter in a language at once full of filigree and backbone.

I hope I am not giving away any military secrets when I reveal that owing to his predilection for destroying motorcycles and, rumor had it, airplanes, the Fleet Air Arm was quite glad to let him go to the Old Vic, where the damage he could do was limited by the architecture. I equally hope that I am not revealing any Hippocratic secrets by disclosing that his running love affair with machines had cost him several teeth, and that by 1945 there was a complicated system of bridgework lodged in that noble mouth, which was a tribute to the unrelenting march of dental science.

On the third day of shooting he appeared on the set in high good humor, half Falstaff and half himself, bellowing his delight at being alive, but whistling like a kettle on certain sibilants, a sound which he evidently attributed to someone other than himself, since he kept looking around him to find its origin. It was clear that he had left the bridgework at home. Mickey and I exchanged a furtive look and controlled our mutual tendency to giggle.

"Why can't we shoot?" asked Ralph with a piercing whistle, by now riled by the delay.

While Mickey slipped off to call Ralph's home, I panicked — a director of twenty-four faced with one of the greatest actors of the age.

"The camera is broken," I said foolishly.

Unfortunately Ralph is not only fascinated by speed and its consequences, but also by fiddling with wreckage in order to resuscitate it. He now approached the camera to see if he could mend it.

"I hear the camera is broken," he said to Jack Hildyard, the cameraman.

"No," replied Jack reasonably, who had heard none of this.

"What sauce!" cried Ralph, with another blast on the whistle, which made Jack Hildyard flinch.

"Why did you tell me the camera was broken? It isn't," he went on, looking me in the eye.

"It's my inexperience, Ralph," I pleaded. "It's the sound-mixing machine."

"The sound-mixing machine!" roared Ralph, with two separate

and well-defined blasts, causing the sound-mixer to turn all the knobs on his machine urgently to zero.

Ralph crossed over to him.

"I hear the sound-mixing machine is out of commission," he said, with a particularly penetrating whistle on the last word.

"Yes. Yes, it is," the sound man confirmed, intelligently.

Just then Mickey returned.

"Your house wants to talk to you on the phone, Mr. Richardson," he said.

"Oh no," Ralph replied, rather petulantly, "I want to work. I don't want to speak to home."

"It may be urgent," I suggested.

"No," he said flatly.

"Since we can't shoot in any case . . ." I said.

"Confound it. All this is quite insufferable," he declared, with one final blast as he went to take the call.

He reappeared a moment later, walking a little unsteadily, his hand to his brow.

"What is it?" I asked, worried.

"It's nothing. Nothing. A migraine. Comes over me suddenly. The consequence of — oh, but why should I bore you with that? I have some powders — a prescription, you understand . . . like a fool, I left them at home . . . they'll bring them out here . . . straightaway, straightaway . . . perhaps if I could lie down a moment . . ."

Mickey walked him gravely to his room as he seemed to sway under the influence of some latent tropical disease from the time he crashed into a palm tree, the whole incident made more menacing by its understatement. The whistles were by now no more than the sighing of the wind in a leafless tree.

Twenty minutes later a Bentley drove up to the studio gates, and a small packet was delivered for Mr. Ralph Richardson.

Ten minutes after that Ralph reappeared, once again in high spirits.

"I feel much better now. *Mens sana in corpore sano*," he announced. All that Latin and not a trace of a sibilant whistle. The sound man turned the knobs on his console back to normal, and we did a good day's work.

The film was a great success, which led people to believe that I was an up-and-coming director. Only I knew that my ambition did not really lie in that direction. I was too wedded to the word by habit and by inclination to allow a purely visual imagination to develop. Nevertheless, the temptations were there.

Before doing another film, I appeared for a limited season in Rodney Ackland's version of *Crime and Punishment*. It was an enormous production with upward of forty actors either waiting to make entrances or exits, and it starred John Gielgud and Edith Evans. Anthony Quayle was our director, and I was engaged to play Porfiry Petrovitch, the police chief who relentlessly tracks down Raskolnikov. It was a formidable challenge for a young actor to play a man of sixty (much more difficult than seventy or eighty), and most interesting to be involved with another of our leading actors so soon after the film with Ralph.

John Gielgud was certainly the idol of the drama students of my generation, and his single-mindedness has been constant, even when challenged in the mentality of superficial assessors by the meteoric energies of Laurence Olivier. It is, of course, vain to talk of who is and who is not the greatest actor. There is simply no such thing as a greatest actor, or painter, or composer (in spite of what I was taught in my prep school about Beethoven).

The great become assets on an artistic stock exchange of their times, or if they are lucky, of all times. They may go up or down a few points as fashion plays its tricks, but they do not predominate, or sink very low; they are merely interdependent in the panorama of their epoch, stones in the mosaic, each contributing his own color, her own patina.

I do not think that Raskolnikov was Gielgud's greatest role. His tremulous voice, so exquisite an instrument in illuminating classical texts with clarity and passion, seemed to me a little highly strung for the sly, down-to-earth subtleties of Dostoevski; in fact, it made it extremely difficult for me to play at cat and mouse. With such a declamatory rodent I had to be a more than normally somnolent feline. My instincts were to arrest him as soon as I set eyes on him, so apparent was his guilt. I only performed the rest of it because the text was written, but by the end of the evening, I had no very high regard for myself as a sleuth.

Never mind; it was an intensely rewarding experience, since I began to know and understand John Gielgud as one of the kindest and most profoundly considerate of men, virtues which are too often a positive disadvantage among the insensitive, for whom *monstres sacrés* are by definition more *monstre* than *sacré*.

Innumerable stories exist about the comic vanity and acidulated repartee of actors, from Sarah Bernhardt to Sacha Guitry, from Mrs. Patrick Campbell to Noël Coward. No such stories exist about John Gielgud, not only because they could not exist but because, in any case, they would be entirely eclipsed by his fame as a master of the faux pas. All of these, true or apocryphal, are part of the public record, and sometimes, I dare say, the apocryphal ones ring truest of all, which is a measure of how John Gielgud's minor talent has captured the imagination as an affectionate adjunct to the major talent we all respect.

I once saw him on a local late-night television interview in St. Louis, Missouri. He was busy playing *The Ages of Man*, his one-man show, in half a ball park, and now he was being interviewed by a long-winded intellectual.

"One final question," the interviewer said. "Sir . . . Sir Gielgud . . . did you . . . oh, you must have had . . . we all did . . . at the start of your very wonderful . . . very wonderful and very meaningful . . . let me put it this way . . . did you have someone . . . a man . . . or . . . or indeed, a woman . . . at whom you could now point a finger and say . . . Yes! . . . this person helped me when I . . ."

By now John understood what was being asked of him, and he prepared to answer, disguising his dislike of the pretentious by a perfect courtesy.

"Yes, I think there was somebody who taught me a great deal at my dramatic school, and I certainly am grateful to him for his kindness and consideration toward me. His name was Claude Rains."

And then, as an afterthought, he added, "I don't know what happened to him. I think he failed, and went to America."

I regard this as the jewel of my collection, since I must have been one of the only ones to hear it and am probably the only one to remember it.

Much later, when John was directing a play of mine, *Halfway up the Tree*, at the Queen's Theatre, I remonstrated with him about a certain scene during rehearsal.

"John," I said firmly, "I just don't think that scene is going to work unless that young woman is *much, much* more aggressive."

John replied by thinking aloud.

"Perhaps I should have allowed her to wear her hat after all . . ."

This gift for blurting out a train of thought without a capacity for censorship can lead either to the celebrated lapses or else to fragments of inspired surrealism, moments at which one is permitted a glimpse into the sorcerer's workshop.

He has always had the gift of a ready tear, and his sensitivity is as evident as his sensibility. After one last night in Manchester, I saw a small pink and white suitcase at the stage door. Since I had a complicated makeup, I always left the theater long after John, and I realized at once that he had forgotten the suitcase. I took it with me to the Midland Hotel, and found him dining alone. I told him I had it, and his face transformed itself into a grimace of gratitude, eyes deflected somewhere above my head and sideways, a vein zigzagging its way up his temple like a mountain highway, mouth forced into a strained smile.

"Won't you join me?" he asked.

I did, for a while, but was tempted, once he had finished, to join another table where Max Bacon, a celebrated Jewish comic, was regaling members of our cast with the riches of his repertoire. I told

John I wouldn't be long, and that I would deliver the suitcase to his room in a little while.

Unfortunately it was not until three in the morning that Max Bacon got around to his first story again, and the second house began. It was only when I was on the way to my room that I remembered the suitcase. Despite the lateness of the hour, I determined to try to deliver it. When I reached John's room, I knocked with the greatest discretion. A voice both clear and brilliant rang out, "Come in!"

The door was on the latch. Because of the timbre of his voice I did not enter the room so much as make an entrance into it. He was lying on his bed as though posing for a sacred picture by El Greco, naked and immobile. He put an end to my confusion by another ringing phrase, this time with a dying cadence and a throb of bitterness.

"My pajamas are in that bag," he cried, and immediately his eyes grew moist.

I was glad I hadn't waited until the morning to deliver the suitcase. Such prudence would have occasioned the longest stage pause in history.

John Gielgud is so shy at first meetings that he makes a normally shy person like myself feel brash, even boorish. And yet, despite this gossamer delicacy, there are the heights to rise to before an anonymous public, and an ego, totally invisible in the drawing room, imperceptibly takes over. As the curtain fell on the first act of *Crime and Punishment* during the first performance, he suddenly trumpeted a message to us all.

"If there are going to have to be all these people in the wings, they *must look at me!*" He found it impossible to play to backs turned in discretion, in order not to break his concentration. To hell with the concentration, once there were people he was hungry for faces!

My domestic life was falling into nerveless and dispassionate ways, in spite of the delightful cavorting of Tamara. It was clear that it could not last. There were arguments. These were never rows but rather wearisome exercises in self-justification which never stuck to any point for very long, but dragged across a whole landscape of differences along prescribed furrows. A kind of tedium enveloped us, made worse by the heedless happiness of our daughter.

All this was the fault of no one, only perhaps that of circumstances. During the heroic days of war, our way of life was everybody's way of life, but now with the coming of peace, I was testing my ability to be myself to the full, making up for lost time; whereas Isolde, more mystical and abstract by nature, seemed to me to be removed from my realities in a numb withdrawal.

The withdrawal was perhaps not quite as numb as it seemed to me, since I noticed the frequent presence at home of a young fellow with a pleasantly pugnacious face. It was a little surprising that I was never introduced to him, but since I am a great believer in personal liberty and I think there are few characters sillier than suspicious husbands, I never asked who he was. I was informed soon enough, however, when Isolde announced that she wished to marry him.

I asked her to reconsider her decision. Her mind, she said, was made up. She was hankering for a steady, undramatic life, removed from the mainstream, a life without stress. She slid silently out of my life, and I hardly more noisily out of hers. My regret was for Tamara, although the positive nature of her disposition boded well for her capacity for survival. All the same, if there is anything I detest in life, it is irresponsibility. I have a puritanical revulsion for the kind of self-indulgence which creates life and then abandons it to fend for itself.

The end of our marriage seemed to me curiously tepid. It was all very English and very reasonable, with the added spice of that ludicrous charade of sending a detective to a prescribed room in a transient hotel where Isolde would be discovered playing cards with a hired adulterer. It all worked like a spell, without a trace of collusion, and soon I was ready for the law courts. One morning my solicitor called me to tell me to hurry up, the hearing was at eleven o'clock, and the judge was Mr. Justice Tudor-Rees.

I sat in my bath with a copy of *Who's Who* on my wet knees. I looked up Mr. Justice Tudor-Rees just to know what I was up against. His credentials seemed overwhelming for a mere divorce, but I did happen to notice that his wife's maiden name was Dorothy Sidebottom, a distinguished, hard-to-forget name in the northern countryside.

I reached the law courts as another divorce was in progress. A pathetic woman faced the judge, wearing a black straw hat adorned with plastic cherries. She smiled doggedly, as though she had been told to create a good impression.

"It was while your husband was away on his battle cruiser that you invited the Pole in question, Jerzy . . ." and here the barrister struggled unavailingly with one of the more complicated Polish surnames, eventually giving up and looking appealingly at the judge. "There is a Pole in question, M'Lud."

The judge, scribbling away, looked up briefly and nodded. "You invited the Pole in question to your rented apartment in Lee-upon-the-Solent . . ."

The barrister nodded at his client, who hissed her assent.

"And it was there, in the living room, on Friday the fourth, that, upon the sofa, connection took place," roared the barrister, in a huge voice, and nodded.

I reflected that I had never heard the act of adultery described more sleazily than in a law court, beneath the Lion and the Unicorn.

Once more, the wretched woman, with rouge on her cheeks like a doll, nodded back and hissed.

"Would you kindly ask your client to speak up," asked the judge suddenly. "I have not yet heard one word of her evidence, and I am not inclined to give judgment in a case I cannot hear."

"I must crave your lordship's indulgence," yelled the barrister, "but as I think I have explained, my client is deaf."

"Yes, but I'm not," said the judge, "and I don't see why I should be submitted to this kind of thing."

So saying, he deferred the hearing until such a time as the

wretched woman could throw a clearer light on the facts of her Polish connection.

I was frankly horrified at the callousness of the procedure, a horror which dissipated into alarm when I found I was next on the agenda.

My lawyer, a Member of Parliament from Ulster, asked me a series of predictable questions, which I answered in an overproduced theatrical voice, so eager was I not to be misunderstood. I was given technical custody of Tamara, although this right was waived owing to the child's age. All seemed to be going swimmingly in the hypocritical ritual when the judge suddenly fixed me with an eye both awake and aware.

"Why?" he asked, without continuing. Emergency was written all over my lawyer's face.

"Why?" repeated the judge again. "Why did you give your daughter the eccentric name of Tamara?"

"I don't consider the name at all eccentric," I replied, not without haughtiness.

The judge flushed with irritation.

"In all my experience," he remarked, "it is among the most eccentric names which have come to my notice."

"You must realize, M'Lud, that my surname is Russian," I said. "It would be ridiculous were I to call my daughter, say, Dorothy."

He looked up in surprise, forgetting for a moment to frighten me.

"Dorothy's a perfectly good name," he said.

"In certain circumstances, M'Lud, it cannot be bettered. Not, however, in mine."

A mischievous smile played about his mouth for a moment. I saw an anecdote forming in his mind. On arriving home that night, he was going to say, "Oh, incidentally, Dorothy, my dear. You'll never guess. I had that actor-fellow Ustinov in court today, and d'you know what happened . . . ?"

Thanks to *Who's Who*, I was through the minefield. I left court a free man, with all that entails, now once more open to burdensome temptations and the unnecessary exhaustion of uncertainty.

My father wasn't in terribly good form either, living alone in a service flat in London while my mother lived in Gloucestershire. It was never clear whether they had separated or not, but he was very active in his bachelor pad cooking meals of extraordinary richness which he shared with those who admired him and whose livers could stand the assault of cream and tarragon.

At the theater I shared my dressing room with an improbable character called Campbell Cotts, whose real name was Sir Campbell Mitchell-Cotts, Baronet. He was a big man, tall and fat, with a low, pomaded hairline, brown eyes at once cool, arrogant, and childish, and a mouth twitching incessantly in a kind of sensuous assessment of nothing in particular. He had fallen into the acting profession by mistake, and his comportment on the stage was identical with his comportment elsewhere. His conversation was bewildering to say the least, since when you laughed at what seemed vaguely amusing, he appeared hurt, and when you listened with careful attention to what was solemn, he appeared equally hurt.

One evening he declared that, although not a Catholic (pronounced Cartholic), he had presented Brompton Oratory (pronounced Brumpton Uratory), with a considerable sum as a penance for having wet his bed. My nascent smile was nipped in the bud by his fixed, fanatical stare and his munching. I tried outstaring him, and he turned away, flushed with annoyance.

My father, now in the full glow of his Englishness, found Campbell absolutely irresistible. He must have sensed in such a man a little fallout from the intransigent majesty of Empire. At all events, he begged me to invite him to lunch, which I did.

They spent their time criticizing my choice of wines, and exchanging obscure anecdotes about the lowest of deeds in the highest of circles. I said not a word, having no word to say. Eventually, as they swilled the brandy around their balloon glasses, Campbell, flushed with wine and good fellowship, slapped my father affectionately on the knee with his free hand, and, as he began to light his Havana, asked the rhetorical question, "What are we, my dear friend, but a couple of old poachers in the hedgerows of society?"

Klop looked at me in some alarm. He had never seen himself as a poacher, nor did he understand to what part of society the hedgerows referred. I could not help him. He seemed crestfallen, as though his inherent foreignness had been discovered owing to the neglect of some finer point, whereas Campbell, rosy and pouting, sat staring at the ceiling with an aura of self-satisfaction, savoring both the cognac and his remark to the dregs.

13

AFTER *The Banbury Nose*, and during the last days of servitude in the Army, I slaved away at my fifth play, a curiosity which had not much chance of commercial success at the time. It was called *The Tragedy of Good Intentions*, and was a story of the First Crusade, in which I was aided by the *Cambridge Mediaeval History*. It was the first of my plays for which research was necessary, and I stretched a fictitious tale on the framework of an authentic historical reality. It was performed by the Old Vic at the Liverpool Playhouse in 1945, and attracted not much attention.

The conviction was growing in me that, whereas Shakespeare was admittedly the greatest of our playwrights, there was a general recognition of the fact that Sir Arthur Pinero was the best of them. To attempt any kind of an emulation of Shakespeare was, of course, foolhardy on a purely artistic level, but quite apart from that, it was also regarded as a form of heresy, an act of shocking self-confidence; but an emulation of Pinero was eminently acceptable. Shaw was regarded as a prattling interloper, tolerated because of his gift of laughter and joy which made his iconoclasm irresistible, but he was certainly not a beacon suitable for a young author at sea.

Had England had the equivalent of those University Chairs for Playwrighting which to this day color minor American criticism, Pinero would have been the supreme example of dramatic carpentry for the fledglings to follow and lose their gifts. The theory that is all too often advanced by the pundits is that there are thousands of wrong ways to write a play, and only one right way. It is nearer the truth to say that, even if there are thousands of wrong ways to write a play, there are hundreds of right ways, on condition that the personality of the writer is allowed to be an ingredient in the result. None of the important dramatists of the century followed the rules laid down by experts. Chekhov would have been told that he lacked action, O'Neill that he must cut, Ionesco that he must clarify, Brecht that he must impose practical limits on his vision.

In other words, the academy is, as ever, the temple of mediocrity, and the ideals it imposes are strictly useful only for those with nothing to say.

With my sixth play, I decided to toy with the criteria imposed by my critics, by writing for once a realistic play in an abundantly realistic set (the rain fell in buckets, literally, in the third act). The theme was mildly provocative at the time. A clash between two clergymen, the one a good man but a third-rate cleric, the other a man of doubtful quality but an excellent cleric. The catalyst, the wife of one and the sister of the other, was Gladys Cooper, who made the part very much her own, even supplying many of the lines, which varied from night to night.

In spite of these frequent surprises and anomalies, she gave a performance of extraordinary power as a woman frustrated by the vacillations of a husband addicted to goodness. There has rarely been an actress who exuded more animal health, even in old age, or who was more fatally attractive, her deep and lovely voice cajoling or cruel or both at once.

The play, entitled *The Indifferent Shepherd* was not a great success, although it had a satisfactory run at the Criterion. It was as though the critics resented the fact that I had, in some measure, heeded their advice. This was encouraging.

Another play followed at the 1949 Edinburgh Festival, called *The Man in the Raincoat*. It was written in one long act, artificially split in order to accommodate drinking habits. It was played by Mary Ellis and George Coulouris, who disliked each other so heartily during rehearsals that there was nothing left over for the performance. Alan Wheatley was the third member of the cast, Percy Cartwright the fourth, and neither of them disliked anybody.

I directed the play myself. Since its theme of a miscarriage of justice was very close to my heart, I evidently thought higher of it than did the public, and it had no subsequent career, except in Oslo where it did very well under the charming title of *Mannen i Regnfrakken*.

I was by now inured to being an *enfant terrible*, although I felt I had been one for rather too long. My second film, *Vice-Versa*, based on the admirable book by F. Anstey, was according to many ahead of its time. With Roger Livesey in the role of the negligent, hypocritical Victorian father who tells his sniveling son, about to return to a hideous seat of learning after the holidays, that schooldays are the happiest days of any man's life, only to find himself transmogrified into his son's body, the film seemed to me to have a good chance of success. For the boy, I engaged a young and extremely precocious fellow named Anthony Newley, for the terrifying headmaster, Dr. Grimstone, an unknown actor who had fought in the Spanish Civil War on the side of unpopular legitimacy, James Robertson Justice, and for his daughter, a sweet little English rosebud, Petula Clark.

Had the film been made by Disney, it would have had fewer rough edges. What am I saying? — no rough edges. But it would have been less ambitious even on the humble level of a farce, and there was one sequence especially close to my questing heart which I still consider among my happier inspirations.

That exquisite actor Robert Edison, playing the romantic sportsmaster with no interest in sports, sat reading a book of poems while twenty-two boys ran riot in a roughhouse of a game of football. Suddenly he looked up. Horrors! The mortarboard of Dr. Grimstone was traveling like a pirate ship on the skyline of a privet hedge, coming his way. In a flash, he was on his feet, exhorting the boys to renewed efforts. The only trouble was, the ball had become mislaid during their extracurricular activities.

The boys entered into the spirit of the emergency, and played as they had never played before, dribbling, heading, shooting, saving goals — all with an imaginary ball. The headmaster observed the scene with evident pleasure, his eyes moving sideways, upward, downward. Only after a considerable time did a doubt begin to cloud that imperious, bearded face, until it had hardened into a hideous conviction.

"Where is the ball?" he thundered.

"That's funny," said Robert Edison, looking around himself and tapping his pockets absently.

Perhaps a degree of surrealism was too abstract for the tastes of the time, but it was one of those films which acquire a handful of fanatical addicts at once, who only serve to annoy even further those closed to its little mysteries.

The same became true in 1949 for my third film, *Private Angelo*, based on the charming book by Eric Linklater about an Italian Private, forever in search of the *"Dono de Corraggio,"* the gift of courage, which is eventually imposed on him by adverse circumstances. It must be said that it was a book hardly calculated to please the Italians, since it was based on prejudices about their warlike qualities, which were distinctly paternalistic. The Italians have always seemed to me to be almost overendowed with courage expressed in the form of personal panache or recklessness. They are nonpareil in the production of condottiere, poisoners, boxers, racing-drivers, stuntmen, popes angelic and diabolic, gangsters, and unflinching martyrs. Place all these disparate elements in a trench, however, and cover them with the same drab uniform and a coat of mud, give them an officer or two they don't necessarily respect, and of course their splendid qualities of individual radiance are tarnished. They prefer not to die under anonymous, or worse, under stupid circumstances.

The proof of this is the outraged Italian Private who leaped on to the parapet in the last days of the war, during a violent German bombardment. "*Mascalzoni*," he cried, "Don't you know there are people here?" only to fall under a hail of bullets.

No sane man can discern a lack of resolution here. He had merely had the sorry genius to find a way to die intelligently and nobly in a situation that was neither intelligent nor noble.

There was, however, not much room for considerations of this nature in a book that was almost pastoral in nature and that derived its poetry from a sort of serene oversimplification of the grave events it grazed on its journey.

I played Private Angelo myself, in retrospect rather too placid for the conventional view of an Italian, and rather too fair also for that unobservant multitude which considers all Italians swarthy. In the film my father (by indiscretion rather than by marriage), the Count Piccolograande, was played by Godfrey Tearle, that most aristocratic of actors, imbued with a certain distant loneliness, like a Saint Bernard with an empty cask of brandy. I always wished to invade his solitude and yet respected it too much to do so. Charming, elegant, yet with the massive vocal possibilities — his diaphragm belonged to a previous generation of classical actors — he performed every role with extraordinary dignity, which was also his greatest limitation.

I once saw him play a dishonest judge and believed it not at all. He did all he could to look dishonest as he was exposed by the police, but all he succeeded in doing was to appear anxious, and once the handcuffs were clamped on him, he immediately looked innocent, and the perfectly polite men from Scotland Yard seemed like brutes.

And yet, when he played the Italian Count, resilient in misfortune, looking up at the Roman balcony where American Generals were posing for American cameramen, British Generals for British cameramen, and a solitary French General for a solitary French cameraman, his face assumed the features of age-old disenchantment as he intoned softly: "Ah, Angelo, what have we learned? A different text for every schoolbook, a different inscription on every tomb. Nothing. We have learned nothing . . ." And his fine face was lost in the carnival of popular rejoicing at the coming of peace.

I used no music in this film, shot largely in the Tuscan village of Trequanda. At least, the music was not written especially for it, as was the habit in those days, but supplied by the village orchestra, the Societa Filodrammatica e Sportiva di Trequanda. The local conductor, an imperious old gentleman with a limp, conducted, among other numbers, the "Miserere" from *Il Trovatore* and "Marcia dei Bersaglieri," and he was as exacting with his ensemble as any great conductor, and twice as unpleasant toward recalcitrant musicians. The moderating influence of the trade unions had not yet penetrated here, and he was not beyond making personal reflections which would have occasioned walkouts anywhere else.

When he transported the orchestra to Rome for the recording sessions, it was rumored that this great maestro, whose crumpled nose was so crowded with constellations of blackheads that at times it appeared like a weathered miniature score, had no use for or knowledge of the sanitary amenities placed at his disposal, and that consequently his presence in the four-star hotel was tantamount to locking a puppy in one of the better rooms.

Nevertheless, he arrived in the recording room as sure of his destiny as ever, clutching a black leather baton case. He withdrew from it an olive branch with which he proceeded to conduct with a precision and a sense of tempo I have never come across even in professional film musicians. Told that the "Miserere" lasted two seconds too long, he immediately, without reference to metronome or stopwatch, produced a "Miserere" exactly two seconds shorter. There was no symbolism attached to his use of an olive branch, however. To achieve his uncanny results, he was just as unpleasant with his orchestra as ever.

The recording session, planned for three days, was completed in just over half a day thanks to the extraordinary ability of this instinctive musician, which was just as well, since it limited the damage to his palatial room.

I spoke previously of the moderating influence of trade unions. I referred, of course, merely to the verbal decorum upon which they quite rightly insist, but not to the pressures they exert, which are too often self-defeating. No one in his right mind could possibly deny the existence of the original grievances which compelled workers to organize themselves. It was an automatic outcome of industrial revolutions everywhere. And yet, in every human endeavor it is success which is the challenge to the highest of aspirations even more than failure.

While directing *School for Secrets*, I had committed the tactical error of offering my film unit a cold lunch out of my slender resources. It was a particularly scorching day on the Thames, and a fashionable riverside hotel was the site of my confusion. Cold salmon and strawberries and cream were eaten with pleasure; hock was drunk. Afterward a shop steward rose and proposed a graceful vote of thanks to me for my generosity and brotherly sentiments, at the same time reminding me officially that I owed them for the hot lunch they had been deprived of. His statement was greeted with prolonged applause as the hock glasses were raised to drink my health.

Once again, in Italy, everything stopped at certain statutory hours for the taking of tea, even though the temperature was well over 100° Fahrenheit and cold drinks were available at all times. The Italian crew looked at us in amazement. They were all stripped to the waist and wore their political convictions on their heads in the form of paper hats made of *L'Unità*, the Communist newspaper.

At first the British crew remonstrated with me to try to force the Italians to stop for tea also. Nothing would induce the Italians to do so. The British searched their moral armory for sanctions. I reminded them that we were in Italy and there was no way in which Italians could be forced to drink tea on their own soil. The British became sullen, as people do when they feel they are up against unfair opposition. Eventually a delegation came to see me. They would forgo their tea so long as it appeared in the books that they had had it. Apparently the whole thing would be difficult to explain in a drafty office in London. The arteries of liberty had hardened already; the careless dictatorship of privilege had been replaced by the careful dictatorship of regulations. Disobedience was the only escape for men of goodwill.

The last problems I had were during the filming of *Billy Budd*, many years later. The shop steward was a small, rakish individual whose dearest wish was evidently to grow a mustache like Clark Gable's to finish off his pleasantly disreputable appearance, but this was a wish unreasonably withheld by nature. Not a hair would grow on his upper lip. Undismayed, he made good nature's lapse with a mauve eyebrow pencil. Unfortunately, however, he was nearsighted, yet too vain to wear glasses, so his mustache was very rarely even remotely symmetrical.

We were in Spain, at sea off the coast near Alicante, rolling about on an eighteenth-century man-of-war, commanded in the film by me (and when filming ceased, by Captain Alan Villiers, who spent his time howling archaic commands to the winds, interspersed with expletives in no recognizable language). It stands to reason that, on such a boat, the toilet arrangements were almost as primitive as they had been in Nelson's day, and this found no favor with the unions.

The shop steward warned me once or twice, and then one fine morning he announced a strike. I knew he was upset by the fact that his mustache was particularly carelessly drawn, as though his mind had wandered over knottier problems before the bathroom mirror.

"It's no good," he said. "You wouldn't heed my warning, and there it is, strike action. I did my best. I'm known as a governor's man — it's no good for my reputation within the movement. Never mind. I stuck my neck out, but it's no good. It's the Spanish boys, you know. They are the straw that broke the camel's back, in a manner of speaking, if you follow. We got definitive news only this morning that three of them reported sick with crabs."

Fortunately for me, the last part of this was being overheard by the delegate of the Spanish union, which was, of course, no union at all in our sense, but a kind of Franco concession in the direction of modernity. This man now flared up with an indignation both righteous and magniloquent. "It is a lie to say that three of our men ha' gone sick wi' crabs," he shouted. "It is an insult to the Spanish labor force, to the quality of Spanish artisans, and it betrays an unfriendly attitude whi' I resent deeply."

The British shop steward became conciliatory, and eventually the Spaniard calmed down, owing more to the limits of his vocabulary in English than for any other reason. Once a degree of peace had been restored, he explained that the truth was that three of the Spanish crew had reported sick with gonorrhea.

"Ah, that's different," agreed the British shop steward. "That's a question of diet, isn't it?"

Thanks to a certain weakness in the British shop steward's diagnostic sense, the ship sailed again with its ancient toilets, and a full crew.

In case it be thought that I am opposed to unions, I hasten to say that I am a member of fourteen of them, which is outrageously expensive, but the reward is that I have never been on strike, simply because it has never happened that all fourteen have gone out at the same time.

Also, at their best, they can even be instruments of enlightenment. When we worked at Trequanda, the unions decided there also that the toilets did not meet the high standards set for the reception of British waste matter, so we built a couple of conveniences at the side of a sandy area used by the local sportsmen for a variety of games.

When we left Trequanda, we formally presented the toilets to the commune, and they were unveiled officially in their civic form by the priest in the course of a simple ceremony, during which he prayed Almighty God to render our labors fertile. I visited Trequanda quite recently, and the toilets are still there, doorless, rusting, and with cracked ceramics, yet stubbornly resisting the passage of time and vandals, still managing to proclaim their purpose to all who pass. Just as the vestiges of Roman sanitation are still found in England — fragments of mosaic, steam pipes, dim outlines of baths — so, thanks to the unions, remnants of British plumbing are still found in Tuscany, their origins gradually lost in mystery as the relentless march of time clouds the truth in theory and speculation. What will the archaeologists of the future make of those tiny chips of porcelain found in a Tuscan wasteland, which, when pieced together, make up the following hieroglyph: "Thomas Crapper and Company, King's Road, London S.W.3."?

Among the actors in the film were two of my particular favorites in that galaxy of distinguished performers England never ceases to turn out: Robin Bailey, one of the greatest comic technicians I have ever worked with, not as well known as he deserves, and Peter Jones, with whom I evolved a comic series for the BBC, which preceded the "Goon Show" and was like chamber music to the orchestral follies which were to follow. Pat Dixon produced these programs, and our guardian angels and consistent inspirers were Denis Norden and Frank Muir, masters of the ridiculous.

Peter and I invented a couple of characters out of the folklore of London — Morris and Dudley Grosvenor, low characters with high ambitions, as their name suggests. They spoke in the lisping accent of London's East End, and had endless wife trouble with their platinum-haired companions, as they did with the wretched character called simply "The Boy," who was sent out on dangerous and sometimes criminal errands in which he consistently failed. These programs were improvised within a certain framework, and often they reached satisfactory heights of comic melancholy. Foolishly asking "How's Zelda?" on one occasion, I received the following exercise in gloom from Peter Jones.

"Zelda? I'll tell you this much, Mowwie, if every evening after work you are hit on the head with a beer bottle with monotonous wegularity, mawwiage soon loses its magic."

Our satire delved into all fields of fiction as well. In our Coronation number, we produced a series of famous lines from the obscure moments of history, such as "Give me ten Grenadiers, and I will give you Harwich," and "What? There are no flags left? Strap *me* to the flagpole!"

It was lighthearted and quietly wicked, and people seemed to like it.

Robin Bailey, Peter Jones, and I, accompanied by Brenda Bruce and Molly Urquhart, also performed a play of Eric Linklater's entitled *Love in Albania*. We started it at the Bath Festival, and made a success of it at the St. James's Theatre in London. It was once again an affectionate kind of literary comedy, and I played one of the more simple-minded purveyors of America's cosmic message, a Military Policeman of Albanian origin searching Europe for his long-lost partisan daughter, "Wounded in the Bosoom for democracy." Peter Jones was a stuttering, exasperated intellectual, and Robin Bailey a suburban husband faced with these lunatic intruders.

It was far-fetched and preposterous, but the situations kept the audience in stitches, which was a hazard for all three of us, since we are all dangerously addicted to helpless laughter on occasion. We are in distinguished company, for John Gielgud too is as fragile in this respect as anyone I have ever played with.

Once the pause imposed by the audience was just too long, and Peter Jones and I were off. We turned our backs to the audience, but it was of no avail. The audience that night had the same dangerous characteristic, and they began to laugh as heartily as we for as little reason. It became an almost sinister form of mass hysteria, like a dance marathon. To make matters worse, we had an excellent stage manager who was a pillar of the Boy Scout movement in his moments of leisure. His head suddenly appeared in the fireplace, upside down behind the false logs, the fire reflecting in his glasses.

"Pull yourselves together!" he snarled.

Thanks to him, we were both now well beyond the point of no return. Only exhaustion enabled us to continue to the end of the play when the worst was over.

I adapted a play during this period, the only one in my career. It was by Ingmar Bergman, then known as a promising playwright rather than as a film director of immense distinction. He had written a film for Alf Sjöberg, entitled *Frenzy* in England and *Torment* in

America, a strange piece about the perils of young love in Swedish schools, a triangle composed of a youthful streetwalker, a schoolboy, and a sadistic schoolmaster. It was absorbing, as a film, perhaps because the background of Swedish scholastic life had to be accepted as genuine by those unacquainted with its traditions; whereas in London, the schoolboys, who included Denholm Elliott and Alan Badel, seemed strangely old for such a school, and the terror imparted by the odious schoolmaster, played by me in rimless glasses, was somewhat damped by having to speak in English. The experience was a curious one, in that it made me realize the enormous value of incomprehensibility in certain works of art, both plastic and dramatic. In removing the exoticism from the text by making it understandable, we had also dispensed with a certain mystery which gave the work its quality, or illusion of quality, there was no knowing which. Perhaps all we had done was to discover the Achilles' heel behind that stout woolen Swedish look. Or perhaps subtitles, habitually accused of inadequacy, are merely the sentinels which guard a work's secrets, or its lack of them? Dispense with a foreign language, and you are suddenly a conjuror without a mirror.

Frenzy made for a passable evening of tension, largely owing to the exquisite Joan Greenwood, whose gritty voice suggested the erosion of innocence by the sad necessities of a flagrantly empty life, but the niceties and above all the nastiness of Scandinavian pedagogy escaped most of the men in the cast, as Mr. Chips might well have left them even colder than usual in Uppsala.

One moment.

Yes?

You seem somehow to be rushing through these years. Your narrative is formless compared to the careful reconstruction of your early years.

That is perhaps because I am, in retrospect, less interested in them than in the years of my relative helplessness, where I could chart a progression from obstacle to obstacle, where I had my parents to complement, to accommodate, to consider. Now I was alone, after the failure of a marriage. More than alone, I was adrift, making up for a time which had never been lost but merely neglected because of ignorance, a lack of curiosity, a certain complacency. Despite the rigors of the British taxes, I had the illusion of a certain transitory wealth for the first time in my life. I bought weird motorcars which spent a great deal of time lifeless by the roadside, with me, as often as not rain-sodden, trying to make sense of the engines.

Among these monsters was a Hispano-Suiza Boulogne with only three seats and the flag of a defunct yacht club on the doors. It had come to England mysteriously at the time of Dunkirk, and had spent the intervening years abandoned on a dock, where the cylinder block had cracked. I drove this vast machine of 1927 with all the assurance of a Michael Arlen rake, and I have been told by reliable witnesses that I was even more sinister at the wheel of my Mercedes-Benz "S"-wagen, a supercharged two-seater, like a propelling pencil on four huge wheels linked by cable brakes, about as unsafe a vehicle as it was possible to conceive, especially as it was capable of Valkyrie rides at over 100 mph, with supercharger howling. I often exceeded this speed on the way to the studio. The car is now safe in the geriatric ward of Lord Montagu's Motor Museum at Beaulieu.

You complain of your solitude, and yet you seem to have enjoyed yourself inordinately.

There are always elements in solitude that are distinctly enjoyable, but they are not usually elements that wear well in retrospect. They are selfish and purposeless. They are ephemeral, often destructive. I flitted from affair to affair as I flitted from car to car. By this I don't mean I was deliberately inconstant, but rather that I was actively searching for the fulfillment of marriage, and that there was a certain desperation in it. I think, you see, that there has always been an atavistic undertow dragging me toward the image of the patriarch I was meant to be by nature and by tradition, but at the same time there was a tumultuous impatience about my work and my life which made me avid in the exploitation of my own youth.

You were pleasure-bent?

Perhaps, but I gave myself no pleasure. As you know, I am by temperament responsible, and I had no patience for the person I was. The characteristics of an aging *enfant terrible* gave me no more solace than it did my critics. Oh, I never stopped learning. I learned what it was to be lovesick, to wait in endless agony for telephone calls which rarely came; and when they came, how suddenly the mood of desperation would change to one of elation. I learned what it was like to be callous, out of sheer mental fatigue, a sense of self-preservation. I learned that women seemed all the same when things went wrong, all different when things went well.

Do you really think that is true?

No longer, because I no longer have to. The relationships between the sexes are so inextricably fouled up by wits, cynics, wise-acres, philosophers, psychologists, psychiatrists, and finally Women's Lib, that it takes the best part of a lifetime to find out that the general has no bearing whatever on the particular. Those who maintain the link exists are like explorers who lose heart in the face of a natural barrier and never penetrate into the hinterland where people are people, and not merely slaves to physical apparatuses that have slanted minds into channels dictated by convention. You are silent. Why?

I just fear you may be a little square for your age.

It is out of fear of what is known as squareness that we rarely say what we really think or feel. After all, what is profundity but a convoluted way of expressing the obvious, in which the matter is disguised by the manner to the satisfaction of intellectuals? It is no error that "To be or not to be, that is the question" is an essay in profundity which has become the property of all, even if the vast majority have not the faintest notion of how the speech continues. And yet, what the hell does it mean? It is merely a key to what follows, which is unknown to most people, and yet it is accepted as the acme of human vision by those who have never bothered to examine it or to open the door to which it is the key. "The evil that men do lives after them"; "Uneasy lies the head that wears a crown"; "To be or not to be." Shakespeare, thank God, was not afraid of squareness.

He wouldn't have known what squareness was.

Exactly. It takes a long time to struggle through to your own being, to uproot all the weeds of a certain kind of education, of a certain kind of locker-room scepticism, which evolves as the barnacles of other people's experiences and of other people's prejudices begin to stick to you and imperceptibly hamper your progress.

You learned that, then?

I have never ceased learning, and I am convinced that it is of primordial importance to learn more every year than the year before. After all, what is education but a process by which a person begins to learn how to learn?

And, perhaps, a process by which a person begins the long journey of discovery of himself?

Precisely. People know themselves when they are children, and then everything is done to integrate them into society as what is pretentiously and erroneously termed "useful members." It is here that they lose themselves, sometimes irrevocably, in a prison of convention, where individual thought is replaced by conditioned reflexes imposed by a sense of propriety and its attendant hypocrisy. The roots of racialism, for example, are planted deep in this fallow soil. Anti-Semitism is one of its bitter fruits, and the excesses of those who hate Arabs with imagined or pseudo-historical acerbity are just as ugly and just as sterile. Old men of quality are those who have fought their way successfully to a rediscovery of themselves in spite of every temptation, and it is no wonder they tend to befriend children. They have their common ground, themselves, the ones not yet lost, the others rediscovered.

Would you say that because of your meticulous ear and gift for imitation, you were very prone to the unconscious influence of others?

I would, yes. My plays were eclectic at this time, with an almost ferocious rejection of any kind of obvious influence. I was utterly determined to be myself without as yet a very clear conception of who I was. I was, if you like, escaping from the pigeonhole with the same application that others preferred to use on concentrating on personal attitudes. This made for obscurity and it disturbed people. Hence the *enfant*, hence the *terrible*.

May I suggest that it was perhaps more difficult for you than it was for others?

You may, of course. Although you must know I hate the idea that anything was more difficult for me than for others.

You are just averse to self-pity, but I do feel that it was difficult with a background as diffuse as yours, with bloodstreams gallivanting to all points of the compass and an empathy with widely divergent attitudes – Russian at one moment, English the next, then French, and Italian, and God knows what. You must, at times, have felt a pang of envy toward those younger dramatists who wrote with the uncomplicated anguish of personal experience about boardinghouses in Nottingham or rented rooms in Croydon. Their authenticity was never in doubt, and their passions rang true.

Envy? I honestly doubt it. Where can you go after a boardinghouse in Nottingham except to another boardinghouse in Nottingham? And nothing is as deeply felt as the first literary explosion. After that, art and artifice take over. Success there may be, and astuteness, but the freshness of the first plunge into public consciousness is gone forever. That is a destiny common to us all.

Ibsen did well enough with his fjord-side houses, as did Chekhov with his slatted mansions. They never left their Nottinghams, their Croydons.

Did they not? Chekhov's next play, had he lived, would have been a symbolical drama about a bird-woman in the Arctic regions. I am convinced it would have been a disaster, since his enormous talent did not stretch to such fin de siècle extroversions. In *The Seagull* he already dabbled with such a theme, and I believe that the play within a play purportedly written by the emotional young poet Konstantin was, in fact, conceived in the utmost earnestness by Chekhov, in order to test a more lyrical style on his audience. With his sophisticated and self-mocking demureness, it was disguised as the immature outpouring of a youthful talent, but it was, I feel sure, a prototype of what was to come if the audience listened in silence. As for Ibsen, his last play, *When We Dead Awaken*, is almost entirely incomprehensible and ends with an avalanche. All who slept in Nottingham or Croydon, Smolensk or Bergen do their best to escape. I needed a special kind of launching pad to crystallize whatever talent I have, and admittedly it was less easy to find than was Nottingham to the talented local boy . . . But I did not despair.

Would you say these were unhappy years?

To live for the moment has its thrills, but the moments have a habit of accumulating and creating time. I drove myself hard, as though life were really as short as it seemed. I remember my adventures with a mixture of amusement and pain, in the hope that I created more amusement than pain in others, but there is no accounting the degree of love invested when one's own sentiments are confused by old-fashioned ideas of permanence, mingled with a latent misgiving which was ever present. I lived in a charming flat on the Thames Embankment, which my then secretary found for me. She is now a busy and successful writer of detective stories under her married name of Patricia Moyes, and I like to think that she discovered her ability while heroically dealing with the many problems of my own creation.

What finally brought this period of public apprenticeship to a close?

A chiding voice calling out of the Heavens "Whither goest Thou?"

Quo Vadis?

Exactly. And the chiding voice was that of the venerable lion of Metro-Goldwyn-Mayer.

14

An exciting proposition came my way when I was twenty-eight years old. M-G-M was going to remake *Quo Vadis*, and I was a candidate for the role of Nero. Arthur Hornblow, Jr., was to be the producer, and I was tested by John Huston. I threw everything I knew into this test, and to my surprise John Huston did little to restrain me, encouraging me in confidential whispers to be even madder. Apparently the test was a success, but then the huge machine came to a halt, and the project was postponed for a year.

At the end of the year, the producer was Sam Zimbalist and the director Mervyn Le Roy. They also approved my test, but warned me in a wire that I might be found to be a little young for the part. I cabled back that if they postponed again I might be too old, since Nero died at thirty-one. A second cable from them read "HISTORI-CAL RESEARCH HAS PROVED YOU CORRECT STOP THE PART IS YOURS."

To celebrate I purchased the first new car in my life, a rather ugly postwar Delage convertible in cream, with a cherry-red top that took three men to open and many more to shut, and cherry-red upholstery, which indelibly stained the clothing of all who sat on it.

I determined to drive around Spain on the way to Rome, where the film was to be shot. I broke down in Granada, Seville, Barcelona, Madrid, Badajoz, Jerez de la Frontera, Lorca, Perpignan, Narbonne, Cannes, San Remo, and at the gates of Rome, where a ball bearing broke in a wheel, causing it to overheat. When the car was raised, I saw a stamping on the underside of the chassis dating it October 1938. The ugly body had been added in 1949 to a chassis which had survived the Occupation in some shed, and now it had been sold to a patsy as a brand new car. I only bought it in order to replace a secondhand one, also built in 1938, which was one of the most agreeable cars I ever owned, and reliable to boot.

Rome was in the throes of Holy Year, and bursting with pilgrims. It was also one of the hottest summers on record. I met Mervyn Le Roy for the first time some hours before we began to shoot. He is an affectionate man of less than average height and of slight build. His blue eyes are friendly, although he has a vocational addiction to shouting, which is the right of any Army commander; and, as I was quick to discover, the production of an American epic is the nearest peacetime equivalent of a military operation, with time as the enemy.

I spoke to him with unaccustomed earnestness about my role, and asked him if he had any observations to make.

"Nero? Son of a bitch," he declared.

I was inclined to agree with him.

"You know what he did to his mother?" he suddenly said, with decent Jewish concern, as though there were something one ought to do about it.

I replied that, yes, I did know what he did to his mother.

"Son of a bitch," repeated Mervyn, almost angry.

I nodded my head. So far we saw eye to eye. "But is there any specific aspect of the man you wish me to bring out?" I asked.

To my surprise, Mervyn replied by doing a tap-dance routine.

I applauded, and he beamed with pleasure.

"I used to be a hoofer," he said.

I said, truthfully, that I didn't know that.

There was a long pause while I wondered uncomfortably if by some hideous chance he expected Nero to tap-dance.

"Nero," said Mervyn.

I pricked up my ears.

"The way I see him . . ."

"Yes?"

"He's a guy plays with himself nights."

At the time I thought it a preposterous assessment, but a little later I was not so sure. It was a profundity at its most workaday level, and it led me to the eventual conviction that no nation can make Roman pictures as well as the Americans.

The Romans were pragmatic, a people of relaxed power with nouveau-riche lapses of taste. They too believed in the beneficence of atrium living, in pampering the body with steam and the laying on of heavy hands after the excesses of a four-star cuisine. They too believed in dressing for comfort, and the intrigues in their senate matched anything in Washington, while their total belief in Roman know-how led to a few ugly surprises, as did the total belief in American know-how in Vietnam. They too garnished their official walls with flags and eagles, and eventually the Roman way of life was all-important, being practiced even when the later emperors were of Iberian or Dalmatian origin; it mattered little. What mattered was a family feeling, a *modus vivendi* that was sometimes gracious, sometimes coarse, sometimes civilized, and sometimes violent and cruel, and yet, ever, unmistakably, Roman.

The inevitable vulgarities of the script contributed as much to its authenticity as its rare felicities. I felt then as I feel today, in spite of the carping of critical voices, that *Quo Vadis*, good or bad according to taste, was an extraordinarily authentic film, and the nonsense Nero was sometimes made to speak was very much like the nonsense Nero probably did speak.

So gargantuan was the production that I was sent to the Rome Opera House for three singing lessons, in the belief that such a crash course might make of me another Mario Lanza as I sang my lament to the burning city.

I arrived at the opera one morning in an atmosphere of high tension. Apparently *Samson et Dalila* had just been hissed the night before, and I was taken to be the new Samson from Paris. I pointed out that I would consider the part after I had had my lessons, but not before. It was on this abrasive and highly operatic note that I was ushered into the presence of my professor.

He confessed to me, after dismissing a distraught soprano who had just waded through the mad scene from *Lucia di Lammermoor*, that in agreeing to teach me how to sing in three lessons he was motivated by financial considerations. I reassured him that such considerations had not been absent from my mind when accepting to play the part of Nero. We drank a toast to M-G-M only with our eyes, and he confessed that his task was hopeless. Three years, perhaps, he said, but three lessons . . .

He sat down disconsolately at a piano which was as hopelessly out of tune in its way as the lately departed soprano had been in hers. It twanged like a guitar on some notes, like a banjo on others, and other yellowed keys produced no sound at all. Almost at once the score, by the Hungarian composer Miklos Rozsa, proved rather too advanced for the professor, who was accustomed to the predictable patterns of Donizetti and Verdi. He berated the music for its inordinate number of flats, and delivered to me the pith of his first year's course in a single lesson.

"Always, as I tell Gobbi, always breathe with the forehead," he declared.

I wrinkled my temple as though it contained a small pulse. He was enchanted. Never, he informed me, had any pupil been quicker on the uptake.

At the start of the second lesson, he asked me what I remembered of the first lesson.

"Breathe with the . . . ?" he asked.

"Forehead," I replied.

"Bravo!" he cried. "What a memory! Really fantastic." Now followed the second lesson, containing all I would learn in the second year, in concentrated form. "As I tell Gobbi, think with the diaphragm," he said.

I adopted a distinctly constipated look, which seemed to me the faithful outward proof that my diaphragm was wrapped in thought. I set the pulse going in my forehead at the same time.

"My God, it's fantastic, fantastic! One at a time, yes, perhaps, but both together, so soon! Fantastic! What a talent!"

Before the third and final lesson, he decided on the usual refresher.

"Da Capo," he said, "Breathe with the . . . ?"

"Forehead."

"Bravo! Think with the . . .?"

"Diaphragm."

"Bravissimo!"

And here followed the third and most difficult lesson.

"As I say to Gobbi, always, in all circumstances, sing . . . with the *eye!*"

I came away as enriched musically as the professor had been enriched financially, and whereas those who saw the film might not have guessed that I was thinking with my diaphragm or indeed breathing with my forehead, I fear it was painfully obvious that I was singing with my eye.

The heat was absolutely tremendous. Among the senators surrounding me on that hallowed balcony from which we were supposed to watch Rome in flames, there were some eminent English actors, among them Nicholas Hannen and D. A. Clarke-Smith. To add to the heat of the sun, braziers were burning all around us, shedding black ash on our togas, and the lights bored into us from above. A gallant lady harpist from the American Academy in Rome sat, drenched in perspiration, on a podium, waiting to accompany my hand movements on the lyre with her daintier sounds. Mervyn Le Roy was shouting orders and counterorders from a crane, and thin green rivers began snaking their way down my face from my laurel wreath, which was made of inferior metal, with a horrible ferrous odor. It was utter misery in this creative cauldron, and I feared for the health of the older actors, as their nostrils grew black with dust from the braziers, and their lungs began heaving in their boiling chests. A miniature of Rome caught fire to add to the inferno, and a back-projection screen came alive with visual pyrotechnics behind us. At last we were ready to shoot. I recalled the words of my crazed song, "O Lambent Flames, O Force Divine," and cleared what throat I could still sense.

Just then Mervyn cried, "Let me down! Let me down, for Christ's sake, will you?"

A sense of exasperated anticlimax set in as Mervyn disappeared from sight. Then the balcony began to shake, indicating that someone was scaling it. Mervyn's head appeared over the battlements, cigar gripped between his teeth, his eyes confident and understanding, like those of a manager telling a half-dead boxer that he's leading on points, and he summoned me to within confidential distance.

Waving his Havana at the burning city, he said quietly, "Don't forget, you're responsible for all this." Mervyn was never a director to leave anything to chance.

The third in the triumvirate of inseparable English actors was Felix Aylmer. They were inseparable only because of the *Times*, and more particularly its crossword puzzle. Whichever of them was called latest would stop on the way to the studio and buy three copies of the airmail edition. They would sit on the set, their glasses on their noses, and solve its riddles.

It didn't take long to notice a curious atmosphere among them, however. Felix Aylmer and D. A. Clarke-Smith would only communicate with one another through Nicholas Hannen. This fact gave rise to odd dialogue, like

CLARKE-SMITH: Revulsion.

AYLMER: Ask him where?

HANNEN: Where?

CLARKE-SMITH: Sixteen across.

AYLMER: Too many letters, tell him.

CLARKE-SMITH: Tell him I already know.

HANNEN: He already knows, he says.

Intrigued by the absurdity of this dialogue, reminiscent of Eugene Ionesco in his English mood, I asked Nicholas Hannen to explain it. He revealed that the two had not spoken since 1924, when Clarke-Smith's wife had left him after a nocturnal argument, and had taken sanctuary at Felix Aylmer's cottage. Hot on her heels, Clarke-Smith banged on Aylmer's door. The two men in pajamas and dressing gowns faced each other.

"I have reason to believe my wife is here," cried Clarke-Smith.

"She's in the spare room, D. A. Let's be reasonable and talk about this in the morning, after a good night's rest."

Those were the last words they had exchanged until "Revulsion," "Ask him where?"

Occasionally they were summoned to work, and they tucked their copies of the *Times* into their togas. Unfortunately D. A. Clarke-Smith was afflicted with a hacking cough, which he successfully suppressed, thereby only making the air mail edition of the *Times* noisier as it was buffeted against his heaving chest, making a sound of someone stamping on a pile of autumn leaves. Immediately the sound man looked up at the eaves.

"Goddam birds nesting up there," he said.

Shooting was frequently held up while technicians attempted to winkle out the imaginary intruders. When nothing was found, they searched for rats, for ticking pipes, for mirages.

I would never give away my friends and their humble enjoyments. After twenty-six years of silence, they deserved a little consideration.

There were, of course, absurdities galore, as there could scarcely fail to be in a production of such magnitude. The fighting bull, enclosed in a freight car of the Portuguese State Railways, was lured out into a corral designed for horses by the ten-gallon-hatted experts, against the considered advice of a diminutive Portuguese bullfighter, with the result that at the height of the luncheon break, an angry bull ambled into the commissary, having butted his way to an easy freedom. Then there was the animal which Buddy Baer as Ursus was supposed to wrestle, then kill by breaking its neck. Out of prudence, the idea of a bull, as specified in the book, was rejected, especially after the company's previous experience with this animal. Consequently a chloroformed cow was selected, placed in such a way that the udders were invisible. Unfortunately every time that Buddy Baer twisted its neck, this had the effect of bringing the poor animal to, and everytime Buddy stood in triumph with his foot on its carcass, the cow looked up at him and mooed pathetically. And let me not forget Mervyn's inspired instruction to a couple of mountainous wrestlers, one Italian, one Turkish, who were supposed to kill each other with savage grunts and groans for my pleasure as I nibbled at larks and fondled my favorites!

"Action! And make every word count!"

I returned to London brimful of new experiences, feeling that I had widened my horizons irrevocably. In any case, no one who spends close to five months in Rome, that glut of overripe peaches in a dish of hills, can ever be quite the same. The emphasis on sin, perhaps inevitable in a place so overtly dedicated to the material majesty of God, and in which the spiritual majesty has to be taken for granted by those less than entirely gullible, gives one a feeling of turpitude and langor. The climate, the sleepy days and wide-awake nights, add to this sentiment of nervous exacerbation and squalid temptation, and one turns away from the city with a kind of weary revulsion, only to be impatient for one's return.

London seemed ordered and proper after Rome. The thefts were methodical, the burglaries routine, with nothing left to brilliant inspirations of the moment. Cops and robbers, like people in the street, moved at a regulation clip, without surprises. There was no darting out of archways, no driving up on the pavement, no midnight bathing and glamorous suicides in the Serpentine, no traces of heroin among the abandoned clothes, no scandal implicating the scions of ancient houses in decay.

And yet, I could work in London, whereas in Rome it had become utterly impossible. Refreshed by my absence and by my enforced abstinence, I began to develop an idea in which the four powers were compelled to administer the Palace of the Sleeping Beauty by means of a commission. Out of this grew a play called *The Love of Four Colonels* which was constructed almost musically in a theme, variations, and a final fugue.

The four Colonels — British, American, French, and Russian — were utterly realistic in the first act, disgruntled men with longings and aspirations beyond their grasp, beyond their means. A wicked fairy comes to tempt them. The Russian fires at him; the fairy scratches his belly, complains of the bullet's itch; the Russian faints. A good fairy arrives to maintain the age-old balance.

In the second act, they move to the enchanted Palace, which has resisted the horrors of war wrapped in its impenetrable foliage. Each Colonel is automatically in love with the Sleeping Beauty, and acts his passion with her in the form of a play within a play, according to his tastes and his nostalgia. The mild and monosyllabic Briton becomes a turbulent romantic in a scene of unrestrained Elizabethan lechery; the Frenchman, more true to himself, changes least to become a petit Marquis of the seventeenth century, all bawdy asides laced with vinegar; the Russian, gruff and bearlike, becomes a nostalgic Czarist officer with epaulets, cradling himself on a Chekhovian swing while he knits a jumper; the American, pill-taking and gaseous, turns into a saccharine fighting father, the founder of "Girls' Town," converting evil-doers to the true faith with a straight left.

In spite of the encouragement of the wicked fairy, and thanks to the intervention of the good fairy, they all fail to seduce Beauty. Then, by magic, they perceive their wives, who have arrived at headquarters to visit their husbands, and the awful reality is revealed to them as the wives speak of them unrestrainedly. Two of them, the romantics, the Frenchman and the American, decide to stay on in the endless pursuit of their ideal, forever destined to fail. The Englishman and the Russian decide to return to reality out of differing senses of obligation, where a pursuit of ideals has ended long ago and can never torture them again.

The play opened at Wyndham's Theatre, London, on May 23, 1951, and was my first great success. For me, it marked a coming of age. From now on I might be terrible, but the *enfant* was gone for ever.

The play was performed in New York by Rex Harrison and Lilli Palmer, directed by Rex Harrison, in sets by Rolf Gerard. Although it did not last nearly as long as it did in London, it won the New York Drama Critics Circle Award as Best Foreign Play of 1953. In Paris it ran for about six years at the little Théâtre Fontaine, and has been revived twice since. In Germany, the meeting place of the control commission was dubbed the "Palace of the Sleeping Beauty" by sections of the press.

Meanwhile *Quo Vadis* appeared, and I was nominated for an Oscar as best supporting actor. The wind was in my sails. I moved from Chelsea Embankment to a house in King's Road which belonged to the Church Commissioners and boasted a plaque informing the passerby that Ellen Terry had lived there. Actually the house, a lovely and rather reticent building dating from 1702, should have displayed another plaque, for I discovered that the composer Dr. Arne had lived there also and, in fact, had written "Rule, Britannia" while in residence. I played the work in many versions and at various volumes, but I was unable to evoke any reaction from the Doctor's ghost.

The house had an enormous studio in lieu of a garden, and I spent most of my time in there with my books, my records, and the few works of art I was beginning to accumulate. My mother, who had done the costumes for *Vice-Versa* and *Private Angelo*, often stayed with me, while my father still occupied his bachelor apartment round the corner. It was a curious arrangement, but I asked no questions, especially since they saw much more of each other now than during my mother's fairly long sojourn in Gloucestershire.

After a time, they announced that they had found a flat not far away, and I was delighted that time had seemed to heal what wounds there were. Like everyone else, I had made myself into a company, which at the time was believed to be the only way to ride out the nightmarish taxation, a sytem which made you the care-taker for money which you had earned, but which wasn't yours to spend. This, I will be told, is normal in the tax structures of free countries, and yet there were few free countries at the time where you were supposed to hold on to up to ninety-five percent of your earnings until asked to surrender it like a good fellow for the government to misspend, because it had more experience than you in the matter.

At all events, despite a fairly frugal existence, my tax affairs were pronounced to be in a sorry state. I discovered this on the death of my tax accountant, who was revealed by his successor to have been somewhat unimaginative in the handling of my affairs. Taking into consideration the almost medieval code of honor which prevents accountants from speaking ill of their peers, one can well guess what word he might have employed if he had not limited himself to unimaginative. All of which raises a very serious point. How does a person like myself distinguish a good tax adviser from a less than good one? Usually, alas, by whether he is agreeable to be with or not, and whereas this may be a social criterion, it is worse than useless with tax advisers. For instance, the unimaginative, deceased one was a very agreeable man indeed, and to cloud the issue even further, so is the imaginative, alive one. This makes nonsense of a nascent theory that probably a corrosive, unpleasant individual tends to inspire confidence in a layman, since taxes are, by their very nature, corrosive and unpleasant inventions. But then, in any case, how would a layman arrive at a definition of a good tax adviser? Probably by considering him good when he takes the same amount in salary as he saves you in taxes. A bad tax adviser is clearly one who takes more in salary than he saves you in taxes. What both good and bad tax advisers take in time is simply unassessable.

When Henry Wallace, then a presidential candidate, recklessly proclaimed this to be "The Century of the Common Man," he was as wide of the mark as only an ambitious politician can be. This is still, and will be to its bitter end, the Century of the Middleman. In the United States, life-style leader at this time, it is advisable to retain a lawyer long before any litigation, as well as an agent to keep your name in the forefront of employers' minds. Then, possibly owing to the population explosion and the need to create jobs, the business manager is created, along with the public relations man. All these people watch each other like hawks on your behalf, but since they are also bound by the highest moral principles, they never warn you in time when things begin to go wrong, since on no account can they permit themselves to be critical of one another. And so, any reasonably good-natured performer sooner or later treats these outsiders as personal friends, and no longer cares much if they are good at their job or not. The fact that they are tax-deductable seems to be sufficient to carry them in overlapping advisory capacities through life.

So it was that my new tax adviser, while tut-tutting a great deal as he deciphered the "unimaginative" mess of his predecessor, asked me, in light of the deplorable state of my finances, what kind of car I drove.

"Aston-Martin," I replied.

"Oh God," moaned my taxman. "Must you?"

I answered with some liveliness. I told him London was full of even more expensive cars, Rolls-Royces and Bentleys. Who bought them? It couldn't all be inherited money. Or was it merely that these proud owners had had more imaginative advice?

He grunted in a noncommittal way, as though overflowing with bitter secrets.

"All right," he said, "what other car have you?"

"I have no other car," I answered.

"Oh, good God," cried the taxman, now really upset.

My first economy measure in the reconstruction of my parlous finances was, therefore, to go out and purchase a Standard Eight which I didn't need, as a personal car, so that I could put the Aston-Martin down to business. I began to learn the nature of the cloud-cuckoo atmosphere in which we were beginning to live, and the gratuities as well as the price of freedom.

One of the directors of my company was my literary agent, an

Australian named Alroy Treeby; another was my cousin, Julius Caesar Edwardes, who ended up at British Petroleum as director of public relations, and my father, who sat there making notes of what was being said, clearing his throat on occasion as though about to speak (but never did), and putting the minutes into a leather portfolio when it was over. I don't think poor Klop had the remotest understanding of what was going on, but once he was on the board of a company for the first and last time of his life, he made the best of a job beyond his comprehension by looking distinguished and even, at times, shrewd. I felt sorry for him because, although I kept myself out of the phone book for obvious reasons, he put himself into it. He was the only Ustinov in the London book, and received a great many inquiries for me. The extent of these inquiries seemed like an endless reminder that I had not turned out the failure of his prophecy, but he never complained and attempted to take all the messages with the thoroughness of a company director; only the theatrical firm of Linnit and Dunfee was consistently beyond his grasp, since he used to inform me with the utmost seriousness that Dunnit and Fifi had called. His quiet efforts on my behalf, his unequal and yet uncomplaining struggle with the complications of a life very different from his own, made me feel like the father, him seem like the son.

He retained his dignity in all this, perhaps because, now more than ever, he was eager not to seem to be "letting the side down."

It was nevertheless my father who first tired of the vanities of town life and hankered for the country. This desire was peculiar and uncharacteristic. Of all the people I have ever known, he was the most blatantly urban in character. Not that he would ever have been a boulevardier, even had the affluence of his youth made such a desire possible. He preferred narrower streets and the freedom to wander unobserved. He liked to browse in shops, buy herbs at greengrocers for his cooking. He liked hailing taxis and using the telephone. I just could not reconcile the abandonment of all this with his real predilections, unless this emigration to a voluntary exile had about it an abandonment of life itself, a relinquishing of his command over the better things of existence. Why? Because living would merely be an echo of what his had been. He saw no sense of achievement in longevity, and old men who asked you to guess their ages with a challenging twinkle seemed to him grotesque. Before he began his long, and by all appearances voluntary, decline, he still had one or two missions abroad on behalf of his wartime employers. Consequently my mother went to the country first, in order to settle them in. Lonely and frightened in the Cotswolds after London, she asked me for a dog — once again a most uncharacteristic request.

I bought a golden retriever puppy somewhere in Knightsbridge, and took it to the theater with me, where its whimpering could be heard on the stage. I named it Colonel, out of deference to its contribution to my play.

The next day I was visited by a rather masculine lady in tweeds, wearing a porkpie hat and a tie. She wished to deliver the pedigree and asked me if I had yet selected a name for the dog. I said rather sheepishly that I was going to call it Colonel.

"Oh, what a rattling good notion," replied the lady, transferring her weight nervously from foot to foot. "The little beggar was sired by Squadron-Leader."

I delivered him to my mother the very next Sunday, and he immediately began chewing everything in sight — carpets, shoes, canvases, and even my mother.

I had no occasion to visit my parents until some time later, by when my father had taken his retirement. I arrived unannounced, and to my surprise found that I had broken into a large cocktail party. What was even stranger than the type of reception my parents were giving was the type of guests they had invited. All the men were elderly, and wore mustaches, either great untidy red entanglements hanging over their mouths like rusting barbed wire or else tidy little clipped things, like a third eyebrow, or white tufts blocking the nostrils, snowballs at the moment of impact. The majority of them had ice-blue eyes, and the wives looked exactly as you would expect, wizened yet friendly, plagued with discreet nervous tics and speaking much louder than necessary in jagged upper-crust cadences.

Not long after my arrival they began to leave in pairs, effusive in their thanks. When the last couple had gone, I asked my father what on earth had prompted such a gathering. He looked at me resentfully, and told me it was my fault, "yours and your mother's."

My mother had evidently been far too busy painting and had not made any effort to train the dog, who was now much larger, less prone to chew, but absolutely undisciplined. Klop, on his return to England, had decided to take the dog in hand, a duty which gave some point to the exercise to which he had been condemned by the doctor, and so he would go out with it for walks.

Naturally, in passing through villages the distractions for a canine nostril grew in variety, and the dog would go streaking off in obedience to some uncontrolled instinct, my father shouting in the distance, "Colonel! Colonel!"

Inevitably the door of a cottage would open, a gentleman in tweeds would appear and say, "Yes? Did I hear my name?"

The encounter would result in some good-natured laughter and an invitation to have a drink.

My father tried to alter his itinerary in order to avoid villages where known Colonels lived, but there were more of them than he had reckoned with, and the day inevitably arrived when he ran out of villages. Now, with Colonel as disobedient as ever, he was repaying all those other Colonels who had answered his call with greater alacrity, by plying them with pink gin and whisky.

"Why does your mother need a dog? And why did you give him the idiotic name of Colonel?" asked my father as he started washing up the glasses.

"I could have called him Vicar," I said as I began drying them.

For two long years *The Love of Four Colonels* continued, exhausting and exhilarating, and it could have gone on considerably longer than its well over eight hundred performances. During that time I spent some weekends seeing it in other countries: in Germany, Denmark, Holland, and Italy. My private life was less erratic than before, but no more settled for that. Although I began to suspect that I was not made for marriage, I knew perfectly well that I was not made for celibacy either. Nor did I care for my profession to the exclusion of all else. I was, in other words, all eggs and precious little basket. And, curiously enough, when all is well these anomalies are far more apparent than when adversity strikes. You look around you at the growing edifice of your life and admit to yourself that it is beautiful, but beautiful to what purpose? What and whom is it for? Solitude is a necessary ingredient in the act of creation, but loneliness is very different — not loneliness while alone, but loneliness in public places, in the midst of gaiety and joy.

My heart did leap once, on the tennis court of all places. I played badly since I kept my eye on my partner instead of on the ball. She was a French girl with an amusing face and a lively temperament, called Hélène. Our mutual attraction was immediate, and we enjoyed one another's company. Then she disappeared to France, leaving me the telephone number of her grandfather, at whose house she lived. He was a Marquis, and his butler sounded like something even higher. The *cordon sanitaire* round my delightful partner was dignified and hermetic. There was nothing I could do.

A little while later, while browsing in Mr. Moroni's newspaper shop in Soho, I saw the photograph of a strikingly beautiful girl on the cover of a pulp magazine. There was a story about her in it, and a teasing phrase appeared under her picture, *"J'adore les contes de fées"* ("I love fairly tales"). Pretending it was for a nonexistent cook, I bought it along with all the other foreign magazines I took regularly. I carried it to the theater.

Three days later, my French agent, André Bernheim, appeared in my dressing room after the performance, accompanied by the very girl on the cover of the magazine. Her name was Suzanne Cloutier, and she was a young French-Canadian actress who had played Desdemona in Orson Welles's film of *Othello*. She was now in England to act in a film of Herbert Wilcox's called *Derby Day*, and André

Bernheim asked if I would kindly look after her when he had gone. She spotted the magazine on my dressing table, and I truthfully told her the circumstances of its purchase. Such providential acts can sometimes rush one into an impression that destiny is at work.

She told me she was on the run from Orson Welles, that his representatives were searching high and low for her to implement a contract for which she had not been paid. Her work in Wilcox's film must therefore be considered clandestine in the extreme. An executive from Paramount Pictures, with whom she had a long-term agreement, and I set her up in a remote but comfortable hotel, and an improbable detective story began, at the culmination of which we ran straight into Orson Welles in a fashionable restaurant.

He was perfectly charming, surprised to see her, and asked kindly how she was. The small talk bore no trace of malice nor of any desire to implement a contract, and all Suzanne's efforts to appear frightened could not turn Orson into the Svengali he patently had no ambition to be.

A little later, while dancing — yes, I had been dragooned into this unsuitable pastime — she told me her mother was a German Jewess called Braun and that her father was descended from an Indian chief with a name I cannot today recall, but that, apart from that, she was British and defiantly French, and as such had been denied the privilege of learning her own language, which she spoke perfectly, by the villainous Anglo-Canadian authorities. All this was said with utter conviction, and even if I found most of it hard to swallow, these tales had an undeniable comic charm, in which the fact that she seemed to take them so seriously was not a minor ingredient.

People were enchanted by her freshness, her extraordinary capacity for invention, and her acumen in pursuing her ends; and I must admit I was among them. And even if one never quite knew when to reach for a pinch of salt, she had said it herself. She loved fairy tales — "J'adore les contes de fées."

15

SUZANNE'S first marriage had been brief. This is no reflection whatsoever on her husband, an eminent doctor, for when he looked around after the wedding reception, Suzanne had gone. Their married bliss had lasted the best part of half a day, and then his bride was on her way to New York to become a Powers model. She had, she told me, undergone all the pomp and splendor of a military wedding (for her husband was then still in the Army, and his father was a General) simply in order to give her parents pleasure. It never seemed to occur to her to equate their happiness with their dismay at her disappearance, a fact which I found troubling, to say the least.

In this perplexity I made a happy choice of legal adviser in Dr. Elio Nissim, an Italian Jew who was the logical choice to represent the Vatican at the See of Canterbury, a tribute to the intelligence of the Catholics and the sensibility of the Protestants.

Nissim managed to arrange a divorce under the law pertaining to wives abandoned in Europe by G.I.'s, which was brilliant by any standard even if this particular case could hardly pretend to be a prototype for such a situation.

There were more surprises on the way, however. Suzanne's

parents had instigated legal proceedings within the Catholic Church to have the marriage annulled, a procedure of immense complication. The decision was eventually handed down many years later, and the news was broken to Suzanne by Monseigneur Leger, the Cardinal Archbishop of Montreal, during a midnight phone call. I sought to burp our son, who was teething and shouting his head off, and to divert our daughter, who had been deprived of her sleep and who was therefore shouting back, while Suzanne, making desperate signs at me to keep the children quiet, was in the process of learning that Mother Church had accorded her request for an annulment on the grounds of nonconsummation. She expressed her gratitude in a voice of pristine wonder that such marvels could come to pass, interspersed with assurances that they didn't have a crossed line.

"*C'est curieux,*" the Archbishop said, "*je pense entendre des enfants pleurer.*"

"*C'est peut-être l'Atlantique, Monseigneur,*" Suzanne suggested reverently.

Elio Nissim is an extraordinary man, tiny, with a shrill voice, and an eggshell pallor, an advocate of the highest order who eventually gave up the law, I suspect because he was too good at it. His disgust with the fallibility of men and the self-imposed misery of the human condition made him abandon the career he had mastered with such gentle eloquence and lacerating skill. He was incapable of bitterness, and so he preferred the clean air of the pasture to the heat and odors of the kitchen.

Harry Truman, another small man of brisk brilliance, once said about politics, "If you can't stand the heat, get out of the kitchen ."

For certain temperaments, it is not the heat but the smell which drives them out.

During the run of *The Love of Four Colonels,* Bill Linnit had presented a serious play of mine, *The Moment of Truth,* at the Adelphi Theatre. It starred Eric Portman and that fine emigré actor Charles Goldmer, the first playing a kind of free paraphrase on both Marshal Pétain and King Lear, whereas Goldmer played a variant on Laval, the man who is a villain, doing a great deal of good in the course of his villainy, and who knows he will have to pay the price. It did not run long, but I consider it one of my good plays. The press was indifferent, except for the *New York Herald Tribune*'s Paris edition which carried a superb notice. This could unfortunately give us but little commercial help, and yet a notice like this gives a dramatist the requisite hope under any kind of adversity.

Do I detect some resentment in what you have just said?

Oh, the beauty of injustice is that it works both ways — without that, it would really take a great deal of getting used to. Let's face it, James Agate and Herbert Farjeon were at least as unjust in our favor as Harold Hobson, Clive Barnes, and Walter Kerr were against us.

Three against two?

That's my prejudice at work. It's probably more like forty against forty. But injustice on our level is largely a matter of opinion, while opinion itself is at the mercy of vogue, whim, camp, chichi, all the little mannerisms which make of the Gadarene swine a cohesive and reasoned entity, endlessly renewed and endlessly rushing down the well-worn path, generation after generation.

Are you hurt by the comments of critics? It sounds as though you are.

I find them hard to forget. When Walter Kerr virtually accuses me of plagiarizing works I have never seen, I consider it careless of a man of undoubted distinction to hazard such wondering in public and I have no burning desire to see him again. When Clive Barnes, in trying to say something agreeable about a work of mine he found feeble, reverts to paying a curious compliment about my earliest play, remembering it as having had a "fleeting honesty," whatever that may mean, I become a little irritated when I find out that he must have made this Olympian judgment when he was fifteen and a half years old. He frowned when I brought this to his attention dur-ing an unsolicited encounter at a New York social gathering. "I always thought we were contemporaries," he said. I urged him to look himself up in Information Please Almanac for all our sakes, not least his own.

In other words, you are hurt by what seem to you careless comments of those who should know better?

Hurt! What does hurt mean? We survive, don't we? Whereas injustice is something we not only have to live with if we are lucky, but which can kill us if we are not. How can one compare a damp little squib from a critic to the kind of injustice we see all around us? I wouldn't dream of ever being other than slightly cold toward those who, to my mind, have behaved in an unpleasant manner toward me and I wouldn't even have brought these matters up at all if this hadn't been *my* autobiography and if I hadn't been put up to it by you.

Just as well to get it out of your system.

I'm not even sure of that, but how can one compare the imperceptible scratches on our hide with the terrible "moments of truth" in which men have been destroyed by the law at the expense of justice?

The Moment of Truth was the name of your play about Pétain and Laval.

It was the title finally chosen because the producers feared that the original one, *King Lear's Photographer*, would sound facetious. On second thoughts, *The Moment of Truth*, a title of magnificent pretension taken from the bullfight when the bull is ceremonially put to the sword at the signal of the president of a court, is perhaps more far-reaching and significant. My play was not only about Pétain and Laval. There are other King Lears on record. Hindenberg, Badoglio, Franco. It was the tragedy of a man who outlives his life, if I may coin a phrase, and of another man who pragmatically exploits the reputation of this living legend. I believe that injustice is tolerable up to a point in the heat of war or of revolution. It is for that reason that I could never be a conscientious objector. I find it impossible to claim for myself a particular delicacy of spirit when there is chaos all around me. At the same time, I regard injustice, or even the risk of injustice, perpetrated in the august precincts of a court of law, with calm consideration and time for reflection, utterly repellent.

What made you write your play?

I think it was the sight of Pétain, sitting expressionless and silent in the courtroom, beyond thought, beyond reaction, merely the catalyst for some high-flown oratory, which branded my mind. On and on went his life in his windswept island prison, forgotten except by some of the most intransigent and retrogressive of his supporters, silent now because the altar of patriotism had been redecorated with other symbols.

You are very tough, you who are usually so bland . . .

I am very tough, especially with those I love. I love the French, I have spent a long time in their midst. I believe that one admires people, collectively or individually, for their virtues, but that one loves people for their faults, if such love is true.

Of all nations, the French seem to me the most vindictive, and the most able to carry their quarrels into the beyond, after death has put a period to their tumultuous eloquence. Ancient hatreds are nurtured like precious flowers in a garden and diatribes about half-forgotten and even historical contentions have all the freshness of a burning topicality.

But these characteristics do not for a moment make them especially prone to injustice; far from it. They merely give French injustice a particular color compared to the multitude of other injustices. Look at poor, dumb, parachuting, ill-informed Rudolf Hess all alone in Spandau prison in his early eighties. Even Louis XVI was never all alone in the Tuileries. And all this because the "great patriotic war" has so scarred the Russian sense of compassion that they must needs force their victim to pretend to drink the bitter dregs of defeat long after the cup is empty.

And what of the trials of Bentley and of Evans, to mention only two very doubtful cases before bewigged and robed British judges, traditionally so liberal in their dispensation of benefits of the doubt? Their wisdom and moderation did not prevent them from perpetrating several proven miscarriages of justice and a host of cases in which doubt has only received its benefit after hanging.

Finally, for the sake of argument, although there can never be a finality in the infinite annals of injustice, what about Chessman, executed nearly twenty years after his crime, after every avenue of delay and appeal had been used up in the legal system the most prodigal in safeguards against abuse? When Chessman eventually died, he was a different man from the one who had been reckless in his youth. He was eloquent and creative.

Apologists for the American legal system will say that the delay in execution was Chessman's own fault. If he had not conducted his own defense with such astuteness, he could have been put to his death earlier. In reply to this atrocious argument, I would merely say that the sentence is not really one of death, for man has no control over what occurs after life. In this sense, it is a careless and pretentious misnomer. In fact, it is a sentence to spend the last days of life as unpleasantly as possible, and over unpleasantness of this sort man's control is only too hideously obvious.

Have you any proof of this?

Certainly. If it were really a sentence of death, why remove shoelaces, neckties, and belts from the prisoner? Suicide is a do-it-yourself, labor-saving form of death, which should meet with the approval of society if such were really the sentence. But no, the prisoner must live out his time and suffer all the hideous little rituals invented by man for his own ostracism — the last wishes; the menu of the ultimate meal; the final cigarette (now no longer particularly dangerous for the health); the embarrassed murmuring of the priest. A president of France once commuted a death sentence on a criminal whose appointment with the guillotine had been delayed for three weeks by appeals and doubts. He understood that after six weeks, life in the shadow of death becomes inhuman and self-defeating. Seen in this light, the eighteen-year vigil of Caryl Chessman becomes not only barbaric, but does no credit whatsoever to the hundreds of wise people who contributed toward this unequal battle.

And would you say that the Army first made you conscious of your feelings about these aspects of life?

National Service is the only dictatorship of the spirit permitted in a democratic society. The Navy has its own particular traditions, the Air Force is by definition more modern and more technical. At the time I was in it, the Army was the least exclusive of the three, a kind of monstrous school for backward adults, in which degrees could be achieved in monstrous disciplines.

Why?

I said before that for some temperaments, a bad education is the best. The Army was deplorable as a finishing school, and therefore I will forever be grateful for all it taught me.

Isn't there a risk that your attitude leads you to be unpleasantly negligent about all those — among them, some good friends of yours — who lost their lives?

Oh come on. I have told you how scandalized I am by death.

By individual death, by calculated death, yes, you have. But how about the others, the six million Jews, the twenty million Russians, the uncounted, uncountable others?

They induce a melancholy in anyone of the remotest sensitivity, but they are not only uncounted but incalculable. We cannot comprehend, as we cannot weep for the thousands who die in traffic. Life was cheap in the Middle Ages. It has become cheaper since. It is only in specific battles for specific lives that our culture is put to the test and with it our humanity.

Could it be that you are a pessimist, after only fifty-five years of precious life?

Precious only to you and me. Cheap as any other on the open market. A pessimist? Not at all. I am an optimist, unrepentant and militant. After all, in order not to be a fool an optimist must know how sad a place the world can be. It is only the pessimist who finds this out anew every day.

Are we advancing at all?

We have fought two wars to end war. In 1976, the nations of this world set aside the same amount of money for its starving children as they lavished on armaments every two hours. Can any right-minded man afford to be a pessimist? That was a luxury for easier days.

Another play, *No Sign of the Dove,* for which my mother did the sets, took place in a large country house in drenching rain and its theme was ambitious despite the angular conventions of a vaudeville. It began on the ground floor, among the guests of a pretentious literary houseparty — a flatulent German philosopher, a poetess, her novelist brother, a sycophant and his wife — prepared for a weekend of intellectual delights. Meanwhile the floods are rising. The second act took place on the second floor, among the bedrooms. Partners changed, and a couple of private detectives attempted to keep abreast of events. Only an old man, the father of the house, and a small waif are busy building an ark in a room, refusing all contact with the other guests. The floods have filled the ground floor. The last act is on the roof. The waters rise, and it becomes clear that it is the second coming of the floods. The curtain falls as the detectives organize community singing to keep the spirits up.

The booing from the gallery began just forty-five seconds after the curtain rose. It was well organized and thorough. Scouts must have seen the play in the provinces, and their smoke signals were observed from afar by those self-appointed arbiters of public taste who used to shout their frustrations from the dark anonymity of the gallery.

I am not defending the play. If it can't do it for itself, it deserves no help, nor do I. It may indeed have been too Continental in flavor for these insular roisterers, its style may have been too deliberate, its edge too sharp (or too blunt), its message too tragic (or too unjustified); but whatever the truth, the fact that the second night audience clapped fast and furiously meant nothing. It was already too late to save the play, and it is possible that the applause was not entirely a mitigation of its qualities, but a generous vote of confidence in me, a balm after the scourge.

Whatever the truth, I suffered a numb feeling of disgust, and then, almost immediately, a sudden upsurge of confidence, a kind of controlled rage with the outward aspect of insolent serenity. This was, after all, no more than the childish initiation into some scholastic lodge, the ritual all new boys must go through if they wish to earn the respect of their fellows. The great virtue of disaster is that it gives a man the possibility of demonstrating his fiber before so many people.

I did what I had to, wrote an article for the *Daily Express* on what it was like to be booed, and forgot the theater for a while. I played the part of George IV in my second American film, *Beau Brummell*, at the M-G-M studios in London, co-starring with Elizabeth Taylor and Stewart Granger. It was selected later as the Royal Command Film because the committee in charge of such events decided that nothing interested royalty more than royalty. It was only when Robert Morley as George III attempted to strangle me — a most realistic performance — that suddenly a hideous doubt sprang up in the minds of those responsible that the sight of one of the Queen's not-too-distant ancestors attempting to strangle another one in a fit of insanity was perhaps not the happiest of diversions for Her Majesty, and the press the next day bubbled with that particular form of pious hypocrisy which has marked all recent British scandals, large or small.

Suzanne and I left for Hollywood immediately after our marriage. I had been contracted to play in the film *The Egyptian*, and I was looking forward to acting with Marlon Brando, who was one of its stars along with Victor Mature, Jean Simmons, Michael Wilding, and other famous names. I had already appeared in a view of ancient Rome seen through Polish eyes in *Quo Vadis*, by Henryk Sienkiewicz, and now I was about to indulge in a view of ancient Egypt as conceived by a Finn, Mika Waltari. In a sense, Rome is already a part of the modern world, whereas the spirit of ancient Egypt is still wrapped in the secrecy of sphinxes and the smiles of cats which make the enigma of the Mona Lisa seem commonplace.

Unfortunately this relative difficulty of discerning a palpable artistic personality for Egypt outside the stilted murals and the pyramids compels designers to go to *Aïda* for inspiration. And this film was no exception. The sheer size of the decor dwarfed everything that stood before it: men, ideas, intelligence itself.

The only element in this elaborate cocktail half as mysterious as ancient Egypt was the director, Michael Curtiz, a tall and upright Hungarian who had come to Hollywood so long ago that he gazed over the palm trees and stucco castellations of its civilization with the blind, all-seeing faith of its prophet. He had never learned American, let alone English, and he had forgotten his Hungarian, which left him in a limbo of his own, both entertaining and wild. His eyes had no pupils visible; they must have been the size of pinpoints, and the irises were of the brightest blue, the blue of innocence.

I was presented to him on arrival, and he greeted me with the complicated grace of an Imperial Corps Commander welcoming a new Lieutenant hot from Budapest. The next day I was presented to him again, with precisely the same result. He had evidently forgotten me in the interim. I reckoned I was introduced to him at least ten times during the first week, each time for the first time. After that a kind of shadow passed across his face, as though he were trying to place me.

I came down on to the floor for my debut to find him filming a tavern scene. Jean Simmons was sweeping the floor with a large besom broom. Victor Mature was very angry about something or other in Ancient Thebes, and he dashed a papier-mâché goblet to the ground.

"No lips of mine shall ever touch this chalice!" he cried out.

In the center of the stage sat my stand-in, dressed identically to me, chewing gum and looking around with a very contemporary kind of detachment. I touched Mike Curtiz's arm. He bridled in irritation, then stared at me, trying to place me.

"Cut," he cried. "Vy you not on set?"

"Nobody called me," I said.

"Gott damn, dat no excuse."

Angrily, I took the place of my stand-in.

"Vy you not bring my attention?" he shouted at the stand-in.

"I tried to, sir," shrugged the stand-in.

"We all did!" cried Jean Simmons.

"That's right," confirmed Victor Mature.

"Ven nobody have interest film in heart, vil suffer only vun ting — film," grumbled Curtiz.

Of course, by now, Marlon Brando was no longer part of the cast. He had taken one look at the final script and pleaded illness, from which he made a miraculous recovery once shooting had begun with his replacement.

Communications with Mike Curtiz were extraordinarily difficult. He seemed to understand absolutely nothing I said, while agreeing with it all and doing just the opposite. There was only one slender ray of hope. In a moment of rare repose, he suddenly spoke, apropos of nothing.

"Vienna," he said, with a fatalistic chuckle, "I remember ven I vos barefoot boy in Vienna mit my broder, selling in the teater sveets und magazine programs. Life!" His eyes looked heavenward a moment in smiling recognition of his fortune, and he retired once again into his more impenetrable abstractions.

It so happened that I had just received a letter from the "Theatre in der Josefstadt" in Vienna, on appropriately heraldic and evocative notepaper. They were about to perform *The Love of Four Colonels* and asked for certain precisions. It was a letter so technical it could mean nothing to anybody but myself, but I thought the letterhead itself might lure the nostalgic Curtiz further out of his lair and expose him to human contact by way of his reminiscences.

The next day, after briefly reminding him who I was, I said, "Mike, you remember yesterday—"

"Of course I remember yesterday," he interrupted as though I had insulted his powers of retention. I refused to be sidetracked.

"You told us of your boyhood in Vienna."

"Dat vos not yesterday," he cried, "a long time ago!"

His expression became suddenly serene.

"Vienna," he said, with a fatalistic chuckle, "I remember ven I vos barefoot boy in Vienna mit my broder, selling in the teater sveets und magazine programs. Life!" His eyes looked heavenward a moment in smiling recognition of his fortune, and before he could retire once again into his more impenetrable abstractions, I nipped in with my letter.

He took it, and to my dismay did not so much as glance at the letterhead, but went straight on to the letter as though it were intended for him.

"We're ready, Mike," said the cameraman.

"Mein Gott, vot manners," cried Curtiz, "to interrüpt van man ven his is reading vun letter!"

The cameraman went away in disgust, and Mike Curtiz returned to his incomprehensible reading matter. Then, to my horror, he stuffed it into his pocket and prepared to direct.

My chief concern was how to recover it, and I waited till the end of the day. I cornered him as he was about to leave the set.

"Mike," I said, "could I have my letter, please?"

"No," he replied gently, on a tone of high morality, "I am not de kind director write letter actors. I know it exist director too scared actors, so dey write letter instead to say vot tink. I not such. If I tink stink, I say. If I think voonderful, I say. Alvays I say. No letter. Alvays say."

I gritted my teeth.

"Mike," I said, "You have a letter *belonging* to *me*."

"I no mailman," he retorted, heatedly. "Ven is letter for you, it vil be post-office, mit your name on, not mine name on."

"Mike," I screamed, "you have a letter belonging to me from *Vienna!*"

"Vienna," he said, with a fatalistic chuckle, "I remember ven I vos barefoot boy in Vienna mit my broder—"

Before he had finished the sentence, I dug into his pocket and removed my letter. He noticed nothing. I made no further attempt to reach a more accessible unity. We were both better off that way.

Curiously enough, he was much more perceptive than he seemed to be, even though extremely absentminded. Rumor had it that he had injured himself badly not long before by stepping out of his Cadillac, while it was in motion, to commit a new idea to paper. Needless to say, he was driving himself.

At the end of *The Egyptian*, a film I never saw since I found it so profoundly silly while I was making it, Mike Curtiz asked me to do another film, with Humphrey Bogart, Aldo Ray, Basil Rathbone, and Joan Bennett, called *We're No Angels*, based on a charming French play by Albert Husson, *La Cuisine des anges*.

It suited our purpose admirably to stay in Hollywood a little longer, since Suzanne was reaching the term of her pregnancy, and she could not travel anymore. She had been to a celebrated pediatrician whose only interest seemed to be the extent of my salary, since, he explained, he took one-tenth of it, which was deductible in my case. I began to have nightmares about being chided by the taxman for not having had twins, so that one of them could be put down to business and leave the other for pleasure.

The pediatrician seemed unable to understand that, being British and resident in Britain, I only had very limited pocket money to spend on luxuries like childbirth, and eventually we found a Canadian doctor who was going to Europe on vacation and was consequently willing to be paid in sterling.

These were not easy times in Hollywood. Some American friends I had made in England, notably Adrian Scott, had virtually disappeared, and asking after them seemed as dangerous as any request for the whereabouts of distinguished colleagues in a dictatorship. The lamentable Senator Joseph McCarthy was on the rampage with his prolonged drumhead court-martial, occupying everyone's attention on television and disseminating a reprehensible panic among those one had thought to be made of sterner stuff, while leading good-natured fools to utter portentous and ignorant pronouncements about the nature of communism and democracy.

McCarthy was investigating the infiltration of subversive ideas into the United States Army, and what he succeeded in illustrating was what I have referred to elsewhere as the lack of moral courage in people of admirable physical courage. To watch one brave, bemedaled façade after another collapse under the specious pummeling of this sinister clown was more than one's sense of workaday decency could stand. It therefore came as a great relief to me to be invited to do a fifteen-minute recording for the BBC on the sole subject of the Army-McCarthy hearings. I still do not believe that the BBC, in their cloistered island freedom, realized the local hazards of what they were asking me to do. They could not know, in the quiet rooms of Broadcasting House, that Americans actually cowered when the subject of McCarthy was brought up and cast a hasty eye around the assembly to assess the nature and position of other guests. It was like one of Hollywood's own films about Nazi Germany.

I went alone to Don Lee Mutual, Channel 5, and a bored technician asked me who my piece was for, CBC? No, I said, BBC.

"What the hell's that?" he asked, marking the as-yet-empty reel with the initials.

"British Broadcasting Corporation."

"British!" He pulled a long face, as though surprised that we had already managed to give up the tom-tom and the hilltop beacon as a means of communication.

I sat down and read my piece, from which I take the liberty of quoting:

> To the outside observer there is nothing particularly striking about the Senator — there is no fire, no perceptible fanaticism, and curiously no oratorical powers. Words come more easily to him than sentences, which is normal; but even words fall grudgingly from his lips — his eyes, meanwhile having all the dispassionate intensity of a lion who is having his own private troubles gnawing a juiceless knuckle. His voice is plaintive by nature, and trembles obediently when a particularly emotional tone is ordered by the brain. On other occasions, it tries the elusive intonations of sarcasm, sounding much like a car with a dying battery, and even attempts the major key of jocularity when bonhomie is called for, but it is a sad laugh, and one which does not invite participation.

It is as though he had cheated the physical restrictions placed on him by nature, and had trained the very shortcomings of his equipment into weapons. His own evident lack of wit makes him impervious to the wit of others; his own inability to listen makes him immune to argument; his own tortuous train of thought wears down the opposition; his crawling reflexes, his unnaturally slow and often muddled delivery force quicker minds to function at a disadvantage below their normal speeds. And yet, cumbersome as is the Senator in action, his changes of direction, like those of the charging rhinoceros, are often executed with alarming ease. A mind trained in all the arts of tactical expediency urges the ponderous machinery on its provocative way.

Whenever he is compelled to admit that he doesn't know, he does so with an inflection suggesting that it isn't worth knowing. Whenever he says he does know, he does so with an inflection suggesting that others don't — and won't. This then is the outward face of the man who has heard voices telling him to go and root out Communists — and this is the face of a man who recognizes his potential enemy in everyone he meets. Like a water-diviner, he treads the desert with a homemade rod and shouts his triumph with every flicker of the instrument, leaving hardworking professional men to scratch the soil for evidence.

No one who has enjoyed an argument, no one who has entertained a challenging doubt, no one who relishes an unfettered view of history and of the current scene, could possibly be a Communist. But anti-Communism is no creed — democracy is no creed — it is a vehicle for the enjoyment of freedom, for the ventilation of thought, for the exercise of mutual respect, even in opposition. This is the heritage which has given debate its laws. This is the heritage which is traditionally so near the heart of this immense republic, and for which so many of her sons have died.

When anti-Communism attempts to become a creed, it fights with the arms of its enemy, and like its enemy, it breeds injustice, fear, corruption. It casts away the true platform of democracy, and destroys the sense of moral superiority without which no ethical struggle is ever won.

This majestic land, these United States, know by instinct — in fact they have often taught us from more venerable parts — that democracy can never be a prison — it is a room with the windows open.

When I raised my eyes off my paper, I saw that where there had been one bored technician at the outset, the control room now looked like a tankful of trout in a restaurant, full of surprised and hypnotized faces glued to the glass. All that was missing were the bubbles.

As I left, there was a chorus of questions. "Hey, did you really mean that?" "D'you work for a group?" "Wow, when's this going out?" "Are they willing to accept this kind of thing in England?"

There must have been one of them who was eager for a fast buck, because a report appeared in one of the less-responsible gossip columns adding all manner of red frills to what I had said, presumably in the interests of freedom of the press. The studio was extremely worried, and asked me to lie low and avoid questions, which was an indication of the wretched atmosphere at the time. They even asked me not to come down to lunch while Hedda Hopper was there. Since time has not been generous with her memory, I had better remind some of the younger readers, and even, thank Heavens, some of the older ones, that Hedda Hopper, in her time a useful starlet, became in her dotage a feared columnist whose virtue was that she said what she thought, and whose vice was that what she thought didn't amount to much.

As it turned out, the request for me not to confront her was occasioned not only by my utterances, but by a conviction she held that "he was so great in *Quo Vadis*, he has to be a fag, and you know what I feel about fags!" Needless to say, I had my meal in the restaurant as usual.

Our daughter Pavla was born at St. John's Hospital in Santa Monica on June 2, 1954, at 3:33 in the afternoon. That evening I was invited to the Bogarts and arrived late, having spent the day at the hospital. Bogie was mixing drinks at a bar on the way to the living room.

"Well?" he said, his eyes anxious.

"It's a girl. Both doing well," I replied.

His face, so human and involuntarily kind turned into the disenchanted mask he was known by.

"What's the matter?" I asked, not without a grain of irony. "You disapprove?"

"No, no," he muttered. "Congratulations, and all that usual crap. I can just hear in my head the noise those women in the living room are going to make when you tell them." And, holding a tray of drinks, he did a wonderfully overdrawn imitation of a roomful of women greeting the news of a childbirth. "Aaaooow—"

We went into the living room together. Bogie said he had an announcement to make, and spoke in the dead tones of a ringside announcer. "Peter's just become the proud father of a baby girl. Both mother and child are doing well."

"Aaaaooow—"

Bogie gave me the filthiest of his enviable repertoire of filthy looks, while he dispensed his martinis. I recognized that his imitation was not overdrawn at all.

When I had finished the film we decided, in spite of the presence of a newborn child, to return to England slowly, by way of Mexico, Cuba, Haiti, and Jamaica. There we caught a French ship, the *Antilles*, which stopped at Guadeloupe, Martinique, Port of Spain, La Guaira, and Vigo on its way to Plymouth.

Hollywood had been exciting, despite a permanent financial stringency. We were young and adventurous, and life in our tiny apartment on Wilshire Boulevard was full of incident, most of it pleasant. Our neighbor was Frank Sinatra, then still a hermit saddened by his worship of Ava Gardner. Morning, noon, and night he sang. I had been writing *Romanoff and Juliet*, and whereas I had been impervious to the German bombs, I frankly found it difficult to concentrate with this insidious serenade going on, hardly deadened by the cardboard wall.

When I mentioned this to my wife, I was lectured. "There is a man who really works at his craft, always honing his instrument in search of the ultimate perfection, driving himself relentlessly toward the pinnacle of his profession. Whereas you—"

Just then the needle stuck in the groove. They were records. All the wall eliminated was the orchestral accompaniment.

Once, when visiting him, the inevitable record was playing. He left the room for a moment to mix some drinks. During his absence,

Judy Garland appeared, clutching a pile of records. She immediately replaced his record with one of hers. He reappeared as though he had heard a burglar. Then he laughed at his own reaction.

Since I was paid in England, we managed our journey by saving money from our expenses. Mexico whetted the appetite for future journeys, especially perhaps Yucatán, quite unlike the rest of the country. The ancient city of Mérida nestles in the heart of a crewcut jungle, an oasis of silence amid the catcalls of jaguars and the cackle of exotic birds. The only noise seemed to come from the groaning of windmills, which are everywhere. The kitchens, with their copper pots, are spotless, reminiscent of Dutch interiors, which go well with the windmills, and since the people, tiny, fragile, and very soft-spoken, look like Indonesians, it is easy to feel that one is in some old colonial outpost in the East Indies.

The Mayan ruins in Chichén Itzá and Uxmal are quite as remarkable as those of the Aztecs and Toltecs.

Cuba was on the eve of elections and Batista seemed to be the only candidate worthy of taking seriously. The city of Havana was lovely, but the atmosphere at the time was disturbing. The place felt as though it was irretrievably impregnated with American influence, which is not at all the same as saying that it was like the United States. Every advertisement was for an American product, and the cards we procured enabling us to swim in the Officer's Club also enabled us to swim and float among some of the most preposterous machos on record. It felt as though the changing room would have a sword rack and a spur bin. I felt and said at the time that such a country could only explode in order to rediscover its identity. Cuban refugees, like Russian refugees, never tire of evoking the elegance of life in the past, which they refer to as free, and plaintively insist that they would have become modern states if only "they had been left alone to develop in their own good time."

Revolutions have never succeeded unless the establishment does three-quarters of the work. It was completing its contribution while we were in Cuba.

Haiti was different. Here there was a feeling of resistance to all outside influence, which is not difficult for a people so hypnotized by its own image and passionate history. The extraordinary figures of Toussaint L'Ouverture, Dessalines, Pétion, and Henri Christophe dominated its early years, with Dessalines and Pétion less known but probably the most effective, whereas Henri Christophe, crowning himself an emperor in the image of Napoleon and in hatred of the French, constituted an English type of court, with the Grand Chamberlain, the Grand Duke of Don-Don, and the two masters of nobility, the Dukes of Limonade and Marmalade.

It would always be difficult for a people with such a colorful sense of both pomp and circumstance to find themselves at home with the dry crackle of Marxist theory. Rather nervously avoiding a voodoo procession in the village of Léogâne, which was far from being for tourists, we drifted into a ramshackle churchyard with simple crosses and mere sticks of wood. In the middle of it was a small and hideous mausoleum, its Grecian roof held up by weeping angels, dedicated to what must have been one of the great families of the Haitian empire, for on it were inscribed the words "Famille Actedoffrande-Milord."

A little later, from one of the wooden houses dating from the colonial period, we heard the strains of a Polish dance which must have been the rage at the time, a courtly Krakowiak hammered out on an old piano, full of crystalline runs with missing notes. Glancing through the windows, we caught sight briefly of a dignified rout in progress in an atmosphere reminiscent of the antebellum South, but with coffee-colored beauties in huge and fanciful costumes performing the steps accurately with their nimble gallants. It seemed as if the throbbing African nostalgia of voodoo was too vulgar for these stately ghosts.

On a walk, I ran into Peter Brook. It was a meeting of two Stanleys, both of us rather unhappy at not being alone in this strange world. Our disappointment was aggravated by the sudden emergence of Livingstone in the shape of Graham Greene. He seemed as horrified at seeing us as we had been at seeing each other. We had lunch together since there seemed nothing else to do. By the time we were ready for coffee, the atmosphere had warmed pleasantly. Instead of regaling each other with tales of distant Haiti in some London club, we were resigned to sitting in distant Haiti and regaling each other with tales of London.

We arrived back in England, which was slightly anticlimatic after our fill of exoticism. The house was beautiful, but hardly practical once there was a child. There were stairs and more stairs, up and down, and a never-ending series of redoubtable nannies, who never lasted longer than a week or two. The tensions in the house were often very difficult to take, and it was becoming abundantly clear that Suzanne had a dislike for many things English because of a particular prejudice which really had nothing to do with the English themselves, but with Canadians of English or Scottish origin.

We went to France, where I had been engaged to appear in Max Ophüls's film *Lola Montes*. We left in my car, taking a nanny wearing a uniform, which included a gray velvet collar, the dirtiest article of clothing I had ever seen except on a recluse. Reluctantly I carried Nanny's largest suitcase to the car and noticed that its center of gravity kept shifting as I walked. I placed it on the pavement and asked her what was inside it. She blushed and refused to say. I reminded her that we would have to go through customs, and she might be forced to open it there. She began to vacillate, and eventually allowed me to open it. It contained a collection of glass milk bottles, inadequately washed out, which now contained London tap water, rendered opaque by the remnants of milk. "Well, I heard up in Edinburgh that the French water is undrinkable," she pleaded. It was quite clear that yet another nanny had outstayed her welcome.

The film of *Lola Montes* was destined to become a classic. There were precious few signs of this destiny during its making. Max Ophüls was a *rara avis* all right, a German giggler who lived in his own particular stratosphere of subtlety, and who protected himself against the instrusion of Philistines into his private world by a grotesque and wonderful perversity. When I had the sad honor of writing his obituary for the *Guardian*, I wrote that he had the gift of manufacturing the smallest wristwatch ever known, and could subsequently insist on suspending it from a cathedral so that passersby could tell the time.

The new "letter-box" format of Cinemascope was imposed on him for commercial reasons by the producers, but he whispered to me with the glee of a court jester that he had found a way of cheating them, and reverting to the beloved intimacy of the old small screen.

"How?" I asked, thinking he must have found some contractual loophole.

He held his hands up, far apart, and brought them slowly closer to one another.

"Two pieces of black velvet," he whispered, and roared with uncontrollable laughter at the simplicity of his act of sabotage.

Max was the first great poet of bad taste, in that he was the first to exploit Art Nouveau as a thing of beauty and style, not merely as a curiosity, the visible cancer of a decadent and dying society as my generation was brought up to believe it to be. He saw in its asymmetrical outbursts elements of controlled imagination that were eminently cinematic, and to borrow a phrase and even an idea from Calder, he made them mobiles with his camera, which never tired of laying pictorial ambushes for the human face.

In his endless search for subtlety, he would ask you to register hatred or brutality without changing the expression of your face and then plunge you into shafts of darkness, or shoot you through a metal banister or a net curtain to obliterate every effect except your presence. He was a dictator in the image of a Prussian Junker, who found the most irresistible of all comic creations in this world, the Junkers of Prussia. His father had been a military tailor in Saarbrücken called Oppenheimer, who, like the Jewish tailor in Zuckmayer's *Der Hauptmann von Köpenick*, kept barking at his studious son to stand up, with his shoulders well back.

"*Halt dich gerade, halt dich gerade, sonst kommst du mie zu Militär!*" ("Stand up, stand up, or you'll never make it in the Army!")

The old man was shrewder politically than the majority of officers he fitted. He believed none of the military optimism of the time that the war would be a short one, and since some cavalry regiments wore black trousers, Max remembered him calling up to his assistants — "Fix red stripes on all our tuxedo trousers; this war's going to go on a long time."

Unfortunately he could not be expected to know that the cavalry would last a much shorter time than the war.

Max loved officers of the Belle Epoque, their utter uselessness, their obligations toward virility, their statutory quick temper over imagined slights, their generous ability to make room for younger men by eliminating each other on the field of honor. And yet his comments were never destructive, and he handled the objects of his attention like rare wines, as though the absurdity of years could be destroyed by an excessive movement of the bottle in which these rare essences were contained. He was a tender despot, more than a little in love with those things his intelligence most disliked.

A most Germanic idea occurred to him during the huge circus scene. The rhythm of Georges Auric's lilting score was taken up by a series of dwarfs and Lilliputians, moving up and down on ropes like pistons or like wooden horses on a gigantic merry-go-round. The dwarfs were fairly comfortable, unless any of them happened to suffer from vertigo, because their massive torsos were firmly implanted in the leather harnesses. The Lilliputians were less serene, however, since they were perfectly formed miniature people and they had some difficulty remaining immobile in belts that had been patently designed for dwarfs. One Lilliputian began to slip dangerously, and the belt tried to become a collar; only his arms preventing him from either sliding right through and dropping some thirty to forty feet, or else being strangled. The pathetic cries of his tiny voice could be barely heard over the caressing waltz. There was a general movement of consternation, nipped in the bud by Max's rasping imitation of a Prussian warlord.

"*Lass hängen die Zwerge!*" ("Let the dwarfs hang!") I looked at him, appalled. He felt my presence, glanced at me with a guilty grin, and dissolved into his uncontrollable fit of silent laughter, taking the time to shout "Cut!" The point was, he had his shot.

During another immensely complicated take — lasting four and a half minutes and involving horses, tumblers, and trapeze artists, and with the camera moving on an endless complicated track, spiraling and dipping — I, as the ringmaster, sent a dwarf off for a glass of water, which was not part of the meticulous planning. Surprised, the dwarf ran off to fetch it. Since he didn't know where to find it, it took rather a long time, and my irritation increased, as did the hoarseness of my throat. At last he brought it, I drank it surreptitiously while shouting out my lines, like a headwaiter having a secret nip, and gave the empty glass to the dwarf, drying my mouth with a large silk handkerchief which was part of my costume. It was as relaxed as the rest was formal. At the end of the take, Max Ophüls expressed both the quality of his despotism and of his magnanimity. Taking me aside, for once rather sad, he said: "Peter, the one thing I regret is that I didn't tell you to do that."

I did one other film at that time, which was shot in Sicily, and its only remarkable feature was that the producers ran out of money after three days, a record even for Italy. But by then, I had already completed *Romanoff and Juliet,* a three-act play absolutely neoclassical in form. I had always remembered the joy of playing in *The Rivals* with Edith Evans, and I wanted to try my hand at something as direct and as undisguisedly theatrical, ignoring the famous "fourth wall" and employing asides whenever expedient. I remembered that *The Rivals* had entertained troops, some of whom had never seen a play before, much more than the low farces specifically aimed at their intellect.

The theme was a variation on the tragic love of Romeo and Juliet, with Romeo as son of the Soviet Ambassador and Juliet the daughter of the American Ambassador. The intractable families, the Capulets and the Montagues, were replaced by the governments of the U.S.A. and the U.S.S.R., and the scene was a small neutral country, cringing in the center of the political arena, its economy largely dependent on printing stamps with deliberate anomalies.

On its way to London, the night of our opening in the suburb of Golders Green, our son Igor was born. It was April 30, 1956. I acted my part euphorically that night, and my father, by all reports, wept tears of quiet joy. Once again, I was grateful to hear, mother and child were doing well.

16

Romanoff and Juliet opened at the Piccadilly Theatre in London on May 17, 1956, and was an immediate success. Even Harold Hobson devoted an unaccustomed amount of space to it — unaccustomed that is, by his standards when they were applied to me. In fairness to those standards, I must admit that there was more emphasis on the success of the evening than on any traces of quality which might have been thinly scattered over it. The hardened professionals of the gallery were still there, but interspersed with drama students and other young people. This time there was no trace of trouble, and I could at last bask in a glow of not just being a one-play man.

May I say a word here? Before you go off along a straight chronological line, I believe there is room for an important tangent. Your imaginary country had no name.

That is correct.

Later on, when you made a film of it, you were compelled, by the realistic nature of the medium, to give your country a name. Concordia.

Yes.

Do you remember how this imaginary country began?
Of course I do. As a small boy of eight or nine, I was walking along a country lane in Sussex — West Chiltington to be precise — when I passed by a farmyard in which a woman was in the process of wringing a chicken's neck. The sudden end of the bird's hysterical shrieking marked a first rendezvous with death and I returned home to the rented cottage sickened by what I had seen.

It was not only your first rendezvous with death, but your first conscious confrontation with a certain aspect of nature.

Of course, that whole terrifying process with which only madmen are ever entirely reconciled. Even the names are changed, out of deference to finer feelings. You don't eat cow, but beef. You don't eat calf, but veal. You don't eat pig, but ham, bacon, or pork. You don't eat deer, but venison. Cold-blooded fish are among the few living entities that retain their identity in death.

Certainly one of the inspirations of vegetarianism is a revulsion at this sinister cycle of survival by killing, the endless sacrifice of the weaker in order to make the strong stronger.

Nature is both magnificent and awful, both sublime in its equilibrium and horrifying in its detail, and a child must somehow reconcile itself to the necessity of refined table manners while digging its teeth into fragments of a mild-mannered creature that had until recently been mooing peacefully in a field and expressing a personality of its own.

There are those who renounce this process altogether, but who still brave the resentful gaze of salmon or the absurd squint of Dover Sole. For the most squeamish, however, there is no escape from the ritual. Roald Dahl knew what he was doing to us when he vented his fantasy about salad screaming in anguish as it is eaten, and since no child starts its life with a hunger strike, we are all irretrievably marked by the corruption of nature by the time our ideas of revulsion are awakened. Hunger has, quite simply, been a more compelling argument than dismay at the equation of existence.

By the time I saw my chicken garroted, I had already suffered various excesses of imagination along these lines. I used to fight shy of drinking water when I was made to eat fish, because I fancied that fish, even masticated into a pulp, might miraculously come together if there was water in my stomach and swim about in there as in a glass bowl. The chicken, however, was the hardest blow to this town child, who had never before consciously associated the leg or wing on a bed of rice with the living nitwits that rushed in front of motorcars like mad golfers in plus-fours.

There was, I found, only one escape from this nightmare, only one way in which I could keep a grip on myself in this vile world of grown-ups, and that was the establishment of an imaginary country, to which I owed total allegiance. The first article in the constitution of this land was that no chicken would have its neck wrung.

Exactly. But with the passage of time, the country changed its character, did it not?

Countries grow, as do humans. What had started as a childish revolt against the casual viciousness of adults became, with the passage of time, a growing reality, and even, I may say, a source of patriotism to me, denied the usual racial sentiments by an excessive admixture of prenatal ingredients.

You mean, of course, that the country still exists.

Yes. It is more real than ever, and eminently useful.

Would you tell us about it?

Certainly not. I will only reveal that it has a geographical position, an outlook of its own, and problems. Many problems. Just as an adult has many problems. It is no Utopia, no Erewhon. Those are countries whose secrets have been betrayed. Immediately you begin to share secrets of this kind, you begin to entertain, and then the utility of such a place, and its reality, are destroyed. All I can tell you is that the mineral wealth and transport are nationalized, whereas free enterprise is encouraged where human ingenuity and acumen are concerned.

How about the fate of chickens?

I am ashamed to say that I haven't given chickens a thought for many years now, and I have no doubt that their poor necks are wrung as they are elsewhere.

Disgraceful. Tell us what you can about your country and tell us why all you cannot tell us must remain a secret.

Our legal system is based on a form of medieval disposition, there being no counsel for the defense and the public prosecutor being given no voice in the proceedings, only being able to answer questions as a witness would. In other words, all drama is drained from the trial — drama which may be exciting, especially when idealized and concentrated in television playlets, but in which the shuttlecock so dramatically bandied hither and thither in this macabre game is nothing but the truth and in which the score may militate against a human life or human career. This is acceptable on television, but not at all, I think, in life.

So that all the judges, the advocates, and the jury are, at the outset, on the same side?

On the side of truth. It is the evidence which may separate them, but never the roles in which they are cast initially. Their devotion to the truth must be absolute, and they can rebuke each other if any deviations from it are noticed and accepted as such. All discussion is open, and everyone, including the prisoner, may make observations, according to a rigorous adherence to the rules of debate.

Do you seriously think such a system would work?

Do you seriously think the alternatives work? Apart from making good TV, that is?

Well, we now know your country's relationship to chicken. How did you come by this idea?

I developed it slowly, over the years — but it came to a head at my club, during the recess of a celebrated murder trial. In the gentlemen's toilet, a great lawyer stood relieving himself into one bowl. I recognized him as the prosecuting counsel. Next to him, engaged in the same relief work, was another distinguished counsel, defending an alleged murderess. They were discussing the morning's work in tones at once jocular and collusive.

I was so shocked that I asked the one I knew better whether they always came to the urinal to discuss matters which were still sub judice.

"Where else can we do it?" he replied, and the other joined in the laughter as he adjusted his dress. Several weeks later the cause of all the levity was hanged.

You actually used such a situation in a short story.

It is wonderful when you can reproduce a scandalous incident and yet have a perfect answer if some august authority seeks to refute your credibility. That is all that I care to say about my country, except that by now whenever a grave international situation develops, I react not as an Englishman, nor as a Russian, nor as one who is sometimes in America, France, Switzerland, or Germany, but as life-President of my own nation. I write protests, démarches, and am always willing to accept apologies, although, up to now, very few have been forthcoming.

But you spoke before of the utility *of such a country. Utility to whom?*

Utility to me. Its influence goes far beyond a mere pastime, a mere mental folly. When I began to work for UNICEF and, at a later stage, for UNESCO, both agencies of the United Nations which come in for more than their share of abuse from the ignorant, I realized that my addiction to my own point of view, or rather, that of my nation helped me beyond all measure to acquire the full neutral stance necessary for such a job.

By neutral, I presume you do not mean free from prejudice, because no man with an attitude can be entirely free from that.

Of course not. I agree with you. The great heresies, however, come from precisely those who believe they *are* free from prejudice. "UNESCO is at it again" read the lead headline in the *Herald Tribune* of Paris, in many ways an admirable paper. The article blamed UNESCO for encouraging so-called Third World nations in wishing to escape from the informational hegemony of the American press agencies by creating press agencies of their own, and it was presumed that they wished this tendentious news of their own creation to supplant the truth. But it would of course not be the truth that they would be supplanting. All news is tendentious, depending on its source, its interpretation, and the temper of the times. And

American news is as tendentious as any other. The fact that it faithfully reflects the tendencies of its readers does not mean that it is
closer to the truth than any other, but merely that it is conscious of
its obligations toward its readers' prejudices and therefore of its own
commercial health.

*Well, naturally opinion is, by definition, tendentious. That is quite
true, but there are so many instances in the modern world in which
there is no effort whatsoever to tell the truth that one can understand all too well a certain American impatience in the face of the
kind of criticism you, or your government, level at them.*

Leave my government out of this. It is as sensitive as any other
and as childish in its reactions. Our only chance of being objective
or indeed honest is by dealing with all subjects as an individual.

Then why bother to have a country?

Don't be ridiculous; everyone must have a country. The only difference between myself and the others is that they seem to be satisfied with what they have been given, whereas I was stranded
with a cricket ball, a caraway seed, a glass of wine, and a copy of
Streuvelpeter, to say nothing of the alloy spoon in my mouth. There
has never been an anthem which sets my foot tapping, never an
occasion which brings a lump to my throat. I can take no allegiance
to a flag if I don't know who's holding it. My only allegiance is to my
own conscience, and who is to tell me that that is not higher than
any flag, or any mediocre tune written by a third-rate bandmaster to
the words of a fourth-rate poet, to which men rise as a mass with a
look of inane piety on their faces? Why have a country, you ask?
How would I understand my fellowmen if I didn't place myself at
the same disadvantage; if I didn't invent problems, how would I
understand real ones? Especially today.

Why especially today?

You registered American impatience with criticism. My God, I
spend my time in America trying to explain the Russians to them to
the best of my ability and I spend my time in Russia trying to
explain the Americans to them. Despite their fiscal and military
collusion, they understand each other not at all. But since I am

devoted to the concept of freedom and consider the American concept to be insanely ambitious and absolutely wonderful, I am saddened by certain shortcomings in the realization of these ideals.
Freedom of the individual is so sacrosanct that, ironically, it is not
sufficiently protected. The individual too often becomes the victim
of the pressure group, the protection racket, the little local law unto
itself. We have already spoken of the dreaded McCarthy and we
know the folklore of the Ku Klux Klan and the fastest gun in the
West, and Watergate, which I suppose might be characterized as
the slowest wits in the East. After each is brought to heel, there are
those superb optimists who maintain that each victory over malig-
nancy is a proof that the system works. Yes, it works indeed, with an
undeniable splendor, in a carnival atmosphere of wisecracks and intrigue and comic hats and streamers, but at what cost to the very intimacy, the very solitude before beliefs, which it is sworn to maintain?

*This has always existed, everywhere, in some form or other. The
British proudly believe that a man is innocent until proved guilty.
You only have to look at the inside of a British law court to be convinced that a man has to be pretty guilty to be there at all. Not only
ideals, but even ideas, have always been greater than men, greater
even than the men who fathered them. You know that. You even
told me you were an optimist, which proves you know that. Why
now suddenly this pessimistic stricture, especially today?*

Why? Let me explain it by another cartoon, by the talented Mr.
Mauldin. Two well-dressed men stare at the United Nations build-
ing. One says to the other: "A First Class Idea, not given a Second
Chance by the Third World."

Well?

Just over two hundred years ago, the United States emerged like
a phoenix from just such a third world. Has she forgotten so quickly
what it was like to be poor and pure and young? Must she so soon
filch the musty robes of power from the wardrobe and behave as the
British and others did when they were the flagellating fathers of the
pupil world? Why this pharisaic impatience with those just fallen

)m the nest? Is it merely the impatience of the young with those
.ill younger, or is it a trap laid by stealthy nature to try and lure
America into a posture that was the cause of her own rebellion, her
own birth?

*She is so much richer than all the rest of us, it is a miracle her
people at least have remained as nice as they undoubtedly are. The
British were never pleasant when a superpower, except as individuals. As colonists they were pretty awful.*

As colonists everyone was pretty awful, and the farther north you
went, the worse they became. Come to that, the Americans weren't
much good at it either. But you are quite right in saying that the
Americans are far nicer than they have any right to be and that in itself is a signal triumph, and it must be accounted as fallout from the
democratic system. To a certain extent they are bound to engender
a degree of animosity, by virtue of their technical accomplishments
and the extraordinary generosity of their soil, but it is sometimes
true that they react according to the animosity they create instead of
in spite of it, and they tend to shout the virtues of their system to
the winds, although if we all adopted it, commercial intercourse
would come to a full stop.

How do you mean?

If we could never take the responsibility for anything we said
without referring it to the ratification of two national assemblies and
a president, it would take years and years for any agreements to be
signed. It is bad enough when one partner is compelled constitutionally to do so, and it does explain, paradoxically, why the United
States prefers to do business with tawdry dictators. It is so much
quicker, and you know where you stand. Equally paradoxically, the
United States is directly responsible for the spread of socialism, a
movement she says she mistrusts and abhors, although she herself
has digested many of its elements.

How is she responsible?

By the lack of restraint on huge supranational corporations who
eventually threaten the existence of many of the proudest companies
in other parts of the world, which are then forced to seek protection

behind the skirts of government. What America preaches and wh[ ]
she makes others practice are often as far apart as can be, and this,
when applied to that developing world, toward which she owes an
immense, a unique moral responsibility, is often very serious indeed.

Was all this inherent in Romanoff and Juliet?

For those who cared to look for it, yes. It all depended on the
habits of the audience. To those who swallowed their pill whole,
there was only the fleeting taste of sugar. To those who let it dis-
solve, the bitter tang of the medicine soon became apparent.

Nevertheless, it did well in America.

They usually swallow their pills instead of sucking them. They are
in a hurry. But there were those who noticed. Harry Truman, for
instance, who wrote me a most perspicacious letter, which I treasure to this day. He knew perfectly well that what you call criticism
is engendered by respect and affection, not by any feelings of aversion.

*I was glad to be able to clear up that point, so often a cause of ir-
responsible comment, against which there is no defense, in the
sacred name of freedom of the press.*

During the run of *Romanoff and Juliet,* I accepted an invitation to
play tennis in the Soviet Embassy in London from the Minister-
Counsellor, Mr. Romanov, who said he wanted his revenge for my
taking his name in vain, thereby demonstrating a rare grace and
humor. My companion was a Conservative Member of Parliament.
We were pitted against Romanov and his doubles partner, Comrade
Korbut.

It was raining that day, a hopeless top-to-bottom rain, without
inflection. I had the impression we were playing in a pointillist picture.

"We can't play in this," muttered the Member of Parliament.

"Isn't that what they're waiting to hear?" I asked, my upper lip
stiff with cold.

"You're right, by Jove," said the M.P., and bravely called across ₁e net to suggest that play should begin.

"We cannot begin," cried Mr. Romanov, "because the umpire has not yet arrived. He has been detained by the Ambassador."

By the time the so-called umpire did arrive, we were ready to be wrung out like flannels. He turned out to be a steely eyed man who stood at the net and quickly became as wet as we were.

"Play!" he barked, as though instructing a firing squad to do its duty.

I was so enervated by his presence that I served a double fault.

"Love-fifteen!" he yelled.

By the time we arrived at deuce, my agitation had given way to a grim determination, and I served an ace.

"Advantage, Great Britain," shouted the umpire.

And so it went on to an eventual victory in a thoroughly bad match.

We went into the shower, and Mr. Romanov wagged a warning finger.

"Today," he said, "you won. But in a year . . ."

Stalin had, at this time, been denounced, but not yet entirely discredited, and there was some doubt as to what to do with him. I noticed, when we had first entered the Embassy, the shape of a large picture on the red brocade wall, a patch darker than the rest. This mystery was resolved in the shower, where we found Stalin in a huge gilt frame, smiling benignly at the naked athletes.

"Today," he seemed to say, "you won. But in a year . . ."

During the match I had leaped for a high ball and landed badly. Two days later I was hardly able to move and had to spend eight weeks on a board with a slipped disc. I came out of *Romanoff and Juliet* and was told by a celebrated doctor that I would have to wear a corset for life and that tennis was out of the question for the same length of time.

I was fitted for the corset by a gentleman in a morning suit who presented me with a card claiming that his firm were "Makers of

Surgical Trusses to His Late Majesty King George the Fifth." He made me lift my pajama top so that he could reach around me with a tape measure, and the poor fellow, who was suffering from the early symptoms of Parkinson's Disease, placed his ice-cold hands on my warm back, and soon I was shaking with uncontrolled laughter in what was one of the most embarrassing and macabre minor episodes of my life.

I still have the corset, which would find immediate favor in the wardrobe of a sadomasochistic transvestite, and which I declined to wear after one atrocious day. Luckily Suzanne had an acquaintance in Paris, a Rumanian lady called Madame Codreanu, who had a great knowledge of things Oriental, and who walked on my spine with all her weight, stubbing out imaginary cigarettes on every vertebra. I grew over an inch, which cost me a pretty penny in having all my trousers lengthened, but I am eternally grateful for the cure. Needless to say, I play tennis whenever I can.

Before performing *Romanoff and Juliet* in America, I shot a film in Paris with the redoubtable Henri-Georges Clouzot. He had a reputation for immense intelligence and for refined cruelty, neither of which I found entirely justified. He certainly betrayed ambitions to be cruel, but frankly lacked the equipment for it; and his intelligence was manifest mainly by his frequent changes of mind.

In order to undermine my confidence, he told me that Gary Cooper would have been the ideal casting for the part I was playing. I answered him by saying that he could never have afforded Gary Cooper. We were all spies in the film: Curt Jürgens wearing dark glasses, even then a tedious cliché for increasing tension; Sam Jaffe, speaking a French as extraordinarily American as Jürgens's was cozily Teutonic and mine sullenly Slavonic; and Martita Hunt, who had studied with Sarah Bernhardt and who spoke a French far better than anyone, including Clouzot. Hers was not a French you expected to hear in a film, however, let alone a spy film. But then, Clouzot's forte was his incongruity. It either came off or it didn't. On this occasion, it didn't.

On one occasion, Clouzot eyed me icily and asked me, "Why do we not get on better?"

"Let us say I am ill in some remote part of the world," I replied, "and I call for a doctor. You arrive and, without saying a word, you open your bag and extract the most sinister galaxy of surgical instruments imaginable — saws, needles, scalpels, and tubes. Meticulously you select the sharpest and thinnest of the needles and sterilize it in a flame. Then you approach my eye with professional resolve. You speak for the first time when I can already feel the heat of the needle.

" 'By the way, what do you do in life?' you inquire.

" 'You ask me? I'm a doctor,' I reply."

Clouzot turned and walked away. It was not the answer he desired.

I did an affectionate film after this neurotic fantasy, the story of a wicked lawyer in New York too avaricious to buy a dog, who barks through his door to rid himself of unwanted visitors. Inevitably, he turns into a dog himself for most of the film. This fable, called, if you please, *Un Angel Volo Sobre Brooklyn*, was shot in Madrid by the Hungarian expatriate director, Ladislao Vajda.

Then we went by ship to America, *en famille*, from Algeciras. On arrival we were met by the press and by a duckbill platypus — I cannot now think why, but it was a publicity stunt thought up by David Merrick. George S. Kaufman, then in his declining years, was going to redirect the play for American taste after Denis Carey's excellent job in London. The sets were by Jean-Denis Malcles.

It was clear quite early on that George Kaufman, a towering figure in the American theater, was by then beyond the chore he had accepted. There was an element of enormous sadness about the man, a pride which preferred a bitter silence to comment, and an inability to rehearse for more than three or four hours a day. He would arrive in an air-conditioned Cadillac and sit around listlessly in the auditorium, looking, I remember, like a deck chair that could never be folded up correctly. His contributions were minimal, because even at the best of times our styles were very different, he being an inspired inventor of comic lines that were comic in their own right, whereas what I wrote could only generate laughter if said by a particular person in a particular situation. Poor George manfully went through the motions of helping until the dress rehearsal, when he announced softly yet savagely that he would have given us notes if he hadn't lost them. It was the last time he spoke to us.

We opened to vaguely favorable notices, but like practically everything else on Broadway, it was touch and go until a veritable bombardment of the airwaves, engineered by David Merrick and carried out by me on every kind of television program, put the show over as though it had been a new and mildly controversial European car. We ran for a season, and then, after the holidays, we resumed on the road.

The holidays were spent in the South of France. During the course of them, I was invited to a cocktail party aboard a sailing boat in Cannes harbor. It was an opportunity to see a business acquaintance and I therefore accepted the invitation, although I had never met my host, a French North African carpet manufacturer resident in Mexico.

Before leaving the party an hour after my arrival, I had bought the boat. It was, and is, a 58-foot ketch built of steel in Amsterdam in 1929 by De Vries Lentsch, as elegant and harmonious a craft as you could wish. Its past history was romantic. It had been ordered by Dr. Boucard, of whom a portrait, test tube in hand, was painted by Tamara de Lempicka; Dr. Boucard had made a fortune with an emetic on a milk base called Lactéol, well known to French babies, and the first name of this svelte racing yacht was none other than *Lactéol*.

By the time I laid my hands on her, she was called *Christina*, which led to endless complications, since that was also the name of Onassis's floating palace. I received a few cryptic messages by mistake, such as: "TIME NOT RIPE BAGHDAD WILLING SUGGEST TWENTY REPEAT TWENTY MILLION ADEQUATE KARAKRISTIDIS," or

"SEND AUTHORIZATION RETURN TWENTY TANKERS CASH ON DE-LIVERY MONROVIA BESTEST PHILEMONOPOULOS."

It was eventually immensely frustrating not to be able to react to some of these messages as I would have wished, and I resolved rather sadly to put an end to this flow of tantalizing information by changing the name of the yacht to *Nitchevo*. *Nitchevo* means "nothing" in Russian, but it is also redolent of *quién sabe?* and *In shā Allāh*. If Allah didn't wish me to make my fortune in tankers by cracking codes, then I would be content with *Nitchevo*, and I have been ever since. My rash, thoughtless purchase has given me some of the happiest times of my life.

Had I been Getty or indeed, Onassis, I could imagine no luxury greater than arriving in Istanbul in my own good time, without the knowledge of Air France or TWA or even of Türk Hava Yokari. To see the minarets floating on a sea mist of pink, the setting sun caressing the golden globes for the last fleeting moments before being engulfed in the rich purple of late evening, while a crescent moon, fragile as a clipping from a baby's fingernail, hangs palely overhead — that is beauty on the scale of personal achievement, in the sense that a runner bean from your garden tastes subtly different to one purchased in a shop.

I have faced high seas and even peril on old *Nitchevo*, with waves breaking on the roof of the deckhouse, arrows of icy water in flight as in medieval battle, little whirlpools scurrying round the calves and pushing at the ankles, seas angry and devious in their malice. All of it, even the moments of fear, was sheer exhilaration. Risk seems to be an intrinsic ingredient in a man's life, a means of sharpening his knowledge of himself, and I had missed its presence, even during the war under impersonal bombs or lost in the sludge of administration.

The sea not only sharpens a sense of beauty and of alarm, but also a sense of history. You are confronted with precisely the sight which met Caesar's eyes, and Hannibal's, without having to strain the imagination by subtracting television aerials from the skyline and filling in the gaps in the Colosseum. And among the islands of

Greece, or off the magical coast of Turkey, or yet again, in the sheltered splendor of Dalmatian waters, you rediscover what the world was like when it was empty, when time itself was the richness that oil is today, and when pleasures were as simple as getting up in the morning.

No fish tastes like fish you catch yourself, and every day is a journey of discovery. *Nitchevo* has been my inspiration in good times, my salvation in bad. The captain who came with it, José Perez Jimenez, is an integral part of his craft. He was aboard when I bought it and we have aged together. His wife, Carmen, a blonde girl with a gentle Spanish beauty, a little doll-like in repose, tinged with both melancholy and humor in animation, sails with us and cooks the fish we catch.

José himself has the aquiline gravity of the bullfighter, and would have inspired confidence in any of the navigators of the golden age. His passion for the sea is contained in an austere secrecy not unlike that of a monk for his God, and his controlled anarchy is utterly and uniquely Spanish. Salvador Dali's answer when asked whether he believed in God would suit this Spanish attitude to the ground, even to the sky.

"*Soy praticante ma non creyente,*" he said ("I practice but I do not believe"), a statement which was greeted with hosannas by the leading clergy of Spain.

Having read in his *Baedeker* that the island of Mykonos possessed something like three hundred churches and chapels for a population of two thousand, José turned to me like a grandee as an impenetrable fog swirled around us off the island, and said, "Three hundred churches, and so little light."

He is a man to whom one can attribute valor without it seeming overblown or eccentric. When dealing with the mundane obligations of earning a living, it is a marvelous consolation to know that in some distant harbor, white and peaceful, a venerable jewel of Dutch craftsmanship awaits my idle moments with a couple of dear friends aboard.

While on this first maritime vacation, I had completely forgotten another obligation which I had undertaken in New York prior to leaving. A certain Mr. Weeks from a magazine called *The Atlantic Monthly* had contacted me asking for a playlet about the Russians and the Americans on the moon. I was none too enthusiastic, since I felt I had exhausted the subject of the Russians and the Americans in *Romanoff and Juliet*, and I also sensed that nothing that might happen on the moon could not happen more effectively and more comprehensibly here on earth.

I mentioned the offer to a few American friends, all of whom blanched visibly when I told them I was thinking of turning it down. "Turn down *The Atlantic Monthly!*" they cried, of one voice. "Why, there are those who struggle for a lifetime only to have a piece turned down by *The Atlantic Monthly*, and they consider *that* an achievement!"

I was made to feel like a kind of peacock, all feathers and no guts, and in a moment of weakness agreed to Mr. Weeks's request. Then, of course, faced with the unsuspected joys of navigation, I forgot all about my holiday task. Back in New York, I suddenly remembered it with horror and then received a phone call from Mr. Weeks asking when he could have it, and then forcing my response by telling me the deadline was in four days' time. I tried to get out of my obligation, but Mr. Weeks was stern and avuncular. "We have held the space, young man, there's no road back now," or more trenchant words to that effect.

I sat down in my hotel room and wrote a short story about the Swiss reaching the moon. I had never written a story before and had a feeling of utter irresponsibility, which was not helped by extreme pangs of hunger. I knew I was back in New York, because every time I ordered a snack from room service, the waiter, an out-of-work actor, sat on my bed to watch television and discuss the prospects of getting a job on a soap opera. I had no alternative but starvation if I was to meet the deadline.

At last I finished it, sent it off to Boston, and awaited the inevitable explosion. It came a few days later in the form of a request for seven more stories. I could not believe it. Mr. Weeks became Edward and shortly after that, Ted, and it was he who gave me the confidence to break out into the tantalizing world of nondramatic writing, where the terrible rigors of playwriting are no longer so stringent, where there is time to snatch a breath and turn a phrase only obliquely necessary to propel the action forward.

I wrote away on the road, in Columbus, Ohio, in St. Louis, in Washington, D.C. The most successful of these stories, which gave its title to the eventual book, *Add a Dash of Pity*, I wrote in the Plankinton House Hotel in Milwaukee.

"Add a Dash of Pity" dealt with the moral and material chaos created by generals who thoughtlessly write their memoirs long after the end of the war, stirring up the doubts, regrets, and sorrows of those who had either participated in action or lost loved ones in the war.

Years later, I heard from a distinguished publisher who had approached Admiral Chester Nimitz with a request for his memoirs. The Admiral had refused to write them, claiming that he was influenced in his decision by my short story. It is an onerous responsibility for one of the war's least effective Private soldiers to have so influenced one of its greatest admirals, and yet it is also an achievement in communications to have touched such a remote luminary on the simple plane of human sensibility.

The year of *Romanoff and Juliet* ended, and we went straight to Hollywood, where I was to act in an epic, by name *Spartacus*.

Spartacus went on for so long that our third child, a daughter, Andrea, who was born during the filming, was able to answer the questions of an inquisitive playmate before I had finished.

"What does your daddy do for a living?" asked the playmate.

"Spartacus," replied Andrea.

17

Spartacus was a film with an extraordinarily rich mixture and as full of intrigue as a Balkan government in the good old days. Kirk Douglas was the producer of this epic, as well as the incarnation of Spartacus, the leader of a slave uprising in ancient Rome. It was based on the celebrated book by Howard Fast, who had been regarded as left wing by the hawks, and the script was being written by Dalton Trumbo, who had also been suspected of Communist sentiments by the same erratic authorities; but to complicate matters, he was no longer on speaking terms with Howard Fast. It was impossible to mention the fact that the author of the script, Sam Jackson, was actually Dalton Trumbo. I found out because Anthony Mann, the director, thought the whole masquerade too ludicrous for words, and took me to see Dalton Trumbo in exile up a side street in Pasadena; from then on, I signed my various memoranda and rewrites Stonewall Ustinov.

Before long Anthony Mann was fired with the peremptory harshness usual in those matters and replaced by a young man with huge eyes who seemed at the time to have none of the vices, and few of the virtues, of youth, but who proved to be biding his time with brilliant political pragmatism and shepherding his gifts through the minefields of concession toward a glorious future career. His name was Stanley Kubrick.

Laurence Olivier had been brought from England, I from God knows where, and Charles Laughton, John Gavin, Tony Curtis, and Jean Simmons from up the road. We had all been sent scripts in order to tempt us, with subtle variations favoring our particular characters. No two scripts, we discovered, were the same. Since Larry Olivier had arrived a week prior to the majority of us, he had already inspired a yet newer version of the script in which his role had somewhat grown in importance. He has played sufficient Shakespearean villains superbly well to have a great confidence in his own powers of persuasion, and it was always amusing to watch him at work in the wings, in the process of getting his own way. When discovered, he would give you a mischievous wink and what had begun as an artifice ended as a performance, simply because he was being watched.

Laughton, whom I had not seen for more than a passing moment since being forced to sit through the *Sign of the Cross* for the second time, was a very different sort of person, almost aggressively vulnerable and sometimes petulant. In this company, he seemed to sit around, waiting to have his feelings hurt, and there was no great love lost between him and Larry, the result of an animosity much older than my career, of which I understood nothing and about which I was singularly uninquisitive.

Knowing that Laughton was shortly to attempt the role of King Lear at Stratford, rather late in life, Larry gave him some hints as to where the dead spots were to be found on that stage as far as acoustics were concerned, a solicitude which Laughton interpreted as veiled hostility in the guise of ostentatious comradeship. Their whole careers had been eminently different, Laughton the man of concessions, who regarded acting as part art and part whoring. He had sold his soul to Hollywood in a way, but had kept a grip on his impenetrable integrity through thick and thin, playing roles as improbable as American admirals in "B" pictures, but, when the oc-

casion demanded it, able to hold an audience spellbound by readings from the Bible with no props apart from the hypnotic calm of
his personality, his eye flicking like the ignition light on a car, an indication that the engine was still running and would spring into action at any moment.

He had a house and a pool, in which he floated like a topsy-turvy
iceberg, only the tip visible above the surface. On one occasion the
toilet flushed and he opened an octopus eye to call, "You do that
deliberately to annoy me when I'm trying to think."

Yes, he had signed his soul away for comfort, and yet, within his
sanctum there was his collection of Renoirs and of Pre-Columbian
art. He was surrounded with things of beauty, which were parts of
his soul translated.

Larry Olivier meanwhile had set up in a rented house with Roger
Furse, the designer, a delightful bearded figure. Like an odd couple
they would make laundry lists and shopping lists, determined to survive within the limits of their living allowance, walking advertisements for Britain's financial embarrassment.

Larry had confided to friends long ago that his ambition was to be
Britain's first theatrical peer and his dexterity in handling a career
unique in its unswerving distinction is beyond praise. He was the
vestal virgin to Laughton's whore, and yet whereas Laughton
feasted his eyes on the work of great painters as he emerged dripping from his pool of contemplation, Larry fretted at arithmetic and
tried to pick holes in the bills of the supermarket. Their ambitions
were utterly different, and each had but scant consideration for the
viewpoint of the other.

For some reason, perhaps availability, I was picked as confidant
for both. Charles was very sensitive to the influence Larry was supposed — rightly or wrongly — to be exerting on Kirk Douglas, and
since he felt he could no longer carry sufficient weight to counteract
this nefarious plotting, he decided to sulk, an activity at which he
was particularly adept. He refused to act the scenes given him, and
I was solicited by the management to try to bridge the gap by finding out what he wanted.

The result of this was that I rewrote all the scenes I had with Laughton, and we rehearsed at his home or mine, often slogging away into the middle of the night. The next day, we rearranged the studio furniture to conform with what we had engineered at home, and presented the company with a fait accompli: Kubrick accepted what we had done more or less without modification, and the scenes were shot in half a day each. Laughton was easy to work with, because he overflowed with an almost carnal glee at the process of acting.

One of my first scenes with Larry Olivier consisted in my rushing up to his horse as it cavorted among a huge mass of prisoners of war, grabbing its bridle, and gazing up at its immaculate rider: "If I identify Spartacus for you, Divinity, will you give me the women and the children?" I said, in the character of the sleazy slave dealer.

There followed the most enormous pause while Larry let his eyes disappear upwards under his half-open lids, licked his lips, pushed at his cheeks from within with his tongue, let his head drop with a kind of comic irony at the quirks of destiny, hardened once again into the mold of mortal divinity, looked away into the unknown as his profile softened from brutal nobility into subtlety. "Spartacus!" he suddenly cried, as though slashing the sky with a razor, and then hissed, "You have found him?"

I was so absolutely staggered at the extent of the pause that I expressed precisely the surprise I felt. Now I gazed over the prisoners with a closed expression, giving nothing away. Then I let a furtive smile play on my lips for a moment at some private thought, chasing it away and seemed about to say something, but changed my mind. I ran the gamut of impertinence, of servility, and of insincerity as he had of vanity, power, and menace. At long last, when he least expected it, I let a practically inaudible "Yes" slip from my mouth.

"Dear boy," said Larry, in a businesslike voice which ill concealed a dawning annoyance, "D'you think you could come in a little quicker with your 'Yes'?"

"No," I said politely.

We both looked at one another straight in the eye and smiled at the same moment.

Larry is, as everyone knows, a magnificent actor, unparalleled in certain roles. His Richard III had a hypnotic power, an evil elegance and wit the like of which I had never seen before and have not seen since, and in certain comic parts his imaginative brio is quite superlative. For my taste, his Hamlet, prefixed as the story of a man "who could not make up his mind," was rather less suited to him, since of all actors he is the most difficult to imagine as one who has not made up his mind.

Everything about him is so superbly stage-managed, so utterly controlled, so immaculately rehearsed that there is very little room for surprise, for the casual or negligent. He can be, and is, a delightful companion. When he was avoiding the press at the time of the breakup of his marriage to Vivien Leigh, I met him at Rome airport, and, with the agreement of the Italian authorities, whisked him off to my rented house in my car, directly from the tarmac. In New York, he and Joan Plowright dined with us before their relationship was suspected, and now, after the harrowing experience of illness, he seems to have found a peace of mind and to have taken the time to bask in his most merited glory, surrounded by very young children and a wife brilliantly talented in her own right.

At that time, however, I must admit that, in spite of enjoying his confidence and trust, and being at pains to merit it, I was never absolutely at ease in his presence, either on or off the stage. He seemed to know so utterly what he was doing at all times, in arrogance or in modesty, in gentleness or in strength, that a mental guard just refused to come down in my defenses. Whereas the scenes with Laughton had some elements of abandon in them, of folly even, those with Larry were more in the spirit of a fencing match.

When I won the Oscar for the best supporting performance in *Spartacus*, Larry sent me a cable thanking me for having supported him so well. It was a joke, of course.

Later, when we were both up for an Emmy award, he for "A

Moon And Sixpence," I for "Barefoot in Athens," I was informed by
the Academy of Television Arts and Sciences that he had sent a message that he could not be present and that if he were to win he
would like me to accept it for him. Being a little superstitious on
such occasions, I prepared a speech of acceptance for him. A few
hours later I had won the award and was only able to give the acceptance speech I had thought of for him, with certain improvised
emendations. I was compelled to reveal the reasons for my hesitations and the laughter made of this a joke as well.

There is no possible doubt of his place in theatrical history, more
especially since his great contemporaries could only have been what
they are, whereas Larry could have been a notable ambassador, a
considerable minister, a redoubtable cleric. At his worst, he would
have acted the parts more ably than they are usually lived.

Our English accountant thought we were gone for a year, and I
must say, so did I at first, but Suzanne had other ideas. The recur-
ring theme was Switzerland, and while I did not much care for the
stigma attached by the press to the so-called tax refugees, I was sufficiently irritated by the greed of the British tax authorities when it
came to those engaged in the liberal professions not to turn an absolutely hostile ear to the idea of emigration. I felt that, if successful,
we were treated as little factories, and I thought then as I think now
that the attitude was disastrously shortsighted and damaging.

As always, there were many ingenious loopholes for those
engaged in commerce — the South of France abounded with luxury
cars with British registration and immense yachts at the times of the
most draconian travel restrictions — and, since I spent less and less
time in Britain anyway, it began to be a form of masochism to expose myself to the endless and ruinous inconvenience of acting as
custodian for monies which would be confiscated, apart from the tip.

Naturally attention was already focused on Noël Coward and
Richard Burton, brain-drain pioneers, today accorded the same
grudging admiration as conscientious objectors. I was in Canada
when I received a call from the *Daily Express*. A supercilious voice

said: "Ah, Mr. Ustinov, there's a rumor going around town that you're about to do a Noël Coward. Is there any truth in this?"

"You mean that I'm going to appear at Las Vegas?" I asked.

There was an appreciative snigger and then: "No. That you are actually going to set up house abroad."

"Oh," I cried, as though my dull head had seen daylight for the first time, "You don't mean doing a Noël Coward, you mean doing a Beaverbrook!"

His tone hardened at the mention of his boss. "What exactly are you suggesting?" he inquired.

"There's a rumor going around here in Canada that he's left to go to England. Is there any truth in this?"

There was a pause. "Fair enough," he said, and hung up.

Naturally the great drawback for a writer is a feeling of being out of touch; but then, if one is a certain kind of writer, one has to ask, out of touch with what? Graham Greene is not out of touch in Antibes with his tortured gentlemen in foreign parts, nor was I out of touch with my secret country, and Noël Coward's great charm was being constantly and defiantly out of touch. Unless you are a writer who, like a weathercock, feeds on every little burp of local wind, there is no compelling reason to be in touch here more than elsewhere. The great resurgence of regional writing in England, accompanied by regional acting, gave sudden impetus to this kind of quasi-journalistic expression, often coarse in texture and therefore seemingly accurate to the ignorant, but since I could at the best of times play no part in this intimist revival, I reflected that it was none of my business.

We began our exile in a rented chalet in Villars-sur-Ollon, which was rather too high for my comfort. Instead of working, I spent most of my time falling down on the ice, hip-deep in snow and distinctly drowsy. It was wonderful that the children took to skiing as I had taken to water long ago, and it was a compensation that I was able to offer them amenities and outdoor pleasures which I have never had, but I felt uncomfortable at this altitude.

Eventually we took a permanent suite in a hotel in Montreux, living an appalling existence, like exiled royalty patiently awaiting assassination out of fatalism and force of habit. The lake created its own kind of mildewed background to the wrought iron of the balconies and the screeching of the ravens that landed like wet face-flannels on the grass.

It was a place of empty bandstands and old ladies in groups and marmalade with people's names on it; shops selling cuckoo clocks and lace. And above us, surprisingly, Vladimir Nabokov, living as we and drawing strength and inspiration from the surrounding deadness.

Now it was no longer Sinatra and his endless songs; it was Nabokov and his perfumed, convoluted English, so dense and intense you can hardly read it without taking deep breaths. "*He* can work here. *He* doesn't complain."

However, for me, it was quite a pleasure to be called away again, this time to Australia, by none other than Fred Zinnemann. It was, alas, always quite a pleasure to be called away by just anyone, which the children resented, but of course I only found this out later. One always imagines, fool that one is, that marriages must be kept going for the sake of the children, and in doing so, one merely reflects the inexperiences of the celibate priests who are so ready with their advice in territories where their moral guesswork is of no practical use. Children are the first to sniff insincerity and the makeshift harmony of moribund unions. They crave a higher standard of honesty than adults are prepared or able to offer.

I fondly imagined that, by removing myself, I was removing the cause of discord, but this proved to be untrue. I merely buried my head in distant sand instead of being content with the pile on my own front porch.

Australia was about as far as one could go from the frictions of family life, and the intense rural existence to which we were subjected in the film *The Sundowners* had something about it reminiscent of a stint with the Foreign Legion. Fred Zinnemann, the director, is a character of the most disarming purity of vision, a man without compromises, endlessly listening for some inner echo to the calls of his observation and unwilling to make a move until absolutely satisfied that he is not betraying his creative juices by hasty judgments. He is, therefore, slow as a conscientious magistrate to arrive at his conclusions. There are fallow days in which nothing works because he will not allow it to, and other days more felicitous when everything is on a propitious wavelength, without static.

He imposes an authority rare among directors by subjecting himself as well as you to the scruples of the oracle hidden at the heart of his consciousness. Working with him is a permanent lesson in integrity, the process one of painful elimination rather than by erratic flashes of genius. A genius Freddie may be, but he mistrusts the word, denying its existence. He used to play the violin; the only composer he never tired of was Bach. Crossword puzzles are too unconstructive for such a mind. Battles exist so that they can be won and they are no use winning unless they are difficult.

He is Austrian and Jewish, but his approach is German in the highest sense of the word. He lacks all traces of Austrian grace or the occasional extremism of Jewish intellectuals, nor has he any visible feelings of superiority, but is timid and open-minded and tight-lipped. No wonder that he made of *The Nun's Story* one of the sexiest films ever, in which abstinence became an erotic barometer and the unrequited longings of the protagonists kept hovering on the brink of obscenity. When Edith Evans, a benign and practical mother superior, casually handed Audrey Hepburn a scourge wrapped in a velvet container, it was one of the truly probing moments of cinema, enervating as no piece of mechanical pornography can ever hope to be.

Freddie made a beautiful film of *The Sundowners*, unfashionable in manner and matter — a Western without gunfire, but with human problems unsugared and devoid of artificial coloring. Robert Mitchum was superb in the role of an Australian, his usual distant look matched by an accent authentic beyond belief, while Deborah Kerr displayed her vibrant femininity, more exquisite even in what was left unsaid than in what was said.

One day, in rehearsal, I went through my part with a cigarette

stuck to my lips. I still smoked then. Suddenly Freddie grabbed the
cigarette and wrenched it out of my mouth, drawing blood.

"You can't concentrate with that," he cried angrily, throwing it
away.

I picked it up, dusted it down, and replaced it in my mouth.

"That's not true," I said. "*You* can't concentrate with that. Then
why not ask me to put it out?"

He flushed. I let a moment of silence pass, and said, "Certainly
Freddie," and stubbed it out.

That was the only contretemps we had, and it was not very
serious, but very typical of the level of earnestness in which his talent flourished. There was a scholastic element in working with him,
an element of homework well or badly done, an element of good or
bad marks at the end of term.

All this time, I had slaved away at a novel, my first, inspired as
ever in my desire to break new ground by the untiring efforts of Ted
Weeks, an author-baiter if ever there was one. I was, and still am,
largely ignorant about the world of publishing, and he calmed my
fears and stimulated my curiosity.

The Loser appeared in 1961 and excited no great eulogies or aver-
sions. It was a picaresque investigation into the Nazi spirit, based on
many of my own experiences with those unfortunate people. One or
two excellent notices in England proved to me that it was liable to
be better understood in Europe than in America, although on its appearance in Germany itself it was categorized as "*sehr bitter*," which
surprised me, although perhaps it should not have.

Universal Pictures, who had been the producers of *Spartacus*,
were very hospitable after my Oscar and the fact that my diplomacy
had smoothed over the difficulties with Laughton. They said they
would be interested in a film version of my play *Romanoff and
Juliet*, so long as it cost no more than $750,000. Those were the
days.

I have always found it difficult to digest the same meal twice, and
perhaps I was too eager to keep those moments which had really
worked in the play intact, even if it was part freewheeling fantasy

and part photographed play. The leads, Sandra Dee and John Gavin, were then Universal contract stars, and they were given me for a small consideration, but although they tried manfully, neither of them was ideally suited to the style of the text and the film suffered from an intrinsic incongruity, although it had many elements I was satisfied with.

After a long absence, I was preparing my return to the theater with a play, *Photo Finish*, which was subtitled "An Adventure in Biography." I wrote it quickly, as I often do, but after much mature consideration and considerable daydreaming.

The sets were doggedly and depressingly realistic in order to give freer reign to the experimental nature of the work. An old man sits in bed in his library, while his old wife, hostile and sarcastic, potters about, enjoying her freedom of motion and his immobility with the same nagging glee. She talks exhaustingly as she tidies up.

"Books," she says. "I don't know what you see in them . . . I can understand a person reading them, but I can't for the life of me see why people have to write them."

It is clear that he is at work on his autobiography. She prattles on in a monologue at times lachrymose, at times vicious, at all time wounding, for a full three minutes. He controls any desire to participate in the scene. At length she fusses over his blankets, straightening them, worrying them into some form of tidiness germane to her.

"You are, without doubt, the silliest, most stubborn, most childish old man the world has ever known . . . and it's just impossible to keep up a normal conversation with you. If you need anything, ring the bell like an ordinary person, don't start shouting. Goodnight, Sam, and sleep well, or whatever it is you do down here."

With that, she kisses him on the forehead, and goes out. It is only when she is gone that he speaks for the first time.

"I enjoyed that chat, Stella . . . thank you very much."

As he prepares to sleep, the door opens and a man enters, opening the secret drawer in the old man's desk with a key only he owns. It is himself at sixty, preparing to seduce a show girl with the undignified aid of a £7,000 necklace from Cartier. Sam at eighty knows that the girl will be the cause of a near-fatal heart attack, but that knowledge only makes him at sixty more dogged in his pursuit. Eventually Sam, forty, puts in an appearance, and Sam, twenty, with a very young and lovely Stella, and, in the second act, even Sam's father, who died relatively young, confronts his very old son in a scene that is one of the best I have ever written.

"In my day," concedes the father, who was a full-bodied vintage Victorian hypocrite, "there were things that were done, and things that were not done, and there was even a way of doing things that were not done."

It is a play which takes place in four different epochs simultaneously, with none of them predominating except at the very end. It is not a flashback or a flashforward, but both and neither. It is a play about forgiveness, about understanding, and finally about courage. And if the portrait of the woman is unflattering, it was perhaps a small symptom of my own personal sadness at the time.

When we played it in Boston, I noticed that at all four matinees the front rows were occupied by rather odd-looking people whose mouths tended to hang open and whose heads tilted at surprising angles. Then a distinguished psychiatrist came around and told me he was using the play as therapy with patients who had never come to terms with their parents, a fact I found both intriguing and disturbing.

In London the play was a considerable success at the Saville Theatre. Thank goodness it also held an appeal for those with no parental problems. In New York we fell foul of a newspaper strike. For once that I had a rave review in the *New York Times*, it had to be passed from hand to hand like a *Samizdat* in Moscow!

What gave me renewed satisfaction was the play's success in Paris, with Bernard Blier superbly crotchety as old Sam and Philippe Noiret divinely opulent as the reprehensible father, and the triumph in Germany, with that remarkable actor Martin Held, and subsequently with Heinz Rühmann.

The play appeared at exactly the same time as my best film, *Billy*

Budd. Based on Herman Melville's long story and a fine dramatization by two American authors, I leaned heavily on that consistently extraordinary battalion of British character actors which are the real backbone of our theater. Robert Ryan, a massive and wicked presence on the screen, agreed to play the part of Claggart, the embodiment of evil, while I gave the part of Billy Budd, the embodiment of good, to an unknown — a hesitant, uncertain young actor named Terence Stamp. Captain Vere, the Pontius Pilate of this Passion, I played myself, not because I thought I was particularly suited to the role but because I could find no one else at the price; and the old Dansker, the Recording Angel, I confided to Melvyn Douglas, who had practically retired and who was by chance vacationing in Spain, where the picture was to be shot.

As it sometimes happens, every stroke of luck militated in our favor, and we felt ourselves blessed from the outset. Behind the leaders stood that cohort of wonderful talent, actors like Paul Rogers, John Neville, John McCallum, Lee Montagu, Niall MacGinnis, others too numerous to mention. Don Ashton designed the scenery, Antony Hopkins wrote the music, Tony Mendelson did the costumes, and Bob Krasker was the cameraman, as he had been in *Romanoff and Juliet.*

It was only when we had finished shooting that my troubles began. Allied Artists, who had financed the film, began looking for a happy ending. I remonstrated with them.

"Would it have helped *Ben Hur* if Christ had not been crucified?" I asked.

Two faces lit up with enthusiasm until convinced of the absurdity of the idea by the head of the company. Their British distributor, ABPC, refused to put the film out, suggesting it should be livened up by stock footage from various pirate films. The parent company sent me a cutter from Hollywood to show me how to make the movie more commercial. The ideas put forward were too awful to contemplate.

I called the film censor, John Trevelyan, a remarkable man, who sat in an office under a picture of the Queen, as in a consulate.

"Tell me about the film," he said. "There are, I suppose, no scenes of violence in it, nothing to justify an X certificate?"

"There's a flogging," I said shyly.

"A flogging?" His eyebrows raised. "Do you really need that flogging?" His head shook negatively in anticipation of a reasonable reply.

"Yes I do, John," I insisted, and explained how Billy Budd is impressed for service aboard his merchantman and arrives on the man-of-war just at the moment a flogging is taking place. His eyes meet those of the victim . . .

"Of course," said John Trevelyan, "everything is said in that look, and for that look to retain its eloquence, that flogging is absolutely *vital*. Right. Now there's no second flogging, I trust."

"Yes there is," I practically whispered.

"*Two* floggings in one family film? Oh come, come, Peter, you are rather stretching my credulity!" And then, with a weary sigh, he added, "All right, suppose you tell me about the second flogging."

I explained how Billy had prevented the murder of Claggart, and that now, because of his intervention, the would-be killer was being flogged, an event for which Billy felt some responsibility.

"Well, there is absolutely no similarity between the two floggings," conceded John Trevelyan. "Both are admirably motivated and entirely different in character despite the rather similar visual quality which, in the nature of things, they both share. Very well, we'll let them both go. Now, I hope you're not going to tell me there's a *third* flogging!"

"No," I said, but added, "there's a hanging."

"A hanging!" gasped Trevelyan in a grave voice and, recovering from his surprise, went on — "However, I presume you have the good taste not to actually show the noose around the neck."

"Oh yes," I said, "His last words, 'God bless you, Captain Vere,' are known to all with the remotest culture. How can you dramatize the greatest of Christian virtues, that of forgiveness, unless the noose is actually around Billy's neck?"

"You can't," he conceded in hushed tones and then added magnanimously, "Very well, you can have your hanging."

It was after this discussion that he saw the film together with a friend he had invited, Fred Thomas from the Rank Organization. Mr. Thomas confessed himself most impressed with the film and stated that Rank would distribute it in England on condition that it could be prized away from ABPC without too much ugliness.

John Trevelyan's black eyes glistened. "This," he said, "is where I come in. I am going to give the film an X rating."

Both Thomas and I began remonstrating. John held up a hand, and we fell silent.

"ABPC will drop the film like a hot brick."

"What then?" we both asked.

"Then you will make the terrible but necessary concession of cutting a single blow from either one of the floggings, I don't care which, and it will be suitable fare for the family."

Billy Budd opened at the Leicester Square Theatre under the aegis of J. Arthur Rank and was a great critical success. The reception in New York was no less cordial. But the morons had not had their last word yet. When I took the splendid review of that most difficult and influential of magazines, *Time,* in to the director of publicity, he withdrew the cigar from his mouth and lisped in his gritty worldly-wise voice, "Oh Jesus, don't say we got a good notice in *Time* magazine. That's the kiss of death."

18

IN giving my impressions of some of the great actors with whom I have been privileged to work, I would be churlish if I left out Paul Rogers, since he is the prototype of that extraordinary tradition of British character actors who have made a contribution to the reputation of the drama and cinema in Britain out of all proportion to their fame. To him and to his kind a sense of responsibility toward the work in hand is primordial. Even if blessed by stardom, he remains first and foremost an actor, for it is only as an actor that he feels safe.

In rehearsal, he will always volunteer to hear your lines, to discuss an artistic matter with you in moments of perplexity, or to give younger members of the cast the benefit of his experience, without for a moment being doctrinaire or officious. He is always learning, which is his greatest strength apart from the sterling solidity of his character.

I remember meeting Paul in New York while he was playing in a work of Harold Pinter's, and it was wonderful to see how exhilarated he was at entering the secret world of this important playwright. A man who had every right to be blasé as an undoubted master of his craft was, on the contrary, bubbling with youthful enthusiasm as he submitted himself to new sensations and new techniques.

I was privileged to work with Paul in both *Photo Finish* and *Billy Budd*, and he enriched my consciousness of my profession as no one else has done, before or since.

The danger of autobiographies is not so much what is written as what is not written. I would be ungrateful not to acknowledge the enormous confidence given me by Noël Coward early in my career, and the subsequent help I received from two very remarkable men of the theater, Sir Peter Daubeny, with whom I shared not only many happy working hours, but also a birthday — we were born on precisely the same day — and Alexander Cohen, who actually seems to find the financial climate of Broadway bracing. Both these men have done extraordinary work in the propagation of good theater, and both have benefited from wives who rose without effort to the height of their visions, Lady Molly and Hildy, part and parcel of these two very different men's success.

It was during my work on *Photo Finish* that I was asked by Sir Georg Solti to direct my first opera — or rather, operas, since he and Sir David Webster envisioned a most curious triple bill, consisting of Puccini's *Gianni Schicchi*, Ravel's *L'Heure Espagnole*, and Schönberg's *Erwartung*. We had five weeks in which to do them, each with a different designer and each with different singers. Since I could not work on matinee days, this cut our rehearsal period down even further.

The Italian designer Clerici, a pale man with glacier-mint rimmed glasses, soft spoken as some power behind the Vatican throne, devised a shallow set for *Gianni Schicchi* on which the singers climbed up and down like insects on a chest of drawers. Sir Geraint Evans gave one of his characteristic performances, in that whatever I did to integrate him into any concept I might have, he seemed to do what he had done successfully many times before and would do many times again elsewhere.

The French designer Ponnelle, today a celebrated director of operas and musicals in his own right, did a wayward sketch of the set for *L'Heure Espagnole* with no indications of the height of doors or the mechanical details of clocks, with the result that I spent one

Sunday in an empty Covent Garden working out the dimensions of clocks within which singers had to conceal themselves. I sat there with a ruler, a pencil, and a thermos of café au lait, reflecting on the unpredictability of life. Ponnelle meanwhile had a dress rehearsal of *Kiss Me, Kate* at Düsseldorf. If that isn't Show Business, at least that's Opera.

Erwartung, whatever its musical qualities, is a piece of bilious inanity conceived in a Vienna sickening for World War I, in which a woman searches for a real or imagined lover in a forest and finds a real or imagined corpse in the course of nineteen minutes of fretful music. Amy Shuard had a voice of extraordinary magnitude, but she was happier singing than acting, so that Herr Schneider-Siemssen and I conceived a set which moved more than she did, a process which included projections by means of slides. Schneider-Siemssen hand-painted the slides, but neglected to use unbreakable glass, with the result that they all cracked when inserted into the lanterna magica. He was in tears of rage until I pointed out that sticking plaster gave them an even more abstract quality than before, and seemed to add to the agony of the meandering soprano a hint of clinical foreboding. He was well satisfied and even enthusiastic about my defense of sticking plaster as a new texture in theatrical design, as were the press, who found that works such as *Erwartung* were exactly what Covent Garden should be doing.

My next operatic venture, some five years later, was once again thanks to Sir Georg Solti, under the aegis of Professor Rolf Liebermann, in Hamburg. The work was *The Magic Flute*. To my mind, Mozart, the divine Mozart, remains to be rediscovered and perhaps needs to be rediscovered by each succeeding generation. It is typical that there should be a prejudice against Schikaneder and a belief that in some way he was unworthy of Mozart, and that therefore, whereas the music is sacrosanct, the text is not. Klemperer even went as far as to record the opera leaving out all dialogue.

My view is entirely opposed to this heresy. Admittedly Schikaneder was a journeyman dramatist, a gag man, a play doctor, an improviser, but if he was good enough for Mozart, he's certainly good enough for me — more especially since *The Magic Flute* is a kind of pantomime, with something of a popular farce and something of *The Tempest*, its grave moments sublimely elevated by Mozart onto a celestial plane, its reassuring moments of contact with a vulgar funny bone entrusted to Schikaneder. The moral of the tale is disarming in its simplicity, masonic or just human. Why then mystify the clear and limpid line by making of the rituals cloistered and fetid mysteries when they are open to the sky, unregimented, free, and democratic? There is nothing more at stake than the eternal struggle between day and night, the sunburst and the moonglow, good and evil, with tiny mortals torn apart and brought together by those elemental forces.

On another level, it is not without dramatic sophistication, which the demands of nineteenth-century taste have eliminated, as is so often the case.

When the rosebushes part, revealing the Queen of the Night in all her evil glitter, Monostatos scampers to the footlights and says, dramatically, "That is the Queen of the Night!"

Well, he doesn't, as I was at pains to point out to some learned musicologists who accused me of tampering with the original. Monostatos scampers to the footlights and says, "That, if I am not mistaken, is the Queen of the Night!"

This is one of many such bowdlerisms, where the wit and color of Schikaneder has been eliminated by the erosion of time and its servers.

The sets of Jean-Denis Malcles were fresh and lovely, and I regard the production as a success.

When it went to the Maggio Musicale in Florence, William Weaver wrote in the *Herald Tribune*, "It was superbly realized, beautifully paced. . . . When it was new, some time ago, this Peter Ustinov staging of *The Magic Flute* came in for some criticism. It is hard now to see why; it is surely respectful of the text and faithful to the music, and yet inventive."

This led to an offer to do *Don Giovanni* at the Edinburgh Festival, with Daniel Barenboim. Peter Diamond suggested I do the sets and the costumes, an offer I somewhat rashly accepted. The theater in Edinburgh is more or less of the dimensions of the theater in Prague where *Don Giovanni* received its original production and its intimacy imposes a certain simplification in both means and methods, which should be all to the good. As with *The Magic Flute*, I insisted on an absolutely continuous action, without those ponderous silences punctuated by the clatter and rumble of scene changes and the sight of scurrying feet with every undulation of the curtain.

Don Giovanni, described by Mozart and Da Ponte as a *"Dramma giocoso,"* has been brainwashed even more thoroughly than *The Magic Flute* by the intervening generations of those who loved their opera unwisely but too well. Nowadays it is treated as a psychological tragedy, in which the advent of Freud and his buddies has added condiment upon condiment until the origin of the meal is practically undistinguishable.

First of all, indiscriminate copulation is not the stuff of tragedy, and all the unjustified theories about Don Giovanni's impotence do nothing to elevate in that direction. They are merely the miserable result of modern psychological research on the story of a joyously inconsiderate cad. The result of all this pretentious nonsense is that the sets are usually as black as ink, that the statue of the Commendatore is left to the imagination, and that even Giovanni's comeuppance is in the form of a self-inflicted death by the bursting of his overcharged conscience. It is one of the baser trials of the human intelligence that it enlarges the field of stupidity; the stupidity of a stupid man is mercifully intimate and reticent, while the stupidity of an intellectual is cried from the rooftops.

We have already been made to stare at empty canvases and listen with reverence to immobile pianists sitting at silent pianos. What we gain or lose from such experiences is our business, but when the mentality of smartness, of vogue, grips an authentic masterpiece, then we have a right to rebel. To perform *Don Giovanni* as I saw it on the French television, designed with the utmost elegance, as though they all — peasants and landlords — had been to their fittings at some sixteenth-century Dior boutique and now glittered as virtually the only sources of light in a mineshaft, is indicative of the confusion of our times. It was highly praised by members of the French government eager to help their ailing opera, and the pundits universally lauded this stylish travesty, in which there was not the smallest trace of "*giocoso.*" To make my evening complete, there was Sir Geraint Evans, his cheeks glowing in the dark, giving the identical performance to the one in my very different production.

His great qualities are a permanent commentary on all that makes opera inviting, and finally impossible, to someone trained in the theater. With his fine eighteenth-century face looking like many of the actors' portraits in the Garrick Club, dark eyes, bulbous nose and chubby cheeks, on the small side, bristling with invention, ferociously energetic, helpful, greedy, understanding, and unscrupulous, he knows from the outset what he intends to do, usually because he has already done it successfully and rehearsals are spent getting his own way by running the whole gamut of techniques, from charm to bluster and back again. His strength is that he is not of this century. His defeat is that he is. Surrounded by singers who can sing but can't act, who can sing and can act, or who cannot do both at the same time, he impregnates himself against these inconsistencies by doing his own thing, and doing it brilliantly, alone. I believe *Don Giovanni* is what it is supposed to be, a *dramma giocoso*, a morality in which the graver moments are dark shadows in the sunlight, not an added intensity to the pervading gloom. The seriousness with which everything is taken is deliciously Spanish, redolent of prie-dieu and crucifix rather than a psychiatrist's couch.

So determined were the contemporaries of Meyerbeer to make this unyielding material tragic that they chopped the end off, bringing the curtain down on Don Giovanni's disappearance into hell, an awful warning to fornicators. This concept has lasted till now, the excuse being that musically the facile coda is not up to the marvelous confrontation between Giovanni, the Commendatore, and Leporello. And yet it is the coda which brings us back to the spirit of the opera.

Oh, you should have heard the outcry from the purists when I brought two policemen on at the end, late as ever, to measure the hole through which Don Giovanni had disappeared in preparation for a long-winded report to Madrid! What was the justification for such a facetious conceit? Quite simply, *signori miei,* that they are in the text if you only bother to look. Don Ottavio, frustrated in his attempt to rid the world of Don Giovanni (largely owing to the influence of the women, who can't bear to see their tormentor dispatched), has recourse to Madrid with a formal charge which he waves about as he swears revenge, and he returns finally, when it is too late to matter, with *"due ufficiali."*

It all makes sense if you treat the work as it was written. If, however, you load the fragile vehicle with all the baggage of contemporary psychoanalytical claptrap, then you get what you deserve — a resounding success, and congratulations for having made something halfway valid out of a work now deemed unplayable.

My next venture in this weird world of compromise was at the behest of Rolf Liebermann, for the Paris Opera. Massenet is no Mozart and his *Don Quichotte* was an attempt to supply Chaliapin with a role worthy of a great Boris Godounov. Now Nicolai Ghiaurov wished to revive this curiosity, a piece of fustian in which Dulcinea becomes a demi-mondaine, devoid of all peasant force, doing a few Iberian gestures on a balcony to the delight of the villagers, who shout *"Anda, Anda!"* in unison, and in which Don Quixote passes among the crowds like Christ among the lepers, dispensing thoughts as profound as those on a calendar.

The trouble began very early on, when I received letters from angry old baritones in retirement and other ornaments of the French musical establishment, denouncing me for thinking I could do justice to an authentic *French* masterpiece, while Duval, Dupont, and Duroc were still alive, to say nothing of Dulac, Dupré, and Duchamps, who, although dead, would have done it better than me alive, and probably better than Duval, Dupont, and Duroc. Rehearsals were like trying to find a porter in an airport, a milling crowd of choristers obliterating the leading singers under the swinging arms of a chorus master who walked backward through anything that barred his way.

Everybody talked at once, even if everybody sang at different times, and nothing was ready when it should have been. A lady of great and evidently bitter experience in this house, who had taken me under her capacious wing, kept prompting me in the usages of the place. *"Maintenant il faut gueuler! Mais menacez, Maître, menacez! Un peu de colère, Maître, voyons!"*

I was incapable by nature of following her instructions since anger is such a rare commodity in my armory that I can never afford to use it tactically to futile ends.

I had to design some windmills, the smallest of which worked well with men inside them, but the largest one had an electric motor placed on top, which propelled the blades at a snail's pace and consistently broke when any weight was placed on them. Since Don Quixote, or rather, a stunt-double, had to be taken up into the flies on one of the blades, the prospect became distinctly depressing after the fourth breakdown, on the eve of the premiere.

I have never worked in such an atmosphere of utter confusion, and they could find nothing better to do than to blame that confusion on me, because some of my designs had been handed in late (months before, for the most) and because I failed to shout as loud as the others. There are more ghosts in that building than in the whole of England and Scotland put together and all of them are ill-natured, discourteous, and malevolent.

All this may sound like sour grapes for the disaster that awaited my production. I swear there is not a sour grape in the whole tiny harvest. My hat is raised higher than ever to Rolf Liebermann for the wonders he managed to achieve with such unpromising material, and I surprised even myself after the gale of booing which broke out at my appearance at the curtain by turning my back on the audience, a gesture which produced a great roar of dismay, and then going out for a very good meal in the highest of spirits. The fever had broken and I was once again in the best of health.

For the record I must add that on the last night the big windmill worked, although its blades rotated in the opposite direction from those of its brethren. I asked why they bothered with such a detail once the harm was done and they replied that under the financial structure of the house, they wouldn't touch the credits for the next opera if they didn't account for every franc in the pre-production projection of this one. I had, indeed, worked in the last blockhouse of the Ligne Maginot.

Ghiaurov and the singers were wonderfully loyal, and as a final error of this whole nonsensical episode I cherish the headline in the Milan evening paper, which said, with a bitchiness in the highest tradition, "At last something worth seeing in the Paris Opera House." It was La Scala galloping to the rescue, but it wasn't true. By some miracle there have been many wonderful productions at the Paris Opera as well as a few indifferent ones.

The miracle is, of course, Rolf Liebermann. Berated by an interrogating critic five years after the event, he defended his choice of me as the director of *Don Quichotte* by saying that he loved it but that perhaps the two of us had been ignorant at the time of the unwritten traditions of French opera, and further declared that his decision to invite me to undertake this production had been prompted by the fact that my *Magic Flute* in Hamburg had been the best he had ever seen. I hope that his critical sense is as acute as his exemplary loyalty and ethical serenity.

This brings me to an artistic confession. I am used to criticism in that I expect it, and by now I feel I am almost sure enough of my taste to be able to make light of it, even if it rankles. No performer can please consistently. There are times when he must swim against the tide in order to progress, in order to grow. That is normal.

So that it is not attacks on my work or even on my person which I find perplexing so much as praise poured on the works of others which I dislike or which I consider unworthy of serious consideration. This, more than anything, makes me aware of changing times and changing climates, forces me as an old fighter to roll with the punch. Books are different. They keep their secrets better than plays. They do not require interpretation, and, most important, make their appeal to one person at a time, in secret, in isolation.

Perhaps it is an illusion typical of one who has worked for a certain length of time in a chosen profession, but I began to feel that standards were no longer as high, that critics were no longer the austere customs officers who asked you what you had to declare and judged you by your appearance, but rather young officers who leaped on to the parapet, encouraging the playwright to charge in the direction of this or that faction or trend. The very word trendy never existed when I was young—

I can't let you go on. You suddenly write as though you are ninety, a toothless, gutless old dodderer.

That's what comes from trying to be sincere.

Look at the facts!

No need to show.

Look at the facts. You merely changed gears, as it were. Things happened to force you to look deeper into yourself. You began to wonder whether you were really doing what you wished to do, what you were meant to do. It is very exciting when this happens in the middle of life instead of at the beginning. It happens often at the beginning.

What happened, apart from the fact that my marriage was drifting inexorably onto the rocks?

Your father died.

Oh. I had not forgotten.

He, who had sworn that he would not reach the age of seventy, died on December 1, 1962, at eight o'clock in the evening, four hours before his seventieth birthday. He had been in a virtual coma for three days before the end, except for a sip of champagne every now and then and an extraordinary moment of lucidity when he looked you straight in the eye with a slightly puzzled expression and said, in French, "Tiens, je te reconnais de mes rêves."

Yes, "I recognize you from my dreams." That must go high on the list of famous last words — and I was the only one to hear them. So vanished a man I never really knew, and whom I, like all sons everywhere, needed to know better. There is no fault attached to this. The need and the awkwardness lie somewhere deep in human nature. The crosscurrents of jealousy, of ambition, of protectiveness, of authority try to shove under the level of consciousness however well they are controlled by breeding and usage.

Our true natures are perhaps best illustrated by the behavior of dogs, ferociously protective of their young for a while, and suddenly, overnight, bitter rivals for bone or bitch. They seem to forget their family obligations and, indeed, their family, whereas we are not permitted to do so by our social and religious habits. Our behavior in this area has no precedent in the animal world from which we have raised ourselves so laboriously. It has therefore no prolonged basis in instinct. It is because we know who our parents are that we treat them as such. If we didn't, we wouldn't. This means that the intellect guides the instincts, with all the confusion that such an awkward compromise automatically entails. Add to this gruel the spices of hypocrisy, filial piety, parental example, duty, amour propre, and the rest, and you have a cuisine ready for the culinary magic of great novelists and playwrights.

Did your father's death bring you closer to your mother?

No. Curiously enough, it brought her closer to him. She who had chided him for his drift into incapacity and death; she who sought to interest him in the life around him; she who did all she could to stimulate and invigorate him, now slowly became as apathetic as he had been, playing Scrabble with her sister Olga, who had settled down with her.

The two sisters were entirely different in character; Olga, who always had a weight problem, wandered around the tiny cottage like a dreadnought. Because she had no abiding interest in life apart from the manufacture of patchwork quilts, which she turned out in vast quantities like a cottage industry, she was also inclined to be insensitive toward the qualms or phobia of lesser folk. She was seventeen years older than Nadia. One day Olga complained to me that my mother had been a most obstinate baby — that on one occasion, she, Olga, had grasped her sister's minute foot, held it aloft, and asked a rhetorical nursery question, "Who does this little foot belong to?"

The baby had apparently withdrawn its foot with some annoyance. Nadia flared up at the memory of the incident.

"What the hell did you always want with my foot?" she growled.

Olga looked resentful and after a moment of silence she limped out of the room, offended.

When a televison crew arrived to talk to Nadia about the publication of her book on my father, Olga insisted on being in the picture, if only to outstare the viewers with her round pebble eyes. She seemed to believe she was being snapped by some Victorian family photographer.

Suddenly, with the cameras running, she interrupted Nadia, who was struggling to give a little coherence to her ideas.

"Your nose is dripping," she announced.

"Let it drip," Nadia snapped and continued with her hesitant narrative.

Once again Olga looked offended and made no secret of her feelings.

Olga was a redoubtable presence in the house and a source of comfort in a way, even if, when she died at the age of 91, Nadia made no secret either of her sorrows or of her relief to be alone once again. But by then, of course, she was very rarely alone. There was a whole team of gallant ladies taking it in turns to look after her, among them her golden-hearted neighbors Mrs. Tovey and Miss Sorrel-Taylour.

Meanwhile the children were growing. They knew her, of course.

Yes, and they took great delight in each other's company. Except for the *idée fixe* of my mother's that it was quite natural that the cycle of love within a family should not be reciprocal, but should gravitate toward the future. In other words, she was resigned to the fact that my interest in my children should be greater than my interest in her, just as her interest in me had been greater than her interest in her own parents. Because of this theory of hers, she was extremely undemanding and, while very warm by nature, rather undemonstrative.

But where did you spend most of your time?

That is difficult to say. I did the film *Topkapi* in Turkey and Greece, with a little of it in France. It was directed by Jules Dassin, a fine, meticulous director with a great sense of humor, who dedicated his career to his wife, Melina Mercouri. It is no reflection on her to suggest that perhaps he could have had a rather more remarkable career if he had not dedicated himself so devotedly to her service. It is, I believe, ever so with husband and wife teams, with the undoubted exception of the Lunts, who possessed an uncannily integrated style in which neither seemed to be making concessions to the other.

Having worked with the Burtons as they have been intermittently called — Elizabeth Taylor and Richard Burton — on two different occasions, once in Peter Grenville's version of Graham Greene's *The Comedians,* and again in a strange film I directed called *Hammersmith Is Out,* I can only confirm my opinion that the chemistry of having them both in a film, regarded as a rare "coup" by financiers, in fact lacked mystery. Love scenes, and even worse, lust scenes, between people who presumably have them anyway in the privacy of their home are inevitably somewhat flat on the screen; and if they happen to be passing through a momentary crisis, such scenes are worse than flat, merely a tribute to their professionalism, and there are few things worse than that.

Richard is a fine actor with a wayward quality women find hard to resist, but the waywardness is somehow stunted by the image of off-screen propriety in opulent wealth. Elizabeth, too, a person of tremendous instinct and surprising intelligence, requires a latitude which the outward appurtenances of the superstar somehow blunts. Now that they are on their own again, it may be a blow for romantics, or merely for those of us who like them both, but it may well be a salutary liberation for their careers.

You received an Oscar for Topkapi.

Oh yes, I was reaching the age of compensation. I had, on my desk, two emasculated gentlemen, and two emasculated ladies as well. These were the Emmy awards, which I received for playing Dr. Johnson and Socrates, and the four of them made for a fine mixed-doubles match. Then I won a third Emmy playing an aged Jewish delicatessen-store owner on Long Island, at grips with racial prejudice in the shape of a proud black boy, in a fine if rather sentimental script by Rod Serling. We now had an umpire as well.

And in spite of all this, you were subject to feelings of mournfulness, of decrescendo?

Well, I also performed an Arab potentate in a film starring Shirley MacLaine, with whom I dearly wanted to work and will always clearly want to work. I knew the script was overblown, overfarcical, and I began to feel, in reading many new scripts and seeing many new films, that we were in a transitional period and that comedy as I conceived it was losing its way. It was all overstated, and mannered, and weird, as though laughter away from the laugh machine was unreliable. Nudity made its appearance, first in shadows, then boldly, then explicitly. After millions of years of life on this planet, human beings were told there had been a breakthrough in that their eyes might now rest on pubic hair for the first time. Just as music was being confused with sound and painting with decoration, so organization was surrendering to happening, order to chaos. Novelty became as ephemeral as a mayfly. Styles were being revived even before they were obsolete. So desperate were we for the lost disciplines that the seventies began reviving not only the twenties, the thirties, the forties, the fifties, but even the sixties. Eventually the seventies will revive the seventies, until December revives January!

You are getting old.

Now it's my turn to upbraid you. There's no need to say that with a sigh. In 1968 I was elected Rector of Dundee University, remember?

Will I ever forget! Half a bottle of whiskey you had to drink out of a silver goblet as you were dragged around the city in a landau, pulled by the University football team in lieu of horses.

Those were just the light-hearted japes of highspirited medics, and they were fun. Perhaps more fun for them than for me, but that was half the point. The six years that followed were the real test. The cool machinations of the social science Marxists, young fellows gazing at you resentfully through the odd gaps in the hair which cascaded down their faces, already well versed in all the low tricks of political chicanery. There was never any trouble from the dental students, the medical students, or the engineers, those who had tremendously difficult disciplines to master and therefore had no time for university politics; but the social sciences were the overflow for all those who had not yet decided what to do with their lives, and for all those whose premature frustrations led them into the sterile alleys of confrontation. They called wildcat meetings among themselves, informing no one else, and in secret passed a vote calling on me to resign. "Forty in favour of your resignation; six against" read the telegram.

That was the time to be tough.

Why did they wish you to resign? I can't remember.

I refused to support them in an illegal strike which took the form of refusing to pay for their lodgings. What they wanted was a higher government grant for students. I wanted this too, but I didn't approve of this slipshod and silly way of going about it, in which the University had the last word if it wished to utter it. No tactical advance is worth it if it entails strategic retreat. No, that's not Clausewitz, that's me.

I asked for a new vote of confidence by secret ballot, sending the forms to the entire student body of the University. There were by now about forty-five in favor of my resignation, but instead of six against, the figure had risen to well over two thousand. There were howls and bleats of unconstitutional behavior on my part. I ignored them, wrote an article for a leading newspaper, and met the lads in a head-on collision on television. They protested to me in private at having gone to such lengths to defeat them. I informed them that what they wanted above all was publicity, and that, as a good Rector, I had acceded to their request.

Now what has all this got to do with growing old?

Everything. There is a tendency in men of my age, and in my profession, to pretend to be younger than they are. In Hollywood I recognize only half my acquaintances. The bald ones have neatly sewn hair; the hirsute ones have their ears covered in cozy mobcaps of russet locks. And they all wear faded jeans, with lumps of gold on chains around their necks. There are no old men anymore. *Playboy* and *Penthouse* have between them made an ideal of eternal adolescence, sunburnt and saunaed, with the gray dorianed out of them.

Gracious.

Yes. Well, the young need old men. They need men who are not ashamed of age, not pathetic imitations of themselves. I have said elsewhere that parents are the bones on which children sharpen their teeth. It is true of rectors too, and teachers. And of what use are those bones if they are soft, if they expose their marrow to the searching tongue, if they are not hard and — why not? — unbreakable? I became, at last, what they needed me to be.

But why this intensity, when you take your plays and films, your failures and even your successes, for granted?

Oh, I still had *Hot Millions* to come, with the splendid Maggie Smith, the most sensitive actress of all that I have worked with; I had three films with Disney, *Blackbeard's Ghost, One of Our Dinosaurs Is Missing*, and *The Treasure of Matacumbe;* I had *Viva Max*, in which I played a Mexican general, and which was banned in Mexico; I had *Logan's Run*, in which I played a man of ninety. Among my plays I still had *Halfway Up the Tree* to come, a lightweight piece which ran a year in London with Robert Morley in the lead, and *The Unknown Soldier and His Wife*, the most ambitious of my works for the theater, brilliantly directed by John Dexter at Lincoln Center in New York, and played by me at Chichester and then in London. In this last production I had the pleasure of working with my eldest daughter, Tamara, now a delicious girl I was beginning to know again after a false start to both our lives as regards our relationship. She married a most talented young director, Christopher Parr, and they spend much of their time in Edinburgh.

I must not forget my second book of short stories, *The Frontiers of the Sea*, and my second novel, *Krumnagel*, which is certainly one of my better works.

Is that all you are going to say about them?

They can, and must, speak for themselves if they are capable of speaking at all. I know, for instance, that *The Unknown Soldier and His Wife* is a difficult play, but that does not mean it needs translation by the author, of all people. All I have done in my life must stand or fall on its own merits or lack of them. There is nothing I can add, except perhaps to cast a little light on the secret person whom I am discovering with your help. That is why childhood and extreme youth are so much easier as a personal archaeological site than maturity and middle age. I have no wish to defend myself again at ages when I was already capable of defending myself. My hope was to analyze myself at an age when I could only submit, or stand aside, or pretend that the opposite of the truth was true.

And this explains your ardor as the Rector of a small Scottish University. You prefer to talk about that than about your plays?

Infinitely. It was a renewal. I did it for six years. Twice elected for periods of three years each. They may have thought of it as a joke, but they did not realize that for me it was a vital moment in my life, when I bent my mind to new problems, to real problems compared to the mere careers of plays or films.

I always thought that the Rectors of Scottish Universities were sinecures.

So did everyone. It so happened, however, that at one and the same time all the Rectors decided it was time for this to stop and that ombudsmen in the modern world were a very sound and a good idea, even if this function had been conceived as long ago as the very beginning of the fifteenth century. The Rectors — Jo Grimond, Kenneth Allsop, John Cleese, and others — began to meet and compare notes, to the extent that our activities created the same alarm as secret meetings among regimental mascots might occasion among Colonels. The Vice-Chancellors always wanted to know what we were up to, and sooner or later they found out.

My time of office was made a pleasure by the many interesting people I met, people I would never have met in the more normal course of events. And I shall always cherish the resilient grace of the Queen Mother during my inauguration, when we were pelted with toilet rolls by the students, which she picked up as though someone had mailed them to the wrong address. She also went beetroot red when the janitor opened a door with a key, and said to me in a fine Scottish brogue, "Rector, there's no way around it, you'll have to share this room with the Queen Mither." She giggled furtively just as she was about to open the fine new dental center, when I pointed out to her on the plan that three contiguous departments were designed in the highest body-snatching "traditions" of Burke and Hare in nearby Edinburgh, the departments being Emergency, Post-Mortem, and Experimental.

And of all the memories I took away from there which gave me a personal glow of satisfaction, the most disarming came from a distracted parent appealing for consideration for his wayward child. The envelope was addressed to "The Lord Rectum of Dundee University," and that is how I have seen myself ever since in moments of self-doubt.

19

You are so reticent about some of the events that interest me most, that I feel I will have to stay with you practically till the end of the book.

You are most welcome, Dear Me, I assure you. After all, we are coming to the most difficult of all parts.

Why?

Oh, you know. People have their image. Hateful word! I once reluctantly appeared on a television talk show in order to propagate a play, to counterattack some critical carping, and it became a habit — in the United States, that is. I discovered, and they discovered, that I have a certain gift of the gab which happens to coincide with a time when television has imposed special demands on the orator — that he destroy his projection, that he become natural, that he act with the same propriety as he would in people's homes.

Explain yourself.

TV may well be the medium on which to address the nation, but it may no longer be treated as such. You are talking to units of one, or two — to lonely old ladies to whom television is the only comfort. Such people are easily frightened. They don't wish a rude fellow pinning them to the wall with his insistence. As a medium, it is basically bland and insidious and yet it is also a kind of lie detector, which ferrets out insincerity with unparalleled efficiency. It was television which destroyed the bad McCarthy. Occasionally it showed him when he was not speaking, but whispering into the ears of his aides, or being whispered at. We saw a man whose mask of sincerity was down, a man relaxing and showing his real self in his corner, between the rounds. Nixon was no more successful when he told bedtime stories to the nation. One was invariably more conscious of the intention than of the achievement.

Do you consider that television has a function of which nobody is apparently aware – as a kind of arbiter of sincerity?

Yes. I believe it has affected priorities more than any other profession, although its influence on us all has been enormous. When before was a runner accompanied on his attempt at a record by a stopwatch visible to all, and when could the results of a close race be judged by everyone? And when before has time, its chance gestures, its gratuitous orchestration, been captured in the form of instant replay? And this instant replay can be used not only for sport but for assassinations, bank robberies, and other daily occurrences.

These are new and wonderful techniques, and yet, to my mind, there is nothing more extraordinary than television's ability to outstare a politician and say to him, "Convince me."

To the experienced eye, every reticence, every avoidance, every joke helps to build a pattern of the man's true state of mind. How lucky were the great men of the past! They could disappear for a while to let dust settle, to let things blow over when they had gone wrong. Today there is no respite. The camera lies in wait in the most unexpected places. We know all our candidates far too well for their own comfort, their own peace of mind. Popularities fluctuate as hysterically as values on the stock exchange, as we notice some detail which displeases us or a casual faux pas is blown into a national calamity by the media.

It seems to me you don't quite know whether to admire television or to condemn it.

Neither and both. It is an instrument, like the telephone. If asked whether you like the telephone, you are liable to reply that that depends entirely who is on it. As the harbinger of news that you have just inherited a million, it is liable to be appeciated. With a crashing bore on the end of the line, it tends to be cursed. But even at the worst of times, there is not much point in condemning it. It is here to stay, in ever-improving form, and personally, I have a great deal to thank it for.

Tell me, before we plunge into the present and glimpse the future. Who were the men and women who have most impressed you in your life? I am not changing the subject, incidentally, since it is really an extension of your concern with politicians, who, in your mature life, seem to have taken the place of the military as your favorite targets.

The military are démodé. It's a far cry from ceremonial parades to the indescribable nightmare of nuclear conflict. In spite of this, there are still romantic toughs about, acting out their pathetic fantasies as mercenaries in developing countries, or as heroes of anonymous resistance, placing bombs in suitcases in public places and reaping casual harvests in the destruction of innocents. These madmen are to be pitied. They belong to the rabid wing of Miss Lonelyhearts and they find their consummation in the company of other crackpots.

By now the difference between the possibilities of total and immediate destruction for all, which is a matter for technicians, not for soldiers, and the small part of the spectrum reserved for what are demonstrations rather than wars with conventional weapons, which are still a matter for soldiers, is so great that it is difficult to see what they have to attract a young person to what used to be referred to as the call to arms.

Politicians are still realities, even if they have become attached to show business because of their compulsive addiction to television. I do not for a moment subscribe to the Communist heresy that political figures are superior to men of other professions, that they have an obligation to oversee the activities of the arts and sciences with a

severe pedagogic eye in the interest of political orthodoxy. That is to
stultify the liberal arts and other professions and to stifle necessary
sources of criticism.

What is interesting about politicians in a democratic society is
that, whereas they are motivated by power as they are in all societies, everything is done constitutionally to make that power an obligation instead of a source of enjoyment. One cannot help noticing
how often a removal from power in a dictatorship entails disgrace,
the end of a career, or even the end of life, whereas in a removal
from power in a democracy the initial disappointment is often mitigated by a huge sigh of relief. This is as it should be. When power
is enjoyed, it is abused.

Starting with politicians, then, I have been impressed by Edward
Heath, the only European who can match Jimmy Carter smile for
smile. I admire him not for his politics, with which I have always
been in some disagreement (except for his championship of Europe,
with which I am in absolute accord), but for his passions. A man
who loves music as he does, not merely as a stealthy purchaser of
records, but as a Walter Mitty who dares to cross the frontier of the
imagination into unfriendly reality, and conduct an orchestra with
precision and verve, is bound to be a person with an extrarodinary
courage and grip of abstractions. If you add to that his accomplish-
ment as a sailor, you realize that he is as good a conductor on a moving platform as on a still one. Alas, he has been a consistent victim of
that miserable prejudice which believes that a prime minister
should be person without visible talent; that talent in high places is
tantamount to a lapse of taste.

That excellent violinist, Jeremy Thorpe, fell victim to a hypocrisy
which one would have hoped Britain to have grown out of; but no,
the bittersweet piety of the Victorian moralist has survived the scorn
of the emancipated, and still succeeds in doing its damage by erosion on those who admit that life has changed beyond recognition
for the multitude, but who insist that a minority, because of the office they hold, must continue to pretend to live as no one ever
could.

One could see the rot propagated in the sad case of Profumo, when it was seriously maintained that a celebrated model could have passed military secrets to a Soviet naval attaché. Such a preposterous idea might have held water in 1914, when a French general, rendered forgetful by the delights of orgasm, could have moaned, "Ten divisions, two of them mounted," into the attentive ear of Mata Hari, but what kind of military secret is it that a model, or practically anyone attentive for that matter, could glean as a result of Mr. Profumo's inattention, and thus pass on, some time later, to a Russian Lieutenant, in the form of idle pillow-talk? Absurdity has a place of honor in contemporary civilization, so long as it does not grow irksome and affect the careers and, indeed, the lives of men.

Ernest Bevin was certainly the most remarkable of the British politicians I knew. I once referred to him as Britain's only peasant, in that he had a wonderful rural quality and an ability to reduce the complexities of foreign affairs to the scale of the farmyard, thereby creating an Orwellian world that was, however, neither frightening nor full of foreboding, but merely understandable.

"I mind me," he used to say, "when we was institutin' trade talks with the Russians, they sent over a young man called Denakosov or maybe Dekanosov, and I put one of my best young men with 'im . . ." He hesitated, and he consulted his wife, Florence, as always when in doubt. "'Oo was it, Floss? Was it Harold Ramsay?"

"No," she piped, "you sent him to the Argentine for the meat, remember?"

"Oh, yes," he grumbled. "'Oo was it then?"

"I think his name begun with a P," Florence suggested.

"You're right!" he called, triumphant. "George Gibbons, that's 'oo it was!"

His tone of gravity returned.

"They was gettin' on like the proverbial 'ouse on fire," he continued, "and just as they was gettin' ready to relegate their findin's to a 'igher level, Dena . . . Kanosov disappears . . . never 'eard of again."

His jaw set grimly as he remembered the event. Then he became casual again.

"Well, next time I saw Molotov, in Lake Succ-ess, over in . . . in. . ." His memory failed again for a moment.

"America?" suggested Florence.

" 'Merica," echoed Ernie, "I said to 'im, look 'ere Molotov, I don't know where your young man's gone and I admit it's none of my business. But nevertheless, in the interests of common courtesy, next time we 'ave trade talks, will you please do me the kindness of tellin' me in advance if your young man is going to disappear before the end — then I won't put one of my best young men with 'im."

Bevin came under tremendous and bitter attack from Zionists because of his reluctance to end the British Mandate in Palestine prematurely. He was determined to a point of stubborness that when the State of Israel did become a reality, it should do so on a firm and equitable basis with its neighbors, and who is to say today that he was entirely wrong? The impatient excesses of the Haganah and Irgun and Stern Gang only strengthened his resolve — and incidentally provided a model for the PLO to follow in later years. To level accusations of anti-Semitism at such a man is to indulge in the facility of extremism and to be about as grossly unfair as it is possible to be. He was a noble person and probably a great foreign minister.

Among his other favorite tales, in which he foresaw some of his country's future troubles, was a fable he told with cozy relish.

"There was three men in a boat, see, a Communist, a Fascist, and a good Union man. All of a sudden, the boat sinks and the three men are thrown in the water. There's people on the river bank. The Fascist does his salute at them, but finds it impossible to swim with one arm, and 'e drowns. The Communist begins shouting slogans at them, exhausts 'imself, and 'e drowns. This leaves only the Union man, swimmin' towards the bank with strong easy strokes. He's almost within 'is depth, when the factory siren goes, and 'e drowns."

An artist is somewhat the same mold as Ernest Bevin is J. B. Priestley, a no-nonsense Northerner who shared with Bevin, the West-Countryman, an extraordinary memory for ancient music-hall routines. Whenever Bevin felt the atmosphere sagging, be it in Bristol or in a private home in London, in the White House or the Kremlin, be began singing old popular songs, long forgotten, for which Floss and he had an infalliable memory. These abrupt out-bursts must have puzzled Stalin.

Jack Priestley, too, with all his appearance of intolerance for the mediocre, the second-rate, has an immense compassion for the lives and problems of uninspired entertainers. He is a proud man, with a magnificent instinctive intelligence tempered occasionally by a de-liberate reversion to small-town hard-headedness.

Invited to his lovely apartment in the Albany, I set eyes on a painting by Sickert hanging over the mantlepiece, depicting the au-dience in a theater gallery.

"My God," I said, "that's a wonderful Sickert!" He gazed at it like a venerable Saint Bernard through the self-generated blue coils of pipe smoke.

"That is the second finest theatrical Sickert in existence, and I have the other one."

At that time, we tried to form an English Playwrights' Company, in emulation of the celebrated American producing organization run by the playwrights themselves: Elmer Rice, Maxwell Anderson, Sid-ney Howard, Robert E. Sherwood, and Marc Connelly. The British team was to be Priestley, Terence Rattigan, James Bridie, Benn Levy, and myself, and we had two meetings in Priestley's flat, under the chairmanship of Benn Levy, the bearded socialist parlia-mentarian and dramatist husband of Constance Cummings.

We arrived at a purely financial consideration in the course of the agenda. Benn Levy said, "I think this is a matter which only applies to highly successful dramatists, but, since we all live and write in hopes, I suppose we should have a ruling." At this point he ad-dressed himself to Rattigan. "Terry, perhaps you would tell us in confidence your solution to this problem?"

Terence Rattigan never had time to answer, for Jack Priestley in-terrupted, his hackles halfway risen. "I think I ought to remind you, gentlemen, that I too have had my share of success. . ."

The second meeting was no more fruitful; it was, in fact, the last.

"I hope it is understood," said Jack Priestley, puffing away at his pipe, "that as a result of this free association of dramatists, we all from now on write plays expressing the right ideas."

I noticed the angular Dr. Mavor wince. He wrote highly personal and capricious plays under the nom de plume of James Bridie. His eyes grew in size and his nose pointed at Jack, while his Scottish voice caressed his words.

"I owe what little success I have known by expressing the wrong ideas, Mr. Priestley, and I think it is really too late in life for me to change now — for any reason, however specious."

That was the end of that, and a very good thing too.

On another occasion, I was chairman of some meeting of the League of Dramatists at Claridge's. I am a very poor chairman at the best of times, most especially in England where I consistently forget that usage forbids guests to smoke before the Queen's health has been drunk. The evening in question was no exception, and I suddenly became aware of Jack Priestley, doubled up as he dodged in and out of the tables, holding his dead pipe like a revolver, like an officer involved in some heroic action in 1914.

Eventually he arrived by my side, convinced that his approach had been inconspicuous.

"I'm as good a republican as the next man," he whispered, fiddling agitatedly with his pipe, "but don't you think it's time for the Royal Toast?"

Finally, there is one story so apocryphal that it has to be true.

"Mr. Priestley," said the gushing interviewer, "we are conducting an enquiry for the magazine. What would you do if you had a million?"

"I've got a million," replied Jack and walked away.

He is a man opulent in his contradictions and sometimes absolutely outrageous in his remarks, but one is always delighted to see him. His robust self-confidence and his gruff rejection of sentimentality are a permanent vote of confidence in human nature.

I notice that your examples are all English, or at least British.

That is quite normal, since I lived there most of my life and the men and women I met during my formative years were almost exclusively British. Later, in New York, however, I was privileged to spend some time with that extraordinary triumverate which guided the destinies of the United Nations during a particularly dangerous period, Dag Hammarskjöld, Andy Cordier, and Ralph Bunche.

I dined and lunched with them on occasion, and it is horrifying to think that they are all gone. Hammarskjöld, shy rather than cold, showed me photographs of Khrushchev beating his shoe on his desk during that famous incident in the General Assembly. If you looked carefully, you could see that he was wearing both his shoes, which meant that he either borrowed the shoe from a hapless aide, or else that he smuggled the shoe in to the General Assembly in a paper bag, disguised as a sandwich.

There is no doubt that Hammarskjöld's northern sense of propriety was deeply shaken by the roughness of the outburst, and ironically, since the Russian code of what is socially permissible comes largely across the Baltic from Sweden, it was precisely this rowdy behavior of Khrushchev's, dubbed *Ne-Kulturny* (uncultured), which eventually proved his undoing at home. Had he lived to know this, Hammarskjöld would have been unexpectedly reassured.

Ralph Bunche was as quiet, as reserved, as Andy Cordier was outspoken. One had to strain at times to hear what Ralph Bunche was saying, whereas Andy's foghorn voice left nothing to the imagination, not even the dynamic force of his character. Of course, the mystery of Ralph's quality of reticence was not far to seek, and yet, what always came as a surprise was the extraordinary toughness which his mild manner concealed. Apparently he had been the protégé of a wonderful old teacher of another generation. He worked hard to bring out all his unique pupil's brilliance, and it was when Ralph was leaving to go to the university, into which he had passed with every manner of commendation, that the old teacher produced the unkindest cut of all, in guise of the greatest compliment he could pay.

"Bunche," he said, with a tear in his eye, "congratulations. And, Bunche . . . I want you to know, I never considered you as a Negro."

Adlai Stevenson was frequently a member of this civilized and glorious team. Accessible and chipper, he was the type of American who is unfortunately no longer called to the greatest heights, as indeed I am convinced that neither Harry Truman nor either of the Roosevelts would be if they had the opportunity of running today. Such manifest intelligence is somehow suspect, as is any outward demonstration of character. It seems to be the habit to elect presidents for their lack of evident vices instead of for their possession of evident virtues. The existence of vices is allowed to become apparent during the incumbency. In such computerized calculations, in which those seeking to be everything to all men end up being precious little to any, there was no possible place for someone as twinkling with minor malice as Adlai Stevenson.

"The work of the Catholic missions in New Guinea," he declared at one of our dinners at the Brussels Restaurant in New York, his voice portentous, "is beginning to pay dividends. Statistics have shown that on Fridays the staple meal is fishermen."

During the enervating days of the Cuban crisis, it was clear that he was left completely in the dark by the Kennedy administration. There were no doubt very good reasons for this embarrassing oversight, in that enough was going on in Washington not to have to bother about New York and the U.N. as well. But it did point to one increasingly obvious discrepancy, and that is whereas small and new countries send their best men to the United Nations, large countries only send those they can spare, since the fountainhead of their policies are not there. In that sense, Adlai Stevenson was far too fine a mind to entrust with the window-dressing of an American presence among the meek.

His isolation led to embarrassment for him and for anybody of the remotest sensitivity. On the second Sunday of the crisis, we were invited to brunch at John Gunther's. Early in the morning, the television announced that the Russians had protested about a new over-flight of their territory by a U-2. There was enough tension in the air without that.

Adlai Stevenson arrived at Gunther's saying how he was looking forward to brunch, the first civilized meal he was going to enjoy for a week. He looked very tired, but the twinkle was there.

"Things seem calmer at last," he said.

"Despite the U-2 flight over Russia?" I asked.

He laughed, but then reined in his reflex.

"You're joking, of course," he replied, giving a distinct impression that, if it was a joke, it wasn't all that amusing.

"No," I said, "I heard it on the TV at about nine o'clock."

"I heard it at ten," said Lord Caradon, who was present.

When Adlai was sure it was "on the level," he asked to use the phone. After a moment he returned and said regretfully that he could not stay for brunch.

It was the last time I saw him.

The Sunday before I had a date to play tennis with Max Blouët, the then manager of the Drake Hotel. We had to wait to begin because our fourth player had not yet turned up. He was none other than Monsieur Kosciusko-Morizet, then French Ambassador to the U.N., since Ambassador to Washington. Our third player was the Ambassador from Cambodia, who waited patiently with us.

When M. Kosciusko-Morizet eventually turned up, he was both apologetic and deeply annoyed about something far beyond tennis. Eventually, as he smashed the third easy ball into the netting surrounding the court, he exploded.

"It is just impossible to be a French Ambassador these days. The Americans tell us nothing. Nothing! Why am I late? Just as I was leaving I had yet another telephone call with disagreeable revelations — and on a Sunday!"

Needless to say we lost, the Cambodian's patient lobbing and drop shots being a subtle foretaste of the style of future hostilities. Later that day I had to go to Washington. The British Ambassador,

Sir David Ormsby-Gore, now Lord Harlech, a personal friend of John Kennedy's, asked me in for a drink.

"Well, it's a grim situation," he said, his fine medieval face reposed and earnest, "but there is one element of consolation — the Americans are keeping us informed of every move."

This was too much for me.

"Oh," I said, "that's curious. I've just been playing tennis with Kosciusko-Morizet — "

The British Ambassador's eyes lit with pleasure.

"How is he?" he inquired.

"Perhaps not as well as he should be," I suggested. "He told me the French are being informed of nothing at all. Nothing, he emphasized."

The life drained from the British Ambassador's eye once again.

"He actually *said* that, did he?" he inquired.

"He actually *said* that," I echoed.

The Ambassador took a deep breath and then said casually, "Well, it's quite true, of course, but we do have to put up *some* kind of appearance."

The incident was a succinct explanation of the relationship between the three countries at the time.

You met de Gaulle, remember?

How could I forget? But I must say that my purpose here is not name-dropping or an acquisition of illusory self-importance, and so I only mention those with whom a contact, however brief, had some meaning which is worth sharing with others. After all, thousands of people knew de Gaulle far better than I, if anyone knew him at all.

Every great man, upon departure, leaves the most unconscionable mess behind him, a confusion of unfinished business, of regrets, of recrimination, of love, of awe — all the ingredients for social and political chaos. Georges Pompidou had the unenviable task of making order out of the loose ends and of imposing a period of quiet growth on his country, still enervated by the absence of its secular pontiff and all the unpredictable excitements of his reign. Pompidou came out of this trial bluff and blunt, but never dull. He somehow exemplified a quiet courage, a discreet yet trenchant wit, very different from the *"superbe"* of de Gaulle, but quite as French. Like Truman after Roosevelt, he began as a disaster, born out of disaster, and ended mourned by all, with a suspicion that he might, at the final stocktaking, run his haughty predecessor very close indeed as a president.

As a man he was certainly most engaging, preserving his initial simplicity with no effort whatsoever. In fact, he was the only person in his position who consistently and plaintively bemoaned the fact that his high office kept him segregated both from his friends and from those he would have liked to have known better.

He had an absolute passion for the arts, and was determined to understand and savor even the most obscure of coeval abstractions, turning certain rooms in the Elysée into exhibitions of unashamedly forward-looking furniture. He believed that France was a haven of the creative senses and that it behoved her chief executive to be as up to the minute as its most advanced pioneer.

I was fortunate to be present at the farewell lunch M. Pompidou gave Christopher Soames, then at the point of relinquishing his post as British Ambassador to Paris in order to take up his new appointment as Commissioner to the EEC in Brussels. There were a mere sixteen people seated at table on this moving occasion. Suddenly the President claimed our attention by tapping his glass. He then, soberly and quietly, proposed the health of Christopher Soames, adding that his sincere hope was to live long enough to see Christopher fill a place to which he would be admirably suited, that of first President of Europe.

The toast came as a quiet bombshell, and bereft Christopher of any suitable answer. In fact, there was no answer suitable for such a patently sincere and magnanimous wish. A year later, at a function in London, Christopher asked me if his memory of the incident was accurate. Had Pompidou actually proposed such a toast or was it all a dream? I was able to confirm that I had heard it too, although until the question was put I too had had vague doubts that I had heard it aright.

Monsieur Pompidou's successor, Valery Giscard d'Estaing, began his presidential career as demurely as Georges Pompidou, but soon noticed that the French, a nation of hero-worshippers, demand men they can look up to, and so he consciously toughened his attitude to become a kind of national examiner, judge and advocate at one and the same time. Like many Frenchmen tired of the ever-changing governments of the past, under the aegis of presidents who were sinecures, he has become fascinated with American "presidentialism," and the idea of an all-powerful president, only limited in his authority by the time span of his incumbency, guiding the destinies of a government whose prime minister is an emasculated figure. The perils of such an arrangement seemed lost on the French, for reasons of novelty and modernity, and they chose the year of Watergate to make their greatest progress in the direction of a transatlantic style. De Gaulle is a convenient precedent, which seems to give credence to an arrangement quite new in French parliamentary history, although it was de Gaulle's personality rather than any constitutional prerogative that created such a possibility in the first place.

Whereas de Gaulle was a military figure, Giscard is a lay figure from the world of the *Grandes Écoles,* answering questions with a finicky clarity of syntax and often categorizing his replies to questions in several numbered sections. It is he who seems to correct France's exam papers, and every session of the cabinet has the odd appearance of a reunion on the first day of term, the ministers refreshed and eager to do well under the temperate yet unforgiving eye of the professor.

One begins to realize the greatness and the accuracy of Molière as France's national playwright par excellence when we discover echoes of his creations in the living. De Gaulle could have been a superb creation of Molière's if he hadn't been a superb creation of his own, and Giscard too, with his conquered timidity, the modulated style of his utterances, his patience with those presumed slightly slow of wit, his prissiness and his gracious nod in the direction of destiny, could have stepped out of a Molière play, his sidelong glances contradicted by the austerity of his habit.

Pompidou would have found less favor with Molière, since he had less to hide and hid it not at all.

I notice, as I am sure others will notice, that there is not a woman among the gallery of those who have left an impression on you.

Women have left great impressions on me, but hardly in a manner I can communicate. They have been remarkable for their constancy, their charm, their courage. I am talking about friends now, mark you, nothing else. Leaving out those I have already mentioned, like Edith Evans, or those who deserve to be mentioned again and again, like Sibyl Thorndike, there is one woman in particular whom I do wish to talk about. Moura Budberg took her name from one of her marriages. She had also been married to a Count Benckendorf. And she had been the mistress and muse of Maxim Gorki, of H. G. Wells, and of Robert Bruce-Lockhart, author of *Memoirs of a British Agent.* A large woman, bearing a striking resemblance to Peter the Great, and born strangely enough at Poltava, scene of his greatest victory over the Swedes, she lived a long life on the fringe of literature, translating, advising, lending her knowledge to the movie industry; but above all she was a great intangible influence on all who came in contact with her.

She was strikingly original. Staying with us in Rome, she said at breakfast, as an afterthought, "You must be careful of burglars in this house."

"Why?" we asked nervously.

We had to wait for the toast and marmalade to be masticated and swallowed before a reply was forthcoming.

"Because I saw a hand reach for my handbag through the window in the early hours of the morning."

"What did you do?" we asked, now thoroughly alarmed.

Once again, the toast and marmalade had precedence.

"The hand was within range of my walking stick. I hope I didn't break the poor man's wrist."

During the war, owing to a circumstance as eccentric as herself, she found herself locked out of her London apartment naked. Instead of doing what most women would have done, which is to call for help while attempting to conceal their modesty, Moura placed a fire-bucket over her head and went down into the street to solicit assistance.

In Moscow I saw her ask a policeman for a taxi. He pointed out that he was a policeman, not a commissionaire. She said that in her day a policeman would not have needed to point out that he was not a commissionaire in order to hail a taxi for an old lady. Eventually the poor man was blowing his whistle desperately and waving aimlessly at all moving vehicles in order to rid himself of this majestic presence.

Despite her long liaison with Maxim Gorki, she was a great friend of Gorki's widow, and they sat in rocking chairs reminiscing about the object of their adoration on the veranda of a dacha near Moscow.

She represented for me an indomitable side to the Russian character, one which, despite the creation of my own nation, consoles and comforts me.

I may have been brought up to accept British thought patterns and to have been exposed to the style of the French, the casualness of the Americans, and the atmospheres of many other peoples, but when I was in Moura's presence, I felt deeply and serenely Russian. It was, and still is, a sentiment which I could not do without from time to time.

Who supplies it now that Moura has left us?

Her memory is as alive as ever. But I am conscious of my Russianness when I am with Russians, even if my knowledge of the language is far from adequate. Nabokov comforts me too, despite his professorial affectations and a spoken English quite other than his highly personal written English and giving every evidence of having been learned at the knee of some Scottish nanny in St. Petersburg.

He has a merry laugh and he is willing to use it. At the same time, his prejudices are sometimes so curious that they are difficult to share even when the imperative is mere politeness. An old hiker with staring eyes turned up in Montreux, revealing himself to be the son of the Russian liberal Prime Minister Stolypin, assassinated in 1911 in Kiev, of whom Lenin had said that if he were allowed to continue his reforms, revolution would become unnecessary. Stolypin Junior was longing to meet Nabokov.

Respectful as ever of the privacy of creative artists, I said he was very busy, but I would nevertheless try. The great man answered the phone himself. I explained the nature of my call.

"Stolypin?" said Nabokov. "No, I do not think I wish to meet him."

"Oh, come on," I urged, "you have something in common at least."

"Oh?"

"His father and your uncle were both assassinated."

"Yes, admittedly, but for different reasons. Tell him I regret, and when he has gone come up for a drink."

He too has something indomitable about him.

And Solzhenitsyn?

I don't know Solzhenitsyn, but I have the gravest misgivings about everything except his courage and his sincerity.

I only brought him up because, once we're on the subject of the indomitable—

I understand. No one can fail to be impressed, even overawed by his extraordinary singleness of purpose and his almost superhuman self-discipline, and yet, although he is an undoubted authority on horror in the camps and on official obtuseness out of them, once he came to the West he was under an overriding obligation to speak. Why? Because he was confronted with that most terrible of all temptations, that of being listened to. He revealed himself quickly to possess a new version of an old cosmic vision and to be a Russian mystic in an ancient tradition, in which acuity and intolerance mingle with the fumes of incense and of wordsmoke. I fear that the Russians were as shrewd in letting him go as he was in accepting their offer.

What makes you say that?

An offer from an American magnate in the South to fly thousands of miles for a handsome wad of dollars, in order to read aloud Solzhenitsyn's Warning to America at a sociopolitical function. My soul too has been open to temptation, but I never thought to recognize Solzhenitsyn among the tempters, but there he was, large as life, among the Southern aristocracy.

You refused?

There are certain things I cannot bring myself to do, even if I am starving. To lend myself to a viewpoint I find unreal and undiscriminating is one.

And yet you lent your name to a wine commerical?

Ah, cruel. I will explain in the next and final chapter.

Do you remember, at the poolside of the Beverly Hills Hotel, an elderly gentleman in a flowered cabana-suit gripping your wrist and saying, in one breath, "I want you to know I admire everying you do and I own Manischewitz"?

I do. I was flattered both as a person and as a wine salesman.

I suppose you know that many people assume that you are Jewish?

Sometimes I wish I were. It would save so much trouble.

Trouble?

Yes. Earlier on I spoke about UNESCO and the press agencies, remember?

Yes.

Well, by means of a reckless canard, the Jewish news agency reported me to have slandered the state of Israel in a highly reputable Dutch newspaper. The item was as incredible in its inaccuracy as it was in its spitefulness, and it ended with the statement, "Mr. Ustinov is of Jewish origin," whatever that may mean by way of nuance. The result was the cancellation of theater parties to a play of mine which was then on the road, and other regrettable consequences. I was, quite clearly, a traitor to a sacred cause.

Did they do nothing to check the truth of your origins or your statement?

Nothing. Whereas the investigators of Watergate went to immense pains to check every detail of their serious allegations, these anonymous creatures did absolutely nothing to substantiate their claims or to enable me to raise my voice in my own defense at such outrageous calumnies.

What is your opinion? Answer now.

I believe that the Jews have made a contribution to the human condition out of all proportion to their numbers. I believe them to be an immense people. Not only have they supplied the world with two leaders of the stature of Jesus Christ and Karl Marx, but they have even indulged in the luxury of following neither one nor the other. If I were Jewish, I would be as proud of it as Jews so naturally are. The fact that I am not Jewish means merely that I have an equal right to be proud of whatever it is I am, and this has taken me over half a century to find out and even now I am far from sure.

Obviously no one can afford to believe in the intrinsic superiority of one people over another. It should be our pride that we are members of the human race rather than of one of its innumerable subdivisions, but I fear we are not ready for this and doubtless never will be. The dog will always be a better friend to man than are other men. But even here the thoroughbred is often more highly prized than the mongrel, which is as tactful an outlet for racialism as any.

Didn't they ask you, in Israel, why you thought the Russians had an aversion to them?

Yes. I replied that the Russians probably found it impossible to forgive the Jews for the Revolution. Lenin and Stalin were two of the very few of the original Bolsheviks who were not Jewish intellectuals — Kamenev, Zinoviev, Trotsky, Joffé, Litvinov, Radek; the list is endless. And I doubt if the Russians would ever have been capable of putting such ideas to the test unassisted by the permanent Jewish fermentation in the world of thought.

What is your connection with Israel then?

My connection is with Palestine. This is not a provocation, merely an historical accuracy. All my family had left by 1917, with the exception of my Aunt Tabitha who had married a Palestinian Arab, Anis Jamal, and who lived in Jerusalem until forced to flee at the time of the creation of the state of Israel. Israeli friends protest that no one was forced to flee, and that all residents could have stayed on and become useful subjects of the new republic. Opinions have varied about such cases in other countries, including Russia and Algeria, and probably they will occur again in the cases of Rhodesia and of South Africa, but it is difficult to see how a country described as a "National Home," a theocracy as well as a democracy, can extend full equality to all its citizens, without regard to race or religion. In any case, with the bullets of hot-headed patriots flying around, it was not the moment to stop and argue. My aunt, now a widow, lives in a small flat in Beirut. Her house in Jerusalem is, I was told there, under the jurisdiction of the Custodian of Enemy Property.

In the words of an enlightened Jewish friend, a noted sociologist and humanitarian with whom I have been honored to serve on many committees, "The Palestinians are the last victims of Hitler."

I will not reveal his name lest he too should become the target of hasty judgment and misrepresentation.

The allegation that some of one's best friends are Jewish is always a cue for a gale of ironic laughter. When an allegation that some of one's best friends are Palestinians produces the same sarcastic guffaw in lieu of the stunned silence of today, we will know that the problems of that tortured corner of our globe are well on their way toward a pacific solution.

20

Your mother died in 1975?

In February. My father had been cremated. My mother had always had a horror of such a process, but at her death, she left a letter asking to be cremated too. Their ashes are buried in a village churchyard, at Eastleach, in Gloucestershire.

I found a mountain of letters in her cupboard, from her to Klop, from Klop to her. Klop was reported never to write to anyone. Now I stumbled onto this secret world. A natural discretion prevented me from glancing at more than one or two. All I managed to discover was that my instincts had been correct. My parents had had no real time to know one another well before I was born. I have kept the letters. Perhaps one day, when I am wiser, and enough time has passed, I may read one more.

Your father murmured in French in his coma, your mother in Russian.

The mysteries of the subconscious. She had never really liked things Russian. Having been born there of foreign heritage, she always hankered for Western ways and means of expression, and yet then, in her last hours, she spoke almost exclusively in Russian. She reacted to Mozart on a small transistor radio, changing her expression according to the subtle moods of the music, and sipped water, where Klop had sipped champagne. There was no hint of sadness. It was part of a functional process almost as old as life itself, and there was a kind of serene complicity between us.

She was happy?

As happy as the awful discomfort of dying would allow.

She had spent so much time and energy worrying about you with her usual discretion. As usual, you only heard about it through other people.

Yes, a diary I discovered was searing evidence of the awful injury she had suffered as the result of events which I have briefly hinted at, and her anxiety for my well-being was both selfless and discreet. Luckily I had time to reassure her as to my spiritual serenity before she died.

In what way?

That is a leading question, and I am not sure I am ready to talk about it yet.

You had better hurry. There are not many pages left.

I will, I promise you. In any case, the book would not be complete without its coda, its bridge to the unrecorded future. Meanwhile, is there anything of more general interest you wish to ask?

Your mother followed your life from a self imposed distance?

She was the opposite of the demanding, pervasive parent. Even if she treated me as being somewhat younger than I ever was at a given time, she wanted a man as a son, not a boy. She followed my career with alternating approval, fear, annoyance, and relief. She could be damning in her criticism, but her expression of it was always polite and gentle. She knew too well the difficulties of creation to be negligent in her condemnation or unstinting in her praise. If she had a fault, it was to laugh too loudly at my jokes and to laugh even louder at her own.

She knew about your extracurricular activities, at the University and with UNICEF?

Oh, yes. She regarded them with a sort of quizzical interest, as though they might deflect me from more suitable work. When she understood that they were food for my soul, however, she wanted to know all about them.

When did you first begin to devote a little time to UNICEF?

I received a telegram back in the late sixties asking me to act as Master of Ceremonies at a UNICEF concert at the Theatre Nationale de L'Odéon, in Paris. At that time I knew nothing about UNICEF, the United Nations International Children's Emergency Fund, and was merely tempted by the extraordinary quality of the participants, the like of which no commercial enterprise could possibly muster for a simple performance. I accepted and during the course of rehearsals met Leon Davičo, a Yugoslav journalist from *Politikr* in Belgrade, seconded to UNICEF.

It was this forthright and winning man who first contaminated me with the happy virus of enthusiasm for this vital cause. Even if I hate galas, which seem to me an incongruous way of raising money, I did help to put together quite a few of them on behalf of UNICEF, in Italy, France, Switzerland, Germany, and Japan. On television they brought quite a handsome revenue, even if it was only a drop in the ocean of children's needs.

This is no place for propaganda, even if the burden on private charity is rendered practically unbearable by the scandalous negligence of governments, but I was impressed from the beginning by the selfless work of those often-maligned international civil servants who have a passionate interest in their work and who are content with the knowledge of its constructive nature as a moral recompense. It is so easy, as I have suggested elsewhere, to attack the United Nations as a futile field for undemocratic or antidemocratic ideas, but such critics conveniently overlook the facts that it was constituted as a democratic forum and that the ideas of the majority cannot be roughly pushed aside just because they happen to be temporarily out of favor in some influential places. Orthodox Communism is under quite as much pressure as is Western capitalist democracy. Everywhere new countries, conceived in rebellion, growing up in poverty, are seeking their own way and their own interdependence in a confusing and often brutal world. The prerequisite for maintaining a clear head in such a world is, of course, a certain modicum of faith in the possibilities of human nature, and it is not the excesses of this African warlord or of that dapper South American General that can sway such a necessary faith any more than the excesses of outriders of the Western bandwagon, the arms manufacturers whose products are loaded with grease for eager palms, or their Eastern counterparts, who still move divisions to silence the voices of legitimate complaint.

The General Assembly and the Security Council are but the shop window in which views are presented and opposed and in which we can be elated or depressed according to our convictions. Within the shop, however, all is different. Nationalities and creed are largely forgotten. Confronted with problems, Christian and Communist, Moslem and Socialist, Buddhist and Conservative do their best within the means at their disposal to solve them. This is a source of confidence even to the most jaded cynic.

Are you sure this is not an idealized picture of what goes on?

Perhaps it is, but it is an idealized picture shared by many of those involved. The esprit de corps of these international organizations never ceases to surprise me, as well as the quality of those in charge.

Who, for instance?

Henry Labouisie is an astonishing American, a career diplomat who keeps his own counsel and has an experience in human affairs on which he continually and mildly draws in order to be tough and outspoken where it matters. As sometimes happens with men of quality, age only reinforces his qualities and makes his vision more acute. He is the head of UNICEF at this time of writing. His wife is the daughter of Rene and Ève Curie.

The director-general of UNESCO, whose task is, if anything, more controversial, is M. M'Bow, a Senegalese educationalist with a splendid and necessary disdain for difficulties and a cool head, utterly negligent of pressures and confident in the irrefutable logic of his neutral but never reticent position.

Why do you say his task is more controversial?

It is easier to raise a tear over babies, even among the hard of heart, then it is to beg sympathy for students, to appeal to Philistines for help in saving ancient monuments.

I see your point.

UNICEF was the only agency of the United Nations to be allowed into Nigeria after the Biafran war, because of its apolitical nature. UNICEF was also the only agency to have an office in Hanoi throughout the hostilities, and in the last days of the war all shades of opinion in Vietnam made urgent appeals to UNICEF to help save the lives and guarantee the well-being of children caught in the tidal wave of battle. This could not be said at the time because of some ruling of Congress that the United States could not support an organization having contact with an enemy. Is it to be believed?

But tell me, honestly, did this sudden interest in the fate of children not coincide with some dramatic events in your private life?

No. I am grateful that my interest grew out of a dissatisfaction with a life of the merely amusing, of the merely diverting. It managed to predate the climax of my personal problems, except of course that these had been growing inexorably over almost twenty years. It may well be, however, that my consciousness of children's needs was fixed by my own observation of a growing family. As I intimated, it was only by watching my own family that I grew aware of many basic relationships among human beings. I became conscious of the need to give affection without an immediate ability to do so. I was too far gone, as it were, in the ways of solitude, to break through the barrier without difficulty. And yet it had to be done. I recognized the necessity.

You have always, if I understand you, mistrusted those who, because of some personal tragedy, suddenly join crusades against that which has afflicted them or their families?

Mistrust is hardly a word I would use in this context. Tragedy is never foreseeable, only sometimes premonitory. When the wind is in our sails, we never think as deeply as when the wind is contrary, and who is to blame us? Nevertheless, I believe that the time for

thanksgiving is when all is going well. Better early than late, even if
better late then never. Most of us are negligent creatures. Things,
even those under our noses, have to be brought to our attention.
I'm glad you said that.
Why?
*Because sooner or later you'll have to talk about yourself again,
instead of pontificating about generalities.*
That is the square Russian in me.
*I recognize it, but you can't put off talking about the end of your
second marriage forever, like a visit to the dentist. The book is
nearly over. Be brave.*
You know perfectly well that my second marriage is the theme for
another book, a book that will never be written. At least, not by me.
If one of the children should take it into his or her head to be as
crisp and objective as their grandmother was about their grandfather, or as I hope their father is with their grandparents, that is a legitimate prerogative of a later generation. They may have at their
disposal by then psychological insights which were denied me,
which could explain the material with greater assurance than I can,
and which could analyze with serenity and precision the sources of
my despair.
Is that all you are going to say?
Yes.
Well, that's that.
Not quite. Whereas I have scruples about imposing my version of
the truth on the living and even on the dead, I have absolutely no
compunction whatsoever in telling about the divorce itself, because it
drifts away from the private and dramatic into the field of light entertainment. It also shows how far we have moved along the path to
a just society in the past twenty years.
You will remember that my first divorce took place in London,
under the aegis of the Lion and Unicorn rampant, in an aura of sanctity. The decor, in other words, was the same as the one in which
men had been sentenced to death for stealing wallets a hundred and
fifty years ago. Poor Isolde, so eager to marry again, had to sit in a

sordid hotel room and play cards with a rented gentleman in underwear, waiting patiently for a detective to break in at an appointed hour and discover them. After such a compromising incident and the subsequent hearing, there was a six-week delay before the issuing of the Decree Nisi so that the King's Proctor might assure himself that there had been no hint of collusion. Ah, divine hypocrisy! With what style was dirty linen laundered in public in those days!

Nowadays, all that is laundered is money. My second divorce proved it. At the risk of pontificating again, I must skip a few generalities in order to place the particular in its context.

In this terrifying world of computers and headlong progress, groups of people demonstrate on behalf of the enfeebled environment and against the installation of nuclear power plants. These are, ironically, the true conservatives of today, although they prefer the term conservationists. In Switzerland, an admirable country in many ways, the banks take the place of the nuclear power plants for the time being. The fallout from the overheated economy seeps out across the green valleys in an imperceptible haze, destiny's secret weapon against the lofty Calvinist conscience. It was never, as Bernard Shaw suggests, a country organized deliberately along the lines of a large hotel, nor is its only title to glory the cuckoo clock, as alleged by Orson Welles.

It produced the toughest mercenaries in Europe in the not-too-distant past. Why else would the pope employ Swiss guards if not to feel adequately protected against the Italian princes? There came a point, however, in which the Swiss found themselves consistently killing each other, albeit for high salaries, and decided to put their instincts for banking to a more constructive use. Their neutrality attracted vast sums of money, unexplained and anonymous, legitimate and corrupt, cold and hot, clean and filthy. They claim, perhaps a little nervously, that money has no personality once it is in a vault. One suspects that the bankers are the victims of this contagion and that while the slumbering money retains its personality the bankers lose theirs in their determination to appear mere custodians of the unknown.

I might have foreseen the disasters which would follow once a group of Swiss lawyers suggested what is known as a *"Divorce, à l'amiable,"* which is merely a private contract between the parties, so that the judge is relieved of the necessity of attributing blame. He has little else to do but register the existence of such an agreement and, after a while, proclaim the divorce to be effective.

It would seem, on the face of it, to be an ideal manner in which to allow two civilized people in discord to go their ways.

I was to pay half a million dollars. I was given three years in which to accomplish this task, which I thought impossible at the then-rate of 4.20 Swiss francs to the dollar.

My lawyers pointed out to me that I owned a tract of land which would fetch very nearly the requisite sum if sold to some derelict chief of state in exile or to some Arabian knight with an eye to the unsteady future. I would consequently scarcely feel the divorce at all. It had been agreed that I was to have custody of the children, so that I was not merely suing for my freedom but for a continuation of a joyous and vital responsibility. I signed the agreement.

The next event was a new Swiss law temporarily preventing the sale of any land to foreigners. In the view of the size of the country and the extent of foreign investment I could understand this law very well, but I hardly expected to become one of its first victims. I suddenly found myself burdened with my broad acres, which for a while threatened to be designated as a "Green Zone" or parkland, my huge debt undiminished.

To render the situation even more unpleasant, the dollar slipped from 4.20 to 2.40. My debt began to approach a million dollars. And you ask me why I did a commercial for Californian wines?

My dear fellow, we lived in a world which fondly believes every man but a fool to have his price. Heads of state are on trial for having accepted bribes in order to push one aircraft at the expense of others. One noble public figure even expressed irritation at the end of a lunch that he was to receive one million dollars instead of the expected six million as a recompense. He deemed his lunch a failure. Such a lunch would have solved all my problems, but then, thank goodness, I am not in a position to push weapons for my well-being.

I stuck to wine and a line of cameras which none other than Lord Olivier had already advertised in America; but he had declined to show himself in the light of a salesman to his peers, so I followed meekly in the steps of the master, stifling my approval of his scruples.

Next, the Union of Swiss Cheese tempted me with a substantial financial reward to be seen guzzling Emmenthaler while dressed as a mountaineer before the background of the Matterhorn, this choice thirty seconds to be seen on all the screens of Western Europe. I declined the offer, feeling that my divorce had already caused me as much humiliation as I could bear, although I do often fancy a piece of Emmenthaler in private.

When I did the wine commercial, I was not to know that my employer was in contention with a trade union of field workers, who were busy boycotting grapes and lettuce, a luxury which only a very rich country can afford, even though European viticulturists have been busy recently dumping grapes on freeways in order to attract attention to their grievances.

The result of all this opulent absurdity was that while I opened in a new play in New Haven, Connecticut, there were pickets outside the theater blaming me for underwriting blackleg lettuce and pirate grapes by doing a commercial, and all this because of the unadulterated amiability of a Swiss court. Now do you understand why I call this divorce light entertainment?

That was the same play that was already suffering cancellations from Zionists who had swallowed unquestioningly what you were supposed to have said about Israel?

Indeed. But I can't really blame the lawyers for that. Suffice it to say that I did many things I had no taste for during this period, simply in order to work my way out of my financial problem.

Was it not a high price to pay?

No price is too high to pay. And, after all, if the children turn out well, is that not an achievement their mother can be proud of too? I would have signed that document if it had cost me twice as much, which indeed it has, since I have over the last six years paid the interest on the money as though it had been delivered, and a little extra to conform with the rising cost of living.

Your nonchalance in the light of this crushing burden is really scarcely credible. I know the facts, but are you seriously asking our readers to believe that you consider all this water off a duck's back?

Sufficient water will sink the duck. Of course, I know, as you know, that my particular sensitivity takes refuge in laughter as other's may take refuge in tears, or in murder, or in suicide. All I do have is an inherent toughness, a refusal to submit, a quality really no more admirable than obstinacy. The more my marriages gravitated toward the rocks, the more insanely idealistic did I become about the sudden possibilities of love, simply expended and deeply felt. As things went wrong, I saw more and more clearly how things should be. And, of course, there is no element in this existence which gives you a clearer sense of responsibility than children, and mine have already given me immense joy of a kind I can never consciously repay.

Tamara is now married. I well remember my first encounter with her husband, the young director Christopher Parr. Had I written the scene in a play, I would, no doubt, have fallen into the trap of tradition and made the young man nervous, and the prospective father-in-law a model of compassionate understanding. The truth was, needless to say, quite other. Young Master Parr was the model of composure, studying me through huge horn-rimmed glasses, whereas I was a bundle of nerves, determined not to let my beloved daughter down at this vital moment in her life.

I cracked a few jokes, to which the young man failed to respond. I became earnest and he smiled wanly. Every now and then I would glance at Tammy, and fancied I could read anxiety behind her usual limpid composure. I ended the encounter utterly demoralized, quite convinced that I had failed an examination and had lost the job, not only for myself, but for those who depended on me.

A few weeks later, by means of the faithful press-cutting agency, I received a cutting from some paper in the North of England. It was an interview with Chris, in which he was asked if he were not a little nervous of becoming the son-in-law of someone vaguely notorious. He was quoted as answering, "No, why should I? He's a rattling good sort." This unexpected piece of archaic flattery made me shudder with incredulous relief, as though I had been elected after all, after a recount.

The other children have not, at this time, put my maturity to a similar test, but they no doubt will. I have eyed various aspirants as they drifted into my sight, some of them with pleasure, some with a relative indifference, some with frank alarm. Pavla has a classic, yet very individual, beauty, although I say so myself. She is a bit of a femme fatale, surprisingly gifted with an acute sense of the comic, of the absurd.

I have now worked with both Tammy and Pavla, and know them to be very differently, yet very distinctly, endowed with the instinct for our particular profession, which gives me great satisfaction. Andrea is the soubrette of the family, with a robust sense of fun and a piercing kind of intelligence which consistently baffles me by its almost surgical capacity for analysis. Igor, who is studying sculpture, biology, and mathematics, may easily take me by surprise tomorrow by sharpening the focus of his vision, while Andrea could quite as easily discover the expressive possibilities of the nuance, the hint. It is while youth is making its choice that it is at its most fascinating and rewarding, even if parents tend to sigh with relief when that choice is made.

Naturally I dwell mainly on their good qualities, not only because I am a very conventional proud father, but also because their virtues seem to be more than a little miraculous, whereas I recognize their shortcomings as old enemies of mine which I have tried to hide in myself by education, manners, and *savoir-faire*, all to no avail.

That's all very well, but are you asking me to believe that you recovered your buoyancy after a particularly long and difficult chapter of your life simply by a ferocious and almost possessive attachment to your children's destinies?

No, of course not. That would be most unhealthy, and even unpleasant. I am not, and never have been, possessive. I consider possessiveness to be the most dangerous and underrated of all human vices.

Curiously enough, I agree with you. Once the human animal must face the terrifying fact of his solitude, it is unnatural to deny him the few advantages attached to being alone.

Such as freedom of choice?

All the freedoms possible.

There aren't that many. Look at America. That must be the greatest and noblest experiment in collective freedom known to man, and yet when such advantages are officially and traditionally encouraged, individuals seem to acquire cold feet and to spend their time imitating a collective image of averageness; their one ambition seems to be to disappear inconspicuously into a human mass as typical and as free as themselves.

It's like growing up. There's nothing like restrictions to give freedom its true flavor, the unattainable perfection, always inches out of reach. The truth is that if we ever could be entirely free, we wouldn't know what to do with it. In a panic, we would reconstruct our prisons. We need the prison of our minds, we need its limits. We could no longer measure distance without a scale; the only real freedom is in order, in an acceptance of boundaries.

Did you not write that once we are destined to live out our lives in the prison of our minds, our one duty is to furnish it well?

Yes, I believe I did.

Have you furnished yours well, in your opinion?

Ah, you have led me to my final confession with all the diabolical refinement a torero employs to lure the bull toward the picador!

I hope with happier results.

Well, I have made many mistakes, and been guilty of many errors of judgment, sometimes while trying too hard to do what I thought was right. And then, when the weight of my cumulative stupidities seemed for a moment to be overwhelming, I discovered, quite by chance, the tennis partner who had deflected my attention from my game so many years ago. A great deal had happened to us both, and neither of us had been extravagantly happy in the intervening years. My friendship with Hélène du Lau d'Allemans matured gradually to a point where we became inseparable. Our mutual attraction has grown with time, and this extended springtime has surprised us both. I would no longer know what to do without her.

Can you say that she is the love of your life?

Comparisons are odious. When I was young I was capable of being lovesick. I could burst into tears for reasons which seem frivolous on retrospect, but which were not so at the time. It is for that reason that I try never to patronize the youthful. I may have gained some experience with the passage of time, but at a price. I have half-forgotten what it was like to be young. I do remember, however, that being young is difficult enough to deserve the greatest respect. I loved my wives with the means at my disposal, only I am older now, and I love Hélène, my third wife, in a manner which seems to have matured like wine.

An example, perhaps, of your vintage loving?

For instance, if you wake up in the night, and as your eyes become used to the dark you begin to make out your favorite features creased with the kind of concentration babies devote to sleep, and you catch yourself smiling at the sight with an unaccustomed warmth, you can be pretty sure you are looking at the woman you love. It gives me an enormous pleasure to watch her when she does not know she is being watched, when she is being publicly engaging or privately thoughtful, buried in a book, before the makeup mirror, or just asleep. And she has the kind of sense of humor that invests trouble with proportion and happiness with grace.

She sounds like the perfect woman.

A perfect woman could have no personality. Hélène is a harmony of delightful imperfections, which is the most flattering thing I could say about anyone. I only hope my imperfections seem half as delightful to her. It is so easy to give if there is someone willing to take; it is so easy to take if there is someone with so much to give. She has made me into something approaching the man I once, privately and secretly, hoped to be. She came to my rescue at a turning point during that exhausting, terrifying, and magnificent journey of self-discovery we call life. And for that, I am endlessly grateful.

That seems to bring us to the end.

The end? We have gone through so much together, Dear Me, and yet it suddenly occurs to me we don't know each other at all.

We discover each other in retrospect, with the passage of time, and it is then that we also discover that we don't know each other very well, which is perhaps a good thing.

Perhaps. For the moment, all that interests me, with a greedy, inquisitive fever, is the future.

I'll be there when you need me. In a few minutes' time, if necessary.

Thank you, remorseless spirit.

Don't mention it, all-too-solid flesh.

Index

to make real solutions to the climate crisis—an existential threat to humanity and the planet."

—ROBERT D. BULLARD, professor of urban planning and environmental policy at Texas Southern University

"*The New Climate War* is engaging, approachable, and ultimately deeply uplifting. Mann outlines a hopeful vision of the transformation we must undertake in order to create a better, brighter future on this planet. He makes the clear case that our species is capable of great change, laying out exactly why and how we can rise to overcome the grave challenges before us."

—SASHA SAGAN, author of *For Small Creatures Such As We*

"A fascinating journey through the minds and motivations of the champions of climate denialism as well as the more recent climate doomists. Along the way, we learn of the unequivocal scientific evidence and the rapid evolution of technological solutions. Most importantly, public opinion finally seems to be at a 'tipping point' to catalyze political will to leave the next generation a sustainable world—and not a moment too soon!"

—ROSINA BIERBAUM, professor, University of Michigan and University of Maryland, and former Acting Director of OSTP

"Blunt, lucid. . . . Consistently displaying his comprehensive command of climate science and the attendant politics. . . . An expert effectively debunks the false narrative of denialism and advocates communal resistance to fossil fuels."

—*Publishers Weekly*

THE NEW CLIMATE WAR

THE NEW CLIMATE WAR

The Fight to Take Back the Planet

MICHAEL E. MANN

PUBLICAFFAIRS

NEW YORK

PublicAffairs
Hachette Book Group
1290 Avenue of the Americas, New York, NY 10104
www.publicaffairsbooks.com
@Public_Affairs

Printed in the United States of America

First Edition: January 2021

Published by PublicAffairs, an imprint of Perseus Books, LLC, a subsidiary
of Hachette Book Group, Inc. The PublicAffairs name and logo is a trademark
of the Hachette Book Group.

The Hachette Speakers Bureau provides a wide range of authors for
speaking events. To find out more, go to www.hachettespeakersbureau.com
or call (866) 376-6591.

The publisher is not responsible for websites (or their content) that are not
owned by the publisher.

Print book interior design by Linda Mark

Library of Congress Cataloging-in-Publication Data
Names: Mann, Michael E., 1965– author.
Title: The new climate war : the fight to take back our planet / Michael E. Mann.
Description: First edition. | New York : PublicAffairs, 2021. | Includes
  bibliographical references and index.
Identifiers: LCCN 2020027822 | ISBN 9781541758230 (hardcover) |
  ISBN 9781541758223 (ebook)
Subjects: LCSH: Environmental policy—Citizen participation. | Climatic
  changes—Government policy—Citizen participation. | Green New Deal.
Classification: LCC GE170 .M365 2021 | DDC 363.738/74—dc23
LC record available at https://lccn.loc.gov/2020027822
ISBNs: 978-1-5417-5823-0 (hardcover), 978-1-5417-5822-3 (ebook)

LSC-C

Printing 1, 2020

Michael Mann dedicates this book to his wife, Lorraine Santy,
and daughter, Megan Dorothy Mann, and to the memory of his
brother Jonathan Clifford Mann and mother, Paula Finesod Mann

Contents

Introduction

"There is general scientific agreement that the most likely manner in which mankind is influencing the global climate is through carbon dioxide release from the burning of fossil fuels. . . . There are some potentially catastrophic events that must be considered. . . . Rainfall might get heavier in some regions, and other places might turn to desert. . . . [Some countries] would have their agricultural output reduced or destroyed. . . . Man has a time window of five to ten years before the need for hard decisions regarding changes in energy strategies might become critical. . . . Once the effects are measurable, they might not be reversible."

YOU MIGHT BE FORGIVEN FOR ASSUMING THOSE PROPHETIC words were spoken by Al Gore in the mid-1990s. No, they were the words of fossil fuel giant ExxonMobil senior scientist James F. Black in recently unearthed internal documents from the 1970s.[1] In the decades since, instead of heeding the warnings of its own scientists, ExxonMobil and other fossil fuel interests waged a public relations campaign contesting the scientific evidence and doing everything in their power to block policies aimed at curbing planet-warming carbon pollution.

As a result, our planet has now warmed into the danger zone, and we are not yet taking the measures necessary to avert the largest global crisis we have ever faced. We are in a war—but before we engage we must first understand the mind of the enemy. What

| 1 |

evolving tactics are the forces of denial and delay employing today in their efforts to stymie climate action? How might we combat this shape-shifting Leviathan? Is it too late? Can we still avert catastrophic global climate change? These are all questions to which we deserve answers, and in the pages ahead, we'll find them.

Our story starts nearly a century ago, when the original denial and delay playbooks were first written. It turns out, the fossil fuel industry learned from the worst.[2] The gun lobby's motto—that "Guns Don't Kill People, People Kill People"—dates back to the 1920s. A textbook example of dangerous deflection, it diverts attention away from the problem of easy access to assault weapons and toward other purported contributors to mass shootings, such as mental illness or media depictions of violence.

The tobacco industry took a similar tack, seeking to discredit the linkage between cigarettes and lung cancer even as its own internal research, dating back to the 1950s, demonstrated the deadly and addictive nature of its product. "Doubt is our Product" read one of the Brown & Williamson tobacco company's internal memos.

Then there's the now iconic "Crying Indian" ad. Some readers may recall the commercial from the early 1970s. Featuring a tearful Indian named "Iron Eyes Cody," it alerted viewers to the accumulating bottle and can waste littering our countryside. The ad, however, wasn't quite what it appeared to be on the surface. A bit of sleuthing reveals that it was actually the centerpiece of a massive deflection campaign engineered by the beverage industry, which sought to point the finger at us, rather than corporations, emphasizing individual responsibility over collective action and governmental regulation. As a result, the global environmental threat of plastic pollution is still with us, a problem that has reached such crisis proportions that plastic waste has now penetrated to the deepest part of the world's oceans.

Finally, we get to the fossil fuel industry. Joined by billionaire plutocrats like the Koch brothers, the Mercers, and the Scaifes, companies such as ExxonMobil funneled billions of dollars into a disinformation campaign beginning in the late 1980s, working to discredit the science behind human-caused climate change and its linkage with fossil fuel burning. This science denial took precedence even as ExxonMobil's own team of scientists concluded that the impacts of continued fossil fuel use could lead to "devastating" climate-change impacts.

And the scientists were right. Decades later, thanks to that campaign, we are now witnessing the devastating effects of unchecked climate change. We see them playing out in the daily news cycle, on our television screens, in our newspaper headlines, and in our social media feeds. Coastal inundation, withering heat waves and droughts, devastating floods, raging wildfires: *this* is the face of dangerous climate change. It's a face that we increasingly recognize.

As a consequence, the forces of denial and delay—the fossil fuel companies, right-wing plutocrats, and oil-funded governments that continue to profit from our dependence on fossil fuels—can no longer insist, with a straight face, that nothing is happening. Outright denial of the physical evidence of climate change simply isn't credible anymore. So they have shifted to a softer form of denialism while keeping the oil flowing and fossil fuels burning, engaging in a multipronged offensive based on deception, distraction, and delay. This is the *new climate war*, and the planet is losing.

The enemy has masterfully executed a deflection campaign—inspired by those of the gun lobby, the tobacco industry, and beverage companies—aimed at shifting responsibility from corporations to individuals. Personal actions, from going vegan to avoiding flying, are increasingly touted as the primary solution to the climate crisis. Though these actions are worth taking, a fixation on voluntary action alone takes the pressure off of the push for governmental policies to hold corporate polluters accountable. In fact, one recent study suggests that the emphasis on small personal actions can actually undermine support for the substantive climate policies needed.[3] That's quite convenient for fossil fuel companies like ExxonMobil, Shell, and BP, which continue to make record profits every day that we remain, to quote former president George W. Bush, "addicted to fossil fuels."

The deflection campaign also provides an opportunity for the enemy to employ a "wedge" strategy dividing the climate advocacy community, exploiting a preexisting rift between climate advocates more focused on individual action and those emphasizing collective and policy action.

Using online bots and trolls, manipulating social media and Internet search engines, the enemy has deployed the sort of cyberweaponry honed during the 2016 US presidential election. They are the same tactics that gave us a climate-change-denying US president in Donald Trump. Malice, hatred, jealousy, fear, rage, bigotry, all of the most base, reptilian brain impulses—corporate polluters and their allies have waged a campaign to tap into all of that, seeking to sow division within the climate movement while generating fear and outrage on the part of their "base"—the disaffected right.

Meanwhile, these forces of inaction have effectively opposed measures to regulate or price carbon emissions, attacked viable alternatives like renewable energy, and advocated instead false solutions, such as coal burning with carbon capture, or unproven and potentially dangerous "geoengineering" schemes that involve massive manipulation of our planetary environment. Hypothetical future "innovations," the argument goes, will somehow save us, so there's no need for any current policy intervention. We can just throw a few dollars at "managing" the risks while we continue to pollute.

With climate progress sidelined by the Trump administration's dismantling of climate-friendly Environmental Protection Agency (EPA) policies such as the Clean Power Plan, along with its rollbacks in regulations on pollutants, its greenlighting of oil and gas pipelines, its direct handouts to a struggling coal industry, and its cheap leases to drill on public lands, the fossil fuel industry has enjoyed free rein to expand its polluting enterprise.

The enemy is also employing PSYOP in its war on climate action. It has promoted the narrative that climate-change impacts will be mild, innocuous, and easily adapted to, undermining any sense of *urgency*, while at the same time promoting the inevitability of climate change to dampen any sense of *agency*. This effort has been aided and abetted by individuals who are ostensible climate champions but have portrayed catastrophe as a *fait accompli*, either by overstating the damage to which we are already committed, by dismissing the possibility of mobilizing the action necessary to avert disaster, or by setting the standard so high (say, the very overthrow of market economics itself, that old chestnut) that any action seems doomed to failure. The enemy has been more than happy to amplify such notions.

But all is not lost. In this book, I aim to debunk false narratives that have derailed attempts to curb climate change and arm readers with a real path forward to preserving our planet. Our civilization can be saved, but only if we learn to recognize the current tactics of the enemy—that is, the forces of inaction—and how to combat them.

My decades of experience on the front lines of the battle to communicate the science of climate change and its implications have provided me with some unique insights. The "hockey stick" is the name that was given to a curve my colleagues and I published in 1998 demonstrating the steep uptick in planetary temperatures over the past century.[4] The graph achieved iconic status in the climate-change debate because it told a simple story, namely, that we were causing unprecedented warming of the planet by burning fossil fuels and pumping greenhouse gases into the atmosphere. Decades later, the hockey-stick curve is still attacked despite the many studies that have not only reaffirmed but extended our findings. Why? Because it remains a threat to vested interests.

The attacks on the hockey stick in the late 1990s drew me—then a young scientist—into the fray. In the process of defending myself and my work from politically motivated attacks, I became a reluctant and involuntary combatant in the climate wars. I've seen the enemy up close, in battle, for two decades now. I know how it operates and what tactics it uses. And I've been monitoring the dramatic shifts in those tactics over the past few years in response to the changing nature of the battlefield. I have adapted to those shifting tactics, changing how I engage the public and policymakers in my own efforts to inform and impact the public discourse. It is my intent, in this book, to share with you what I've learned, and to engage you, too, as a willing soldier in this battle to save our planet from a climate crisis before it is too late.

Here's the four point battle plan, which we'll return to at the end of the book:

Disregard the Doomsayers: The misguided belief that "it's too late" to act has been co-opted by fossil fuel interests and those advocating for them. It's just another way of legitimizing business-as-usual and a continued reliance on fossil fuels. We must reject the overt doom and gloom that we increasingly encounter in today's climate discourse.

A Child Shall Lead Them: The youngest generation is fighting tooth and nail to save their planet, and there is a moral authority and clarity in their message that none but the most jaded ears can fail to hear. They are the game-changers that climate advocates have been waiting for. We should model our actions after theirs and learn from their methods and their idealism.

Educate, Educate, Educate: Most hard-core climate-change deniers are unmovable. They view climate change through the prism of right-wing ideology and are impervious to facts. Don't waste your time and effort trying to convince them. But there are many honest, confused folks out there who are caught in the crossfire, victims of the climate-change disinformation campaign. We must help them out. Then they will be in a position to join us in battle.

Changing the System Requires Systemic Change: The fossil fuel disinformation machine wants to make it about the car you choose to drive, the food you choose to eat, and the lifestyle you choose to live rather than about the larger system and incentives. We need policies that will incentivize the needed shift away from fossil fuel burning toward a clean, green global economy. So-called leaders who resist the call for action must be removed from office.

It is easy to become overwhelmed by the scale of the challenge ahead of us. Change is always hard, and we are being asked to make a journey into an unfamiliar future. It is understandable to feel paralyzed with fear at the prospect of our planet's degradation. It's not surprising that anxiety and fear abound when it comes to the climate crisis and our efforts to deal with it.

We must understand, though, that the forces of denial and delay are using our fear and anxiety against us so we remain like deer in the headlights. I have colleagues who have expressed discomfort in framing our predicament as a "war." But, as I tell them, the surest way to lose a war is to refuse to recognize you're in one in the first place.[5] Whether we like it or not, and though clearly not of our own choosing, that's precisely where we find ourselves when it comes to the industry-funded effort to block action on climate.

So we must be brave and find the strength to fight on, channeling that fear and anxiety into motivation and action. The stakes are simply too great.

As we continue to explore the cosmos, we are finding other planetary systems, some with planets that are even somewhat Earth-like in character. Some are similar in size to ours, and roughly the right distance from their star to reside in the so-called "habitable zone." Some may harbor liquid water, an ingredient that is likely essential for life. Yet we have still not encountered any evidence of life elsewhere in our solar system, our galaxy, or indeed the entire universe. Life appears to be very rare indeed, complex life even more so. And intelligent life? We may, at least for all intents and purposes, be alone. Just us drifting aboard this "Spaceship Earth." No other place to dock, no alternative ports at which to sojourn, with air to breathe, water to drink, or food to consume.

We are the custodians of an amazing gift. We have a Goldilocks planet, with just the right atmospheric composition, just the right distance from its star, yielding just the right temperature range for life, with liquid-water oceans and oxygen-rich air. Every person we will ever know, every animal or plant we will ever encounter, is reliant on conditions remaining just this way.

To continue to knowingly alter those conditions in a manner that threatens humanity and other life forms, simply so a few very large corporations can continue to make record profits, is not just unacceptable, or unethical—it would be the most immoral act in the history of human civilization: not just a crime against humanity, but a crime against our planet. We cannot be passive bystanders as polluters work toward making that eventuality come to pass. My intent with this book is to do everything within my power to make sure we aren't.

CHAPTER 1

The Architects of Misinformation and Misdirection

Doubt is our product, since it is the best means of competing with the "body of fact" that exists in the minds of the general public.
—Unnamed tobacco executive, Brown and Williamson (1969)

THE ORIGINS OF THE ONGOING CLIMATE WARS LIE IN DISINFORMATION campaigns waged decades ago, when the findings of science began to collide with the agendas of powerful vested interests. These campaigns were aimed at obscuring public understanding of the underlying science and discrediting the scientific message, often by attacking the messengers themselves—that is, the scientists whose work hinted that we might have a problem on our hands. Over the years, tactics were developed and refined by public relations agents employed to undermine facts and scientifically based warnings.

KILL THE MESSENGER

Our journey takes us all the way back to the late nineteenth century, to Thomas Stockmann, an amateur scientist in a small Norwegian town. The local economy was dependent on tourism tied to the town's medicinal hot springs. After discovering that the town's water supply was being polluted by chemicals from a local tannery, Stockmann was thwarted in his efforts to alert the townspeople of the threat, first when the local paper refused to publish an article he had written about his findings, then when he was shouted down as he attempted to announce his findings at a town meeting. He and his family were treated as outcasts. His daughter was expelled from school, and the townspeople stoned his home, breaking all the windows and terrifying his family. They considered leaving town but decided to stay, hoping—in vain—that the townspeople would ultimately come around to accepting, and indeed appreciating, his dire warnings.

That's the plot of the 1882 Henrik Ibsen play *An Enemy of the People* (made into a film in 1978 that starred Steve McQueen in one of his final and arguably finest performances). The story is fictional, but it depicts a conflict that would be familiar to audiences in the late nineteenth century. The eerie prescience of this tale today, when an anti-science president dismisses the media as an "enemy of the American people," and conservative politicians knowingly allow an entire city to be endangered by a lead-poisoned water supply, has not been lost on some observers.[1] *An Enemy of the People* is the canonical cautionary tale of the clash between science and industrial or corporate interests. And it serves as an apt metaphor for the climate wars that would take place a century later.

But before we get there, let us next flash-forward to the mid-twentieth century, where we encounter the granddaddy of modern industry disinformation campaigns. This campaign was orchestrated by tobacco industry leaders in their effort to hide evidence of the addictive and deadly nature of their product. "Doubt is our product," confessed a Brown and Williamson executive in 1969.[2] The memo containing the admission was eventually released as part of a massive legal settlement between the tobacco industry and the US government. This and other internal documents showed that the companies' own scientists had established the health threats of smoking as early as the 1950s. Nevertheless, the companies chose to engage in an elaborate campaign to hide those threats from the public.

Tobacco interests even hired experts to discredit the work of other researchers who had arrived at the very same conclusions. Chief among these attack dogs was Frederick Seitz, a solid-state physicist who was also the former head of the US National Academy of Sciences and a recipient of the prestigious Presidential Medal of Science. Those impressive credentials made him a valuable asset for the tobacco industry. Tobacco giant R.J. Reynolds would eventually hire Seitz and pay him half a million dollars to use his scientific standing and stature to attack any and all science (and scientists) linking tobacco to human health problems.[3] Seitz was the original science-denier-for-hire. There would be many more.

Pesticide manufacturers adopted the tobacco industry's playbook in the 1960s, after Rachel Carson warned the public of the danger that DDT (dichlorodiphenyltrichloroethane) posed to the environment. Her classic 1962 book *Silent Spring* ushered in the modern environmental movement.[4] Carson described how DDT was decimating populations of bald eagles and other birds by thinning their eggs and killing the embryos within. The pesticide was accumulating in food webs, soils, and rivers, creating an increasingly dire threat to wildlife—and ultimately, humans. Eventually, the United States banned DDT, but not until 1972.

Carson was awarded for her efforts with a full-on character assassination campaign by industry groups who denounced her as "radical," "communist," and "hysterical" (with all its misogynist connotations—misogyny, and racism as well, as we will see, have become inextricably linked to climate-change denialism). The president of Monsanto, the largest producer of DDT, denounced her as "a fanatic defender of the cult of the balance of nature."[5] Her critics even labeled her a mass murderer.[6] Even today, the industry front group known as the Competitive Enterprise Institute (CEI) continues to defame the long-deceased scientist by insisting that "millions of people around the world suffer the painful and often deadly effects of malaria because one person sounded a false alarm. That person is Rachel Carson."[7] What Carson's posthumous attackers don't want you to know is that Carson never called for a ban on DDT, just an end to its indiscriminate use. It was ultimately phased out not because of the environmental damages that Carson exposed but because it had steadily lost its effectiveness as mosquitoes grew resistant to it. That was something that Carson, ironically, had warned would happen as a result of overuse.[8] And here we are thus afforded an early example of how the short-sighted practices of greedy corporations looking to maximize near-term profits often prove self-defeating.

Credibility and integrity are a scientist's bread and butter and greatest asset. It is the currency that allows scientists to serve as trusted communicators to the public. That's why the forces of denial targeted Carson directly, accusing her of all manner of scientific misconduct. In response to the controversy, President John F. Kennedy convened a committee to review Carson's claims. The committee published its report in May 1963, exonerating her and her scientific findings.[9] Science denialists are never deterred by pesky things like "facts," however. And so the attacks continue today. Consider a 2012 commentary that appeared in conservative *Forbes* magazine entitled "Rachel Carson's Deadly Fantasies," by Henry I. Miller and Gregory Conko. Miller and Conko are Fellows at the aforementioned Competitive Enterprise Institute. Miller is also a scientific advisory board member of an industry front group known as the George C. Marshall Institute (GMI), and, unsurprisingly, a tobacco industry advocate.[10] In the piece, they accuse Carson of "gross misrepresentations," "atrocious" scholarship, and "egregious academic misconduct," despite the fact that her scientific findings have been overwhelmingly affirmed by decades of research.[11] Though bird populations continue to be imperiled by pesticides, more sonorous springs did largely return. And for that, we owe a great debt of gratitude to Rachel Carson.[12]

Due to the work of Carson and other scientists studying the effects of industrial toxins on humans and the environment, awareness of other threats emerged in the 1970s. Lead pollution generated by the gasoline and paint industries, for example, came under scrutiny. Enter Herbert Needleman, whose story is disturbingly reminiscent of Thomas Stockmann's from Ibsen's play. Needleman was a professor and researcher at the University of Pittsburgh School of Medicine. His research identified a link between environmental lead contamination and childhood brain development. Sounding a familiar note, lead industry advocates sought to discredit him and his research, engaging in a character assassination campaign that included unfounded accusations against him of scientific misconduct.[13] He was exonerated—*twice*. The first exoneration was the result of a thorough investigation by the National Institutes of Health. Then, in what might sound like the scientific equivalent of double jeopardy, there was a separate investigation by his university, during which he was locked out of his own files, with bars placed on his file cabinets. No evidence of impropriety ever emerged. His research on how to detect chronic lead exposure—validated by numerous independent studies in the intervening decades—likely has saved thousands of lives and prevented brain damage in thousands more.[14] "Enemy of the People" indeed.

DENIAL GOES GLOBAL

In the 1970s and 1980s we begin to see the emergence of truly *global* environmental threats, including acid rain and ozone depletion. Industry groups whose bottom line might be impacted by environmental regulations began to significantly step up their attacks on the science demonstrating these dangers, and of course on the scientists themselves.

Frederick Seitz—the granddaddy of denialism who was enlisted by the tobacco industry in its war on science—was provided lavish industry funding in the mid-1980s to create the George C. Marshall Institute.[15] Seitz recruited as partners astrophysicist Robert Jastrow (founder of the venerable NASA Goddard Institute for Space Studies) and oceanographer William Nierenberg (onetime director of the revered Scripps Institution for Oceanography in La Jolla, California). These three individuals, as Naomi Oreskes and Erik M. Conway noted in their 2010 book *Merchants of Doubt*, were what could be called *free-market fundamentalists*. None of them had training in environmental science. What they *did* possess was an ideological distrust of efforts to limit what they saw as the freedom of individuals or corporations. As such, they played willfully into the agenda of regulation-averse special interests.[16] Borrowing from the very same tactics Seitz had cut his teeth on as a tobacco industry attack dog a decade earlier, the GMI crew would sow doubt in the areas of science that proved threatening to the powerful vested interests they represented.

One of these scientific issues was acid rain, a phenomenon I'm intimately familiar with, having grown up in New England during the 1970s. At that time, lakes, rivers, streams, and forests throughout eastern North America were being destroyed by increasingly acidic rainfall. The scientist Gene Likens and others discovered the origins of the problem: midwestern coal-fired power plants that were producing sulfur dioxide pollution. Likens would later become the "environmental sustainability czar" for the University of Connecticut.

In April 2017, I gave a lecture at the University of Connecticut in which I revealed some of my own experiences in the crosshairs of the climate-change-denial machine. At the dinner following the lecture, Likens was seated next to me. He turned to me and said, "Your stories sound a lot like mine!" As we ate our salads, he regaled me with stories that were disturbingly familiar: nasty letters and complaints to his bosses; hostile reception by conservative politicians; attacks from industry-funded hatchet men and politicians seeking to discredit his scientific findings. As Likens said some years ago in an interview, "It was bad. It was really nasty. I had a *contract* put out on me."

Likens was referring to a coal industry trade group known as the Edison Electric Institute that had offered nearly *half a million dollars* to anybody willing to discredit him.[17] William Nierenberg, the aforementioned member of the GMI trio, in essence took up that challenge when Ronald Reagan appointed him to chair a panel investigating the acid rain issue. The facts, however, proved stubborn, and the panel's conclusions, published in a 1984 report, largely reaffirmed the findings of Likens and other scientific experts. But hidden away in an appendix written by a contrarian scientist, S. Fred Singer, was a passage suggesting that, as Oreskes and Conway put it, "we really *didn't* know enough to move forward with emissions controls." The passage was just dismissive enough to allow the Reagan administration to justify its policy of inaction.[18]

Fortunately, the forces of denial and inaction did not prevail. Americans recognized the problem and demanded action, and politicians ultimately responded. That's precisely how things are supposed to work in a representative democracy. In 1990, it was a Republican president, George H.W. Bush, who signed the Clean Air Act, which required coal-fired power plants to scrub sulfur emissions before they exited the smokestacks. He even introduced a vehicle known as "cap and trade," a market-based mechanism that allows polluters to buy and sell a limited allotment of pollution permits. Cap-and-trade policy is, ironically, now pilloried by most Republicans. It was the brainchild of Bush's EPA administrator, William K. Reilly, a modern environmental hero whom I'm proud to know and call my friend.

My family frequently goes on vacation to Big Moose Lake in the western Adirondacks. My wife's family has been going there for seventy years. Her parents remember back in the 1970s when the lake was so acidic you literally didn't need to take any showers. A jump in the lake would clean you right off. The waters were crystal clear, because they were lifeless. The wildlife has returned now—I see and hear it when we're there, from the bugs to the fish and frogs to the ducks and snapping turtles, along with the haunting sound of the loons. You sometimes see small teams of scientists out in boats collecting samples of the water in the various lakes, examining its chemistry and contents. The affected ecosystems still haven't recovered completely. Environmental pollution can disrupt food chains, forest ecosystems, and water and soil chemistry in a way that can persist for decades or centuries even after the pollutants themselves are gone. But we are on the road to recovery in the Adirondacks, thanks—dare I say it—to *market-based* mechanisms for solving an environmental problem.

In the 1980s, scientists recognized that chlorofluorocarbons (CFCs), used at the time in spray cans and refrigerators, were responsible for the growing hole in the ozone layer in the lower stratosphere that protects us from damaging, high-energy ultraviolet radiation from the Sun. The erosion of the ozone layer brought with it an increasing incidence of skin cancer and other adverse health impacts in the Southern Hemisphere. My friend Bill Brune, former head of the Department of Meteorology at Penn State, was one of the original scientists researching the relevant atmospheric chemistry. As he has written, "Some of the scientists who carried out this seminal research decided to become advocates for action to mitigate the likely harm from a depleted ozone layer. These scientist-advocates were subjected to intense criticism."[19] That criticism, as Bill noted, took several forms: "Manufacturers, users, and their government representatives initiated public relations campaigns designed not to illuminate but to obscure, to throw doubt on the hypothesis and the weight of scientific evidence, and to otherwise convince lawmakers and the public that the data were too uncertain to act upon." He added, "When results inevitably began to refute their views, or whenever their own work was proven wrong or rejected for publication, these contrarian scientists, government representatives, and industry spokesmen then changed tactics, to denigrate the entire peer-review process." Among those contrarian scientists was the very same S. Fred Singer we encountered in the context of acid rain denial. Get used to that name.

Disregarding the naysayers, in 1987 forty-six countries—including the United States under Reagan—signed the Montreal Protocol, banning the production of CFCs. Since then, the ozone hole has shrunk to its smallest extent in decades. Environmental policy *actually* works. But, with both acid rain and ozone depletion, policy solutions came only because of unrelenting pressure on policymakers by citizens combined with continued bipartisan good faith and support on the part of politicians for systemic solutions to environmental threats. That good faith all but disappeared with the advent of the Trump administration. Indeed, after his 2016 election, Trump appointed individuals to important positions who not only denied the reality and threat of climate change but had played critical roles decades ago in industry-led efforts to deny both ozone depletion and acid rain. Think of them as all-purpose deniers-for-hire.[20]

You might also call them spiritual successors of the George C. Marshall Institute, Frederick Seitz's science-denying think tank. By the late 1980s, the GMI was largely focused on environmental issues. But as it happens, it was not acid rain or ozone depletion that brought the institute into existence in the first place. It was instead the threat that the findings of science posed to an entirely different vested interest: the military-industrial complex. During the late cold war, leading defense contractors, such as Lockheed-Martin and Northrop Grumman, were profiting from the escalating arms race between the United States and the Soviet Union. They stood to benefit in particular from Reagan's proposed Strategic Defense Initiative, otherwise known as Star Wars, an antiballistic missile program designed to shoot down nuclear missiles in space. Standing in their way, however, was, quite literally, one lone scientist.

SCIENTIST AS WARRIOR

Carl Sagan was the David Duncan Professor of Astronomy and Space Sciences and director of the Laboratory for Planetary Studies at Cornell University. He was a respected, accomplished researcher with an impressive record of achievement in earth and planetary science. Sagan did seminal work on the "Faint Young Sun Paradox," the surprising fact that Earth was habitable more than three billion years ago despite the fact that the Sun was 30 percent dimmer then. The explanation, Sagan realized, must be a magnified greenhouse effect. This work is so fundamental that it constitutes the first chapter in the textbook I've used to teach first-year Penn State students about Earth history.[21]

Sagan, however, was far more than a scientist. He was cultural phenomenon. He had an unmatched ability to engage the public with science. Not only could he explain it to the person on the street, he could get people excited about it. I can speak to this matter on a personal level. It is Carl Sagan who inspired *me* to pursue a career in science.

I had always had an aptitude for math and science, but it had constituted a path of least resistance, not a passion. Then Sagan's popular PBS series *Cosmos* premiered at the start of my freshman year in high school. Sagan showed me the magic of scientific inquiry. He revealed a cosmos that was more wondrous than I could have imagined, and the preciousness of our place in it as simple inhabitants of a tiny blue dot just barely discernible from the outer reaches of our solar system. And the questions! How did life form? Is there more of it out there? Are there other intelligent civilizations? Why haven't they contacted us? I pondered these questions and so many more that Sagan raised in the epic thirteen-part series. Sagan made me realize it was possible to spend a lifetime satisfying one's scientific curiosity by posing and answering such fundamental existential questions.

Sadly, I never got a chance to meet my hero. I finished my PhD in geology and geophysics in 1996, the very same year Sagan passed away. Being in the same field as Sagan, I almost certainly would have met him at meetings or conferences had I entered the profession just a few years earlier. But I have had the pleasure of getting to know him through his writings, and to make the acquaintance of some who knew him well. That includes his daughter, Sasha, a writer who is continuing her father's legacy of inspiring us about the cosmos and our place in it.[22]

Sagan was so compelling and charismatic a personality that he quickly became the voice of science for the nation. On Johnny Carson's *The Tonight Show*, he would mesmerize national audiences with his observations, insights, and often amusing anecdotes. In so doing, he literally knocked Carson's previous go-to science guy out of the lineup for good.[23] That was none other than astrophysicist Robert Jastrow, the aforementioned GMI cofounder. Which brings us back to the main thrust of our story.

Carl Sagan became increasingly political in the 1980s as he recognized the mounting threat of a nuclear arms raise. He used his public prominence, media savvy, and unrivaled communication skills to raise awareness about the existential threat posed by a global thermonuclear war. Sagan explained to the public that the threat went well beyond the immediate death and destruction and the resulting nuclear radiation. The massive detonation of nuclear warheads during a thermonuclear war, Sagan and his colleagues argued in the scientific literature, might produce enough dust and debris to block out a sufficient amount of sunlight to induce a state of perpetual winter, or, as they termed it, "nuclear winter."[24]

Humanity, in short, might suffer the same fate the dinosaurs encountered following a massive asteroid impact: a sunlight-blocking dust storm that ended their reign sixty-five million years ago. Sagan helped bring about public understanding of that scenario through his various media interviews and in an article for the widely read Sunday newspaper insert *Parade* magazine.

Sagan feared that Reagan's Strategic Defense Initiative, which many cold war hawks and military contractors supported, would lead to an escalation of tensions between the United States and the Soviet Union and a dangerous buildup in nuclear arms, portending the very nuclear winter scenario he so feared. But, as Oreskes and Conway noted in *Merchants of Doubt*, the cold war–era physicists at GMI saw these legitimate concerns about SDI as scare tactics employed by Soviet-sympathizing peaceniks.[25] In their eyes, the very concept of nuclear winter was a threat to our security. Working with conservative politicians and industry special interests, the GMI trio sought to discredit the case for concern by going directly after the underlying science—first by discrediting the scientist, Carl Sagan, personally. The attacks took place in congressional briefings and in the pages of mainstream newspapers, where they solicited and wrote articles and op-eds to debunk the findings of Sagan and his colleagues. This campaign even included intimidating public television stations that considered running a program on nuclear winter.[26]

Here's why Sagan's anti-SDI campaign is germane to the central topic of this book: The nuclear winter simulations that Sagan and his colleagues conducted were based on early-generation global *climate models*. So if you didn't like the science of nuclear winter, you *really* weren't going to like the science of climate change, which revealed the culpability of the same powerful polluting interests that groups like GMI were defending. With the collapse of the cold war in the late 1980s, the GMI crew, as Oreskes and Conway noted, needed another issue to focus on. Acid rain and ozone depletion would keep them busy through the early 1990s. But as these matters faded from view (in substantial part because even *Republicans*—as noted earlier—ultimately supported action), GMI and like-minded critics needed another scientific boogeyman to justify their existence. Climate change surely fit the bill.

CHAPTER 2

The Climate Wars

There's no war that will end all wars.
— HARUKI MURAKAMI

When the rich wage war, it is the poor who die.
— JEAN-PAUL SARTRE

AND SO, IT BEGINS

In the early 1990s I was a graduate student working on my PhD in the field of climate science within the Department of Geology and Geophysics at Yale University. I had been lured away from the Physics Department, where I had been studying the behavior of matter at the quantum scale. Instead, I would now study the behavior of our climate system at the global scale. For an ambitious young physicist, climate science was the great western frontier. There were still big, wide-open questions where a young scientist with math and physics skills could make substantial contributions at the forefront of the science. This was my opportunity to realize the vision that Carl Sagan had instilled in me as a youth—a vision of science as a quest to understand our place in the larger planetary and cosmic environment.

My PhD adviser was a scientist named Barry Saltzman, who played a key role in the discovery of the phenomenon of "chaos"— one of the great scientific developments of the twentieth century.

Chaos is responsible, among other things, for the fact that one cannot predict the precise details of the weather beyond a week or so out. Barry was a skeptic—in the true and honest sense of the word. He was unconvinced in the early 1990s that we could establish the human impact on our climate. This was a tenable position then, given that the climate models being used were still quite crude and that the warming signal in the roughly one century of global temperature data was only perhaps just beginning to peek out from the background noise of natural variability.

There were other scientists, such as James Hansen, the prominent director of the NASA Goddard Institute for Space Studies (yes—the same institute that had previously been directed by none other than Robert Jastrow), who had a different view. Hansen felt that we could already demonstrate that human activity—specifically, the generation of greenhouse gases such as carbon dioxide from the burning of fossil fuels like oil, coal, and natural gas—was warming the planet. On a record hot June day in Washington, DC, in 1988, Hansen had testified to Congress, saying, "It is time to stop waffling. . . . [T]he evidence is pretty strong." The Reagan administration had become increasingly unhappy with Hansen's public statements even before that June day. As a NASA civil servant, he was subject to having his written congressional testimonies vetted by the administration, and starting in 1986, the White House's Office of Management and Budget had repeatedly edited them in such a way as to downplay their impact. Exasperated, Hansen finally announced in bombshell 1989 testimony that his words were being altered by White House.[1]

As I began to study climate science in the early 1990s, my own position was closer to Barry Saltzman's than to Hansen's. My research involved the study of natural climate variability based on the use of theoretical climate models, observational data, and long-term paleoclimatic records, including tree rings and ice cores. This work suggested that there were important mechanisms that led to natural climate fluctuations with time scales of fifty to seventy years, almost as long as the instrumental temperature record itself. Such natural

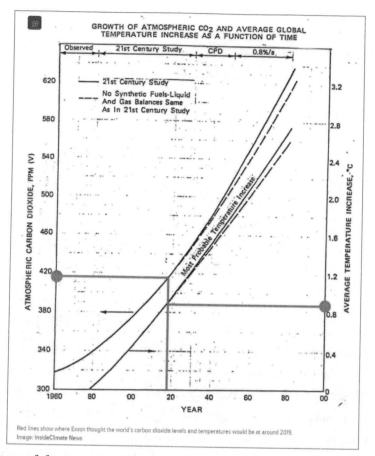

GROWTH OF ATMOSPHERIC CO₂ AND AVERAGE GLOBAL
TEMPERATURE INCREASE AS A FUNCTION OF TIME

Red lines show where Exxon thought the world's carbon dioxide levels and temperatures would be at around 2019.
Image: InsideClimate News

Prediction of future CO_2 rise and temperature increase from an internal 1982 ExxonMobil document. The current observed CO_2 level and global temperature increase are indicated by the thick horizontal and vertical lines. The actual values are 415 parts per million (ppm) CO_2 and a temperature increase of 0.8°C (1.44°F) since 1960, both within the range of the predictions. Figure 3 in Exxon report of November 12, 1982, subject line "CO_2 'Greenhouse' Effect," 82EAP 266, under Exxon letterhead of M. B. Glaser, manager, Environmental Affairs Program, posted by *Inside Climate News* at http://insideclimatenews.org/sites/default/files/documents/1982%20Exxon %20Primer%20on%20CO2%20Greenhouse%20Effect.pdf, p. 7.

long-term climate fluctuations, at the very least, obscured the impacts of human-caused climate change.[2]

It's important to keep some perspective here. Although scientists were still debating whether we had yet detected a human impact on the climate, there was a broad consensus on the basics—i.e., that burning fossil fuels and increasing the concentration of greenhouse gases in the atmosphere would substantially warm the planet, something that had been established by the great Swedish scientist Svante Arrhenius in the late 1800s. And it is worth recalling, from the introduction, the words of ExxonMobil's own experts in the 1970s: *"There is general scientific agreement that . . . mankind is influencing the global climate . . . through carbon dioxide release from the burning of fossil fuels"* (emphasis added.)[3] The famous Danish physicist Niels Bohr is reported to have once said, "Predictions are hard. Especially about the future." Well, Exxon's own scientists made an impressive one back in 1982, more or less predicting spot-on the increase in CO_2 concentrations and the resulting warming we would now see given business-as-usual burning of fossil fuels.[4] The coal industry also knew, as far back as the 1960s, that their carbon emissions were warming the planet.[5]

Nonetheless, the fact that there was still some real division within the climate research community on a matter as seemingly fundamental as whether we had yet firmly detected a human influence on climate meant there was a preexisting cleavage into which the forces of denial could attempt to drive a wedge and generate uncertainty and controversy about the science. For the fossil fuel industry, time was of the essence, because policy action aimed at addressing the problem appeared imminent.

During the presidential election of 1988, George H.W. Bush had pledged to meet the "greenhouse effect with the White House effect." He appointed as his science adviser a physicist named David Allan Bromley. Bromley was a professor from the Yale Physics Department, where I was doing my degree at the time, and I still remember him returning to New Haven to give a special departmental seminar on climate change and climate modeling. Bromley was no left-leaning environmentalist. But he understood the irrefutable physics behind climate change. Meanwhile, Bush's EPA administrator, the aforementioned William K. Reilly, *was* an environmentalist, and he strongly supported action on climate. By 1991, Bush had signaled that he would sign the United Nations Framework Convention on Climate Change (UNFCCC).

But there was some dissent within the administration. Bush's chief of staff, a Massachusetts Institute of Technology (MIT)–trained engineer named John Sununu, was—and remarkably enough, remains today—a climate-change denier. He drew heavily from an unpublished 1989 white paper by the GMI trio of Jastrow, Seitz, and Nierenberg (published the following year as a book, *Global Warming: What Does the Science Tell Us?*) that blamed global warming on solar activity. In his capacity as a representative of GMI, Nierenberg secured a meeting with White House staff, where he presented their dismissive view of climate change. At the very least, this helped create a schism within the Bush administration and blunted the momentum behind climate action.[6]

With the advent in 1988 of the United Nations Intergovernmental Panel on Climate Change (IPCC), the task of refuting the scientific evidence for human-caused global warming became too great for a single small organization like GMI. The cavalry would soon arrive, however. A consortium of fossil fuel interests known as the Global Climate Coalition, which included ExxonMobil, Shell, British Petroleum (BP), Chevron, the American Petroleum Institute, and others, came together in 1989, joining forces with other industry think tanks and front groups, including the genteel-sounding "Heartland Institute" and "Competitive Enterprise Institute." Collectively they constituted what Oreskes and Conway analogized in *Merchants of Doubt* as a "Potemkin Village," a facade of impressive-sounding organizations, institutions, and individuals who would challenge—through newspaper op-eds, public debates, fake scientific articles, and any other means available—the basic science of climate change. They would seek to carry the argument that the science was too uncertain, the models too unreliable, the data too short and too error-ridden, the role of natural variability too unknown to establish any clear human role in global warming and climate change.

David and Charles Koch, otherwise known as the "Koch brothers"—the owners of the largest privately held fossil fuel interest (Koch Industries)—are best known for their highly visible role in funding climate-change denialism in recent years. But they played a key early role here as well, something that has only recently come to light.[7] Under the auspices of the Cato Institute, the libertarian think tank that they founded and funded, they held the very first known climate-change-denial conference back in June 1991. Titled "Global Environmental Crisis: Science or Politics?," it was a sort of Council of Elrond of climate-change denialism. It featured two scientists in particular who would join the ranks of Seitz, Jastrow, and Nierenberg, leveraging their scientific and academic credentials to grant an air of legitimacy to broadsides aimed at discrediting mainstream climate science.

Among the invited speakers was Richard S. Lindzen of MIT, who was quoted in the brochure advertising the conference as saying there was "very little evidence at all" that climate change was a threat. His credentials, like Seitz's, were impressive. He was a chaired professor of meteorology at MIT and a member of the National Academy of Sciences. Like Seitz, he has also received money from fossil fuel interests for his advocacy on their behalf.[8] Scientifically speaking, Lindzen is best known for his controversial insistence that climate models overestimate the warming effect of increasing greenhouse gas concentrations because of processes—related to clouds or atmospheric moisture—that he continues to claim are either missing or poorly represented in the models. Such processes in principle can either tend to increase warming (in a "positive feedback") or decrease warming (in a "negative feedback"). Lindzen, however, has remained focused only on the latter. It seems, indeed, that he has never met a negative feedback he didn't like. He has spent much of his professional career arguing for supposedly missing negative feedbacks, only to have other scientists continually shoot them down.[9] Lindzen has even been so bold as to argue that a doubling of CO_2 concentrations (which we will reach in a matter of decades, given business-as-usual burning of fossil fuels) would raise global temperatures only a very minimal 1°C (1.8°F). The claim strains credulity, given that the planet has now *already* warmed up more than that after only a roughly 50 percent increase in CO_2 concentrations. Indeed, a vast array of evidence, including the response of the climate to volcanic eruptions, the coming and going of the ice ages, and past warm periods, such as the early Cretaceous, when dinosaurs roamed the planet, all point toward warming that is roughly three times (3°C, or 5.4°F) as large as Lindzen predicted.

Also among the speakers at this influential early conference was S. Fred Singer, whom we can now begin to recognize as a sort of all-purpose denier-for-hire. Like Seitz's, Singer's origins were as an academic and a scientist, and like Seitz, he would leave the academic world in the early 1990s to advocate against what he called the "junk science" of acid rain, ozone depletion, tobacco health threats, and, of course, climate change, receiving substantial industry funding for his efforts.[10]

Singer's most significant role relates to the legacy of the revered atmospheric scientist Roger Revelle. Revelle made fundamental contributions to our current understanding of human-caused climate change, providing key evidence in the 1950s that the burning of fossil fuels was increasing greenhouse gas concentrations. He made some of the early projections of future warming. Revelle is also credited with having inspired Al Gore's concern about climate change when Gore was a student at Harvard.

Shortly before Revelle passed away in 1991, Singer added him as a coauthor to a paper he had written for the journal *Cosmos*, published by the Cosmos Club, a Washington, DC, intellectual society. The paper was nearly identical to an earlier dismissive article by Singer. It disputed the evidence that climate change is human caused. Both Revelle's secretary and his former graduate student Justin Lancaster have suggested that Revelle was uncomfortable with the manuscript and that the dismissive framing was added after Revelle, who was gravely ill (and died just months after the paper's publication), had an opportunity to see the final version. Lancaster has stated that Singer hoodwinked Revelle into adding his name to the article and that Revelle was "intensely embarrassed that his name was associated" with it. Lancaster characterized Singer's behavior as unethical and, furthermore, said he had a strong suspicion of Singer's ultimate objective: to discredit Al Gore and his campaign in the early 1990s to raise public awareness about the threat of climate change. Lancaster stands by these charges despite legal threats against him by Singer.[11]

THE BATTLEFIELD TAKES SHAPE

We now fast-forward a few years, to late 1995, when it would all come to a head. The scientific evidence for human-caused climate change had grown ever more compelling. The observations, the model simulations, all seemed to be coming into clear alignment. My once skeptical PhD adviser Barry Saltzman and I were coauthors on an article making this very case.[12] Industry-funded resistance to the science, however, had grown proportionately. Dozens of front groups and scientist deniers-for-hire now occupied an increasingly fortified Potemkin Village of industry-funded climate-change denial. The battlefield had taken shape, the forces were mobilized. Climate change was the defining political issue of the time.

By late November 1995, the Intergovernmental Panel on Climate Change would hold its final plenary in Madrid for its Second Assessment Report. The purpose of the report was to summarize the current consensus among the world's scientists on climate change. As remarked earlier, that consensus was rapidly converging toward acceptance of the reality and threat of climate change. Nonetheless, a fierce dispute arose between the scientists authoring the report and government delegates representing a small subset of countries—Saudi Arabia and Kuwait, in particular, two major oil-exporting nations that profited greatly from the continued extraction and sale of fossil fuels. As science journalist William K. Stevens put it, these nations "made common cause with American industry lobbyists to try to weaken the conclusions of the report."[13]

The question was whether one could state with confidence that human-caused climate change was now detectable. The scientist with primary responsibility for the relevant section of the report was Ben Santer, a climate researcher at the US Department of Energy's Lawrence Livermore National Laboratory in California who had published a series of important articles on the topic. The recipient of a MacArthur "genius award" in recognition of his fundamental contributions to our understanding of climate change, Santer and his IPCC coauthors concluded, based on the existing climate literature, concluded that "the balance of evidence suggests an *appreciable* human influence on climate."[14]

The Saudi delegate complained that the word "appreciable" was too strong. For two whole days, the scientists haggled with the Saudi delegate over this single word in the "Summary for Policy Makers" of the report—the part of the report most likely to be read by politicians and most likely to be reported upon by journalists. They purportedly debated nearly thirty different alternatives before IPCC chair Bert Bolin found a mutually acceptable word: "discernible." The term acknowledged that human activity played at least some role in observed climate change, as the scientists had argued, while making it sound like one almost had to squint to see it, conceding a level of uncertainty that no doubt pleased the oil-rich Saudis.

The fact that two entire days at the final plenary were devoted to debating a single word in the report's summary gives you some idea of how politically charged the debate over climate change had become by late 1995. Ben Santer was the scientist most directly connected to the emerging scientific consensus. In the tradition of Rachel Carson, Herbert Needleman, and Gene Likens, he would be savaged by industry groups and their now familiar attack dogs in an effort to undermine his credibility.

Just a few months after the IPCC plenary, in February 1996, S. Fred Singer published a letter in the journal *Science* attacking Santer. He disputed the key IPCC finding that model predictions matched the observed warming, claiming that the observations instead showed cooling. This was, of course, wrong. They showed nothing of the sort.

They demonstrated clear evidence of warming. But climate-change deniers would cling to one curious dataset—a satellite-derived estimate of atmospheric temperatures produced by two contrarian scientists from the University of Alabama at Huntsville, John Christy and Roy Spencer—that appeared to contradict all the other evidence of warming. The cooling claimed by Christy and Spencer would later be shown to be an artifact of serial errors on their part. But not before climate-change deniers would milk it for all it was worth.[15]

Singer went on to claim that inclusion of Santer's work in the report somehow violated IPCC rules because the work hadn't yet been published. In fact, most of the work had been published, and in any case, the IPCC rules did not require a work cited to be published at the time of the report, but simply that the work be available to reviewers upon request.

Meanwhile, the aforementioned Global Climate Coalition circulated a report to Washington, DC, insiders repeating these false allegations and accusing Santer of "political tampering" and "scientific cleansing." The latter charge, echoing language of the Third Reich, was especially odious given that Santer had lost relatives in Nazi Germany. The claims were of course false. At the request of the IPCC leadership, Santer had simply removed a redundant summary to ensure that the structure of the chapter on which he was lead author would conform to that of the other chapters. A few months later, Frederick Seitz published an op-ed in the *Wall Street Journal* repeating the same false allegations against Santer.[16]

Climate-change deniers were able to spread false charges about Santer faster (and in more prominent venues) than he—or the rest of the scientific community—could possibly hope to refute them. Santer's integrity was impugned, and his job and his life were threatened. It's an example of what I later termed the "Serengeti Strategy," in which industry-funded attackers go after individual scientists just as predators on the Serengeti plain of Africa hunt their prey: attempting to pick off vulnerable individuals by isolating them from the rest of the herd. When my work was prominently featured in the next IPCC report, Ben Santer commented, "There are people who believe that if they bring down Mike Mann, they can bring down the IPCC."[17] They thought I was easy prey.

THE SEITZ DECEPTION

Fast-forward a couple more years, to 1997. The Kyoto Protocol, an addition to the United Nations Framework Convention on Climate Change, had just been adopted. It would commit the countries of the world to substantial reductions in carbon emissions with the aim of avoiding "dangerous anthropogenic interference with the climate system."[18] The pressure on policymakers was mounting. The forces of denial and delay would need to marshal additional forces if they were to forestall action on climate.

In so doing, they would find common cause with some increasingly odd characters. Consider Arthur B. Robinson, a chemist with admittedly impressive credentials. A onetime protégé of Nobel Prize–winning chemist Linus Pauling, Robinson heads up a family-run outfit in Cave Junction, Oregon, that calls itself the Oregon Institute of Science and Medicine. Robinson has advanced some very odd scientific hypotheses over the years, including the discredited claim that vitamin C causes cancer. He has also shown an interest in collecting and analyzing other people's urine. And yes—I know you're wondering—Robinson is also a climate-change denier, a position that has more recently ingratiated him with the right-wing climate-change-denying Mercer family as well as the Trump administration.[19]

In 1998, one year after Kyoto, Robinson joined forces with our old friend Frederick Seitz to undermine support for the protocol. The two organized a petition drive opposing the international agreement. To this day, the "Oregon Petition," with thirty-one thousand nominal "scientist" signatories, is touted as evidence of widespread scientific opposition to the research underlying models of human-caused climate change. This is in spite of the fact that few of the supposed signatories were actually *scientists* (the list included the names Geri Halliwell, one of the Spice Girls; and B. J. Hunnicutt, a character from the TV series *M*A*S*H*). Not to mention that a majority of signatories who actually *were* scientists indicated they no longer supported the petition or couldn't remember signing the petition, or were deceased, or failed to respond when they were contacted by *Scientific American*.[20]

The petition was mailed out to an extensive list of scientists, journalists, and politicos along with a cover letter and an "article" attacking the scientific evidence for climate change. The article, titled "Environmental Effects of Increased Atmospheric Carbon Dioxide," was coauthored by Robinson, his son Noah, and climate-change contrarian Willie Soon. It was formatted to appear as if it had been published in the prestigious *Proceedings of the National Academy of Sciences* (PNAS), the official journal of the hallowed National Academy of Sciences (NAS). Seitz even signed the enclosed letter using his past affiliation as NAS president. The NAS, in response, took the extraordinary step of publicly denouncing Seitz's efforts as a deliberate deception, noting that its position on the issue—that there was now a consensus that climate change is real and human caused—was very much the opposite of what Seitz was saying.

The entire episode, coincidentally enough, played out just days before the publication of our "hockey-stick" article, which appeared in the journal *Nature* on April 22 (Earth Day), 1998.[21] The curve demonstrated the unprecedented nature of modern global warming. It would become a symbol in the climate-change debate. It—and I— would soon become a major target of attack.

THE HOCKEY FIGHT

Let us skip ahead a few more years, to 2002, where we encounter the now infamous "Luntz Memo." Frank Luntz is a professional pollster who has long advised the GOP on matters of policy based on insights derived from polling and focus groups. In a 2002 memo that was leaked by an organization known as the Environmental Working Group, Luntz warned his fossil-fuel-industry-coddling Republican clients that "Should the public come to believe that the scientific issues are settled, their views about global warming will change accordingly."[22] He advised using less threatening language in characterizing the phenomenon, favoring "climate change" over "global warming." Ironically, the very same scientific community that climate-change deniers accuse of being alarmist would increasingly favor the use of that term as well, simply because it's a more comprehensive description of the problem. Climate change involves not only the warming of Earth's surface, but the melting of ice, sea-level rise, the shifting of rainfall and desert belts, altered ocean currents, and so on. Luntz also suggested that Republicans "reposition global warming as theory [rather than fact]." This, too, is ironic, for a *theory* is the most powerful of scientific entities. Gravity is just "a theory." That hardly makes it safe to jump off a cliff.

Luntz warned that "the scientific debate is closing [against Republicans] but not yet closed. There is still a window of opportunity to challenge the science," by which he meant to insert doubt into the public mindset. Following Luntz's prescription, fossil fuel interests and the politicians and attack dogs doing their bidding doubled down in their assault on the science, engaging in a "shoot the messenger" strategy designed to discredit the science underpinning concern over human-caused climate change. I found myself at the center of the attack because of the hockey-stick curve, which soon took on an iconic status in the climate debate. It would be featured in the "Summary for Policy Makers" of the 2001 Third Assessment Report of the IPCC as *the* key new piece of climate-change evidence, supporting the conclusion that recent warmth was unprecedented over at least the past one thousand years.[23]

In reality, it was only one of many independent pillars of evidence that now existed. Human influence on the climate had already been established, as readers will recall, with the publication of the IPCC's Second Assessment Report in 1995. But the hockey stick was far more compelling to the layperson than the rather abstract statistical work behind the key findings of the previous report. One didn't need to understand the physics, mathematics, or statistics underlying climate research to understand what the striking visual was telling us.

The long, gentle cooling trend that characterizes the descent from the relatively warm conditions of the eleventh century into the so-called Little Ice Age of the seventeenth to nineteenth centuries resembles the downturned "handle" of a hockey stick, and the abrupt warming spike of the past century is the upturned "blade." The fact that this dramatic recent warming accompanies the rapid increase in atmospheric carbon dioxide concentrations from the industrial revolution conveys an easily understood, unmistakable conclusion: the warming we are experiencing is unprecedented in modern history. Fossil fuel burning and other human activities are the cause.

That the hockey stick rose to prominence at precisely the same time that climate-change deniers were planning renewed and heightened attacks on the science was a coincidence of timing that had profound implications for my own career. In *The Hockey Stick and the Climate Wars*, I describe the efforts by fossil fuel interests and their hired guns to discredit the hockey stick and me personally.[24] Those efforts included attacks against me and my work by right-wing media outlets like Fox News and the *Wall Street Journal* as well as hostile congressional hearings and investigations by climate-change-denying politicians such as Oklahoma senator James Inhofe, former Texas congressman Joe Barton, and former Virginia attorney general Ken Cuccinelli. All were Republicans. All were recipients of substantial fossil fuel largesse. I was subject to legal assaults by fossil-fuel-industry front groups seeking to abuse open records laws to obtain my personal emails—in the hope of finding something embarrassing with which to discredit me, or something that could be taken out of context and misrepresented to cast doubt on my research. Most of the people and groups behind the effort—the Koch brothers, the Heartland Institute, the George C. Marshall Institute, Fred Singer—are familiar by now.

The good thing about science is that it possesses what the great Carl Sagan described as "self-correcting machinery." The processes of peer review, replication, and consensus, mixed with a healthy dose of skepticism—real skepticism, not the fake kind that is passed off as such by climate-change deniers—keeps science on a path toward truth. If a scientific claim is wrong, other scientists will demonstrate it to be so. If it's right, other scientists will reaffirm it, perhaps improve it and extend it. Climate-change deniers like to claim that scientists simply seek to reaffirm the prevailing paradigm, because that's how you secure funding and get published in the leading journals. As with most things climate-change deniers assert, the opposite is in fact true. *Disproving* the conventional wisdom, refuting a landmark study—that's the path to fame and glory in the world of science.

Accordingly, challenges to the hockey-stick curve in leading scientific journals, such as *Nature* and *Science*, have helped launch the careers of ambitious young scientists. Yet the hockey stick has withstood those and other challenges. Two decades of research by dozens of independent teams, using different data and methods, has time and again reaffirmed our findings. There is now a veritable hockey league of studies that not only confirm our original conclusion—that the recent warming is unprecedented over the past millennium—but in fact extend it to at least the past two millennia and, more tentatively, at least the past twenty thousand years.[25] Our basic finding has stood the test of time and the scrutiny of skeptical scientists. Accordingly, it has now been incorporated into the scientific consensus, and the scientific investigations have moved on, extending our findings and providing additional context. That's how science works.

That is not at all to say that efforts to discredit the hockey stick have ceased. And here we must distinguish between the world of science and the world of politics. The former is driven by the self-correcting machinery that Sagan so eloquently spoke of, in that scientific findings are always subject to appropriate scrutiny and (largely) good-faith challenges. The latter obeys no such rules. The hockey stick continues to be attacked in the conservative media based on the most cynical and disingenuous misrepresentations of the facts.[26] In the world of politics today, almost anything—it seems—goes; reality and logic have gone out the window, replaced by ideologically and agenda-driven "alternative facts."

Nearly two decades ago, in his book *The Demon-Haunted World*, Sagan presaged with some trepidation the world we now live in:

> I have a foreboding of an America in my children's or grandchildren's time—when the United States is a service and information economy; when nearly all the manufacturing industries have slipped away to other countries; when awesome technological powers are in the hands of a very few, and no one representing the public interest can even grasp the issues; when the people have lost the ability to set their own agendas or knowledgeably question those in authority; when, clutching our crystals and nervously consulting our horoscopes, our critical faculties in decline, unable to distinguish between what feels good and what's true, we slide, almost without noticing, back into superstition and darkness.[27]

Sagan's fears have no doubt been realized when it comes to the climate wars, if not our societal discourse writ large. And there is no better example of this pathology than the pseudo-scandal manufactured by the fossil fuel industry that came to be branded as "Climategate," a last gasp, if you will, of hard-core climate-change denial.

CLIMATEGATE—A LAST GASP?

In a more recent counterpart to the infamous 1972 Watergate affair that brought down the presidency of Richard M. Nixon, hackers with links to Russia and WikiLeaks broke into an email server and released stolen emails in a massive, carefully orchestrated disinformation campaign designed to impact the course of American politics.[28]

You could be forgiven for thinking that I'm talking about the now well-established conspiracy between Russia and the campaign of Donald Trump to steal the US presidential election of 2016, a scandal that has since been branded *Russiagate*. But no. I'm talking about the affair in November 2009 that would come to be known as *Climategate*.

Advocates for climate action anticipated an opportunity for meaningful action on climate heading into the United Nations Climate Change Conference in Copenhagen in December 2009. A successor to the Rio and Kyoto conferences, Copenhagen was a source of great hope to climate campaigners; indeed, many referred to it as *Hopenhagen*. With the growing public recognition of the climate threat, thanks to ever greater clarity about the impacts of climate change (the unprecedented disaster of Hurricane Katrina was still fresh in the memory of Americans) and Al Gore's wildly successful documentary *An Inconvenient Truth*, it seemed we were turning a corner. Perhaps, finally, the world was ready to act on climate.

The forces of denial and delay, however, would intercede once again, manufacturing a fake "scandal" in the weeks leading up to the summit. Even the name they successfully attached to the affair— "Climategate"—was the product of a carefully crafted narrative foisted on the public and policymakers in a collaborative effort by fossil-fuel-industry front groups, paid attack dogs, and conservative media outlets. Thousands of emails between climate scientists (including me) around the world were stolen from a university computer server in Great Britain late that summer. Bits and pieces of the emails were disingenuously rearranged and taken out of context by climate-change deniers to misrepresent both the science and the scientists.[29]

Before long, climate deniers had combed through the emails and organized them into a searchable archive. Taking individual words and phrases out of context to distort the original meanings, they claimed to have found the "smoking gun" that revealed climate change to be an elaborate hoax. Terms that were entirely innocent in context—for example, the word *trick*, which mathematicians and scientists use to denote a clever shortcut to solving a problem—were extracted and deliberately misinterpreted.

Climate-change deniers used these misrepresentations to claim that scientists were cooking the books, engaged in an elaborate scheme to *trick* the public! Front groups connected with the Koch brothers and industry-funded critics wanted the public to distrust the climate science by suspecting the climate scientists. Right-wing media outlets—especially the Murdoch media empire (e.g., Fox News and the *Wall Street Journal*) and conspiracy-theory-promoting bottom-feeders such as the *Drudge Report*, Breitbart "News," and Rush Limbaugh—served as a megaphone for outrageous untruths, filling the airwaves, television screens, and Internet with false allegations, smears, and innuendo.

Right-wing politicians joined the fray. James Inhofe, who had famously dismissed the overwhelming scientific evidence of climate change as "a hoax," embraced, with no sense of irony, the *true* hoax that was Climategate. Based on the untruthful Climategate allegations, he called for the criminal investigation of seventeen climate scientists, including Presidential Medal of Science recipient Susan Solomon of MIT, Michael Oppenheimer of Princeton, and Kevin Trenberth of the National Center for Atmospheric Research (NCAR). And yes, I was honored to be on that list as well.

Two years later, roughly a dozen (depending on how you count) different investigations in the United States and the United Kingdom had exonerated the scientists. There had been no data fudging, no attempt to mislead the public about climate change. The only wrongdoing that was established was the criminal theft of the emails in the first place—another cruel case of irony, given that the Watergate scandal, the origin of the "-gate" suffix, was about the theft of documents, not their content.[30]

In the meantime, however, climate-change deniers milked the fake scandal for all it was worth. Readers might recall Saudi Arabia's efforts to dilute the conclusions of the IPCC's Second Assessment Report back in 1995. Here, fifteen years later, the Saudis were still up to their usual mischief, attempting to sabotage the already delicate negotiations at the Copenhagen Summit. The lead Saudi climate-change negotiator, Mohammad al-Sabban, insisted that the pilfered emails would have a "huge impact" on the negotiations. Fifteen years after the IPCC had concluded that there was a discernible human influence on climate, Sabban, remarkably, asserted that "it appears from the details of the scandal that there is no relationship whatsoever between human activities and climate change." Somehow, a few misrepresented emails managed to negate more than a century of physics and chemistry and the overwhelming consensus of the world's scientists.

In understanding the role that both Saudi Arabia and the Murdoch media empire played in promoting Climategate smears and lies, it is worth noting that there is a curious connection between the two. Prince Alwaleed bin Talal of the Saudi royal family and Rupert Murdoch are close allies, and the two have financial ties. Until recently, Prince Alwaleed owned, via his company (Kingdom Holding), 7 percent of News Corporation's shares, making him the second-largest shareholder after Rupert Murdoch and his family (Alwaleed sold off his shares when he was arrested for corruption in 2017, knowing his assets would likely be frozen). Murdoch, News Corp, and the Saudi royal family all share a motive for opposing climate action.[31]

The Climategate thieves were never caught. What we do know is that Russia and Saudi Arabia both played roles in hosting and helping to distribute the stolen emails. Saudi Arabia made direct use of the false Climategate allegations in its efforts to halt progress toward a meaningful global climate treaty in Copenhagen. Recent evidence suggests that the "hacker" who broke into the server did so from Russia.[32] In light of Russia's tampering in the 2016 US presidential election, it seems relevant that Climategate used the same modus operandi and involved some of the same actors (WikiLeaks and Julian Assange) who were part of that campaign. Indeed, it could be argued that it was the very same *motive*.[33]

Vladimir Putin had an interest in Hillary Clinton's defeat in the 2016 election not just for geopolitical reasons, but because fossil fuels are Russia's primary asset, with much of the Russian economy dependent on fossil fuel exports. A prospective Trump presidency was of mutual benefit to both Russia and the world's largest fossil fuel company, ExxonMobil, offering the prospect of a collaborative venture between ExxonMobil and the Russian state oil company Rosneft to develop the largest currently untapped oil reserves in the world—Arctic, Siberian, and Black Sea petroleum reserves worth an estimated $500 billion.

The two companies signed a partnership in 2012 that was stymied when the Obama administration placed economic sanctions on Russia in 2014 for its annexation of part of the Ukraine (Crimea). It is almost certain that Hillary Clinton would have kept those sanctions in place. But not Donald Trump. At the July 2016 Republican National Convention, with Trump the presumptive Republican presidential nominee, his campaign, led by Paul Manafort—an individual who had worked for more than a decade as a lobbyist for Viktor Yanukovych, the Russian-backed former president of Ukraine—altered the official Republican platform to remove language supporting the sanctions.

Once in office, Trump appointed ExxonMobil CEO Rex Tillerson as his secretary of state. His administration attempted (unsuccessfully, thanks to some vestigial backbone among Senate Republicans) to lift the sanctions that stood in the way of the ExxonMobil–Russia oil partnership. We now know, thanks to the special counsel investigation led by former FBI director Robert Mueller, that Russia attempted to influence the election in favor of Donald Trump. It is plausible, if not probable, that a half-trillion-dollar oil deal was the primary impetus. Quid meet quo.

That brings us back to Climategate, which involved the use of stolen emails to influence the Copenhagen Summit of December 2009. It, too, advanced the agenda of fossil fuel interests, including ExxonMobil and Rosneft, by attempting to undermine the single greatest argument against continued fossil fuel exploitation—the threat of human-caused climate change. With regard to Russia's motivations, it is also worth noting that Vladimir Putin is on record dismissing the notion of any human causality to climate change, arguing that the solution is to simply adapt to the changes anyway, and asserting that global warming would actually be a good thing for Russia.[34]

Climategate was, in fact, an early test run for the larger assault on climate action by a small coalition of petrostates that is underway today. "US and Russia Ally with Saudi Arabia to Water Down Climate Pledge," read the headline in *The Guardian* on December 9,

2018, roughly eight years after Copenhagen.[35] Those three countries (and Kuwait for good measure) formed a small coalition opposing a UN motion to welcome the conclusions of a recent IPCC special report warning of the dangers of planetary warming in excess of 1.5°C (2.7°F).[36] And while we're at it, what about Brexit? Or the "Yellow Vest" carbon tax protests in France? Or similar revolts in Australia, Canada, and the state of Washington? Might these episodes, too, be tied to the efforts of rogue state actors to block international climate policy progress? We will return to that question later.

YOU CAN'T FOOL MOTHER NATURE

Climategate could in fact be viewed as the opening skirmish in the new climate war. It marked the critical juncture wherein the forces of denial and inaction all but conceded that they could no longer make a credible, good-faith case against the basic scientific evidence. So they would instead deploy new, more nefarious strategies in their effort to block action on climate.

One of the strategies is simply *lying*. That's what Climategate was all about. Prevarication has become so normalized in the era of Trump (who lies so often that journalists have a hard time keeping up with the count[37]) that climate-change deniers have felt emboldened to dissemble with abandon. With a majority of the public now accepting the reality of climate change, their efforts are targeted at a shrinking minority of people who are motivated by ideology and tribal political identity over fact—a subset of the "conservative base." Polling from 2019 suggests that the percentage of these so-called dismissives in American society now number only in the single digits.[38] But their apparent prominence in the public sphere appears far greater thanks to the megaphone provided by the fossil-fuel-funded climate-change denial machine. The megaphone includes Fox News and the rest of the Murdoch media empire as well as bot armies that are deployed online to flood our social media with misinformation and disinformation. The collective effect is to make extreme positions appear more popular than they actually are. The problem also encompasses fake reports and public debates sponsored by fossil-fuel-industry front groups intended to lend a veneer of credibility to climate-change denial.[39] These efforts provide right-wing politicians with talking points and political cover as they continue to do the bidding of the fossil fuel interests who fund their campaigns instead of the people's business.

It is important to combat this rear-guard assault on the basic facts, not because we are likely to convince the diminishing and increasingly irrelevant denialist fringe—we're not. But they still threaten to infect the larger public discourse. As a result of the denialist echo chamber, people tend to *perceive* that a far greater proportion of the public denies climate change than actually does.[40] That flawed perception, in turn, inhibits people from engaging their friends, neighbors, and acquaintances on climate. If we perceive a topic as contentious and likely to raise conflict with our prospective interlocutors, we often shy away from it entirely. The less we talk about the issue, the less prominent it is in our larger public discourse, and the less pressure that is brought to bear on policymakers to act.

To the extent climate denial persists, it tends to be more in the form of downplaying the *impacts* rather than outright denial of the basic physical evidence. To be specific, much of the residual promoted denialism involves dismissal not of climate change itself, but of the negative impacts that it is having now and will have in the near future. One of the best examples involves the extensive wildfires that have recently afflicted California. Contrarians sought to divert attention from the clear role that climate change—in the form of unprecedented heat and drought—was playing in these record wildfires.[41] Denier-in-chief Donald Trump infamously disparaged state officials by blaming them for "gross mismanagement" of the forests, attributing the problem specifically to an absence of "raking" of forests.[42] In an ironic twist, given the false Climategate accusations that climate scientists had been subject to a decade earlier, released emails in 2020 actually *did* indicate data manipulation—by the Trump administration—to downplay the linkage between climate change and the devastating California wildfires.[43]

Other denialist heads of state have followed suit. President Jair Bolsonaro of Brazil tried to blame environmentalists, rather than his pro-deforestation policies (and climate change), for the widespread Amazon wildfires in 2019. But perhaps an even better illustration lies in the events I witnessed during my sabbatical in Australia during late 2019 and early 2020. As I wrote at the time, "Take record heat, combine it with unprecedented drought in already dry regions, and you get unprecedented bushfires like the ones . . . spreading across the continent. It's not complicated."[44]

The conservative prime minister of Australia, Scott Morrison, is dismissive of climate change. He has promoted Australian coal interests, helped sabotage the 25th Conference of the Parties (COP25) of the United Nations Framework Convention on Climate Change, in Madrid in December 2019, and vacationed in Hawaii while Australians were suffering the impacts of unprecedented heat and wildfires.[45] He and other conservative politicians and pundits sought to deflect attention from the true underlying cause, instead blaming greens for supposedly preventing the government from thinning out forests. The Murdoch media machine, including *The Australian* (described by the independent media watchdog SourceWatch as a paper that "promotes climate change denial in a way that is sometimes . . . so astonishing as to be entertaining"[46]), the *Herald Sun*, and Sky News television, meanwhile, promoted the myth that the massive bushfires engulfing Australia were a result of arson. Rupert Murdoch's own son James chose to speak out, publicly stating that he was "particularly disappointed with the ongoing denial" by his father's media empire.[47]

The impacts of climate change have become too obvious for a reasonable, honest person to deny. They are lapping at our feet—quite literally, when it comes to flooding and coastal inundation by sea-level rise and supercharged hurricanes, and figuratively when it comes to unprecedented droughts, heat waves, and wildfires. Climate change has touched my own life numerous times in recent years. The record flooding in the summer of 2016 where I live in central Pennsylvania was one. Watching my alma mater, the University of

California, Berkeley, shut down in late October 2019 by a historic wildfire in the East Bay hills was another. But my sabbatical during the Australian summer of 2019/2020 was when I truly came face to face with the climate crisis.

Climate change now threatens our economy to the tune of more than a trillion dollars a year.[48] A recent study commissioned by the Pentagon warns of a scenario in which electricity, water, and food systems might collapse by midcentury as a result of the effects of climate change.[49] What was once largely perceived as an *environmental* threat is now viewed as an *economic* and *national security* threat. That reality is bringing increasing numbers of political conservatives to the table—people like Bob Inglis, former Republican congressman from South Carolina, who now heads up an organization called republicEn that promotes free-market climate solutions.

There is also a growing bipartisan Climate Solutions Caucus in the US House of Representatives. Thanks largely to the efforts of the Citizens' Climate Lobby, an international grassroots movement that trains volunteers to engage their representatives on climate issues, there are now twenty-three Republican members of the caucus who support taking action to mitigate climate risk. Even some of the most conservative Republicans in the House of Representatives—including Matt Gaetz of Florida, often regarded as Donald Trump's pit bull in Congress—recognize that the people of their states don't have the luxury of debating the science of climate change, because they are suffering its consequences *now*. Indeed, Gaetz has chided fellow Republicans who still deny the science.[50]

There are indications that some of the leaders of the conservative movement are moderating their stance on climate. There is antitax crusader Grover Norquist, for example, who has at least alluded to the possibility of support for a revenue-neutral carbon tax.[51] I met with Norquist in the fall of 2019 and found him to be informed and thoughtful about the climate issue. And then there is Charles Koch, the remaining "Koch brother," his brother David having passed away in August 2019. In a November 2019 interview, Charles Koch was quoted as saying, "What we want them to do is to find policies that will actually work, actually do something about reducing CO_2 emissions, manmade CO_2 emissions, and at the same time not make people's lives worse."[52] Those words sound encouraging, but until the sole remaining Koch brother calls off his attack dogs—the front groups and dark-money outfits that continue to attack the science and scientists—and demonstrates a good-faith willingness to entertain real climate solutions, it is appropriate to remain skeptical.

Indeed, the "solutions" being advanced by conservatives are often not real solutions. Consider, for example, Marco Rubio's suggestion that the people of Florida can simply "adapt" to the impacts of sea-level rise (What does that mean? Growing gills and fins?).[53] But it is a welcome sea change (forgive the pun) that Republicans seem to be moving on from outright science denial to a more worthy debate over climate policy.

The forces of inaction—that is, fossil fuel interests and those doing their bidding—have a single goal—inaction. We might henceforth call them *inactivists*. They come in various forms. The most hard-core contingent—the *deniers*—are, as we have seen, in the process of going extinct (though there is still a remnant population of them). They are being replaced by other breeds of *deceivers* and *dissemblers*, namely, *downplayers, deflectors, dividers, delayers*, and *doomers*—willing participants in a multipronged strategy seeking to deflect blame, divide the public, delay action by promoting "alternative" solutions that don't actually solve the problem, or insist we simply accept our fate—it's too late to do anything about it anyway, so we might as well keep the oil flowing. The climate wars have thus not ended. They have simply evolved into a new climate war. The various fronts on which this war is being waged constitute the subject of subsequent chapters.

CHAPTER 3

The "Crying Indian" and the Birth of the Deflection Campaign

Good actions give strength to ourselves and inspire good actions in others.
—PLATO

But our energy woes are in many ways the result of classic market failures that can only be addressed through collective action, and government is the vehicle for collective action in a democracy.
—SHERWOOD BOEHLERT (R-NY), former chair of the
House of Representatives Science Committee

VESTED INTERESTS HAVE OFTEN EMPLOYED WHAT'S KNOWN AS a *deflection* campaign in their efforts to defeat policies they perceive as disadvantageous to their cause. Deflection campaigns seek to divert attention from—and dampen enthusiasm for—calls for regulatory reforms to rein in bad industry behavior posing threats to consumers and the environment. The onus is instead placed on personal behavior and individual action. There are numerous examples from recent US history involving the tobacco industry and the gun lobby, but the archetypal deflection campaign is undoubtedly the Crying Indian public service announcement (PSA) of the early 1970s.

Past deflection campaigns set the stage for understanding the current debate over the relative roles of individual and collective action in addressing the climate crisis. Deflection is a critical component of the multipronged strategy now being employed by the fossil fuel industry in its battle against efforts to regulate their activities, and an important front in the new climate war.

DEFLECTION CAMPAIGNS

The slogan "Guns Don't Kill People, People Kill People," used by the National Rifle Association (NRA), provides a textbook example of deflection. Its intent is to divert attention away from the problem of easy access to assault weapons toward other purported contributors to mass shootings, such as mental illness or media depictions of violence. The campaign based on this sloganeering has been remarkably effective in forestalling commonsense gun-law reform. A recent poll indicated that 57 percent of the public believes that mass shootings reflect "problems identifying and treating people with mental health problems," while only 28 percent attribute the phenomenon to overly lax gun laws. A whopping 77 percent believe that the tragic 2018 Parkland High School shooting in Florida could have been prevented by more effective mental health screening.[1]

As gun violence expert Dennis A. Henigan has explained, "the gun lobby's political power will never be overcome until these myths are destroyed. . . . The source of the NRA's disproportionate political power is not simply its money and the intensity of its supporters' beliefs; it is also its effective communication of several simple themes that resonate with ordinary Americans and function to convince them that gun control has little to do with improving the quality of their lives." He noted that the "Guns Don't Kill People" slogan "has been remarkably effective in diverting attention from the issue of gun regulation to the endless, and often fruitless, search for more 'fundamental' causes of criminal violence."[2] Or, as journalist Joseph Dolman put it, it is "about the power of an interest group to impede what looks to most of us like genuine public progress." Thanks in substantial part to the gun lobby's successful deflection campaign, roughly forty thousand Americans die from gun violence every year.[3]

Equally craven, if less well known, is the tobacco industry's effort to divert attention from the dangers of cigarette-initiated house fires by pointing the finger instead at *flammable furniture*. "It wasn't that they argued that cigarettes don't cause fires, they just argued that the better way to address the problem was to have flame retardant furniture," according to Patricia Callahan and Sam Roe, a pair of *Chicago Tribune* journalists. They wrote a series of articles about this classic deflection campaign by the tobacco industry (in concert with the chemical industry).[4]

Burn victim and firefighter groups had been campaigning for laws requiring the tobacco industry to develop fire-safe cigarettes, which would stop burning when not being smoked. Tobacco executives insisted this would be an onerous requirement that would diminish the quality of the smoking experience and the appeal of their product. So they instead sought to neutralize the efforts of firefighting organizations, and, even more audaciously, to co-opt them. Charles Powers, a top executive at the Tobacco Institute—a tobacco-industry front group—boasted that "many of our former adversaries in the fire service defend us, support us and carry forth our federal legislation as their own."[5]

How did the tobacco industry accomplish such a seemingly Herculean task? Through the classic tool of all successful deflection campaigns—subterfuge. Industry supporters infiltrated fire safety organizations to influence their messaging, buying off many of the people working for genuine reform. Tobacco Institute vice president Peter Sparber initiated the effort in the mid-1980s. By the late 1980s, he had left the institute to run his own lobbying firm while still representing the Tobacco Institute, which became a major client. In this capacity, he continued to advance the institute's interests while maintaining plausible deniability with regard to any ostensible *direct* ties to Big Tobacco.

Sparber's crowning achievement was organizing (and ultimately weaponizing) a group of governor-appointed state fire marshals into the National Association of State Fire Marshals (NASFM). He volunteered to serve as the group's legislative consultant and serve on its executive board (it is noteworthy that a somewhat similarly themed group, the Association of State Climatologists, was later weaponized by the forces of climate-change denial[6]). Sparber was even listed on the NASFM's official letterhead and shared its Washington, DC, office.

Among its first actions under Sparber's leadership, the NASFM endorsed an industry-backed federal bill calling for further study of fire-safe cigarettes—in place of a competing bill that would have actually required them. Sparber sought to redirect attention to the ostensible need for flame-proof furniture. Enter *flame retardants*.

Flame retardants are chemicals—to be specific, they are polybrominated diphenyl ethers (PBDEs) that are added to products such as televisions, computers, infant car seats, strollers, textiles, and, yes, furniture, to inhibit flammability. They are also toxic and accumulate in the human body over time. Studies show that PBDEs may inhibit brain development in children and impair sperm development and thyroid function. They have been banned in several states.[7] Here we had a marriage made in heaven (or, rather in hell) between Big Tobacco and the chemical industry, whose interests were suddenly aligned. The tobacco industry needed a scapegoat—flammable furniture. And the chemical industry provided a putative solution—flame retardants.

Another classic tool of deflection campaigns is the use of front groups masquerading as grassroots efforts. Americans for Prosperity, for example, is a Koch brothers front group that advances the agenda of the fossil fuel industry by attacking climate science and blocking action on climate (it also advocates for the tobacco industry[8]). Citizens for Fire Safety was a front group for the chemical industry. It actively opposed legislation seeking to ban the use of hazardous fire retardants in furniture. Its executive director, Grant Gillham, came out of the tobacco industry. The group's mission, according to tax records, is to "promote common business interests of members involved with the chemical manufacturing industry," and most of its money goes toward lobbying efforts in state legislatures where bans on flame retardants are being considered.

Another player in this effort was the scientific-sounding "Bromine Science and Environmental Forum," funded by chemical manufacturers for the purpose of "generating science in support of brominated flame retardants."[9] The Madison Avenue advertising and public relations firm of Burson-Marsteller represented the group. Burson-Marsteller also represented a chemical-industry front group calling itself the Alliance for Consumer Fire Safety in Europe, which, among other things, preyed on instinctive fears of fire by touting an "interactive burn test tool," with which visitors could envision, with horror, their sofas catching on fire. Remember the name Burson-Marsteller. It's not the last time we'll hear it.

Seemingly compelling but inauthentic storytelling is a common theme in deflection campaigns. And here, as detailed by Callahan and Roe, we have one of the very best examples. Dr. David Heimbach was a retired Seattle doctor and burn surgeon; he was also a former president of the American Burn Association. And he, too, preyed on fear. He repeatedly testified, often to the gasps of audiences, about the horrific child burn victims of flame-retardant-free furniture. Among these victims, he said, was a nine-week-old patient who died in a candle fire in 2009. In Alaska, he told lawmakers about a six-week-old patient who was fatally burned in her crib in 2010. Then there was a seven-week-old baby girl who was burned in a candle-ignited fire as she lay on a flame-retardant-free pillow. "Half of her body was severely burned," Heimbach told California lawmakers. He went on to describe how "she ultimately died after about three weeks of pain and misery in the hospital." "Heimbach's passionate testimony about the baby's death made the long-term health concerns about flame retardants voiced by doctors, environmentalists and even firefighters sound abstract and petty," as Callahan and Roe put it.[10]

"But there was a problem," Callahan and Roe noted, "with his testimony." The stories weren't true. There was no evidence of any dangerous pillow or candle fires like the ones he described. None of the victims existed—not the nine-week-old, the six-week-old, or the seven-week-old. The only thing that seemed to be true was that

Heimbach was indeed a burn doctor. He was also, it turns out, a shill for industry, helping bolster the dubious claim that chemical retardants save lives.

It was the Citizens for Fire Safety that sponsored Heimbach and his lurid testimonies about burned babies. Its website featured a photo of smiling children standing in front of a red brick fire station, brandishing a handmade banner reading "Fire Safety" with a heart dotting the "i." Heimbach referred to the image when claiming to lawmakers that Citizens for Fire Safety was "made up of many people like me who have no particular interest in the chemical companies: numerous fire departments, numerous firefighters and many, many burn docs."[11] One person's Astroturf, after all, is another person's grassroots. Who's to say?

As a result of the joint efforts of the tobacco and chemical industries, fire retardants have proliferated broadly throughout the environment—indeed, so much so that these dangerous chemicals can now be detected in North American kestrels and barn owls, in bird eggs in Spain, in fish in Canada, and even in Antarctic penguins and Arctic killer whales. They have been found in honey, in peanut butter—and in human breast milk.[12] And it's all the result of an industry-promoted deflection campaign.

THE CRYING INDIAN

My most vivid early memories date back to the early 1970s, when I was five or six years old. I would like to tell you they are fond remembrances of meaningful moments from my youth: a summer family vacation at the Maine seashore, a holiday gathering with my grandparents and cousins, my first sleep-away camp. But no, my most lucid early memories are of television. Commercials, to be precise.

"I'd like to buy the world a Coke." I can still hear the jingle promising that world peace could be achieved if only everyone would just choose to drink Coca-Cola. It's as if it played on the radio just this morning. Imprinted, too, in my memory is Smokey Bear's stern admonition: "Only you can prevent forest fires." This PSA helped instill in me an early appreciation for nature and the importance of preserving it.

But *one* of those ultra-sticky ads became embedded in my very soul. If you're close to my age, and you grew up in the United States, you know the ad. You can perhaps still picture it: A chiseled, traditionally clothed Native American is paddling his canoe down a river. Slightly ominous music plays in the background, accompanied by a steady drumbeat. As he proceeds down the river, he encounters an increasing volume of flotsam and jetsam. Behind him factories belch smog into the air. The music grows louder and more foreboding. He finally lands his canoe along the river's edge, where it is inundated with more strewn litter.

The man (named "Iron Eyes Cody") makes his way onto land, trampling through yet more discarded refuse, and approaches the edge of a highway. A passenger in a passing car throws a bag of trash out the window, the contents of which splatter at his feet and onto his clothing. He looks down at the mess as we hear a voiceover. It's authoritative and stern, reminiscent of the *Twilight Zone*'s Rod Serling. "*Some* people have a deep abiding respect for the natural beauty that was once this country," it tells us in an almost admonishing tone. "Some people don't." It goes on: *"People start pollution. People can stop it."* As the camera closes in on the man's sullen face, a tear drips from the corner of his eye and down his cheek. He looks sadly at the camera, a polluted American landscape in the background.

His tears were our tears. His pain was our pain. Our great land— and the legacy of indigenous peoples—was now imperiled by our own profligate behavior. Could we save our rivers, fields, and forests before it was too late? *Were we willing to change?*

You *bet* we were. As the newly commissioned stewards of the environment we now were, we knew our mission. No scrap of litter would escape our seizure. Thus was born a new generation of *litter* scoopers. To this day, I have difficulty letting a piece of strewn trash lie there on the roadside. I instinctively look for a nearby receptacle where I can dispose of it. That commercial changed me—and so many people of my generation—for the better, it would seem reasonable to argue.

The ad harnessed the power of an incipient environmental movement. Part of the larger "Keep America Beautiful" campaign, the PSA premiered on the first anniversary of the inaugural Earth Day, April 22, 1971.[13] The famous Cuyahoga river fire in Ohio was a recent memory, ingrained in the collective American psyche. That event arguably triggered a tipping point in public consciousness, spurring a new era of environmental awareness and a flurry of new environmental policies: the creation of the Environmental Protection Agency, the Clean Water Act, the Clean Air Act. This was the dawning of the Age of Aquarius—a new age of environmentalism.

The "Crying Indian" ad, as it came to be known, was the right message at the right time, simple and empowering. You and I can solve this problem. We just need to put our minds to it, get our act together, roll up our sleeves. It's been rated one of the most effective ads in history. Environmental organizations such as the Sierra Club and the Audubon Society embraced the ad, and even served on the advisory council for the campaign. Cody soon made his way onto highway billboards. He became an icon of the modern environmental movement.

But if you're looking for a feel-good story here, you'd better get used to disappointment. Some things aren't quite what they seem. Scratch beneath the surface of the Crying Indian, as historian Finis Dunaway did in a 2017 commentary in the *Chicago Tribune*, and a different picture—indeed, a *dramatically* different picture—begins to emerge.[14]

FALSUS IN UNO, FALSUS IN OMNIBUS

Dunaway emphasized the role that Native Americans played in the early 1970s counterculture. The Crying Indian tapped into that ethos, drawing upon the peace movement in much the same way that the "Buy the World a Coke" jingle did, airing around the same time. (We will see later that the connection with Coca-Cola is not just incidental.) Two of the most memorable films from my childhood, both released in 1971, drew upon these same themes. *Billy Jack* tells the story of a man who was half American Navajo. His pacifist aspirations are at odds with his temper and his penchant for vigilante justice, and he defends a counterculture school of peaceniks and hippies, many of whom are from indigenous tribes, from hostile, bigoted towns-people. *Bless the Beasts and Children* tells the story of a group of teen misfits who find meaning, validation, and empowerment by freeing a herd of buffaloes that are being hunted by ruthless men for sport. It isn't just the buffaloes that are being destroyed; it is the spirit of the Native Americans, for whom the American buffalo is an enduring symbol. The underlying themes in both films were unmistakable: the struggle between peace and empowerment, and *the central symbolic role* in that struggle played by indigenous peoples and their plight. In playing on that very same symbolism, the Crying Indian captured the zeitgeist of the early 1970s. It harnessed all that power.

And it is in the Native American symbolism of the Crying Indian PSA where we encounter our first betrayal, if a seemingly minor and superficial one. For, as it turns out, "Iron Eyes Cody" was not a member of a Native American tribe. He wasn't even Native American at all. Born Espera Oscar de Corti, he was an Italian American who often portrayed Indians in Hollywood films, including "Chief Iron Eyes" in the 1948 Bob Hope film *The Paleface*. This was not, as we shall see, the only sleight of hand in the Crying Indian ad. Nor was it the most significant.

The Crying Indian PSA must be viewed through the prism of the growing problem of highway litter, from bottles and cans in particular, that followed the construction of the interstate highway system in the 1950s. The problem had reached crisis proportions by the late 1960s. It had become noticeable and disturbing. Who wouldn't want to "Keep America Beautiful," after all? It was clear we had a problem. But *how* best to fix it? And *who* pays the cost?

Consumer advocate Ralph Nader founded Public Interest Research Groups (PIRGs), a network of groups throughout the United States focused on consumer and environmental advocacy, in 1971, the same year the Crying Indian first aired. The PIRGs would play a critical role in advancing one particular vision of how to fix the problem and who should pay, namely, *the bottle bill*. The bottle bill was legislation that placed a deposit on bottles and cans (typically five or ten cents) that would be refunded to consumers upon their return, promoting returnable and refillable bottles and encouraging consumers to recycle rather than toss. The legislation placed an additional burden on supermarkets, grocery stores, and package stores, but the *beverage industry*—i.e., Coca-Cola, Anheuser-Busch, PepsiCo, and so on—would bear the brunt of the responsibility and costs, as they would be required to process the returned bottles and cans. That would add to their expenses and decrease their profits.

Now, fast-forward to the summer of 1984, thirteen years after the PIRGs were founded and the Crying Indian first aired. I had just graduated from high school and I needed a summer job. MassPIRG, which had a base in my hometown of Amherst, Massachusetts, seemed like a perfect opportunity to make some money; I could learn about modern environmental and consumer history and help the environment all at the same time.

MassPIRG—the Massachusetts PIRG affiliate—was best known for its efforts to help pass a bottle bill in the state of Massachusetts. During my training, a veteran canvasser accompanied me as I went door to door soliciting contributions from the residents of a small western Massachusetts town. Among other things, my trainer worked with me as I refined my "rap"—the short statement a canvasser quickly recites during that awkward but pivotal moment between when someone has answered the door and when they've had a chance to say anything other than "hello." My trainer expressly discouraged me from mentioning, in my rap, the *bottle bill*—MassPIRG's signature achievement. At least not when canvassing blue-collar and conservative neighborhoods. Instead, I was encouraged to talk about the *lemon law*—a less prominent piece of legislation MassPIRG had sponsored that protects car buyers from defective car purchases. How odd, I thought at the time, that MassPIRG wouldn't take every opportunity to tout its crowning achievement.

The story of the Massachusetts bottle bill dates back to 1973, when I was eight years old. Working together with the Massachusetts

Audubon Society and other environmental organizations, MassPIRG helped lobby the state legislature to place a five-cent deposit on bottles and cans. After several failed attempts to pass the bill, they were eventually able to get it on the ballot as a referendum. They were opposed, however, by a $2 million ad campaign funded by the beverage industry, funneled through two front groups: the Committee to Protect Jobs, and Use of Convenient Containers. The beverage industry succeeded in defeating the bill, albeit by a very narrow margin (less than 1 percent). In 1977, bottle-bill legislation garnered majority support in the state House of Representatives but failed in the state Senate. In 1979, the bill cleared both House and Senate, but was immediately vetoed by Governor Edward King (who was a Democrat at the time, but would later become a Republican).

Perhaps sensing the growing support behind the bottle bill, King proceeded to help push an alternative to the bill, promoted by the beverage industry, through a front group calling itself the Corporation for a Cleaner Commonwealth. It involved hiring kids to pick up bottle and can litter. The solution, you see, isn't regulation of industry. It's individual action. You've just been introduced to the *deflection campaign*. You'll get to know it much better soon enough.

The bottle bill once again passed both the House and the Senate in 1981. King exercised his veto a second time, calling the bill an embodiment of "everything that is wrong with big government." He claimed it imposed an undue financial burden on individuals and would have adverse impacts on the state's economy. This type of argument—that regulatory solutions to environmental problems are supposedly bad for the economy—will also become all too familiar by the time our story is over.

Subject to an intense lobbying campaign from MassPIRG and others, the state legislature, both the House and the Senate, voted to override King's veto. The bill officially became law on November 16, 1981. But the beverage industry wasn't simply going to roll over. It funded a campaign to repeal the bottle bill, getting a referendum onto the ballot. The referendum failed, but 40 percent of voters were in favor of repeal. The bottle bill was implemented on January 17,

1983, with divided public support, after a bruising battle with millions of dollars of negative advertising spent against it. A little more than a year later, during the summer of 1984, I would be discouraged from talking about the bottle bill in all but the most progressive neighborhoods as I canvassed for MassPIRG.

Similar dramas played out in other states. Oregon was actually the first state to enact a bottle bill, in 1971. Next was the very green New England state of Vermont in 1973. The relatively progressive states of Connecticut, Delaware, Iowa, Massachusetts, Maine, Michigan, and New York all followed suit by the early 1980s. Bottle bills failed in numerous other states, however, once again as a result of intensive lobbying and campaigning by the beverage industry. One ad even depicted a group of sad kids in scout uniforms searching in vain for bottles and cans (to the chagrin of the Boy Scouts and Campfire Girls of America, who complained about their brands being appropriated for dubious political motives without their approval). The bottle bill, you see, would put a damper on their money-making recycling efforts. *Deflection* again.

The beverage industry, in other words, employed a crafty, multipronged strategy in opposing the passage of bottle bills. It fought them by lobbying state legislatures and through advertising campaigns aimed at voters depicting such bills as costly for consumers and bad for the business community.

Through the advertising campaigns, the industry did its best to make sure the bottle bills were bruised and battered into marginal popularity, if not toxicity, in the states where they did pass—enough so that any attempts at a national bottle bill, such as the ones proposed by Edward Markey (D-MA) in the US House of Representatives in 2007 and 2009, would be dead in the water. But there was one more critical task—the industry needed to dampen the enthusiasm of the "base," that is, environmentalists intent on action. The week of the very first Earth Day, in April 1970, environmental activists dumped a huge pile of nonreturnable Coke bottles in front of the Coca-Cola headquarters in Atlanta, Georgia, as a means of pressuring the company into supporting a bottle bill.[15] The beverage industry knew it would be difficult to convince those folks and their growing number of followers that a bottle bill wasn't a good thing for the environment. But you *might* be able to convince them that a bill wasn't necessary, or that it wouldn't be effective. That's where the Crying Indian came in.

Putting aside the Native American imagery for now, consider the larger message of the Crying Indian ad: Those bottles and cans that were littering our countryside? They were the result of our bad personal behavior. That's a convenient message to promote if you're an industry whose practices generate massive metal and plastic pollution and you're trying to fight regulations aimed at requiring you to package and process that waste.

Enter Coke and Madison Avenue. The consortium of American corporations behind the "Keep America Beautiful" campaign included Coca-Cola, Pepsi, Anheuser-Busch, and tobacco giant Philip Morris. They had been collaborating with the Ad Council—a nonprofit organization that produces and promotes PSAs on behalf of various sponsors, including environmental groups. In 1971, they worked with New York advertising giant Marsteller (whose public relations firm is Burson-Marsteller, whom you may recall from our earlier discussion of tobacco flame retardants) to create the Crying Indian PSA.

Environmental groups like the Sierra Club and the Audubon Society were initially partners in the campaign, believing it would be a powerful way to raise awareness around littering. But they ultimately distanced themselves from the effort when they realized they'd been had. That's because they realized the "Crying Indian" was, in fact, a public relations ploy hatched by beverage industry groups.

That campaign, part of the multipronged effort to defeat the bottle bill, achieved its primary objective. As we know, only a limited number of blue states passed bottle bills, and a national bottle bill is nowhere on the horizon even decades later. Meanwhile, the growing mass of discarded plastic bottles has given rise to another great environmental crisis of our time—global plastic pollution. It's no longer just littering the countryside: today plastic pollution is so extensive that it has been found in the Mariana Trench, thirty-six

thousand feet underwater. Indeed, it's even in the air: *Wired* magazine ran a story in June 2020 proclaiming, "Plastic Rain Is the New
Acid Rain." *Wired* cited research finding that many tons of micro-
plastics are falling onto wilderness areas every year.[16]

In 2006, ironically, the Ad Council would run another PSA, this
time about ocean plastic pollution. Featuring the title character from
Disney's *The Little Mermaid*, the message was all about how individuals can act by properly disposing of trash. There was no mention of
the beverage industry's role in plastic pollution. Environmental organizations—like the Environmental Defense Fund—were cosponsors. Fool me once . . .

Reflecting on the true story behind the Crying Indian, it's hard
for me not to feel *personally* betrayed, as if the innocence of our
youth was an illusion, as if I—and everyone else of my generation—
was led astray by a false prophet, for the motive of corporate profit.

When it comes to the wider legacy of the Crying Indian, Finis
Dunaway offered this assessment:

> The answer to pollution, as Keep America Beautiful would have it,
> had nothing to do with power, politics or production decisions; it was
> simply a matter of how individuals acted in their daily lives. Ever since
> the first Earth Day, the mainstream media have repeatedly turned
> big systemic problems into questions of individual responsibility. Too
> often, individual actions like recycling and green consumerism have
> provided Americans with a therapeutic dose of environmental hope
> that fails to address our underlying issues.[17]

Which leads us back to the issue of climate change.

WHAT TO DO?

The dual epigraphs that begin this chapter embrace the duality of
the lever arms of action in a functioning democracy. Progress requires individual action—what is a collective, after all, but a group
of individuals? Doing the right thing sets an example for others to

follow and creates a more favorable environment for change. But we also need systemic change, which requires collective action aimed at pressuring policymakers who are in a position to make decisions about societal priorities and government investment.

There are plenty of lifestyle changes that should be encouraged, many of which make us happier and healthier, save us money, and decrease our environmental footprint. Demand-side pressure by consumers can certainly influence the market (indeed, millennials have been accused of killing off various traditional products and services, including landline phones, men's suits, and fast-food chains, with their purchasing decisions[18]). But consumer choice doesn't build high-speed railways, fund research and development in renewable energy, or place a price on carbon emissions. Any real solution must involve both individual action and systemic change.

We must beware of efforts to make it seem as if the former is a viable alternative to the latter. Studies suggest that a solitary focus on voluntary action may actually undermine support for governmental policies to hold carbon polluters accountable.[19] So there is a delicate middle ground—which we must seek out—that encourages personal responsibility and individual action while continuing to use all of the lever arms of democracy (including voting!) to pressure politicians to support climate-friendly governmental policies.

Those who mount deflection campaigns are not truly interested in solving problems—if they were, they'd advocate for multipronged approaches that benefit society at large. Instead, their intent is to sabotage systemic solutions that might be disadvantageous to moneyed interests through subterfuge and misdirection. We can see this in the gun lobby's efforts to deflect the focus away from gun control reform, by shifting attention from the large number of poorly regulated weapons in the country to the mental health of individual perpetrators of gun violence. Big Tobacco, with help from the chemical industry, denied us safe-burning cigarettes but gave us toxic peanut butter and breast milk. The beverage industry largely defeated efforts to pass bottle bills and gave us the problem of global plastic pollution.

And today, fossil fuel interests and the climate inactivists working on their behalf are seeking to block policies aimed at regulating carbon emissions by employing a Crying Indian–like deflection campaign. It is instructive to note some of the striking parallels between the current campaign and deflection campaigns in the past. The silly contention by right-wing figures that climate advocates "want to take away your burgers," for example, sounds a lot like the NRA's admonition that gun-law reform advocates "want to take away your guns." Both reflect an attempt to prey upon fears of big government and limitations on liberty that are prevalent among political conservatives.

The climate action deflectors, moreover, as we shall see, are also attempting to drive a wedge into preexisting rifts within the climate activist community. That includes rifts arising from the ongoing debate over the role of personal behavior versus systemic change. (It also includes rifts involving the politics of identity, and matters of gender, age, and race.) When the climate discourse devolves into a shouting match over diet and travel choices, and becomes about personal purity, behavior-shaming, and virtue-signaling, we get a divided community unable to speak with a united voice. We lose. Fossil fuel interests win.

In June 2019, I made these points in a *USA Today* op-ed I coauthored with my Penn State colleague Jonathan Brockopp.[20] In it, we noted the similarity between the Crying Indian deflection campaign of the 1970s and current efforts to equate climate action almost exclusively with personal responsibility. A prominent state politician from Vermont who campaigns against air travel responded angrily to the comparison. "You do realize that ten states have bottle bills?" he asked, seeming to think he was disproving my point. In debating, this is sometimes referred to as an "own goal." The fact that fewer than a dozen (all *deep blue*) states have a bottle bill—and the fact that a national bottle bill is nowhere on the horizon—speaks to the success of that past deflection campaign. It serves as a cautionary note when it comes to the current deflection campaign on climate, which is the focus of the next chapter.

CHAPTER 4

It's YOUR Fault

A house divided against itself cannot stand.
—ABRAHAM LINCOLN

DEFLECTION IS A PARTICULARLY DEVIOUS STRATEGY FOR INAC-
tivists. In addition to directing attention away from the need for collective action—such as pricing or regulating carbon, removing fossil
fuel subsidies, or providing incentives for clean energy alternatives—
it divides the community of climate advocates by generating conflict
and promoting finger-pointing, behavior-shaming, virtue-signaling,
and purity tests. It also provides a means for tarring leading climate
advocates as hypocrites and firing up political conservatives by emphasizing the purported personal sacrifice and loss of personal liberty
that climate action demands. It all starts with a simple deflection . . .

DEFLECTION COMES TO CLIMATE CHANGE

The current preoccupation with personal behavior didn't arise in a
vacuum. Much like the Crying Indian's focus on the role of individuals in cleaning up bottle and can litter, the focus on the individual's
role in solving climate change was carefully nurtured by industry.

The concept of a "personal carbon footprint" was something that
the oil company BP promoted in the mid-2000s. Indeed, BP launched
one of the first personal carbon footprint calculators, arguably as part

of a larger public relations effort to establish the company as *the* environmentally conscious oil company.[1] I still recall the inspiring ads BP ran at the time billing itself as "Beyond Petroleum." Whether this reflected a genuine embrace of green energy or a cynical "greenwash" gambit, we'll never know. The Deep Horizon oil spill in the Gulf of Mexico in April 2010 would seem to have ended any hope of BP carving a niche out for itself as the green oil company, though it has recently been trying to talk a good game on climate again anyway.[2]

As environmental author Sami Grover opined, "contrary to popular belief, fossil fuel companies are actually all too happy to talk about the environment. They just want to keep the conversation around individual responsibility, not systemic change or corporate culpability."[3] And as Malcolm Harris wrote in *New York Magazine*, "these companies aren't planning for a future without oil and gas, at least not anytime soon, but they want the public to think of them as part of a climate solution. In reality, they're a problem trying to avoid being solved."[4]

It's thoroughly unsurprising, given the emphasis on deflection, that an oil industry site, for example, promoted an article titled "Is Eating Meat Worse Than Burning Oil?"[5] A bit more surprising is the fact that none other than the *New York Times* has been trafficking in messaging that deflects responsibility from fossil fuel interests and their abettors.

In August 2018, the *Times* heavily promoted an article by Nathaniel Rich titled "Losing Earth: The Decade We Almost Stopped Climate Change."[6] It was the cover story for the *New York Times Magazine*, and the entire issue was devoted to just this one story. The *Times* even produced a video trailer to go with it. In the piece, which focuses on the period from 1979 to 1989, Rich dismisses the fossil fuel industry as a mere "boogeyman" when it comes to climate policy inaction. He absolves the Republican Party of blame as well. And he does so through the transparently tenuous argument that the fossil fuel disinformation campaign didn't really ramp up until the 1990s, so the failure of the climate movement, which began in the 1980s, cannot be tied to it. Robinson Meyer of *The Atlantic* argued that Rich's thesis was wrong—and irrelevant anyway. As we saw in Chapters 1 and 2, the basic infrastructure behind the climate disinformation campaign was already in place in the mid-1980s. The lengthy subtitle of Meyer's piece provides a cogent summary: "By portraying the early years of climate politics as a tragedy, the [*New York Times Magazine*] lets Republicans and the fossil-fuel industry off the hook."[7] The penultimate line in Rich's piece is classic deflection: "Human nature has brought us to this place; perhaps human nature will one day bring us through."

Since the publication of Rich's story, the *Times* has published dozens of pieces emphasizing the role of individual behavior in combatting climate change. That includes what we eat ("The Facts About Food and Climate Change"), how we move around ("One Thing We Can Do: Drive Less"), whether we should vacation ("If Seeing the World Helps Ruin It, Should We Stay Home?"), and how we view our overall role in tackling the climate crisis ("I Am Part of the Climate-Change Problem. That's Why I Wrote About It").[8]

During the heightened meat safety concerns of the coronavirus pandemic in the spring of 2020, the *Times* promoted one particular commentary ("The End of Meat Is Here") with the tagline, "If you care about the working poor, about racial justice, and about climate change, you have to stop eating animals."[9] For those in the back, what the *Times* was trying to tell us, in not-so-subtle terms, is that we can't really claim to care about climate change (or racial justice, or really, just about anything) if we choose to eat meat. That's some weapons-grade psychological meat-shaming manipulation there, *New York Times* editors!

In an unusual move during the lead-up to the 2020 Democratic primaries, the *New York Times* endorsed *two* candidates, Minnesota senator Amy Klobuchar and Massachusetts senator Elizabeth Warren. Both candidates supported action on climate (great!), but the *Times* editorial board couldn't resist making this (not so great) critique of one of them: "Ms. Warren often casts the net far too wide, placing the blame for a host of maladies from climate change to gun violence at the feet of the business community when the onus is on society as a whole."[10] If it looks like deflection, sounds like deflection, and smells like deflection, it's probably deflection.

All of this is not to say that the *Times* has been acting as a willing coconspirator in spreading fossil-fuel-industry propaganda; rather, it has been, at the very least, an unintentional enabler of deflection by buying into framing that overwhelmingly emphasizes individual responsibility over systemic change. Perhaps the *Times* and other mainstream media outlets are victims of "seepage"—the infiltration of contrarian framing into the mainstream climate discourse—arguably a consequence of the fossil fuel industry's constant barrage of dis-informative propaganda.[11]

Sami Grover noted how successful the deflection campaign has proven to be: "Ask your average citizen what they can do to stop global warming, and they will say 'go vegetarian,' or 'turn off the lights,' long before they talk about lobbying their elected officials."[12] My graduate institution, Yale University, has bought into this logic. In defending its decision not to divest of fossil fuel holdings, the Yale Corporation issued a statement arguing that "ignoring the damage caused by *consumers*, is misdirected," blaming individuals over corporate behavior.[13]

In an essay titled "The Futility of Guilt-Based Advocacy," ethicist Steven D. Hales argued that the entire discipline of philosophical ethics has been hijacked by such misleading framing. Hales reported that he "recently attended an international ethics conference, and the overwhelming take-away was the realization that philosophical ethics remains obsessed with individuals . . . what you should do, how you should act, who you should become. It is not appreciated that all the really serious moral issues of our time are collective action problems. . . . The talks that did address collective action issues were keen on making them ultimately a matter of individual responsibility or blame."[14]

It is possible that behavior-shaming—about dietary preference, for example—is fed by a sense of powerlessness, despair, and doom—a pervasive sense of inevitability that is promoted by a form of inactivism we will call *doomism*. After all, pointing fingers is something we can all do, even if we perceive climate mitigation as a lost cause. Climate scientist Daniel Swain wondered aloud on Twitter "why so many people apparently think [personal shaming and advocacy of extreme austerity] is somehow helpful." *New York Times* climate reporter John Schwartz replied, "For a lot of people, shaming is its own reward: that feeling of standing on the moral high ground is a hell of a drug."[15] Is behavior-shaming the modern opiate of the climate-anxiety-stricken masses? And are the inactivists the pushers?

Climate-messaging expert Max Boycoff of the University of Colorado agrees that the focus on individual behavior is a product, at least in part, of the seemingly "overwhelming" nature of the challenge and of our failure thus far to have engaged in the kind of collective response that is needed. He argues, however, that framing the problem solely as one of individual responsibility does little to address it, and that "flight-shaming," for example, "is one of the more unproductive ways to have a conversation." He noted that all shaming does is make people feel bad; it's "blaming other people while not actually talking about the structures that give rise to the need or desire to take those trips."[16]

The messaging from some climate pundits, however, has actually played *into* the individual-behavior deflection campaign. Consider David Victor, a policy researcher at the University of California, San Diego. Victor has been criticized for having taken funding from fossil fuel interests (BP and the electric-utility-backed Electric Power Research Institute, to be specific), for serving as a witness for the Trump administration in opposing the Our Children's Trust lawsuit against fossil-fuel-industry polluters, and for his opposition to the use of actionable warming targets in guiding climate policy.[17] In December 2019, he wrote an op-ed in the *New York Times* downplaying the responsibility of leading emitters for the failure of international climate summits, including COP25, to achieve substantial emissions reductions.[18] Dr. Genevieve Guenther, founder and director of the media watchdog organization End Climate Science, characterized Victor's op-ed as "a master class" in inactivist "tropes," from "downplaying the responsibility of the US, to exaggerating the costs of action, to focusing on the hard-to-decarbonize sectors, to calling climate policy . . . 'a religion.'"[19]

Victor has also raised eyebrows by insisting that climate advocates should avoid the rhetoric of "corporate guilt" and accept the fact that "we're all guilty." This language echoes that of the fossil fuel companies. In 2018, for example, Chevron argued in court that "it's the way people are living their lives" that's driving climate change.[20] I cannot speak to Victor's intent or motives. What I *can* speak to is how this sort of framing—deflecting responsibility from corporate polluters to individual behavior—is seized upon and exploited by the inactivists. Victor's comments precipitated a particularly heated argument between climate advocates on social media, which leads us to an important related discussion: how deflection plays into the inactivists' efforts to sow division within the climate community.[21]

ANTISOCIAL MEDIA AND BOTS OF WAR

At the center of the acrimonious debate over individual action versus systemic change is a false dilemma. *Both* are important and necessary. But this debate is increasingly being used to drive a wedge within the community of climate advocates. This is what's known as a wedge campaign, and it's nothing new. It has its origins in decades-old disinformation campaigns.

This style of information warfare was first called "the wedge strategy" more than two decades ago by the Discovery Institute, a religious organization devoted to undermining public acceptance of the theory of evolution.[22] The Discovery Institute sought to introduce the teaching of creationism in schools, driving a wedge into the scientific community by appropriating scientific terminology (including the use of the scientific-sounding term "intelligent design" to describe what is actually thinly veiled young Earth creationism) and articulating an agenda that reasonable science educators might buy into.

As with any broad and diverse community, there are natural divisions within the climate movement that fall along lines, for example, of age, gender, ethnicity, political identity, and, of course, *lifestyle* choices—we'll come back to that. Taking advantage of these preexisting fault lines, a particular subclass of the inactivists, whom we shall call the *dividers*, employ the wedge strategy to sow division and discord within the climate community. The principle is simple: divide climate advocates so they cannot speak with one voice, and use this internal division to distract, disable, preoccupy, and nullify.

Today we know that state actors—Russia, in particular—manipulated social media by promoting fake news articles and deploying trolls and bot armies during the 2016 US presidential election.[23] Their mission was to divide Democratic voters by siphoning off potential supporters of Democratic candidate Hillary Clinton and convincing them to support alternative candidates like Bernie Sanders (in the primaries) or Jill Stein (in the general election), or else discouraging voters so they simply stayed home and didn't vote at all. All they needed to do was depress Democratic turnout enough to tip the election to their preferred candidate, Donald Trump. They were successful.

Some of the fiercest online attacks against Hillary Clinton in 2016 appeared to come from the environmental left, criticizing her climate policies (for example, her position on fracking). We now know that many of those attacks were actually Russian trolls and bots seeking to convince younger, greener progressives that there was no difference between the two candidates (so they might as well stay home). As an adviser to the Clinton campaign on energy and climate, I can attest that there was a *world* of difference between Trump and Clinton when it came to climate.[24] But the fact that younger voters remained under the false impression that Clinton was no better than Trump on climate almost certainly played a role in keeping them from voting, effectively handing the election to Trump—and Russia.[25]

We have seen that Russia's efforts were likely motivated—in part, if not entirely—by an agenda of fossil fuel extraction—in particular, a half-trillion-dollar partnership between Russian state oil company Rosneft and American oil giant ExxonMobil. That partnership was stymied by US sanctions against Russia over its 2014 invasion of Ukraine. A President Clinton would have continued to support the sanctions. A President Trump would not. The scandal that has come to be known as Russiagate might actually be so simple it can be summarized in two words: *fossil fuels*.

The fact that Russia is continuing to use social media to manipulate the American public is well known. What has gotten less attention is *why*. And again, the answer may be the same two words. The Russian economy is dependent on the continued extraction and monetization of Russia's primary economic asset—oil reserves. And we know that Vladimir Putin has made dismissive comments about climate change, misguidedly arguing that Russia might actually benefit from it.

Seen in this light, it would be surprising if Russia did *not* use the tactics it has honed over the past decade to continue to manipulate public opinion on climate change to its advantage in the United States and beyond. As a *Chicago Tribune* reporter summarized it, a 2018 congressional report found that "Russian trolls used Facebook, Instagram and Twitter to inflame U.S. political debate over energy policy and climate change, a finding that underscores how the Russian campaign of social media manipulation went beyond the 2016 president election."[26] Their efforts continue to bear fruit.

The deeply flawed notion that there is no difference between Trump and the Democrats on climate remains pervasive among green progressives.[27] In December 2019, when I posted a link to a *New York Times* op-ed emphasizing the role the Republican Party has played in enabling climate-change denial and inaction, I received a number of angry responses insisting that both parties were equally to blame.[28] One user, whose Twitter home page was emblazoned with an image of Bernie Sanders, insisted, "Climate denial is absolutely bipartisan. Frankly, establishment Democrats are worse because they say it's real and still pursue policies that will kill us all." A pile-on ensued: "This establishment Democratic partisan absolutely proves your point," and, "What difference does it make if Democrats believe the science, but then still promote fracking, drilling." A defender did enter the fray (my climate scientist colleague Eric Steig of the University of Washington), tweeting, "There's so much wrong with your way of thinking about this, I don't even know where to start. I'll just make one point: Democrats were in the [2015] Paris agreement. Trump took us out. Yes, this matters." But have no fear, nihilism always finds a way. Responded one final interlocutor, "But the Paris agreement isn't doing anything and isn't strong enough to halt warming even if everyone fully participated, so . . ." Wrong and misguided. And just what the *dividers* ordered.[29]

Of course, it's not just bad state actors who are involved. Fossil fuel interests and their front groups are known to be using similar methods to manipulate public opinion, and the collective effect is a poisoning and weaponization of social media to advance the cause of denial, deflection, doomism, and delay. The basic strategy is as follows: Use professional trolls to amplify a particular meme on social media, and send in an army of bots to amplify it further, baiting genuine individuals to join the fray. The idea is to create a massive food fight (the term is apropos, given that many of the online tussles, as we will see, are actually *about* individual food preferences) and thereby generate polarization and conflict. A favored approach is to seed a prospective online discussion with trolls or bots aggressively advocating opposite positions and acrimoniously attacking each other. Pretty soon a melee unfolds. This has, of course, been done specifically in the climate arena.[30]

Christopher Bouzy is a software developer and founder of Bot Sentinel, a platform that estimates how likely a specified Twitter account is a "bot" based on an evaluation of its pattern of tweeting. *Inside Climate News* reported an episode that Bouzy observed in the wake of CNN's climate forum in early September 2019. An unusually high number of mentions of the term "climate change" (seven hundred) were made over a twenty-four-hour period by the roughly one hundred thousand Twitter accounts Bot Sentinel was tracking as "trollbots" (bots that have been programmed to engage in divisive trolling behavior). According to Bouzy, whenever a particular phrase like "climate change" is trending among trollbots, there is likely some amount of coordination involved: "What we are noticing is these phrases are more than likely being pushed by accounts that have an agenda," he said, adding, "It's fascinating to see this stuff happen in real time. Sometimes we can see literally 5 or 10 accounts able to manipulate a hashtag because they have so many people following them. It doesn't take that many accounts to get something going."[31] *The Guardian* reported that "the social media conversation over the climate crisis is being reshaped by an army of automated Twitter bots." It estimated that "a quarter of all tweets about climate on an average day are produced by bots," with the effect of "distorting the online discourse to include far more climate science denialism than it would otherwise."[32]

DIVIDE AND CONQUER

When it comes to polarizing rhetoric, there is no greater opportunity to divide people than when it comes to lifestyle choices, for they are tied directly to one's sense of identity. Since individual action is tied directly to lifestyle choices, it provides a perfect opportunity for in-activists. They are more than happy to weaponize individual action and deflection in an effort to generate a wedge within the climate movement.

Social media, as we have already seen, provides a perfect tool for dividers to generate a "personal behavior" wedge. Some of our more combative inclinations—finger-pointing, behavior-shaming, virtue-signaling, and grievance-airing—are on full display on social media, and the bots and trolls exploit them to turn minor fissures into major rifts. Aggressive guilt-based engagement is known to be counterac-tive to progress, as a result of something known as the "boomerang effect." One study concluded, for example, that when it comes to reducing household energy use, "it is particularly important to focus on positive norms (desirable behaviors) rather than negative norms (undesirable behaviors)." Behavior-shaming of individuals may even be counteractive to climate action. Think of this as a "bonus" for the inactivists.[33]

Behavior-shaming isn't *always* a bad thing. When it is directed at the inactivist politicians, industry shills, and climate-change deniers seeking to block action on climate, it is wholly appropriate. Which brings us to Greta Thunberg, the seventeen-year-old Swedish girl who has become the leader of a global youth climate movement. Thunberg has chided politicians and opinion leaders who fail to support climate-friendly policies. But interestingly—and relevant to our larger thesis here—much of the media and social media emphasis has been on her *personal* behavior—in particular, her refusal to fly (owing to the carbon footprint of commercial flight), which resulted in her much-publicized transatlantic crossing by sailboat to participate in the September 2019 United Nations Climate Change Summit in New York City.

Thunberg seems to be a favorite target for those looking to create polarization. Consider the former Fox News executive Ken LaCorte, who operates a website called Liberal Edition News. According to the *New York Times*, it uses "Russian tactics" by feeding readers "a steady diet of content guaranteed to drive liberal voters further left or to wring a visceral response from moderates." One example of LaCorte's divisive content, according to the *Times*, was a story that "singled out an Italian youth soccer coach who called Greta Thunberg, the teenage climate activist, a 'whore.'" It is thoroughly unsurprising that inactivists have employed Thunberg in their wedge-generation efforts.[34]

I have even found myself at the center of those efforts. I have repeatedly emphasized in my public outreach that *both* individual and collective action are important when it comes to climate-change mitigation.[35] I've been outspoken in my support of Thunberg's efforts, for she exemplifies this view in her own actions. But facts be damned if there's a wedge that can be created.[36]

In November 2019, two academics wrote a click-bait commentary on the *Forbes* website with the leading title "Does Greta Thunberg's Lifestyle Equal Climate Denial? One Climate Scientist Seems to Suggest So."[37] Yes, that "climate scientist" was purportedly me. The authors sought to manufacture a fake conflict between Thunberg and me by misrepresenting statements I had made in an interview with *The Guardian*.[38] In the interview, I had criticized inactivists for deflecting attention from systemic solutions to personal action. The authors of the *Forbes* piece claimed, without any evidence, that my criticism was directed at Greta Thunberg, brazenly insisting that "Thunberg v. Mann is now the debate to watch!" The accusation, as others noted, was absurd.[39]

Ironically, in the very same *Guardian* interview, I had warned, "We should also be aware how the forces of denial are exploiting the lifestyle change movement to get their supporters to argue with each other." Mission accomplished! While there's no evidence that these authors were working directly on behalf of inactivists, their efforts were indeed exploited by them.

If you're thinking such disingenuous claims are a one-off, a fluke, an isolated incident, think again. Just a few months earlier, Anthony Watts, a climate-change denier affiliated with the Koch brothers–funded Heartland Institute, leveled a very similar attack against Katharine Hayhoe, a leading climate science communicator. Watts posted a commentary falsely claiming that Hayhoe had attacked Greta Thunberg's "Climate 'Shaming' Crusade."[40] Hayhoe responded immediately on Twitter, saying, "[I] don't normally bother to call out liars on Twitter but I will here, as they're trying to invent a disagreement to drive a wedge between us. @GretaThunberg is not personally shaming anyone: she is acting according to her principles."[41]

The above examples show how the inactivists are seeking to pit climate scientists against climate advocates. They are indisputably also drawing upon generational and cultural divides, seeking, for example, to pit the ivory-towered Baby Boomer and Gen X academics against the down-in-the-trenches, upstart millennial, Gen Z youngsters. Such divisive efforts appear to be catching on ("Okay, boomer," anyone?).[42]

The clashes have spilled out into the streets. Consider this example involving former California governor Jerry Brown. Brown made climate change the signature issue of his final term. He spearheaded the most ambitious climate target in history with an executive order committing California to total, economy-wide carbon neutrality by 2045.[43] He led the opposition to the Trump administration's threat to withdraw from the 2015 Paris Agreement, leading the "we're still in" coalition of states, municipalities, corporations, and businesses that vowed to uphold their commitments. When rumors emerged shortly after the 2016 election that Trump was planning to defund climate data-collecting satellites, Brown famously said, "California will launch its own damn satellite." I was there and heard him say it.[44]

While I will concede that I'm a bit biased—I am both an adviser to, and a friend of, former governor Brown—I was genuinely taken aback to see him vilified as the *enemy* by youth and social justice protesters at the Global Climate Action Summit that Brown held in San Francisco in September 2018. One journalist described the protesters as "part of the environmental justice movement, many people of color from less well-off, more polluted places. . . . They want the fight for climate change to result in cleaner air for them right now," adding, "The people they are protesting (Governor Brown and his allies) are part of the mainstream environmental movement, which is often wealthier and whiter."[45] The protesters attacked Brown for failing to ban oil and natural gas drilling (sometimes called fracking) in California. One banner read, "Climate Leaders Don't Frack." If ever there was a case of the perfect being the enemy of the good, this was it. As Brown pointed out, "We're trying to do more . . . but we have a legislature; we have courts; we have a federal Congress and federal courts. . . . We've got a lot of elements in the political landscape that in a free society we have to deal with."[46]

You might argue that this was a clash between youthful idealism on one side and jaded pragmatism and realpolitik on the other, but there were elements of race and culture and perhaps gender undergirding the confrontation. One former Green Party candidate for the US Senate and Congress, Arn Menconi, posed the rhetorical question, "Have you noticed the other hit pieces coming from our own side that when you don't agree with them you're a sexist and racist?"[47]

Though inactivists are constantly looking for wedges they can use to divide the climate movement, sometimes the climate movement makes it easy for them. Consider, for example, the recent remarks of Roger Hallam, cofounder of the climate activist group Extinction Rebellion, who downplayed the Holocaust. Combined with his controversial past statements on sexism, racism, and democracy, his statements have led to the German branch of Extinction Rebellion distancing itself from the cofounder of the very organization with which they're affiliated.[48]

Let us return, however, to the matter of individual action versus systemic change, for this is at the very center of the wedge campaign. Here we have seen even the most well-meaning of environmental organizations contribute to the growing schisms within the climate movement. The Sierra Club has played a key role in promoting climate action in recent years under the leadership of its executive director, Michael Brune. But readers may also recall that the Sierra Club was one of the (presumably unwitting) initial supporters of the infamous beverage-industry-hatched "Crying Indian" deflection campaign. It appears that the Sierra Club has more recently, at least at times, also fallen victim to the broader climate-change deflection campaign.

In an editorial in the organization's magazine, *Sierra*, titled "Yes, Actually, Individual Responsibility Is Essential to Solving the Climate Crisis," the magazine's editor, Jason Mark, commented on a *USA Today* op-ed I wrote in June 2019 with my Penn State colleague Jonathan Brockopp.[49] In the piece, called "You Can't Save the Climate by Going Vegan. Corporate Polluters Must Be Held Accountable," we opined that *both* individual action and systemic change are important, and that the former cannot be a substitute for the latter. Jason Mark implied that we had presented a "half-truth"—that we had "traded lifestyle scolding for now being scolded if you mention the importance of personal lifestyle." What we had *actually* said was that an *exclusive* focus on individual action, to the point of neglecting systemic change, is problematic: "Though many of these actions are worth taking, and colleagues and friends of ours are focused on them in good faith, a fixation on voluntary action *alone* takes the pressure off of the push for governmental policies to hold corporate polluters accountable" (emphasis added). To be fair, Mark did subsequently revise the online version of his commentary to clarify that we had not in fact argued against the role of lifestyle change.

The Sierra Club has been and remains an important ally in the climate wars. This example serves as a reminder that even allies can buy into unhelpful framing, especially when inactivists are so intent on nurturing that framing.

FOOD FIGHT

Down in the trenches of social media, the wedge campaign is clearly bearing fruit. The dividers have successfully generated a veritable "food fight"—in fact, a literal one, getting people to argue about their dietary preferences, as well as their preferred means of transportation, how many children they have, and other matters of lifestyle and personal choice. "If nobody is without carbon sin, who gets to cast the first lump of coal?" I asked in a commentary for *Time* magazine. "Who is truly walking the climate walk? The carnivore who doesn't fly? The vegan who travels to see family abroad?" The opportunities for finger-pointing seem endless.[50]

Meat, however, is central to the food fight. Especially the meat that so many seem to have a beef with—beef. Though beef consumption is responsible for only 6 percent of total carbon emissions, it often seems to fill close to 100 percent of my Twitter feed.[51] The meat melee was fed by a highly successful and influential 2014 documentary, *Cowspiracy*, which promoted the false notion that meat-eating is the primary contributor to human-caused climate change. *Cowspiracy* diverted—you might even say *deflected*—attention from the real conspiracy on the part of fossil fuel interests to confuse the public about the role of fossil fuel burning. Billed as "The Film That Environmental Organizations Don't Want You to See," *Cowspiracy* maintained that the livestock industry has conspired with leading environmental organizations to hide the fact that meat consumption, not the burning of fossil fuels, is responsible for the lion's share of warming.

But that thesis isn't the product of incisive research and investigative journalism: it's a product of dubious non-peer-reviewed claims built on bad math, amplified by a polemic film.[52]

As a result, there is now a seemingly limitless and very animated community of vegan activists who are convinced that meat-shaming is the solution to climate change. I myself have been attacked on social media for my ostensible lust for meat—despite being up front about the fact that I don't eat it.[53] Animal rights activists often attack climate scientists simply for pointing out that the contribution from meat-eating is small compared to that from the burning of fossil fuels. Such hostility toward fact-based discourse from the ostensible left finds much in common, ironically, with the attacks on climate scientists from the climate-change-denying right. Unwittingly or not, a sizable number of vegan activists have been weaponized by the dividers and deflectors for their cause.

As I frequently point out, I get my electricity from renewables, have one child, drive a hybrid vehicle, and don't eat meat.[54] I have chosen a meat-free lifestyle for several reasons—solidarity with my daughter (who has chosen a meat-free diet), ethical considerations, and a desire to minimize my environmental footprint. I think it's important to set a good example. But I do not attempt to police others' lifestyles. We have already seen that this can be counteractive to climate progress. Gentle encouragement, and, most importantly, incentives for lifestyle change, are a better path.

There are many worthwhile societal problems to confront—animal rights, a cleaner environment, social justice, income inequality, the list goes on. I respect and appreciate those who advocate for tackling these pressing challenges. But I am wary of individuals who seem to be trying to hijack the climate discourse for the cause of worldwide veganism (or, for that matter, the abandonment of market economics—something we'll discuss later). It represents another form of deflection and plays right into the agenda of the inactivists.

Of course, personal behavior isn't limited to food choices. Methods of travel, particularly flight, are another source of great contention. Unlike overland transportation (automobiles, buses, trains), which can be electrified and powered by renewable energy, flight requires moving great amounts of mass over large distances, and at present it is very difficult to decarbonize. There is promising research into high-density biofuels, and with better battery technology, electrification of aviation should eventually become possible. In the meantime, those who rely on air travel have no choice right now but to keep emitting carbon—and, for those of us, like myself, who have the luxury of being able to pay for it, purchasing verifiable carbon offsets.

Still, flying receives a disproportionate amount of shaming, considering its carbon contribution. Air travel only accounts for about 3 percent of global carbon emissions. It is dwarfed by emissions from the rest of the transportation sector, as well as the power sector and industry. In fact, alternatives can sometimes incur a greater carbon footprint than flying—one study has found that when a full life-cycle analysis is performed (i.e., accounting for construction and maintenance of vehicles and required infrastructure), train travel can sometimes come with a higher carbon footprint than air travel.[55] It might also be noted that taking three days off work to travel to a destination by train, or three weeks to travel by boat, is a luxury most working people can't afford. Insisting they do it anyway could be argued to be laden in implicit privilege.

So why does flying, like meat-eating, elicit such passion and so much attention when it comes to our individual carbon footprints? Perhaps deflectors want us to focus on the purported hypocrisy of elites—jet-setting celebrities and conference-attending scientists—who advocate for climate action. We'll return to this point later. Perhaps class warfare is at work. Like age, gender, and ethnicity, class is something that divides us, and it provides a natural wedge for those who want people to fight with each other rather than working together to improve things. Part of the opposition to flight seems to be that it is mostly well-off people who do it. Business-related air travel is a matter of routine for businesspeople, and their companies and corporations pay for it. The greater someone's disposable income, the more likely that person is to fly to distant locations for vacations. Flight-shaming is a good fit with those who see capitalism itself as the enemy. We'll return to this point later, too.

Meanwhile, let's recognize one other matter of personal choice that has substantial implications for our individual carbon footprints: having children. All other things being equal, doubling your family size doubles your collective carbon footprint. It is, of course, possible to raise a child in a carbon-friendly manner—in fact, a friend of mine wrote a book called *The Zero-Footprint Baby* on how to do just that.[56] But doing so requires even more diligence than managing your own carbon footprint—if you're not very good at the latter, it's exceedingly unlikely you'll be any good at the former.

Responding to the criticism she gets from behavior-shamers about her own personal behavior—why she flies to conferences or why she had children—climate scientist Katharine Hayhoe responded that "flying and eating and having children is often framed as a purity test. It's like, 'So you say you care about climate change. But if you have a child or eat meat or, heaven forbid, have ever stepped in an airplane, then you are not one of our allies. You are one of our enemies.'" Hayhoe noted that the sorts of attacks on climate scientists that used to come from climate-change deniers now come from "people who are not only concerned but are part of the fight."[57] Jonathan Foley, a climate scientist who is now executive director of Project Drawdown, an organization devoted to societal decarbonization, calls flight-shaming "the climate movement eating its own."[58]

I must confess that I share the concern and bewilderment of my climate scientist peers. We've chosen to devote our lives to raising awareness about the climate crisis, and yet many ostensible climate advocates would gladly throw us under the bus because we're not living our lives as off-the-grid vegan hermits. Who, today, can truly afford to live without carbon "sin"? The flightless vegan with four children? The childless vegetarian whose job requires transcontinental air travel? The childless, flightless celiac sufferer who relies upon meat for protein? We all face real-world challenges and tough choices that complicate the effort to completely decarbonize our lives in a system that is still reliant on fossil fuel infrastructure. We must change that system. Individual efforts to reduce one's carbon footprint are laudable. But without systemic change, we will not achieve the massive decarbonization of our economy that is necessary to avert catastrophic climate change.

Would Hayhoe and other leading climate scientist-advocates be as effective as they are if they chose to operate entirely outside the system that exists? While some have argued so, I think a compelling argument can be made that advocates for change have the greatest reach, as measured by media accessibility, public speaking opportunities, and engagement with policymakers and stakeholders, working *within* the system that exists.

Nonetheless, many prominent climate advocates continue to advance the "individual action" primacy frame. *Guardian* columnist George Monbiot, known for his advocacy for climate action and his efforts to call out bad corporate actors in the climate space, has insisted that "we are all killers" (that is, those of us who continue to fly are killing the planet).[59] Meteorologist Eric Holthaus, the former editor of the *Wall Street Journal*'s weather blog, decided back in 2013 to swear off air travel for good, insisting "there is no other way that makes sense" when it comes to reducing carbon emissions. He reportedly also considered taking the extraordinary measure of having a vasectomy to guard against his own contribution to population growth.[60]

Holthaus, who garnered a fair amount of media coverage at the time for his no-flying pledge (some of it rather mixed[61]) went further, however. He demanded that others, too, refuse to fly, scolding science writer Andrew Freedman when he said that "those of us that report on weather & climate . . . should be the ones leading by example. There is no neutrality anymore."[62] He also excoriated Jason Rabinowitz, a travel aficionado and host of an aviation podcast, when Rabinowitz shared his plans to fly to Madrid, despite having no particular reason to go, because he had found cheap tickets. Holthaus equated Rabinowitz's pleasure trip to "taking a gun and just firing blindly into the air towards a crowd just because you think it's fun to shoot a gun." Holthaus didn't stop there, going on to call Rabinowitz a "selfish, entitled a**hole," adding, "You don't care who you're hurting. You just care about yourself." He capped off this diatribe with the statement that "unexamined privilege like this is literally causing the biggest existential threat we've ever faced as a species." Note the insertion of yet another wedge issue—socioeconomic class—into the conversation. Conservative media outlets seemed to delight in reporting on the fracas.[63]

Holthaus's critiques afford us a window into how wedge-generation seems to feed on itself, beginning with one form (e.g., behavior-shaming), and expanding to others (e.g., identity politics). In June 2019, I found myself at the center of Holthaus's criticism over my association with the climate-change-themed documentary *Ice on Fire*. The basis of the critique? I—as a white male scientist—had appeared in a trailer for the film (produced by HBO) that he felt didn't have enough gender and racial diversity. It is worth noting that I had no editorial role in either the trailer or the film, that the director was a respected woman filmmaker (Leila Connors), and that the film itself featured a diversity of voices and near equal balance with respect to gender.

Indeed, I have frequently found myself immersed in the toxic online environment that prevails in the climate space today, and my own experiences are representative of a much broader pattern in today's online discourse. The dividers, as we have seen, will feed on any organic disagreement, amplifying divisive messages with bot armies and professional trolls. The friendly fire from ostensible climate advocates provides them with more than ample fodder.

YOU HYPOCRITE!

Dividers have sought to target influential experts and public figures in the climate arena as "hypocrites" by accusing them of hedonistic lifestyles entailing huge carbon footprints. It's a brilliant strategy, because it associates concern about climate with social elites, creating a class/culture wedge and discrediting critical thought leaders, which in turn limits the effectiveness of their messaging efforts. All the while, it once again places the emphasis on the *behavior of individuals*, deflecting attention away from the need for systemic change and policy action. It's a perfect storm of divide, discredit, and deflect.

In many cases, the accusations are false and misleading. But what if they were accurate? What if these thought leaders really did have outsized carbon footprints? Would the "hypocrite" accusation be fair? As cogently articulated by environmental writer David Roberts, "there's a hidden premise here . . . that personal emission reductions are an important part of the fight against climate change—if you take climate seriously, you take on an obligation to reduce your own emissions." But, as we have already seen, personal action means little without systemic change. As Roberts noted, individuals targeted as hypocrites typically "are not advocating sacrifice or asceticism" but instead articulating the case for systemic change. "If they advocate for, and are willing to abide by, taxes and regulations designed to reduce emissions, then such folks are being true to their beliefs. You might think they are wrong . . . but they are not hypocrites."[64]

Take Al Gore, the public figure most closely associated with the climate crisis. Gore has for years been pilloried by the right-wing press, including Fox News and the rest of the Murdoch media empire, for the size of his home, his electricity bills, and even his weight. It's all part of an effort to portray him as a gluttonous hypocrite who doesn't practice what he preaches when it comes to his personal carbon footprint.

Now consider what happened upon the release of Gore's breakthrough documentary *An Inconvenient Truth* in 2006. Credited for raising international public awareness about climate change, the film pulled no punches, pointing the finger directly at polluting interests for society's collective failure to act on climate. Shortly after the film was released, a Koch brothers dark-money interest front group, the Tennessee Center for Policy Research (now the Beacon Center of Tennessee), issued a "report" claiming that the former vice president's home used twenty times more energy than the average American home.[65]

Never mind that the "twenty times" number was inflated (it was probably closer to twelve), or that, as Gore's spokespeople pointed out, his residence was also his office, which was staffed with employees, and that Gore paid a premium to get his electricity from green energy sources.[66] There was a smear to be had! The story was promoted by the right-wing media; indeed, the "hypocrite" narrative ultimately proved irresistible even to mainstream media outlets like ABC News, which ran the headline, "Al Gore's Inconvenient Truth: a $30,000 Energy Bill."[67]

Betraying the true agenda behind the smear campaign—to discredit a key climate messenger at a critical moment *and* to deflect attention from systemic change toward individual behavior—the Tennessee Center's twenty-seven-year-old "president," Drew Johnson, gleefully quipped that "as the spokesman of choice for the global warming movement, Al Gore has to be willing to walk the walk, not just talk the talk, when it comes to home energy use."[68]

As the most prominent celebrity climate activist, Leonardo DiCaprio has been similarly targeted for attack, being portrayed as a jet-setting hedonist by the conservative media. "Hollywood Hypocrite's Global Warming Sermon," read one headline in the Murdoch-owned *Herald Sun* of Australia.[69] Another Murdoch-owned paper, the *New York Post*, ran an article titled "Leo DiCaprio Isn't the Only Climate Change Hypocrite," which also name-checked actor-turned-climate-activist Mark Ruffalo, President Barack Obama, and . . . Pope Francis.[70] Yes, not even the pope is above being smeared by Rupert Murdoch when fossil fuels are on the line. In case those headlines seem too subtle, Britain's right-wing *Daily Mail*, which has attacked DiCaprio as a supposed hypocrite numerous times, gives us "Eco-Warrior or Hypocrite? Leonardo DiCaprio Jets Around the World Partying . . . While Preaching to Us All on Global Warming."[71] You get it? DiCaprio is a *hypocrite*, because he has a *large carbon footprint*, and so we shouldn't be concerned about *global warming*.

Absurd, you say? And yet it's an incredibly effective message, and not just with conservatives, but with the privilege-averse environmental left as well. There is something about perceived hypocrisy—and the sense that someone else is getting more than their fair share—that seems to tap directly into the reptilian part of our brains, bypassing the logic circuits and eliciting instinctive outrage and anger. The intent is to focus that outrage and anger on climate champions—and, ideally, the entire climate movement.

So are the charges fair? As the journalist David Roberts pointed out in a 2016 article for *Vox*, there is not "any evidence that DiCaprio has advocated personal emission reductions or told anyone they ought to forgo planes or boats." Roberts noted that "his focus is on [the need for] political leadership. . . . So the 'hypocrisy' charge fails. You're not a hypocrite for not doing things you haven't said anyone else should do either."[72]

But what about the claim that figures like DiCaprio should simply do better, and that, as an opinion leader devoted to raising awareness about climate change, he should "walk the walk," signaling to others the behavioral changes that are necessary? Roberts answers that charge as well: "If signaling is the issue, well, DiCaprio is supporting electric cars and pushing for clean energy in the film industry and building eco-resorts and supporting clean energy campaigns and starting a friggin' climate charity. Oh, and making heartfelt appeals in front of 9 million people at the Academy Awards. That's a lot of signaling! . . . DiCaprio has a long history of serious work on this issue. By any measure, he's doing better on signaling than the vast majority of wealthy, influential people."[73]

In spite of her extraordinary actions to reduce her carbon footprint, even Greta Thunberg has become a favorite target of these types of attacks. Inactivists have been doing their best to dismiss her and her fellow youth climate activists as hypocrites. After Thunberg famously crossed the Atlantic in a boat to participate in events surrounding the September 2019 UN Climate Change Summit in New York City, Anthony Watts posted an article on his website pouncing on her for, among other things, traveling in a boat that was made partly of "non-recyclable plastic"—really![74]

On September 20, 2019, Thunberg marched with thousands through the streets of New York City. Millions more in other cities around the world joined into this Global Youth Climate Strike, an event seeking to draw attention to the climate crisis. In an effort to undermine the message of the strike, a hoax photo was promoted on Facebook by a dubious group calling itself the Australian Youth Coal Coalition. It claimed to show trash strewn by climate strikers in Sydney's Hyde Park. The caption read, "Look at the mess today's climate protesters left behind in beautiful Hyde Park. So much plastic. So much landfill. So sad." The post was shared nineteen thousand times in twelve hours, and thousands more times by copycats, both on Facebook and on other social media platforms. Unsurprisingly, the image wasn't from the climate strike; it wasn't even from Australia. It was taken in April 2019 at London's Hyde Park following a marijuana festival. In fact, it had already been falsely used before to smear a previous climate protest by the climate activist group Extinction Rebellion—ironically, the Extinction Rebellion folks had actually tried to *clean up* the mess left behind from the festival.[75]

Alleged "hypocrisy" is often the weapon of choice, and it has been wielded against numerous leading public figures in the climate arena. Murdoch's *Herald Sun*—and, of course, Anthony Watts—attacked Bill McKibben, a leading climate activist and founder of the international activist organization 350.org, for his use of air travel.[76] In fact, a Republican Party opposition group had him trailed, trying to get photographs of him—god forbid—using plastic grocery bags.[77] Murdoch's *New York Post* found fault with Green New Deal advocate and freshman congresswoman Alexandria Ocasio-Cortez (AOC) of New York for having the temerity to use an automobile.[78] The Murdoch press criticized the mayor of Sydney, Australia, Clover Moore, for flying. But she was wise to what was going down, tweeting, "This isn't about flights . . . The underlying issue is what climate scientist @MichaelEMann refers to as 'deflection.' While those against action on climate change used to flatly deny climate science, their tactics have matured. Now they don't deny; they deflect."[79]

Sometimes we witness the buckshot approach. Katie Pavlich of the Young America's Foundation—a Koch brothers–supported outfit—managed to get *The Hill*, an ostensibly mainstream media outlet, to publish an op-ed hit piece ("The Frauds of the Climate Change Movement") invoking all the classic hypocrisy tropes, going after the youth climate protesters, Al Gore, and Barack and Michelle Obama, too, for good measure. Pavlich argued that the Obamas' interest in purchasing a seaside home contradicted their belief in climate change and sea-level rise. I kid you not: "If the former president is truly concerned about sea levels rising as a result of climate change . . . his latest real estate purchase places doubts on his sincerity."[80]

Climate scientists, too, as we have already seen, have been deemed fair game for such assaults. I am frequently subject to specious criticisms about my individual lifestyle choices by those looking to discredit my messaging on climate action. Back in November 2018, in response to a widely misunderstand and misrepresented statement by AOC about how much time is left to avert dangerous warming, I tweeted, "We have ZERO years left to take action. Ten years is (an overly conservative estimate of) when we cross into dangerous territory in the absence of immediate action on climate."[81] One critic replied, "Is @MichaelEMann vegan or vegetarian? Does he drive an EV and have solar at home?"—critiques that, as we've already seen, are misguided in my case.[82]

During my sabbatical in Sydney, Australia, in early 2020, the Australian Broadcasting Corporation invited me onto a news program to discuss the unprecedented heat and bushfire outbreak that Australia was experiencing at the time. Tweeted one critic, "So Michael, you flew over on a jet plane to criticise the democratically elected Australian government on its Climate Policy?"[83] It was a deft use of deflection, behavior-shaming, and hypocrisy-leveling all at the same time by an anonymous user who had just joined Twitter, followed nobody, was followed by nobody, and had only ever tweeted a single thing—that reply to me. Dark money meet dark Twitter.

Why would dividers go after *scientists*? The public perceives scientists to possess both authority and integrity; they rank as the most trusted messengers in society.[84] Undermine the public's trust in scientists, and you undermine their message. That premise underlies the "kill the messenger" strategy by climate-change deniers that we encountered in Chapter 1. The problem the deniers face is that the evidence is so overwhelming that attacks on the science itself aren't credible. Exposing scientists as supposed "hypocrites," however, is a relatively effective way of undermining their perceived integrity along with their credibility as climate messengers.

One might think that scientists would push back fiercely against these cynical and exploitive charges of hypocrisy. Yet the response of many climate scientists and climate communicators has been to internalize the criticism. It's an example of the aforementioned phenomenon of "seepage," a kind of academic twist on the Stockholm syndrome. In short, scientists and communicators absorb the bad-faith criticisms of hypocrisy leveled against them by their adversaries and make dramatic changes in their lifestyle, unwittingly *affirming* the flawed and misleading premise that it's all about personal action rather than policy. Leonardo DiCaprio—a hero in my book—has nonetheless spearheaded a global publicity campaign pointing the finger at the eating of meat.[85] A whole bevy of climate scientists and advocates now advertise the fact that they no longer fly, have turned to vegan diets, or have chosen not to have children. These individuals are trying to do what they believe to be the right thing, and attempting to lead by example. But they seem surprisingly unaware that when they seem to make it all about personal choices and the need for sacrifice, they are in fact unwittingly playing into the inactivist agenda. The Crying Indian PSA redux.

This framing was furthermore encouraged by a peer-reviewed study in the journal *Climatic Change* purporting to demonstrate that scientists who didn't "walk the walk" in limiting their personal carbon emissions were less likely to be believed or trusted than those who did. More specifically, the authors claimed that "the communicators' carbon footprint massively affect their credibility and intentions of their audience to conserve energy," and, "their carbon footprint also affects audience support for public policies advocated by the communicator." Or, as the study's lead author, Shahzeen Attari, put it, "It's like having an overweight doctor giving you dieting advice."[86]

Here's the problem: The study didn't actually demonstrate *any* of these things. The protocol of the study was akin to what is known in political polling as a "push poll," that is, a poll that poses a question in such a way as to elicit a particular response. Specifically, at the beginning of the study, the researchers presented respondents with information about a hypothetical communicator's carbon footprint. That, of course, planted the seed in the respondent's mind that personal carbon footprints are the important thing to be focusing on when it comes to climate solutions. I have done thousands of media interviews about climate change during the past few years and I cannot recall a single instance when the interviewer asked me about my personal carbon footprint (other than the one or two cases when the article itself was actually *about* individual carbon footprints). Rarely, if ever, would viewers or readers have any information about my individual carbon footprint. So how could it possibly influence their appraisal of what I have to say? Only in the very artificial laboratory created by this study's protocol could a communicator's personal behavior so directly influence the impact of their message.

Furthermore, the advice the study offered was completely impractical. If climate advocates had to live off the grid, eat only what they could grow themselves, and wear only the clothes they'd knitted from scratch, there wouldn't be much of a climate movement. That level of sacrifice is unacceptable to most. Climate communicators must operate within the system that exists to be effective while articulating the case for changing that system.

Finally, and perhaps most importantly, the study neglected a growing body of research demonstrating that an inordinate focus on individual action can erode support for systemic solutions to the climate-change problem—that is, governmental climate policy.[87] Given that effective policy is far more critical than individual behavior in actually achieving the necessary carbon emissions reductions to stave off catastrophic climate change, the case could easily—I would even say *convincingly*—be made that attempts to redirect focus to communicators' individual carbon footprints are antithetical to action on climate.

The impact of the *Climatic Change* article and its framing has nonetheless reached well beyond the scientific and academic communities. There is now a popular myth, for example, that it is youth climate activist Greta Thunberg's lifestyle decisions (for example, her unwillingness to use air travel and her vegan diet) that are responsible for her outsized impact on the climate conversation. One commentator in *Forbes* argued that the *Climatic Change* study "may explain why Greta Thunberg has succeeded more than others at communicating the climate crisis and galvanizing social action."[88] Science historian Cormac O'Rafferty took issue with the assertion, however, writing, "The authors . . . assert that Greta's lifestyle may be one reason for her great impact. No evidence in the paper is presented to support this hypothesis. It doesn't hurt of course, but I suspect there are many reasons for the impact of Greta in particular."[89] Indeed, I think it's much more defensible to argue that it is Greta Thunberg's fearlessness in speaking truth to power and her steadfast demand that policymakers support the needed systemic changes that make her so powerful and compelling a figure.

RED MEAT FOR THE BASE

There is another adverse consequence of the "individual responsibility" deflection campaign that I have thus far only alluded to.[90] Requiring climate activists to live ascetic lives gives the appearance that they expect everyone else to give up meat, or travel, or other pleasures. And that is politically dangerous: it plays right into the hands of the inactivists who want to portray climate champions as freedom-hating totalitarians. In other words, there is the danger that efforts appearing to place constraints on individual behavior unduly antagonize and energize the conservative opposition to climate action.

Anger can be stirred up among both progressives and conservatives. With progressives, it's typically about issues of perceived injustice. With conservatives, it often involves the perceived loss of personal liberty. Making climate action all about personal sacrifice reinforces the dominant conservative framing: "They'll take away your hamburgers and plastic straws . . . then your guns, too." Predictably, this very notion has become a tribal rallying call for conservatives.

Observe the messaging by trolls and trollbots promoting this framing. I encounter it constantly in my own Twitter feed. One example, which occurred in the lead-up to the September 2019 UN Climate Change Summit in New York City, was initiated by denier-for-hire Patrick Moore.[91] (Moore is perhaps most famous for saying that the Monsanto-produced weed killer glysophate was safe enough that "you can drink a whole quart of it and it won't hurt you." When presented with a cup of it during a live interview, he refused to drink it and stormed off the set.[92]) Moore, in a characteristically distasteful ad hominem attack, referred to me as a "death-wish cultist" for noting that stabilizing warming below dangerous levels will require us to eventually reach zero net carbon emissions (which can be achieved through both decarbonization of our economy and use of technologies to capture and sequester carbon). Replied one account with a "problematic" (65 percent) trollbot rating from Bot Sentinel, "With the anti red meat brigade you wont even be allowed to wear animal skins when you return to the stone age."[93]

Marianne Lavelle of *Inside Climate News* documented eerily similar messaging patterns by trollbots ahead of the 2019 UN Climate Change Summit. "Democrat #Socialists want to ban:—everything made from plastic—red meat—nuclear power . . . I don't think even Venezuelans have ever been this brainwashed!" tweeted an account with an 84 percent trollbot rating. "The Dems position is ban straws, portion our meat, take our guns, take our cars, abort on a massive scale for population control, and all so we can die from climate change in 11 years!!" tweeted another account with a suspicious rating.[94]

Here's why this is important: Climate change is no longer a wedge issue in and of itself. Climate dismissives poll in the single digits, and recent polling shows that most conservatives are on board with clean energy solutions.[95] So the inactivists need something else to mobilize conservatives for their cause. Framing action on climate as a big-government "they'll take away your burgers" power grab that threatens personal freedom is tailor made, ideologically speaking, for this purpose.

Unfortunately, climate messengers often play right into this agenda when they characterize action on climate in terms of "sacrifice." Energy and climate author Ramez Naam put it this way: "I think a focus on personal sacrifice . . . turns off many in the middle. It makes getting political action on climate harder rather than easier."[96] The reason that conservative media outlets like *Twitchy* and *Conservative Edition News* were so delighted to report on Eric Holthaus's flight-shaming episode was that it fed the narrative of environmental extremists trying to dictate how other people should lead their lives.[97] It was a gift from deflectionist heaven.

The premise that climate action demands sacrifice is itself deeply flawed. If anything, the opposite is actually the case. The cost of *inaction* on climate, as measured in the damage done by devastating wildfires, heatwaves, wildfires, floods, and superstorms, is far greater than the cost of taking action. The real sacrifice would be if we *fail* to act, and subject ourselves to ever more dangerous and damaging climate-change impacts. *That's* the appropriate frame to be using here.

Instead we see climate advocacy organizations often reinforcing the notion of a need for "personal sacrifice" in their messaging. Consider again the Sierra Club article by Jason Mark about the importance of individual action. The subtitle for the article? "Personal Sacrifices Are Necessary, and Greens Should Be Honest About That."[98]

Climate scientists, too, can inadvertently play into this unhelpful framing when they emphasize the sacrifices they have chosen to make in an effort to decrease their personal carbon footprints. In an Associated Press article, journalist Seth Borenstein observed, "Some climate scientists and activists are limiting their flying, their consumption of meat and their overall carbon footprints to avoid adding to the global warming they study." Borenstein focused primarily on one particular climate scientist, Kim Cobb, explaining that, "she is about to ground herself. . . . Cobb will fly just once next year, to attend a massive international science meeting in Chili. . . . This year she passed on 11 flights, including Paris, Beijing and Sydney."[99]

Borenstein emphasized that "there's a cost," noting that "Cobb was invited to be the plenary speaker wrapping up a major ocean sciences conference next year in San Diego. It's a plum role. Cobb asked organizers if she could do it remotely," but "they said no. . . . Conference organizers withdrew the offer." Cobb is a colleague and a friend of mine, and there's no doubt in my mind that she's earnest in her efforts to be a positive force for change and to set a good example for other scientists. But do we want to be sending the message that scientists (and by implication, others) must make career sacrifices for the sake of their individual carbon footprints?

Shahzeen Attari, author of the "scientists must walk the walk" study, seems to think so. Attari said that while she doesn't "want to clip [Cobb's] wings," she will be "judged" by her audience on how much energy she uses.[100] We've already discussed why that is unlikely to be true. And to the extent that "sacrifice" is emphasized in scientists' messaging, it might have the unintended effect of alienating moderate and conservative audiences, playing into the notion that climate action is just an excuse to impose a Spartan lifestyle upon the populace.

There is a sizable contingent within the conservative base that frankly seems predisposed to aversion when it comes to a strong, smart, bold, young, powerful Latina. New York City congresswoman Alexandria Ocasio-Cortez fits the bill—and thus served as the perfect foil when she became the principal proponent of the Green New Deal (GND). But the GND has been used to erode conservative support for climate action in more substantive ways, too.

The GND is a nod to President Franklin Roosevelt's New Deal, a major government initiative of the 1930s that used massive government stimulus spending in an effort to lift the United States out of the Great Depression. The New Deal did this primarily by boosting employment through major construction projects, including highways, dams, national park infrastructure, and so on. As originally conceived in the Obama era, the GND also embraced market mechanisms, such as carbon taxes and subsidies for green energy, to tackle environmental challenges.[101]

As reinvented by AOC (and Senator Ed Markey), however, the GND has taken on a considerably larger agenda with an additional focus on diverse social programs. The formal resolution, introduced by AOC and cosponsors on February 7, 2019, supports a "10-year national mobilization over the next 10 years," which includes among its planks the following:

- "Guaranteeing a job with a family-sustaining wage, adequate family and medical leave, paid vacations, and retirement security to all people of the United States."
- "Providing all people of the United States with—(i) high-quality health care; (ii) affordable, safe, and adequate housing; (iii) economic security; and (iv) access to clean water, clean air, healthy and affordable food, and nature."
- "Providing resources, training, and high-quality education, including higher education, to all people of the United States."[102]

Though I broadly support the GND's goals, I have some concerns about the ambitious scope of this specific proposal, as I expressed in a commentary in *Nature* magazine: "Saddling a climate movement with a laundry list of other worthy social programmes risks alienating needed supporters (say, independents and moderate conservatives) who are apprehensive about a broader agenda of progressive social change."[103]

I'm hardly alone in this view. In a January 2020 op-ed in *The Guardian*, Harvard economist Jeffrey Frankel expressed very similar concerns, writing, "In the US, the 'green new deal' signals commitment to the climate cause. But I fear that the legislative proposal that its congressional supporters have introduced will do more harm than good. It includes extraneous measures such as a federal jobs guarantee. This proposal creates a factual basis for a lie that US climate-change deniers have long been telling: that global warming is a hoax promoted as an excuse to expand the size of government."[104]

In my *Nature* commentary, I also questioned the conspicuous absence in the proposal of support for market mechanisms such as carbon pricing, noting that, too, might alienate political centrists who could otherwise be brought on board. We'll have much more to say on this topic in the next chapter.

Some advocates of climate-change action have gone further, including author and activist Naomi Klein. As I stated in the *Nature* commentary, "[Klein's] thesis is that neoliberalism—the prevailing global policy model, predicated on privatization and free-market capitalism—must be overthrown through mass resistance [and that] climate change can't be separated from other pressing social problems, each a symptom of neoliberalism: income inequality, corporate surveillance, misogyny and white supremacy."[105] Such framing fans the flames of the conservative fever swamps, reinforcing the right-wing trope that environmentalists are "watermelons" (green on the outside, red on the inside) who secretly want to use environmental sustainability as an excuse for overthrowing capitalism and ending economic growth.[106] Consider, for example, the admonition by one conservative commentator who said that the climate movement aims to cause "the decline of growth in world economies."[107] That's irresistible bait for many conservatives.

I want to draw attention to one additional plank in the GND resolution, which suggests "working collaboratively with farmers and ranchers in the United States to eliminate pollution and greenhouse gas emissions from the agricultural sector as much as is technologically feasible." Lest we underestimate the creativity of Murdoch's Fox News presenters when it comes to misrepresentation and bad-faith arguments, consider their translation of this rather reasonable proposal. "No more steak. I guess government-forced veganism is in order," said Fox News firebrand Sean Hannity.[108] "They want to take your pickup truck, they want to rebuild your home, they want to take away your hamburgers. . . . This is what Stalin dreamt about but never achieved," said paid Fox News contributor and (extremely) amateur Sovietologist Seb Gorka at a conservative conference.[109]

Fox News waged war against AOC and the GND, with headlines like "AOC Accused of Soviet-Style Propaganda with Green New Deal Art Series" and "Stealth AOC 'Green New Deal' Now the Law in New Mexico, Voters Be Damned," among others.[110] Unsurprisingly, studies show that Fox News weaponized the GND through such framing, dramatically eroding support for the proposal among conservative Republicans from 57 percent to 32 percent in just a matter of months.[111]

The inactivists, of course, have been more than happy to play both sides here. A leaked document that emerged in June 2020 revealed that fossil fuel companies, including Chevron, were behind a PR campaign aimed at exploiting the spring 2020 Black Lives Matter protests to sow racial division within the climate movement.[112] CRC Advisors, the conservative PR firm enlisted to conduct the campaign, had been circulating an email to journalists encouraging them to focus on how environmental groups supporting the Black Lives Matter movement supposedly advocated "policies which would hurt minority communities," and specifically, on how the GND would supposedly hurt minority communities. Caught red-handed were the forces of inaction in their effort to drive yet another wedge, this time involving issues of racial justice and equity, into the climate movement.

WHAT TO DO?

So what can we do to blunt the impact of the deflection campaign currently underway? First of all, realize when you're being played. "Don't feed the trolls" is a popular refrain in social media circles. Learn to recognize trolls and bots and report them when you come across them. They are engaged in a divide-and-conquer strategy against climate advocates, and you become an enabler of that strategy when you get taken in. Be constructive and engage meaningfully with others. Don't let yourself get dragged into divisive spats with those who are on the same side as you. As someone who is actively engaged in social media, I constantly have to remind myself of the very advice I'm giving you right now. When dangerous lies threaten to poison our public discourse, we must do our best to correct the record. But we must avoid traps set by trolls and bots looking to divide us. There's no hard-and-fast rule here. We each must just remain vigilant and use our best judgment.

We should all engage in climate-friendly individual actions. They make us feel better and they set a good example for others. But don't become complacent, thinking that your duty is done when you recycle your bottles or ride your bicycle to work. We cannot solve this problem without deep systemic change, and that necessitates governmental action. In turn, that requires using our voices, demanding change, supporting climate-focused organizations, and voting for and supporting politicians who will back climate-friendly policies—which includes putting a price on pollution—the topic of the next chapter.

CHAPTER 5

Put a Price on It. *Or Not.*

The stock market is roaring and planet Earth is wailing.
—STEVEN MAGEE

AS MY FRIEND BILL MCKIBBEN LIKES TO POINT OUT, THE FOSSIL fuel industry has been granted the greatest market subsidy ever: the privilege to dump its waste products into the atmosphere at no charge.[1] That's an unfair advantage over climate-friendly renewable energy in the playing field that is the global energy marketplace. We need mechanisms that force polluters to pay for the climate damage done by their product—fossil fuels—tilting the advantage to those forms of energy that aren't destroying our planetary home.

Such mechanisms can take the form of tradable emissions permits, also known as *cap and trade*. In this policy, government allocates or sells a limited number of permits to pollute, and the polluters can buy and sell these permits. This strategy limits pollution by providing economic incentives for polluters to reduce emissions. Another policy is a *carbon tax*, wherein a tax is levied at the point of sale on the carbon content of fuels or any other product yielding greenhouse emissions. Additionally, *carbon credits* can be granted for activities that take carbon out of the atmosphere and bury or store it, thus offsetting carbon emissions.

Fossil fuel interests and right-wing anti-regulation plutocrats have fought tooth and nail against any legislation aimed at pricing carbon emissions, for this would diminish their profits. In 2009, they torpedoed a carbon-pricing bill in the United States and similar legislation in Australia and elsewhere. Moreover, a coalition of petrostate actors, including Russia and Saudi Arabia, joined in the United States by the Trump administration, has also conspired to block carbon-pricing initiatives. Ironically, some environmental progressives are now providing them an unintentional assist.

DISOWNING THEIR OWN

As you may recall, former *Republican* president George H.W. Bush signed a cap-and-trade amendment to the Clean Air Act in 1990 that required coal-fired power plants to scrub sulfur emissions before they exited smokestacks. Between 1990 and 2004, sulfur emissions from coal-fired plants fell 36 percent, even as power output increased by 25 percent. The roughly nine-million-ton cap on sulfur emissions was reached in 2007 and fell to about five million tons in 2010. Lakes, streams, and forests in the Northeast—including the western Adirondacks where my family and I often vacation in the summer—recovered. It was a true environmental success story. You might think Republicans would want to own it—and build on this legacy by tackling the climate crisis using the very same market approach.[2] Instead, the GOP disowned its own brainchild.

Presumably expecting some buy-in from moderate Republicans, a cap-and-trade bill sponsored by Democratic congressmen Henry Waxman of California and Edward Markey of Massachusetts (then in the House) was proposed in 2009 to regulate carbon emissions. It passed, but largely on a party-line vote. Opposition from fossil fuel interests and their front groups—which attempted to brand it "cap and tax"—was perhaps predictable.[3] But there was also opposition from some in the environmental community, who argued that the problem was that it *wasn't* a tax. They favored an explicit carbon tax over a system of tradable emission permits.[4]

Nobel Prize–winning economist and progressive *New York Times* columnist Paul Krugman argued that while either a carbon tax or a cap-and-trade policy could achieve the needed reductions in carbon emissions, "in practice, cap and trade has some major advantages, especially for achieving effective international cooperation." He thought the House bill was likely the best compromise possible given the prevailing politics: "After all the years of denial, after all the years of inaction, we finally have a chance to do something major about climate change. Waxman-Markey is imperfect, it's disappointing in some respects, but it's action we can take now. And the planet won't wait."[5]

Further confusing the politics of the matter was the fact that some Republicans actually supported a carbon tax. But with a catch—it had to be "revenue neutral," which is to say, it couldn't increase the overall taxation on the American people, so other taxes, such as income taxes, would have to decrease. South Carolina congressman Bob Inglis and Jeff Flake of Arizona—both fiscally conservative Republicans—made the case for such a vehicle as an alternative to cap and trade.[6]

Fossil fuel interests and their abettors now faced a grave threat. A climate bill was one house of our bicameral legislative branch away from being the law of the land and even some Republicans supported a price on carbon. The inactivists kicked into high gear. First, the Koch brothers used their tremendous wealth and influence to wage a massive disinformation campaign to defeat the climate bill.[7] They had shills such as Myron Ebell of the Koch-funded Competitive Enterprise Institute misrepresent the cap-and-trade bill as a "tax" bill that would hurt our economy and everyday citizens. Even the *New York Times* was hoodwinked into promoting that interpretation. Describing him as "a strong advocate of the acid rain cap-and-trade program," *Times* reporter John M. Broder quoted C. Boyden Gray, who had been White House counsel during the first Bush administration, saying that "opponents were largely correct in labeling the Waxman-Markey plan a tax."[8] The *Times* failed to note that Gray had worked with the Koch brothers as a member of the board of directors for Citizens for a Sound Economy, a conservative think tank the Kochs had founded in 1984. Citizens for a Sound Economy would lead to Freedomworks and Americans for Prosperity.[9]

Americans for Prosperity was in fact a Koch brothers front group. The Kochs employed it as a vehicle for sponsoring a "hot-air" bus tour around the country promoting climate-change denial and fear-messaging about how regulating carbon emissions would supposedly destroy the economy.[10] They even constructed an Astroturf movement that became known as the "Tea Party" to create the illusion of widespread grassroots opposition to the climate bill, marshaling a rabble of disaffected citizens resentful of a changing fiscal, racial, and social landscape that seemed to have left them behind.[11]

Meanwhile, the Kochs served notice to any Republican legislators who might think about supporting climate legislation by making an example of Congressman Bob Inglis (R-SC), who, as noted earlier, had supported a carbon tax bill. Christopher Leonard, author of *Kochland*, described what happened during Inglis's reelection bid in 2010: "Koch Industries stopped funding his campaign, donated heavily to a primary opponent named Trey Gowdy and helped organize teams of Tea Party activists who traveled to town hall meetings to protest against Mr. Inglis. Some of the town hall meetings devolved into angry affairs, where Mr. Inglis couldn't make himself heard above the shouting. Mr. Inglis lost re-election, and his defeat sent a message to other Republicans: Koch's orthodoxy on climate rules could not be violated."[12]

The Kochs' efforts were successful. Democrats were unable to achieve filibuster-proof support (that is, a minimum of sixty votes) in the Senate, and the bill never went forward to President Obama's desk. Even with both houses of Congress under their control and a president in favor of climate action, Democrats were unable to pass a climate bill. While one might blame them for fecklessness, there is little doubt that cap and trade, as Broder at the *Times* put it, "ran into gale-force opposition from the oil industry [and] conservative groups that portrayed it as an economy-killing tax."[13] Tens of millions of dollars from the Koch brothers and dark-money spending aimed at sinking the bill didn't help matters. Nor did a beleaguered president who had already expended considerable political capital fighting a war with the right over health-care reform. And thus ended, with little fanfare, what had once seemed a promising prospect, finally, for a climate bill in the United States.[14] (A noteworthy postscript: Bob Inglis, who in full disclosure is a personal friend, now leads an organization aimed at bringing Republicans on board with climate action. He travels around to speak to conservative audiences about free-market approaches to pricing carbon, and in 2015 he received the JFK Profile in Courage Award.[15])

Similar episodes played out in the other major industrial nations. Australia provides perhaps the most striking example.[16] In some sense, what transpired down under was even more disillusioning than what had occurred in the United States: The Aussies *did* have a national price on carbon, and they lost it. In 2011, after a long, drawn-out battle that dated back several governments, Julia Gillard, prime minister of the ruling labor government, passed an emissions trading scheme, or ETS (another name for a cap-and-trade system). Drawing from the very same textbook that inactivists used to sink the US cap-and-trade bill, Australia's center-right opposition party (the "Liberals"—who are actually *conservatives*) misrepresented the measure as a "carbon tax" that would hurt individuals. This was particularly problematic for Gillard, who had made a campaign promise not to pass a carbon tax but had not ruled out an emissions trading measure.[17]

The usual suspects—Koch-funded front groups combining forces with coal interests and the Murdoch media (which dominate the Australian media landscape)—went to work, savaging Gillard and the Labor Party.[18] The attacks, as described by the *New York Times*, "coalesced around the promise and the tax." The ETS was portrayed "as a burden that would hurt businesses and cost households, instead of one that would cut pollution and ensure a more secure future for our children." There was only the smallest grain of truth to that claim. In principle, some of the cost to polluters of a cap-and-trade policy can be passed on to consumers. But in practice, these costs would have been minimal.[19]

Foreshadowing the attacks on AOC and the Green New Deal that were detailed in the previous chapter, Gillard's critics made not-so-subtle misogynistic appeals to voters in accomplishing their objectives. The *Times* noted that "the heat, anger and vitriol directed at her as a leader—and as Australia's first woman to be prime minister . . . grew strangely nasty."[20]

Liberal Party fossil-fuel advocate and climate-change denier Tony Abbott won the subsequent general election and was eventually able to revoke the ETS. Today the conservative Liberal National Party (LNP), a coalition of the Liberal Party and the National Party, remains in power, with a like-minded prime minister in Scott Morrison who has coddled coal, played a destructive role in international climate negotiations, and downplayed the impacts of climate change even as Australians have suffered through devastating and unprecedented heat, drought, and bushfire outbreaks. It is worth noting that, as in the United States, not all of Australia's conservative politicians were on the wrong side of the climate issue. Former Liberal prime minister Malcolm Turnbull was attacked by the Murdoch press and ousted from office in 2018 in large part because of his support of carbon pricing. He now plays a similar role in Australia to that played by Inglis in the United States, seeking to convince conservatives to come back into the climate tent.[21]

It is instructive, in light of the timeline of these attacks on climate policy, to reconsider the role played by the manufactured "Climategate" controversy. You may recall how that pseudo-scandal played out in late November 2009, just in time to have a detrimental impact on the all-important Copenhagen Summit that December. But we know that it was several months in the making, which means that the plan was likely hatched around the time the Waxman-Markey bill passed the US House of Representatives (late June 2009). The pseudo-scandal dominated conservative media and even some mainstream outlets, including CNN, well into 2010, as the US Senate was taking up the ill-fated cap-and-trade bill. Pretty darned good timing by the inactivists!

In 2009, the Labor Party was in power in Australia, with Kevin Rudd as prime minister. Rudd had attempted to pass a cap-and-trade measure, slated to take effect in July 2010. But an odd coalition of the opposition Liberals (led by Tony Abbott at the time) and the Greens opposed him. According to *The Guardian*, "the Liberal opposition argued that [consideration of the ETS] should all be put off until after the Copenhagen climate conference scheduled for the end of 2009, a tactic that helped to delay the day of reckoning within the Liberal party room."[22] The tactic accomplished more than that. It also postponed consideration of any climate pricing measure until after the "Climategate" pseudo-scandal had broken. With nothing more to go on, I still wonder if Liberal Party insiders were somehow privy to knowledge the rest of us didn't have.

Rudd had anticipated a more favorable political environment for climate action following the Copenhagen Summit. But that was not to be. The proceedings became mired in disputes between developing nations (including China) and the developed world. And the political atmosphere had been poisoned by the climate inactivists' full-on assault, including the ammunition that trumped-up Climategate rhetoric provided.

As we have seen, two petrostates—Russia and Saudi Arabia—are known to have played an important role in the spread of Climategate propaganda. Indeed, Saudi Arabia attempted to sabotage the entire Copenhagen Summit based on the false Climategate claims. This bloc of climate-denying petrostates has since welcomed two additional members: the United States under Trump, and oil-soaked Kuwait. This "coalition of the unwilling" attempted to thwart the findings of the UN Intergovernmental Panel on Climate Change during the December 2018 UN Climate Change Conference in Poland. The IPCC report concluded that rapid and immediate reductions in global carbon emissions were necessary to avert catastrophic planetary warming. The four countries were the only member nations that refused to support a motion to "embrace" the findings of the new report (instead they agreed only to "note" the report's findings—a far weaker measure that is much easier for policymakers to ignore). The delegate for St. Kitts and Nevis—a West Indian island nation threatened by sea-level rise and increasingly dangerous hurricanes—told the UN plenary that it was "ludicrous" for this minority of countries to hold up the critical proceedings over two words.[23]

Based on recent behavior, the coalition of the unwilling now includes Brazil under Jair Bolsinaro and Australia under Scott Morrison. Russia, by far, though, remains the most active member of the coalition of inactivist states. As we have already seen, it was implicated in efforts to influence recent US elections in a manner that was disadvantageous for climate policy. It also appears to have interfered in recent elections in the United Kingdom, working with the climate-change-denying UK Independence Party (UKIP), for example, to pass "Brexit" (the withdrawal of the United Kingdom from the European Union). Brexit is expected to erode the power of the European Union—including its influence on climate policy.[24]

Russia is also believed to have played a role in instigating the 2018 "Yellow Vest" revolts in France that sabotaged governmental efforts to introduce a carbon tax there.[25] In that movement, Russian trolls helped incite protests and rioting in the streets using messaging that played upon class conflict and perceived economic injustice. Ironically, although most of the protesters actually supported action on climate, they opposed a proposed fuel tax, which they were led to believe would be financed by the working class and poor to the benefit of multinational corporations.[26]

Russia has also tampered in Canadian politics. Russian bot farms have been used, for example, in an effort to convince environmental progressives in Canada that Prime Minister Justin Trudeau, who supported carbon pricing, was in fact against taking meaningful action on climate.[27] Trudeau's environment minister, Catherine McKenna, who was responsible for implementing Canada's new carbon tax program, has been subject to an onslaught of Russia-style troll- and bot-based social media attacks since taking office in 2015. Many are tinged with misogyny, dismissing her as a "climate Barbie," and ridden with slurs like "bitch," "c—t," "slut," and "twat."[28] Going into the 2019 Canadian federal election, Russian Twitter trolls attempted to stoke anger against the Trudeau government by focusing on issues such as immigration, employment, the economy, and, of course, climate policy.[29]

What might Russia and other petrostate bad actors be trying to accomplish through these sorts of activities? For one thing, a few early carbon-pricing political disasters in countries like France and Canada might cause other governments considering climate policy to get cold feet, much as the failure in the 1970s and 1980s of many of the efforts to pass bottle bills in individual states in America sank any chance of a national bottle bill. So the theory might be to nip any promising new efforts at carbon pricing in the bud before they have a chance to succeed. And to make a price on carbon toxic, all they have to do is associate it with social unrest, disruption, and economic pain.

We can see how these efforts have paid off for the inactivists when it comes to recent climate policy efforts in the United States. Consider the defeat of a climate tax initiative by voters in Washington state in November 2016. Sure, there was massive opposition and a flood of advertising from fossil fuel interests. But ironically, those opposing the initiative got an assist from environmental organizations such as the Sierra Club, which argued that the carbon tax would violate principles of social justice. This leads to our next discussion: the ironic alienation of environmental progressives from pricing carbon.[30]

PIPELINES, NOT PRICING

From a market vantage point, the fossil fuels we burn are a consequence of both supply and demand. And so there are two basic, complementary approaches to regulating fossil fuels: control *supply* and/or control *demand*. Pricing carbon (or, alternatively, incentives for renewables) reflects an effort to diminish demand, while fossil fuel divestment campaigns and opposition to pipelines, offshore oil drilling, or mountain-top-removal coal mining constitute efforts to diminish supply. Leading climate advocates like Bill McKibben and Senator Bernie Sanders of Vermont at least originally endorsed both approaches.[31]

Despite the natural duality between demand-side and supply-side measures, there is also an asymmetry—at least when it comes to political organizing. It's easy to motivate activists to protest a pipe-line or mountain-top removal. Or to attend demonstrations at college campuses demanding that administrators divest of fossil fuel holdings. These events are visual, involve conflict, bring out A-list celebrities, and generate front-page headlines and graphic photos. Think the Dakota Access Pipeline demonstrations at the Standing Rock Indian Reservation, or Darryl Hannah and James Hansen being arrested protesting Massey Energy's coal processing plant in West Virginia.[32] Or Harvard and Yale student protesters joining forces to disrupt the 2019 Harvard/Yale football game, demanding that both institutions divest of fossil fuel holdings.[33]

Carbon pricing, by comparison, seems wonkish and abstract, and it's hard to capture it in a front-page image or on a television screen. Moreover, while both carbon pricing and pipeline protests reflect efforts to influence the underlying market economics of fossil fuel use, carbon pricing is more readily *seen* as buying into market economics. As a result, carbon pricing has been vulnerable not just to attacks from the right but also to attacks from the left. We've seen how conservatives have been led to oppose carbon pricing—by fear messaging that warns of infringements to personal liberty and heavy-handed governmental mandates. But progressives have also been led to oppose carbon pricing—for them, it has been portrayed as an ostensible mechanism of neoliberal economics that discounts social justice.

One argument that seems to have resonated with the environmental left is that a price on carbon amounts to a regressive tax that selectively hurts low-income workers. This was the claim that was used to foment the Yellow Vest uprising.[34] It is telling that Donald Trump, in his role as patsy for the fossil fuel interests that write his energy and environmental policies, insisted that the Yellow Vest violence was proof that people oppose environmental protection (as noted earlier, it showed nothing of the sort).[35]

In reality, whether a carbon tax is progressive or regressive depends on how it is designed. A fee-and-dividend method, for example, returns any revenue raised back to the people. Such a plan could be designed to be progressive, returning revenue to the poor and those most impacted through an appropriately constructed dividend.

In fact, the carbon-pricing schemes that have been successfully instituted have been *progressive* in nature. With the ETS scheme implemented by Australian prime minister Julia Gillard, the government compensated low-income earners, who ended up *benefiting* financially. Under Canada's carbon tax-and-rebate system, most households actually save money.[36] No less than Pope Francis, a champion of social justice and a true advocate for the poor and downtrodden, has called carbon pricing "essential" for tackling the climate-change "emergency."[37]

Another argument is that carbon pricing would represent a sort of political zero-sum game for climate action, with any carbon tax coming at the expense of losing legal avenues for holding polluters accountable. More specifically, some in the climate movement believe that passage of a carbon tax would shield fossil fuel companies from legal liability for their actions. This simply isn't true.

Much as the tobacco industry was finally held liable for its efforts to hide the dangers of its products from the public, so, too, are there efforts today to use the legal system to bring polluters to justice for hiding the dangers of their product—fossil fuels—to the entire planet.[38] A number of lawsuits against fossil fuel companies are currently working their way through the legal system.[39] Two states have launched fraud investigations targeting ExxonMobil (one went to trial in 2019 and failed). Nine cities and counties, including New York and San Francisco, have used the courts to seek compensation from fossil fuel companies for the climate damages they have caused. Perhaps best known, however, is *Juliana v. U.S.*, brought by twenty-one children who sued the federal government for violating their right to a safe climate. The suit was thrown out but is currently under appeal.[40]

The belief that a carbon tax would somehow end legal liability on the part of fossil fuel interests is premised on mistaking what fossil fuel interests might *want* for what they're actually going to *get*. Some climate activists have breathlessly warned that climate pricing legislation is a "fossil-fuel-funded Trojan Horse" that would amount to "letting oil, gas, and coal companies off the hook" by "exempting fossil fuels companies from . . . lawsuits."[41] While fossil fuel companies have lobbied for a bill that would do just that, none of the climate bills that have been introduced in Congress have proposed to absolve fossil fuel companies of liability.[42] It is simply a fallacy to equate carbon pricing with releasing fossil fuel interests from legal liability.

Another argument frequently made by progressive critics is that a carbon tax cannot achieve the needed emissions reductions. But that depends on the magnitude of the tax.[43] Consider, for example, what transpired in Australia between 2012 and 2014, when Gillard imposed a modest price on carbon through the ETS that ended up costing polluters about $23 per metric ton of emitted CO_2. Emissions in the electricity sector dropped more than 9 percent during the first six months of implementation. And what happened when the Abbott government repealed the ETS in 2014? Emissions recorded their single greatest annual gain (more than 10 percent).[44] Of course, a carbon tax is just one tool in the climate action toolbox and must be combined with other demand-side and supply-side measures in any comprehensive climate plan.

Nonetheless, because of objections from some on the environmental left, the version of AOC's Green New Deal endorsed by leading environmental organizations advocates *against* a price on carbon. A letter signed by 626 groups, including Greenpeace and 350. org, was delivered to every member of Congress in early 2019 laying out support for a Green New Deal, while stating that the groups "will vigorously oppose any legislation that . . . promotes corporate schemes that place profits over community burdens and benefits, *including market-based mechanisms . . . such as carbon and emissions trading and offsets*" (emphasis added).[45] There are other recent cases in which environmental progressives and green groups have opposed carbon-pricing efforts. As we learned earlier, for example, the Sierra Club helped defeat a 2016 climate tax initiative in Washington because its leaders felt it didn't satisfy principles of social justice.[46]

Then there's the Carbon Pollution Reduction Scheme (CPRS) that former Australian Labor prime minister Kevin Rudd proposed back in 2009. Rudd's government had negotiated a package with climate-policy-friendly Liberal leader Malcolm Turnbull that could pass Parliament. Turnbull, however, was replaced as Liberal leader by fossil fuel flack Tony Abbott. On Abbott's first full day as Liberal leader, the members of Parliament (MPs) for the *Green Party*—yes, the party whose very name bespeaks ostensible prioritization of environmental preservation—voted with Abbot *against* the CPRS, purportedly because its members wanted *more ambitious* reduction targets. This fateful decision by the greens, as Mark Butler explained in *The Guardian*, "allowed Abbott to begin to build the momentum that has hamstrung long-term climate action for almost a decade." According to Butler, "had the CPRS passed the parliament in 2009, an emissions trading scheme would likely have been operating for some years before Abbott was able to become prime minister. And it's likely that Abbott would not have been able to build a platform to tear down such a large reform after that time."[47]

Prominent spokespeople within the scientific community, too, sometimes fan the flames of progressive opposition to carbon pricing. Consider the words of Australian environmental scientist Will Steffen, executive director of the Australian National University Climate Change Institute and lead author of a controversial "Hothouse Earth" commentary in the *Proceedings of the National Academy of Sciences*.[48] Asked what could be done to prevent a Hothouse Earth scenario, Steffen said the "obvious thing we have to do is to get greenhouse gas emissions down as fast as we can. . . . *You have got to get away from the so-called neoliberal economics* . . . [and shift to something] more like wartime footing [to decarbonize society] at very fast rates" (emphasis added).[49] While Steffen is no doubt an expert in environmental science, his statements about economics and policy here are ill informed. If we are to achieve rapid decarbonization of our economy, carbon pricing (which one suspects he is lumping in with "neoliberal economics") is essential—it's the main lever arm we have available to us in a market economy.[50]

Among the most market-economics-averse of proponents of a Green New Deal is social activist Naomi Klein, who has long argued that modern-day capitalism—which is to say, neoliberal market economics—is fundamentally at odds with basic human rights and environmental sustainability. According to Adam Tooze, in his article "How Climate Change Has Supercharged the Left" in *Foreign Policy* magazine, "the denunciation of neoliberalism in Naomi Klein's *This Changes Everything* gave a manifesto to the new green left."[51]

I published a commentary in *Nature* that recommended Klein's latest book on the GND but questioned her critique of market mechanisms, pointing out that—as we've already seen—there is no reason that carbon pricing has to be either regressive or inadequate.[52] Her followers immediately took to social media to expressly denounce me. I can understand that some of her supporters might have been disappointed that I had some points of disagreement with her and didn't endorse her precise vision of the Green New Deal. But we are on the same side. And I didn't expect the vitriolic personal attacks of the sort I'm used to getting from the climate-denying right coming instead from the left.

One reader dismissed my commentary as "mansplaining trash from myopic white bros who do not speak for those on the front lines." Now, I'll humbly submit that I *do* know a thing or two about being on the front lines. For two decades I've been in the cross hairs of the attack machine funded by the fossil fuel industry, and I have devoted my professional life to study and activism relating to climate change.[53] Eric Holthaus jumped in to express his disapproval as well, tweeting "Ladies, does he . . . leverage his platform to write op-eds in prominent magazines disparaging the Green New Deal? He's not your climate hero, he's a gatekeeper."[54] These responses—from both strangers and people who are ostensibly on the same side of the issue as I am, seemed to exemplify once again the divisive way that race, gender, and callout culture are being used to divide the climate movement.[55]

The takeaway message from this particular episode, however, is that there is a fairly aggressive effort underway by some on the environmental left to turn support for the GND *in its current form* (including *opposition to carbon pricing*) into a purity test. Even questioning it can lead to massive, mob-like online assaults and ugly accusations that somehow become framed in identity politics and tinged with issues of race, gender, and ageism. We have already seen that the inactivists seize upon such internal conflict and amplify it to sow dissent and divide the climate community. They are surely doing that here. Fortunately, as we've seen, there are also many committed climate advocates who recognize this threat and are willing to push back against needlessly divisive rhetoric. That will remain critical if we are to find some degree of common ground, as a society, when it comes to climate action—including carbon pricing. That leads us to our next topic.

PRICING AIN'T PARTISAN

Despite the divisiveness that has arisen around the role of carbon pricing, there is nothing intrinsically divisive or partisan about it. As we have seen, market mechanisms for dealing with pollution actually have their origins in the Republican Party. Carbon pricing is supported by all former Republican chairs of the president's Council of Economic Advisers. But carbon pricing is also widely supported by Democrats. Nine of the ten leading candidates for the Democratic presidential nomination supported it as of July 2019. The one exception as well as one subsequent major "flip" are rather interesting, and we will discuss them later.[56]

It is only relatively recently, as efforts to implement carbon pricing have actually started to move forward—that we've seen support for carbon pricing start to erode on *both* sides of the political spectrum. That's convenient for fossil fuel interests, whose spokespeople might publicly claim, for public relations purposes, that their companies and organizations support carbon pricing, but behind the scenes still fund groups working to undermine it.[57]

It's hardly surprising that Donald Trump, who has outsourced his policymaking to polluting interests, is dismissive of carbon pricing, which he has derided as "protectionism."[58] But the fact that some environmental *progressives* have grown apprehensive of carbon pricing has almost certainly influenced recent decisions by other climate-friendly politicians to steer clear of it. Consider New York governor Andrew Cuomo. Cuomo has been a leader in many respects when it comes to climate action. He has supported supply-side measures to restrict fossil fuel extraction, becoming only the second governor to ban natural gas drilling via hydraulic fracturing (fracking).[59] And he has promoted at least *one* type of demand-side measure, namely, governmental incentives for renewable energy (the topic of the next chapter). What he has proposed for New York is that it require 70 percent of the state's electric power supply to come from renewable energy sources by 2030 and mandating that it be free of carbon emissions by 2040. But Cuomo has not endorsed a price on carbon—as yet.[60]

Others have nonetheless called upon him to do so. Richard Dewey is the president and CEO of the New York Independent System Operator (NYISO), a not-for-profit corporation responsible for operating New York State's bulk electricity grid, administering its competitive wholesale electricity markets, conducting comprehensive long-term planning for its electric power system, and advancing the technological infrastructure of its electric system.[61] Dewey has insisted that Cuomo cannot achieve these goals without imposing a price on carbon: "These goals are really going to come fast," he has stated, adding that carbon pricing "is a necessary element in meeting them."[62]

The conclusion that we need carbon pricing is also supported by the International Monetary Fund (IMF), hardly a left-leaning organization. The IMF exists to "secure financial stability, facilitate international trade," and "promote high employment and sustainable economic growth."[63] It has estimated that there is an effective global average price of roughly $2 per metric ton, given the various carbon-pricing systems that are in place around the world. It has warned, however, that the world needs an average price of $75 per metric ton if we are to meet the Paris Agreement goal of keeping warming below 2°C (3.6°F). (An even higher price would be needed to keep warming below 1.5°C [2.7°F]—a level of warming increasingly considered to constitute dangerous climate change.[64])

These are examples of objective, moderate, nonpartisan institutions, with no particular axe to grind, that have called for carbon pricing. There are both Democrats and Republicans who support carbon pricing. Why is it proving so difficult to find political common ground here? Part of the answer, of course, is that fossil fuel interests, and the forces of inaction doing their bidding, have worked hard to poison the well (look no further than Donald Trump's threats to retaliate against the European Union over its proposed carbon tax[65]). But frankly, progressive scientists and thought leaders have at times made it easy for them, helping to create a political economy that is toxic for bipartisan compromise.

Let me relate an episode involving David Mastio, the deputy editorial page editor of *USA Today* and a self-avowed "libertarian conservative." In June 2019, I coauthored an op-ed about the dangers of the new climate "deflection campaign" discussed in this book.[66] I was sure the *New York Times* would publish it, but it did not. I was sure the *Washington Post* would then publish it. It didn't. I then went to *USA Today*. David not only embraced the piece and offered to publish it, but encouraged me to keep *USA Today* in mind for any future op-eds. He's precisely the sort of conservative we need on board.

Well, I was crestfallen to read a controversial statement David made some months later when he tweeted this: "Why I remain skeptical of the climate change consensus. If this was a real emergency, the scientists would be in favor of mobilizing the power of capitalism, not government control."[67] I wondered what could have set him off? Clicking through, I saw that it was a tweet paraphrasing a letter signed by eleven thousand scientists: "11,000 scientists have declared we are in a climate emergency. Among other things, *we need to move away from capitalism* . . ."[68] I've intentionally eliminated the rest of the tweet (you can find it in the endnotes) because I want you to read only as far as David would have had to read before becoming suspicious that the declaration of a climate emergency is just a tool—at least to some—for overthrowing capitalism. The "watermelon" fears, revisited.

A parochiality has emerged among environmental progressives that is unhelpful to the process of building consensus for climate action. Here's an example. In January 2020, George P. Shultz, secretary of state under President Ronald Reagan, and Ted Halstead, chairman and chief executive of the nonpartisan Climate Leadership Council, coauthored an op-ed in the *Washington Post* titled "The Winning Conservative Climate Solution."[69] In it, they advocated for a revenue-neutral carbon tax, or, more specifically, a fee-and-dividend system, similar to what is advocated by the nonpartisan Citizens Climate Lobby. In such a system, a fee is charged to carbon polluters, and the revenue is distributed, through a dividend, to the people (for example, in the form of quarterly checks sent by the government to individuals).

Now consider the response to the op-ed by David Roberts, a writer for *Vox*. Roberts tweeted, "I'll never get used to the bizarre convention of calling a policy that the GOP has repeatedly rejected & the vast bulk of conservatives oppose . . . a 'conservative solution.'" He went on to add, "The conservatives who are actually attracted to this policy are conservative centrists & conservative Democrats. This is an intra-left dispute in which one side is fraudulently claiming to be able to count on the right's support."[70]

Roberts often has keen insights into climate politics. But here, he is misguided. He fails to distinguish between traditional conservatives—that includes Reagan conservatives, like George Shultz, who, as we have seen, not only supported but actually *gave us* market-based approaches to reducing pollutants—and the current-day Republican Party, which has indeed been cowed into complicity with the Koch brothers, the Murdoch media, and the fossil fuel industry.

These old-school conservatives—George Shultz, Hank Paulson, Bob Inglis, Arnold Schwarzenegger, or, in the United Kingdom, former prime minister David Cameron—not only support climate action, but are passionate about it. Nevertheless, they are apprehensive about what they perceive to be heavy-handed governmental regulatory approaches, including the GND in its current form. As Shultz and Halstead put it, "the climate problem is real, the Green New Deal is bad."[71] According to Schwarzenegger, who as governor of California led efforts to cut back carbon emissions, and has roundly criticized Donald Trump's efforts to roll back environmental protections, the Green New Deal is "a slogan" and "marketing tool" that is "well intentioned" but "bogus."[72] Cameron has implored his fellow conservatives not to abandon the matter: "Don't leave the issues of climate and the future of the planet . . . These are natural conservative issues, don't leave this to the left or you'll get an anti-business, anti-enterprise, anti-technology response."[73]

We are unlikely to see a climate bill resembling the current version of the GND pass both houses of Congress in the United States. There will need to be some degree of bipartisan compromise, which means bringing along moderate conservatives. Rather than alienating them through partisan rhetoric, we need to create space for them and welcome them into the fold. There *is* a legitimate wedge to be formed, and it's between moderate conservatives, who are on board with climate action, and the recalcitrant deniers, delayers, and deflectors.

Nobody said it would be easy to pass climate legislation with the fossil fuel interests and the Koch brothers doing their best to enforce Republican Party purity. But fissures are starting to form, particularly as a result of generational shifts that favor action. Republican pollster Frank Luntz found that Republican voters under the age of forty favor a fee-and-dividend carbon-pricing policy by a whopping six-to-one margin.[74] The same generational trends that led to a tipping-point-like response on marriage equality during the Obama years will soon reach a tipping point on climate, too. But we don't have a decade to wait, and the most viable path forward toward comprehensive climate legislation in the United States involves market mechanisms, including carbon pricing. It would be sadly ironic—and indeed tragic—if progressives, rather than conservatives, became the greatest obstacle to climate progress by refusing to engage in compromise, cooperation, and consensus building.

Ironically, not only is there in an increasing tendency among progressives to oppose seeking a middle ground when it comes to climate policy, but we've arrived in a "bizarro" world where the climate-change talking points employed on the political left are sometimes virtually indistinguishable from those on the political right. Adam Tooze reported in *Foreign Policy* what transpired at a conference of the UK Labour Party in September 2019: "The general secretary of the GMB trade union, Tim Roache, warned that a crash program of decarbonization would require the 'confiscation of petrol cars,' 'state rationing of meat,' and 'limiting families to one flight for every five years.' He concluded: 'It will put entire industries and the jobs they produced in peril.'"[75] Other labor leaders have an arguably more enlightened view of carbon pricing. In March 2020, James Slevin, president of the Utility Workers Union of America, coauthored an op-ed with Senator Sheldon Whitehouse (D-RI) articulating the case for carbon pricing. They advocated measures to ensure that the revenue raised is rebated to consumers and used to help individuals and communities—particularly coal workers and their families—with support for health plans, pensions, and educational opportunities.[76]

Or consider Kevin Anderson, a climate scientist in the United Kingdom who has criticized the mainstream climate research community for understating the degree of the threat posed by climate change and overstating the progress that has been made. In critiquing a report by the Committee on Climate Change (an independent committee created to advise the UK government on matters of climate mitigation) on what measures are required to meet commitments under the Paris Agreement, Anderson stated that "it is designed to fit with the current political and economic status quo." Then he went further, accusing the entire climate research community of complicity: "The overall framing is firmly set in a politically-dogmatic stone with academia and *much of the climate community running scared of questioning this for fear of loss of funding*, prestige, etc." (emphasis added).[77] That charge is virtually indistinguishable from the shopworn accusation by climate-change deniers that climate scientists invented the climate crisis to bring in loads of grant money.[78]

Indeed, the prevailing politics of climate change today sometimes resemble the metaphorical snake biting its tail, with some on the left end of the spectrum promoting the positions on climate typically found on the right. Consider this characterization of Democratic presidential candidate Tulsi Gabbard by Brian Boyle in the *Los Angeles Times*: "Gabbard is a tricky candidate to pin down. Her domestic policy positions graft rather cleanly with Bernie Sanders' and Elizabeth Warren's progressive platforms—in fact, she was one of Sanders' fiercest supporters in 2016."[79] Sounds "left" doesn't it? But Boyle goes on to point out that Gabbard has taken curiously pro-Russian positions on any host of issues, and indeed, her candidacy was promoted by Russian bot armies. Is it a coincidence that she also happens to be the one Democratic candidate who went on record during the primaries to oppose a price on carbon—a position that aligned suspiciously with Putin's Russia and the Trump administration?[80] This contradiction speaks to the breakdown in our conventional descriptions of "right" and "left" in the current geopolitical environment.

An even more extreme example of the blurring of the political boundaries is the British Internet magazine *Spiked*, which purports to reflect the views of the Marxist far left. *Spiked* frequently engages in what it sees as "pushback against the protected hysteria of modern environmentalism," including rejection of climate science (for example, dismissing IPCC reports as "often over-the-top" and "scare mongering").[81] The magazine also promotes caricatures of the climate movement. It insists, for example, that climate advocates claim "that we have 12 years to save the planet."[82] This is a bastardization of the scientifically backed estimate that we only have around twelve years to bring carbon emissions down (by a factor of two) if we are to avert a dangerous 1.5°C (2.7°F) warming.[83] *Spiked* also promoted Brexit, which, as we know, will help derail EU climate pricing efforts. It was a confusing mix of positions for a far-left magazine, but it all became clear thanks to the work of British columnist George Monbiot. In an exposé for *The Guardian*, Monbiot revealed that among the funders of *Spiked* is in fact the foundation of fossil fuel billionaire (and apparently secret Marxist) Charles Koch.[84] Far right posing as the far left? Can you say *Manchurian Candidate*—backward? If there's a lesson in all of this, it's that inactivists are working hard to generate conflict within the climate movement, literally infiltrating the environmental "left" in an effort to turn climate identity politics on their head. They'll seemingly stop at nothing in their efforts to block climate progress and carbon pricing. Forewarned is forearmed.

ACCELERATING THE TRANSITION

Climate action requires a fundamental transition in our global economy and massive new infrastructure, but there is no reason to think we can't accomplish it—and accomplish it rapidly—with the right market incentives. Those incentives, as we've seen, must involve both supply-side and demand-side measures.

Supply-side measures take the form of blocking pipeline construction, banning fracking, stopping mountain-top-removal coal mining, divesting in fossil fuel companies, and putting a halt to most new fossil fuel infrastructure. These actions obviously lend themselves to activism, protests, and media-ready conflict and publicity. But they *can* also have a material impact. Consider, for example, the Keystone XL Pipeline, which promised to deliver huge amounts of the dirtiest, most carbon-intensive petroleum from the Canadian tar sands to the open market. It's a scenario that climate scientist James Hansen exclaimed would be "game over for the climate."[85] In response to massive protests and pressure from environmental organizations, former president Obama ultimately blocked the construction of the pipeline in 2015, arguing that it would "undercut" his administration's "global leadership" in "taking serious action to fight climate change."[86] Combined with the clean power plan and tighter fuel-efficiency standards imposed by his administration, blocking Keystone XL gave Obama a strong hand in negotiating a bilateral climate agreement with China in 2015 that would, in turn, lay the groundwork for the monumental Paris Agreement later that year.[87]

But, just as personal action is no substitute for systemic change, supply-side efforts are no substitute for demand-side approaches. Both are necessary. Demand-side measures attempt to level the playing field, so that climate-friendly energy, transportation, and agricultural practices outcompete fossil fuels in the marketplace. Carbon pricing is one of the most powerful tools we have to do that. Taking it off the table would constitute unilateral disarmament in the climate wars.

That is literally what happened in Australia. A successful carbon-pricing program that both progressives and conservatives initially supported was nixed by a climate-change-denying, fossil-fuel-flacking prime minister in Tony Abbott. Fatefully, Australia, in the record hot, dry, bushfire-plagued summer of 2019/2020, morphed into a dystopian hellscape resembling a scene from the 1979 Australian film *Mad Max*. Once a shining example of climate leadership in the industrial world, Australia has now become a poster child for the cost of climate inaction. Yet it is not too late for Australians to reclaim leadership by voting in a government that promises to act on climate in the next election.

Nor is it too late in the United States. As I write, the fate of carbon-pricing remains uncertain. The election of Donald Trump in 2016 was a major setback. A Biden presidency would put carbon pricing back on the table. Still there are signs, as we've seen, that some on the political left are also hostile to this policy. During the 2020 Democratic primaries, for instance, Bernie Sanders flipped on the issue of carbon pricing sometime between July 2019, when he supported it (albeit with qualifications), and November 2019, when, in response to direct questioning by the *Washington Post*, he indicated he no longer favored such policies. A cynic might imagine that this concession reflected an effort to wrest carbon-pricing-averse Green New Deal supporters from his chief primary campaign challenger, Elizabeth Warren. The great irony is that, as a result of this flip-flop, *both* major party candidates for the 2020 presidency could have ended up opposed to this important mechanism for climate action.[88]

Of course, a truly comprehensive strategy for leveling the playing field involves more than simply forcing corporate polluters to pay for the damage they're causing. That's the stick. But we need the carrot, too. That means incentives for energy providers to replace fossil fuels with cleaner, safer, carbon-free energy (and, conversely, eliminating the perverse existing subsidies that are provided to fossil fuel energy producers). The inactivists, naturally, as detailed in the next chapter, have opposed these measures, too.

CHAPTER 6

Sinking the Competition

We are like tenant farmers, chopping down the fence around our house for fuel, when we should be using nature's inexhaustible sources of energy—sun, wind, and tide.

—THOMAS EDISON

WE SAW IN THE PREVIOUS CHAPTER THAT CARBON PRICING IS A means of leveling the playing field in the energy market, so that those sources of energy that are not warming the planet (i.e., renewable energy) can compete fairly against those that are (i.e., fossil fuels). A complementary approach is to introduce explicit incentives for renewable energy (and eliminate those for fossil fuels). Here again, the inactivists have put their thumbs on the scale by promoting programs that favor fossil fuel energy while sabotaging those that incentivize renewables, and engaging in propaganda campaigns to discredit renewable energy as a viable alternative to fossil fuels.

SELECTIVE SUBSIDIES

The fossil fuel industry loves subsidies and incentives. When *they* receive them. According to the International Monetary Fund, the industry receives about half a trillion dollars globally in explicit subsidies, such as in the form of assistance to the poor for the purchase of fossil-fuel-generated electricity, tax breaks for capital investment, and public financing of fossil fuel infrastructure. It's a lot of money.

But when *implicit* subsidies are included—that is to say, the health costs and damage born by citizens for the associated environmental pollution, including the damage done by climate change—the estimate rises to a whopping $5 trillion.[1] These perks didn't arise by accident—the industry used its immense wealth and influence to obtain them. In the 2015–2016 election cycle alone, fossil fuel companies spent $354 million in campaign contributions and lobbying.[2]

Fossil fuel interests have also done everything possible to *block* subsidies and incentives for their competition—renewable energy—and they've had a lot of success doing so. That has led to a perverse incentive structure in the energy marketplace through which we are artificially boosting the very energy sources that are hurting the planet, while devaluing those that can save it. Industry front groups like the American Legislative Exchange Council (ALEC) and the Heartland Institute have been particularly active in sabotaging efforts at the national and state levels to promote renewable energy.

The watchdog group SourceWatch describes ALEC as a "corporate bill mill" through which "corporations hand state legislators their wish lists to benefit their bottom line."[3] In recent years, fossil fuel corporations such as ExxonMobil, Shell, and BP have pulled out of ALEC, concerned about increased public scrutiny of their funding activities. But the privately held fossil fuel giant Koch Industries has remained steadfast in its funding of the group.[4] In one year alone, ALEC helped push through seventy bills in thirty-seven states designed to disadvantage clean energy. ALEC has proposed legislation that would undermine state policies mandating that a fraction of the energy produced come from renewable sources (so-called Renewable Portfolio Standards).[5] One bill sponsored by Wyoming Republicans in 2020 was a caricature of these efforts. It would have required utilities to provide 100 percent of electricity from coal, oil, and natural gas by 2022. It failed.[6]

ALEC has also promoted legislation that penalizes those who choose to install solar panels on their homes. This would be accomplished by placing a surtax on homeowners with solar panels who attempt to sell power they don't need back to electric utilities.[7] Such

efforts, ironically, managed to earn the Koch brothers—apparently against intrusive state interference only until their bottom line is threatened—the ire of members of the Tea Party they helped create.

The Koch-funded Heartland Institute has been engaged in similar attacks on renewable energy.[8] Beginning in 2012, it sponsored ALEC's Electricity Freedom Act, model legislation aimed at repealing state renewable energy standard programs. Fortunately, these efforts have largely failed at the state level—with only Ohio halting its program, and only for one year (2014). These efforts have failed at the national level as well. Heartland has also tried to block state-level programs incentivizing solar energy.[9]

The goal of these efforts is to undermine the decarbonization of the power sector. But no assault on renewable energy would be complete without an attack on electric vehicles (EVs), for they are the path to decarbonizing the transportation sector as well. If you get your electricity from renewables and charge your car off an outlet in the garage, you're no longer driving off fossil fuels. That's a threat to the oil industry, which profits off the sale of gasoline, and to Koch Industries, which profits off the refining and distribution of oil and gasoline. Recognizing the threat to their bottom line, agents of the Koch brothers met with oil-refining and marketing companies in 2015 to pitch a "multi-million-dollar assault on EVs."[10]

Central to the plan was one of their bought-and-sold politicians, Republican senator John Barrasso of Wyoming, who was the third-highest recipient of Koch brothers dollars during the 2018 election cycle.[11] Barrasso, as chair of the Senate Environment and Public Works Committee, introduced the Fairness for Every Driver Act in 2019. It would not only end federal tax credits for EVs, but in addition would create an annual "highway user fee" for all "alternative fuel vehicles." It might not surprise you to learn that Barrasso, in his efforts to sell this bill to voters, used talking points that were taken directly from Koch brothers propaganda (for example, that the tax credit "disproportionately subsidizes wealthy buyers," and that "hard-working Wyoming taxpayers shouldn't have to subsidize wealthy California luxury-car buyers"). He and his fellow Republican proponents also used talking points manufactured by the Koch-funded Manhattan Institute (for example, the bogus claim that ending the electric vehicle tax credit would save roughly $20 billion in taxpayer funds over the next decade). These arguments have been characterized as resting on "every conceivable kind of error: data dredging, wishful thinking, truculent, and dogmatism."[12]

Tesla may be the greatest threat of all to the fossil fuel industry. Not only do Teslas compete with the sleekest of conventional automobiles performance-wise, but Elon Musk and his company have also literally redefined what an electric automobile can be. In North Carolina, American-made Teslas were outselling high-performance conventional vehicles, including foreign brands like BMWs, Mercedes, and Audis. The company's success was a triumph of American innovation, industry, and free markets! So the Republican state senate stepped in and tried to pass a bill that would prohibit the sale of Teslas.[13] (While the bill failed, Tesla sales were nonetheless banned in one major city, Charlotte.[14]) Soon thereafter, Republican governor Chris Christie tried to do the same thing in New Jersey.[15] Other red states—Texas, Utah, West Virginia, and Arizona—followed suit.[16] So much for "free-market" Republicans!

Meanwhile, the conservative media, doing the bidding of fossil fuel interests, have promoted mythologies designed to undermine public support for renewable energy. Solyndra was a California manufacturer of thin-film solar cells that used unusual, innovative technology. Plummeting silicon prices, however, led to the company being unable to compete with conventional solar panels, and it went bankrupt in September 2011.[17] The company defaulted on a $535 million loan it had received from the US Department of Energy under President Barack Obama's 2009 economic stimulus package. The vast majority (98 percent) of the funds provided under the federal program went to companies that have *not* defaulted on their loans; in fact, the Department of Energy projects a profit of more than $5 billion over the next two decades, with twenty of the program's thirty enterprises operating and generating revenue.[18]

The overall success of the program notwithstanding, inactivists have sought to make Solyndra the poster child for the supposed failings of renewable energy. They also used Solyndra scandal-mongering to attack Obama's proposed budget in 2015. Presumably what they *really* didn't like about the budget was that it would repeal nearly $50 billion in tax breaks for the oil, natural gas, and coal industries.[19] So in a masterful display of propagandistic jujitsu, Fox News and the *Daily Caller* (a Koch brothers front group masquerading as a media outlet), among others, sought to use Solyndra to tie the Obama budget to an ostensibly failed renewable energy agenda.[20] Despite what they claimed, Solyndra had not received the clean energy tax credits included in the president's 2015 budget. The budget didn't even increase funding for the largely successful loan guarantee program that had supported Solyndra in 2009.[21] But facts be damned when there's an opportunity to simultaneously both smear renewables and protect fossil fuel subsidies.

CROCODILE TEARS

Another line of attack by the inactivists is to cry crocodile tears over the purported threat posed by renewable energy. It's once again the classic tactic of dividing the environmental community, in this case by convincing them that renewables—which actually promise environmentally safe and reliable energy—are instead somehow a threat to our health and the environment.

So we get myths and distortions that seek to create a false dilemma for the environmentally minded, namely, that decarbonizing our economy will somehow come at the expense of environmental peril. None is more prominent than the supposed threat wind turbines pose to birds. Robert Bryce of the aforementioned Koch-funded Manhattan Institute has been out in front promoting this myth, both on the editorial pages of the *Wall Street Journal* and in ultra-right-wing venues like the *National Review*.[22] Do we really think that Bryce cares a feather about the birds whose supposed turbine-driven demise he laments? More birds are killed every year by housecats. Why aren't Bryce and the Murdoch media crusading to rein in our felines? Might they—and other fossil fuel water carriers advancing the "wind is a threat to birds" myth—be crying crocodile tears?

When it comes to the welfare of our feathered friends, I put more trust in the Audubon Society, whose *actual* mission is to "protect birds and the places they need, today and tomorrow." The Audubon Society has stated that climate change is a far greater threat than wind turbines. According to an Audubon Society report, hundreds of bird species in the United States—including our national symbol, the bald eagle—are at "serious risk" due to climate change, with the ranges for some species predicted to be diminished by 95 percent by 2080. Bird catch by wind turbines can be minimized by siting wind farms away from bird migration routes. Accordingly, Audubon supports "properly sited wind power as a renewable energy source that helps reduce the threat posed to birds and people by climate change."[23]

The inactivists have even managed to invent an imaginary health affliction in their efforts to scare people away from wind power—"wind turbine syndrome." Anti-wind advocates have claimed that a whole array of afflictions, including lung cancer, skin cancer, hemorrhoids, and both the gain and loss of weight, are somehow caused by proximity to wind farms. It is just one example of how Sagan's worst fears about "pseudo-science" have come to pass.[24] With absolutely no scientific evidence behind the phenomenon, the fact that some honest actual individuals have claimed to suffer from the imaginary syndrome is a classic example of a "communicated disease"—that is to say, people who might be experiencing any number of maladies and happen to live near a wind farm hear others talk about the putative syndrome and, looking for someone or something to blame, embrace this pseudoscientific but seemingly plausible explanation.[25]

It should come as no surprise that Koch-affiliated groups, fossil fuel interests, and the Murdoch media empire have sought to spread the myth of "wind turbine syndrome" far and wide.[26] Consider the utterings of Fox Business network's Eric Bolling: "Turbines are popping up all across America, as the demand for the usage of wind energy is increasing. But at what cost? Residents close to them have reported everything from headaches to vertigo to UFO crashes."[27] Yes, you read that right: "UFO crashes," too! The anti-wind brigade even managed to recruit President Donald Trump to the cause. Among his long list of ridiculous claims about wind turbines, he suggested they "cause cancer."[28]

Trump, in fact, used a fundraising address on April 2, 2019, to promote fears that allowing wind farms in communities causes financial damage, warning Americans, "If you have a windmill anywhere near your house, congratulations, your house just went down 75 percent in value."[29] Actual studies have found no evidence for the claim that wind turbines affect property values.[30]

Crocodile tears have also been shed over the supposed environmental impact of solar energy. That isn't to say that solar farms and solar panels have no environmental footprint—there are valid issues regarding land use and habitat loss, water use, and the potential release of hazardous materials in manufacturing.[31] But that footprint is tiny compared to the environmental impact of coal, natural gas, and petroleum. And that's not even considering the damages from climate change!

Enter the so-called Breakthrough Institute (BTI), a group originally linked to fossil fuel interests that has more recently been called a "nuclear [industry] front group."[32] Public ethics expert Clive Hamilton has accused BTI of "misrepresenting data on the energy savings of investment in energy efficiency, [criticizing] almost every proposed measure to reduce America's greenhouse gas emissions [and allying] with anti-climate science organizations."[33] Thomas Gerke, writing for *Clean Technica*, noted BTI's propensity for articles "discrediting renewable energy on the one hand and on the other preaching about nuclear energy as the solution for the global energy crisis of the 21st century."[34]

BTI cofounder Michael Shellenberger promotes the myth that solar energy poses a major threat to the environment. In May 2018 he penned a column for *Forbes* soaked with plaintive tears over the supposed toxicity of chemicals in solar photovoltaic cells.[35] Curiously unmentioned in his piece is the fact that (1) solar panel manufacturers in the United States must follow laws to ensure that workers are not harmed by exposure to toxic chemicals, and that chemical waste products are disposed of properly, and (2) manufacturers have a strong financial incentive to ensure that valuable and rare materials are recycled rather than disposed of.[36]

Just months later, Shellenberger followed up with another *Forbes* piece in which he asserted, presumably in all seriousness, that "nuclear is the safest source of electricity," that "low levels of radiation are harmless," and that "nuclear waste is the best kind of waste."[37] You see, nuclear = safe, solar = dangerous. Black = white. Up = down. Welcome to the bizarro world of soft denial.

Fox News has regularly subjected its viewers and readers to anti-solar propaganda warning of the dire environmental threats posed by solar energy. It has given us headlines like "Solar Energy Plants in Tortoises' Desert Habitat Pit Green Against Green."[38] It's an inactivist two-fer, combining feigned environmental concern with environmentalism wedge creation, all in one headline! Other examples include "Environmental Concerns Threaten Solar Power Expansion in California Desert," "Massive East Coast Solar Project Generates Fury from Neighbors," and my favorite: "World's Largest Solar Plant Scorching Birds in Nevada Desert."[39] It's touching to behold once again Rupert Murdoch's deep and abiding empathy for our avian cousins. Which makes total sense when you realize that birds are the modern descendants of dinosaurs.

Oddly, though, I don't recall seeing any Fox News headlines like "Mountain-Top-Removal Coal Mining Kills Off Fish and Amphibians," or "Deep Oil Drilling Destroys the Gulf of Mexico," or "Our Dependence on Fossil Fuels Is Scorching the Planet." Fox News and conservative media display curiously selective outrage over impacts on people and the environment where renewable energy, rather than fossil fuels, is concerned.

Some of the solar scare tactics used by the right-wing media border on the comical. Just as wind turbines supposedly cause cancer, solar panels will apparently cause you to freeze to death in cold climates. Or so claimed Fox News host Jesse Watters as he attempted to discredit the Green New Deal and its architect Alexandria Ocasio-Cortez: "They have this new green deal or whatever. Ok, where they want to eliminate all oil and gas in 10 years. If you're in the polar vortex, how are you going to stay warm with solar panels?"[40]

Of course, the fine art of scaring the public about renewables isn't confined to the United States. Australian prime minister Scott Morrison, known, among other things, for having brandished a lump of coal on the floor of Parliament as a testament to his idea of "clean energy," has also demonstrated some facility in this department. In April 2019, Morrison launched an attack on the Labor Party's proposed target that EVs constitute 50 percent of all new car sales by 2030. Admonishing Labor leader Bill Shorten, he said that pro-EV policies would "end the weekend" for Australians. Morrison warned, "You've got Australians who love being out there in their four-wheel drives. [Shorten] wants to say see you later to the SUV when it comes to the choices of Australians." Ironically, Morrison's own government (the Liberal-National coalition) had proposed policies that were only slightly less bullish on electric vehicles, setting a goal that 25 percent of all new car sales by 2030 be EVs. Noting the irony, Shorten responded that Morrison and the coalition government were "so addicted to scare campaigns, they're even scaring you with their own policies."[41]

"LET THEM BURN COAL"

If the inactivists have shed a few crocodile tears when it comes to the supposed threat posed by renewable energy to our health and the environment, they've cried a whole river when it comes to their supposed concern for the plight of the poor. They've appealed to the logical fallacy known as "you can't chew gum and walk at the same time," or, to be more specific, the idea that promoting renewable energy over ostensibly cheaper fossil fuel energy will somehow divert essential resources from efforts to fight third-world poverty. Welcome to the contrived concept of "energy poverty."

The energy-poverty conceit rests on the flawed premise that lack of access to energy (rather than to, say, food, water, health care, and so on) poses the primary threat to people in the developing world, and, moreover, that fossil fuels are the only viable way to provide that energy. In other words, if you are concerned about the disadvantaged of the world, you should be promoting fossil fuels. It's a truly brilliant, if cynical and manipulative, strategy by fossil-fuel-promoting inactivists to recruit political progressives and moderates to their cause.

Among the promoters of the concept is the aforementioned BTI, whose mission, as stated on its website, is "[to make] clean energy cheap through technology innovation to deal with both global warming and energy poverty."[42] Also among the ranks of energy-poverty adherents are Microsoft CEO Bill Gates and former ExxonMobil CEO Rex Tillerson. Tillerson once posed, without any apparent sense of irony, the question, "What good is it to save the planet if humanity suffers?"[43]

Indisputably the most enthusiastic of energy-poverty crusaders, however, is Bjorn Lomborg. A self-styled "skeptical environmentalist," Lomborg is neither—skepticism, remember, involves good-faith scrutiny of tenuous-seeming claims, not indiscriminate rejection of well-established science. The charismatic Lomborg brandishes a Greenpeace T-shirt to prove his environmental bona fides.

Dig a bit deeper, however, and a rather different story emerges. Lomborg's Copenhagen Consensus Center has been funded by the Randolph Foundation, whose main trustee, Heather Higgins, is also the president of the Koch-funded International Women's Forum.[44] The center is in fact a virtual entity, with an official address at a Lowell, Massachusetts, parcel service. The conservative Abbott government in Australia attempted to provide it with a permanent home, offering $4 million in taxpayer funds to the University of Western Australia if it would provide a home for the center. The university ultimately walked away from the offer.[45]

Lomborg frequently pens commentaries in leading newspapers, including the *Wall Street Journal*, the *New York Times*, and *USA Today*, downplaying the impacts of climate change, criticizing renewable energy, and promoting fossil fuels. With a smile and a professed concern for the environment and the poor, he scolds those who would misguidedly wean us off fossil fuels and promote clean energy.[46]

For someone with such professed sympathy for the plight of the developing world, Lomborg displays a remarkable dismissiveness toward those most vulnerable to the devastating impacts of climate change. In one op-ed he warned that "a 20-foot rise in sea levels . . . would inundate about 16,000 square miles of coastline, where more than 400 million people currently live." An alarming fact. But Lomborg couldn't quit while he was ahead. He continued: "That's a lot of people, to be sure, but hardly all of mankind. In fact, it amounts to less than 6% of the world's population—which is to say that 94% of the population would not be inundated."[47]

Conservatives apparently now study Lomborg's talking points. This type of "big picture" thinking cropped up again in the middle of the coronavirus crisis of early 2020. Take, for example, right-wing Wisconsin senator Ron Johnson's message to his constituents over the Trump administration's failure to take meaningful actions in the early stages of the pandemic. "Right now, all people are hearing about are the deaths," Johnson complained. "Sure the deaths are horrific," he conceded, but "the flip side of this is the vast majority of people who get coronavirus do survive." He cheerily added that, in the end, the coronavirus would kill "no more than 3.4 percent of our population."[48] What's a few hundred million people among friends, after all, Bjorn/Ron?

When it comes to the plight of the poor, I must confess that my own bias is to take Pope Francis more seriously than Bjorn Lomborg. And the pope has rejected the energy-poverty myth, pointing out that distributed, renewable energy in the form of solar power and hydropower is far more practical than fossil fuel use in most of the developing world.[49] Even the fossil-fuel-friendly *Wall Street Journal* has acknowledged as much, noting that "renewable energy could offer a . . . solution for remote areas, because it is created and consumed in the same region and doesn't require massive power plants and hundreds of kilometers of power lines."[50] If you've lost the *Wall Street Journal*, Bjorn, well . . .

There is an even deeper problem, of course, with the premise that climate action detracts from the concerns of the poor. As Pope Francis emphasized in his papal encyclical on the environment, climate change *aggravates* other societal challenges—food, water and land scarcity, health, and national and international security. The US Department of Defense agrees.[51] The irony of the energy-poverty myth is that climate-change impacts will actually place far more people in poverty than are in poverty today. In a scenario of climate collapse, there *is* no economy. Don't take my word for it, though. A World Bank study from 2015 concluded that climate change could "thrust 100 million into deep poverty by 2030." Even Fox News reported it.[52]

IT'S THE JOBS, STUPID!

Another tactic the inactivists use is to scare people into thinking that climate action and renewable energy will take away their jobs. A group connected to the Koch Foundation that calls itself Power the Future has sought to blame Tom Steyer—a climate activist and philanthropist, and perhaps not coincidentally, from the standpoint of being an eligible boogeyman, a Jewish billionaire—for the steady, decades-long decline of the coal industry and the demise of coal communities across America. The organization has even attempted to brand collapsing coal towns as "Steyervilles." Their "proof" is the fact that Steyer's philanthropic spending has increased as coal jobs have decreased—not exactly the sort of iron-clad argument that would pass muster in the peer-reviewed literature, or the pages of a reputable newspaper, or even a fortune-cookie fortune.[53]

Yes, coal jobs are disappearing. And there are now far more jobs in the burgeoning renewable energy industry (hundreds of thousands in solar alone) than there are in the dying coal industry (which currently has less than fifty thousand coal-mining jobs).[54] But these job losses have more to do with increased mechanization and automation of coal mining and competition from cheaper fossil fuels (namely, natural gas) than they do with competition from renewable energy, let alone climate activism itself.

Despite job retraining programs and other efforts to help those displaced by the demise of coal, there are inevitably those—especially older workers—who will encounter difficulty finding subsequent employment. Labor leaders representing the energy sector, such as James Slevin, president of the Utility Workers Union of America, have thus argued that climate policies must include measures to help coal workers and their families by providing financial support for their health plans, pensions, and educational opportunities.[55]

Technological transitions are never easy, and there are always winners and losers. But it is no more appropriate to blame the renewable energy industry for lost coal jobs than it is to blame the fossil fuel industry for destroying the whaling industry, which provided much of the lamp oil that was replaced by kerosene and then coal-powered electrical lighting.

ET TU, MICHAEL MOORE?

File this one under the category of "with friends like this . . ." None other than liberal icon Michael Moore has now joined the ranks of the renewable energy bashers. Working with director Jeff Gibbs, his longtime collaborator on left-of-center polemics like the anti-NRA *Bowling for Columbine* and the anti-Bush, anti–Iraq War film *Fahrenheit 9/11*, Moore, in his 2020 film *Planet of the Humans* (*POTH*), has promoted a full-on assault on renewable energy. Though Gibbs directed the documentary, Moore put the full weight of his celebrity into the project, doing the talk-show circuit and flacking the film like next month's rent depended on it.[56]

POTH had no sooner been screened at film festivals when the negative reviews started to come in.[57] The film, in fact, proved to be so toxic that Moore couldn't get a major distributor to adopt the film. Nor would Netflix or any other major streaming platform show it. So he ended up posting it for free on YouTube on Earth Day 2020, as if his intention were to launch a hand grenade that would produce maximum collateral damage to action on climate.[58]

The fatal flaws in the film, enumerated in excruciating detail by a number of energy and climate experts, comprise a laundry list of deceptive facts and bad-faith arguments.[59] They include: (1) the misleading use of data, photographs, and interviews that are a decade old to dramatically overstate the limitations of renewable energy and understate the efficiency and capacity of current-day renewable energy sources and storage technology; (2) complaints that a still largely fossil-fuel-driven electricity grid is used in the construction of solar panels and wind turbines, without noting that the life-cycle carbon emissions are tiny compared to either coal or gas, and that decarbonization of the grid is precisely what the renewable energy transition is about; and (3) grossly inflated estimates of the carbon footprint of biofuels and biomass (which is tiny compared to that of fossil fuels), while failing to note that biomass accounts for only 2 percent of domestic electricity generation (though Moore and Gibbs spend about 50 percent of the film complaining about it).[60]

The film, disappointingly, promotes the sorts of myths about renewable energy that one expects to hear on Fox News rather than in a Michael Moore–produced film. For example, it decries electric vehicles as not being green because they're fueled off the grid, which is still driven substantially by fossil fuel energy. But this argument neglects the fact that a fundamental component of any meaningful green energy transition is the electrification of transport in concert with the *decarbonization of the electric grid*.[61] To focus on the former without acknowledging the latter is to entirely miss the point, unintentionally or otherwise.

We are treated once again to the now familiar crocodile tears over the ostensible horrible environmental impacts of renewable energy—the large tracts of land required for solar and wind farms, the reliance on mining for metals used in solar panels, and so on. It's odd that Michael Moore seems far more concerned by fields dotted with wind turbines and solar panels than by his newfound concern about climate change. Shortly after the release of the film, he tweeted that "the public knows we're losing the climate battle, thanks to profit & greed & leaders who led us wrong."[62] First of all, we're not "losing the climate battle." As we will see later, substantial progress is now being made. And while profit and greed are certainly part of the problem, so, too, are misguided attacks on renewable energy and the false prophets who bear them. Which brings us back to Michael Moore and Jeff Gibbs.

They are shocked, for example, to learn that the United States gets some of its renewable energy from the burning of biomass (mostly, organic refuse). But in what stands out as a blatant untruth in an already a gratuitously error-ridden film, they claim that power generation from biomass exceeds that of solar and wind. The actual numbers indicate just the opposite, with biomass providing only 1.4 percent and solar and wind providing 9.1 percent of total power generation.[63] Adding insult to injury, they repeat the outrageously misleading claim that "biomass releases 50 percent more carbon dioxide than coal and more than three times as much as natural gas." The erroneous claim is the by-product of the very same bad math we encountered in an earlier chapter with the 2014 film *Cowspiracy*.

Cowspiracy, as readers may recall, falsely asserted that livestock are responsible for 51 percent of carbon emissions. This figure is based on bad accounting coupled with poor scientific understanding. The scriptwriters appear to have been unaware of the simple fact that the carbon produced by cows when they exhale (in the form of carbon dioxide, through what we call "respiration") comes from consumed plant matter that had extracted the carbon from the atmosphere in the first place (through the process of "photosynthesis"). When cows, or any animals—including us—exhale, we're not adding net carbon dioxide to the atmosphere, we're simply helping circulate the carbon through the atmosphere/biosphere system.[64] The actual contribution of livestock to carbon emissions comes from entirely different processes: fermentation, manure management, feed production, and energy consumption. Cows do also belch *methane*, which is itself a potent greenhouse gas, but its lifetime in the atmosphere is much shorter than that of CO_2. The true net contribution to carbon emissions from livestock (15 percent), curiously enough, corresponds to a simple reversal of the two digits in the number (51 percent) cited in *Cowspiracy*.

Moore and Gibbs make essentially the same error in *POTH*, failing to inform their audience that the carbon dioxide produced by burning biomass (with the exception of old-growth forests) is carbon dioxide that recently came from the atmosphere anyway. Biomass is therefore largely "carbon neutral"—far from perfect when we are trying to reduce the amount of carbon in the atmosphere, but still better than releasing CO_2 from the Carboniferous era, as we do when we burn coal or gas. Burning biomass itself doesn't increase carbon dioxide levels in the atmosphere. There are, of course, some carbon emissions associated with processing and transportation, and that's simply a result of the fact that much of our basic infrastructure still relies upon a fossil-fuel-energy economy—a fact that is less true every day as a *result* of the renewable energy revolution! But the carbon emissions are tiny—about ten grams of carbon pollution per kilowatt-hour. For comparison, natural gas yields about five hundred grams and coal nine hundred grams per kilowatt-hour! Much as animal rights activists have overstated the role of meat-eating in climate change to advance their (admittedly worthy) agenda of decreasing meat consumption, so, too, have some forest preservation activists overstated their (admittedly worthy) goal of stopping deforestation.[65]

It's important to get the facts right. The wood chips used in biomass are generally a by-product of already-existing forestry practices, not the result of cutting down trees for fuel as some imply. And biomass is a broad category. While we certainly shouldn't be turning forests into wood chips for burning, it does make sense to burn some forms of organic waste, which can provide a near carbon-neutral source of energy, while we transition to cleaner renewable energy.

POTH reinforces so many of the tropes we've encountered that it almost serves as a poster child for the new climate war. One challenge we face in this new war on climate action is, as we saw in the previous chapter, the wedge that has emerged within the climate movement itself when it comes to market-driven climate solutions. Moore and Gibbs attempt to pry that wedge wide open. The fact that wind and solar energy are increasingly profitable is somehow an indication, to them, that they're "bad." In the words of the editorial board of the *Las Vegas Review-Journal*, Moore seems "particularly aghast to discover that . . . any transition to green energy will require massive investment from evil industrialists and capitalists who might turn a profit. Who knew?"[66]

So heroes become villains—and villains, ironically, become heroes. Climate champion Bill McKibben is vilified for having once, long ago, supported the limited use of biomass energy.[67] Al Gore is attacked for supposedly being "more focused on cashing in than saving the planet."[68] (Couldn't a similar argument be made about Michael Moore and his $50 million net worth?[69]) Moore and Gibbs were apparently "shocked to find a company owned by Charles and David Koch receiving solar tax credits." Now, there are *many* reasons to dislike the Koch brothers—but the fact that they invested in solar energy is not one of them. Only in the Trumpian era of gaslighting could a progressive filmmaker produce a polemic premised on the absurd notion that ultra-right-wing plutocrats are secretly behind the effort to end our dependence on fossil fuels. And get progressives to actually fall for it.

Then there is defeatism and despair-mongering (a topic we'll explore in detail in Chapter 8). As *The Guardian* put it, "most chillingly of all, Gibbs at one stage of the film appears to suggest that there is no cure for any of this, that, just as humans are mortal, so the species itself is staring its own mortality in the face."[70] Writing for *Films for Action*, an award-winning longtime environmental filmmaker, Neal Livingston, had an even harsher critique: "SHAME on these filmmakers for making a film like this, full of misinformation and disinformation, to intentionally depress audiences, and make them think there are no alternatives. . . . Let me make it absolutely clear that the new documentary, *Planet of the Humans*, by Jeff Gibbs—with executive producer Michael Moore, is inaccurate, misleading and designed to depress you into doing nothing."[71] Doomism and the loss of hope can lead people down the very same path of inaction as outright denial. And Michael Moore plays right into it.

Then there is the classic deflection of the sort we've encountered before. Technically, Moore and Gibbs do advance one "solution." Rather than focusing on the systemic source of the problem—our reliance on fossil fuels, they deflect attention toward individual behavior, which, as we have seen, is a classic new-climate-war tactic. The twist here is that it's all about the behavior of *others*. Environmental author Ketan Joshi remarks that Moore "ends up at population control—a cruel, evil and racist ideology that you can see coming right from the start of the film."[72] Brian Kahn, writing in *Earther*, noted, "Over the course of the movie, [Gibbs] interviews a cast of mostly white experts who are mostly men to make that case. . . . There's a reason that Breitbart and other conservative voices aligned with climate denial and fossil fuel companies have taken a shine to the film. It's because it ignores the solution of holding power to account and sounds like a racist dog whistle."[73] It is worth noting, by the way, that people in the developing world, where the main population growth is taking place, have a tiny carbon footprint in comparison with those in the industrial world. The world's richest 10 percent produce half of global carbon emissions.[74] The problem isn't so much "too many people" as it is "too many people who burn a lot of carbon." As environmental sociologist Grant Samms put it, Moore and Gibbs spend the entire film oscillating between "ecological nihilism and ecological fascism."[75]

Conservative foundations and media outlets, on the other hand, loved Moore's film. And it wasn't just Breitbart News that was "full of gratitude and admiration that they should have made this bold, brave documentary."[76] Fossil-fuel-funded groups like the Competitive Enterprise Institute and the Heartland Institute (and their payed attack-dog Anthony Watts) lapped it up.[77] CEI encouraged people to "Hurry, see *Planet of the Humans* before it's banned," while the Heartland Institute promoted the film in a podcast series.[78] Watts advertised it as an "Earth Day Epic," linking to it directly on his blog.[79] Industry-funded denier-for-hire Steve Milloy insisted that "EU politicians should be forced to watch Michael Moore's *Planet of the Humans* . . . with their eyes clamped open if necessary."[80] Other fossil-fuel-industry shills, including Marc Morano of the Committee for a Constructive Tomorrow (CFACT), promoted the film and attacked its critics on Twitter, which also became a predictable venue for manufactured outrage by right-wing trollbots.[81] And yes, even the Koch brothers got in on some of the action. An anti-renewables Koch brothers front group known as the American Energy Alliance spent thousands of dollars promoting the film.[82]

We are left, in the end, to wonder why Michael Moore ever produced this film. Politics can make for strange bedfellows. Moore was a huge supporter of Bernie Sanders during his campaign for president. Sanders made his support for the Green New Deal a centerpiece of his platform, and the GND, at its core, supports renewable energy. But Moore has also been a supporter of Julian Assange for years.[83] The WikiLeaks leader has collaborated closely with Russia in its efforts to attack climate science and undermine action on climate.

Moreover, Moore has been a longtime advocate for blue-collar workers and the unionization movement, beginning with his breakout 1989 film *Roger and Me*, which denounced General Motors' crackdown on union workers. It is hardly unprecedented for the labor left to find itself in conflict with the environmental left. Recall from Chapter 5 that the general secretary of the GMB trade union, Tim Roache, warned that climate action would lead to the "confiscation of petrol cars," "state rationing of meat," and "limiting families to one flight for every five years," placing "entire industries and the jobs they produced in peril."[84]

Does Moore see decarbonization of our economy as a threat to workers? Had Moore struck a secret deal with the fossil fuel industry? Or had he simply lost his mind? Had the Trump presidency somehow caused him to "flip"? Or did Moore simply care more about being provocative than about being right? With his most successful films now more than a decade behind him and his relevance increasingly in question, was he simply looking for a dramatic way to attach himself to the defining issue of the day? Once a polemicist, after all, always a polemicist.

Maybe this is simply a manifestation of what environmental journalist Emily Atkin has referred to as the phenomenon of "first-time climate dudes."[85] It's the tendency for members of a particular, privileged demographic group (primarily middle-aged, almost exclusively white men) to think they can just swoop in, surf the Internet, interview a few hand-selected "experts," and solve the great problems that others have spent decades unable to crack. It is almost inevitable that the product, in the end, is a hot mess, consisting of fatally bad takes and misguided framing couched in deeply condescending mansplaining. On climate change, we've seen it with Bill Gates, *FiveThirtyEight*'s Nate Silver, and now with Michael Moore.[86]

The fact is that we may never know the motives behind this ill-premised, intellectually dishonest stunt by Michael Moore and Jeff Gibbs. What we *do* know is that their misguided polemic furthers the agenda of fossil fuel interests and their tactic of denial, delay, distraction, and deflection by buying into misleading and false narratives about renewable energy. It appears they will go down in history as having ironically sided with wealthy, powerful polluters, rather than "the people" they purport to care about, in the defining battle of our time.

"YOU'RE NOT GONNA HAVE IT!"

Finally, when all other arguments fail, we're left with "Well—it just won't work. You can't do it!" Inactivists in fact twist themselves into veritable pretzels to explain why there's no way we can possibly power our economy with renewable energy. There are fundamental obstacles, they say. Intermittency! Insufficient batteries!

Yes, the wind isn't always blowing, and the sun isn't always shining. And batteries don't have infinite storage capacity. But these challenges are, if you will forgive the pun, overblown. Smart grid technology that adaptively combines various renewable energy sources can overcome these limitations—not in the future, but right now. Utility-scale "big battery" systems like those produced now by Tesla are outperforming and outcompeting fossil fuel generators in providing grid stability to blackout-prone regions like South Australia.[87]

Peer-reviewed research demonstrates authoritatively that even without any technological innovation—that is, using current renewable energy and energy-storage technology—we could meet up to 80 percent of global energy demand by 2030 and 100 percent by 2050. This would be accomplished through increased energy efficiency, electrification of all energy sectors, and decarbonization of the grid through a mix of generation sources, including residential rooftop solar and solar plants, onshore and offshore wind farms, wave energy, geothermal energy, and hydroelectric and tidal energy. The precise mix of technologies would depend on the location, season, and time of day.[88] Sorry, Bill Gates, but we don't "need a miracle."[89] The solution is already here. We just need to deploy it rapidly and at a massive scale. It all comes down to political will and economic incentives.

A renewable energy transition would create millions of new jobs, stabilize energy prices in the absence of fuel costs, reduce power disruption, and increase access to energy by decentralizing power generation.[90] But that's not what we hear from Koch-funded groups like the Heartland Institute. Instead we get supposed experts like coal-industry shill and climate-change denier David Wojick penning pieces with titles like "Providing 100 Percent Energy from Renewable Sources Is Impossible."[91] In dismissing the viability of a renewable energy transition, Wojick engages in a classic game of denial bingo, harping on the ostensible fatal problems of "intermittency" (largely already solved, as discussed earlier), "scalability" (that's simply a matter of government incentives—the very incentives that Wojick's bosses, the Kochs, have worked so hard to game in favor of the fossil fuel industry and against renewable energy), and "expense" (he grossly overestimates battery storage costs; ignores that there are multiple storage options aside from batteries, like pumped-storage hydroelectric power; and pretends that places like Colorado have no sun).

Wojick ends by offering us some revisionist history, dismissing as "false claims" the dramatic success stories that have been told of towns and municipalities that have already transitioned to 100 percent renewable energy. Pay no attention to Greensburg, Kansas—the town that was leveled by an EF5 tornado and rebuilt 100 percent renewable by its conservative Republican mayor.[92] Really, it doesn't exist! Fake news! The critics have gone beyond denial of climate change to denial of reality itself.

Speaking of denial of reality, let's again talk about Fox News and its take on solar energy in the United States. In a 2013 segment attacking the Obama administration's support for renewable energy, Fox News host Gretchen Carlson questioned Fox business reporter Shibani Joshi on why solar power was so much more successful in Germany than in the United States. "What was Germany doing correct?" Carlson asked. "Are they just a smaller country, and that made it more feasible?" Carl Sagan surely rolled over in his grave after hearing the response: "They're a smaller country," Joshi said, *"and they've got lots of sun. Right? They've got a lot more sun than we do"* (emphasis added). Perhaps sensing she had just said something absurd, Joshi doubled down in an effort to explain herself. "The problem is it's a cloudy day and it's raining, *you're not gonna have it*" (emphasis added). Conceding that California actually gets just a bit of sunlight now and then, she elaborated, "Here on the East Coast, it's just not going to work."[93]

Of course, it's only in the mythological universe of Fox News where the East Coast of the United States gets less sun than Germany. As Media Matters pointed out in its response to the segment, estimates from the US Department of Energy National Renewable Energy Laboratory (NREL) show that nearly the entire continental United States gets more sun on average than even the most sun-laden regions of Germany.[94] In fact, as one NREL scientist pointed out, "Germany's solar resource is akin to Alaska's." (Alaska receives by far the least average sunlight of any US state.[95]) But, returning to Carlson's original question: What's the real reason that German's solar industry is doing so much better than the solar industry in the United States? Simple: It doesn't have Fox News, the rest of the Murdoch media, the Koch brothers, and fossil fuel interests all joining forces to destroy it.

FALSE SOLUTIONS

We have seen that there is a dual attack underway by inactivists in the form of efforts to both block carbon pricing and blunt or at least slow the renewable energy transition now underway. Fight back. When you encounter myths about the supposed environmental threat of wind turbines and solar panels, push back against them. Correct the misinformation. If you have friends or family or colleagues who have been taken in by the crocodile tears, hand them a handkerchief and explain to them they've been had. When someone cites "energy poverty" or "lost jobs" as arguments against renewable energy, point out that the opposite is true: the safest and healthiest path to economic development in the third world is access to clean, decentralized, renewable energy, and the greatest opportunity for job growth in the energy industry comes with renewables, not fossil fuels.

But also be prepared for the next line of attack: There is yearning now among the public for a meaningful climate solution. If it's not renewable energy, it must be something else. So inactivists seek to fill that void with reassuring, plausible-sounding alternative "solutions" that do not pose a threat to the fossil fuel juggernaut. And they have done so by introducing a new, seemingly empowering lexicon: "geo-engineering," "clean coal," "bridge fuels," "adaptation," "resilience." Welcome to our next chapter—the *non-solution solution*.

CHAPTER 7

The Non-Solution Solution

It is a wholesome and necessary thing for us to turn again to the earth and in the contemplation of her beauties to know the sense of wonder and humility.
—RACHEL CARSON

When I am working on a problem, I never think about beauty but when I have finished, if the solution is not beautiful, I know it is wrong.
—R. BUCKMINSTER FULLER

THE INACTIVISTS HAVE SOUGHT TO HIJACK ACTUAL CLIMATE progress by promoting "solutions" (natural gas, carbon capture, geo-engineering) that aren't real solutions at all. Part of their strategy is using soothing words and terms—"bridge fuels," "clean coal," "adaptation," "resilience"—that convey the illusion of action but, in context, are empty promises. This gambit provides plausible deniability: inactivists can claim to have offered *solutions*. Just not good ones. They are delay tactics intended to forestall meaningful action while the fossil fuel industry continues to make windfall profits—what noted climate advocate Alex Steffen has referred to as "predatory delay."[1] It is essential that we recognize and expose these efforts for the sham they are, for the clock is ticking. We cannot afford any further delay when it comes to the climate crisis.

A BRIDGE TO NOWHERE

Let me sell you a bridge to a fossil-fuel-free future. Beware of a bait-and-switch, however, for it is actually a bridge to nowhere. It's called natural gas, a naturally occurring gas composed primarily of methane—the same methane that, as we learned earlier, is belched by cows, contributing to greenhouse gas emissions. This particular source of methane isn't biogenic, however. It is a fossil fuel formed from ancient organic matter—plants and animals that died and were buried beneath Earth's surface millions of years ago. They eventually made it down deep into Earth's crust, where, subjected to great pressure and heating, they eventually turned into an admixture of hydrocarbon molecules residing in either the solid, liquid, or gaseous state (coal, oil, or natural gas, respectively). Like other hydrocarbons, natural gas is energy rich, and it is readily burned for heating, cooking, or electricity generation. Or it can be cooled into a liquid (liquefied natural gas, or LNG) that can be used as a fuel for transportation.

Natural gas reservoirs can be found in sedimentary basins around the world, from Saudi Arabia to Venezuela to the Gulf of Mexico, from Montana and the Dakotas to the Marcellus Shale spanning the Appalachian Basin. That includes my home state of Pennsylvania, where the discovery of extensive natural gas deposits has led to an explosion in natural gas drilling over the past decade and a half. Pennsylvania is now responsible for more than 20 percent of all the natural gas produced in the United States.

The fracking boom has generated billions of dollars in revenue for the state. It has also generated a heated debate, forgive the pun, about the role Pennsylvania should be playing in expanding fossil fuel extraction at a time when we are increasingly dealing with the negative impacts of climate change (and that's not even accounting for the other serious potential environmental threats from natural gas extraction, including the impact of fracking chemicals on the safety of water supplies).[2]

The debate is playing out over an increasingly large stage. Australia's natural gas boom is threatening its agreed-upon carbon emissions targets.[3] Indeed, before the devastating bushfires of the summer of 2019/2020 had even ended, Australia's conservative, pro-fossil-fuel prime minister, Scott Morrison, had eagerly announced a $2 billion plan to boost the domestic natural gas industry.[4] The tragic irony was apparently lost on him.

The Trump administration, meanwhile, heavily promoted natural gas in the United States, attempting to improve its image by re-branding it as "freedom gas."[5] The implication that it will somehow help spread freedom evokes propaganda campaigns from days of yore. The tobacco industry used the phrase "Torches of Freedom" in the early twentieth century in an effort to encourage women to smoke, convincing them it was a source of empowerment during the first wave of feminism in the United States.[6]

Natural gas has often been characterized as a bridge fuel, a way to slowly wean us off more carbon-intensive fuels like coal and gently nudge us toward a renewable energy future. The rationale is that, nominally, natural gas produces about as half as much carbon dioxide as coal for each watt of power generated. Indeed, the "coal to gas switch," as it's called, is partly responsible for the flattening of global carbon emissions as natural gas displaces more carbon-intensive coal. In the United States, for example, it has been tied to a 16 percent decrease in carbon emissions from the power sector during the 2007–2014 period.[7]

What is unique about natural gas among fossil fuels, however, is that it is not only a fossil fuel. It's also a greenhouse gas. In fact, methane is nearly one hundred times more potent as a greenhouse gas than carbon dioxide on a twenty-year time frame.[8] That means it can cause warming not only when we burn it for energy, and it re-leases carbon dioxide, but when the methane itself escapes into the atmosphere. The process of hydraulic fracturing, or fracking, that is used to break up the bedrock to get at natural gas deposits inevitably allows some of the methane to escape directly into the atmosphere (what's known as "fugitive methane").

The Obama administration sought to limit fugitive methane emissions by requiring natural gas interests to curb methane releases from drilling operations, pipelines, and storage facilities. The Trump administration disbanded these regulations, claiming it would save industry millions of dollars.[9]

The rest of us pay the price. Research from 2020 has demonstrated that the spike in atmospheric methane levels in recent decades is coming from natural gas extraction (as opposed to farming and livestock, or natural sources such as peat bogs and melting permafrost).[10] Moreover, the rise in methane is responsible for as much as 25 percent of the warming during this period.[11] Connecting the dots, it is reasonable to say that fugitive methane emissions from fracking are contributing substantially to warming—enough that they may well offset, at least in the near term, the nominal decrease in carbon dioxide emissions from the coal-to-gas switch.

There are other problems with the bridge-fuel framing. Perhaps the most obvious is that we don't have decades to get this right. If we are to avert warming beyond the 1.5°C (2.7°F) danger limit, we've got *one decade* to decrease global carbon emissions by a factor of two.[12] That's a very short bridge. And increased use of natural gas for power generation is likely to crowd out investment in a true, zero-carbon solution in the power sector: renewable energy. Ultimately, the predicament with natural gas is that the solution to a problem created by fossil fuels cannot be a fossil fuel.

UNCLEAN COAL

Why not just gather the carbon dioxide released from coal burning at a coal-fired power plant before it makes it to the atmosphere? Then contain it, burying it somewhere beneath Earth's surface (or below the ocean floor)? There's a name for that—it's called carbon capture and sequestration, or CCS, and it's already being implemented.

As I first drafted the paragraph above, the TV was on in the background. Playing was an ExxonMobil commercial promoting CCS. The advertisement conjured an enticing vision of technology overcoming our problems: coal power without carbon pollution—at last, the promise of "clean coal"! Problem solved, right? Not quite. There are in reality a number of fundamental problems with the feasibility, cost, and reliability of CCS.

With CCS, typically, the carbon dioxide released during the burning of coal is scrubbed from emissions and captured, compressed, and liquefied. It is then pumped deep into the Earth, several kilometers beneath the surface, where it is reacted with porous igneous rocks to form limestone. This approach mimics the geological processes that bury carbon dioxide on geological time scales and provides a potential means of long-term geological sequestration of carbon dioxide.

The first full-scale proof of concept for CCS was built in Illinois. Called FutureGen, it was designed to provide data about efficiency, residual emissions, and other matters that would enable scientists to evaluate CCS performance. If CCS were to be deployed commercially at a larger scale in the future, that data would be vital. The project was funded by an alliance of the US Department of Energy and coal producers, users, and distributors. It was ultimately canceled in 2015 as a result of difficulties acquiring public funds.[13] Other CCS projects followed, however, including the large-footprint Petra Nova project in Texas.

Despite its failure, FutureGen did provide some useful insights into the viability of CCS. The scientists involved in the project estimated that they could bury roughly 1.3 million tons of carbon dioxide annually, equivalent to roughly 90 percent of the carbon emitted by the plant's coal burning.[14] But the FutureGen site was chosen in part for its favorability, as it is located above geological formations that are suited to carbon sequestration. This might not be true for many existing coal-burning sites.

The Global CCS Institute reports that there are today fifty-one CCS facilities globally in some stage of development that plan to capture nearly 100 million tons of carbon dioxide per year. (Nineteen facilities are currently in operation, and another thirty-two are either under construction or in development.) Of these, eight are in the United States.[15]

CCS might sound like a foolproof way to mitigate coal-based greenhouse emissions, but there are real questions about its scalability. It simply isn't feasible to bury the *billions* of tons per year of carbon pollution currently produced by coal burning. Many coal-fired power plants are not located at CCS-favorable sites. Moreover, given unforeseen factors, such as earthquakes and seismic activity, or groundwater flow, the efficacy of CCS in any particular location could be compromised. Carelessly sequestered carbon could easily end up becoming mobilized and belched back into the atmosphere.

Economically there is a problem as well. Coal is currently not competitive with other forms of energy in the marketplace. It is, as we have already seen, a dying industry. Requiring that coal plants capture and sequester their carbon will only make it more expensive and hasten the collapse of the industry. Unless, of course, government (that is, taxpayers like you and me) pays for it. In that case, we would be subsidizing dirty energy that still carries climate risk, rather than the cheaper, clean energy that can mitigate it, a true perversion of the economic incentive structure.

Finally, there is the more fundamental limitation that CCS is not even carbon neutral in the best of circumstances. Even if the 90 percent rate of sequestration estimated by FutureGen scientists is correct, and representative more generally of CCS, that would mean that 10 percent of the carbon dioxide would still escape to the atmosphere. CCS-equipped coal-fired power plants would continue to emit tens of millions of tons of carbon dioxide every year. Moreover, most of the carbon dioxide that is captured in CCS is placed into tapped oil wells for enhanced oil recovery. The oil that is recovered, when burned, yields several times as much carbon dioxide as was sequestered in the first place by CCS. So much for carbon-friendliness!

Despite all the talk these days about "clean coal technology," such technology—in the sense of coal-based energy that is free of polluting greenhouse gases—does not yet exist. Until data from experimental sites have been collected and studied, a process that would take years, it will be unclear how much carbon dioxide is actually being sequestered by CCS. It could be decades before the efficacy of true long-term carbon burial could be established. Yet, we have seen that even a decade of additional business-as-usual greenhouse gas emissions could commit us to catastrophic climate change. As Michael Barnard, chief strategist for TFIE Strategy, Inc., a think tank focused on clean energy solutions, aptly put it, "we're in a hole that we've created by shoveling carbon out of the ground and into the sky. The first thing to do is stop shoveling. All CCS does is take teaspoons out of massive scoops of carbon and puts them back in the hole."[16]

CCS is attractive to fossil fuel companies, as it provides them with a license to continue extracting and selling fossil fuels. It is anathema to climate activists, however, because its claim to carbon neutrality is dubious. CCS, unsurprisingly, has been at the very center of the policy debate surrounding the Green New Deal.

Readers may recall from Chapter 5 a letter signed by leading environmental organizations proposing a particular version of AOC's Green New Deal warning that the groups "will vigorously oppose any legislation that . . . promotes corporate schemes that place profits over community burdens and benefits, *including market-based mechanisms . . . such as carbon and emissions trading and offsets.*"[17] What was obscured by those ellipses was the additional inclusion in the blacklist of "carbon capture and storage" (as well as "nuclear power" and "waste-to-energy and biomass energy"). Such overly restrictive language appears to have kept a number of prominent mainstream environmental organizations, including the Sierra Club, the Audubon Society, and the Environmental Defense Fund from signing the letter.[18]

One prominent group that *did* sign the letter, however, was the Sunrise Movement, the youth-led activist group that came to prominence in late 2018. It was in the news in particular over its efforts to pressure House Majority Leader Nancy Pelosi (D-CA) into creating a committee to draft a Green New Deal. Sunrise demanded that any potential plan must fund "massive investment in the drawdown and capture of greenhouse gases," which would seem to conflict with the restrictive language about carbon capture in the letter they had signed. But Sunrise now omits "capture," speaking only of the "draw-down of greenhouse gases," which would seem to indicate support for natural drawdown via reforestation and regenerative agriculture, but, by omission, not CCS.[19]

James Temple, senior editor for energy at the centrist *MIT Technology Review*, took issue with the environmentalists' letter in a piece he penned titled "Let's Keep the Green New Deal Grounded in Science." Temple argued that the sort of "rapid and aggressive action" the letter claims is necessary to avert the dangerous warming of 1.5°C (2.7°F) is likely incompatible with policies that take key options like carbon capture off the table.[20]

What has emerged here is a battle between climate progressives and climate moderates on the role of industry and market-driven mechanisms. And while my assessment of the science and economics leads me to side with climate moderates on the merit of climate pricing, for reasons outlined previously, I tend to side with the progressives on the dubious merit of CCS schemes for all the reasons discussed above (with the possible exception of currently difficult-to-decarbonize sectors like cement production).

GEOENGINEERING, OR "WHAT COULD POSSIBLY GO WRONG?"

So, if "clean coal" and natural gas "bridge fuels" aren't the solution, is there some other way we can engineer our way out of the climate crisis? Perhaps we should consider *geoengineering*—schemes that employ global-scale technological intervention with the planet in the hope of offsetting the warming effects of carbon pollution.

Many of these proposed schemes sound like they're taken right out of science fiction. And as with science fiction films, bad things tend to happen when we start tampering with Mother Nature. We might not get a planet run by apes, giant fire-breathing dinosaurs, or institutionalized cannibalism, but we could get worse droughts, more rapid ice-sheet melt, or any number of unpleasant surprises. When it comes to a system we don't understand perfectly, the principle of unintended consequences reigns supreme. If we screw up this planet with botched geoengineering attempts, there is no "do over." And, as they say, "there is no planet B."

Consider, for example, proposals to shoot reflective particulates—sulfate aerosols—into the stable upper part of the atmosphere known as the stratosphere, where they would reside for years. This human-produced effect would mimic the way volcanic eruptions cool the planet. An explosive tropical volcanic eruption can put enough reflective sulfate particles into the stratosphere to cool the planet for a while. (The Mount Pinatubo eruption of 1991 in the Philippines, for example, cooled the planet by 0.6°C [1°F] for about fifteen months.)[21]

This scheme has the *advantage* of being feasible. It would use custom-designed cannons to fire substantial amounts of sulfate aerosols into the stratosphere, easily as much as was released during the Pinatubo eruption. Doing the math, all it would take is a Pinatubo-size injection of particles every few years to offset the current warming effect of carbon emissions. It would also be relatively cheap to do (compared to other means of mitigation).[22]

The scheme has the distinct *disadvantage*, however, of potential major adverse climate side effects. First of all, we would get a very different climate from the one we're used to. The spatial pattern of the geoengineering-induced cooling isn't the mirror image of the pattern of greenhouse gas warming. That's because the physics is different. In the former case, we're reducing the incident sunlight, while in the latter case, we're blocking the escape of heat energy from Earth's surface. Those effects have very different spatial patterns. On average, the globe may not warm under the sulfate aerosol plan, but some regions would cool while others warmed. Indeed, some regions would likely end up warming even faster than they would have without the geoengineering. We could conceivably end up, for example, accelerating the destabilization of the West Antarctic or Greenland ice sheet and speeding up global sea-level rise. Climate model simulations indicate that the continents would potentially get drier, worsening droughts.[23]

There are other potentially nasty environmental side effects as well. It was, after all, the production of sulfur dioxide and the resulting sulfate aerosols in the lower atmosphere from coal-fired power plants that gave us the acid rain problem in the 1960s and 1970s, prior to passage of the clean air acts. The sulfate particles from geo-engineering would be higher up—in the stratosphere—but they would ultimately still make it down to the surface, where they would acidify rivers and lakes. And then there's the "ozone hole." Though it has mostly recovered, there are enough ozone-depleting chemicals still in the stratosphere that, with the extra kick they would get from the injected sulfate aerosols, we would likely see continued destruction of the protective ozone layer.

As with any "cover-up" approach to climate change that doesn't deal with the root cause of the problem (continued carbon emissions), carbon dioxide would continue to build up in both the atmosphere and the ocean. The problem of ocean acidification, sometimes called "global warming's evil twin," would continue to get worse, further threatening the world's coral reefs and calcareous sea life such as shellfish and mollusks and wreaking havoc on ocean food chains.

Sulfate aerosol geoengineering is a Faustian bargain: it would require us to continue to inject sulfate aerosols into the stratosphere while carbon dioxide continued to accumulate in the atmosphere. Were there a major war, a plague, an asteroid collision, or anything else that might interfere with the regular required schedule of sulfate injections, the cooling effect would disappear within a few years. We would experience decades' worth of greenhouse warming in a matter of years, giving new meaning to the concept of "abrupt climate change."

One of the cruelest ironies of all with this prospective technofix is that it would likely render *less* viable one of the most important and safest of climate solutions: solar power. The sulfate aerosols would reduce the amount of sunlight reaching Earth's surface that is available to produce solar energy, making the already tough challenge of weaning ourselves off the fossil fuels at the root of the climate-change problem even more difficult.

Another widely discussed geoengineering scheme is ocean iron fertilization. Over much of the world's oceans, iron is the primary limiting nutrient for algae, or phytoplankton, which take up carbon dioxide when they photosynthesize. It is therefore possible to generate phytoplankton blooms by sprinkling iron dust into the ocean, which in turn metabolizes carbon dioxide. When the phytoplankton die, they tend to sink to the ocean bottom, burying their carbon with them.

One of the advantages of ocean iron fertilization is that it is solving the problem at its source, taking carbon out of the atmosphere. That means it also prevents the worsening of ocean acidification. It's an example of what is termed "negative emissions technology"—it actually takes carbon *out of* the atmosphere. The idea is appealing enough that a number of companies tried to commercialize the scheme more than a decade ago. One company even sold carbon credits, promising to bury a ton of carbon dioxide for only $5, a bargain for any organization or company seeking to lower its carbon footprint.

Subsequent experiments, however, showed that the scheme doesn't really work. Iron fertilization leads to more vigorous cycling of carbon in the upper ocean, but no apparent increase in deep carbon burial, which means no permanent removal of atmospheric carbon. To make matters worse, studies showed that it could actually favor harmful "red tide" algae blooms that create oceanic dead zones. Lacking evidence of efficacy, and with growing concern about unintended consequences, support for iron fertilization geoengineering has dissipated.[24]

Sticking with this theme, though, might there be other negative emissions technology that could be implemented safely and cost effectively? Trees do it, after all. They take carbon out of the atmosphere as they photosynthesize, and they store it in their trunks, branches, and leaves. Then they bury carbon in the ground, in their roots, and in the leaf and branch litter that falls and gets deposited onto the forest floor and buried in the soil.

Perhaps we can learn from the trees. Maybe even improve upon them. Trees, after all, don't do a perfect carbon burial job. Like us, they respire—putting carbon dioxide back into the atmosphere. And when they die and decompose, some of their carbon escapes back to the atmosphere. It's part of the long-term balance of the terrestrial carbon cycle.

We might try to make a more perfect (from a climate standpoint) "tree"—a tree that takes carbon out of the air more efficiently than regular trees and doesn't give any of it back to the atmosphere. Rather than dying and decomposing, synthetic trees (with "leaves" treated with sodium carbonate) could turn the carbon they extract from the atmosphere into baking soda, which can be buried for the long term. Such a scheme has not only been suggested by scientists, but its viability has already been demonstrated through proof-of-concept trials. It is calculated that an array of ten million synthetic trees around the world could take up a significant chunk, perhaps as much as 10 percent, of our current carbon emissions.[25] But this so-called direct air capture would be difficult and expensive to do, perhaps costing more than $500 per ton of carbon removed. A related approach that has been suggested recently, which involves atmospheric CO_2 removal through the artificial enhancement of weathering by rocks, might be less expensive—somewhere in the range of $50 to $200 per ton of carbon. But its proponents concede that it could remove, at the very most, only about two billion tons of carbon dioxide per year, a veritable drop in the bucket compared with current carbon emissions.[26]

These limitations mean that at present, it is far easier and cheaper to prevent the buildup of carbon dioxide in the atmosphere in the first place, by limiting fossil fuel burning. But the cost of this direct air capture could be brought down substantially with additional research and through the economies of scale of mass production. And if, after doing everything possible to reduce our carbon emissions, we still find ourselves headed toward catastrophic warming, we might need a stopgap solution.

Of all of the geoengineering schemes, direct air capture seems the safest and most efficacious. Unlike CCS, which continues our reliance on fossil fuels, this form of carbon burial could, along with natural reforestation (discussed later), be an important component of broader efforts to "draw down" carbon from the atmosphere, a strategy that arguably belongs in any comprehensive climate abatement program. But since we're only talking about 10 percent, at most, of current carbon emissions, it is obvious this cannot be a primary strategy for mitigation.

People have suggested many other schemes, from putting reflective mirrors in space to seeding low clouds over the oceans. All of them are fraught with political and ethical complications. For one, who gets to set the global thermostat? For low-lying island nations, current carbon dioxide levels are already too high—their people are already threatened with the loss of their land and their rich cultural heritages by the several feet of sea-level rise that is likely baked in. While the industrial world debates whether we can still avoid dangerous warming of 1.5 or 2°C (2.7 or 3.6°F), dangerous warming is already here for many. Some might want to set the thermostat at a lower temperature than others. Who gets to make the decision?

One could easily imagine a whole new form of global conflict wherein rogue states employ geoengineering to control the climate in a way that is optimal for themselves. A climate model simulation might show, for example, that sulfate aerosol injection could relieve the drought that plagues a particular nation. Yet, it would do so at the expense of causing a drought elsewhere. The perpetual conflict in the Middle East has arguably always been fundamentally about access to scarce freshwater resources.[27] Would geoengineering provide yet another weapon to fuel this ongoing battle?

A fundamental problem with geoengineering is that it presents what is known as a moral hazard, namely, a scenario in which one party (e.g., the fossil fuel industry) promotes actions that are risky for another party (e.g., the rest of us), but seemingly advantageous to itself. Geoengineering provides a potential crutch for beneficiaries of our continued dependence on fossil fuels. Why threaten our economy with draconian regulations on carbon when we have a cheap alternative? The two main problems with that argument are that (1) climate change poses a far greater threat to our economy than decarbonization, and (2) geoengineering is hardly cheap—it comes with great potential harm.

But despite the caveats, disadvantages, and risks, geoengineering has proven to be appealing to fossil fuel interests and those advocating for them.[28] They can have their cake and eat it too, claiming to support a putative climate "solution," but one that poses no threat to the fossil fuel business model. A 2019 report on geoengineering by the Center for International Environmental Law (CIEL) explains how "the most heavily promoted strategies for carbon dioxide removal and solar radiation modification depend on the continued production and combustion of carbon-intensive fuels for their viability." CIEL noted that "the hypothetical promise of future geoengineering is already being used by major fossil fuel producers to justify the continued production and use of oil, gas, and coal for decades to come."[29]

Geoengineering also appeals to free-market conservatives, as it plays to the notion that market-driven technological innovation can solve any problem without governmental intervention or regulation. A price on carbon, or incentives for renewable energy? Too difficult and risky! Engaging in a massive, uncontrolled experiment in a desperate effort to somehow offset the effects of global warming? Perfect!

It is thoroughly unsurprising, for example, that someone with as much skin in the carbon game as Rex Tillerson, former CEO of the world's largest fossil fuel company, ExxonMobil, has argued that climate change is "just an engineering problem."[30] Nor is it surprising that some of the now familiar inactivist players, such as Bjorn Lomborg and the Breakthrough Institute, have promoted geoengineering as a primary means of climate mitigation.[31]

Perhaps more eye-opening, though, is the fact that business magnates like former Microsoft CEO Bill Gates have embraced the concept. Writing in *Fortune*, journalist Marc Gunther reported that "Gates has been convinced that the risk of global warming is worse than most people think. He can see that the world's governments have failed to curb the emissions caused by burning coal, oil, and natural gas. . . . So the Microsoft billionaire and philanthropist has stepped into the breach to become the world's leading funder of research into geoengineering—deliberate, large-scale interventions in the earth's climate system intended to prevent climate change and its repercussions."

Gates gave millions of dollars to two climate scientists, David Keith of Harvard University and Ken Caldeira of Stanford University, to perform research and engage in experimentation with geoengineering. That includes relatively safe direct air capture but also potentially harmful stratospheric sulfate aerosol injection.[32] Perhaps relevant, in their *Guardian* commentary "The Fossil Fuel Industry's Invisible Colonization of Academia," Benjamin Franta and Geoffrey Supran singled out these two centers of geoengineering research—Stanford and Harvard—as exemplars of how "corporate capture of academic research by the fossil fuel industry is an elephant in the room and a threat to tackling climate change."[33]

Harvard's Keith has "done as much as any single researcher to push the touchy topic of geoengineering toward the scientific mainstream," according to James Temple of *Technology Review*.[34] Keith is affiliated with the Breakthrough Institute and a signatory of the "Ecomodernist Manifesto," a techno-optimist, pseudo-environmentalist polemic that *Guardian* columnist George Monbiot characterized as "generalisations, . . . ignorance of history, . . . unexplored prejudices . . . an astonishing lack of depth," and a "worldview that is, paradoxically, nothing if not old-fashioned."[35] Keith helps lead a for-profit venture financed by Bill Gates to implement geoengineering and is currently planning to do real-world experimentation testing the viability of sulfate aerosol stratospheric injection.[36]

Keith spearheaded a 2019 study of the ostensible impact of sulfate aerosol geoengineering on the global climate, which included a modeling experiment to simulate the effects.[37] He took to Twitter to promote his team's findings, claiming he and coauthors had demonstrated that "no region is made worse off" by solar geoengineering. Other leading climate scientists contested that claim. Chris Colose, a climate researcher at the NASA Goddard Institute for Space Studies, pointed out that the modeling experiment is a bit of a bait-and-switch: "They don't actually put aerosols in the atmosphere. They turn down the Sun to mimic geoengineering. You might think that is relatively unimportant . . . [but] controlling the Sun is effectively a perfect knob. We know almost precisely how a reduction in solar flux will project onto the energy balance of a planet. Aerosol-climate interactions are much more complex." Colose went on to point out the numerous other ways in which the modeling experiment they had done was a gross idealization of actual real-world implementation of their geoengineering scheme, emphasizing a number of the well-established flaws and caveats that we encountered earlier in our discussion of sulfate aerosol geoengineering.[38]

Ken Caldeira, the other of the two Gates-funded geoengineering scientists (who has now left his position at Stanford to work directly for Bill Gates), later weighed in, asserting, "The evidence is that solar geoengineering would be expected to reduce climate damage."[39] Again, many leading climate scientists begged to differ. Climate researcher Daniel Swain from the University of California at Los Angeles weighed in that he finds it "strange" that the regional details of climate model simulations are "taken pretty literally" in these idealized geoengineering experiments, "but are subject to huge caveats otherwise," adding that while there's "lots of evidence" that sulfate aerosol geoengineering would indeed reduce the global average temperature, "that's not all that matters!"[40] Jon Foley, executive director of Project Drawdown, added that relying on such idealized experiments is "a big gamble, especially when models have a hard time" reproducing detailed temperature patterns.[41] Matthew Huber, a leading climate researcher at Purdue University, expressed two concerns: whether humans could properly administer the highly structured geoengineering protocol required, and whether the models are reliable enough to capture some of the potential surprises that might be in store.[42]

One gets the distinct feeling that scientists like Keith and Caldeira suffer from some degree of hubris when it comes to leaping from the results of their highly idealized modeling experiments to sweeping conclusions about the real world. One also gets the feeling that their attitude toward real-world geoengineering potentially crosses the line from dispassionate inquiry to advocacy. As a scientist, that's okay as long as you're up front about it. I've argued as much in the *New York Times*.[43] But both of them seem uncomfortable acknowledging that they're engaged in advocacy. I can speak to this directly. Keith and Caldeira each responded rather defensively to a tweet of mine in which I stated that many "geoengineering *advocates* . . . see geoengineering as an excuse for continued business-as-usual burning of fossil fuels" (emphasis added).[44] At the time, I was bemused by the fact that they thought the tweet was directed at them (it wasn't), and I wondered aloud whether they *do* indeed consider themselves to be "geoengineering advocates." Each equivocated, drawing a distinction between advocacy for research and advocacy for implementation.[45] I would argue that their words and actions blur any such distinctions.

Finally, let's discuss the role here of climate *doomism*, a topic we will explore in depth in the next chapter. Geoengineering advocates have increasingly found common cause with climate-change doomsayers—those who believe that the situation is now so dire that truly desperate action is required, or that we're beyond the point where any effective action is possible.

Such misguided framing was beautifully captured in a December 2019 *Washington Post* op-ed, "Climate Politics Is a Dead End. So the World Could Turn to This Desperate Final Gambit."[46] In it the author, Francisco Toro, a Venezuelan political commentator, promotes a bleak climate policy outlook, articulating the view of some climate activists "that only a drastic push toward net-zero carbon emissions can save the world. But . . . the politics to achieve this don't exist." As an example he cites "the events of the past decade, including the failure of the climate conference in Madrid [COP25 in 2019]."

Toro then uses this defeatist narrative to justify the implementation of potentially dangerous geoengineering schemes ("Yes, a geoengineered future may be scary. But unchecked climate change is absolutely terrifying. And attempts to prevent it aren't working"). No inactivist polemic would be complete without deflection and a free pass for polluting interests ("Climate activists typically blame the failure to cut emissions on greedy corporations and crooked politicians. . . . The regrettable reality is that people around the world demand cheap energy"). He misleadingly invokes the "Yellow Vest" protests as evidence that people will "punish leaders who threaten their access to it."

This commentary exemplifies how climate doomism is being exploited to support dangerous technofixes that might be favored by polluters but could leave us worse off. It demonstrates the deep hypocrisy of polluting interests and the inactivists doing their bidding, who first sabotage climate negotiations like those in Madrid, and then proclaim that the *failure* of those negotiations is grounds for their proposed "solution" (geoengineering technofixes).[47]

The fundamental problem with geoengineering, in the end, is that tinkering with a complex system we don't fully understand entails monumental risk. Geoengineering expert Alan Robock of Rutgers University believes that geoengineering is too risky to ever try. "Should we trust the only planet known to have intelligent life to this complicated technical system?" Robock wondered. "We don't know what we don't know."[48] The CIEL report discussed earlier notes "the stark contrast between the . . . narrative that geoengineering is a morally necessary adjunct to dramatic climate action" and the reality that geoengineering is "simply a way of avoiding or reducing the need for true systemic change, even as converging science and technologies demonstrate that shift is both urgently needed and increasingly feasible." It highlights, furthermore, "the growing incoherence of advocating for reliance on speculative and risky geoengineering technologies in the face of mounting evidence that addressing the climate crisis is less about technology than about political will."[49]

GREENING THE PLANET

We've seen that one type of geoengineering that has been proposed—direct air capture—mimics what trees do naturally by capturing carbon through photosynthesis, storing it in their trunks and limbs, and burying it in their roots and branches and leaf litter. So why not just engage in the massive planting of trees—that is, large-scale reforestation of the vast regions of the planet that have been deforested (or *afforestation*—foresting regions that were previously something else). Such efforts could be supplemented by land use and agricultural practices that sequester additional carbon in soils.

What is appealing about this particular negative emissions option is that it's a "no regrets" path forward. After all, by planting trees we can get better-functioning ecosystems; maintain and even increase biodiversity; improve the quality of our soils, air, and water; and better insulate ourselves from the damaging impacts of climate change. Could efforts to "green the planet" make a major dent in our carbon emissions? Or mitigate them altogether? It's certainly proven to be convenient for some, who, to deflect attention away from the subject of what polluters should be doing, present "tree planting" as the solution and treat it as evidence of bold action on climate. Hence Donald Trump's "politically safe new climate plan" (promoted originally by some of his Republican congressional colleagues) of supporting efforts to plant hundreds of millions of new trees.[50] Is there actually merit to the suggestion?

Let's take a look at the prospects for reforestation and afforestation. One study claimed that an additional 0.9 billion hectares of the planet's surface is available for this purpose. That translates to billions of new trees that collectively could capture just over 200 billion tons of carbon over the next couple of decades.[51] That's a rate of carbon sequestration of roughly 11 billion tons of carbon dioxide per year. Other scientists have questioned the assumptions of the study and argued for much lower levels of potential carbon sequestration. In fact, the most recent IPCC report (2019) estimated that roughly only 60 billion tons of carbon dioxide could be sequestered through reforestation by the end of the century, which translates to less than 1 billion tons of carbon dioxide per year.[52] Nonetheless, let us, for the sake of argument, accept the much higher 11 billion number.

Regenerative agriculture based on recycling farm waste and using composted materials from other sources, combined with land use practices that enhance soil carbon sequestration, could potentially bury somewhere in the range of 3.5 to 11 billion tons of carbon dioxide emissions per year. Let us once again take the very optimistic upper limit of 11 billion tons per year.

Adding together these contributions gives us 22 billion tons of carbon dioxide per year. That sounds like quite a bit, but we are currently generating the equivalent of roughly 55 billion tons per year of carbon dioxide through fossil fuel burning and other human activities.[53] That means that even if we accepted estimates from the very upper limits of the uncertainty range, the combined effect of reforestation and agriculture and land use practices would at most only slow the buildup of carbon dioxide in the atmosphere by a factor of 44 percent. In other words, atmospheric carbon dioxide levels would continue to rise, just at a rate that is roughly half as fast.

That estimate, of course, is overly optimistic. We cannot ignore the massive demands on available land of 7.7 billion (and growing) people competing for space for settlement, agriculture, and livestock. When real-world economic constraints are taken into account, the actual land area available for reforestation may be only about 30 percent of the technically available land area assumed in the recent study.[54]

Climate change itself, furthermore, is likely to diminish the ability of forests to sequester carbon. The bushfires in the summer of 2019/2020 doubled Australia's total carbon emissions in the year that followed and were likely to cause a 1 to 2 percent increase in global carbon dioxide concentrations.[55] And Australia is not the only place that is burning. Wildfires taking place from the Amazon to the Arctic are releasing billions of tons of carbon dioxide a year.[56] A study reported in 2020 in the journal *Nature* demonstrated that the peak carbon uptake by tropical forests occurred during the 1990s and has declined ever since as a result of logging, farming, and the effects of climate change. The authors found that the Amazon could go from a sink (a net absorber of carbon) to a source (a net producer of carbon) within the next decade, which is decades ahead of schedule based on former climate model predictions.[57]

Such findings underscore one of the potential pitfalls of relying upon reforestation as a primary means of climate mitigation (or, for that matter, as the basis for carbon offsets or credits). Any carbon that is sequestered could easily be lost, perhaps in rapid bursts, because of forest burning. Ironically, the problem becomes worse as the planet continues to warm and conditions become more conducive to massive forest burning.

Moreover, as with geoengineering, there are potential unintended consequences. The coauthor of a recent government report on forest carbon burial told the BBC that "we would be crazy to undertake the massive scale of planting being considered if we did not also consider the wider effects upon the environment including impacts on wildlife, benefits in terms of reducing flood risks and effects on water quality, improvements to recreation and so on." The report noted that careless tree planting, ironically, could actually lead to increased carbon emissions. As the BBC noted, "carpeting upland pastures with trees would reduce the UK's ability to produce meat—which may lead to increasing imports from places that produce beef by felling rainforests."[58]

Finally, no discussion of natural carbon drawdown is complete without addressing proposals for using biomass for energy followed by the capture and sequestration of any carbon dioxide produced. This is known as "bioenergy with carbon capture and storage," or BECCS. The IPCC has emphasized this technology in its scenarios for stabilizing carbon dioxide concentrations that assume zero total effective emissions within a matter of decades. The IPCC does this by relying upon the presumption that BECCS can actually yield negative carbon emissions, which would offset some residual fossil fuel burning and other carbon-generating practices to achieve the needed zero net emissions.

How could this work? Readers may recall from the previous chapter Michael Moore's false claim, in his film *Planet of the Humans*, that "biomass releases 50 percent more carbon dioxide than coal and more than three times as much as natural gas." In reality, biofuels (neglecting the fossil fuel energy that might be used in processing and transportation) are carbon neutral, having taken as much carbon dioxide out of the atmosphere when they were plant matter as they release when they're burned. They are therefore far more carbon-friendly than fossil fuels, yielding energy with little or no carbon pollution. In fact, they can—in a sense—be made even *more carbon-friendly than renewables*, providing energy and drawing down carbon from the atmosphere *at the same time*.

This might seem like it violates some law of physics, but it doesn't. The idea is that you burn the biofuels to get energy as you would coal or natural gas. The process, as we have explained, is carbon neutral to start. Now, if you capture the carbon dioxide and bury it, then you're doing even better than carbon neutrality—you're actually drawing down carbon that came from the atmosphere and capturing and burying it. Of course, all of the concerns we encountered previously with carbon sequestration in the context of coal or natural gas apply here as well—namely, you have to be able to bury it efficiently, safely, and effectively permanently, and that's not easy to do. Moreover, as we already saw with CCS, capture is unlikely to be complete, so some of the carbon does make it back into the atmosphere.

As alluded to earlier, negative emissions technologies—and particularly BECCS—are assumed in the various IPCC emissions scenarios or "pathways," including those that allow us to stay below critical warming thresholds such as 1.5 or 2.0°C (2.7 or 3.6°F). Given the fact that BECCS has not yet been demonstrated to be commercially viable at the scale assumed in these scenarios, the IPCC could rightly be criticized for, in essence, "kicking the can down the road"—putting forth scenarios that allow substantial near-term carbon emissions and still avert dangerous planetary warming only by assuming massive negative emissions in future decades using currently unproven technology. What if that technology does not emerge? The "Faustian bargain" again rears its head.[59]

THE NUCLEAR OPTION

All reasonable options should be on the table as we debate how to rapidly decarbonize our economy while continuing to meet society's demand for energy. There is no easy solution, and there are important and worthy debates to be had in the policy arena as to how we accomplish this challenging task.

There is a good-faith argument to be made, for example, that nuclear energy should be part of the solution, and I have colleagues whom I deeply respect who are bullish on the role it might play as part of a comprehensive plan to tackle climate change. I myself remain skeptical that nuclear energy should play a central role in the required clean, green energy transition. Let me explain why.

There are a number of major obstacles, first of all, to safe, plentiful nuclear power. There is the risk of nuclear proliferation, and the danger that fissile materials and weapons-applicable technology could make it into the hands of hostile nations with militaristic intentions or terrorists. There is the challenge of safe long-term disposal of radioactive waste. And there are some profound examples of the acute environmental and human threat posed by nuclear power, most recently highlighted, for example, by the Fukushima Daiichi nuclear disaster north of Tokyo in March 2011.

Hitting closer to home—for me, literally—was the historic Three Mile Island nuclear disaster of March 1979. It took place in my home state of Pennsylvania on a long, narrow island in the Susquehanna River near Harrisburg, less than a hundred miles southeast of the Happy Valley, in which I currently reside. I'm reminded of the incident—a partial meltdown that led to the release of harmful radiation—every time I fly into the Harrisburg Airport over the plant's eerily iconic cooling towers. (The plant is now closed but not yet decommissioned.)

No means of energy production is without environmental risk, but nuclear power carries with it unique dangers. As noted by Robert Jay Lifton and Naomi Oreskes in a 2019 *Boston Globe* op-ed, improvements in design cannot eliminate the possibility of deadly meltdowns.[60] Nuclear power plants will always be vulnerable to natural hazards such as earthquakes, volcanoes, or tsunamis (like the one that triggered the Fukushima meltdown), or technical failure and human errors (like the ones responsible for Three Mile Island).

Climate change itself, ironically, increases the risk. As Lifton and Oreskes pointed out, extreme droughts have led to reactors being shut down as the surrounding waters become too warm to provide the cooling necessary to convey heat from the reactor core to the steam turbines and remove surplus heat from the steam circuit.[61] Some of my own research has shown that climate change is leading to less reliable flow for the very river—the Susquehanna—that supplied the Three Mile Island nuclear plant with needed cooling water.[62] A similar threat looms for many other active plants.

Some have argued in favor of a role for small modular reactors (SMRs), which, as the name implies, are considerably smaller than the massive reactors in Fukushima or Three Mile Island. They also require less up-front capital, and arguably they allow for better security of nuclear materials. Energy experts, however, have raised serious concerns about SMRs, including "locating sites for multiple reactors, finding water to cool these reactors, and the higher cost of electricity generation."[63] SMRs, in short, are not an obvious nuclear power "magic bullet."

Still others argue that the answer is so-called "next generation" or "generation IV" nuclear power plants, such as molten-salt reactors that automatically cool down when they get too hot, or very-high-temperature reactors (VHTR), which could be coupled to a neighboring hydrogen production facility for significantly reduced cost.[64] But as University of California, Berkeley, energy expert Dan Kammen noted, it "could easily take the advanced nuclear projects 30 years to get through regulatory review, fix the unexpected problems that crop up . . . and prove that they can compete." In the meantime, we could see a breakthrough in other technologies, such as electric storage and fusion. Kammen added that while "ultimately on a planet with 10 billion people, some amount of large, convenient, affordable, safe baseload power—like we get from nuclear fission, or fusion—would be just hugely beneficial," there are "other competitors in view on the straight solar side that 10 years ago sounded like science fiction—space-based solar, transparent solar films on every window. That world works, too."[65]

Some would argue that our energy choices amount to balancing different risks. True, nuclear energy has risks, they acknowledge, but they are worth it in the balance. They would say that though nuclear accidents are acute, they are rare. And while the damage can be fatal and long-lasting, it is regionally localized. Compare that to the risks posed by climate change, which are pervasive, global, and slowly but steadily growing. If we are forced into a choice between one risk or the other, a reasonable argument could be made that there's a significant role to be played by nuclear energy. The problem with this argument is that it buys into the fallacy that nuclear power is necessary for us to decarbonize our economy. Although it may well make sense to continue with the operation of *existing* nuclear power plants until they are retired (after twenty to forty years, their typical lifetime), given that the embodied carbon emissions associated with their construction is a "sunken" carbon cost, it makes little sense to build new ones.

As we have already seen, electrification of the various energy sectors in conjunction with decarbonization of the grid can already be achieved using renewables such as residential rooftop solar and solar plants, onshore and offshore wind farms, wave energy, geothermal energy, and hydroelectric and tidal energy. Researchers have shown how these existing renewable energy technologies could be scaled up to meet 80 percent of global energy demand by 2030 and 100 percent by 2050. To those who argue that nuclear is a cheaper option, the numbers indicate otherwise. As Lifton and Oreskes noted, the average nuclear power generating cost is about $100 per megawatt-hour, compared with $50 for solar and $30 to $40 for onshore wind. Renewable energy costs are now competitive with fossil fuels—even with the incentives that are currently skewed against them—and much lower than for nuclear.[66]

So if the math and logic don't obviously favor a nuclear solution, why do advocates fight so fiercely for it? For some, no doubt, it's a matter of principle. As I mentioned earlier, I have colleagues whom I respect deeply who are convinced that nuclear energy is critical to solving the climate crisis.[67] But for many, alas, it appears to be all about ideology and political tribalism. "Hippie punching"—establishing one's conservative bona fides by opposing perceived leftist environmentalists—has become de rigueur, as a common target for attack serves to unite conservatives in the climate arena. Consider, for example, the attacks on global-warming icon and conservative punching bag Al Gore. My friend Bob Inglis, a former Republican congressman from South Carolina, has said, "In my first six years in Congress from 1993 to 1999, I had said that climate change was hooey. I hadn't looked into the science. All I knew was that Al Gore was for it, and therefore I was against it."[68]

Support for nuclear energy has become a shibboleth for conservatives in the climate policy arena. It's easy to understand why. It was the left, after all, that protested nuclear power in the 1970s. While I was growing up in Massachusetts, and protests of the Seabrook nuclear plant were taking place in nearby New Hampshire, it was all granola-crunching tree-huggers, scruffy college students and aging flowerchildren.

"The enemy of my enemy is my friend" might not be a very satisfying explanation for the unusual amount of support for nuclear energy among conservatives, but it's difficult otherwise to explain it. Solar *should be* the preferred solution for conservatives: it can be deployed locally, and if installed privately it can help liberate users from dependency on overly regulated centralized utilities. Meanwhile, nuclear power plants require huge up-front capital investments and are not viable without governmental subsides, so they are hardly the free-market solution conservatives purport to favor.[69] Bob Inglis is of course famous as a conservative climate crusader. He is all about free-market solutions to the climate crisis. He also happens to have a nuanced view of the role of nuclear energy as a climate solution: "It used to be convenient for us as conservatives to blame enviros for why we're not building nuclear power plants," he told a reporter, "but if we update our rhetoric to the actual facts, what we find is it's more a question of economics."[70]

Inglis is the exception to the rule. Conservatives (and "conservative liberals" such as CNN commentator Fareed Zakaria) love big fixes like nuclear energy and geoengineering.[71] What do these "solutions" have in common? They divert resources and attention away from the more obvious solution—renewable energy. Indeed, a cynic might wonder whether some who staunchly advocate for these options are more interested in dampening enthusiasm for a renewable energy revolution than in actually solving the climate problem. The Breakthrough Institute promotes both nuclear energy and geoengineering. So do the "ecomodernists."[72] Former Democratic presidential candidate Andrew Yang promoted nuclear energy and geoengineering as well, as he sought, during his campaign, to thread the needle of maintaining credibility on climate while courting conservative Democrats.[73]

"ADAPTATION" AND "RESILIENCE"

The last refuge of the false solutionists is the language of "adaptation" and "resilience." That is not to say that both aren't important—they are. We have no choice but to adapt to those climate-change impacts that are now inevitable, and we need to establish greater resilience in the face of the heightened climate risk that already exists. The Global Commission on Adaptation, for example, has recommended pursuing five key areas of climate-change adaptation over the next decade: early warning systems, climate-resilient infrastructure, altered agricultural practices, protection of coastal mangrove ecosystems, and more resilient water resource management.[74]

But much as exclusive focus on individual action has been used in a deflection campaign to undermine systemic change, exclusive focus on adaptation and resilience has become a favored tactic of inactivists. It's another way of sounding like one is taking proactive steps to address the climate crisis while enabling business-as-usual burning of fossil fuels and the continued profits that go with it.

We see this language in the messaging of Republicans who are still trying to navigate a course between flat-out denial and indefinite delay. Consider Republican senator Marco Rubio of Florida, the state arguably most on the frontlines of climate-change impacts. In August 2018, he wrote an opinion piece in *USA Today* citing innovation and adaptation as the key to combating climate change.[75] In it, he insisted that the impacts of sea-level rise could be managed through restoration of the Everglades. Costly projects aimed at slowing the encroachment by the ocean of Florida's coastline might buy some of the wealthier communities some time, but, as a colleague and I responded in a commentary, without the ability to move to higher ground, coastal populations will become increasingly vulnerable to frequent flooding and toxic floodwaters, and coastal tourism and industry will suffer.[76]

There is no way to engineer our way out of sea-level rise. If we continue to emit carbon, warm the oceans, and melt the ice sheets, the oceans will ultimately prevail in this battle between humans and nature.

In early 2019, after Democrats had taken back the House of Representatives, there was both good news and bad news when it came to the Republican stance on climate. The good news was that Republicans were no longer contesting the basic scientific evidence—they'd finally, it seems, given hard denial a rest. The bad news was that they were still promoting inaction, only this time dressed up in the language of "innovation," "conservation," and "adaptation."[77]

The Republican approach to climate change resembled a person trying to fix a leak in his ceiling with buckets, towels, and mops, but no mention of repair or a handyman. As the *Washington Post*'s Steven Mufson reported in early 2020, "the GOP is still hammering out details, but some critics say the new Republican approach to climate change looks a lot like the old one. In addition to [proposals to plant] trees, senior Republicans are said to be considering tax breaks for research, curbs on plastic waste and big federally funded infrastructure projects in the name of *adaptation* or *resilience*. The already well-worn buzzword '*innovation*' will be their rallying cry, and natural gas, despite its carbon emissions, will be embraced" (emphasis added).[78] What's missing here? Any discussion of carbon emissions, fossil fuels, or renewable energy.

A week later, Republicans on the House Energy and Commerce Committee, Greg Walden of Oregon, Fred Upton of Michigan, and John Shimkus of Illinois, wrote an op-ed in which they acknowledged that "climate change is real," adding that they "are focused on solutions."[79] Their commentary predictably emphasized the belief that "America's approach for tackling climate change should be built upon the principles of *innovation, conservation,* and *adaptation*" (emphasis added). They promoted the usual conservative favorites of carbon capture and nuclear power. And where they mentioned renewable energy, they emphasized research and innovation with regard to clean energy technologies, batteries, and storage. There was no discussion about actual *deployment* of renewable energy or market mechanisms—such as incentives for renewables or a price on carbon—that might level the playing field and enable the rapid transition away from fossil fuels necessary to avoid a crisis.

This phenomenon is not unique to the United States. In Australia, with the massive shift in public sentiment that took place in the aftermath of the historic bushfires of summer 2019/2020, there was a grudging acceptance by conservatives of the climate threat.[80] Former deputy prime minister and National Party leader Barnaby Joyce, who had previously gone to great lengths to deny climate change, conceded in a *60 Minutes* special on the Australian bushfires (in which we were both co-panelists) not only that "the climate is changing," but that the bushfires were a consequence of climate change.[81] Even climate-change-denying columnist Andrew Bolt of the Murdoch-owned *Herald Sun* has now admitted the reality of human-caused climate change.[82]

Unfortunately, in spite of this grudging acceptance of the problem, there is no will in the current Australian government to do anything about it other than promoting "adaptation" and "resilience."[83] Such framing has been front and center in the messaging of Australia's fossil-fuel-industry-coddling prime minister, Scott

Morrison. When it comes to the record heat and drought that Australia has experienced, the collapse of major river systems (such as the Murray-Darling) that provide critical freshwater resources, the death spiral of the Great Barrier Reef, catastrophic flooding events, and unprecedented, widespread, intense, fast-spreading bushfires, the solution, Morrison seems to think, is simply to "build . . . resilience for the future."[84] That policy was satirically summarized as "get fucken used to it" in a mock governmental public service announcement produced by Juice Media of Melbourne that went viral in early February 2020.[85]

It's important once again to recognize that resilience does play a role. There is no doubt that the communities, individuals, and brave firefighters who battled the devastating Australian bushfires displayed remarkable resilience, courage, and fortitude, not only in fighting the fires but in dealing with the resulting death, loss, and destruction. But the political discourse of "resilience" does them— and indeed, everyone else—a disservice. In emphasizing "adaptation" and "resilience," Morrison was engaged in a rhetorical, rather than substantive, response, both to the immediate crisis of the bushfires and to the longer-term underlying crisis of human-caused climate change. The community-wide anger that resulted was therefore understandable.

The Morrison government had neglected a previous request by fire chiefs that would have funded a fleet of water-bombing aircraft— precisely the sort of equipment needed in the face of worsening firestorms.[86] When it came to action, all the Morrison government could muster were hasty, reactive announcements of government funding initiatives to deal with the bushfire crisis after it was already underway.[87]

Those actions amounted to political spin aimed at distracting the public from the serious conversation that is needed, not only about the underlying cause of the unprecedented extreme weather disasters, but about the need to decarbonize our economies. For Australia, dangerous climate change has arguably *already* arrived at roughly 1°C (1.8°F) of warming, and dramatic reductions in carbon emissions are necessary to avoid double that much warming. Yet, in the wake of the epic bushfires, Morrison announced a $2 billion plan to promote natural gas while his coalition partners were busy advocating for new coal-fired power stations. They also wanted to open new export-oriented coal basins.[88]

In the rhetoric that fossil-fuel-promoting politicians typically use in the aftermath of climate-change-fueled disasters, we encounter another form of deflection. Talk of reducing carbon emissions, blocking new fossil fuel infrastructure, and embracing renewable energy remain off limits. Instead, those defending the fossil fuel hegemony display a softer form of denial. Don't worry about mitigation and decarbonization, we'll just adapt to the "new normal." Perhaps we'll evolve to develop gills and fins. And fireproof skin. The onslaught of damaging extreme weather events in Australia and around the rest of the world reminds us that there are limits to adaptation and resilience in a rapidly warming world. There is no amount of resilience or adaptation that will be adequate if we fail to get off fossil fuels.

REAL CLIMATE SOLUTIONS . . .

A viable path forward on climate, as we have seen, involves a combination of energy efficiency, electrification, and decarbonization of the grid through an array of complementary renewable energy sources. The problem is that fossil fuel interests lose out in that scenario, and so they have used their immense wealth and influence to stymie any efforts to move in that direction. These interests, and those advocating for them, have attempted to deflect attention from these real climate solutions, promoting in their place ostensible alternatives. Their favored options include supposedly climate-friendly forms of fossil fuel burning, uncontrolled planetary-scale manipulation of the climate, and reliance on technologies such as massive reforestation and nuclear power whose viability as true climate solutions is dubious. Their other favored option is to engage in hollow rhetoric about "adaptation" and "resilience" that neglects the fundamental source of the problem—the burning of fossil fuels.

There are false prophets who promote these non-solutions. They come with progressive-sounding names, like the Breakthrough Institute or the "ecomodernists." But don't be fooled—what they're peddling is business-as-usual dressed up as progress. And don't fall for their crocodile tears over "divisiveness" whenever someone attempts to call out bad-faith efforts to promote false solutions and deflect attention from real ones.

Consider the plaintive lament by ecomodernist Breakthrough Institute affiliate Matthew Nisbet, who wrote that "those specializing in the dark arts of social media 'engagement' have used these platforms to hack our brains, training our focus on conservatives and the evildoings of the fossil fuel industry while the end times loom."[89] Nisbet asks us to accept an alternative reality in which social media, rather than having been exploited by denialists and inactivists, has somehow been gamed *against* them by some shadowy band of environmental activist "dark arts" practitioners. This outrageous claim is perhaps unsurprising coming from Nisbet, given that he authored a heavily criticized, un-peer-reviewed report some years ago that others have characterized as employing highly questionable accounting to level the rather absurd claim that green groups have outspent fossil fuel interests in the climate propaganda wars.[90]

But what about Nisbet's claim that climate activists might be governed by the fear that "end times loom"? Here he's at least partly right, but for the wrong reason. The false prophets have been successful, at least in part, in convincing some climate activists that desperate measures—like geoengineering—might be called for. Desperate times, after all, call for desperate measures, and there is a growing contingent within the climate movement that buys into a narrative of doom-and-gloom and desperation, a narrative that can, ironically, lead them down the very path of inaction that inactivists have laid out for them. It is the final front in the new climate war, a front that we explore in the next chapter.

CHAPTER 8

The Truth Is Bad Enough

The only thing we have to fear is . . . fear itself—nameless, unreasoning, unjustified terror which paralyzes needed efforts to convert retreat into advance.
—FRANKLIN DELANO ROOSEVELT

The word "catastrophe" is not permitted as long as there is danger of catastrophe turning to doom.
—CHRISTA WOLF

AN OBJECTIVE ASSESSMENT OF THE SCIENTIFIC EVIDENCE IS adequate to motivate immediate and concerted action on climate. There is no need to overstate it. Exaggeration of the climate threat by purveyors of doom—we'll call them "doomists"—is unhelpful at best. Indeed, doomism today arguably poses a greater threat to climate action than outright denial. For if catastrophic warming of the planet were truly inevitable and there were no agency on our part in averting it, why should we do anything? Doomism potentially leads us down the same path of inaction as outright denial of the threat. Exaggerated claims and hyperbole, moreover, play into efforts by deniers and delayers to discredit the science, posing further obstacles to action.

DANGER IS HERE

There is no one well-defined threshold that defines dangerous human interference with our climate. There is no cliff that we fall off at

1.5°C (2.7°F) warming or 2°C (3.6°F) warming. A far better analogy is that we're walking out onto a minefield, and the farther we go, the greater the risk. Conversely, the sooner we cease our forward lurch, the better off we are.

Dangerous climate change has in fact already arrived for many: for Puerto Rico, which was devastated by an unprecedented Category 5 hurricane with Maria in September 2017; for low-lying island nations like Tuvalu and coastal cities like Miami and Venice, which are already facing inundation by rising seas; for the Amazon, which has seen massive forest burning and climate-change-induced drought; for the Arctic, too, which has seen unprecedented wildfires in recent years; and for California, which has experienced unprecedented death and destruction from wildfires that now occur year-round. And those are just a few examples. The United States, Canada, Europe, and Japan have collectively witnessed unusually persistent, damaging weather extremes in recent years. Africa has been subject to drought, floods, and plagues of locusts. Australia has witnessed virtually every possible form of weather and climate disaster in recent years. And the list goes on.

We often hear that climate change is a "threat multiplier" when it comes to conflict, national security, and defense, for it heightens the competition that already exists over critical resources—food, water, space. But that framing applies equally to other domains, including human health. As I was writing this paragraph in the isolation of my sabbatical residence in Sydney in mid-March 2020, overlooking a serene Pacific Ocean that took my mind off the ever-worsening coronavirus (COVID-19) pandemic rapidly spreading outside the confines of my apartment, I couldn't help but think about the lessons the crisis might offer us. Our infrastructure is already burdened by climate-related challenges. Australia hadn't yet recovered from the catastrophic weather disasters of the 2019/2020 austral summer. Along comes yet another assault on its basic societal infrastructure. Soon any capacity to cope and adapt is exceeded. I was forced to cut my sabbatical short and head back to the States. Things were even worse there.

So yes, it's fair to say that dangerous climate change has already arrived and it's simply a matter, at this point, of how bad we're willing to let it get. While climate-change deniers, delayers, and deflectors love to point to scientific uncertainty as justification for inaction, uncertainty is not our friend here. It is cause to take even more concerted action. We already know that projections historically have been too optimistic about the rates of ice-sheet collapse and sea-level rise.[1] They also appear to be underestimating the incidence and severity of extreme weather events.[2] The consequences of doing nothing grow by the day. The time to act is now.

Recognizing that dangerous climate change is here already is, in an odd way, empowering. For there is no "danger" target to worry about missing. It is too late to prevent harmful impacts—they're already here. *But how much* additional danger we encounter is largely up to us. There is agency in the actions we take. The latest science tells us that, to a good approximation, how much the surface of the planet warms is a function of how much carbon we've burned up until that point. It is our decision-making henceforth that will determine how much additional warming and climate change we get (with some important exceptions we'll discuss later).

It is for this reason that a "carbon budget" is a meaningful notion. We can only burn a finite amount of carbon to avoid 1.5°C warming. And if we exceed that budget, which seems quite possible at this point, there is still a budget for avoiding 2°C warming. Every bit of additional carbon we burn makes things worse. But conversely, every bit of carbon we *avoid* burning prevents additional damage. There is both urgency and agency.

There is a role for voicing concern. It is important to recognize the risks of unmitigated climate change, including the potential for unpleasant surprises. We must consider worst-case scenarios when assessing our vulnerability, particularly given the fact that we have historically underestimated the rate and magnitude of key climate-change impacts. It is appropriate to criticize those who downplay the threat.

But there is *also* a danger in overstating the threat in a way that presents the problem as unsolvable, feeding into a sense of doom, inevitability, and hopelessness. Some seem to think that people need to be shocked and frightened to get them to engage with climate change. But research shows that the most motivating emotions are worry, interest, and hope.[3] Importantly, fear does not motivate, and appealing to it is often counterproductive, as it tends to distance people from the problem, leading them to disengage from, doubt, or even dismiss it.

Max Boycoff of the University of Colorado is a recognized leader in the study of climate messaging. He has argued that "if there isn't some semblance of hope or ways people can change the current state of affairs, people feel less motivated to try to address the problems." Boycoff has a T-shirt (inspired by the work of climate communication expert Ed Maibach of George Mason University) that reads: "It's real; it's us; experts agree; it's bad; there's hope."[4] Note once again the carefully calibrated balance of urgency ("it's bad") and agency ("there's hope").

DOOMISM

On one hand, inactivists—as we have seen—attempt to downplay the threat of climate change, or even argue that it will be "good for us." Consider Bjorn Lomborg, who, as you'll recall, glibly writes off the displacement of nearly half a billion people by sea-level rise as "less than 6% of the world's population."[5] Or consider the pleadings of Trump's former EPA administrator (and Koch brothers lackey) Scott Pruitt, who infamously claimed that climate change would help "humans flourish."[6] And there's tone-deaf Murdoch media minion Andrew Bolt, who, in the wake of the devastating climate-change-fueled Australian bushfires of the summer of 2019/2020, insisted on the front page of the Melbourne *Herald Sun* that "warming is good for us."[7]

But if the inactivists tend to *understate* the threat from climate change, there is a segment of the climate activist community that not

(Tom Toles)

only *overstates* it, but displays a distinct appetite for all-out doomism—portraying climate change not just as a threat that requires urgent response, but as an essentially lost cause, a hopeless fight. From the standpoint of climate action, that's problematic on several levels.[8] First, it provides a useful wedge for inactivists to employ as they attempt to divide climate advocates by raising the very emotional question of whether it is too late to act.

Doomism is a form of "crypto-denialism," or, if you like, "climate nihilism." The boundary between what constitutes denialism and what constitutes nihilism is fuzzy. As clean-tech author Ketan Joshi put it, "Doomism is the new denialism. Doomism is the new fossil fuel profit protectionism. Helplessness is the new message."[9] So it has been stoked by inactivists, primarily because it breeds disengagement.

This is hardly the first time it's been used in that way. In his 2011 book *Winston's War*, British historian Max Hastings made a compelling case that doomist framing was employed rather effectively by isolationists opposed to US involvement in World War II.[10] Hastings described how those opposing US involvement in the war transitioned rapidly from the argument that "our involvement isn't necessary" to the argument that "it's too late for our involvement to make a difference." The parallels with climate inactivism are compelling, and indeed, rather chilling. And the metaphor is worth extending, because it is arguable that what is needed to combat the climate crisis is in fact a World War II–like mobilization effort.

Climate doomism can be paralyzing. As one observer noted, "[climate] doomism has been used as a tool to turn people off action and to pervert election results."[11] That makes it a potentially useful tool for polluting interests looking to forestall or delay action. With many on the political right already opposed to meaningful climate action for ideological and tribal reasons, doomism provides a means for co-opting those on the left. It's a brilliant strategy for building a truly *bipartisan* coalition for inaction.

It is easy to understand why climate advocates have become somewhat disillusioned. In the space of a few years, we saw the United States go from playing a leading role in international climate negotiations to being the sole nation to renege on its commitment to the 2015 Paris Agreement. It is in this environment that doomism has flourished. Indeed, a September 2019 CBS News poll found that 26 percent of those who don't feel climate change should be addressed cite the belief that there is "nothing we can do about it," a larger percentage than those citing the belief that "it's not happening."[12] Doomism, it seems, now trumps denialism as a cause for inaction.

Doomist thinking has become widespread today even among ostensible environmental advocates. Consider in this vein the words of Morgan Phillips, codirector of The Glacier Trust, a not-for-profit organization that aims "to help communities at altitude adapt to and mitigate climate change."[13] Responding on Facebook to my June 2019 *USA Today* op-ed on the importance of systemic climate solutions, Phillips wrote, "You can't save the climate. . . . [T]he political, cultural and technological change required is impossible now. . . . We're very likely in the midst of a mass extinction event. . . . [I]t looks to me to be far too late to avoid runaway warming now."[14]

There is *no* scientific support whatsoever for such a claim. The state-of-the-art climate model simulations used, for example, in the IPCC's Fifth Assessment Report (2014) provide no support at all for a runaway warming scenario at even 4° or 5°C (7.2° or 9°F), let alone 3°C (5.4°F), which is where current policies (i.e., "business-as-usual") are now likely taking us as we slowly begin to decarbonize the economy.[15] As for "mass extinction," the most comprehensive study to date, published in April 2020 in the premier journal *Nature*, found that less than 2 percent of species assemblages will undergo collapse (what the authors call "abrupt ecological disruption") from climate change if we keep planetary warming below 2°C (3.6°F). The number rises to 15 percent if warming reaches 4°C. That is certainly very troubling, but it doesn't constitute a "mass extinction" event of the sort that is evident in the geological record.[16]

Now look where these false prophecies of doom lead Phillips. He continued: "There isn't a bottomless pit of resources available to spend on responses . . . to climate and ecological breakdown. Trade offs [*sic*] need to be made, we have to ask whether we want to spend billions on spurious 'green tech' silver bullets, or billions on disaster risk reduction in the global south." To summarize his argument: (1) there's nothing we can do to prevent catastrophic, "runaway" climate change, and (2) efforts to act will somehow siphon away critical resources from helping people adapt to the inevitable coming apocalypse. So doomism literally undermines his support for climate mitigation.

The flames of doomism are being fanned by polluting interests who don't want to see us change. We must fight back every bit as fiercely as we fight outright climate-change denial. Unsurprisingly, trolls and bots are being used to promote doom and inevitability. Doomist messaging has become omnipresent in my own Twitter feed. Let's consider a couple of particularly salient examples.

Canadian prime minister Justin Trudeau and his administration, as we have seen, have been targeted by trollbots over their implementation of carbon pricing. In response to a fairly anodyne tweet by Trudeau about Canadian governmental priorities, a Twitter user quoted a previous statement by me that "meeting our Paris obligations alone doesn't get us to where we need to be . . ."[17] An account named "DarleneLily," with a 66 percent Bot Sentinel trollbot score, replied, *"There's no way you can control the planets temperature.* You can't stop other countries from polluting and using up their own natural resources. Truth the world is overpopulated. And *you can't stop the Supreme deity. The world is ending"* (emphasis added).[18] It's perfectly disabling doomist messaging.

A link I posted to my June 2019 *USA Today* op-ed touting the importance of systemic solutions and the dangers of only emphasizing individual behavior triggered doomist troll-like responses.[19] One Twitter user tweeted, "All-out war on climate change made sense only as long as it was winnable. *Once you accept that we've lost it, other kinds of action take on greater meaning . . ."* (emphasis added).[20] A few days later, the same person tweeted, "Carbon tax caused yellow vest protests in France. Who can afford to buy a new electric car. #MagicalThinking Too little, too late!"[21] Note the combination of doomist thinking with an effort to undermine agency—the Twitter user both discredited the role of electrification of transportation and invoked the "Yellow Vest" canard that inactivists so often employ to throw damp water on carbon pricing. That's some pretty sophisticated and savvy inactivist messaging.

Doomist social-media messaging is in fact often combined with "both-siderism": that is, there is no hope because both major parties in the United States are equally bad on climate (readers will recall that Russia used this trope to suppress enthusiasm for Democratic candidate Hillary Clinton in the 2016 election). In response to my tweet of a link to Paul Krugman's *New York Times* op-ed titled "The Party That Ruined the Planet: Republican Climate Denial Is Even Scarier Than Trumpism," one user tweeted back, "Obama was literally bragging this year about oil exports at an all time [*sic*] high after his presidency. This is absurd. *Climate denial is absolutely bipartisan.* Frankly, *establishment Democrats are worse because they say it's real and still pursue policies that will kill us all"* (emphasis added).[22] There are countless other examples in my Twitter feed from the past few years of doomist messaging being used to suppress climate activism.

MESSENGERS OF DOOM

The problem can be as simple as the headline that is chosen by an editor. Consider, for example, the recent *Nature* study cited earlier showing that ecosystem collapse can be avoided by limiting warming to 2°C. On Twitter, the Pulitzer Prize–winning *Inside Climate News* instead said, "A new study warns that climate change will soon lead to massive ecosystem collapse as key species go extinct."[23] Note how agency, unintentionally perhaps, is stolen by not properly contextualizing the claim—namely, by not acknowledging that such a scenario can be avoided through concerted action. I coyly suggested a rewrite of their tag line: "Comprehensive new *Nature* Study Shows that Massive Ecosystem Collapse Can be Averted if Warming is Limited to 2C—Which is Still Possible."[24] The award-winning editor Bruce Boyes of the Australian *KM Magazine* concurred, explaining that "the reporting can spin science findings into the negative, with headlines that disengage rather than engage."[25] Another observer commented, "Turn away from climate doom and catastrophism, and suddenly a better future seems very possible."[26]

The New Yorker might as well be the member newsletter of America's liberal elite. Get a featured article there and you achieve the equivalent, with the progressive intelligentsia, of appearing on the cover of *Rolling Stone*. That's where Jonathan Franzen—known largely as a fiction writer—found himself in September 2019 with one of the most breathtakingly doomist diatribes that has ever graced a magazine's pages. In an article titled "What If We Stopped Pretending? The Climate Apocalypse Is Coming. To Prepare for It, We Need to Admit That We Can't Prevent It," Franzen gave inactivists one of the greatest gifts they've received in years.[27]

The reviews were decidedly negative. Ula Chrobak of *Popular Science* summarized Franzen's thesis thusly: "He's claiming that those advocating for climate action are practically delusional, and that renewable energy projects and high speed trains are futile efforts to stop a planet 'spinning out of control.'"[28] *Climate Nexus* executive director Jeff Nesbit explained that "this sort of 'climate doomism' is as much a trap as 'personal sacrifice' is. Both are clever narrative plots by forces opposed to any real action on climate."[29] Science journalist John Upton opined, "It's hard to imagine major outlets publishing essays declaring efforts to reduce poverty hopeless. Or telling cancer patients to just give up. Yet this Climate Doomist trope flourishes—penned, best I can tell, exclusively by older, comfy white men."[30] End Climate Silence founder Genevieve Guenther, too, was decidedly unimpressed: "This piece is completely incoherent: the apocalypse cannot be stopped due to 'human nature' (so says the white man) but we can endure it. . . . Jonathan Franzen has no particular authority on climate, and the NYer shouldn't run trash." And Project Drawdown executive director Jon Foley described the article as "a shallow, poorly researched, self-indulgent piece. Probably one of the worst climate pieces I've ever read outside the denier's camp."[31]

The fundamental problem with the article is that it attempts to build a case for doom on a flimsy foundation of distorted science. I can speak to this directly, because I was contacted by the *New Yorker*'s fact-checkers to evaluate a passage in an earlier draft of the article. The passage read, "To project the rise in the global mean temperature, scientists rely on complicated atmospheric modeling. They take a host of variables and run them through supercomputers to generate, say, ten thousand different simulations for the coming century, in order to make a 'best' prediction of the rise in temperature. What then gets reported in the media isn't the likeliest rise in temperature. It's the lowest temperature that shows up in ninety-three percent of all scenarios. When a scientist predicts a rise of two degrees Celsius, she's merely naming a number about which she's very confident: the rise will be at least two degrees. The likeliest rise is far higher."

I told the fact-checker: "This doesn't look correct to me. When scientists generate an ensemble (spread) of temperature projections, the quantity that is generally communicated is the *average* or *median* warming. There is roughly an equal likelihood that the true value is either less than or greater than that value. And most scientists do their best to communicate the spread itself, i.e. the uncertainty range, and not just the middle value."

Even after Franzen had been informed of his error, he ended up keeping the incorrect statement that "the rise will be *at least* two degrees" (albeit changing 'The likeliest rise is far higher" to 'The rise might, in fact, be higher"). The final wording still falsely implied that the model averages preferentially underestimate the warming, despite my having communicated to the fact-checker that there's an equal likelihood that they underestimate or overestimate the warming. The uncorrected error conveniently supported Franzen's doomist narrative. Alas, I had only been allowed to see this one passage.

The whole article, it turned out, was riddled with basic science errors. *Business Insider* summarized experts' assessment of his piece thusly: "Scientists blast Jonathan Franzen's 'climate doomist' opinion column as 'the worst piece on climate change.'"[32] The critical problem is one we've already encountered and discussed. Franzen argued that we will fail to limit warming to below 2°C. That in itself is not objectively defensible—it is certainly still within our ability to avert 2°C warming given rapid decarbonization efforts. But more problematically, he invoked the strawman that we will then fall off a climate cliff, with supposed runaway feedback loops that kick in, rendering mitigation efforts useless. To quote Franzen directly: "In the long run, it probably makes no difference how badly we overshoot two degrees; once the point of no return is passed, the world will become self-transforming." We've already seen that there is no objective scientific support for such runaway warming scenarios. Yet they form the entire basis for Franzen's false prophecy of doom.[33]

Franzen's feelings were apparently hurt by the overwhelmingly negative response to his article. In fact, he has blamed it—or at least online critiques of his brand of doomist prophesizing—for the lack of progress on climate. In an interview with *The Guardian* he complained of the "Twitter rage" against him, arguing that "online rage is stopping us tackling the climate crisis."[34] He insisted that the "messenger was being attacked even if the facts of the message were not being challenged." While I'm sympathetic to his concern about online rage, which—as I have noted myself—can be counterproductive to action, the critiques of his commentary were in fact, as detailed above, grounded in his fundamental misrepresentations of climate science.

One of the more baleful aspects of doomism is the way it endorses intergenerational inequity—that is to say, its total dismissiveness when it comes to the interests of future generations. Rupert Read is an academic from the University of East Anglia in the United Kingdom and a self-avowed spokesperson for Extinction Rebellion. He's also a messenger of doom. After Read delivered a particularly fatalistic public lecture, climate scientist Tamsin Edwards blasted him: "I am shocked at this talk. Please stop telling children they may not grow up due to climate change. It is WRONG . . ."[35] It certainly is.

There is something especially disturbing when middle-aged men scold teenage girls fighting for a livable future. It's even worse when other middle-aged men stand by and applaud. Perhaps I'm taking just a bit of poetic license here, but that's essentially what happened with provocateur and author Roy Scranton and *Vox* climate pundit David Roberts in an episode I'll now recount.

Scranton is the ultimate doomist. In 2018 he literally wrote a book titled *We're Doomed*.[36] He snidely criticizes youth climate activists, dismissing their efforts as "Pure Disney." Though he has since deleted his Twitter account, back in December 2018 he took to the social media outlet to castigate youth climate activists as unwitting tools: "Enlisting children to carry the message of catastrophic climate change is at the same time a *reprehensible* abdication of responsibility and an embarrassing display of sentimentality and magical thinking. Pure Disney logic" (emphasis added).[37]

Scranton uses "Disney" so often, in fact, I'm surprised he doesn't have to pay them royalties. He invoked the multinational entertainment conglomerate's name once again to dismiss the writing of environmental author and 350.org founder Bill McKibben.[38] Scranton's flippant language suggests he thinks this is all somehow funny. But in fact, it's dead serious, and others aren't laughing. In response to his reprehensible attack on the youth climate movement and its de facto leader Greta Thunberg, youth climate activist Alexandria Villaseñor retorted, "Greta sparked a movement that has thousands of youth learning about climate change and realizing they have power. What have you done @RoyScranton? besides tell us we're doomed . . ."[39]

What I found especially disappointing in this particular affair was the reaction of *Vox*'s David Roberts, a pundit whose views about environmental matters are often insightful. Roberts weighed in on a piece Scranton had written for the *Los Angeles Review of Books* that dismissed Bill McKibben and others for their efforts to present a viable path forward on climate.[40] Roberts glibly endorsed Scranton's doomist take: "I like this piece from @RoyScranton & agree that the forced hortatory uplift at the end of climate books/articles is always the worst part." He then contemptuously scorned those who rightfully push back on such doomism, saying it was "fascinating" to him "to watch how fiercely, even angrily," people responded to Scranton's piece.[41] It appears that Roberts has since deleted this tweet. I don't blame him.

People *should* be angry at anyone engaged in self-righteous and self-serving (yeah—doom porn *sells!*) propagandizing at the expense of our children and grandchildren's future. As a scientist who studies the projections and numbers, let me affirmatively state, for the record, that Scranton—and Roberts and Read and Franzen and other doomist men—are dead wrong. Our demise is only assured if we follow their lead and surrender. If your midlife crisis has caused you to give up on the future, then step aside. Get out of the way. But please don't obstruct others stepping forward to do battle.

DOCTOR DOOM

Guy McPherson, a retired ecology professor from Arizona, is arguably the scientific leader of the doomism movement, a cult figure of sorts. McPherson, like other doomists, argues that we have already triggered irreversible vicious cycles (for example, the massive release of frozen methane) that will render the planet lifeless in a matter of years. There's nothing we can do about it. What he calls "exponential climate change" will render human beings and all other species extinct within ten years owing to supposed runaway warming—something for which there is, as we have already seen, no shred of scientific evidence. But, if you like, mark December 2026 on your doomsday calendar—that's when McPherson said we will meet our collective demise.[42] (In the wake of the COVID-19 crisis in early 2020, McPherson provisionally moved his doomsday estimate all the way up to November 1, 2020. So if you're reading this, you can breathe a sigh of relief now!)[43]

According to science journalist Scott Johnson, "McPherson is a photo-negative of the self-proclaimed 'climate skeptics' who reject the conclusions of climate science. He may be advocating the opposite conclusion, but he argues his case in the same way. The skeptics often quote snippets of science that, on full examination, don't actually support their claims, and this is McPherson's modus operandi. . . . Both malign the IPCC as 'political' and therefore not objective. And both will cite nearly any claim that supports their views, regardless of source—putting evidence-free opinions on par with scientific research."[44]

McPherson is prolific, writing books, doing countless lectures, and appearing in online videos where he trumpets his message of imminent doom. He counsels us to grieve for our demise and find solace in "love," ending each of his videos the same way: "At the end of extinction, only love remains." His message has spread like a virus through environmentally aware regions of the Internet, with copycats writing pieces like "Are We Heading Toward Extinction? The Earth's Species—Plants, Animals and Humans, Alike—Are Facing Imminent Demise. How We Got Here, and How to Cope" (this from the progressive *Huffington Post*).[45] Greenpeace cofounder Rex Weyler has even echoed McPherson's doomsaying of imminent extinction in a commentary posted on Greenpeace's website.[46]

This sort of framing, again, plays right into the hands of the forces of delay and inaction. It is readily used to suppress activism and reduce enthusiasm for action. If we're doomed, then why expend time and effort pushing for action on climate? Such efforts are curiously reminiscent of the way Russia sought to suppress democratic turnout in the 2016 presidential election by convincing enough Democratic voters that there was essentially no difference between Hillary Clinton and Donald Trump. If your vote doesn't matter, then why bother?

Russia used online social media campaigns to drive a wedge between supporters of Bernie Sanders, who promoted hard-core climate policies (such as the outright banning of fracking), and the ultimate Democratic nominee, Hillary Clinton, who favored more "centrist" climate policies.[47] It was a deeply cynical and indeed sinister campaign on Russia's part, for, as we know, Russia is opposed to international climate action and has used social media campaigns to promote climate contrarianism.[48] Russia clearly didn't support Sanders's aggressive climate stance. But its leaders understood that he was a spoiler, and so they ran a massive social media campaign to exaggerate and exploit perceived climate policy differences between him and Clinton. The objective was to make Clinton unacceptable to Sanders supporters and not worth voting for—to convince a large enough number of progressives to simply sit out the election. And they did, helping hand the presidency to Russia's preferred candidate: climate-change denier and fossil fuel stooge Donald Trump.[49]

The Trump connection is an interesting one. McPherson frequently does interviews on a webcast network called American Freedom Radio that features on its page a virtual smorgasbord of right-wing conspiracy theories.[50] McPherson posted a commentary on his website supporting Donald Trump in the 2016 presidential election. Quoting from it directly: *"Donald Trump is another manifestation of the cleansing fire. . . . [H]e has secured my vote* to quicken the demise—sparking the flame. If you are one of those folks going through an earlier stage of grief and still finding it hard to accept our fate . . . it's becoming more and more obvious that the jig is up and time is short. In context, my goals for today include being kind to someone, smiling at a stranger, and *calling a few friends to convince them to vote for The Donald*" (emphasis added).[51]

So with McPherson and other doomists we find ourselves in a very odd corner of the universe where right meets left and doom meets denial. Whether climate change is a hoax (as Donald Trump would have us think) or beyond our control (as McPherson insists), there is no reason to cut carbon emissions. It doesn't matter how we get there. To the inactivist agenda, only the destination matters.

Doomists will attack upon the mere suggestion that disaster can still be averted. As one observer noted, "I've seen people post links to apocalyptic films scorning climate activists for even trying to avert catastrophe."[52] I've experienced this personally. In early September 2019, I appeared on Ali Velshi's MSNBC show to discuss the findings of the IPCC's new "Special Report on the Ocean and Cryosphere in a Changing Climate." I was subsequently berated on Twitter by an individual describing himself as a New Green Deal–supporting "Ecotopian Berniecrat." He was upset that I had cited the report's apparently insufficiently doomist prognosis of five to six feet of sea-level rise by the end of the century under business-as-usual fossil fuel burning.[53]

Why would I and other leading climate scientists be lying to understate the climate threat? Climate doomists, like climate denialists, often subscribe to conspiracy theories about scientists. But in the doomist version, the scientists aren't conspiring to promote a massive hoax. Instead, they are engaged in a massive cover-up to hide how bad climate change really is. Scott Johnson noted that "the skeptics dismiss science they don't like by saying that climate researchers lie to keep the grant money coming," while doomists insist that "scientists are downplaying risks because they're too cowardly to speak the truth and flout our corporate overlords."[54] Commenting on the recent trend, my climate scientist colleague Eric Steig perhaps put it best when he asked, "Where did this 'climate scientists are lying to us—telling us it isn't so bad—because of grant money' come from? Is this a real 'movement,' or just a bunch of Russian bots?," adding, "I miss the days of arguing with climate deniers."[55]

Taking the conspiracy theory to its absurd limit, if climate scientists are lying to maintain their employment, then only unemployed climate scientists can be trusted. That was literally the argument made by one purveyor of climate doom whose Twitter account no longer exists: "I suggest reading Guy McPherson who is unemployed and so tells the truth (working academics are funded by big biz and can't—crowd control), Sam Carana who posts under a pseudonym and Peter Wadhams who is also unemployed—ice expert from Cambridge. All are in the imminent camp." (Actually, McPherson and Wadhams are both professors emeriti.) Note that "imminent" means "doomist."[56]

We've already learned about McPherson. What about these other two individuals? As noted by Dana Nuccitelli in *The Guardian*, Peter Wadhams predicted back in 2012 that we would see an ice-free Arctic by the summer of 2016.[57] It is 2020 and we are nowhere close to that point. Like McPherson, Wadhams insists that Arctic warming will lead to massive releases of trapped methane and abrupt resulting warming. Sam Carana isn't even a real person—it's a pseudonym—so we know nothing about his actual qualifications. What we *do* know is that, as Scott Johnson has stated, he "posts a great deal of strange and unscientific claims" about . . . you guessed it, Arctic methane.[58]

Why do the doomists seem to be inordinately obsessed with Arctic warming and methane? We know that methane is a very potent greenhouse gas. And some of the best-known natural examples of catastrophic past warming events appear to have involved substantial releases of methane trapped either in permafrost or in the so-called methane hydrate along the sea floor. For example, warming of roughly 14°C (25°F) occurred at the end of the Permian period 250 million years ago, resulting in one of the greatest mass extinction events in Earth's history: 90 percent of all life was wiped out. At the boundary of the Paleocene and Eocene epochs (what is known as the Paleocene-Eocene Thermal Maximum, or PETM) roughly 56 million years ago, Earth experienced warming of as much as 7°C (13°F), with, again, widespread extinction.[59]

So if you're looking for a dramatic, doomsday-like climate-change scenario, it's very tempting to look toward methane. More specifically, you might focus on mechanisms whereby warming of the Arctic releases massive amounts of methane previously frozen in the permafrost, leading to more warming, more melting ice, more methane release, and a runaway warming scenario. The problem is that, aside from the questionable claims of a handful of contrarian scientists, there's simply no evidence that the projected warming could lead to such an event. Authoritative reviews of the scientific literature on the topic reveal "no evidence that methane will run out of control and initiate any sudden, catastrophic effects."[60]

That hasn't stopped the methane catastrophists from looking for any scrap of data that might support their narrative. Back in September 2019, they were hyping a momentary spike recorded by one isolated methane measurement station in Barrow, Alaska. At the time, I explained that this was almost certainly an isolated blip, perhaps reflecting contamination of the site—and that there was no evidence it was part of a larger pattern or trend.[61] Sure enough, methane levels at that site subsequently returned to normal. At least one media outlet that had uncritically reported the putative methane spike issued a correction, noting that the data had not been "validated," were impacted by "local pollution," and may be "subject to change."[62]

There's another important point to be made here. Although there has been a global uptick in methane, as we noted in the previous chapter the evidence suggests it's coming from natural gas extraction and not natural sources such as melting permafrost.[63] The doomists thus have it completely backward here. Rather than it being out of our hands, with appropriate policies governing natural gas extraction and fugitive methane emissions we can likely prevent the continued buildup of methane in the atmosphere. There is *agency* on our part.

While doomism itself might be dismissed as a rather fringe movement, there is some evidence of "seepage" of doomist conspiracy-mongering into the mainstream climate discourse. Consider, for example, an exchange that took place between climate experts back in January 2020. It started with Kevin Anderson, a climate scientist who has been critical of the mainstream climate science community for what he perceives to be complacency and a lack of urgency in the face of a crisis.

Anderson is no doomist, but he's at the far end of the aggressiveness scale within the climate science community. He has, for example, publicly chastised scientists who continue to use air travel, going so far as to travel on a container ship to a scientific conference to make his point (long before this sort of thing became fashionable à la Greta). Going further, he has argued that even scientists engaged in fieldwork in remote locations should only travel this way: "People have gone to the Amazon for years without flying."[64] Let's leave aside any discussion of how presumptuous it is to tell scientists engaged in laborious and logistically challenging fieldwork that they must take several additional weeks out of their schedules to travel by boat to remote locations. Anderson obviously buys heavily into the "personal action" framing of climate solutions. But he has also blamed his fellow scientists for a failure of systemic action, which leads us back to our story.

In January 2020, Anderson criticized a report by the United Kingdom's Committee on Climate Change (CCC), an "independent, statutory body established under the Climate Change Act 2008 . . . to advise the UK Government . . . on emissions targets and report to Parliament on progress made in reducing greenhouse gas emissions and preparing for climate change."[65] Anderson plaintively asked, "Why is there so little critique of [the CCC's] 'net-zero' report by academics & the wider climate community? It is designed to fit with the current political & economic status quo, & in so doing proposes cuts in CO_2 far smaller than those needed to meet our Paris 1.5–2°C commitments!"[66] Defending the CCC, one commenter pointed out that they "are mandated to fulfil the Paris Agreement but would most likely welcome more analysis of their work."[67]

It was then that Anderson leveled an accusation against the entire scientific community, responding, "I wish I had your confidence in the process of scrutiny. Fine to argue around the edges, but the overall framing is firmly set in a politically-dogmatic stone with academia & much of the climate community running scared of questioning this for fear of loss of funding, presitige [sic], etc."[68]

If that sounds like the sort of accusation we expect from climate deniers and doomists, it's because that's the sort of accusation we expect from climate deniers and doomists. The chief executive of the CCC, understandably perturbed by Anderson's attack, responded, "It's not a politically dogmatic stone. It's the UK's Climate Change Act, which we're obliged [to] follow."[69] UK climate scientist Tamsin Edwards objected to the collective smear against the climate science community, tweeting, "That's quite an accusation about academics. . . . On what basis do you make the claim that 'much' of the community are mendaciously or cynically silent to protect their own interests?"[70] Anderson's unsatisfyingly vague response? "Repeated discussion over many years with many academics (and others) who work speciifcally [sic] on mitigation."[71] A more likely explanation, in my view? Too much exposure to doomist rhetoric. Or perhaps its more civilized close cousin, *soft doomism*.

"DEEP ADAPTATION"

Doomism sometimes masquerades under a nom de plume. Consider what has come to be known as "Deep Adaptation," introduced and promoted by Jem Bendell, an academic from the University of Cumbria in the United Kingdom. In February 2019, Bendell published an article that *Vice* characterized as "The Climate Change Paper So Depressing It's Sending People to Therapy."[72] But it is not an academic article in the usual sense. It was rejected by scientific journals, and Bendell ultimately self-published it on his website.[73] That means it lacks the rigor of a peer-reviewed scientific article. It has nonetheless been viewed far more than any typical peer-reviewed scientific article—by one estimate, more than 100,000 people have read it.

Although Bendell's article is, at least on the surface, less hard-core than the doomist "all life will end in a decade" messaging of Guy McPherson, Bendell nonetheless argues that near-term "climate-induced *societal collapse*" (a somewhat more murky concept) "is now inevitable in the near term," which he clarifies to mean "about a decade" (emphasis added).[74] Bendell bases this prognostication on the now all-too-familiar (but discredited) claims of a supposed Arctic "methane bomb" that will precipitate runaway warming, the collapse of agriculture, exponential increases in infectious disease, near-term societal collapse, and *possibly*—he at least seems to imply in places—human extinction. Bendell exaggerates both the projected climate change and its impacts.[75]

Equally problematic, his prescription for how we might address this looming threat involves no real mitigation. There's no mention of reducing carbon emissions, just some vague language about "restorative agriculture" and "resilience" and the insistence that we must "adapt" to the inevitable demise of civilization as we know it.

The BBC interviewed a number of scientists, asking them to comment on the merit of Bendell's assertions.[76] Among them was Myles Allen, professor of geosystem science at the University of Oxford, who asserted that "predictions of societal collapse in the next few years as a result of climate change seem very far-fetched." Allen noted, moreover, that "lots of people are using this kind of catastrophism to argue that there's no point in reducing emissions."

I too was quoted. I described the Bendell paper as "a perfect storm of misguidedness and wrongheadedness," since "it is wrong on the science and its impacts." I said, "There is no credible evidence that we face 'inevitable near-term collapse,'" and I emphasized that Bendell's doomist framing was "disabling" and would "lead us down the very same path of inaction as outright climate change denial." I added that "fossil fuel interests love this framing."

And indeed they must, for it breeds disengagement from the climate battle. One alarmed reader of Bendell's article is quoted in *Vice* as saying, "We're fucked. . . . Climate change is going to fuck us over. . . . Should I just accept the deep adaptation paper and move to the Scottish countryside and wait out the apocalypse?'"[77] Another individual, quoted by the BBC, said that "a few months after reading the Deep Adaptation paper," he and his wife decided to sell their home and move out to the country. "When the crunch comes," he said, "there'll be a lot of people in a small area and it's going to be mayhem—and we'll be safer if we move further north because it's colder."[78] We have terms for such folks, like "doomsday preppers" and "survivalists."

If you take the most environmentally aware progressives, lead them to despair, and convince them to dissociate from civilization, they're not out there on the front lines participating in the political process, demonstrating and fighting for the needed systemic changes. Bendell's paper is a more powerful tool for disengagement than any article ever written by a climate-change denier.

SOFT DOOMISM

If outright doomism is generally too shrill to gain much currency in mainstream climate discourse, what we shall henceforth refer to as *soft doomism* has found its way to the very center of the conversation. Soft doomists don't quite argue for the inevitably of our demise as a species, but they typically imply that catastrophic impacts are now unavoidable and that reducing carbon emissions won't save us from disaster. It's doomism dressed up, you might argue, in more respectable clothing.

Soft doomists tend to use terms like "panic." "Time to Panic" was the headline on a 2019 *New York Times* op-ed by David Wallace-Wells, author of *The Uninhabitable Earth* (which I will discuss later).[79] According to Sheril Kirshenbaum, executive director of the nonprofit organization Science Debate and host of the National Public Radio podcast *Serving Up Science*, "stoking panic and fear creates a false narrative that can overwhelm readers, leading to inaction and hopelessness."[80]

"Panic" is a word that conjures images of people running screaming through the streets with their hands over their heads. It evokes irrational, desperate, rash behavior rather than considered, well-thought-out, deliberate action. The latter is helpful. The former is not. And it can lead us to very strange and uncomfortable places.

Let's concede that the "p" word is appropriate in some contexts. Consider, for example, Greta Thunberg. In her message to world leaders gathered at Davos, Switzerland, in January 2019 for the World Economic Forum, she chastised the crowd for having failed to act meaningfully on the climate crisis, telling them, "I want you to panic." In that context, it is reasonable to interpret her comments as suggesting that the attending politicians and opinion leaders deserve to feel the scorn of young people like herself calling for action. Indeed, her subsequent statement was "And then I want you to act."[81]

But unfocused and diffuse "panic" messaging can lead to counterproductive actions. As we have seen, it has led to support for potentially dangerous geoengineering schemes, which have been sold as a necessary last-ditch means of averting climate devastation. Read no further than the headline of the December 2019 *Washington Post* op-ed "Climate Politics Is a Dead End. So the World Could Turn to This Desperate Final Gambit."[82]

Soft doomism has become increasingly widespread. Its basic tenets have been adopted by groups like the aforementioned Extinction Rebellion, which takes the position that "we are facing an unprecedented global emergency. Life on Earth is in crisis. . . . [W]e have entered a period of abrupt climate breakdown, and we are in the midst of a mass extinction of our own making."[83] In mid-January 2020, a curious online article was making the rounds, ironically well-titled "Climate Fatalism."[84] While the article was unsigned, it was sponsored by an organization called the Freedom Lab, which describes itself as an "innovation hub" and "thinktank" that produces "actionable insights," which it shares "through regular publications and public events."[85]

The article embodies the ambivalence and internal contradictions that have come to characterize soft doomism. "Last year," it begins, "several alarming reports made it clear that immediate and radical action is needed to prevent disastrous levels of global warming." It's a promising start, acknowledging the problem and entreating the reader to action. However, in the very next line, the author writes, "Action is nowhere to be found and we are bound to hit the tipping points of global warming that will render any further action irrelevant." It's an abrupt turn toward doomism and futility that is made even more confusing by the sentence that follows, which warns of the threat of the very sort of fatalism that the article is promoting: "As this notion spreads, 2019 could see many of us falling prey to climate fatalism and a shift in political focus towards climate adaptation."

Despite the contradictions, the piece has an agenda. It concludes with a prescriptive statement masquerading as a predictive one: "We will see a shift from preventing climate change to adapting to (and battling) the effects. Much of this will entail engineering, to build dams and extreme-weather-proof buildings, for instance. It's likely that governments will shift funding from preventive measures to these kinds of adaptive solutions." The message is that climate change is bad—very bad, but we will fail to act to solve it, so we might as well just adapt, be more resilient, and, oh yeah—explore technofixes. We've heard this story before. It is the "non-solution solution" of the previous chapter.

Soft doomism in a sense plays the same role among progressives that soft denial plays among conservatives. That is to say, it is a form of doomist rhetoric that is tolerated in polite company. And unsurprisingly, some prominent progressive climate and environment pundits have engaged in its rhetoric. Consider again the otherwise generally insightful David Roberts of *Vox*. In late December 2019, Roberts tweeted, "We're not going to limit temp to 1.5C. The weird social pressure to continue pretending we can, or might, is weird to me. The situation is tragic. The people & institutions responsible deserve all the anger in the world. But it is what it is."[86]

Climate and energy policy pundit Jon Koomey chided Roberts: "Dave, please stop the defeatist pessimism. Not helpful, and probably not even right. We are able to do this, and given a sufficient shift in the politics, we will do it. But the longer we wait the more stranded assets there will be and the more costly it will be."[87] That comment, of course, precipitated its own feeding frenzy of doomist commentary. One individual wrote, "I know it is technically feasible. It is not socially and psychologically feasible."[88]

That comment, while misguided, usefully betrays an underlying point of confusion—a fallacy that is in fact commonly encountered in these sorts of discussions. The fallacy is conflating physics and politics. While the laws of physics are immutable, human behavior is not. And dismissiveness based on perceived political or psychological barriers to action can be self-reinforcing and self-defeating. Think World War II mobilization or the Apollo project. Had we decided a priori that winning the war or landing on the moon was impossible, these seemingly insurmountable challenges would never have been met. We have encountered compelling evidence that a clean energy revolution and climate stabilization are achievable with current technology. All we require are policies to incentivize the needed shift. That doesn't violate the Newtonian laws of motion, or the laws of thermodynamics. It only challenges us to think boldly. Scratch beneath the surface and we find that most soft doomism is premised not in the physical impossibility of limiting warming, but in a cynical, pessimistic belief that we lack the willpower to act. It's giving up before we have even tried. And once again, the inactivists are smiling all the way to the bank.

In this vein, let's talk about the so-called "Hothouse Earth" article mentioned in Chapter 5. It was published in August 2018, with Australian environmental scientist Will Steffen as the lead author.[89] In a sense, this article helped lay the groundwork for other doomist and soft doomist accounts like those by Scranton, Franzen, and Bendell. Like the Bendell paper, it went viral. Also like the Bendell paper, it wasn't peer-reviewed research, but simply a "perspective," more of an opinion piece than a scientific article. One important difference was that "Hothouse Earth" was published in the high-profile, prestigious *Proceedings of the National Academy of Sciences*, lending the imprimatur of the US National Academy of Sciences—the highest scientific authority in the land—to the study's findings.

Steffen, the principal author, is executive director of the Australian National University (ANU) Climate Change Institute. Readers may recall from Chapter 5 Steffen's unusually aggressive and prescriptive views on climate action: *"You have got to get away from the so-called neoliberal economics* . . . [and shift to something] more like wartime footing [to decarbonize society] at very fast rates" (emphasis added).[90]

The "Hothouse Earth" article makes similar claims to those we've encountered before among doomists and soft doomists—indeed, it is the likely inspiration for their thinking. But it is more nuanced and employs more caveats than other accounts, arguing that even if we keep warming under the oft-cited "dangerous" limit of 2°C, hypothesized amplifying feedbacks, such as "permafrost thawing" and "decomposition of ocean methane hydrates," *could* lead to climate change spiraling out of control. The article asserts that "even if the Paris Accord target of a 1.5°C to 2.0°C rise in temperature is met, we cannot exclude the risk that a cascade of feedbacks *could* push the Earth System irreversibly onto a 'Hothouse Earth' [4–5°C warming] pathway," with massive ice loss, sea-level rise, megadroughts, and other dire impacts.

Mainstream climate research, as already noted, doesn't support these claims—at least for the near term. Thus, rather than a summary of our current understanding, the "Hothouse Earth" article is "speculative" and more of an "interesting think piece," according to UK climate scientist Richard Betts.[91] Betts emphasized that there is "large uncertainty" in the "Hothouse Earth" authors' estimate of 2°C as the trigger point for cascading feedbacks, noting that it reflects "risk averse" assumptions, and that "even if the self-perpetuating changes do begin within a few decades, the process would take a long time to fully kick in—centuries or millennia."

The combination of the authority of a prestigious journal, high-profile authors, and dramatic claims nonetheless ensured that "Hothouse Earth" would get a huge amount of media attention—and naturally, all the nuance was lost in the media frenzy that ensued. A very similar follow-up commentary, coauthored by many of the principals of the earlier article, was published a year later in the prestigious journal *Nature*, triggering yet another round of publicity.[92] Collectively, the two reports were covered by hundreds of media outlets, including CNN, *Newsweek*, *The Guardian*, *National Geographic*, the BBC, the *Daily Mail*, the *Sydney Morning Herald*, the *New York Post*, and many others. With over-the-top headlines, like "Climate Change Driving Entire Planet to Dangerous 'Tipping Point'" (*National Geographic*), and "Scientists Warn Earth at Dire Risk of Becoming Hellish 'Hothouse'" (*New York Post*), the collective coverage suggested that we face imminent and unavoidable catastrophic climate change. It all played into a doomist narrative of helplessness—and, as we shall see later, fueled conservative efforts to caricature and discredit climate predictions.[93]

UNINHABITABLE EARTH?

There is one rendering of climate doomism that stands out above all others. It has been so influential that it deserves its own section. Albeit more nuanced than most of the doomist genre, "The Uninhabitable Earth," a July 2017 article by David Wallace-Wells that he later developed into a best-selling book, had a profound impact on the larger conversation about climate change.[94] The article, published in *New York Magazine*, predated "Hothouse Earth," Roy Scranton, Jonathan Franzen, Jem Bendell, and the rest of the lot. It was to climate doom porn what Shakespeare is to modern literature. It defined the genre, and its success generated considerable additional demand for more of the same. And make no mistake: climate doom porn *does* sell. "The Uninhabitable Earth" was the most read article in the history of *New York Magazine*.[95] Perhaps it's for the same reason people ride rollercoasters, engage in bungee jumping, or go skydiving—they sometimes just want to be scared out of their wits. Climate doom ostensibly gives them that same rush of adrenaline. Am I calling it a drug? I guess so. Am I calling its purveyors pushers? I guess, in a sense, I am.

It is perhaps redundant to say that an article entitled "The Uninhabitable Earth" presents an overly bleak view of our climate future. And the subtitle doubles down on the doom: "Famine, Economic Collapse, a Sun That Cooks Us: What Climate Change Could Wreak—Sooner Than You Think." But extraordinary claims, as Carl Sagan famously said, require extraordinary evidence. Does the article deliver?

I expressed my concern about the article initially in a Facebook post. "The evidence that climate change is a serious problem that we must contend with now," I wrote, "is overwhelming on its own. There is no need to overstate the evidence, particularly when it feeds a paralyzing narrative of doom and hopelessness. I'm afraid this latest article does that. That's too bad. The journalist is clearly a talented one, and this is somewhat of a lost opportunity to objectively inform the discourse over human-caused climate change."[96] I expanded on my critique in an op-ed I coauthored for the *Washington Post* warning against the threat of doomist thinking, using "The Uninhabitable Earth" as the central example.[97]

My fundamental point of contention will be familiar to readers by now because it reflects a recurrent problem: the overly pessimistic and bleak depiction of our prospects for averting catastrophic climate change based on overstatement of climate-change impacts. "Uninhabitable Earth" exaggerates, for example, the near-term threat of climate "feedbacks" involving the release of currently trapped methane. The scientific evidence, as we have already seen, doesn't support the notion of a game-changing, planet-melting methane bomb of the sort the article envisions.

The article incorrectly asserts that the planet is warming "more than twice as fast as scientists had thought." That statement was false. The study the article refers to simply showed that one particular satellite temperature dataset that had tended to show *less* warming than other datasets has now been brought in line with them after some problems were corrected for.[98] In fact, recent research (including work I was involved in) shows that past climate model simulations actually slightly *overpredicted* the warming during the first decade of the twenty-first century.[99] Once appropriate corrections are made, it turns out the models and observations are pretty much in line. While some climate-change impacts, like ice melt and sea-level rise, are indeed proceeding faster than the models predicted, the warming of the planet's surface is progressing pretty much as forecast. And that is plenty bad enough.

One could dismiss isolated mischaracterizations of the scientific evidence as innocent and innocuous oversights. But when there are many of them, and they all seem to point in the same direction—toward exaggerating the magnitude and pace of climate change—it suggests a cherry-picking of the evidence to support a particular narrative: a narrative of doom, in this case.

Even the story about the Svalbard seed vault that opens the article is, at best, misleading. Wallace-Wells begins his piece with "This past winter, a string of days 60 and 70 degrees warmer than normal baked the North Pole, melting the permafrost that encased Norway's Svalbard seed vault—a global food bank nicknamed 'Doomsday,' designed to ensure that our agriculture survives any catastrophe, and which appeared to have been flooded by climate change less than ten years after being built."

It's a nice story. But it's not true. I actually saw the vault a year after Wallace-Wells had written his piece, in October 2018, while attending a climate-change workshop on "Navigating Climate Risk" in Svalbard.[100] The vault was just fine. One of its founders explained that there really never was any flood. Rather, every year when the snow melts on the mountain, they get some water coming in at the top of the tunnel that leads to the seed vault. It's happened every year since it's been open, and they're working to address it.[101]

I'm just one scientist, and perhaps you might dismiss my concerns about the article as biased. After all, I was interviewed by Wallace-Wells at length and not mentioned or quoted. Perhaps there are sour grapes on my part?[102] Fortunately, you don't have to take my word for it. Climate Feedback is a climate-scientist-run website that evaluates the factual basis, reliability, and credibility of climate-themed articles that appear in the media based on evaluation by a panel of leading experts. Climate Feedback evaluated "Uninhabitable Earth."[103]

To be more specific, Climate Feedback had the article evaluated by fourteen climate scientists chosen for their expertise across the range of issues covered by the article (three more were added after the initial deadline, bringing the total to seventeen). The article earned an average scientific credibility score of –0.7 on a scale that goes from –2 (very low) to +2 (very high). A score of –0.7 puts it just above –1 (low). Climate Feedback provided the following summary: "Seventeen scientists analyzed the article and estimated its overall scientific credibility to be 'low.' A majority of reviewers tagged the article as: Alarmist, Imprecise/Unclear, Misleading."[104] It's one thing to be *alarmed*—and we should be given the evidence. It's something else to be *alarmist*—a term that implies an unfounded, potentially harmful exaggeration of risk or danger.

Some felt this critique was unfair. David Roberts, who, as we have seen, occasionally weighs in with pessimistic and doomist-sympathetic views of his own, dismissed the criticisms by scientists like myself as "off-base scientific niggling."[105] Does he have a point? Scientists, after all, are biased toward, well, the science. They might not, for example, appreciate the poetic license sometimes required for effective journalism. In November 2017, I participated in an event that was part of the New York University Arthur L. Carter Journalism Institute's Kavli Conversations on Science Communication. The host was Dan Fagan, professor of journalism and director of NYU's Science, Health and Environmental Reporting Program. The event was called "The 'Doomed Earth' Controversy" and billed as "The author of the controversial *New York Magazine* cover story about worst-case climate scenarios in conversation with a prominent critic."[106] Yes, that's Wallace-Wells and me, respectively. The discussion was moderated by Robert Lee Hotz, a science writer at the *Wall*

Street Journal and a Distinguished Writer in Residence at the NYU Journalism Institute.

After having listened to the roughly forty-five-minute discussion between the three of us (where there was actually more agreement than disagreement), host Dan Fagan took the floor and issued his verdict. He began by expressing his appreciation of a "great discussion" and went on to note that a journalist's "first obligation is to reflect reality." While he "salute[d] David for his piece because . . . all pieces of the bell curve . . . should be written about," he also criticized it. His main concern was that while it "had . . . boilerplate [language] . . . about likelihood, it felt . . . tossed in and it certainly wasn't part of the overall framing of the piece." The piece wasn't clear on "Is this happening in five years? Is this happening in a century?" and as a result it "violated some of the rules that I've been teaching." Namely, the article was "inadequately contextualized," though Fagan appreciated that Wallace-Wells was "operating from the frustration that many of us feel."

Wallace-Wells seemed to have taken the criticism to heart. In August 2018 he asked me to comment on the full-length book version of the article, also to be titled *The Uninhabitable Earth*. The way he described it gave me optimism: "The book is . . . in part a revision and expansion of [the] article," he said. It was "focused less on worst-case scenarios, and in part [was] a more essayistic meditation on what it will mean, for politics and culture etc., to live in a world transformed by climate change in the coming decades." He asked me to review the prologue in particular, which, as he put it, "frames the whole project." He told me to be "ruthless" in my assessment. I appreciated the opportunity and was happy to oblige. I read it over and reported back to him a few days later. I told him that "the science is solid," but that I had "a number of minor comments" (nine of them, to be specific) that I felt should be addressed. I outlined them for him.

Among my main points, I said that "the claim that 'few experts think we'll hit' the 2C target seems misleading. . . . Many experts have pointed out a viable path to 2C. . . . There are no physical obstacles to 2C stabilization. Only political ones—at this point." I also said, "The claim that none of the industrial nations are on track to meet their Paris commitments is questionable. Some analyses suggest that the U.S. is very much on target to do so . . . and China, the world's largest emitter (!) is on course to exceed its targets. That's the world's two largest emitters right there." Finally, I pointed out, "You say that scenarios exceeding 2C warming are shrouded, delicately, from view. By whom? Certainly not the scientific community. 'Business as Usual' warming scenarios of 4–5C are prominent in the IPCC reports, other scientific assessments, and many popular articles about climate change. If you mean that *journalists* (and the media) are shrouding these scenarios from view then [you] should say so."

The book came out in February 2019. I was disappointed to find that no substantive changes were made in the prologue in response to the points I had raised. As far as the rest of the book is concerned, while the sorts of blatant errors that marred the original article were largely gone, the pessimistic—and, at times, downright doomist—framing remained, as did exaggerated descriptions that fed the doomist narrative. Consider, for example, this passage:

> Some [climate feedbacks] work in [the] direction [of] moderating climate change. But many more point toward an acceleration of warming, should we trigger them. And just how these complicated, countervailing systems will interact—what effects will be exaggerated and what undermined by feedbacks—is unknown, which pulls a dark cloud of uncertainty over any effort to plan ahead for the climate future. We know what a best-case outcome for climate change looks like, however unrealistic, because it quite closely resembles the world as we live on it today. But we have not yet begun to contemplate those *cascades that may bring us to the infernal range of the bell curve* [emphasis added].[107]

The prose gives a reader the impression that there are all sorts of positive feedbacks that climate scientists haven't even "contemplated." And if "cascades that may bring us to the infernal range of the bell curve" isn't a doomist dog whistle for unjustified "runaway warming" scares, I don't know what is. This passage—and many others in the book—would lead readers to assume that we are completely flying blind with regard to climate change. It implies that climate projections are completely unreliable (reminiscent of the claims made by climate-change deniers). A reader would never suspect that, in fact, climate models (1) have done a remarkable job predicting the increase in global temperature over the past half century, and (2) show no evidence of the sort of "infernal cascade" Wallace-Wells asks us to fear.[108]

The publisher (Penguin Random House) features quotations from a variety of impressed reviewers on its webpage for the book. It's hardly surprising that most of these reviewers expressed alarm over what the book describes. One said "*The Uninhabitable Earth* hits you like a comet, with an overflow of insanely lyrical prose about our pending Armageddon." Another said, "*The Uninhabitable Earth* is the most terrifying book I have ever read." Yet another said "its mode is Old Testament" and called it a "white-knuckled tour through the cascading catastrophes that will soon engulf our warming planet."[109] This is climate doom porn. And, as I said before, climate doom porn sells. After its release on February 20, the book was on the *New York Times* Hardcover Nonfiction Best Sellers List for six weeks in a row.

If you still can't get enough of it, then have no fear, for the doom will be televised. HBO is turning *The Uninhabitable Earth* into a series. Well, sort of. According to Yessenia Funes of *Gizmodo*, it will "influence a fictional anthology series that examines what our future may look like as climate change progresses." The director, Adam McKay, "will help visualize the gloom and doom in all its horrible glory for the show's first episode." Funes doesn't hide her enthusiasm: "I am here for it. Let's freak everyone the hell out."[110] If you thought you just heard me groan, it's because you just heard me groan.

I was invited to appear with Wallace-Wells on the MSNBC *Morning Joe* program shortly after the publication of the book.[111] One of the show's hosts, Mika Brzezinski, opened with, "It could be a world of . . . mass extinctions and economic calamity. Our next guest argues that *fear* may be the only thing that saves us." Asked about how bad things are going to get, the first words out of Wallace-Wells's mouth were, "It looks pretty bleak." What ensued, however, was a more balanced and nuanced discussion about both the costs of inaction and the need to take action. I imagine that my participation in the segment helped steer the conversation in that direction.

During the commercial break, host Willie Geist turned to Wallace-Wells and said, "Isn't there any good news?" I joked, "I think that's what I'm here for." Then, back on the air, Geist turned to me and asked, in closing, "What's the good news you can tell people about climate change right now?" I pointed out that "there is urgency, as David has said, but there's also agency" (my first use of that framing). I went on to talk about how the conversation is now changing, with even some Republicans starting to come to the table. (We'll talk more about that in the next chapter.)

Wallace-Wells nonetheless continued with rather doomist language in his engagement with the public. A few days after the MSNBC segment, he did an interview with a reporter from *Vox*, Sean Illing. Illing titled his piece "It Is Absolutely Time to Panic About Climate Change: Author David Wallace-Wells on the Dystopian Hellscape That Awaits Us." Wallace-Wells told Illing, "As someone who was awakened from complacency into environmental advocacy through alarm, I see real value in fear."[112]

Wallace-Wells occasionally weighs in on Twitter with alarmist commentary that requires correction by climate scientists. For example, in September 2019 he tweeted that "the world could hit 1.5C—the target of all global climate action—as soon as 2021. It could hit 2C—'catastrophic warming' by 2025."[113] That's wrong. It's the result of an erroneous extrapolation of a claim someone had tweeted that "temperatures [are] up . . . 0.2°C just between 2011 and 2015."[114] No climate scientist would ever try to measure the warming trend based on a five-year period because of the huge amount of "noise" in measuring temperature differences from year to year. Things like El Niño and volcanic eruptions can skew short-term readings.

The true warming rate is about 0.2°C (~0.4°F) per *decade*. Since current warming stands at about 1.2°C (~2.2°F), it would at current rates take a decade and a half to reach 1.5°C (2.7°F) warming, and another two and a half decades to reach 2°C (3.6°F) warming. But even if we used the incorrect estimate of 0.2°C per five years, Wallace-Wells's math is still wrong. We wouldn't reach 1.5°C for the better part of a decade, and we wouldn't reach 2°C for another twenty years. So it's puzzling how Wallace-Wells came up with his numbers in the first place. What's clear is that it fits with a narrative of impending doom.

Climate scientists immediately corrected Wallace-Wells. Richard Betts noted, "Even if this extrapolation were correct (it isn't), a single year at 2C is not going to be 'catastrophic.' 2C above pre-industrial for decades would indeed bring profound & possibly self-reinforcing changes, but simply hitting 2C for the first time will not make it all kick off."[115] Eric Steig was more blunt: "This is the kind of thing that makes me want to say . . . 'leave the science communication to scientists' . . . it's utterly irresponsible and wrong."[116]

Wallace-Wells also continues to mischaracterize the progress that is being made on the policy front. In a December 2019 article in *New York Magazine*, referring to the Conference of the Parties in Madrid, he wrote, "It was, of course, the 25th COP, and judging by the only metric that matters—carbon emissions, which continue to rise—the conference followed 24 consecutive failures. Emissions set a new record in 2018, and are poised to set another again in 2019. Just three years since the signing of the Paris accords, no major industrial nation on Earth is on track to honor the commitments it made in Paris."[117] There are *all kinds of* wrong here.

First of all, he's just wrong. Emissions remained flat in 2019, with power-sector emissions actually dropping, and total emissions are poised to drop in 2020 (though in the latter case that's at least in part due to the COVID-19 pandemic). To quote the International Energy Agency (IEA), "Emissions trends for 2019 suggest clean energy transitions are underway, led by the power sector. Global power sector emissions declined by some 170 Mt [million metric tons], or 1.2%, with the biggest falls taking place in advanced economies where CO_2 emissions have dropped to levels not seen since the late 1980s (when electricity demand was one-third lower)."[118] We would like to be seeing them not just flattening but declining. However, it's wrong to claim they are rising or to ignore the transition that is clearly underway toward a renewable-energy-driven economy.

What about Wallace-Wells's assertion that no major industrial nations are on track to honor their 2015 Paris Agreement commitments? I challenged him on this very matter when reviewing the draft prologue of his book. He failed to make any changes, and he repeats the misleading claim here. China, the world's largest emitter, is on course to meet its Paris target early.[119] The United States may meet its obligations in spite of the Trump administration's policies.[120] While there are criticisms to be made about the limits of the Paris Agreement, and there are certainly countries that are failing to live up to their commitments, it's simply not the case that no major industrial nation is on track to honor its Paris obligations.

These errors and mischaracterizations aren't innocuous—they are in service of the doomist narrative Wallace-Wells continues to promote. He argues that the existing framework (the United Nations Framework Convention on Climate Change, or UNFCC, and the annual Conferences of the Parties) for global climate negotiations has failed us and should be abandoned. Instead, he insists, it should be replaced with something akin to an international version of the Green New Deal. He points to the perceived failure of the most recent climate negotiations in Madrid as motivation for this position.

This argument is misguided on several levels.[121] Not only does it engage in unhelpful despair-mongering, but it takes entirely the wrong message away from what transpired in December 2019 at the COP25 in Madrid. A small number of nations led by fossil-fuel-friendly regimes, including Australia, in essence conspired to sabotage the negotiations. Blaming the "COP model" and attributing blame broadly provides cover for, and enables, the relatively small number of bad state actors that are attempting to poison the well.

This current obstacle is a consequence of an unfavorable geopolitical playing field that has allowed oligarchs and demagogues to rise to power in those countries in recent years. No alternative model for international climate cooperation is likely to circumvent that obstacle. Certainly not one based on, as Wallace-Wells is suggesting, a globalized version of the Green New Deal, which already carries ideological baggage and comes with so much opposition already baked in.

Wallace-Wells, moreover, by dismissing the entire history of efforts by the UNFCC and previous COPs, based on disappointment with COP25, is truly throwing the baby out with the bathwater. He is neglecting, for example, the highly successful COP21 Paris meeting in 2015, in which the nations of the world committed to substantial carbon emissions reductions. While those reductions don't alone solve the problem (they get us almost halfway to limiting warming below 2°C), and not every nation will meet its targets, the Paris Agreement was a monumental achievement. It put a framework in place for ratcheting up commitments as international negotiations proceed in subsequent COPs.[122]

Wallace-Wells, perhaps unsurprisingly, objected to these criticisms. He tweeted, "I haven't given up on the COP/UN model, but I don't think considering whether alternate approaches might be more effective is 'doomist.' We need to make progress wherever we can, and the European Green Deal (for instance) suggests at least one hopeful alternative (as I mention)."[123] Kalee Kreider is the head of communications at the National Geographic Society, former communications director for Al Gore, and a senior adviser to the United Nations Foundation. She took some offense to Wallace-Wells's dismissive comments about decades of climate policy efforts by the United Nations that she and so many others had contributed to. She replied to his tweet, sardonically, "*Cough*, the Paris Agreement was a US-China deal that then the rest of the world followed. *Cough*. That was how it got done" (emphasis added). In a subsequent tweet she linked to a November 2014 bilateral agreement between the United States and China, the world's two largest emitters, that laid the groundwork for the highly successful Paris international climate agreement.[124]

It is important that we hold our policymakers accountable for taking concerted action on climate, as activists like Greta Thunberg have done. But it's not constructive to dismiss the real progress that is being made, for it plays into the agenda of the inactivists, who have attempted to sabotage climate progress—including the 2019 COP25 negotiations. They would like nothing more than to see us throw up our hands in defeat and declare international climate negotiations dead.

I fear that defeatist rhetoric like Wallace-Wells's not only throws climate leaders who have spent their lives pushing for climate progress under the bus but also rewards the bad-faith efforts of inactivists. I suspect, moreover, that the attitude is contagious. Greta Thunberg not only follows Wallace-Wells on Twitter but retweets his often pessimistic missives.[125] In her January 2019 speech at the World Economic Forum in Davos, she declared that "pretty much nothing has been done" on climate change.[126] Not *enough* is being done, for sure, but to say that "nothing has been done" is simply false. It is dismissive of the actions that countries, states, cities, companies, and individuals are taking every day to help move us off fossil fuels, and it is dispiriting to the individuals who have worked so hard to improve the situation. It also neglects the hard data from the International Energy Agency demonstrating that we are indeed making progress toward decarbonizing the global economy.

In what can only be described as a case of journalistic whiplash, just days after his pessimistic December 16, 2019, *New York Magazine* article, Wallace-Wells published another piece in in the same magazine expressing a rather glowingly optimistic outlook. Titled "We're Getting a Clearer Picture of the Climate Future—and It's Not as Bad as It Once Looked," the piece, which came out on December 20, had the tag line: "Good News on Climate Change: Worst-Case Looks Unrealistic."[127] The basis of the article was an opinion piece that had just been published in *Nature,* the subtitle of which almost sounded like it was intended specifically for Wallace-Wells: "Stop Using the Worst-Case Scenario for Climate Warming as the Most Likely Outcome."[128] The piece didn't actually cast doubt on worst-case climate responses. It didn't in any way provide new evidence ruling out climate surprises or aggravating feedback mechanisms. It simply argued that the "business-as-usual" trajectory now points toward lower carbon emissions. Why? Because of the *policy progress* that is being made in decarbonizing our economy. The commentary, in short, challenged Wallace-Wells's basic thesis.

DOOMISM MEETS ALARMISM

The inactivists promote doomism for at least two different reasons. First, it leads to disengagement. It's another way to dampen enthusiasm among climate advocates and activists—simply convince them it's too late to do anything. But there's actually another reason that inactivists seek to promote doomism. To the extent that it can be portrayed as *alarmism,* it feeds a basic anti-environmental trope that has been a staple of inactivists for decades. As environmental author Alistair McIntosh succinctly put it, "by exceeding the consensus expert science whilst claiming to be based on it, [doomism] feeds denialists by discrediting real science . . . and it sets followers up for disillusion."[129]

Recall the attacks on Rachel Carson by industry groups back in the 1960s. She was denounced as "radical," "communist," "hysterical," "a fanatic defender of the cult of the balance of nature," and a mass murderer.[130] These slanders continue to this day: the fossil-fuel-funded Competitive Enterprise Institute currently claims that "millions of people around the world suffer the painful and often deadly effects of malaria because one person sounded *a false alarm* . . . that person is Rachel Carson" (emphasis added).[131]

Similar accusations were made against Paul Ehrlich, of *The Population Bomb* (1968) fame, whose early warnings of the impact of unrestricted resource depletion have ultimately proven prophetic;

against scientist and science communicator extraordinaire Carl Sagan; and against early climate messengers Stephen Schneider and James Hansen.[132] I myself am regularly dismissed as an "alarmist" by right-wing groups. Indeed, on the day that I wrote this paragraph I was called "the *most* staunch climate alarmist scientist" (emphasis added) in a commentary by CNS News, which is a project of the Media Research Center, a front group for fossil fuel interests and the right-wing Scaife family.[133]

For decades, "false alarm" and "alarmism" have been the rallying calls of conservative interest groups looking to discredit environmental concern—including climate change—as henny-pennyism. A favorite claim relates to the late great climate scientist and science communicator Stephen Schneider. In the early 1970s, when there was still some uncertainty about the relative impacts of warming from greenhouse gases and cooling from sulfur dioxide aerosol pollution, Schneider and coauthor S. Ichtiaque Rasool speculated that the latter effect might win out if sulfur emissions continued to accelerate. That didn't happen because the United States and other industrial nations passed clean air acts in response to the growing acid rain problem. These measures required sulfur dioxide to be "scrubbed" from smokestack emissions prior to entering the atmosphere.[134]

The fact that some scientists—like Schneider—were still wrestling with the competing effects of aerosol cooling and greenhouse warming in the early 1970s has nonetheless given rise to a widespread canard: the notion that "climate scientists were predicting an ice age in the 1970s." The implication is that if scientists so completely botched their predictions back then, why should we trust them now? The reality is (1) they didn't botch the predictions (they just couldn't predict the passage of the clean air acts), and (2) there was no scientific consensus about cooling in the 1970s, just a few scientists, like Schneider, speculating about that possibility.[135] But the notion of a discredited "1970s global cooling scare" has proven an enduring myth that denialists have continued to seize upon. During congressional testimony I gave in July 2006, for instance, climate-change-denying congresswoman Marsha Blackburn (R-TN) attempted to lecture me about how she "remembered" when she was growing up in the 1960s that climate scientists were worried about another ice age. She had obviously failed to study her denialist talking points closely enough, since the claim is supposed to be about the 1970s.[136]

It's hardly surprising that the forces of inaction would still be exploiting doomist narratives today. They can easily be caricatured as alarmism. "Prophets of doom" is the way Donald Trump described those who were advocating action on climate at the January 2020 World Economic Forum in Davos. Ideally, the accusation of alarmism is paired with the shopworn claim that climate scientists are promoting climate doom only to line their pockets with grant money.[137] There's nothing that fires up the conservative base more than right-wing pundits calling out "alarmist scientists who get . . . $89 billion in US government research money" by promoting doomist prophecies.[138] The doomists have made it all too easy for them.

Consider, for example, Jem Bendell's over-the-top "Deep Adaptation" article, which was the inspiration for Alistair McIntosh's warning about how doomism can feed denialism by playing into the agenda of the forces of anti-science.[139] McIntosh referred to a 1956 book, *When Prophecy Fails*, which uses the example of one particular doomsday cult to demonstrate the phenomenon. But a very specific example is at hand here.

Ronald Bailey, the author of *Global Warming and Other Eco Myths: How the Environmental Movement Uses False Science to Scare Us to Death*, reviewed Bendell's article for the libertarian magazine *Reason* in a piece titled "Good News! No Need to Have a Mental Breakdown over 'Climate Collapse.'"[140] In his commentary, Bailey invoked Paul Ehrlich, one of the inactivists' favored punching bags, to ridicule Bendell: "Ehrlich is still predicting an imminent ecological apocalypse and I suspect that Bendell will be doing the same thing in the year 2065." Bailey used Bendell's "concocted case for collapse fatalism" quite effectively to mock concern about climate change.

The "Hothouse Earth" article has also been used to caricature climate concern as an alarmist charade. The *Daily Caller*—which I've called "a Koch front group masquerading as a media outlet"—regularly features attacks on climate science and climate scientists.[141] "Scientists Issue 'Absurd' Doomsday Prediction," read its headline about "Hothouse Earth."[142] The *Caller*'s climate contrarian "energy editor," Michael Bastasch, proceeded to exploit the actual alarmist excesses of the article as an excuse to launch into boilerplate attacks on climate science (for example, "climate models have regularly over-predicted temperature rise"—no, as we have already seen, they haven't) and climate action (quoting, for example, climate contrarian Roger Pielke Sr., who said that an "absurd" emphasis on climate-change impacts "[harm] actual effective policies with reducing risks from extreme weather and other threats"[143]). Bastasch ends by warning of personal sacrifice, attempting to scare his conservative readers into thinking that the *true* threat is aggressive climate action and the dramatic lifestyle changes it will purportedly demand, which "means no fossil fuels . . . reducing consumption and a whole host of other activities." (The reality, of course, is that climate *inaction* is the greater threat to the economy and our way of life.)

Naturally, the Murdoch media is replete with "false-alarm" climate framing. Consider climate-change denier Miranda Devine, formerly of the Murdoch-owned Australian *Daily Telegraph*, *Sunday Telegraph*, and *Herald Sun*, who now pens columns for the Murdoch-owned *New York Post*. In the wake of the devastating Australian bushfires of the summer of 2019/2020, Devine wrote a column for the *Post* titled "Celebrities, Activists Using Australia Bushfire Crisis to Push Dangerous Climate Change Myth."[144] In the piece, she proceeded to dismiss the well-established linkages between climate change and the unprecedented wildfires based on the standard denialist canards. This included attributing the fires to "arson," "green groups," misguided "hazard protection," and "biodiversity" preservation policies. But her core message was summed up in this single sentence, "Whether or not you believe the most dire predictions of climate alarmists makes no difference. We can't dial down the Earth's temperature any more than we can lock up every teenage arsonist." Such a neat little package of denial, doomism, and deflection wrapped up and topped off with charges of alarmism. To err is Devine. To forgive is . . . well, difficult, in this case.

I have seen my own words misrepresented and weaponized by denialist media figures in an effort to portray the climate science community as doomist alarmists. A case in point involves the *Boston Globe*'s resident climate-change denier, Jeff Jacoby. His mischaracterizations of climate science have some scientists howling. They are so egregious that MIT climate scientist Kerry Emanuel, a Republican and political conservative, wrote a letter to the *Globe* in which he chastised Jacoby for presenting "a false choice between panic and the denial of risk." He went on to admonish the *Globe* for publishing a particular commentary that Jacoby had written: "Assessing and dealing with climate risk in an environment of highly uncertain science and expensive options is challenging enough without having to entertain the flippancy of your columnist."[145]

In a *Globe* column from March 15, 2020, "I'm Skeptical About Climate Alarmism, but I Take Coronavirus Fears Seriously," Jacoby quoted me in a way that implied that I myself had accused the climate science community of alarmism.[146] He wrote, "The horrors of pandemics have been documented and depicted often. Yet while climate activists have been forecasting world-ending doomsday scenarios since the 1960s, the apocalypse never seems to materialize." To support his claim, Jacoby then pointed to "facts" from the fossil-fuel-funded, climate-change-denying Competitive Enterprise Institute (rather than legitimate archival evidence). "Although climate is always in flux," he wrote, "unmitigated anthropogenic warming would doubtless lead to cataclysm. But human societies have a genius for mitigating and adapting their way out of existential threats. Which is why it's dangerous, as climatologist Michael Mann has written, to overstate the science of global warming 'in a way that presents the problem as unsolvable, and feeds a sense of doom, inevitability, and hopelessness.'" The source of this quote was my Facebook post criticizing David Wallace-Wells's doomist 2017 *New York Magazine* "Uninhabitable Earth" column.[147]

My actual position was, of course, very much the opposite of what Jacoby had implied. In a letter to the *Globe*, I responded,

> The truth is bad enough when it comes to the devastating impacts of climate change, which include unprecedented floods, heat waves, drought, and wildfires that are now unfolding around the world. . . .
>
> The evidence is clear that climate change is a serious challenge we must tackle now. There's no need to exaggerate it, particularly when it feeds a paralyzing narrative of doom and hopelessness.
>
> There is still time to avoid the worst outcomes, if we act boldly now, not out of fear, but out of confidence that the future is still largely in our hands. That sentiment hardly supports Jacoby's narrative of climate change as an overblown problem or one that lacks urgency.
>
> While we have only days to flatten the curve of the coronavirus, we've had years to flatten the curve of CO_2 emissions. Unfortunately, thanks in part to people like Jacoby, we're still currently on the climate pandemic path.[148]

A PATH FORWARD

It is important to communicate both the threat and the opportunity in the climate challenge. I learned this the hard way. For years my standard public lecture on climate change focused only on the science and the impacts, because I am a scientist. I would then pay lip service to "climate solutions," with the obligatory final slide depicting a montage of recycling efforts, wind turbines, solar panels, and the like. I was fortunate that my audiences were made up of thoughtful and sharing folks. And when they would linger afterward to talk with me, I heard the same thing over and over: "That was a great presentation. But it left me so *depressed*!"

My vanity led me to hear only the compliment and not the admonition that followed it. But the fact is that my presentation, by definition, was not *great*. It was *deficient*. I hadn't thought deeply about our predicament, and as a result I wasn't in a position to report on it responsibly. But I was inspired to do my due diligence and to inform myself about where we really stood, and what was truly necessary to avert catastrophe—to study the literature, crunch the numbers, and figure out how far down the climate-change highway we've gone and what exit ramps are still realistically available to us.

I can tell you that those who are paying attention are worried, as they should be, but there are also reasons for hope. The active engagement of many cities, states, and corporations, and the commitments of virtually every nation (with the United States currently a wildcard as this book goes to press), are very hopeful signs. The rapid movement in the global energy market toward cleaner options is another sign of hope. Experts are laying out pathways to avoid disastrous levels of climate change, and clearly expressing the urgency of action.[149] There is still time to avoid the worst outcomes if—to repeat myself—we act boldly now, not out of fear, but out of confidence that the future is largely in our hands.

What is the antidote to irrational, disabling, doom-and-gloom "futility messaging"? Motivating hope that is grounded in entirely legitimate and defensible reasons for cautious optimism that the worst can still be averted. Recognizing that some harm has already occurred, and that some additional harm is inevitable, provides some needed perspective. It's not a matter of whether we're "effed," after all. It's a matter of *how* "effed" we are.

Let us in this context revisit the two epigraphs that began this chapter, for they address the challenge we face. First is the famous Franklin D. Roosevelt quote: *"The only thing we have to fear is . . . fear itself—nameless, unreasoning, unjustified terror which paralyzes needed efforts to convert retreat into advance."* Roosevelt's famous admonition describes our climate predicament to a T; the surest path to catastrophic climate change is the false belief that it's too late to act.

Then there is the second quote, by the German literary critic, novelist, and essayist Christa Wolf: *"The word 'catastrophe' is not permitted as long as there is danger of catastrophe turning to doom."* It has become fashionable in the climate discourse to use terms like "catastrophe," "emergency," and even "extinction." We must not allow the policing of language to be used as wedge to divide us. But we cannot let words be used in a manner that robs us of agency. Once again it is important to convey both *urgency* and *agency* in talking about the challenge we face. Personally, I like to speak of the "climate crisis," as it embraces both elements (a "crisis," after all, is defined as "a time when a difficult or important decision must be made").

We do not face a scenario of near-term societal collapse or human extinction. The only assurance of such scenarios would be our abject failure to act. If there were not still a chance of prevailing in the climate battle, I would not be devoting my life to communicating the science and its implications to the public and policymakers. I know we can still avert catastrophe. And I speak with some authority on the matter. As a scientist who is still engaged in climate research, my views are informed by hard numbers and facts. In the final chapter of the book, we confront the remaining front in the new climate war—ourselves, our own self-doubt that we have it within ourselves as a species to meet the challenge at hand.

CHAPTER 9

Meeting the Challenge

The darkest hour is just before the dawn.
— THOMAS FULLER

Hope is a good thing, maybe the best of things, and no good thing ever dies.
— ANDY DUFRESNE (in *The Shawshank Redemption*)

DESPITE THE CHALLENGES DETAILED IN THIS BOOK, I AM CAU-
tiously optimistic—that is to say, neither Pollyannaish, nor dour, but
objectively hopeful—about prospects for tackling the climate crisis
in the years ahead. The reason for that optimism is a confluence of
developments, a "perfect storm," if you will, of eye-opening events
that are helping to prepare us for the task ahead. First, there have
been a series of unprecedented, extreme weather disasters that have
vivified the climate-change threat. Second, a global pandemic has
now taught us key lessons about vulnerability and risk. And finally,
we've seen the reawakening of environmental activism, and, in particular, a popular uprising by children across the world that has
framed climate change as the defining challenge of our time.

The thesis of this book is that these developments—along with the
collapse of plausible climate-change deniability—have provided us
with an unprecedented opportunity for progress. The inactivists have
been forced into retreat from "hard" climate denial to "softer" denial:
downplaying, deflecting, dividing, delaying, and despair-mongering.
These are the multiple fronts of the new climate war. Any plan for

victory requires recognizing and defeating the tactics now being used by inactivists as they continue to wage war.

With immensely powerful vested interests aligned in defense of the fossil fuel status quo, it won't come without a fight. We will need the active participation of citizens everywhere aiding in the collective push forward. And we need to believe that it is possible. And it is. We can win the battle for our planet.

THE DENIAL DEATH SPIRAL

When *Washington Post* editorial cartoonist Tom Toles and I published our book *The Madhouse Effect* in the early fall of 2016, colleagues criticized us for writing a book about climate-change denial.[1] The age of denial, they said, was over. The discussion from here on out would be all about *solutions*.

But subsequent history did not cooperate. Climate-change denier Donald Trump was then elected leader of the world's most powerful country. During his administration we've seen the United States go from a leader in worldwide efforts to combat climate change to the only country threatening to withdraw from the 2015 Paris Agreement. We saw a veritable dismantling of fifty years' worth of environmental policy progress in the United States. The intransigence of the United States gave other polluters, such as China, an excuse to ease off on their own efforts. As a result, after flatlining for several years, and appearing to be poised to decline, carbon emissions rose for several years instead.

Something else happened around the same time. We witnessed unprecedented climate-change-fueled weather disasters in the United States and around the world. They came in the form of record floods, wildfires, heat waves, droughts, and superstorms. Damaging, deadly weather extremes drove home the fact that climate change is no longer theoretical and distant. It's here and now. The damaging impacts of climate change had arrived. We know the litany by now: Hurricane Maria in Puerto Rico; flooding in Houston and the Carolinas; wildfires in California; historic drought, flooding, and plagues of locusts in Africa; flooding, heat, drought, and bushfires in Australia. The list goes on. And on. And on.

To quote Groucho Marx, "Who ya gonna believe, me or your lying eyes?"[2] Denial simply isn't viable when people can see the unprecedented impacts playing out in real time on their television scenes, their newspaper headlines, their social media feeds, and their backyards. And as a result, we are now seeing the last gasps of hard climate denial. We see it in the virtual disappearance of "false balance" in the mainstream media—the practice, widespread in the past, in which climate-change deniers were treated on a par with mainstream climate researchers when it came to journalistic climate coverage.[3]

Hard denial, today, is mostly confined to the media outposts of the fringe right, shoved to the edges of our discourse by a sliding "Overton window" driven toward reality by the stark facts on the ground. Climate denial operations are waning as fossil fuel interests and plutocrats reject their services in favor of the "kinder, gentler" forms of inactivism that make up the new climate war. The conservative Cato Institute, for example, closed up its climate-denial shop in 2019.[4]

The climate-denying Heartland Institute is increasingly ignored and unable to garner mainstream coverage.[5] Their 2019 "conference," held at the Trump International Hotel in Washington, DC, was reduced from the sprawling three days of its earlier incarnations to just a single-day affair. While it had attracted more than fifty sponsors in past years, it drew just sixteen in 2019—fifteen if you account for the fact that one was fake. Attendance was limited to a couple hundred attendees—predictably, given that the declining demographic of denialists is mostly older white men. Despite holding their "conference" at a Trump property and in Washington, DC, "no one from the Trump administration" was in attendance, a fact bemoaned by Heartland's "science director" (and convicted criminal) Jay Lehr.[6] Lehr insisted that this was "a huge loss" for the administration, since the conference would "reveal that neither science nor economics back up the climate scare." Heartland was forced to lay off staff in 2019.[7]

Even soft denial no longer seems to be getting the traction it once did. In June 2020, Michael Shellenberger, cofounder of the Breakthrough Institute, published a commentary titled "On Behalf of Environmentalists, I Apologize for the Climate Scare." Adopting the schtick of self-styled "Skeptical Environmentalist" Bjorn Lomborg, the piece engaged in the usual inactivist tropes of downplaying climate-change impacts and dismissing renewable energy, all out of alleged "concern" from an ostensibly reformed erstwhile "alarmist." The commentary was panned by the expert evaluators at Climate Feedback, who gave it an average credibility score of –1.2 (between "low" and "very low").[8] Shellenberger originally published the piece at *Forbes*, but they removed it within hours for violating their policies on self-promotion (he was essentially plugging his new book *Apocalypse Never: Why Environmental Alarmism Hurts Us All*). The commentary was subsequently republished by Murdoch's *Australian*. Shellenberger received coverage from the usual nexus of inactivism-promoting organizations and outlets (the Heartland Institute, Glenn Beck, Breitbart News, *Russia Today*, the *Daily Telegraph*, and the *Wall Street Journal*). But other than a critique by *The Guardian*, he got little mainstream coverage.[9]

Shortly thereafter, in mid-July, Bjorn Lomborg published his *own* book, *False Alarm*, once again offering up the same tired tropes. Nobel Prize–winning economist Joseph E. Stiglitz wrote a blistering review of the book for the *New York Times*, which ends thusly: "As a matter of policy, I typically decline to review books that deserve to be panned. . . . In the case of this book, though, I felt compelled to forgo this policy. Written with an aim to convert anyone worried about the dangers of climate change, Lomborg's work would be downright dangerous were it to succeed in persuading anyone that there was merit in its arguments. This book proves the aphorism that a little knowledge is dangerous. It's nominally about air pollution. It's really about mind pollution." There now seems to be little appetite for inactivist diatribes.

Republican communication experts recognize a sinking ship when they see one. Frank Luntz, the GOP messaging guru we encountered earlier, who coached climate-change-denying Republicans and fossil fuel interests on how to undermine public belief in human-caused climate change, has now flipped. In the summer of 2019 he testified to the US Senate's Special Committee on the Climate Crisis that "rising sea levels, melting ice caps, tornadoes, and hurricanes [are] more ferocious than ever. It is happening." He told the committee that he was "here before you to say that I was wrong in 2001"; now, he hoped to put "policies ahead of politics." He proceeded to advise the senators, based on wisdom derived from his polling and focus groups, on how best to frame the climate crisis to get buy-in from the electorate.[10]

Luntz is hardly alone. Douglas Heye, a former communications director at the Republican National Committee, warned of the threat to Republicans who continue to deny the climate crisis: "We're definitely sending a message to younger voters that we don't care about things that are very important to them. . . . This spells certain doom in the long term if there isn't a plan to admit reality and have legislative prescriptions for it."[11]

Republican policymakers seem to be getting the message, too. *Inside Climate News* noted that "an increasing number of Republican politicians have sought to distance themselves from climate denial." It cited the examples of House Minority Leader Kevin McCarthy of California, who recently "introduced a package of bills to promote carbon capture and sequestration technology," and Alaska senator Lisa Murkowski, who "has been attempting to lead a bipartisan effort to pass energy efficiency and technology investment."[12]

Even the fossil fuel industry has turned a corner, no longer denying that its product is warming the planet and changing the climate. In 2018, the cities of San Francisco and Oakland sued the oil companies BP, Chevron, ConocoPhillips, ExxonMobil, and Shell for the damages (due to sea-level rise) that they've caused, indirectly, through the extraction and sale of planet-warming fossil fuels. Citing the reports of the IPCC, a lawyer for Chevron, Theodore Boutrous Jr., assented unambiguously to the strength of the underlying science: "From Chevron's perspective, there is no debate about the science of climate change." The oil companies had admitted, in court, that, as *Grist* put it, "fossil fuels are the problem."[13]

You may have already guessed what came next. As *Grist* described it, Boutrous "twice read a quote from the IPCC that climate change is caused 'largely by economic and population growth.' Then, [he] added his interpretation. 'It doesn't say that it's the production and extraction that's driving the increase,' he said. 'It's the way people are living their lives.'" If you thought you heard a "ping" sound, that's because of the massive deflection we just witnessed.

If these proceedings were a bellwether, and I surely think they were, deniers have essentially thrown in the towel. When it comes to the war on the science—that is, the *old* climate war—the forces of denial have all but conceded defeat. But the new climate war—the war on *action*—is still actively being waged.

TIPPING POINTS—THE *GOOD* KIND

There is reason to be optimistic on the political side as well. The 2018 midterm elections in the United States resulted in a historic swing toward Democrats, ushering in prominent political "rock star" newcomers like Alexandria Ocasio-Cortez, who ran on a Green New Deal platform. Significantly, during the first climate-change hearing held by the House of Representatives' Science Committee under fresh new Democratic leadership, Republicans—seemingly aware of the dramatic shift in public perception—no longer sought to challenge the basic scientific evidence behind human-caused climate change. They instead argued for policy solutions consistent with their political ideology. We can argue over whether they are optimal solutions, but they go beyond the diversionary and deflective proposals we've seen from Republicans in the past, including mechanisms such as carbon pricing. There does now seem to be real political movement toward meaningful action on climate.

House Democrats put forward a bold climate plan in June 2020 that included incentives for renewables and support for carbon pricing.[14] Given an even modestly favorable shift in political winds, one could envision this passing the House and moving on to the Senate with a half dozen or more moderate conservatives crossing the aisle, joining with Senate Democrats to pass the bill within the next year or two. Indeed, it is a well-kept secret in Washington, DC, that many Republicans are quietly supportive of climate action but have been afraid to "come out of the closet" for fear of retribution from powerful ideological purists such as the Kochs and Mercers. *New York Times* columnist Justin Gillis met with one highly placed Republican operative who, requesting anonymity, acknowledged that "we are going to have to do a deal with the Democrats. We are waiting for the fever to cool."[15] I have also had amicable and productive anonymous meetings with prominent conservatives, including a well-known columnist for a Murdoch-owned Australian newspaper. That numerous Republican politicians and conservative opinion leaders *would* support climate action if they felt they were granted the license to do so by party power brokers adds to the notion that a climate-action tipping point could be looming in our near future.

This is not to say that it will be easy to pass climate legislation. Fossil fuel interests, ideologically driven plutocrats like Charles Koch, members of the Mercer and Scaife families, and the global Murdoch media empire are still doing all they can to muddy the waters and block progress. But, as we have seen, there are dramatic demographic shifts underway that favor action on climate. Frank Luntz's recent polling shows that Americans in general support carbon pricing by a four-to-one margin, and Republicans under the age of forty by an amazing six-to-one margin.[16] In short, climate denial is increasingly a liability, while the promise of climate action is an opportunity to win over younger voters.

History teaches us that social transitions are often not gradual but instead sudden and dramatic, and they don't even require a majority in support of change. A committed vocal minority can potentially push collective opinion past a "tipping point." A 2018 study suggested that "opinion of the majority [can] be tipped to that of the minority" once the latter reaches about 25 percent of the public.[17] We appear to have witnessed this phenomenon in action with the rather sudden, dramatic increase in support for marriage equality by Americans during the Obama years. According to Pew Research, public support for same-sex marriage rose from under 40 percent when Obama was elected to over 60 percent when he left office.[18]

Triggered by the horrific killing, captured on video, of a forty-six-year-old black man, George Floyd, by Minneapolis police, a similar tipping point on attitudes toward racial justice seems to have taken place in early summer 2020. One poll showed that the percentage of Americans who think that police are more likely to use excessive force against African Americans jumped from 33 percent to 57 percent. Public awareness and outrage led to massive demonstrations over the unjustified killing. Pollster Frank Luntz commented, "In my 35 years of polling, I've never seen opinion shift this fast or deeply. We are a different country today than just 30 days ago."[19]

It is not unreasonable to speculate that we might be close to such a tipping point on climate as well. According to a Pew Research poll in 2019, 67 percent of the public thinks we're doing too little to reduce the effects of climate change.[20] That, of course, doesn't mean that they prioritize it, or that they're actively pushing for action on climate. But another 2019 poll, conducted by CNN, found that "82 percent of registered voters who identified as Democrats or Democratic-leaning independents consider climate change a 'very important' top priority they'd like to see get the focus of a presidential candidate."[21] Let us account for the fact that roughly 80 percent of eligible citizens are registered, and that 40 percent of voters are Democrats and about 30 percent independent (which we'll conservatively assume split equally into 15 percent and 15 percent when it comes to which direction they lean).[22] That yields at least 36 percent of American citizens $(0.80 \times 0.55 \times 0.82)$ who reasonably define the "issue public" for climate action—that is, the set of people who prioritize the issue. That percentage exceeds the 25 percent theoretical threshold required for generating a societal tipping point. It is comparable to the percentage of the American public that supported marriage equality at the beginning of the Obama era, just before that tipping point was reached.

In other words, there's reason to believe that we are currently primed for a marriage-equality-like tipping point with climate action. There is still opposition, but the opposing forces in this case—which include the world's most powerful industrial sector, fossil fuels—are considerably stronger and better funded than those that opposed marriage equality (the religious right). That means that the forward push to get us past the tipping point has to be all that much harder. Fortunately, the forces of progress appear to be aligning in a favorable manner: the visceral evidence of a climate crisis is now before us; we are seeing the demise of denial and the rise of climate activism, particularly from the children's climate movement; and we are learning critical lessons even now from another global crisis, the 2020 coronavirus pandemic.

One group of climate experts has in fact published a set of "concrete interventions to induce positive social tipping dynamics." They propose, as key ingredients, "removing fossil-fuel subsidies and incentivizing decentralized energy generation, building carbon-neutral cities, divesting from assets linked to fossil fuels, revealing the moral implications of fossil fuels, strengthening climate education and engagement, and disclosing greenhouse gas emissions information."[23] A lot of these basic ingredients indeed seem to be in place, or close to being in place.

First of all, as we have already seen, the fossil fuel industry is starting to "feel the heat." Oil-rich Saudi Arabia has "shifted its strategy in the era of decarbonization" by lowering the price of oil exports in a desperate attempt to maintain demand.[24] Coal, the most carbon-intense fossil fuel, is in a death spiral. The state of New York, for example, has retired its last coal-fired power plant.[25] The Canadian mining giant Teck Resources has withdrawn plans for its $20 billion tar sands project.[26] Natural gas is increasingly being recognized not as a "bridge to the future," but as a liability to local communities.[27]

And now, the banking and finance industry is rethinking its role in funding new fossil fuel infrastructure. The primary reason is what is known as *transition risk*. As we choose to decarbonize our economy, demand for fossil fuels will wane. That makes fossil fuel extraction, production, refining, and transport all bad investments. The finance and investment community increasingly fears a bursting of the so-called carbon bubble.

As *Guardian* correspondent Fiona Harvey explained, "investments amounting to trillions of dollars in fossil fuels—coal mines, oil wells, power stations, conventional vehicles—will lose their value when the world moves decisively to a low-carbon economy. Fossil fuel reserves and production facilities will become stranded assets, having absorbed capital but unable to be used to make a profit." Harvey also pointed out that "this carbon bubble has been estimated at between $1tn and $4tn, a large chunk of the global economy's balance sheet. . . . Investors with high exposure to fossil fuels in their portfolios will be hurt, as those companies and assets cease to be profitable." Especially worrying, "If the bubble bursts suddenly, as [experts suggest] it might, rather than gradually deflating over decades, then it could trigger a financial crisis."[28]

There is another reason investors are rethinking their fossil fuel investments, however. It is a generalized notion of *fiduciary responsibility*, which can be defined as "the legal and ethical requirement [of a financial adviser] to put your best interest before their own."[29] An expansive view of this responsibility would require that portfolio managers not make decisions that will mortgage the planet for their clients' children and grandchildren.

Under Australian law, such an expansive view of fiduciary responsibility already applies to pension (or so-called superannuation) fund managers.[30] And it turns out that this has broad international implications, because Australia is home to the world's third-largest net pension holdings, worth just under $2 trillion (a consequence also of Australian law, which requires employers to contribute at least 9 percent of a worker's salary to a superannuation fund[31]). That means that the decisions of Australian "superfund" managers substantially leverage global investment. If Australian superfund managers choose not to invest in fossil fuel companies, it will have reverberations for the fossil fuel industry writ large.

I participated in meetings with several groups of Australian superfund managers in Sydney and Melbourne during my sabbatical in Australia in early 2020. Repeatedly they told me that they now view their investment decision-making through the lens of their larger responsibilities to their clients—in particular, their responsibility not to laden them with risky long-term fossil fuel investments, and their responsibility not to invest in an industry that threatens future livelihood and livability. These audiences were as hungry for detailed facts, figures, and assessments of risk as any I've ever encountered. I left those meetings with the sense that "it may be banking & finance, rather than national governments, that precipitate a climate action tipping point."[32]

There is considerable evidence to support that conjecture. Investors are already taking preemptive actions. According to Axel Weber, the chairman of Swiss multinational investment bank UBS, the finance sector is on the verge of "a big change in market structure" because investors are increasingly demanding that the sector account for climate risk and embed a price on carbon in their portfolio decisions.[33] Mark Carney, governor of the Bank of England, said in early 2020 that because climate change could make fossil fuel financial assets worthless in the future, he is considering imposing a "penalty" capital charge on them.[34]

Insurance giant The Hartford, Sweden's central bank, and Black-Rock, the world's largest asset manager, have indicated they will stop insuring or investing in Alberta's carbon-intensive tar sands oil production.[35] BlackRock has gone even further, announcing it will no longer make investments that come with high environmental risks, including coal for power plants.[36] Goldman Sachs, Liberty Mutual, and the European Investment Bank—the largest international public bank in the world—are among the numerous banks and investment firms that are now pulling away from fossil fuel investments.[37] In the space of a few days in early July 2020, three multibillion-dollar oil and natural gas pipeline projects in the United States—Atlantic Coast, Dakota Access, and Keystone XL, were at least temporarily halted due to what the *Washington Post* characterized as "legal defeats and business decisions."[38] The carbon bubble sure appears ready to pop.

Younger investors, who are far more likely to prioritize action on climate, are playing a particularly vital role here. Consider the actions of twenty-four-year-old Mark McVeigh, an environmental scientist who works for the Brisbane City Council. McVeigh has sued his pension fund for failing to account for climate-change-related damages in its investment decisions. The case is currently working its way through the court system.[39]

While we're talking about the role of young folks, let us consider the impact of fossil fuel divestment, a college-student-led movement. I think back to my first semester at UC Berkeley in the fall of 1984. I had not been politically active in high school. My choice to matriculate to Berkeley had nothing to do with its legacy as a fount of political activism. It had nothing to do with the role it played in the protests of McCarthyism in the 1940s and 1950s, in the civil rights and free-speech movements in the 1960s, or in the Vietnam War protests of the late 1960s and early 1970s. As an aspiring young scientist, I was attracted to UC Berkeley because of its reputation as one of the leading institutions for scientific education and research.

The mid-1980s marked the "Reagan Revolution." Shortly after my arrival that fall, on the night that Ronald Reagan was elected to his second term as president, I watched the Berkeley College Republicans march triumphantly across campus. Complacency had replaced activism even at Berkeley. But activism wasn't dead. It was simply dormant. The anti-apartheid movement—opposing the South African government's brutal and violent policy of discrimination against nonwhites—however, was brewing.

It came to a full boil in 1985. The UC Regents had nearly $5 billion invested in the South African government, more than any other university in the country, helping prop up this system of discrimination. UC Berkeley students demanded the university divest of its holdings. When the Regents resisted, the students held increasingly large and well-publicized sit-ins and protests on famous Sproul

Plaza, the very place where Berkeley students before them had protested in decades past. The students were unrelenting. And in July 1986, under great pressure from the student body, the Regents finally agreed to divest of holdings in the apartheid government and companies doing business with them. That triggered a nationwide divestment movement, and by 1988, 155 institutions of higher learning had chosen to divest.[40] In 1990, five years after the protests had begun at Berkeley, South Africa initiated the dissolution of apartheid. Students at Berkeley—and all across the nation—had helped "change the world."[41] I was part of it.

In 2014, more than two decades later, Berkeley students would once again stage protests in Sproul Plaza. This time it was to demand that the UC Regents divest of fossil fuel holdings. The argument was twofold. First, fossil fuel companies, through the extraction and sale of their product, were causing dangerous planetary warming. Therefore, as with apartheid, there was an obvious moral argument to be made—that the university shouldn't be encouraging harmful activities with their investments. But there was another, more pragmatic reason the student protest made sense: simply put, fossil fuel companies are now bad, risky investments. Their main assets—known but as yet untapped fossil fuel reserves—must ultimately be left stranded.

Fossil fuel divestment has now spread across the country. More than a thousand college campuses and other institutions throughout the United States (accounting for more than $11 trillion in holdings) have divested of fossil fuel stocks.[42] The UC Regents are among them. In September 2019, roughly thirty-three years after their fateful decision to divest from the South African apartheid government, they announced they were divesting of fossil fuel holdings.[43] If past is indeed prologue, we might just speculate that *perhaps* we're just a few years from the bursting of the carbon bubble.

It has been said that "the stone age didn't end for want of stones."[44] Nor is the fossil fuel age ending for want of fossil fuels. It's ending because we recognize that the burning of fossil fuels poses a threat to a sustainable future. But it's also ending because something better has come along: renewable energy. As we have seen, even in the absence of widespread carbon pricing or adequate subsidies, renewable energy is surging owing to the fact that people are embracing clean sources of energy that are ever more competitive with dirty fossil fuel energy.

There is increasingly a sense of inevitably now in the clean energy revolution. The International Energy Agency, as we learned earlier, reported that "clean energy transitions are underway." The IEA attributed the fall in power-sector carbon emissions and the flattening of overall carbon emissions in 2019 to a combination of wind, solar, and other renewable energy sources. Clean energy collectively saved 130 Mt of carbon dioxide from being emitted that same year.[45] This global picture is encouraging.

What we see at the national level is no less promising. In the United States we've crossed a critical milestone. Renewable energy capacity has now reached 250 gigawatts (a gigawatt is a billion watts), amounting to 20 percent of total power generation, a consequence of growth in installed wind and solar voltaic capacity, enhanced energy storage, and an increase in electric vehicle sales.[46] Renewables, for the first time, outcompeted coal in power generation during the first quarter of 2020.[47] In Australia a similar story is underway. Tesla's big batteries are now outperforming fossil fuel generators on both performance and cost.[48] South Australia is now on its way to 100 percent renewable energy.[49] Similar success stories can be told around the world. We are ready to turn the corner. We are approaching a tipping point of the good kind.

THE *REAL* PANDEMIC

Opportunity can arise from tragedy. Such seemed to be the case with the COVID-19 outbreak of early 2020. Nature had afforded us a unique teaching moment. Watching the pandemic unfold, both the impacts and the response, was like watching a time lapse of the climate crisis.[50] Was this a climate-change practice run?

Though the climate crisis is playing out considerably more slowly than the pandemic, there is much to be learned about the former from the latter. These important lessons have to do with the role of science and fact-based discourse in decision-making; the dangers of ideologically driven denial, deflection, and doomism; the roles played by individual action and government policy; the threats posed by special interests hijacking our policy machinery; the fragility of our societal infrastructure; and the distinct challenges of satisfying the needs of nearly eight billion (and growing) people on a finite planet. Will we take away the right lessons?

What can we learn, for example, about the role of science? As with climate change, scientists had warned of the threat of a pandemic many years in advance.[51] They had designed theoretical models for just that scenario that proved essential for anticipating what would happen with the novel coronavirus. The initial spread occurred at an exponential rate, just as models predicted.[52] This meant we could anticipate that more and more people would become infected in the weeks and months ahead, which they did. We knew that the major- ity of those infected by COVID-19 would experience mild or no symptoms while remaining highly contagious, and we knew that for others, COVID-19 would create the need for emergency medical supports that are not available in sufficient supply.

A popular Internet meme is that "every disaster movie starts with the government ignoring a scientist." And the coronavirus pro- vided some striking examples. Prime Minister Boris Johnson in the United Kingdom initially disregarded what the world's scientists were telling him and instead advocated for "herd immunity"—that is, simply letting the disease spread rampantly among the popula- tion, building collective resistance in the remaining population but needlessly sacrificing lives in the process.[53] This decision was based on what turned out to be a faulty analysis by his advisers.[54] Johnson then not only contracted COVID-19 himself but likely spread it to others through irresponsible personal behavior, becoming a poster child for the dangers of disregarding scientific predictions.[55]

The coronavirus outbreak also taught some important lessons about the cost of delay. The United States paid a terrible price by not acting quickly and decisively enough to avoid danger—more than 200,000 deaths at the time this book went to press. It is beginning to dawn on many that we are paying a similar price with the climate crisis. If we had acted decades ago, when a scientific consensus had been reached that we were warming the planet, carbon emissions could have been ramped down gently and much of the damage that we are now seeing could have been avoided. Now they must be lowered dramatically to avert ever more dangerous warming. With COVID-19, there is a two-week delay between intervention actions and changes to the rate of growth in transmissions and deaths. Both the United States and the United Kingdom were slow to take meaningful preventive measures. Whereas deaths had plateaued in most industrial countries by early April 2020, they continued to climb for these two countries.[56] For both climate change and coronavirus, taking appropriate action pays future dividends. Conversely, the slower we are to act, the higher the cost, as measured by both economic losses and deaths.

The parallels weren't lost on other observers. "By the time the true scale of the problem becomes clear, it's far too late," wrote Patrick Wyman in *Mother Jones*. "The disaster—a crisis of political legitimacy, a coronavirus pandemic, a climate catastrophe—doesn't so much break the system as show just how broken the system already was."[57] *The Guardian*'s Jonathan Watts weighed in, too, with a headline reading, "Delay Is Deadly: What Covid-19 Tells Us About Tackling the Climate Crisis."[58]

As with climate change, unwarranted doomism reared its head. Jem Bendell sought to connect the two phenomena explicitly, blaming the coronavirus on rising temperatures. Saijel Kishan at Bloomberg News reported, "Bendell is . . . willing to make the connection between coronavirus and climate change. He says that a warmer habitat may have caused the bats to alter their movements, putting them in contact with humans."[59] I know of no scientific evidence for that claim.

Lessons about the dangers of ideologically driven denial were of course in great abundance. The same individuals, groups, and organizations that have for years served as purveyors of climate-change denial were quick to attack and undermine public faith in the science of the coronavirus crisis. This strategy makes sense, given the common underlying ideology and politics. Climate-change denial serves the agenda of powerful corporations and the Trump administration. COVID-19 denial did the same, with corporate profits, near-term economic growth, and Trump's reelection prospects all threatened by large-scale lockdowns.

So we saw the standard denialist modus operandi in play. Russian trolls early on promoted disinformation and conspiracy theories.[60] Right-wing organizations pumped out anti-science propaganda. A dark-money-funded group called the Center for American Greatness published a commentary mocking the hockey-stick-like projections of coronavirus cases by epidemiologists, comparing them to the supposedly "widely refuted"—you guessed it—climate-change hockey-stick graph that my coauthors and I published more than two decades ago.[61] Even the subtitle of the article ("There's Still Time to Find a Balance Between Public Health and the Economy") cried false dilemma.

The usual denialist suspects were rounded up. Benny Peiser and Andrew Montford—two climate-change deniers—were given substantial real estate on the editorial pages of Rupert Murdoch's *Wall Street Journal* to insist that "scary" coronavirus projections were based on "bad data" and that we must not take "draconian measures" that might harm the economy.[62] As it was published on April 1, you could be forgiven for thinking it was an April Fool's joke. At that very moment, coronavirus cases in New York were surging toward their peak, as subsequent weeks would prove. The climate-change-denying Heartland Institute insisted that social-distancing measures should be lifted.[63] Online, meanwhile, a rogues' gallery of climate-change contrarians, including Judith Curry, Nic Lewis, Christopher Monckton, Anthony Watts, Marcel Crok, and William Briggs, all joined in on the frenzy.[64]

Trump himself emerged early on as a leading source of disinformation. As with climate change, he initially dismissed concerns about COVID-19 as a "hoax."[65] With both COVID-19 and climate change, "Trump . . . employed similar tactics—namely cherry-picking data, promoting outright falsehoods and using anecdotal experience in place of scientific data," reported *Energy and Environment News*.[66] And in both cases Trump depended upon agenda-driven anti-science contrarians to justify his course of inaction.[67] Writing for Pulitzer Prize–winning *Inside Climate News*, Katelyn Weisbrod described "6 Ways Trump's Denial of Science Has Delayed the Response to COVID-19 (and Climate Change)," with a subtitle noting that "Misinformation, Blame, Wishful Thinking and Making Up Facts are Favorite Techniques."[68]

Fearing a slowdown of the economy and threat to his reelection hopes, Trump repeatedly dismissed the public threat and discouraged people from taking the actions recommended by health experts, such as social distancing and mask-wearing. Jeff Mason wrote, in an article for Reuters, "Early on he said that the virus was under control and repeatedly compared it to the seasonal flu," and in late March "he argued the time was coming to reopen the U.S. economy, complaining that the cure was worse than the problem and setting a goal of economic rebirth by Easter on April 12." In early April, furthermore, Dr. Deborah Birx, leading the White House task force on the pandemic, told Americans they needed to "do better at social distancing." But, as Mason put it, "President Donald Trump didn't like the message."[69]

As time went on, and Trump's desperation with the lockdown grew, his anti-scientific and pseudoscientific response to the COVID-19 crisis itself constituted a mounting public health threat. There were his entirely unfounded and irresponsible suggestions that the virus could be cured by ultraviolet light or disinfectants. After having initially issued an emergency authorization in March 2020 for the use of two antimalarial medications, hydroxychloroquine and chloroquine, in response to pressure from Trump, the US Food and Drug Administration reversed that decision in June 2020, noting that the medications "were unlikely to be effective" for treating COVID-19, and that any potential benefits were outweighed by safety risks, including heart problems.[70]

Trump discouraged the use of face masks, a simple measure known to greatly reduce transmission of coronavirus. In June 2020, he held dangerous indoor political rallies in Tulsa, Oklahoma, and Phoenix, Arizona, that defied all public health measures (masks were not encouraged, and staff were even ordered to remove the social-distancing stickers on chairs in Tulsa). And he held a crowded "4th of July" event at Mount Rushmore that represented not only a public health threat but an environmental one as well, featuring a fireworks display that experts warned posed a severe fire hazard due to climate-change-fueled heat and drought conditions.[71]

Other conservatives aided and abetted Trump's efforts. At times, it would have been almost comical if it were not so dangerous. Indeed, the *Daily Show* was compelled to compile a "best of" reel it called the "Heroes of the Pandumic."[72] It featured assorted right-wing personalities, Republican talking heads, and politicians dismissing the threat of the virus. On Fox News, Sean Hannity complained that the "media mob" wanted people to think the pandemic was "an apocalypse," and Rush Limbaugh dismissed it as "hype," insisting that "the coronavirus is the common cold folks." Lou Dobbs on Fox warned, "The national left-wing media [is] playing up fears of the coronavirus." Commentator Tomi Lahren, also on Fox, mocked those who were concerned as crying, "The sky is falling because we have a few dozen cases," adding that she was "far more concerned with stepping on a used heroin needle."

The disdain for science and public health concern went on and on. Fox News personalities Jeanine Pirro, Dr. Marc Siegal, and Geraldo Rivera all dismissed coronavirus as no worse than the flu in what could readily be seen as a coordinated Fox News talking point. Other Fox personalities insisted they were not "afraid" of the virus, that it was "very difficult to contract," and that it was "milder than we thought." A Fox panel told viewers, "It's actually the safest time to fly."

Fox News and other right-wing media even resorted to orchestrated character attacks against the nation's top infectious disease expert, simply because he refused to act as a rubber stamp for Trump's most misguided coronavirus policy gambits. Media Matters described the phenomenon: "Dr. Anthony Fauci, director of the National Institute of Allergy and Infectious Diseases for the past 36 years, is a widely respected immunologist and major public face of the Trump administration's response to COVID-19. Despite his credibility established over decades as a public health official, right-wing media have begun to launch attacks against [him], blaming the medical expert for allegedly harming the economy and undermining President Donald Trump."[73] In what might sound all too familiar, the Trump administration even went so far as to circulate an opposition research document cherry-picking and misrepresenting Fauci's statements to try to discredit him as a scientist and as a messenger.[74]

Republican politicians followed suit, too. Trump's most loyal, fiercest bulldogs in Congress treated the pandemic like it was a joke. Congressman Devin Nunes (R-CA) told viewers to "just go out and go to a local restaurants." Matt Gaetz (R-FL) wore a gas mask on Capitol Hill to mock concern about coronavirus. When a reporter questioned James Inhofe (R-OK), the leading climate-change denier in the US Senate, about what precautions he was taking, Inhofe extended his arm and dismissively asked, "Wanna shake hands?" Eight governors—all Republicans—collectively ignored the words of Dr. Anthony Fauci, who had expressed concern about the lack of adequate lockdown.

Conservative coronavirus denial turned ever more deadly as a coordinated effort emerged among Republican politicians and talking heads to convince the elderly to "take one for the team." Texas lieutenant governor Dan Patrick said on Fox News that grandparents should be willing to die to save the economy for their grandchildren.[75] Conservatives doubled down on this talking point, with other leading personalities, like Fox News's Brit Hume, arguing that it was an "entirely reasonable viewpoint" for the elderly to risk their lives

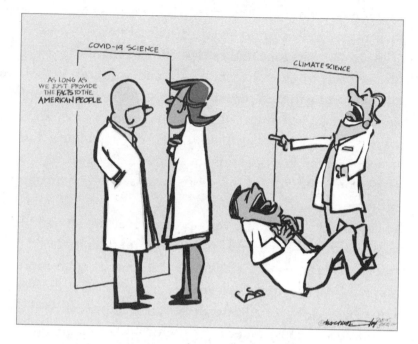

to help the stock market.[76] One right-wing talk-show host took this progression to its logical extreme, insisting that "while death is sad for the living left behind, for the dying, it is merely a passage out of this physical body."[77]

Herein we see yet another remarkable parallel with climate-change inactivism: the transition over time from denial to false solutions, and then, eventually, to "it's actually good for us." This transition took more than a decade with climate inactivists; with the coronavirus deniers it happened in a matter of weeks.[78] Climate scientist Mike MacFerrin explained, "The right wing's instantaneous flip from 'it's a hoax' to 'let millions die in service to the "market"' is the same script they play with climate change, to a tee. They want you to do nothing."[79] And former CBS News anchor Dan Rather put it this way: "After years when we should have learned of the dangers of 'false equivalence' it baffles me that we are seeing a framing that pits the health of our citizens against some vague notion of getting back to work."[80] I noted, in turn, that it's "not unlike the false equivalence . . . that pits the health of our entire planet against some vague notion of economic prosperity."[81] The right-wing response to coronavirus was, indeed, a précis of the climate wars.

While it took years for the threat of climate change to crystallize, with the impacts of epic storms, floods, and wildfires, it took only weeks for the reality of the coronavirus to set in as people witnessed colleagues, friends, and loved ones contract the disease, and sadly, in some cases, perish from it. Under such circumstances, the consequences of denial and inaction became readily apparent to the average person on the street (or, more aptly, safely self-quarantined in their home).

The coronavirus pandemic thus provided an unexpected lesson on the perils of anti-science. As I told *Energy and Environment News*, the pandemic "exposes the dangers of denial in a much more dramatic fashion. We may look back at the coronavirus crisis as a critical moment where we were all afforded a terrifying view of the dangerous and deadly consequences of politically and ideology-driven science denial. We looked into the abyss, and I hope we collectively decide that we don't like what we saw."[82] Tweeted Steve Schmidt, former presidential campaign co-adviser for the late senator John McCain, "The injury done to America and the public good by Fox News and a bevy of personalities from Limbaugh to Ingraham . . . will be felt for many years in this country as we deal with the death and economic damage that didn't have to be."[83]

There were other key lessons to take away from the pandemic that had broad implications for the climate crisis. We were provided with more examples of the concept of a "threat multiplier"—that is, the compounding nature of multiple simultaneous threats. The damage already wrought by climate change in some places affected their ability to respond to the coronavirus threat. So extensive was the damage to Puerto Rico's health-care infrastructure after Hurricane Maria that vital equipment was lacking when coronavirus came along. A thirteen-year-old named Jaideliz Moreno Ventura was just one of the resulting casualties: she died because Vieques, where she lived, lacked the medical equipment to treat her.[84] Many others were similarly affected, and the tragedy was a legacy of the devastating, climate-change-fueled impacts of Hurricane Maria, along with the insufficient federal support for Puerto Rico under President Trump and his failure to send aid for hurricane recovery, including for critical public health infrastructure.[85]

The pandemic also crystallized the dual roles played by both individual action and government policy when it comes to dealing with a societal crisis. While containment required individuals to act responsibly by practicing social distancing, using masks, and following other advice regarding mitigative behavioral actions, it also required government action in the form of policies (like stay-at-home orders, restrictions on public gatherings, and so on) that would *incentivize* responsible behavior.

The coronavirus crisis, in fact, underscored the importance of government. The need for an organized and effective response to a crisis, after all, is one of the fundamental reasons we have governments in the first place. Crises, whether in the near term like COVID-19 or in the long term like climate change, remind us that government has an obligation to protect the welfare of its citizens by providing aid, organizing an appropriate crisis response, alleviating economic disruption, and maintaining a functioning social safety net.[86]

Citizens, in turn, have a responsibility to hold politicians accountable whenever government fails to uphold its end of the "social contract." In a democratic society, political action and individual action are inextricably linked. We need to deal with problems such as COVID-19 and climate change, and we need competent, science-driven leaders to do that. Consider the contrast between the United States and the United Kingdom, under Donald Trump and Boris Johnson, respectively, on the one hand—two politicians who dismissed the need for lockdown and social distancing—and, on the other hand, New Zealand and Germany, which saw limited impact under their respective leaders Jacinda Ardern and Angela Merkel, who instead embraced such measures.

As I'm writing, we don't yet know the outcome of the upcoming presidential election that will determine the fate of climate policy in the United States, and indeed the world, for years to come. But is seems plausible that voters will recognize the shortcomings of a president who had "received [his] first formal notification of the outbreak of the coronavirus in China" at the beginning of January 2020, including "a warning about the coronavirus—the first of many—in the President's Daily Brief," and "yet . . . took 70 days from that initial notification . . . to treat the coronavirus not as a distant threat or harmless flu strain . . . but as a lethal force . . . poised to kill tens of thousands of citizens."[87] It seems equally plausible that an administration that exploited the pandemic by stripping away environmental protections at the behest of big polluters, greenlighting the construction of controversial new fossil fuel infrastructure, and criminalizing climate protests while the public was distracted will see a reckoning come the election.[88]

The most important question of all, though, is this one: Can an event like the coronavirus crisis become a turning point, an opportunity to bring needed focus to an even greater crisis—the climate crisis? The climate crisis is, after all, the greatest long-term health threat we face. Even as we battled the pandemic, climate change continued to loom in the background. "Earth Scorched in the First 3 Months of 2020," reported *Mashable*.[89] In Australia, where I was residing in early 2020 when the COVID-19 epidemic was just beginning to unfold, Australians were still recovering from the calamitous bushfires of the summer of 2019/2020. Meanwhile, the Great Barrier Reef was beginning to suffer the third major bleaching event in five years, an unprecedented and foreboding development.[90]

The COVID-19 pandemic spoke to the fragility of our expanding, resource-hungry civilization and our reliance on massive but fragile infrastructure for food and water on a planet with finite resources. Some argued that this crisis might be sounding the death knell of resource-extractive neoliberalism.[91] I myself am not so sanguine.[92] But I do think it has generated a long-overdue discussion about the public good and environmental sustainability.

Some ecologists believe that our resource-hungry modern lifestyle—in particular, the destruction of rain forests and other natural ecosystems—may be an underlying factor favoring the sorts of pandemics we have just witnessed.[93] That raises some disturbing possibilities, but to appreciate them, we must take a brief scientific digression into the concept of *Gaia*, the ancient Greeks' personification of Earth herself.

Put forward by scientists Lynn Margulis and James Lovelock in the 1970s, the Gaia hypothesis says that life interacts with Earth's physical environment to form a synergistic and self-regulating system.[94] In other words, the Earth system in some sense behaves like an organism, with "homeostatic" regulatory mechanisms that maintain conditions that are habitable for life. Although the concept has often been taken out of context and misrepresented—for example, to depict Earth as a sentient entity—it is really just a heuristic device for describing a set of physical, chemical, and biological processes that yield stabilizing "feedback" mechanisms maintaining the planet within livable bounds. There is no consciousness or motive. It's simply the laws of physics, chemistry, and biology at work in a fascinating and fortuitous manner.

There is evidence that the hypothesis holds within the range of its assumptions. Earth's *carbon cycle*, which governs the amount of CO_2 greenhouse gas in the atmosphere, is heavily influenced by life on Earth. Photosynthetic organisms, such as cyanobacteria (blue-green algae) and plants, for example, take in CO_2 and produce oxygen, which is needed by animals like us. There is evidence that as the Sun has become brighter over Earth's lifetime of the past 4.5 billion years, the carbon cycle has intensified, decreasing atmospheric CO_2 levels and helping keep Earth from becoming inhospitably hot. A specific example is the famous Faint Young Sun Paradox—the surprising finding that Earth was habitable to basic lifeforms more than 3 billion years ago despite the fact that the Sun was 30 percent dimmer—which we encountered back in Chapter 1. Readers may recall that the great Carl Sagan proposed an explanation: namely, there must have been a considerably larger greenhouse effect at the time. (Incidentally, Sagan and Margulis were married for about seven years. I often wonder what other scientific synergies must have emerged in their daily dinner-table conversations.)

During the height of the COVID-19 crisis, air traffic, transportation, and industrial activity greatly diminished, and pollution, including carbon emissions, was reduced. I couldn't help but pose a rhetorical question.[95] Are pandemics such as coronavirus, metaphorically speaking, acting like Gaia's immune system, fighting back against a dangerous invader? Aren't *we*—through the damage we are inflicting on the planet, its forests, its ecosystems, and its oceans and lakes, actually the metaphorical *virus*?[96] I wasn't the only one asking such questions.[97] My question was intentionally provocative, and I was sensitive about even asking it, since such thinking can easily be misconstrued and abused for misanthropic and ecofascist purposes.[98]

Here's the point, though. Unlike microbes, human beings have agency. We can choose to behave like a virus that plagues our planet, or we can choose a different path. It's up to us. Our response to the coronavirus pandemic shows it's possible for us to change our ways when we must. The COVID crisis was acute and immediate, and the penalty of inaction was swift. Climate change may seem slower than coronavirus and farther away, but it is very much here, and it requires many of the same behavioral changes. In this case our commitment must be sustained rather than fleeting. We must flatten the curve—of carbon emissions—to get off the climate pandemic path.[99]

While the coronavirus pandemic was truly a tragedy, we must consider the opportunities it has brought along in its wake as we attempt to work our way back to normal life and governments implement economic stimulus plans to jump-start their economies. The pandemic has given us an opening to get off the path of climate distress and onto a healthier path. We must work even harder to decarbonize our economy and minimize our environmental footprint. There are clear side benefits to an economy that is less vulnerable to disruptions in the production and transport of fuel. Regardless of what else happens, the sun will still shine, and the wind will still blow. Renewable energy is both safer and more reliable than fossil fuels. We were already seeing the decoupling of our global economy from fossil fuels before the pandemic. (We had substantial economic growth in 2019 without a rise in carbon emissions.) Why not take this opportunity to accelerate the transition from fossil fuels to renewable energy?

The good news is that this seems to be happening, despite the Trump administration's best efforts to impede this transition by seeking to fast-track the further dismantling of climate and environmental protections.[100] *Inside Climate News* reported in July 2020 that two of the world's largest oil companies, Shell and BP, were lowering their outlooks for demand for their products and slashing the value of their assets by billions, saying the coronavirus pandemic could accelerate a shift to clean energy.[101] In early April 2020, a group of state officials from agencies such as the California Energy Commission, collectively representing more than 25 percent of total US power generation, announced a new coalition dedicated to 100 percent clean energy. In doing so, they explicitly acknowledged both the challenges and the opportunities for change in the wake of the pandemic.[102] New York State, the world's eleventh-largest economy, put forward a COVID-19 recovery plan centered on renewable energy.[103] ClimateWorks Australia had a stimulus-ready plan already in place for Australia to move toward net-zero carbon emissions.[104] It appears we may, indeed, be turning a corner. That's just one reason to be optimistic. There are others.

THE WISDOM OF CHILDREN

The Bible prophesied that "a little child shall lead them" (Isaiah 35:9). And such has been the case with climate action. Over the past few years, we have witnessed the rise to prominence of Greta Thunberg, a teenager from Sweden, who achieved by the age of sixteen an iconic global cultural status typically reserved for pop stars and Hollywood celebrities. She has been nominated for the Nobel Peace Prize and was featured on the cover of *Time* magazine. Thunberg has been diagnosed as having Asperger syndrome, but instead of seeing it as a liability, she calls it her "superpower."[105] Now seventeen, she possesses a remarkable ability to speak truth to power in strong, laser-focused, perfectly delivered language.

In 2018, at age fifteen, she began protesting outside the Swedish parliament to raise awareness about the threat of climate change. Her efforts garnered increasing levels of media attention. She went on to speak at the 2019 United Nations Climate Change Summit, to the British and European Parliaments, and, perhaps most famously, to the attendees of the 2019 World Economic Forum in Davos, where she chided the politicians and other influential individuals gathered there for their failure to address the existential challenge of our time, warning them "our house is on fire."

Thunberg's efforts have been infectious. She has sparked a global youth movement called "Fridays For Future," with literally millions of children around the world marching, striking, and protesting for climate action weekly. Kids in the United States wear T-shirts bearing her likeness. Adults are now mobilizing to support the movement, too. Inactivists have become so worried that they've even manufactured and promoted an "anti-Greta," a teenager who dismisses the climate crisis, in a desperate and feeble attempt at distraction and misdirection.[106]

They *should* be worried. In response to this popular uprising, the UK and Irish parliaments have now both declared a "climate emergency."[107] The majority of UK voters now support dramatic action to lower greenhouse gas emissions to nearly zero by 2050 regardless of cost.[108] There is clearly a sense of urgency. But there is also recognition of *agency*—a sense that action is possible, that our future is, to a great extent, still in our hands.

While Thunberg has garnered the lion's share of attention, there are other leaders of this movement. Among them is Alexandria Villaseñor, who, beginning in December 2018, at the age of fourteen, skipped school every Friday to protest against lack of climate action in front of United Nations Headquarters in New York City. She cofounded the US Youth Climate Strike and Earth Uprising youth climate activist groups. Then there's Jerome Foster, who as of 2020 was eighteen years old. An activist from Washington, DC, he is founder and editor in chief of *The Climate Reporter*. I joined Villaseñor and Foster in Easthampton, Long Island, in August 2019 in a panel event called "The Youth Climate Movement Could Save the Planet"—a sentiment with which I agree.[109] Afterward, the two even *inducted* me "officially" into the youth climate movement after I was able to demonstrate competency in Instagram technique.

It was a light moment, but the topic couldn't be more serious. The local paper, summarizing the discussion, said of the youth leaders, "Despite little meaningful movement to address a growing emergency, they have hope. Their generation, they said, is mobilizing to preserve a livable world."[110] These kids have helped accomplish what seemingly nobody else could. They've helped place climate change on the front page of the papers and at the center of our public discourse. They are the main reason I'm optimistic that we're finally going to win this battle.

In solidarity with these youths, a group of just under two dozen climate scientists, myself included, published a letter in *Science* magazine that was ultimately cosigned by thousands of other scientists around the world. The letter offered support to them for their efforts.[111] It read, in part, "The enormous grassroots mobilization of the youth climate movement . . . shows that young people understand the situation. We approve and support their demand for rapid and forceful action. We see it as our social, ethical, and scholarly responsibility to state in no uncertain terms: Only if humanity acts quickly and resolutely can we limit global warming . . . and preserve the . . . well-being of present and future generations. This is what the young people want to achieve. They deserve our respect and full support."

They deserve not only our respect and support but our protection as well.[112] We saw earlier, back in Chapter 4, how leaders of the youth climate movement like Greta Thunberg and Alexandria Villaseñor have been targeted by trolls and bots and even heads of state, including Donald Trump and Brazilian president Jair Bolsonaro.

The attacks on Thunberg reached fever pitch in the lead-up to the high-profile, high-stakes events of September 2019: the Global

Youth Climate Strike and the UN Climate Change Summit in New York City. Andrew Bolt, the Australian climate-change-denying propagandist at Murdoch's *Herald Sun*, attacked Thunberg, then sixteen, as "strange" and "disturbed."[113] Christopher Caldwell, a Senior Fellow and contributing editor for the right-wing Scaife-funded Claremont Institute, was granted space in the *New York Times* to attack her in a piece titled "The Problem with Greta Thunberg's Climate Activism: Her Radical Approach Is at Odds with Democracy."[114] Patrick Moore, chairman of the board of directors of the CO2 Coalition, a climate-change-denying Koch brothers front group that is the modern-day successor to the infamous George C. Marshall Institute we encountered back in Chapter 2, went so far as to tweet "Greta = Evil."[115]

The Eye of Sauron is focused upon these kids. The most powerful industry in the world, the fossil fuel industry, sees them as an existential threat and has them firmly in its sights. Consider the recent actions of the Organization of the Petroleum Exporting Countries (OPEC), a trillion-dollar international organization founded in 1960 by five petrostates—Iran, Iraq, Kuwait, Saudi Arabia, and Venezuela. It now consists of fourteen oil-exporting countries that own 80 percent of the world's proven oil reserves.

In July 2019, OPEC's secretary general, Mohammed Barkindo, referred to the youth climate movement as the "greatest threat" the fossil fuel industry faces. He expressed concern that the pressure being brought to bear on oil producers by the mass youth movement was "beginning to . . . dictate policies and corporate decisions, including investment in the industry." Barkindo acknowledged that even the children of OPEC officials were now "asking us about their future because . . . they see their peers on the streets campaigning against this industry."[116]

Unintimidated, members of the youth climate movement actually welcomed the comments "as a sign the oil industry is worried it may be losing the battle for public opinion." The criticism, as *The Guardian* characterized it, "highlights the growing reputational concerns of oil companies *as public protests intensify along with extreme weather"* (emphasis added).[117] Note, by the way, the acknowledgment here of the role played by a synergy of underlying factors—in this case both the youth climate movement and mounting weather disasters. It is indeed no single factor—but a convergence of them—that has led both to intensified attacks by inactivists and an unprecedented opportunity for change.

The kids are at the center of it all. And they are being attacked simply for fighting for their future. It is morally incumbent upon the rest of us to do more than just pat them on the back. Communication expert Max Boycoff expressed the worry, in a September 2019 op-ed, "that we adults, who got us into this mess, are not doing enough. . . . Adult utterances about 'legacies' and 'intergenerational' generally ring hollow when the scale of engagement and action pales in comparison to the scale of the ongoing challenge."[118]

The children have created an opportunity that didn't exist before—they've gained a foothold for the rest of us. It is time for us to take the opportunity we've been given as we prepare for battle—the battle to preserve a livable planet for our children and grandchildren.

THE FINAL BATTLE

Though they are on the run, the forces of climate-change denial and inaction haven't given up. Nor are they, as Malcolm Harris wrote in *New York Magazine*, "planning for a future without oil and gas." "These companies," Harris observed, after attending a fossil-fuel-industry planning meeting, "want the public to think of them as part of a climate solution. In reality, they're a problem trying to avoid being solved."[119]

Climate inactivists are now engaged in a rear-guard action as their defenses start to crumble under the weight of the evidence and in the face of a global insurgency for change. But let us also recognize that they are still in possession of a powerful arsenal as they wage the new climate war. It includes an array of powerful *D*s: disinformation, deceit, divisiveness, deflection, delay, despair-mongering, and doomism. The needed societal tipping point will not easily be reached as long as these immensely powerful vested interests remain aligned in defense of the fossil fuel status quo and in possession of these formidable weapons. It will only happen with the active participation of citizens everywhere aiding in the collective push forward.

It is the goal of this book to inform readers about what is taking place on this front and to enable people of all ages to join together in the battle for our planet. With that goal in mind, let's revisit the four-point battle plan outlined at the very start, reflecting now on everything we've learned:

Disregarding the Doomsayers: We have seen how harmful doomism can be. It is disabling and disempowering. And it is readily exploited by inactivists to convince even the most environmentally minded that there's no reason to turn out for elections, lobby for climate action, or in any other way work toward climate solutions. We must be blunt about the very real risks, threats, and challenges that climate change *already* presents to us. But just as we must reject distortions of the science in service of denialism, so, too, must we reject misrepresentations of the science—including unsupported claims of runaway warming and unavoidable human extinction scenarios— that can be used to promote the putative inevitability of our demise.

Unfortunately, *doom sells*! That's why we've seen a rash of high-profile feature articles and best-selling books purveying what I call "climate doom porn"—writing that may tap into the adrenaline rush of fear but actually inhibit the impulse to take meaningful action on climate. It's why we see headlines with an overly doomist framing of what the latest scientific study shows (or at least plays up the worst possible scenarios).[120]

Feeding doomism is the notion that climate change is just too big a problem for us to solve. Especially pernicious in this regard is the dismissal of climate change as a "wicked problem." While definitions vary, what's relevant here is how it is defined in common parlance. Wikipedia defines a wicked problem as "a problem that is difficult *or impossible to solve* because of incomplete, contradictory, and changing requirements that are often difficult to recognize" (emphasis added).[121]

The idea that the climate problem is fundamentally unsolvable is itself deeply problematic. Jonathan Gilligan, a professor in earth and environmental science at Vanderbilt University, agrees, explaining, in a Twitter thread, "There are profound problems with the 'wicked problem' idea, that tend to produce a sense of helplessness because wicked problems are, by their definition, unsolvable."[122]

Others weighed in on how the "wicked problem" framing can constitute a form of soft denial. Paul Price, a policy researcher in Dublin City University's Energy and Climate Research Network, explained, "Social science use of 'wicked' & 'super-wicked' too often seems a form of 'implicatory denial,' a rhetorical fence to avoid physical reality."[123] Atmospheric scientist Peter Jacobs added, "There is almost literally no environmental problem that one couldn't successfully reclassify as 'wicked' at the outset if one wanted to, even topics where we've successfully mitigated much of the harm (ozone depletion, acid rain, etc.)."[124]

In any case, the "wicked problem" framing is convenient to polluting interests, which have worked hard to sabotage action on climate. And it's wrong. The truth is, if we took the disinformation campaign funded by the fossil fuel industry out of the equation, the climate problem would have been solved decades ago. The problem is not hopelessly complicated.[125]

Nevertheless, the forces of doomism and despair-mongering remain active, and we must call them out whenever they appear. In March 2020, as I was writing the final section of this book, social media was abuzz: Bernie Sanders had dropped out of the Democratic presidential primaries, leaving Joe Biden the presumptive nominee. Some Sanders supporters were particularly aggressive in insisting that this spelled climate Armageddon. A commenter tweeted at me, "If we don't reduce carbon output by 50% of 2018 by 2030 climate change becomes a run away [*sic*] process that cannot be stopped."[126] I responded, "That's false. . . . Climate-change deniers distort the science. Let's not resort to their tactics."[127] The commenter continued, "Biden's plan doesn't come close to accomplishing that. There is no reason to vote in this election because it's apocalypse either way."[128]

It was a perfectly toxic brew of misguided thinking, consisting of distortions of the science in the service of doomist inevitability and false equivalence—between a president who has done notable damage to international climate efforts and a candidate whom Politifact calls "a climate change pioneer."[129] The cherry on top is the overt and cynical nihilism—the notion that there is nothing we can do, so we might as well simply give up. It would be easy to dismiss this as a one-off comment. But in fact it is reflective of a hostile online atmosphere that has been fueled by bad state actors. Bernie Sanders had said just a month earlier, "In 2016, Russia used Internet propaganda to sow division in our country, and my understanding is that they are doing it again in 2020. Some of the ugly stuff on the Internet attributed to our campaign may well not be coming from real supporters."[130]

This sort of propaganda may be more harmful now than climate-change denial itself. It must be treated as every bit as much of a threat to climate action. Those who promote it should be called out in the strongest terms, for they threaten the future of this planet. When you encounter such doomist and nihilistic framing of the climate crisis, whether online or in conversations with friends, coworkers, or fellow churchgoers, call it out.

Don't forget, once again, to emphasize that there is both *urgency* and *agency*. The climate crisis is very real. But it is *not* unsolvable. And it's *not* too late to act. Every ounce of carbon we don't burn makes things better. There is still time to create a better future, and the greatest obstacle now in our way is doomism and defeatism. Journalists and the media have a tremendous responsibility here as well.

A Child Shall Lead Them: Back in 2017, I coauthored a children's book, *The Tantrum That Saved the World*, with children's book author and illustrator Megan Herbert.[131] It told the story of a girl, Sophia, who is frustrated by the animals and people—including a polar bear, a swarm of bees, a Pacific Islander, and others—who continue to show up at her door. They've been displaced from their homes by climate change. Sophia becomes increasingly frustrated by this disruptive activity and throws a tantrum. But she ultimately redirects her anger and frustration—and the tantrum itself—in an empowering way. She becomes the change she wishes to see in the world, starting a whole movement that demands accountability by the adults of the world to act on the climate crisis. Less than a year later, Greta Thunberg would rise to prominence and the youth climate movement would take the world by storm. Yes, life does indeed sometimes imitate art—in this case, in a most profound way.

The children speak with a moral clarity that is undeniable to all but the most jaded and cynical. It is a game-changer. But, as we've seen, that's what makes them such a threat to vested interests—the heads of petrostates and the fossil fuel industry itself. They have attacked the children because the children pose a serious threat to the industry's business-as-usual model. Fossil fuel interests rely on that model continuing for record profits.

Some colleagues of mine blithely dismiss the notion that we are, even if involuntarily on our part, in a "war" with powerful special interests looking to undermine climate action. Ironically, they are engaged in a form of denial themselves. The dismissiveness of soothing myths and appeasement didn't serve us well in World War II, and it won't serve us well here either. Especially when we are dealing with an enemy that doesn't observe the accepted rules of engagement. To carry the analogy one step further, the attacks on child climate activists most surely constitute a metaphorical violation of the Geneva Conventions. So yes, we are in a war—though not of our own choosing—and our children represent unacceptable collateral damage. That is why we must fight back—with knowledge, passion, and an unyielding demand for change.

This problem goes well beyond science, economics, policy, and politics. It's about our obligation to our children and grandchildren not to leave behind a degraded planet. It is impossible now not to be reminded of this threat whenever I have an opportunity to share the wonders of this planet with my wife and fourteen-year-old daughter. In December 2019, before I began my sabbatical in Australia, I traveled with my family to see the Great Barrier Reef. Within a month after our visit the third major bleaching event of the past five years, the most extensive yet, was underway. Some experts fear that the reef won't fully recover.[132]

It fills me with an odd sort of "survivors' guilt" to have seen the reef with my family just in the nick of time. The next stop on our vacation was no less sobering. We went to the famous Blue Mountains of New South Wales. Unfortunately, the majestic vistas were replaced by a thick veil of smoke from the unprecedented bushfires that were spreading out across the continent.

I feel some wistfulness about the fact that my daughter, when she grows up, may not be able to experience these same natural wonders with her children or grandchildren. It's appropriate to feel grief at times for what is lost. But grief about that which is wrongly presumed to be lost yet can still be saved—and which is used, under false pretenses, in the service of despair and defeatism—is pernicious and wrong. Since I have already used at least one *Lord of the Rings* metaphor in this book, you'll forgive me if I use another. I'm reminded of the Steward of Gondor, who wrongly presumes his son to be dead and his city to be lost, telling the townspeople to run for their lives, and his assistants to take his still-living son off to be burned. Fortunately, Gandalf whacks him upside the head with his staff before his orders can be carried out. Sometimes I feel that way about doomists who advocate surrender in the battle to avert catastrophic climate change.

Educate, Educate, Educate: As we have discussed, the battle to convince the public and policymakers of the reality and threat of climate change is *largely* over. The substantive remaining public debate is over how bad it will get and what we can do to mitigate it. So online, don't waste time engaging directly with climate-change-denying trolls and bots. And where appropriate, report them. Those who seem to be *victims* of disinformation rather than *promoters* of it deserve special consideration. Try to inform them. When a false claim appears to be gaining enough traction to move outside the denialist echo chamber and infect honest, well-meaning folks, it should be rebutted.

You have powerful tools at your fingertips. A personal favorite resource of mine is Skeptical Science (skepticalscience.com), which rebuts all the major climate-change-denier talking points and provides responses that you can link to online or via email. Inform yourself about the latest science so you are armed with knowledge and facts, and then be brave enough to refute misinformation and disinformation. Online there are Twitter accounts you can follow that provide up-to-date information about the science, impacts, and solutions. A few personal favorites of mine are @ClimateNexus, @TheDailyClimate, @InsideClimate, and @GuardianEco. Feel free to follow yours truly (@MichaelEMann), too, if you don't mind the occasional cat video!

Climate-change deniers constantly complain about language and framing. Don't fall for it. Don't make concessions to them. In sports parlance, they're trying to "work the refs." The classic example is the shedding of crocodile tears over use of the term "climate-change denier" itself. In point of fact, it's an appropriate, accepted term to describe those who reject the overwhelming evidence. The goal of the critics in this case is to coerce us into granting them the undeserved status of "skeptics," which actually *rewards* their denialism. Legitimate skepticism is, as we know, a good thing in science. It's how scientists are trained to think. Indiscriminate rejection of evidence based on flimsy, ideological arguments is not.

When we falsely label climate-change denialism as "skepticism," it legitimizes disinformation and muddies the climate communication waters. It makes concessions to those who have no interest at all in good-faith engagement, are unmovable in their views, and are intentionally trafficking in doubt and confusion. What is so pernicious is that at the same time it actually *hinders* efforts to convince and motivate the "confused middle"—those who are liable to throw up their hands in frustration when presented with the apparent predicament of a debate between two ostensibly legitimate camps.

But enough about climate-change deniers. They are increasingly a fringe element in today's public discourse, and our efforts to educate are best aimed at those in the confused middle. These folks accept the evidence but are unconvinced of the urgency of the problem and are unsure whether we should—or can—do anything about it.

My advice is to spend your time on those who are reachable, teachable, and movable.[133] They need assistance. As we have seen, far too many have fallen into climate despair, having been led astray by unscientific, doomist messaging, some of it promoted by the in-activists in a cynical effort to dispirit and divide climate activists. Others are victims of other types of climate misinformation. When you encounter, for example, the claim that it's too expensive to act, point out that the opposite is true. The impacts of climate change are already costing us far more than the solutions. And indeed, 100 percent green energy would likely pay for itself.[134]

Call out false solutions for what they are. We've seen that many of the proposed geoengineering schemes and technofixes that have been proposed are fraught with danger. Moreover, they are being used to take our eye off the ball—the need to decarbonize our society. Even some of the fiercest climate hawks are sometimes way off base here. Elon Musk, for instance, has suggested that nuclear bombs could be used to make Mars's atmosphere habitable. While such proposals seem almost amusingly flippant, they are dangerous—not because we might expose little green men to nuclear radiation, but because they offer false promise for a simple escape route, providing fodder for those who argue "we can just find another planet if we screw up this one."

Climate change is arguably the greatest threat we face, yet we speak so little about it. Silence breeds inaction. So look for opportunities to talk about climate change as you go about your day—that's the gateway to all of the solutions we've discussed. Unlike corona-virus, we cannot look forward to a literal vaccine for the planet. But in a metaphorical sense, knowledge *is* the vaccine for what currently ails us—denial, disinformation, deflection, delayism, doomism, you know the litany by now. We must vaccinate the public against the efforts by inactivists to thwart climate action, using knowledge and facts and clear, simple explanations that have authority behind them. That's empowering, because it means we can *all* contribute to the cure.

Changing the System Requires Systemic Change: Inactivists, as we have seen, have waged a campaign to convince you that climate change is *your* fault, and that any real solutions involve individual action and personal responsibility alone, rather than policies aimed at holding corporate polluters accountable and decarbonizing our economy. They have sought to *deflect* the conversation toward the car you drive, the food you eat, and the lifestyle you live.

And they want you arguing with your neighbor about who is the most carbon pure, dividing advocates so they cannot speak with a unified voice—a voice calling for change. The fossil fuel industry and the inactivists who do their bidding fear a sober conversation about the larger systemic changes that are needed and the incentives they will require. And it's for one simple reason: it means the end of their reign of power.

Make no mistake. Individual action is part of the solution. There are countless things we can do and ought to do to limit our personal carbon footprint—and indeed our total environmental impact. And there are many reasons for doing them: they make us healthier, save us money, make us feel better about ourselves, and set a good example for others to follow. But individual action can only get us so far.

We were recently afforded a cautionary tale about the limits of behavior change alone in tackling the climate crisis. The dramatic reduction in travel and consumption brought about by the global lockdown response to the coronavirus pandemic reduced global carbon emissions by only a very modest amount.[135] Referencing this fact, Glen Peters, research director on past, current, and future trends in energy use and greenhouse gas emissions at the Center for International Climate Research (CICERO), posed a question: "If such radical social change leads to (only) a 4% drop in global emissions, then how do we get a 100% drop by ~2050? Is #COVID19 just going to show how important technology is to solve the climate problem?"[136] It's a valid point.

The answer is that there *is* no path of escape from climate-change catastrophe that doesn't involve polices aimed at societal decarbonization. Arriving at those policies requires intergovernmental agreements, like those fostered by the United Nations Framework Convention on Climate Change (UNFCCC), that bring the countries of the world to the table to agree on critical targets. The 2015 Paris Agreement is an example. It didn't solve the problem, but it got us on the right path, a path toward limiting warming below dangerous levels. To quote *The Matrix*, "There's a difference between knowing the path and walking the path." So we must build on the initial progress in future agreements if we are to avert catastrophic planetary warming.

The commitments of individual nations to such global agreements can only, of course, be met when their governments are in a position to enforce them through domestic energy and climate policies that incentivize the needed shift away from fossil fuel burning and other sources of carbon pollution. We won't get those policies without politicians in office who are willing to do our bidding over the bidding of powerful polluters. That means that we must bring pressure to bear on politicians and polluting interests. We do that through the strength of our voices and the power of our votes. We must vote out politicians who serve as handmaidens for fossil fuel interests and elect those who will champion climate action. That brings us full circle, because we are now back to talking about the responsibility of individuals—but now, it's about the responsibility to vote and to use every other means we have to collectively influence policy.

Herein we have encountered a new challenge. Opposition to key policy measures is now coming not just from the right, as traditionally expected, but from the left, too. While a vast majority of liberal democrats (88 percent) support carbon pricing, there is a movement underway, as we have seen, among some progressive climate activists to oppose it. Their opposition is based on the perception that it violates principles of social justice (though there's no reason that needs to be the case), or that it buys into market economics and neoliberal politics.[137] Others insist that it can't pass because it's unpopular with voters (the opposite is actually true), or that it could too easily be reversed by a future government (which one could say of any policy that isn't codified as a constitutional amendment).[138]

Some climate opinion leaders are in denial of this development. In early April 2019, I complained that "the greatest trick the devil ever pulled was getting progressives to oppose carbon pricing." I was referring not to the majority of self-identifying progressives, but to the small number of progressive climate activists who now oppose such measures.[139]

The often vituperative pundit David Roberts defensively tweeted in response that "the number of progressives who outright oppose carbon pricing is tiny & utterly insignificant in US politics. Just another example of phantom leftists against when [sic] Reasonable People can define their own identities."[140] This argument ignores the most prominent progressive in modern American politics, Bernie Sanders, who, in response to direct questioning by the *Washington Post* in November 2019, indicated he didn't support carbon pricing.[141]

It's not just Sanders. Roberts was immediately contradicted by Twitter users who came out of the woodwork to demonstrate my very point.[142] One self-avowed Unitarian Universalist (a religion known for its progressive philosophical and political outlook[143]) responded to Roberts, "I'm an advocate for climate action thru [Citizens Climate Lobby] & other groups. Almost ALL progressive folks I encounter (friends, Twitter, EJ) reflexively oppose carbon price of all sorts. They generally retreat to 'just ban FFs' as more likely & better. There's a lot of work to do."[144]

This opposition to carbon pricing seems to be tied to a larger trend on the left against "establishment" politics. This development has been fueled at least in part by state-sponsored (Russian) trolls and bots looking to sow division in Democratic politics in an effort to elect fossil-fuel-friendly plutocrats like Donald Trump to power. That tactic was successful in the 2016 presidential election and was very much still in play during the 2020 election, as detailed by the *Washington Post* in a February 2020 article.[145]

The same witches' brew that helped bring Donald Trump to power in 2016—interference by malevolent state actors, cynicism, and outrage, including among some on the progressive far left—appears, as this book goes to press, to be a potent threat to climate action today.

Let's recognize, though, that while some of the outrage has been manufactured by bad actors who have magnified and then weaponized divisions, some legitimate underlying grievances have also played a role. Some environmental progressives profess a distrust of neoliberal economics. And why not? It's gotten us into this mess. Some prominent figures, such as Naomi Klein, have openly challenged the notion that environmental sustainability is compatible with an underlying neoliberal political framework built on market economics. It's entirely conceivable she's right.

Some progressives feel that current policies don't do enough to address basic societal injustices. At a time when we see the greatest income disparity in history, along with a rise in nativism and intolerance, surely they have a point. They argue that any plan to address climate change must address societal injustice, too. But I would argue that social justice is *intrinsic* to climate action. Environmental crises, including climate change, disproportionately impact those with the least wealth, the fewest resources, and the least resilience. So simply *acting* on the climate crisis is acting to alleviate social injustice. It's another compelling reason to institute the systemic changes necessary to avert the further warming of our planet.

Yes, we have other pressing problems to solve. And climate change is just one axis in the multidimensional problem that is environmental and societal sustainability. I don't purport to propose, in this book, the solution to all that ails us as a civilization. I do, however, offer what I see as a path forward on climate.

As we pass the milestone of the fiftieth anniversary of the very first Earth Day (April 22, 1970), I believe that we are at a critical juncture. Despite the obvious political challenges we currently face,

we are witnessing an alignment of historical and political events—
and acts of Mother Nature—that are awakening us to the reality of
the climate crisis. We appear to be nearing the much-anticipated
tipping point on climate action. In a piece titled "The Climate Crisis
and the Case for Hope" published in September 2019, my friend
Jeff Goodell, a writer for *Rolling Stone*, posited that "a decade or so
from now, when the climate revolution is fully underway and Miami
Beach real estate prices are in free-fall due to constant flooding, and
internal combustion engines are as dead as CDs, people will look
back on the fall of 2019 as the turning point in the climate crisis."[146]
We can debate the precise date of the turning point. But I concur
with Jeff's larger thesis.

It is *all* of the things we have talked about—behavioral change,
incentivized by appropriate government policy, intergovernmental
agreements, and technological innovation—that will lead us forward
on climate. It is not any one of these things, but *all of them* working
together, at this unique moment in history, that provides true reason
for hope. To repeat one of the epigraphs that began this final chapter, "Hope is a good thing, maybe the best of things." Alone it won't
solve this problem. But drawing upon it, we will.

Acknowledgments

I am grateful to the many individuals who have provided help and support over the years. First and foremost are my family: my wife, Lorraine; daughter, Megan; parents, Larry and Paula; brothers, Jay and Jonathan; and the rest of the Manns, Sonsteins, Finesods, and Santys.

I give special thanks to Bill Nye, "The Science Guy," for his friendship, leadership, inspiration, and support over the years.

I am indebted to all those who have inspired me, mentored me, and served as role models, including, but not limited to, Carl Sagan, Stephen Schneider, Jane Lubchenko, John Holdren, Paul Ehrlich, Donald Kennedy, Warren Washington, and Susan Joy Hassol. I thank leaders of the youth climate movement, including Greta Thunberg, Alexandria Villaseñor, Jerome Foster, and Jamie Margolin, for the inspiration they have provided.

I am greatly indebted to the various politicians on both sides of the political spectrum who have stood up against powerful interests to support and defend me and other scientists against politically motivated attacks and who have worked to advance the cause of an informed climate policy discourse. Among them are Sherwood Boehlert, Jerry Brown, Bob Casey Jr., Bill Clinton, Hillary Clinton,

Peter Garrett, Al Gore, Mark Herring, Bob Inglis, Jay Inslee, Edward Markey, Terry McAuliffe, John McCain, Christine Milne, Jim Moran, Alexandria Ocasio-Cortez, Harry Reid, Bernie Sanders, Arnold Schwarzenegger, Arlen Specter, Malcolm Turnbull, Henry Waxman, Sheldon Whitehouse, and their various staffs.

I thank my colleagues in the Departments of Meteorology and Geosciences and elsewhere at Penn State for the supportive environment they have helped foster. Among them are President Eric Barron, former president Graham Spanier, Dean Lee Kump, Earth and Environmental Systems Institute (EESI) director Sue Brantley, department head David Stensrud, and former department head Bill Brune, as well as the ever-helpful staffs in the Department of Meteorology, the College of Earth and Mineral Sciences, and EESI.

I also want to thank my agents, Jodi Solomon, Rachel Vogel, and Suzi Jamil; PublicAffairs editorial staff members Colleen Lawrie, Jeff Alexander, and Brynn Warriner; publicity team Brooke Parsons and Miguel Cervantes; and copyeditor Kathy Streckfus for all their hard work and support with this project.

I wish to thank the various other friends, supporters, and colleagues past and present for their assistance, collaboration, friendship, and inspiration over the years, including John Abraham, Kylie Ahern, John Albertson, Ken Alex, Richard Alley, Yoca Arditi-Rocha, Ed Begley Jr., Lew Blaustein, Doug Bostrom, Christian Botting, Ray Bradley, Sir Richard Branson, Jonathan Brockopp, Bob Bullard, James Byrne, Mike Cannon-Brookes, Elizabeth Carpino, Nick Carpino, Keya Chaterjee, Noam Chomsky, Kim Cobb, Ford Cochran, Michel Cochran, Julie Cole, John Collee, Leila Conners, John Cook, Jason Cronk, Jen Cronk, Heidi Cullen, Hunter Cutting, Greg Dalton, Fred Damon, Kert Davies, Didier de Fontaine, Brendan Demelle, Andrew Dessler, Steve D'Hondt, Henry Diaz, Leonardo DiCaprio, Paulo D'Oderico, Pete Dominick, Finis Dunaway, Brian Dunning, Andrea Dutton, Bill Easterling, Matt England, Kerry Emanuel, Howie Epstein, Jenni Evans, Morgan Fairchild, Chris Field, Frances Fisher, Patrick Fitzgerald, Pete Fontaine, Josh Fox, Al Franken, Peter Frumhoff, Jose Fuentes, Andra Garner, Peter Garrett, Peter Gleick, Jeff Goodell, Amy Goodman, Nellie Gorbea, David Graves, David Grin-spoon, David Halpern, Thom Hartmann, David Haslingden, Susan Joy Hassol, Katharine Hayhoe, Tony Haymet, Megan Herbert, Michele Hollis, Rob Honeycutt, Ben Horton, Malcolm Hughes, Jan Jarrett, Paul Johansen, Phil Jones, Jim Kasting, Bill Keene, Sheril Kirshenbaum, Barbara Kiser, Johanna Köb, Jonathan Koomey, Kalee Kreider, Paul Krugman, Lauren Kurtz, Deb Lawrence, Stephan Lewandowsky, Diccon Loxton, Jane Lubchenko, Scott Mandia, Joseph Marron, John Mashey, Roger McConchie, Andrea McGimsey, Bill McKibben, Pete Meyers, Sonya Miller, Chris Mooney, John Morales, Granger Morgan, Ellen Mosely-Thompson, Ray Najjar, Giordano Nanni, Jeff Nesbit, Phil Newell, Gerald North, Dana Nuccitelli, Miriam O'Brien, Michael Oppenheimer, Naomi Oreskes, Tim Osborn, Jonathan Overpeck, Lisa Oxboel, Rajendra Pachauri, Blair Palese, David Paradice, Rick Piltz, James Powell, Stefan Rahmstorf, Cliff Rechtschaffen, Hank Reichman, Ann Reid, Catherine Reilly, James Renwick, Tom Richard, David Ritter, Alan Robock, Lyndall Rowley, Mark Ruffalo, Scott Rutherford, Sasha Sagan, Jim Salinger, Barry Saltzman, Ben Santer, Julie Schmid, Gavin Schmidt, Steve Schneider, John Schwartz, Eugenie Scott, Joan Scott, Drew Shindell, Randy Showstack, Hank Shugart, David Silbert, Peter Sinclair, Dave Smith, Jodi Solomon, Richard Somerville, Amanda Staudt, Alex Steffen, Eric Steig, Byron Steinman, Nick Stokes, Sean Sublette, Larry Tanner, Jake Tapper, Lonnie Thompson, Sarah Thompson, Kim Tingley, Dave Titley, Tom Toles, Lawrence Torcello, Kevin Trenberth, Fred Treyz, Leah Tyrrell, Katy Tur, Ana Unruh-Cohen, Ali Velshi, Dave Verardo, David Vladeck, Nikki Vo, Bob Ward, Bud Ward, Bill Weir, Ray Weymann, Robert Wilcher, John B. Williams, Barbel Winkler, Christopher Wright.

Notes

INTRODUCTION

1. Neela Banerjee, Lisa Song, and David Hasemyer, "Exxon: The Road Not Taken. Exxon's Own Research Confirmed Fossil Fuels' Role in Global Warming Decades Ago," *Inside Climate News*, September 16, 2015, https://insideclimatenews.org/news/15092015/Exxons-own-research-confirmed-fossil-fuels-role-in-global-warming.

2. Naomi Oreskes and Erik M. Conway, *Merchants of Doubt: How a Handful of Scientists Obscured the Truth on Issues from Tobacco Smoke to Global Warming* (New York: Bloomsbury Press, 2010), 6.

3. David Hagmann, Emily Ho, and George Loewenstein, "Nudging Out Support for a Carbon Tax," *Nature Climate Change* 9, no. 6 (2019): 484–489.

4. M. E. Mann, R. S. Bradley, and M. K. Hughes, "Global-Scale Temperature Patterns and Climate Forcing over the Past Six Centuries," *Nature* 392 (1998): 779–787.

5. Michael E. Mann (@MichaelEMann), Twitter, April 5, 2020, 2:53 p.m., https://twitter.com/MichaelEMann/status/1246918911989334016.

CHAPTER 1: THE ARCHITECTS OF MISINFORMATION AND MISDIRECTION

1. Rachel Shteir, "Ibsen Wrote 'An Enemy of the People' in 1882. Trump Has Made It Popular Again," *New York Times*, March 9, 2018, www.nytimes.com/2018/03/09/theater/enemy-of-the-people-ibsen.html.

2. David Michaels, *Doubt Is Their Product* (New York: Oxford University Press, 2008).

3. See Mark Hertsgaard, "While Washington Slept," *Vanity Fair*, May 2006; "Hot Politics," PBS Frontline, April 3, 2006, www.pbs.org/wgbh/pages /frontline/hotpolitics/interviews/seitz.html; "Smoke, Mirrors and Hot Air: How ExxonMobil Uses Big Tobacco's Tactics to Manufacture Uncertainty on Climate Science," Union of Concerned Scientists, January 2007, www.ucsusa .org/sites/default/files/2019-09/exxon_report.pdf.

4. Rachel Carson, *Silent Spring* (Boston: Houghton Mifflin, 1962).

5. Quoted in Christopher J. Bosso, *Pesticides and Politics: The Life Cycle of a Public Issue* (Pittsburgh: University of Pittsburgh Press, 1987), 116.

6. Naomi Oreskes and Eric M. Conway, *Merchants of Doubt: How a Handful of Scientists Obscured the Truth on Issues from Tobacco Smoke to Global Warming* (New York: Bloomsbury Press, 2010).

7. "Rachel Carson's Dangerous Legacy," Competitive Enterprise Institute, SAFEChemicalPolicy.org, March 1, 2007, www.rachelwaswrong.org.

8. Clyde Haberman, "Rachel Carson, DDT and the Fight Against Malaria," *New York Times*, January 22, 2017.

9. Robin McKie, "Rachel Carson and the Legacy of Silent Spring," *The Guardian*, May 26, 2012.

10. "Henry I. Miller," Competitive Enterprise Institute, https://cei.org /adjunct-scholar/henry-i-miller; "Gregory Conko Returns to CEI as Senior Fellow," Competitive Enterprise Institute, https://cei.org/content/gregory-conko -returns-cei-senior-fellow.

11. Henry I. Miller and Gregory Conko, "Rachel Carson's Deadly Fantasies," *Forbes*, September 5, 2012, reprinted at Heartland Institute, www.heartland .org/_template-assets/documents/publications/rachel_carsons_deadly _fantasies_-_forbes.pdf.

12. For a description of a recent peer-reviewed article demonstrating the threat to bird populations associated with a class of pesticides known as neonicotinoids, see "Controversial Insecticides Shown to Threaten Survival of Wild Birds," *Science Daily*, September 12, 2019, www.sciencedaily.com /releases/2019/09/190912140456.htm.

13. Joseph Palca, "Get-the-Lead-Out Guru Challenged," *Science* 253 (1991): 842–844.

14. Benedict Carey, "Dr. Herbert Needleman, Who Saw Lead's Wider Harm to Children, Dies at 89," *New York Times*, July 27, 2017.

15. While the group no longer lists its funders, a screen capture from some twenty years ago shows present or past funding from Exxon as well as the Sarah Scaife Foundation. See "George C. Marshall Institute: Recent Funders," George C. Marshall Institute, on Internet Archive Wayback Machine, 14 captures from August 23, 2000, to December 17, 2004, http://web.archive.org /web/20000823170917/www.marshall.org/funders.htm.

16. Oreskes and Conway, *Merchants of Doubt*, 6–7, 249. Oreskes and Conway used the term "free-market fundamentalism" to describe blind faith in the

ability of the free market to solve any problem without the need for government intervention.

17. "Whatever Happened to Acid Rain?," *Distillations* radio program, hosted by Alexis Pedrick and Elisabeth Berry Drago, Science History Institute, May 22, 2018, www.sciencehistory.org/distillations/podcast/whatever -happened-to-acid-rain.

18. Osha Gray Davidson, "From Tobacco to Climate Change, 'Merchants of Doubt' Undermined the Science," *Grist*, April 17, 2010, https://grist.org /article/from-tobacco-to-climate-change-merchants-of-doubt-undermined -the-science/full; Oreskes and Conway, *Merchants of Doubt*, 82.

19. William H. Brune, "The Ozone Story: A Model for Addressing Climate Change?," *Bulletin of the Atomic Scientists* 71, no. 1 (2015): 75–84.

20. See Andrew Kaczynski, Paul LeBlanc, and Nathan McDermott, "Senior Interior Official Denied There Was an Ozone Hole and Compared Undocumented Immigrants to Cancer," CNN, October 8, 2019, www.cnn .com/2019/10/08/politics/william-perry-pendley-blm-kfile/index.html.

21. Lee R. Kump, James F. Kasting, and Robert G. Crane, *The Earth System*, 2nd ed. (New York: Pearson, 2004).

22. Sasha Sagan's first book, *For Small Creatures Such as We: Rituals for Finding Meaning in Our Unlikely World*, was published in October 2019 by G. P. Putnam's Sons. The publisher describes it as "a luminous exploration of Earth's marvels that require no faith in order to be believed."

23. Keay Davidson, *Carl Sagan: A Life* (Hoboken, NJ: John Wiley and Sons, 1999).

24. Sagan coauthored a peer-reviewed article in the leading scientific journal *Science* on December 23, 1983, presenting the scientific case for nuclear winter based on computer modeling. The article has become known as "TTAPS," after the first letters of the various authors' last names. The full reference is R. P. Turco, O. B. Toon, T. P. Ackerman, J. B. Pollack, and Carl Sagan, "Nuclear Winter: Global Consequences of Multiple Nuclear Explosions," *Science* 222, no. 4630 (1983): 1283–1292.

25. In *Merchants of Doubt*, Oreskes and Conway detailed how cold war hawks distrusted the scientists questioning the efficacy and appropriateness of developing missile defense systems like the Reagan administration's Strategic Defense Initiative.

26. Oreskes and Conway, *Merchants of Doubt*, chap. 2.

Chapter 2: The Climate Wars

1. See Mark Bowen, *Censoring Science: Inside the Political Attack on Dr. James Hansen and the Truth of Global Warming* (New York: Dutton, 2007), 224–227.

2. Michael Mann, *The Hockey Stick and the Climate Wars: Dispatches from the Front Lines* (New York: Columbia University Press, 2013).

3. Neela Banerjee, Lisa Song, and David Hasemyer, "Exxon: The Road Not Taken. Exxon's Own Research Confirmed Fossil Fuels' Role in Global Warming Decades Ago," *Inside Climate News*, September 16, 2015, https://insideclimatenews.org/news/15092015/Exxons-own-research-confirmed-fossil-fuels-role-in-global-warming.

4. See Kyla Mandel, "Exxon Predicted in 1982 Exactly How High Global Carbon Emissions Would Be Today," *Climate Progress*, May 14, 2019, https://thinkprogress.org/exxon-predicted-high-carbon-emissions-954e514b0aa9. The internal Exxon report, dated November 12, 1982, with the subject line "CO_2 'Greenhouse' Effect," 82EAP 266, under the Exxon letterhead of M. B. Glaser, manager, Environmental Affairs Program, was obtained by *Inside Climate News* and is posted at http://insideclimatenews.org/sites/default/files/documents/1982%20Exxon%20Primer%20on%20CO2%20Greenhouse%20Effect.pdf.

5. Élan Young, "Coal Knew, Too: A Newly Unearthed Journal from 1966 Shows the Coal Industry, Like the Oil Industry, Was Long Aware of the Threat of Climate Change," *Huffington Post*, November 22, 2019, www.huffpost.com/entry/coal-industry-climate-change_n_5dd6bbebe4b0e29d7280984f.

6. Naomi Oreskes and Eric M. Conway, *Merchants of Doubt: How a Handful of Scientists Obscured the Truth on Issues from Tobacco Smoke to Global Warming* (New York: Bloomsbury Press, 2010), 186.

7. Jane Meyer, "'Kochland' Examines the Koch Brothers' Early, Crucial Role in Climate-Change Denial," *New Yorker*, August 13, 2019, www.newyorker.com/news/daily-comment/kochland-examines-how-the-koch-brothers-made-their-fortune-and-the-influence-it-bought.

8. According to Ross Gelbspan, Lindzen admitted in an interview to receiving (as of 1995) roughly $10,000 per year from fossil fuel industry consulting alone. Gelbspan noted that Lindzen "charges oil and coal interests $2,500 a day for his consulting services; his 1991 trip to testify before a Senate committee was paid for by Western Fuels, and a speech he wrote, entitled 'Global Warming: The Origin and Nature of Alleged Scientific Consensus,' was underwritten by OPEC." Ross Gelbspan, "The Heat Is On: The Warming of the World's Climate Sparks a Blaze of Denial," *Harper's*, December 1995, https://harpers.org/archive/1995/12/the-heat-is-on. Lindzen's official bio lists him as a member of the Science and Economic Advisory Council of the Annapolis Center for Science-Based Public Policy. "Richard S. Lindzen," Independent Institute, www.independent.org/aboutus/person_detail.asp?id=1215. According to the *DeSmog* blog, the Annapolis organization received funding from ExxonMobil. "Annapolis Center for Science-Based Public Policy," *DeSmog* (blog), n.d., www.desmogblog.com/annapolis-center-science-based-public-policy.

9. Mann, *The Hockey Stick and the Climate War*.

10. See Gelbspan, "The Heat Is On," 46–47; James Hoggan, with Richard Littlemore, *Climate Cover-Up: The Crusade to Deny Global Warming* (Vancouver: Greystone, 2009), 30, 80, 138–140, 156–157.

11. Keith Hammond, "Wingnuts in Sheep's Clothing," *Mother Jones*, December 4, 1997, www.motherjones.com/politics/1997/12/wingnuts-sheeps-clothing. See also J. Justin Lancaster, "The Cosmos Myth," OSS: Open Source Systems, Science, Solutions, updated July 6, 2006, http://ossfoundation.us/projects/environment/global-warming/myths/revelle-gore-singer-lindzen; "A Note About Roger Revelle, Justin Lancaster and Fred Singer," *Rabett Run* (blog), September 13, 2004, http://rabett.blogspot.com/2014/09/a-note-about-roger-revelle-julian.html (contains a comment by Justin Lancaster stating his views about these matters).

12. S. Marshall, M. E. Mann, R. Oglesby, and B. Saltzman, "A Comparison of the CCM1-Simulated Climates for Pre-Industrial and Present-Day CO_2 Levels," *Global and Planetary Change* 10 (1995): 163–180.

13. An excellent account of these events can be found in Chapter 6 of Oreskes and Conway, *Merchants of Doubt*.

14. See Intergovernmental Panel on Climate Change, *IPCC Second Assessment: Climate Change 1995*, available at IPCC, www.ipcc.ch/site/assets/uploads/2018/06/2nd-assessment-en.pdf.

15. Mann, *The Hockey Stick and the Climate Wars*, 181–183.

16. These events are summarized in Mann, *The Hockey Stick and the Climate Wars*.

17. Fred Pearce, "Climate Change Special: State of Denial," *New Scientist*, November 2006.

18. "Kyoto Protocol to the United Nations Framework Convention on Climate Change," Chapter 27, section 7.a, December 11, 1997, United Nations Treaty Collection, https://treaties.un.org/pages/ViewDetails.aspx?src=TREATY&mtdsg_no=XXVII-7-a&chapter=27.

19. See Daniel Engber, "The Grandfather of Alt-Science," *FiveThirtyEight*, October 12, 2017, https://fivethirtyeight.com/features/the-grandfather-of-alt-science.

20. "Skepticism About Skeptics," *Scientific American*, August 23, 2006.

21. M. E. Mann, R. S. Bradley, and M. K. Hughes, "Global-Scale Temperature Patterns and Climate Forcing over the Past Six Centuries," *Nature* 392 (1998): 779–787.

22. See "The Environment: A Cleaner, Safer, Healthier America," Luntz Research Companies, reproduced at SourceWatch, www.sourcewatch.org/images/4/45/LuntzResearch.Memo.pdf.

23. J. T. Houghton, Y. Ding, D. J. Griggs, M. Noguer, P. J. van der Linden, X. Dai, K. Maskell, and C. A. Johnson, "Climate Change 2001: The Scientific Basis," Contribution of Working Group I to the Third Assessment Report of the Intergovernmental Panel on Climate Change, 2001, www.ipcc.ch/site/assets/uploads/2018/03/WGI_TAR_full_report.pdf.

24. Mann, *The Hockey Stick and the Climate Wars*.

25. In 2012, a team of seventy-eight leading paleoclimate scientists representing the PAGES 2k Consortium, drawing on the most widespread paleoclimate database that has been assembled, published a new reconstruction

of large-scale temperature trends. PAGES 2k Consortium, "Continental-Scale Temperature Variability During the Past Two Millennia," *Nature Geoscience* 6 (2013): 339–346, https://doi.org/10.1038/NGEO1797. They concluded that global temperatures have reached their greatest levels in at least 1,300 years. A direct comparison by a German paleoclimatologist reveals their temperature reconstruction to be virtually identical to the original hockey-stick reconstruction. Stefan Rahmstorf, "Most Comprehensive Paleoclimate Reconstruction Confirms Hockey Stick," *Think Progress*, July 8, 2013, https://archive.thinkprogress.org/most-comprehensive-paleoclimate-reconstruction-confirms-hockey-stick-e7ce8c3a2384. In 2019, a group of scientists extended the conclusion, with similar levels of confidence, back to the past two thousand years. See, for example, George Dvorsky, "Climate Shifts of the Past 2,000 Years Were Nothing Like What's Happening Today," *Gizmodo*, July 24, 2019, https://earther.gizmodo.com/climate-shifts-of-the-past-2-000-years-were-nothing-lik-1836662680. A more tentative pair of peer-reviewed studies has extended this conclusion back to at least the past twenty thousand years. See, for example, "Real Skepticism About the New Marcott 'Hockey Stick,'" *Skeptical Science*, April 10, 2013, https://skepticalscience.com/marcott-hockey-stick-real-skepticism.html.

26. Consider a recent article in the right-wing *Telegraph* of London: Sarah Knapton, "Climate Change: Fake News or Global Threat? This Is the Science," *Telegraph*, October 15, 2019, www.telegraph.co.uk/science/2019/10/15/climate-change-fake-news-global-threat-science. This article promoted a number of discredited criticisms advanced by climate-change deniers against the hockey stick. A panel of experts evaluated the article for the independent climate media watchdog group Climate Feedback and gave the article a negative rating for accuracy, noting the inaccurate claims made about the hockey stick. "Telegraph Article on Climate Change Mixes Accurate and Unsupported, Inaccurate Claims, Misleads with False Balance," Climate Feedback, October 18, 2019, https://climatefeedback.org/evaluation/telegraph-article-misleads-with-false-balance-mixing-in-unsupported-and-inaccurate-claims-sarah-knapton.

27. Carl Sagan, *The Demon-Haunted World* (New York: Random House, 1996).

28. Michael Mann and Tom Toles, *The Madhouse Effect: How Climate Change Denial Is Threatening Our Planet, Destroying Our Politics, and Driving Us Crazy* (New York: Columbia University Press, 2016).

29. These events are described in detail in Mann, *The Hockey Stick and the Climate Wars*, chap. 14.

30. Mann, *The Hockey Stick and the Climate Wars*.

31. Kenneth Li, "Alwaleed Backs James Murdoch," *Financial Times*, January 22, 2010, www.ft.com/content/c33aad22-06c8-11df-b058-00144feabdc0; Sissi Cao, "Longtime Murdoch Ally, Saudi Prince Dumps $1.5B Worth of Fox Shares," *Observer*, November 9, 2017, https://observer.com/2017/11/longtime-murdoch-ally-saudi-prince-dumps-1-5b-worth-of-fox-shares.

32. See Iggy Ostanin, "Exclusive: 'Climategate' Email Hacking Was Carried Out from Russia, in Effort to Undermine Action on Global Warming," *Medium*, June 30, 2019, https://medium.com/@iggyostanin/exclusive-climategate

-email-hacking-was-carried-out-from-russia-in-effort-to-undermine-action
-78b19bc3ca5a.

33. The evidence is laid out in Mann and Toles, *Madhouse Effect*, 164–166.

34. "Putin Says Climate Change Is Not Man-Made and We Should Adapt to It, Not Try to Stop It," Agence France-Presse, March 31, 2017, www.scmp .com/news/world/russia-central-asia/article/2083650/trump-vladimir-putin -says-climate-change-not-man-made.

35. Jonathan Watts and Ben Doherty, "US and Russia Ally with Saudi Arabia to Water Down Climate Pledge," *The Guardian*, December 9, 2018, www.theguardian.com/environment/2018/dec/09/us-russia-ally-saudi-arabia -water-down-climate-pledges-un.

36. "Special Report: Global Warming of 1.5°C," Intergovernmental Panel on Climate Change (IPCC), October 8, 2018, www.ipcc.ch/sr15.

37. Daniel Dale, "Lies, Lies, Lies: How Trump's Fiction Gets More Dramatic over Time," CNN, October 27, 2019, www.cnn.com/2019/10/27/politics /fact-check-lies-trump-fiction-obama-kim-jong-un/index.html.

38. Abel Gustafson, Anthony Leiserowitz, and Edward Maibach, "Americans Are Increasingly 'Alarmed' About Global Warming," Yale Program on Climate Change Communication, February 12, 2019, https://climate communication.yale.edu/publications/americans-are-increasingly-alarmed -about-global-warming.

39. Consider, for example, the 2009 "NIPCC" climate-change-denying report put out by the Heartland Institute, funded by the Koch brothers and the fossil fuel industry: S. Fred Singer and Craig Idso, "Climate Change Reconsidered: 2009 NIPPC Report," Nongovernmental International Panel on Climate Change, 2009, http://climatechangereconsidered.org/climate-change -reconsidered-2009-nipcc-report. The report was formatted to mimic the IPCC report itself. Or the "debate" staged by the Heartland Institute in New York on September 23, 2019, in an attempt to blunt the growing momentum for climate action arising from the United Nations Climate Change Summit of September 2019 and surrounding public awareness campaigns: "Videos: Climate Debate in NYC on Sept. 23—Moderator, John Stossel," Heartland Institute, www.heartland.org/multimedia/videos /climate-debate-in-nyc-on-sept-23---moderator-john-stossel.

40. See, for example, this summary of a study of Australian public opinion on climate change: Naomi Schalit, "Climate Change Deniers Are Rarer Than We Think," *The Conversation*, November 11, 2012, https://theconversation .com/climate-change-deniers-are-rarer-than-we-think-10670.

41. Natacha Larnaud, "'This Will Only Get Worse in the Future': Experts See Direct Line Between California Wildfires and Climate Change," CBS News, October 30, 2019, www.cbsnews.com/news/this-will-only-get-worse -in-the-future-experts-find-direct-line-between-california-wildfires-and -climate-change.

42. Mary Tyler March, "Trump Blames 'Gross Mismanagement' for Deadly California Wildfires," *The Hill*, November 10, 2018, https://thehill.com /homenews/administration/416046-trump-blames-gross-mismanagement

-for-deadly-california-wildfires; Patrick Shanley and Katherine Schaff-stall, "Late-Night Hosts Mock Trump's 'Weird' Trip to California Following Wildfires," *Hollywood Reporter*, November 20, 2018, www.hollywoodreporter.com/live-feed/late-night-hosts-mock-trump-fire-comments-california-trip-1162958.

43. Emily Holden and Jimmy Tobias, "New Emails Reveal That the Trump Administration Manipulated Wildfire Science to Promote Logging: The Director of the US Geological Survey Asked Scientists to 'Gin Up' Emissions Figures for Him," *Mother Jones*, January 26, 2020, www.motherjones.com/environment/2020/01/new-emails-reveal-that-the-trump-administration-manipulated-wildfire-science-to-promote-logging.

44. Michael E. Mann, "Australia, Your Country Is Burning—Dangerous Climate Change Is Here with You Now," *The Guardian*, January 2, 2020, www.theguardian.com/commentisfree/2020/jan/02/australia-your-country-is-burning-dangerous-climate-change-is-here-with-you-now.

45. Indeed, I gave a number of interviews at the time making that connection for viewers and listeners, including ABC Australia. See "'A Tipping Point Is Playing Out Right Now' Says Climate Scientist Michael Mann," YouTube, posted January 2, 2020, ABC Australia, www.youtube.com/watch?v=OYtAGTe9MjY&feature=youtu.be; "Australian Fires: Who Is to Blame?," BBC, January 6, 2020, www.bbc.co.uk/sounds/play/p07zns45.

46. See "The Australian," SourceWatch, www.sourcewatch.org/index.php/The_Australian, accessed January 8, 2020.

47. Lachlan Cartwright, "James Murdoch Slams Fox News and News Corp over Climate-Change Denial," *Daily Beast*, January 14, 2020, www.thedailybeast.com/james-murdoch-slams-fox-news-and-news-corp-over-climate-change-denial.

48. Fiona Harvey, "Climate Change Is Already Damaging Global Economy, Report Finds," *The Guardian*, September 25, 2012, www.theguardian.com/environment/2012/sep/26/climate-change-damaging-global-economy.

49. Nafeez Ahmed, "U.S. Military Could Collapse Within 20 Years Due to Climate Change, Report Commissioned by Pentagon Says," *Vice*, October 14, 2019, www.vice.com/en_us/article/mbmkz8/us-military-could-collapse-within-20-years-due-to-climate-change-report-commissioned-by-pentagon-says.

50. Geoff Dembicki, "DC's Trumpiest Congressman Says the GOP Needs to Get Real on Climate Change," *Vice*, March 25, 2019, www.vice.com/en_us/article/zma97w/matt-gaetz-congress-loves-donald-trump-climate-change.

51. Philip Bump, "Anti-Tax Activist Grover Norquist Thinks a Carbon Tax Might Make Sense—with Some Caveats," *Grist*, November 13, 2012, https://grist.org/politics/anti-tax-activist-grover-norquist-thinks-a-carbon-tax-might-make-sense-with-some-caveats.

52. "Charles Koch—CEO of Koch Industries (#381)," *Tim Ferris Show* (podcast), August 11, 2019, https://tim.blog/2019/08/11/charles-koch.

See also "Charles Koch Talks Environment, Politics, Business and More," Koch Newsroom, August 12, 2019, https://news.kochind.com/news/2019 /charles-koch-talks-environment,-politics,-busi-1.

53. Andrea Dutton and Michael E. Mann, "A Dangerous New Form of Climate Denialism Is Making the Rounds," *Newsweek*, August 22, 2019, www.newsweek.com/dangerous-new-form-climate-denialism-making-rounds -opinion-1455736.

CHAPTER 3: THE "CRYING INDIAN" AND THE BIRTH OF THE DEFLECTION CAMPAIGN

1. James Downie, "The NRA Is Winning the Spin Battle," *Washington Post*, February 20, 2018, www.washingtonpost.com/blogs/post-partisan/wp/2018 /02/20/the-nra-is-winning-the-spin-battle.

2. Dennis A. Henigan, *"Guns Don't Kill People, People Kill People": And Other Myths About Guns and Gun Control* (Boston: Beacon Press, 2016).

3. Joseph Dolman, "Mayor's Promise on Guns Is Noble," *Newsday*, February 15, 2006. In 2017, the most recent year for which we have complete data, 39,773 people died from gun-related injuries in the United States, according to the Centers for Disease Control and Prevention. See John Gramlich, "What the Data Says About Gun Deaths in the U.S.," Pew Research Center, August 16, 2019, www.pewresearch.org/fact-tank/2019/08/16 /what-the-data-says-about-gun-deaths-in-the-u-s.

4. See Patricia Callahan and Sam Roe, "Big Tobacco Wins Fire Marshals as Allies in Flame Retardant Push," *Chicago Tribune*, May 8, 2012, www .chicagotribune.com/lifestyles/health/ct-met-flames-tobacco-20120508-story .html; Patricia Callahan and Sam Roe, "Fear Fans Flames for Chemical Makers," *Chicago Tribune*, May 6, 2012, www.chicagotribune.com/investigations /ct-met-flame-retardants-20120506-story.html.

5. Callahan and Roe, "Big Tobacco Wins Fire Marshals."

6. See, for example, Juliet Eilperin and David A. Fahrenthold, "Va. Climatologist Drawing Heat from His Critics," *Washington Post*, September 17, 2006, www.washingtonpost.com/archive/local/2006/09/17/va-climatologist -drawing-heat-from-his-critics/1bd66873-9fcc-40af-b9af-6e5808649af3.

7. James Pitkin, "Defying a Chemical Lobby, Oregon House Passes Fire-Retardant Ban," *Willamette Week*, June 18, 2009.

8. "Americans for Prosperity," SourceWatch, www.sourcewatch.org/index .php/Americans_for_Prosperity.

9. Callahan and Roe, "Fear Fans Flames."

10. Callahan and Roe, "Fear Fans Flames."

11. Callahan and Roe, "Fear Fans Flames."

12. Deborah Blum, "Flame Retardants Are Everywhere," *New York Times*, July 1, 2014, https://well.blogs.nytimes.com/2014/07/01/flame-retardants-are -everywhere.

13. "Pollution: Keep America Beautiful—Iron Eyes Cody," Ad Council, www.adcouncil.org/Our-Campaigns/The-Classics/Pollution-Keep-America-Beautiful-Iron-Eyes-Cody.

14. Finis Dunaway, "The 'Crying Indian' Ad That Fooled the Environmental Movement," *Chicago Tribune*, November 21, 2017, www.chicagotribune.com/opinion/commentary/ct-perspec-indian-crying-environment-ads-pollution-1123-20171113-story.html. See also Finis Dunaway, *Seeing Green: The Use and Abuse of American Environmental Images* (Chicago: University of Chicago Press, 2015).

15. See Dunaway, *Seeing Green*, 86.

16. Matt Simon, "Plastic Rain Is the New Acid Rain," *Wired*, June 11, 2020, www.wired.com/story/plastic-rain-is-the-new-acid-rain.

17. Dunaway, "'Crying Indian' Ad."

18. "These Things Are Disappearing Because Millennials Refuse to Pay for Them," *Buzznet*, June 27, 2019, www.buzznet.com/2019/06/millennials-refuse-to-buy.

19. David Hagmann, Emily H. Ho, and George Loewenstein, "Nudging Out Support for a Carbon Tax," *Nature Climate Change* 9 (2019): 484–489.

20. Michael E. Mann and Jonathan Brockopp, "You Can't Save the Climate by Going Vegan: Corporate Polluters Must Be Held Accountable," *USA Today*, June 3, 2019, www.usatoday.com/story/opinion/2019/06/03/climate-change-requires-collective-action-more-than-single-acts-column/1275965001.

CHAPTER 4: IT'S YOUR FAULT

1. See Sami Grover, "In Defense of Eco-Hypocrisy," *Medium*, March 21, 2019, https://blog.usejournal.com/in-defense-of-eco-hypocrisy-b71fb86f2b2f.

2. "BP Boss Plans to 'Reinvent' Oil Giant for Green Era," BBC, February 13, 2020, www.bbc.com/news/business-51475379.

3. See Grover, "In Defense of Eco-Hypocrisy."

4. Malcolm Harris, "Shell Is Looking Forward: The Fossil-Fuel Companies Expect to Profit from Climate Change. I Went to a Private Planning Meeting and Took Notes," *New York Magazine*, March 3, 2020, https://nymag.com/intelligencer/2020/03/shell-climate-change.html.

5. Charles Kennedy, "Is Eating Meat Worse Than Burning Oil?," OilPrice.com, October 22, 2019, https://oilprice.com/The-Environment/Global-Warming/Is-Eating-Meat-Worse-Than-Burning-Oil.html.

6. Nathaniel Rich, "Losing Earth: The Decade We Almost Stopped Climate Change," *New York Times Magazine*, August 1, 2018, www.nytimes.com/interactive/2018/08/01/magazine/climate-change-losing-earth.html.

7. Robinson Meyer, "The Problem with *The New York Times*' Big Story on Climate Change," *The Atlantic*, August 1, 2018, www.theatlantic.com/science/archive/2018/08/nyt-mag-nathaniel-rich-climate-change/566525.

8. Hannah Fairfield, "The Facts About Food and Climate Change," *New York Times*, May 1, 2019, www.nytimes.com/2019/05/01/climate/nyt-climate

-newsletter-food.html; Tik Root and John Schwartz, "One Thing We Can Do: Drive Less," *New York Times*, August 28, 2019, www.nytimes.com/2019/08/28 /climate/one-thing-we-can-do-drive-less.html; Andy Newman, "If Seeing the World Helps Ruin It, Should We Stay Home?," *New York Times*, June 3, 2019, www.nytimes.com/2019/06/03/travel/traveling-climate-change.html; Andy Newman, "I Am Part of the Climate-Change Problem. That's Why I Wrote About It," *New York Times*, June 18, 2019, www.nytimes.com/2019/06/18 /reader-center/travel-climate-change.html.

9. Jonathan Safran Foer, "The End of Meat Is Here," *New York Times*, May 21, 2020, www.nytimes.com/2020/05/21/opinion/coronavirus-meat -vegetarianism.html.

10. Editorial Board, "The Democrats' Best Choices for President," *New York Times*, January 19, 2020, www.nytimes.com/interactive/2020/01/19/opinion /amy-klobuchar-elizabeth-warren-nytimes-endorsement.html.

11. S. Lewandowsky, N. Oreskes, J. S. Risbey, B. R. Newell, and M. Smithson, "Seepage: Climate Change Denial and Its Effect on the Scientific Community," *Global Environmental Change* 33 (2015): 1–13, https://doi.org/10 .1016/j.gloenvcha.2015.02.013.

12. Grover, "In Defense of Eco-Hypocrisy."

13. Jennifer Stock and Geremy Schulick, "Yale's Endowment Won't Divest from Fossil Fuels. Here's Why That's Wrong," *American Prospect*, March 8, 2019, https://prospect.org/education/yale-s-endowment-divest-fossil-fuels.-wrong.

14. Steven D. Hales, "The Futility of Guilt-Based Advocacy," *Quillette*, November 23, 2019, https://quillette.com/2019/11/23/the-futility-of-guilt -based-advocacy.

15. John Schwartz (@jswatz), Twitter, November 14, 2019, 8:38 a.m., https://twitter.com/jswatz/status/1195018223621754880.

16. Clay Evans, "Ditching the Doomsaying for Better Climate Discourse," *Colorado Arts and Sciences Magazine*, December 18, 2019, www.colorado.edu /asmagazine/2019/12/18/ditching-doomsaying-better-climate-discourse.

17. Brad Johnson, "Pete Buttigieg Climate Advisor Is a Fossil-Fuel-Funded Witness for the Trump Administration Against Children's Climate Lawsuit," *Hill Heat*, November 18, 2019, www.hillheat.com/articles/2019/11/18/pete -buttigieg-climate-advisor-is-a-fossil-fuel-funded-witness-for-the-trump -administration-against-childrens-climate-lawsuit; David G. Victor and Charles F. Kennel, "Climate Policy: Ditch the 2°C Warming Goal," *Nature*, October 1, 2014, www.nature.com/news/climate-policy-ditch-the-2-c-warming-goal -1.16018.

18. David G. Victor, "We Have Climate Leaders. Now We Need Followers," *New York Times*, December 13, 2019, www.nytimes.com/2019/12/13/opinion /climate-change-madrid.html.

19. Dr. Genevieve Guenther (@DoctorVive), Twitter, December 13, 2019, 10:38 a.m., https://twitter.com/DoctorVive/status/1205557572528410628.

20. Nathanael Johnson, "Fossil Fuels Are the Problem, Say Fossil Fuel Companies Being Sued," *Grist*, March 21, 2018, https://grist.org/article/fossil -fuels-are-the-problem-say-fossil-fuel-companies-being-sued.

21. See this Twitter thread initiated by journalist Emily Atkin (@emorwee), November 20, 2019, 6:01 a.m., https://twitter.com/emorwee/status /1197152947282612225.

22. See the Discovery Institute's self-described five-year "wedge strategy," archived at AntiEvolution.org, www.antievolution.org/features/wedge .html.

23. Aja Romano, "Twitter Released 9 Million Tweets from One Russian Troll Farm. Here's What We Learned," *Vox*, October 19, 2018, www.vox.com /2018/10/19/17990946/Twitter-russian-trolls-bots-election-tampering.

24. Lucy Tiven, "Where the Presidential Candidates Stand on Climate Change,"Attn.com,September6,2016,https://archive.attn.com/stories/11189/ presidential-candidates-stance-on-climate-change; Brad Plumer, "On Climate Change,the Difference Between Trump and Clinton Is Really Quite Simple," *Vox*, November 4, 2016, www.vox.com/science-and-health/2016/10/10/13227682 /trump-clinton-climate-energy-difference.

25. Rebecca Leber, "Many Young Voters Don't See a Difference Between Clinton and Trump on Climate," *Grist*, July 31, 2016, https://grist.org/election -2016/many-young-voters-dont-see-a-difference-between-clinton-and-trump -on-climate.

26. Craig Timberg and Tony Romm, "Russian Trolls Sought to Inflame Debate over Climate Change, Fracking, Dakota Pipeline," *Chicago Tribune*, March 1, 2018, www.chicagotribune.com/nation-world/ct-russian-trolls-climate-change -20180301-story.html.

27. See Nancy LeTourneau, "The Gaslighting Effect of Both-Siderism," *Washington Monthly*, October 8, 2018, https://washingtonmonthly.com/2018 /10/08/the-gaslighting-effect-of-both-siderism.

28. Paul Krugman, "The Party That Ruined the Planet: Republican Climate Denial Is Even Scarier Than Trumpism," *New York Times*, December 12, 2019, www.nytimes.com/2019/12/12/opinion/climate-change-republicans.html.

29. The entire conversation can be found at Michael E. Mann (@MichaelEMann), Twitter, December 12, 2019, 5:04 p.m., https://twitter.com /MichaelEMann/status/1205292356208979968.

30. Sandra Laville and David Pegg, "Fossil Fuel Firms' Social Media Fightback Against Climate Action," *The Guardian*, October 11, 2019, www .theguardian.com/environment/2019/oct/10/fossil-fuel-firms-social-media -fightback-against-climate-action; Craig Timberg and Tony Romm, "Russian Trolls Sought to Inflame Debate over Climate Change, Fracking, Dakota Pipeline," *Chicago Tribune*, March 1, 2018, www.chicagotribune.com/nation-world /ct-russian-trolls-climate-change-20180301-story.html.

31. Marianne Lavelle, "'Trollbots' Swarm Twitter with Attacks on Climate Science Ahead of UN Summit," *Inside Climate News*, September 16, 2019, https://insideclimatenews.org/news/16092019/trollbot-Twitter-climate -change-attacks-disinformation-campaign-mann-mckenna-greta-targeted.

32. Oliver Milman, "Revealed: Quarter of All Tweets About Climate Crisis Produced by Bots," *The Guardian*, February 21, 2020, www.theguardian.com /technology/2020/feb/21/climate-tweets-Twitter-bots-analysis.

33. Elisha R .Frederiks, Karen Stenner, and Elizabeth V. Hobman, "Household Energy Use: Applying Behavioural Economics to Understand Consumer Decision-Making and Behaviour," *Renewable and Sustainable Energy Reviews* 41 (2015): 1385–1394, www.sciencedirect.com/science/article/pii/S1364032114007990.

34. Nicole Perlroth, "A Former Fox News Executive Divides Americans Using Russian Tactics," *New York Times*, November 21, 2019, www.nytimes.com/2019/11/21/technology/LaCorte-edition-news.html.

35. See Michael E. Mann and Jonathan Brockopp, "You Can't Save the Climate by Going Vegan. Corporate Polluters Must Be Held Accountable," *USA Today*, June 3, 2019, www.usatoday.com/story/opinion/2019/06/03/climate-change-requires-collective-action-more-than-single-acts-column/1275965001; Michael E. Mann, "Lifestyle Changes Aren't Enough to Save the Planet. Here's What Could," *Time*, September 12, 2019, https://time.com/5669071/lifestyle-changes-climate-change.

36. See, for example, my commentary "Greta Thunberg, Not Donald Trump, Is the True Leader of the Free World," *Newsweek*, September 24, 2019, www.newsweek.com/greta-thunberg-donald-trump-true-leadership-climate-change-free-world-1461147.

37. Nives Dolsak and Aseem Prakash, "Does Greta Thunberg's Lifestyle Equal Climate Denial? One Climate Scientist Seems to Suggest So," *Forbes*, November 14, 2019, www.forbes.com/sites/prakashdolsak/2019/11/14/does-greta-thunbergs-lifestyle-equal-climate-denial-one-climate-scientist-seems-to-suggest-so (subsequently edited by *Forbes*). See also thread at Jerome Foster II (@JeromeFosterII), Twitter, November 15, 2019, 6:35 p.m., https://twitter.com/JeromeFosterII/status/1195530789334798338.

38. Robin McKie, "Climate Change Deniers' New Battle Front Attacked," *The Guardian*, November 9, 2019, www.theguardian.com/science/2019/nov/09/doomism-new-tactic-fossil-fuel-lobby.

39. Dr. Lucky Tran (@luckytran), Twitter, November 15, 2019, 9:28 a.m., https://twitter.com/luckytran/status/1195393067764699137; John Upton (@johnupton), Twitter, November 15, 2019, 8:20 a.m., https://twitter.com/johnupton/status/1195375914365919232.

40. See "Anthony Watts," SourceWatch, www.sourcewatch.org/index.php/Anthony_Watts; "Heartland Institute," SourceWatch, www.sourcewatch.org/index.php/Heartland_Institute; Eric Worrall, "Katharine Hayhoe Attacks Greta Thunberg's Climate 'Shaming' Crusade," *Watts Up with That*, August 19, 2019, https://wattsupwiththat.com/2019/08/19/katharine-hayhoe-attacks-greta-thunbergs-climate-shaming-crusade.

41. The tweet in question is Prof. Katharine Hayhoe (@KHayhoe), Twitter, August 20, 2019, 9:34 a.m., https://twitter.com/KHayhoe/status/1163851874921005057.

42. See, for example, Dictionary.com, www.dictionary.com/e/slang/ok-boomer: "*OK boomer* is a viral internet slang phrase used, often in a humorous or ironic manner, to call out or dismiss out-of-touch or close-minded opinions associated with the baby boomer generation and older people more generally."

43. See, for example, David Roberts, "California Gov. Jerry Brown Casually Unveils History's Most Ambitious Climate Target: Full Carbon Neutrality Is Now on the Table for the World's Fifth Largest Economy," *Vox*, September 12, 2018, www.vox.com/energy-and-environment/2018/9/11/17844896/california-jerry-brown-carbon-neutral-2045-climate-change.

44. Brown made the announcement at the December 2016 annual meeting of the American Geophysical Union in San Francisco—a conference I attended (I spoke at the meeting).

45. Emily Guerin, "Jerry Brown Is Getting Heckled at His Own Climate Conference," LAist, September 12, 2018, https://laist.com/2018/09/12/la_environmentalists_heckling_jerry_brown_at_climate_conference.php.

46. Mark Hertsgaard, "Jerry Brown vs. the Climate Wreckers: Is He Doing Enough?," *The Nation*, August 29, 2018, www.thenation.com/article/jerry-brown-vs-the-climate-wreckers-is-he-doing-enough.

47. See Arn Menconi (@ArnMenconi), Twitter, November 17, 2019, 6:43 a.m., https://twitter.com/ArnMenconi/status/1196076331269681152.

48. Kate Connolly and Matthew Taylor, "Extinction Rebellion Founder's Holocaust Remarks Spark Fury," *The Guardian*, November 20, 2019, www.theguardian.com/environment/2019/nov/20/extinction-rebellion-founders-holocaust-remarks-spark-fury.

49. Jason Mark, "Yes, Actually, Individual Responsibility Is Essential to Solving the Climate Crisis," Sierra Club, November 26, 2019, www.sierraclub.org/sierra/yes-actually-individual-responsibility-essential-solving-climate-crisis; Mann and Brockopp, "You Can't Save the Climate by Going Vegan."

50. Mann, "Lifestyle Changes Aren't Enough."

51. According to the World Resources Institute, total annual emissions from animal agriculture (production emissions plus land-use change) are about 14.5 percent of all human emissions, of which beef contributes about 41 percent. Richard Waite, Tim Searchinger, and Janet Ranganathan, "6 Pressing Questions About Beef and Climate Change, Answered," World Resources Institute, April 8, 2019, www.wri.org/blog/2019/04/6-pressing-questions-about-beef-and-climate-change-answered.

52. See Jonathan Kaplan, "There's No Conspiracy in Cowspiracy," Natural Resources Defense Council, April 29, 2016, www.nrdc.org/experts/jonathan-kaplan/theres-no-conspiracy-cowspiracy; Doug Boucher, "Movie Review: There's a Vast Cowspiracy about Climate Change," Union of Concerned Scientists, June 10, 2016, https://blog.ucsusa.org/doug-boucher/cowspiracy-movie-review.

According to the latter, "the 51% figure is key to the film's conspiracy theory. . . . Ironically, in light of *Cowspiracy*'s thesis that environmental NGOs are hiding the science, this study proposing this figure on which they rely so heavily was not published in a scientific journal, but in a report by an environmental organization, the Worldwatch Institute. The report's authors, Jeff Anhang and the late Robert Goodland, were not named in the movie but were described simply as 'two advisers from the World Bank.'"

53. In response to a tweet of mine stressing the urgency of reducing carbon emissions, one vegan or vegetarian activist posed the presumably rhetorical question, "Is @MichaelEMann vegan or vegetarian? Does he drive an EV and have solar at home?" I replied "I don't eat meat, I drive a hybrid, and have a wind-only energy plan. I also think that trying to shame people over lifestyle is presumptuous and unproductive." See Trees (@SolutionsOK), Twitter, November 14, 2018, 10:43 a.m., https://twitter.com/SolutionsOK /status/1062778092345679872.

54. Seth Borenstein, "Climate Scientists Try to Cut Their Own Carbon Footprints," Associated Press, December 8, 2019, https://apnews.com/dde2bf 108411ecd973de60bfda5250aa. See also Michael E. Mann (@MichaelEMann), Twitter, November 20, 2019, 8:39 a.m., https://twitter.com/MichaelEMann /status/1197192725445185536.

55. Catherine Brahic, "Train Can Be Worse for Climate Than Plane," New Scientist, June 8, 2009, www.newscientist.com/article/dn17260-train-can-be -worse-for-climate-than-plane.

56. Kaya Chatterjee, The Zero-Footprint Baby: How to Save the Planet While Raising a Healthy Baby (New York: Ig Publishing, 2013).

57. Maxine Joselow, "Quitting Burgers and Planes Won't Stop Warming, Experts Say," Climatewire, E&E News, December 6, 2019, www.eenews.net /stories/1061734031.

58. Seth Borenstein, "Climate Scientists Try to Cut Their Own Carbon Footprints," Associated Press, December 8, 2019, https://apnews.com /dde2bf108411ecd973de60bfda5250aa.

59. George Monbiot, "We Are All Killers," February 28, 2006, www .monbiot.com/2006/02/28/we-are-all-killers.

60. David Freedlander, "The Meteorologist's Meltdown: Eric Holthaus on Deciding to Quit Flying," Daily Beast, October 1, 2013, www.thedaily beast.com/the-meteorologists-meltdown-eric-holthaus-on-deciding-to-quit -flying.

61. See, for example, Eric Berger, "Who Is Eric Holthaus, and Why Did He Give Up Flying Today?," Houston Chronicle, September 27, 2013, https:// blog.chron.com/sciguy/2013/09/who-is-eric-holthaus-and-why-did-he-give -up-flying-today; Jason Samenow, "Meteorologist Eric Holthaus' Vow to Never to [sic] Fly Again Draws Praise, Criticism," Washington Post, October 1, 2013, www.washingtonpost.com/news/capital-weather-gang/wp/2013/10/01 /meteorologist-eric-holthaus-vow-to-never-to-fly-again-draws-praise -criticism; Will Oremus, "Meteorologist Weeps over Climate Change, Fox News Calls Him a 'Sniveling Beta-Male,'" Slate, October 3, 2013, https://slate .com/technology/2013/10/sniveling-beta-male-fox-news-greg-gutfeld-slams -eric-holthaus-for-giving-up-flying.html.

62. See, for example, Berger, "Who Is Eric Holthaus?"; Eric Holthaus (@ EricHolthaus), Twitter, October 1, 2013, 7:22 a.m., https://twitter.com /EricHolthaus/status/385047176851644417, quoted in Samenow, "Meteorologist Eric Holthaus' Vow"; Oremus, "Meteorologist Weeps."

63. "U. Minnesota Scholar Criticizes Air Travel," *Conservative Edition News*, n.d., https://conservativeeditionnews.com/u-minnesota-scholar-criticizes -air-travel; "Doug P.," "Meteorologist Eric Holthaus SHAMES Aviation Buff over Unnecessary Commercial Flight Because It's 'Just as Deadly as a Gun' and 'Should Be Outlawed,'" *Twitchy*, July 25, 2019, https://twitchy.com/dougp -3137/2019/07/25/meteorologist-eric-holthaus-shames-aviation-buff-over -unnecessary-commercial-flight-because-its-just-as-deadly-as-a-gun-and -should-be-outlawed.

64. David Roberts, "Rich Climate Activist Leonardo DiCaprio Lives a Carbon-Intensive Lifestyle, and That's (Mostly) Fine," *Vox*, March 2, 2016, www .vox.com/2016/3/2/11143310/leo-dicaprios-carbon-lifestyle.

65. See "Beacon Center of Tennessee," SourceWatch, www.sourcewatch .org/index.php/Beacon_Center_of_Tennessee.

66. See David Mikkelson and Dan Evon, "Al Gore's Home Energy Use: Does Al Gore's Home Consume Twenty Times as Much Energy as the Average American House?," Snopes, February 28, 2007, www.snopes.com/fact-check /al-gores-energy-use.

67. Jake Tapper, "Al Gore's 'Inconvenient Truth'?—A $30,000 Utility Bill," ABC News, February 27, 2007, https://abcnews.go.com/Politics/Global Warming/story?id=2906888.

68. See Mikkelson and Evon, "Al Gore's Home Energy Use."

69. Rita Panahi, "Hollywood Hypocrite's Global Warming Sermon," *Herald Sun*, October 7, 2016, www.heraldsun.com.au/blogs/rita-panahi/hollywood -hypocrites-global-warming-sermon/news-story/b4cc2e4b6034c032998 fb3c13e6df4a6.

70. Andrea Peyser, "Leo DiCaprio Isn't the Only Climate Change Hypocrite," *New York Post*, May 26, 2016, https://nypost.com/2016/05/26/leo-di -caprio-isnt-the-only-climate-change-hypocrite.

71. Alison Boshoff and Sue Connolly, "Eco-Warrior or Hypocrite? Leonardo DiCaprio Jets Around the World Partying . . . While Preaching to Us All on Global Warming," *Daily Mail*, May 24, 2016.

72. Roberts, "Rich Climate Activist Leonardo DiCaprio."

73. Roberts, "Rich Climate Activist Leonardo DiCaprio."

74. Eric Worrall, "Doh! Climate Messiah Greta Thunberg's Plastic Boat Trip Will Require Four Transatlantic Flights," *Watts Up with That*, August 18, 2019, https://wattsupwiththat.com/2019/08/18/doh-climate-messiah-greta -thunbergs-plastic-boat-trip-will-result-in-two-airline-flights.

75. Naaman Zhou, "Climate Strikes: Hoax Photo Accusing Australian Protesters of Leaving Rubbish Behind Goes Viral," *The Guardian*, September 21, 2019, www.theguardian.com/environment/2019/sep/21/climate-strikes -hoax-photo-accusing-australian-protesters-of-leaving-rubbish-behind-goes -viral.

76. Andrew Bolt, "Look, in the Sky! A Hypocrite Called McKibben," *Herald Sun*, April 8, 2013, www.heraldsun.com.au/blogs/andrew-bolt /look-in-the-sky-a-hypocrite-called-mckibben/news-story/164435dd3

d4447ba60bcea92c349edda; Anthony Watts, "Bill McKibben's Excellent Eco-Hypocrisy," *Watts Up with That*, October 5, 2013, https://wattsupwiththat .com/2013/10/05/bill-mckibbens-excellent-eco-hypocrisy.

77. Bill McKibben, "Embarrassing Photos of Me, Thanks to My Right-Wing Stalkers," *New York Times*, August 5, 2016, www.nytimes.com/2016/08 /07/opinion/sunday/embarrassing-photos-of-me-thanks-to-my-right-wing -stalkers.html.

78. Isabel Vincent and Melissa Klein, "Gas-Guzzling Car Rides Expose AOC's Hypocrisy Amid Green New Deal Pledge," *New York Post*, March 2, 2019, https://nypost.com/2019/03/02/gas-guzzling-car-rides-expose-aocs -hypocrisy-amid-green-new-deal-pledge.

79. Clover Moore (@CloverMoore), Twitter, December 4, 2019, 10:47 p.m., https://twitter.com/CloverMoore/status/1202479544172630016.

80. Katie Pavlich, "The Frauds of the Climate Change Movement," *The Hill*, October 1, 2019, https://thehill.com/opinion/katie-pavlich/463930-katie -pavlich-the-frauds-of-the-climate-change-movement. The Young America's Foundation has received a substantial amount of money from the Koch brothers and the Koch brothers–funded Donors Trust. See "Young America's Foundation," SourceWatch, www.sourcewatch.org/index.php/Young_America%27s _Foundation.

81. Michael E. Mann (@MichaelEMann), Twitter, November 13, 2018, 1:30 p.m., https://twitter.com/MichaelEMann/status/1062457643313315840.

82. Trees (@SolutionsOK), Twitter, November 14, 2018, 10:43 a.m., https://twitter.com/SolutionsOK/status/1062778092345679872; Michael E. Mann (@MichaelEMann), Twitter, November 14, 2018, 10:47 a.m., https:// twitter.com/MichaelEMann/status/1062779071770300418.

83. Ben Penfold (@BenPenfold7), Twitter, January 2, 2020, 8:24 p.m., https://twitter.com/BenPenfold7/status/1212952842656370688.

84. "It's a Fact, Scientists Are the Most Trusted People in World," Ipsos, September 17, 2019, www.ipsos.com/en/its-fact-scientists-are-most-trusted -people-world; Boshoff and Connolly, "Eco-Warrior or Hypocrite?"

85. DiCaprio produced the documentary *Cowspiracy* discussed earlier in this chapter.

86. Shahzeen Z. Attari, David H. Krantz, and Elke U. Weber, "Climate Change Communicators' Carbon Footprints Affect Their Audience's Policy Support," *Climatic Change* 154, no. 3–4 (2019): 529–545; Borenstein, "Climate Scientists Try to Cut Their Own Carbon Footprints."

87. Joselow, "Quitting Burgers."

88. Jeff McMahon, "Greta Is Right: Study Shows Individual Lifestyle Change Boosts Systemic Climate Action," *Forbes*, November 19, 2019, www .forbes.com/sites/jeffmcmahon/2019/11/19/greta-is-right-study-shows -individual-climate-action-boosts-systemic-change/#67fc82e64a54.

89. Cormac O'Rafferty (@CormacORafferty), Twitter, November 21, 2019, 7:08 a.m., https://twitter.com/CormacORafferty/status/1197532349078163456.

90. Mann, "Lifestyle Changes Aren't Enough."

91. Moore has been funded by a number of corporate interests to attack science that proves disadvantageous to them. See "Patrick Moore," SourceWatch, www.sourcewatch.org/index.php/Patrick_Moore, accessed January 5, 2020.

92. Helen Regan, "Watch a GMO Advocate Claim a Weed Killer Is Safe to Drink but Then Refuse to Drink It," *Time*, March 27, 2015, https://time.com/3761053/monsanto-weed-killer-drink-patrick-moore.

93. Paul Wogden (@WogdenPaul), Twitter, September 11, 2019, 10:58 p.m., https://twitter.com/WogdenPaul/status/1172026602374533120.

94. Lavelle, "'Trollbots' Swarm Twitter."

95. Abel Gustafson, Anthony Leiserowitz, and Edward Maibach, "Americans Are Increasingly 'Alarmed' About Global Warming," Yale Program in Climate Change Communication, February 12, 2019, https://climatecommunication.yale.edu/publications/americans-are-increasingly-alarmed-about-global-warming; "Climate Change Opinions Rebound Among Republican Voters: Bipartisan Support for Climate and Clean Energy Policies Remains Strong," Yale Program in Climate Change Communication, May 8, 2018, https://climatecommunication.yale.edu/news-events/climate-change-opinions-rebound-among-republican-voters-bipartisan-support-for-climate-clean-energy-policies-remains-strong.

96. Ramez Naam (@ramez), Twitter, September 30, 2019, 12:53 p.m., https://twitter.com/ramez/status/1178759746075054080.

97. "U. Minnesota Scholar Criticizes Air Travel"; "Doug P.," "Meteorologist Eric Holthaus SHAMES Aviation Buff."

98. Mark, "Yes, Actually, Individual Responsibility Is Essential."

99. Borenstein, "Climate Scientists Try to Cut Their Own Carbon Footprints."

100. Borenstein, "Climate Scientists Try to Cut Their Own Carbon Footprints."

101. See, for example, Jeremy Lovell, "Climate Report Calls for Green 'New Deal,'" Reuters, July 21, 2008, www.reuters.com/article/us-climate-deal/climate-report-calls-for-green-new-deal-idUSL204610020080721.

102. Salvador Rizzo, "What's Actually in the 'Green New Deal' from Democrats?," *Washington Post*, February 11, 2019, www.washingtonpost.com/politics/2019/02/11/whats-actually-green-new-deal-democrats.

103. Michael E. Mann, "Radical Reform and the Green New Deal," *Nature*, September 18, 2019, www.nature.com/articles/d41586-019-02738.

104. Jeffrey Frankel, "The Best Way to Help the Climate Is to Increase the Price of CO_2 Emissions," *The Guardian*, January 20, 2020, www.theguardian.com/business/2020/jan/20/climate-crisis-carbon-emissions-tax.

105. Mann, "Radical Reform and the Green New Deal."

106. Such was indeed the premise of the right-wing shock jock Glenn Beck's "novel" *Agenda 21*, reviewed by yours truly for *Popular Science*: Michael E. Mann, "What Does a Climate Scientist Think of Glenn Beck's Environmental-Conspiracy Novel?," *Popular Science*, December 12, 2012, www.popsci.com/environment/article/2012-12/what-does-climate-scientist-think-glenn-becks-environmental-conspiracy-novel.

107. Gary Anderson, "Negative Rates, Climate Science and a Fed Warning," Talk Markets, November 21, 2019, https://talkmarkets.com/content

/economics—politics-education/negative-rates-climate-science-and-a-fed
-warning?post=241500#.

108. Dominique Jackson, "The Daily Show Brutally Ridicules Fox's Sean Hannity for Whining AOC's Green New Deal Will Deprive Him of Hamburgers," *Raw Story*, February 14, 2019, www.rawstory.com/2019/02/watch -the-daily-shows-trevor-noah-brutally-mocks-sean-hannity-over-thinking-aoc -wants-outlaw-hamburgers-with-green-new-deal.

109. Antonia Noori Farzan, "The Latest Right-Wing Attack on Democrats: 'They Want to Take Away Your Hamburgers,'" *Washington Post*, March 1, 2019, www.washingtonpost.com/nation/2019/03/01/latest-right-wing-attack -democrats-they-want-take-away-your-hamburgers.

110. Sam Dorman, "AOC Accused of Soviet-Style Propaganda with Green New Deal 'Art Series,'" Fox News, August 30, 2019, www.foxnews.com/media /aoc-green-new-deal-art-series-propaganda; Daniel Turner, "Stealth AOC 'Green New Deal' Now the Law in New Mexico, Voters Be Damned," Fox News, May 27, 2019, www.foxnews.com/opinion/daniel-turner-stealth-version -of-aoc-green-new-deal-now-the-law-in-new-mexico-voters-be-damned.

111. Tom Jacobs, "Did Fox News Quash Republican Support for the Green New Deal?," *Pacific Standard*, May 13, 2019, https://psmag.com/economics/did -fox-news-quash-republican-support-for-the-green-new-deal.

112. Brian Kahn, "Big Oil Is Scared Shitless," *Gizmodo*, June 18, 2020, https://earther.gizmodo.com/big-oil-is-scared-shitless-1844084649.

CHAPTER 5: PUT A PRICE ON IT. OR NOT.

1. "Bill McKibben: Actions Speak Louder Than Words," *Bulletin of the Atomic Scientists* 68, no. 2 (2012): 1–8.

2. Justin Gerdes, "Cap and Trade Curbed Acid Rain: 7 Reasons Why It Can Do the Same for Climate Change," *Forbes*, February 13, 2012, www.forbes .com/sites/justingerdes/2012/02/13/cap-and-trade-curbed-acid-rain-7 -reasons-why-it-can-do-the-same-for-climate-change/#6e920874943a.

3. John M. Broder, "'Cap and Trade' Loses Its Standing as Energy Policy of Choice," *New York Times*, March 25, 2010, www.nytimes.com/2010/03/26 /science/earth/26climate.html.

4. For example, environmental organizations like Greenpeace and climate scientist and advocate James Hansen. See Paul Krugman, "The Perfect, the Good, the Planet," *New York Times*, May 17, 2009, www.nytimes.com/2009/05 /18/opinion/18krugman.html.

5. Krugman, "The Perfect, the Good, the Planet."

6. Eric Zimmermann, "Republicans Propose . . . a Carbon Tax?," *The Hill*, May 14, 2009, https://thehill.com/blogs/blog-briefing-room/news/35719 -republicans-proposea-carbon-tax.

7. Christopher Leonard, "David Koch Was the Ultimate Climate Change Denier," *New York Times*, August 23, 2019, www.nytimes.com/2019/08/23 /opinion/sunday/david-koch-climate-change.html.

8. Broder, "'Cap and Trade' Loses Its Standing."

9. "C. Boyden Gray," SourceWatch, www.sourcewatch.org/index.php/C ._Boyden_Gray, accessed January 15, 2020.

10. "Americans for Prosperity Foundation (AFP)," Greenpeace, www .greenpeace.org/usa/global-warming/climate-deniers/front-groups/americans -for-prosperity-foundation-afp.

11. Terry Gross, "'Kochland': How The Koch Brothers Changed U.S. Cor-porate and Political Power," National Public Radio, *Fresh Air*, August 13, 2019, www.wuwm.com/post/kochland-how-koch-brothers-changed-us-corporate -and-political-power#stream/0.

12. Christopher Leonard, "David Koch Was the Ultimate Climate Change Denier," *New York Times*, August 23, 2019, www.nytimes.com/2019/08/23 /opinion/sunday/david-koch-climate-change.html.

13. Broder, "'Cap and Trade' Loses Its Standing."

14. Haroon Siddique, "US Senate Drops Bill to Cap Carbon Emissions," July 23, 2010, www.theguardian.com/environment/2010/jul/23/us-senate-climate -change-bill.

15. "Bob Inglis," John F. Kennedy Presidential Library and Museum, 2015, www.jfklibrary.org/events-and-awards/profile-in-courage-award/award -recipients/bob-inglis-2015.

16. For an excellent review, see Marc Hudson, "In Australia, Climate Policy Battles Are Endlessly Reheated," *The Conversation*, April 9, 2019, https://theconversation.com/in-australia-climate-policy-battles-are-endlessly -reheated-114971, and for a discussion of the comparative politics of climate denial in the United States, Australia, and other Western nations, see Christo-pher Wright and Daniel Nyberg, "Corporate Political Activity and Climate Co-alitions," in *Climate Change, Capitalism, and Corporations: Processes of Creative Self-Destruction* (Cambridge: Cambridge University Press, 2015).

17. Mark Butler, "How Australia Bungled Climate Policy to Create a De-cade of Disappointment," *The Guardian*, July 5, 2017, www.theguardian .com/australia-news/2017/jul/05/how-australia-bungled-climate-policy-to -create-a-decade-of-disappointment.

18. See Graham Readfearn, "Australia's Place in the Global Web of Climate Denial," Australian Broadcasting Corporation, June 28, 2011, www.abc.net .au/news/2011-06-29/readfearn—australia27s-place-in-the-global-web-of -climate-de/2775298; Graham Readfearn, "Who Are the Australian Backers of Heartland's Climate Denial?," *DeSmog* (blog), May 21, 2012, www.desmogblog .com/who-are-australian-backers-heartland-s-climate-denial.

19. Julia Baird, "A Carbon Tax's Ignoble End," *New York Times*, July 24, 2014, www.nytimes.com/2014/07/25/opinion/julia-baird-why-tony-abbott-axed -australias-carbon-tax.html; Butler, "How Australia Bungled Climate Policy."

20. Baird, "A Carbon Tax's Ignoble End."

21. See, for example, Turnbull's commentary "Australia's Bushfires Show the Wicked, Self-Destructive Idiocy of Climate Denialism Must Stop," *Time*, Jan-uary 16, 2020, https://time.com/5765603/australia-bushfires-prime-minister -essay. I had a chance to get to know Turnbull during my sabbatical in Sydney

in early 2020. I found him to be thoughtful, earnest, and honorable—in general, and in his efforts at climate policy. I'm sure he's frustrated that he was unable to convince fellow Liberals to support meaningful action on climate while he was in office. Like Inglis, he seems committed to doing what he can to further the cause of climate action in Australia.

22. Butler, "How Australia Bungled Climate Policy."

23. Jonathan Watts and Ben Doherty, "US and Russia Ally with Saudi Arabia to Water Down Climate Pledge," *The Guardian*, December 10, 2018, www.theguardian.com/environment/2018/dec/09/us-russia-ally-saudi-arabia -water-down-climate-pledges-un.

24. Manuel Roig-Franzia, Rosalind S. Helderman, William Booth, and Tom Hamburger, "How the 'Bad Boys of Brexit' Forged Ties with Russia and the Trump Campaign—and Came Under Investigators' Scrutiny," *Washington Post*, June 28, 2018, www.washingtonpost.com/politics/how-the-bad-boys-of -brexit-forged-ties-with-russia-and-the-trump-campaign--and-came-under -investigators-scrutiny/2018/06/28/6e3a5e9c-7656-11e8-b4b7-308400242c2e _story.html; Richard Collett-White, Chloe Farand, and Mat Hope, "Meet the Brexit Party's Climate Science Deniers," *DeSmog* (blog), May 1 2019, www .desmog.co.uk/2019/05/01/brexit-party-climate-science-deniers.

25. Roman Goncharenko, "France's 'Yellow Vests' and the Russian Trolls That Encourage Them," *Deutsche Welle*, December 15, 2018, www.dw.com/en /frances-yellow-vests-and-the-russian-trolls-that-encourage-them/a-46753388.

26. Emily Atkin, "France's Yellow Vest Protesters Want to Fight Climate Change: Trump Says the Violence Is Proof That People Oppose Environmental Protection. He Couldn't Be More Wrong," *New Republic*, December 10, 2018, https://newrepublic.com/article/152585/frances-yellow-vest -protesters-want-fight-climate-change.

27. Alexander Panetta, "Notorious Russian Troll Farm Targeted Trudeau, Canadian Oil in Online Campaigns," *The Star*, March 18, 2018, www.thestar .com/news/canada/2018/03/18/notorious-russian-troll-farm-targeted-trudeau -canadian-oil-in-online-campaigns.html.

28. Fatima Syed, "The Abuse Catherine McKenna Receives on Twitter Exploded the Day the Carbon Tax Started," *National Observer*, October 25, 2019, www.nationalobserver.com/2019/10/25/news/abuse-catherine-mckenna -receives-Twitter-exploded-day-carbon-tax-started.

29. Ahmed Al-Rawi and Yasmin Jiwani, "Russian Twitter Trolls Stoke Anti-Immigrant Lies Ahead of Canadian Election," *The Conversation*, July 23, 2019, https://theconversation.com/russian-twitter-trolls-stoke-anti-immigrant -lies-ahead-of-canadian-election-119144.

30. Nathalie Graham, "Looks Like Out-of-State Money DID Sway Your Vote, Washington," *The Stranger*, November 7, 2018, www.thestranger.com /slog/2018/11/07/35182424/a-big-night-for-corporate-money-and-a-dismal -display-for-the-carbon-fee; "Sierra Club Position on Carbon Washington Ballot Initiative 732," Sierra Club, September 2016, www.sierraclub.org/washington /sierra-club-position-carbon-washington-ballot-initiative-732; Kate Aronoff, "Why the Left Doesn't Want a Carbon Tax (Or at Least Not This One): The

Battle over a Washington State Ballot Initiative Previews the Future of the Climate Debate," *In These Times*, November 3, 2016, http://inthesetimes.com /article/19592/why-the-left-doesnt-want-carbon-tax-washington-i-732-climate -change-ballot.

31. A good discussion of the relative merits and complementary nature of the two approaches is provided in Fergus Green and Richard Denniss, "Cutting with Both Arms of the Scissors: The Economic and Political Case for Restrictive Supply-Side Climate Policies," *Climatic Change* 150 (2018): 73–87.

32. Lorraine Chow, "These Celebrities Take a Stand Against Dakota Access Pipeline," EcoWatch, September 9, 2016, www.ecowatch.com/justice-league -dakota-access-pipeline-2000093607.html; "Hansen and Hannah Arrested in West Virginia Mining Protest," *The Guardian*, June 24 2009, www.theguardian .com/environment/2009/jun/24/james-hansen-daryl-hannah-mining-protest.

33. Emily Holden, "Harvard and Yale Students Disrupt Football Game for Fossil Fuel Protest," *The Guardian*, November 24, 2019, www.theguardian .com/us-news/2019/nov/23/harvard-yale-football-game-protest-fossil-fuels.

34. See, for example, Rachel M. Cohen, "Will Bernie Sanders Stick with a Carbon Tax in His Push for a Green New Deal?," *The Intercept*, July 3, 2019, https:// theintercept.com/2019/07/03/bernie-sanders-climate-change-policy-carbon-tax.

35. Atkin, "France's Yellow Vest Protesters."

36. "Most Canadian Households to Get More in Rebates Than Paid in Carbon Tax: PBO," *Global News*, February 4, 2020, https://globalnews.ca/news /6504187/canada-carbon-tax-rebate-pbo.

37. Robert W. McElroy, "Pope Francis Brings a New Lens to Poverty, Peace and the Planet," *America: The Jesuit Review*, April 23, 2018, www .americamagazine.org/faith/2018/04/23/pope-francis-brings-new-lens-poverty -peace-and-planet; "Pope Francis Backs Carbon Pricing and 'Radical Energy Transition' to Act Against Global Warming," Australian Broadcasting Corporation, June 14, 2019, www.abc.net.au/news/2019-06-15/pope-backs-carbon -pricing-to-stem-global-warming/11212900.

38. Geoff Dembick, "Meet the Lawyer Trying to Make Big Oil Pay for Climate Change," *Vice*, December 22, 2017, www.vice.com/en_us/article/43qw3j /meet-the-lawyer-trying-to-make-big-oil-pay-for-climate-change.

39. David Hasemyer, "Fossil Fuels on Trial: Where the Major Climate Change Lawsuits Stand Today," *Inside Climate News*, January 17, 2020, https:// insideclimatenews.org/news/04042018/climate-change-fossil-fuel-company -lawsuits-timeline-exxon-children-california-cities-attorney-general.

40. Umair Irfan, "21 Kids Sued the Government over Climate Change. A Federal Court Dismissed the Case," *Vox*, January 17, 2020, www.vox.com /2020/1/17/21070810/climate-change-lawsuit-juliana-vs-us-our-childrens-trust -9th-circuit.

41. For a representative account, see Daryl Roberts, "Nature Conservancy Endorses Fossil Fuel Funded Trojan Horse," Alt Energy Stocks, May 27, 2019, www.altenergystocks.com/archives/2019/05/nature-conservancy-endorses -trojan-horse-tort-liability-waiver.

42. Dana Drugmand, "New Carbon Bills Won't Let Oil Companies Off the Hook for Climate Costs," *Climate Liability News*, July 31, 2019, www.climateliabilitynews.org/2019/07/31/carbon-bills-climate-liability-waiver.

43. I made these arguments in a review of Naomi Klein's book *On Fire* that I wrote for *Nature* in 2019: Michael E. Mann, "Radical Reform and the Green New Deal: Michael E. Mann Examines Naomi Klein's Collection on the Proposed US Policy Aiming to Curb Climate Change," *Nature*, September 19, 2019, www.nature.com/articles/d41586-019-02738-7.

44. See Brad Plumer, "Australia Repealed Its Carbon Tax—and Emissions Are Now Soaring," *Vox*, November 6, 2014, www.vox.com/2014/11/6/7157713/australia-carbon-tax-repeal-emissions-rise; Brad Plumer, "Australia Is Repealing Its Controversial Carbon Tax," *Vox*, July 17, 2014, www.vox.com/2014/7/17/5912143/australia-repeals-carbon-tax-global-warming.

45. Brian Kahn, "More Than 600 Environmental Groups Just Backed Ocasio-Cortez's Green New Deal," *Gizmodo*, January 10, 2019, https://earther.gizmodo.com/more-than-600-environmental-groups-just-backed-ocasio-c-1831640541; "Green New Deal Letter to Congress," January 10, 2019, Scribd, www.scribd.com/document/397201459/Green-New-Deal-Letter-to-Congress.

46. "Sierra Club Position on Carbon Washington Ballot Initiative 732," Sierra Club, September 2016, www.sierraclub.org/washington/sierra-club-position-carbon-washington-ballot-initiative-732.

47. Butler, "How Australia Bungled Climate Policy."

48. Will Steffen, Johan Rockström, Katherine Richardson, Timothy M. Lenton, Carl Folke, Diana Liverman, Colin P. Summerhayes, et al., "Trajectories of the Earth System in the Anthropocene," *Proceedings of the National Academy of Sciences* 115, no. 33 (2018): 8252–8259, https://doi.org/10.1073/pnas.1810141115.

49. Kate Aronoff, "'Hothouse Earth' Co-Author: The Problem Is Neoliberal Economics," *The Intercept*, August 14, 2018, https://theintercept.com/2018/08/14/hothouse-earth-climate-change-neoliberal-economics.

50. At this point, you might reasonably be asking what authority I speak with when it comes to such matters. I would simply point out that, while I'm not an economist myself, I have coauthored peer-reviewed research with environmental economists on the topic of carbon pricing and I have attained some degree of familiarity with the discipline. See S. Lewandowsky, M. C. Freeman, and M. E. Mann, "Harnessing the Uncertainty Monster: Putting Quantitative Constraints on the Intergenerational Social Discount Rate," *Global and Planetary Change* 156 (2017): 155–166, https://doi.org/10.1016/j.gloplacha.2017.03.007.

51. Adam Tooze, "How Climate Change Has Supercharged the Left: Global Warming Could Launch Socialists to Unprecedented Power—and Expose Their Movement's Deepest Contradictions," *Foreign Policy*, January 15, 2020, https://foreignpolicy.com/2020/01/15/climate-socialism-supercharged-left-green-new-deal.

52. Mann, "Radical Reform and the Green New Deal."

53. I hasten to mention that I know a thing or two about being "on the front lines." See, for example, my book *The Hockey Stick and the Climate Wars: Dispatches from the Front Lines* (New York: Columbia University Press, 2013).

54. Eric Holthaus (@EricHolthaus), Twitter, November 7, 2019, 9:03 a.m., https://twitter.com/EricHolthaus/status/1192487740279066629.

55. The full thread can be found at Nathalie Molina Niño (@NathalieMolina), Twitter, November 6, 2019, 8:50 p.m., https://twitter.com/NathalieMolina /status/1192303192756936704. For example, one post, from "Patricia," said, "@MichaelEMann has more scientific knowledge in his cerebellum than you have in a hundred Trump heads. Deniers are done. Thanks to people of integrity, like Michael, we are moving on with solutions, including dismantling the fossil fuel industry." "Tenny" posted, "Michael Mann has been on the front lines doing all he can to get the public to understand what's going on, and taking threats of jail from congress critters and the VA AG, been sent white powder in an envelope, etc." "Ursula" tweeted, "As if we don't have enough on our plates. More than not helpful, backdoor approach to aiding and abetting deniers. You are the Front line and have battle scars to prove it. Wonder what her real issue is."

56. Tim Cronin, "Where 2020 Democrats Stand on Carbon Pricing," *Climate X-Change*, November 15, 2019, https://climate-xchange.org/2019/11/15 /where-2020-democrats-stand-on-carbon-pricing.

57. Gillian Tett, "The World Needs a Libor for Carbon Pricing," *Financial Times*, January 24, 2020, www.ft.com/content/20dd6b82-3dd1-11ea-a01a -bae547046735; "Exxon and Friends Still Funding Climate Denial and Obstruction Through IPAA, FTI, Energy in Depth," Climate Investigations Center, December 20, 2019, https://climateinvestigations.org/exxon-and-friends-still -funding-climate-denial-and-obstruction-through-ipaa-fti-energy-in-depth.

58. Tett, "The World Needs a Libor."

59. Thomas Kaplan, "Citing Health Risks, Cuomo Bans Fracking in New York State," *New York Times*, December 17, 2014, www.nytimes.com/2014/12/18 /nyregion/cuomo-to-ban-fracking-in-new-york-state-citing-health-risks.html.

60. Peter Behr, "Grid Chief: Enact Carbon Price to Reach 100% Clean Energy," *Energy and Environment News*, January 23, 2020, www.eenews.net /energywire/2020/01/23/stories/1062152903.

61. "What We Do," New York Independent System Operator, www.nyiso .com/what-we-do.

62. Behr, "Grid Chief."

63. "About the IMF," International Monetary Fund, www.imf.org/en /About.

64. Tett, "The World Needs a Libor"; "Special Report: Global Warming of 1.5°C," Intergovernmental Panel on Climate Change (IPCC), October 8, 2018, www.ipcc.ch/sr15.

65. Gillian Tett, Chris Giles, and James Politi, "US Threatens Retaliation Against EU over Proposed Carbon Tax," *Irish Times*, January 26, 2020, www.irishtimes.com/business/economy/us-threatens-retaliation-against -eu-over-proposed-carbon-tax-1.4151974.

66. Michael E. Mann and Jonathan Brockopp, "You Can't Save the Climate by Going Vegan. Corporate Polluters Must Be Held Accountable," *USA Today*, June 3, 2019, www.usatoday.com/story/opinion/2019/06/03/climate-change -requires-collective-action-more-than-single-acts-column/1275965001.

67. David Mastio (@DavidMastio), Twitter, November 6, 2019, 6:57 a.m., https://twitter.com/DavidMastio/status/1192093712400171011.

68. The full tweet is "11,000 scientists have declared we are in a climate emergency. Among other things, we need to move away from capitalism and instead prioritize 'sustaining ecosystems and improving human well-being by prioritizing basic needs and reducing inequality.'" Nora Biette-Timmons (@biettetimmons), Twitter, November 5, 2019, 7:21 a.m., https://twitter.com /biettetimmons/status/1191737368132366339.

69. George P. Shultz and Ted Halstead, "The Winning Conservative Climate Solution," *Washington Post*, January 16, 2020, www.washingtonpost.com /opinions/the-winning-republican-climate-solution-carbon-pricing/2020/01 /16/d6921dc0-387b-11ea-bf30-ad313e4ec754_story.html.

70. David Roberts (@drvox), Twitter, https://twitter.com/drvox/status /1218316952956997636.

71. Shultz and Halstead, "The Winning Conservative Climate Solution."

72. "Believe It or Not, a Republican Once Led the California Charge on Climate Change," KQED, September 13, 2018, www.kqed.org/science/1931206 /californias-a-team-on-climate-moonbeam-and-the-governator; Edward Helmore, "Angry Schwarzenegger Condemns Trump for Wrecking Clean-Air Standards," *The Guardian*, September 9, 2019, www.theguardian.com/us -news/2019/sep/09/schwarzenegger-trump-california-clean-air-emissions -climate-crisis; J. Edward Moreno, "Schwarzenegger Says Green New Deal Is 'Well Intentioned' but 'Bogus,'" *The Hill*, January 17, 2020, https://thehill .com/homenews/news/478847-schwarzenegger-says-green-new-deal-is-well -intentioned-but-bogus.

73. Myles Wearring and Emily Ackew, "Don't Leave Climate Change Action to the Left, David Cameron Urges Conservatives," Australian Broadcasting Corporation, January 30, 2019, www.abc.net.au/news/2020-01-29 /david-cameron-says-dont-leave-climate-change-action-to-the-left/11907804.

74. Shultz and Halstead, "The Winning Conservative Climate Solution."

75. Tooze, "How Climate Change Has Supercharged the Left."

76. Sheldon Whitehouse and James Slevin, "Carbon Pricing Represents the Best Answer to Our Climate Danger," *Washington Post*, March 10, 2020, www .washingtonpost.com/opinions/carbon-pricing-represents-the-best-answer-to -our-climate-danger/2020/03/10/379693ae-62fb-11ea-acca-80c22bbee96f _story.html.

77. See Kevin Anderson (@KevinClimate), Twitter, January 28, 2020, 12:53 a.m., https://twitter.com/KevinClimate/status/1222080140383080448.

78. This is one of the leading climate denial myths documented at Skeptical Science.com. See "Climate Scientists Would Make More Money in Other Careers," Skeptical Science, https://skepticalscience.com/climate-scientists-in -it-for-the-money.htm.

79. Brian A. Boyle, "Tulsi Gabbard May Not Be a Russian Asset. But She Sure Talks Like One," *Los Angeles Times*, October 25, 2019, www.latimes.com /opinion/story/2019-10-25/tulsi-gabbard-russian-asset-republican.

80. Tim Cronin, "Where 2020 Democrats Stand on Carbon Pricing," *Climate X-Change*, November 15, 2019, https://climate-xchange.org/2019/11/15 /where-2020-democrats-stand-on-carbon-pricing.

81. "Brendan O'Neill, Why Extinction Rebellion Seems So Nuts," *Spiked*, November 11, 2019, www.spiked-online.com/2019/11/07/why-extinction -rebellion-seems-so-nuts; Ben Pile, "Apocalypse Delayed: The IPCC Report Does Not Justify Climate Scaremongering," *Spiked*, October 18, 2019, www .spiked-online.com/2018/10/18/apocalypse-delayed.

82. O'Neill, "Why Extinction Rebellion Seems So Nuts."

83. "Special Report: Global Warming of 1.5°C."

84. George Monbiot, "How US Billionaires Are Fuelling the Hard-Right Cause in Britain," *The Guardian*, December 7, 2018, www.theguardian.com /commentisfree/2018/dec/07/us-billionaires-hard-right-britain-spiked -magazine-charles-david-koch-foundation.

85. James Hansen, "Game over for the Climate," *New York Times*, May 9, 2012, www.nytimes.com/2012/05/10/opinion/game-over-for-the-climate.html.

86. Quoted in Coral Davenport, "Citing Climate Change, Obama Rejects Construction of Keystone XL Oil Pipeline," *New York Times*, November 6, 2015, www.nytimes.com/2015/11/07/us/obama-expected-to-reject-construction -of-keystone-xl-oil-pipeline.html.

87. I made that argument in an interview. See "Dr. Michael Mann on Paris and the Clean Power Plan: 'We're Seeing Real Movement,'" *Climate Reality*, October 27, 2017, www.climaterealityproject.org/blog/dr-michael-mann-paris -and-clean-power-plan-were-seeing-real-movement.

88. Fred Hiatt, "How Donald Trump and Bernie Sanders Both Reject the Reality of Climate Change," *Washington Post*, February 23, 2020, www .washingtonpost.com/opinions/how-donald-trump-and-bernie-sanders-both -reject-the-reality-of-climate-change/2020/02/23/cc657dcc-54de-11ea-9e47 -59804be1dcfb_story.html.

CHAPTER 6: SINKING THE COMPETITION

1. Jocelyn Timperley, "The Challenge of Defining Fossil Fuel Subsidies," *Carbon Brief*, June 12, 2017, www.carbonbrief.org/explainer-the -challenge-of-defining-fossil-fuel-subsidies.

2. Dana Nuccitelli, "America Spends over $20bn per Year on Fossil Fuel Subsidies. Abolish Them," July 30, 2018, www.theguardian.com/environment /climate-consensus-97-per-cent/2018/jul/30/america-spends-over -20bn-per-year-on-fossil-fuel-subsidies-abolish-them.

3. "American Legislative Exchange Council," SourceWatch, www.source watch.org/index.php/American_Legislative_Exchange_Council.

4. See, for example, Kert Davies, "ALEC Lost Membership Worth over $7 Trillion in Market Cap," Climate Investigations Center, November 28, 2018, https://climateinvestigations.org/alec-lost-membership-worth-7-trillion.

5. "ALEC's Latest Scheme to Attack Renewables," *Renewable Energy World*, December 16, 2013, www.renewableenergyworld.com/2013/12/16/alecs-latest-scheme-to-attack-renewables.

6. Camille Erickson, "Bill to Penalize Utilities for Renewable Energy Returns to Wyoming Legislature, Quickly Fails," *Caspar Star-Tribune*, February 12, 2020, https://trib.com/business/energy/bill-to-penalize-utilities-for-renewable-energy-returns-to-wyoming/article_aafdd7cd-5012-5b8d-bf94-28341cea657f.html.

7. Suzanne Goldenberg and Ed Pilkington, "ALEC's Campaign Against Renewable Energy," *Mother Jones*, December 6, 2013, www.motherjones.com/environment/2013/12/alec-calls-penalties-freerider-homeowners-assault-clean-energy; Editorial Board, "The Koch Attack on Solar Energy," *New York Times*, April 26, 2014, www.nytimes.com/2014/04/27/opinion/sunday/the-koch-attack-on-solar-energy.html.

8. Suzanne Goldenberg, "Leak Exposes How Heartland Institute Works to Undermine Climate Science," *The Guardian*, February 15, 2012, www.theguardian.com/environment/2012/feb/15/leak-exposes-heartland-institute-climate.

9. "Heartland Institute," Energy and Policy Institute, www.energyandpolicy.org/attacks-on-renewable-energy-policy-by-fossil-fuel-interests-2013-2014/heartland-institute.

10. Carolyn Fortuna, "The Koch Brothers Have a Mandate to Destroy the EV Revolution—Are You Buying In?," *Clean Technica*, August 22, 2019, https://cleantechnica.com/2019/08/22/the-koch-brothers-have-a-mandate-to-destroy-the-ev-revolution-are-you-buying-in.

11. Ben Jervey, "Senator John Barrasso Parrots Koch Talking Points to Kill Electric Car Tax Credit," *DeSmog* (blog), February 5, 2019, www.desmogblog.com/2019/02/05/senator-john-barrasso-koch-talking-points-electric-car-tax-credit.

12. Fortuna, "The Koch Brothers Have a Mandate."

13. Will Oremus, "North Carolina May Ban Tesla Sales to Prevent 'Unfair Competition,'" *Slate*, May 13, 2013, https://slate.com/technology/2013/05/north-carolina-tesla-ban-bill-would-prevent-unfair-competition-with-car-dealerships.html.

14. Bruce Brown, "Confusing! North Carolina Bans Tesla Sales in Charlotte, Allows Them in Raleigh," *Digital Trends*, May 26, 2016, www.digitaltrends.com/cars/tesla-north-carolina-sales-charlotte-raleigh.

15. Will Oremus, "Free-Market Cheerleader Chris Christie Blocks Tesla Sales in New Jersey," *Slate*, March 12, 2014, https://slate.com/technology/2014/03/new-jersey-tesla-ban-chris-christie-loves-free-market-blocks-direct-car-sales.html.

16. The one "blue state" exception is Connecticut. See Union of Concerned Scientists, "Why You Can't Buy a Tesla in These 6 States," EcoWatch, February 26, 2017, www.ecowatch.com/states-cant-buy-tesla-2278638949.html.

17. Melissa C. Lott, "Solyndra—Illuminating Energy Funding Flaws?," *Scientific American*, September 27, 2011, https://blogs.scientificamerican.com /plugged-in/solyndra-illuminating-energy-funding-flaws.

18. Denise Robbins, "Study: How Mainstream Media Misled on the Success of the Clean Energy Loan Program," Media Matters, April 10, 2014, www.mediamatters.org/new-york-times/study-how-mainstream-media -misled-success-clean-energy-loan-program; Henry C. Jackson, "Program That Funded Solyndra Failure Producing Success Stories," *Washington Post*, December 30, 2014, www.washingtonpost.com/politics/program-that-funded-solyndra -failure-producing-success-stories/2014/12/30/3e896b46-9074-11e4-a900 -9960214d4cd7_story.html.

19. Amy Harder, "Obama Budget Would Pour Funds into Climate, Renewable Energy," *Wall Street Journal*, February 3, 2015, www.wsj.com/articles /obama-budget-would-pour-billions-into-climate-renewable-energy -1422903421.

20. See "The Daily Caller," SourceWatch, www.sourceWatch.org/index.php /The_Daily_Caller.

21. Robbins, "Study: How Mainstream Media Misled."

22. Elliott Negin, "The Wind Energy Threat to Birds Is Overblown," *Live Science*, December 3, 2013, www.livescience.com/41644-wind-energy-threat -to-birds-overblown.html.

23. Wendy Koch, "Wind Turbines Kill Fewer Birds Than Do Cats, Cell Towers," *USA Today*, September 15, 2014, www.usatoday.com/story /money/business/2014/09/15/wind-turbines-kill-fewer-birds-than-cell-towers -cats/15683843.

24. See, for example, my review of Sagan's *The Demon-Haunted World* in "Summer Books," *Nature*, August 3, 2017, www.nature.com/articles /548028a.

25. Simon Chapman, "How to Catch 'Wind Turbine Syndrome': By Hearing About It and Then Worrying," *The Guardian*, November 29, 2017, www .theguardian.com/commentisfree/2017/nov/29/how-to-catch-wind-turbine -syndrome-by-hearing-about-it-and-then-worrying.

26. Sharon Zhang, "Fossil Fuel Knocks the Wind out of Renewable Energy Movement in Ohio," *Salon*, January 5, 2020, www.salon.com/2020/01/05/fossil -fuel-knocks-the-wind-out-of-renewable-energy-movement-in-ohio_partner.

27. Fox Business, *Follow the Money*, November 12, 2010, quoted in Jill Fitzsimmons, "Myths and Facts About Wind Power: Debunking Fox's Abysmal Wind Coverage," *Think Progress*, May 31, 2012, https://archive.thinkprogress .org/myths-and-facts-about-wind-power-debunking-foxs-abysmal-wind-cov erage-e314b70c4059.

28. Philip Bump, "Trump Claims That Wind Farms Cause Cancer for Very Trumpian Reasons," *Washington Post*, April 3, 2019, www.washingtonpost .com/politics/2019/04/03/trump-claims-that-wind-farms-cause-cancer-very -trumpian-reasons.

29. Bump, "Trump Claims That Wind Farms Cause Cancer."

30. John Rodgers, "The Effect of Wind Turbines on Property Values: A New Study in Massachusetts Provides Some Answers," Union of Concerned Scientists, January 22, 2014, https://blog.ucsusa.org/john-rogers/effect-of-wind-turbines-on-property-values-384.

31. "Environmental Impacts of Solar Power," Union of Concerned Scientists, March 5, 2013, www.ucsusa.org/resources/environmental-impacts-solar-power.

32. Noel Wauchope, "A Radioactive Wolf in Green Clothing: Dissecting the Latest Pro-Nuclear Spin," *Independent Australia*, September 20, 2017, https://independentaustralia.net/environment/environment-display/a-radioactive-wolf-in-green-clothing-dissecting-the-latest-pro-nuclear-spin,10735. Among the Breakthrough Institute's original primary funders were the Cynthia and George Mitchell Foundation, which is tied to George Mitchell's fortune derived from natural gas extraction and fracking. "Who Funds Us," Breakthrough Institute, http://thebreakthrough.org/about/funders, accessed July 9, 2015. The foundation advocates for the continued extraction of natural gas. "Shale Sustainability," Cynthia and George Mitchell Foundation, www.cgmf.org/p/shale-sustainability-program.html, accessed July 29, 2015.

33. Clive Hamilton, "Climate Change and the Soothing Message of Luke-Warmism," *The Conversation*, July 25, 2012, https://theconversation.com/climate-change-and-the-soothing-message-of-luke-warmism-8445.

34. Thomas Gerke, "The Breakthrough Institute—Why the Hot Air?," *Clean Technica*, June 17, 2013, https://cleantechnica.com/2013/06/17/the-breakthrough-institute-why-the-hot-air.

35. Michael Shellenberger, "If Solar Panels Are So Clean, Why Do They Produce So Much Toxic Waste?," *Forbes*, May 23, 2018, www.forbes.com/sites/michaelshellenberger/2018/05/23/if-solar-panels-are-so-clean-why-do-they-produce-so-much-toxic-waste.

36. "Environmental Impacts of Solar Power."

37. Michael Shellenberger, "The Real Reason They Hate Nuclear Is Because It Means We Don't Need Renewables," *Forbes*, February 14, 2019, www.forbes.com/sites/michaelshellenberger/2019/02/14/the-real-reason-they-hate-nuclear-is-because-it-means-we-dont-need-renewables.

38. "Solar Energy Plants in Tortoises' Desert Habitat Pit Green Against Green," Fox News, February 20, 2014, www.foxnews.com/us/solar-energy-plants-in-tortoises-desert-habitat-pit-green-against-green.

39. Associated Press, "Environmental Concerns Threaten Solar Power Expansion in California Desert," Fox News, April 18, 2009, www.foxnews.com/story/environmental-concerns-threaten-solar-power-expansion-in-california-desert; Alex Pappas, "Massive East Coast Solar Project Generates Fury from Neighbors," Fox News, February 15, 2019, www.foxnews.com/politics/massive-east-coast-solar-project-generates-fury-from-neighbors-in-virginia; "World's Largest Solar Plant Scorching Birds in Nevada Desert," Fox News, February 15, 2014, www.foxnews.com/us/worlds-largest-solar-plant-scorching-birds-in-nevada-desert.

40. Lee Moran, "Fox News' Jesse Watters Gets Schooled over Nonsensical Winter Solar Panels Claim," *Huffington Post*, February 1, 2019, www.huffpost.com/entry/fox-news-jesse-watters-solar-panels_n_5c540aa7e4b043e25b1b2168.

41. Amy Remeikis, "'Shorten Wants to End the Weekend': Morrison Attacks Labor's Electric Vehicle Policy," *The Guardian*, April 7, 2019, www.theguardian.com/australia-news/2019/apr/07/shorten-wants-to-end-the-weekend-morrison-attacks-labors-electric-vehicle-policy.

42. As noted at "Breakthrough Institute," Wikipedia, https://en.wikipedia.org/wiki/Breakthrough_Institute, accessed February 24, 2020.

43. See, for example, Bill Gates, "Two Videos That Illuminate Energy Poverty," GatesNotes, June 25, 2014, www.gatesnotes.com/Energy/Two-Videos-Illuminate-Energy-Poverty-Bjorn-Lomborg. Tillerson is quoted in Michael Babad, "Exxon Mobil CEO: 'What Good Is It to Save the Planet If Humanity Suffers?,'" *Globe and Mail*, May 30, 2013, www.theglobeandmail.com/report-on-business/top-business-stories/exxon-mobil-ceo-what-good-is-it-to-save-the-planet-if-humanity-suffers/article12258350.

44. Graham Readfearn, "The Millions Behind Bjorn Lomborg's Copenhagen Consensus Center US Think Tank," *DeSmog* (blog), June 24, 2014, www.desmogblog.com/2014/06/25/millions-behind-bjorn-lomborg-copenhagen-consensus-center; "Independent Women's Forum," SourceWatch, www.sourcewatch.org/index.php/Independent_Women%27s_Forum; "Donors Trust: Building a Legacy of Liberty," *DeSmog* (blog), www.desmogblog.com/who-donors-trust; "Claude R. Lambe Charitable Foundation," Conservative Transparency, http://conservativetransparency.org/donor/claude-r-lambe-charitable-foundation; Pete Altman, "House Committee to Vote on Fred Upton's Asthma Aggravation Act of 2011," Natural Resources Defense Council, March 15, 2011, www.nrdc.org/experts/pete-altman/house-committee-vote-fred-uptons-asthma-aggravation-act-2011.

45. "UWA Cancels Contract for Consensus Centre Involving Controversial Academic Bjorn Lomborg," Australian Broadcasting Corporation, May 8, 2015, www.abc.net.au/news/2015-05-08/bjorn-lomborg-uwa-consensus-centre-contract-cancelled/6456708.

46. Graham Readfearn, "Is Bjorn Lomborg Right to Say Fossil Fuels Are What Poor Countries Need?" *The Guardian*, December 6, 2013, www.theguardian.com/environment/planet-oz/2013/dec/06/bjorn-lomborg-climate-change-poor-countries-need-fossil-fuels.

47. Bjorn Lomborg, "Who's Afraid of Climate Change?," Project Syndicate, August 11, 2010, www.project-syndicate.org/commentary/who-s-afraid-of-climate-change.

48. Jonathan Chait, "GOP Senator Upbeat Coronavirus May Kill 'No More Than 3.4 Percent of Our Population,'" *New York Magazine*, March 18, 2020, https://nymag.com/intelligencer/2020/03/gop-senator-no-more-than-3-4-of-our-population-may-die.html.

49. Pope Francis, "Address of His Holiness Pope Francis to the Members of the Diplomatic Corps Accredited to the Holy See," The Holy See, January

13, 2014, http://w2.vatican.va/content/francesco/en/speeches/2014/january /documents/papa-francesco_20140113_corpodiplomatico.html.

50. R. Jai Krishna, "Renewable Energy Powers Up Rural India," *Wall Street Journal*, July 29, 2015, www.wsj.com/articles/renewable-energy-powers-up -rural-india-1438193488.

51. Pope Francis, "Address of His Holiness Pope Francis"; "DoD Releases Report on Security Implications of Climate Change," US Department of Defense, DOD News, July 29, 2015, www.defense.gov/news/newsarticle .aspx?id=129366. The Defense Department report notes that "global climate change will aggravate problems such as poverty, social tensions, environmental degradation, ineffectual leadership and weak political institutions that threaten stability in a number of countries."

52. "World Bank Says Climate Change Could Thrust 100 Million into Deep Poverty by 2030," Fox News, November 8, 2015, www.foxnews.com /world/2015/11/08/world-bank-says-climate-change-could-thrust-100-million -into-deep-poverty-by.

53. "Koch Alum's Dark Money Group, 'Power the Future,' Denies Its Own Lobbying Status," *DeSmog* (blog), April 16, 2018, www.desmogblog.com/2018 /04/16/koch-alum-s-dark-money-group-power-future-denies-its-own-lobbying -status.

54. Nadja Popovich, "Today's Energy Jobs Are in Solar, Not Coal," *New York Times*, April 25, 2017, www.nytimes.com/interactive/2017/04/25/climate /todays-energy-jobs-are-in-solar-not-coal.html.

55. Sheldon Whitehouse and James Slevin, "Carbon Pricing Represents the Best Answer to Our Climate Danger," *Washington Post*, March 10, 2020, www .washingtonpost.com/opinions/carbon-pricing-represents-the-best-answer -to-our-climate-danger/2020/03/10/379693ae-62fb-11ea-acca-80c22 bbee96f_story.html.

56. Sam Haysom, "Michael Moore Talks to Stephen Colbert About His New Climate Change Documentary," *Mashable*, April 22, 2020, https:// mashable.com/video/michael-moore-planet-of-the-humans.

57. See, for example, Lindsey Bahr, "New Michael Moore-Backed Doc Tackles Alternative Energy," Associated Press, August 8, 2019, https://abcnews .go.com/Entertainment/wireStory/michael-moore-backed-doc-tackles -alternative-energy-64844048; "Editorial: Michael Moore-Backed Film Criti- cizes Renewable Energy," *Las Vegas Review-Journal*, August 18, 2019, www .reviewjournal.com/opinion/editorials/editorial-michael-moore-backed-film -criticizes-renewable-energy-1829377.

58. "Michael Moore Presents: Planet of the Humans," Full Documentary, Directed by Jeff Gibbs, YouTube, posted April 21, 2020, www.youtube.com /watch?v=Zk11vI-7czE.

59. See, for example, Ketan Joshi, "Planet of the Humans: A Reheated Mess of Lazy, Old Myths," April 24, 2020, https://ketanjoshi.co/2020/04/24/planet -of-the-humans-a-reheated-mess-of-lazy-old-myths; Leah H. Stokes, "Michael Moore Produced a Film About Climate Change That's a Gift to Big Oil," *Vox*,

April 28, 2020, www.vox.com/2020/4/28/21238597/michael-moore-planet-of
-the-humans-climate-change. A compendium of critical responses is available
at "Moore's Boorish Planet of the Humans: An Annotated Collection," Get Energy Smart Now!, April 25, 2020, http://getenergysmartnow.com/2020/04/25
/moores-boorish-planet-of-the-humans-an-annotated-collection.

60. See Michelle Froese, "Renewables Exceed 20.3% of U.S. Electricity
and Outpace Nuclear Power," *Windpower Engineering*, July 29, 2019, www
.windpowerengineering.com/renewables-exceed-20-3-of-u-s-electricity-and
-outpace-nuclear-power.

61. Mark Z. Jacobson, Mark A. Delucchi, Zack A.F. Bauer, Savannah C.
Goodman, William E. Chapman, Mary A. Cameron, Cedric Bozannat, et al.,
"100% Clean and Renewable Wind, Water, and Sunlight All-Sector Energy
Roadmaps for 139 Countries of the World," *Joule* 1, no. 1 (2017): 108–121,
https://doi.org/10.1016/j.joule.2017.07.005.

62. Michael Moore (@MMFlint), Twitter, April 24, 2020, 6:26 p.m., https://
twitter.com/MMFlint/status/1253857924750999552.

63. See "Frequently Asked Questions: How Much Carbon Dioxide Is Produced per Kilowatthour of U.S. Electricity Generation?," US Energy Information Administration, www.eia.gov/tools/faqs/faq.php?id=74&t=11.

64. Doug Boucher, "Movie Review: There's a Vast Cowspiracy About Climate Change," Union of Concerned Scientists, June 10, 2016, https://blog
.ucsusa.org/doug-boucher/cowspiracy-movie-review.

65. See Biofuelwatch (@biofuelwatch), Twitter, April 27, 2020, 3:42 a.m.,
https://twitter.com/biofuelwatch/status/1254722596530241537.

66. "Editorial: Michael Moore-Backed Film Criticizes Renewable Energy."

67. See Bill McKibben, "Response: Planet of the Humans Documentary,"
350.org, April 22, 2020, https://350.org/response-planet-of-the-humans
-documentary.

68. "Editorial: Michael Moore-Backed Film Criticizes Renewable Energy."

69. "Michael Moore Net Worth," Celebrity Net Worth, www.celebrity
networth.com/richest-celebrities/directors/michael-moore-net-worth.

70. Peter Bradshaw, "Planet of the Humans Review—Contrarian Eco-
Doc from the Michael Moore Stable," *The Guardian*, April 22, 2020, www
.theguardian.com/film/2020/apr/22/planet-of-the-humans-review-environment
-michael-moore-jeff-gibbs.

71. Neal Livingston, "Forget About Planet of the Humans," *Films for Action*, April 24, 2020, www.filmsforaction.org/articles/film-review-forget-about
-planet-of-the-humans.

72. Joshi, "Planet of the Humans: A Reheated Mess."

73. Brian Kahn, "Planet of the Humans Comes This Close to Actually Getting the Real Problem, Then Goes Full Ecofascism," *Gizmodo*, April 20, 2020,
https://earther.gizmodo.com/planet-of-the-humans-comes-this-close-to
-actually-getti-1843024329.

74. AFP, "World's Richest 10% Produce Half of Global Carbon Emissions, Says Oxfam," *The Guardian*, December 2, 2015, www.theguardian

.com/environment/2015/dec/02/worlds-richest-10-produce-half-of-global -carbon-emissions-says-oxfam.

75. Grant Samms (@grantsamms), Twitter, April 23, 2020, 9:05 a.m., https://twitter.com/grantsamms/status/1253354390943076352.

76. James Delingpole, "Michael Moore Is Now the Green New Deal's Worst Enemy," Breitbart, April 23, 2020, www.breitbart.com/entertainment/2020/04 /23/delingpole-michael-moore-is-now-the-green-new-deals-worst-enemy.

77. "Competitive Enterprise Institute," SourceWatch, www.sourcewatch .org/index.php/Competitive_Enterprise_Institute, accessed April 29, 2020; "Heartland Institute," SourceWatch, www.sourcewatch.org/index.php /Heartland_Institute, accessed April 29, 2020; "Anthony Watts," SourceWatch, www.sourcewatch.org/index.php/Anthony_Watts, accessed April 29, 2020.

78. Myron Ebell, "Hurry, See 'Planet of the Humans,' Before It's Banned," Competitive Enterprise Institute, April 24, 2020, https://cei.org/blog/hurry -see-planet-humans-it%E2%80%99s-banned; Donny Kendal, Justin Haskins, Isaac Orr, and Jim Lakely, "In the Tank (Episode 240)—Review: Michael Moore's Planet of the Humans," Heartland Institute, April 24, 2020, www .heartland.org/multimedia/podcasts/in-the-tank-ep240--review-michael -moores-planet-of-the-humans.

79. Anthony Watts, "#EarthDay EPIC! Michael Moore's New Film Trashes 'Planet Saving' Renewable Energy—Full Movie Here!," Watts Up with That, April 22, 2020, https://wattsupwiththat.com/2020/04/22/earthday-epic -michael-moores-new-film-trashes-planet-saving-renewable-energy-full -movie-here.

80. "Steven J. Milloy," SourceWatch, www.sourcewatch.org/index.php /Steven_J._Milloy, accessed April 29, 2020; Steve Milloy (@JunkScience), Twitter, April 27, 2020, 6:55 a.m., https://twitter.com/junkscience/status /1254771076870975491.

81. "Marc Morano," SourceWatch, www.sourcewatch.org/index.php/Marc _Morano, accessed April 29, 2020; Marc Morano (@ClimateDepot), Twitter, June 5, 2020, 4:35 p.m., https://twitter.com/ClimateDepot/status /1269050171809120260.

82. Emily Atkin, "A Party for the Planet('s Destruction): A Powerful Anti-Climate Group Spent Thousands to Promote Michael Moore's Climate Documentary on Facebook This Week," Heated, May 19, 2020, https://heated .world/p/a-party-for-the-planets-destruction.

83. "Film-Maker Michael Moore Visits Julian Assange at Embassy," Irish Independent, June 10, 2016, www.independent.ie/style/celebrity/celebrity -news/film-maker-michael-moore-visits-julian-assange-at-embassy-34788794 .html.

84. Adam Tooze, "How Climate Change Has Supercharged the Left: Global Warming Could Launch Socialists to Unprecedented Power—and Expose Their Movement's Deepest Contradictions," Foreign Policy, January 15, 2020, https://foreignpolicy.com/2020/01/15/climate-socialism-supercharged -left-green-new-deal.

85. Emily Atkin, "The Wheel of First-Time Climate Dudes. Or, Alternatively: Why I Don't Want to Review Michael Moore's Climate Change Documentary," *Heated*, April 23, 2020, https://heated.world/p/the-wheel-of-first-time-climate-dudes.

86. Laura Geggel, "Bill Gates 'Discovers' 14-Year-Old Formula on Climate Change," *Live Science*, February 26, 2016, www.livescience.com/53861-bill-gates-climate-formula-not-new.html; Michael E. Mann, "FiveThirtyEight: The Number of Things Nate Silver Gets Wrong About Climate Change," *Huffington Post*, November 24, 2012, www.huffpost.com/entry/nate-silver-climate-change_b_1909482.

87. Giles Parkinson, "How the Tesla Big Battery Has Smoothed the Transition to Zero Emissions Grid," Renew Economy, March 1, 2020. See also Randell Suba, "Tesla 'Big Battery' in Australia Is Becoming a Bigger Nightmare for Fossil Fuel Power Generators," Teslarati, February 28, 2020, www.teslarati.com/tesla-big-battery-hornsdale-australia-cost-savings.

88. Jacobson et al., "100% Clean and Renewable Wind, Water, and Sunlight All-Sector Energy Roadmaps."

89. "Bill Gates Q&A on Climate Change: 'We Need a Miracle,'" *Denver Post*, February 13, 2016, www.denverpost.com/2016/02/23/bill-gates-qa-on-climate-change-we-need-a-miracle.

90. Jacobson et al., "100% Clean and Renewable Wind, Water, and Sunlight All-Sector Energy Roadmaps."

91. "David E. Wojick," SourceWatch, www.sourcewatch.org/index.php?title=David_E._Wojick; David Wojick, "Providing 100 Percent Energy from Renewable Sources Is Impossible," Heartland Institute, February 12, 2020, www.heartland.org/news-opinion/news/providing-100-percent-energy-from-renewable-sources-is-impossible.

92. Patrick Quinn, "After Devastating Tornado, Town Is Reborn 'Green,'" *USA Today*, *Green Living* magazine, April 13, 2013, www.usatoday.com/story/news/greenhouse/2013/04/13/greensburg-kansas/2078901.

93. Will Oremus, "Fox News Claims Solar Won't Work in America Because It's Not Sunny Like Germany," *Slate*, February 7, 2013, https://slate.com/technology/2013/02/fox-news-expert-on-solar-energy-germany-gets-a-lot-more-sun-than-we-do-video.html.

94. Max Greenberg, "Fox Cedes Solar Industry to Germany," Media Matters, February 7, 2013, www.mediamatters.org/fox-friends/fox-cedes-solar-industry-germany.

95. Oremus, "Fox News Claims Solar Won't Work in America."

CHAPTER 7: THE NON-SOLUTION SOLUTION

1. Eillie Anzilotti, "Climate Change Is Inevitable. How Bad It Gets Is a Choice," *Fast Company*, March 12, 2019, www.fastcompany.com/90318242/climate-change-is-inevitable-how-bad-it-gets-is-a-choice.

2. Paul Muschick, "Pennsylvania Is Heating Up Because of Climate Change. Let's Do Something About It," *Morning Call*, November 15, 2019, www .mcall.com/opinion/mc-opi-climate-change-costs-pennsylvania-muschick -20191115-mxaqyumnzfdctnictlskzb6sc4-story.html.

3. Jane Bardon, "How the Beetaloo Gas Field Could Jeopardise Australia's Emissions Target," Australian Broadcasting Corporation, February 29, 2019, www.abc.net.au/news/2020-02-29/beetaloo-basin-gas-field-could-jeopardise -paris-targets/12002164.

4. "Scott Morrison Announces $2 Billion Energy Deal to Boost Gas Use," SBS News, January 31, 2020, www.sbs.com.au/news/scott-morrison -announces-2-billion-energy-deal-to-boost-gas-use.

5. Luke O'Neil, "US Energy Department Rebrands Fossil Fuels as 'Molecules of Freedom,'" *The Guardian*, May 30, 2019, www.theguardian.com/business /2019/may/29/energy-department-molecules-freedom-fossil-fuel-rebranding.

6. Amanda Amos and Margaretha Haglund, "From Social Taboo to 'Torch of Freedom': The Marketing of Cigarettes to Women," *Tobacco Control* 9, no. 1 (2000): 3–8.

7. "What Is the Emissions Impact of Switching from Coal to Gas?," *Carbon Brief*, October 27, 2014, www.carbonbrief.org/what-is-the-emissions-impact -of-switching-from-coal-to-gas.

8. Gayathri Vaidyanathan, "How Bad of a Greenhouse Gas Is Methane?," *ClimateWire*, December 22, 2015, www.scientificamerican.com/article/how -bad-of-a-greenhouse-gas-is-methane.

9. Emily Holden, "Trump Administration to Roll Back Obama-Era Pollution Regulations," *The Guardian*, August 30, 2019, www.theguardian .com/environment/2019/aug/29/trump-administration-roll-back-methane -regulations.

10. Andrew Nikiforuk, "New Study Finds Far Greater Methane Threat from Fossil Fuel Industry," *The Tyee*, February 21, 2020, https://thetyee .ca/News/2020/02/21/Fossil-Fuel-Industry-Far-Greater-Methane-Threat -Study-Finds.

11. Jonathan Mingle, "Atmospheric Methane Levels Are Going Up— And No One Knows Why," *Wired*, May 5, 2019, www.wired.com/story /atmospheric-methane-levels-are-going-up-and-no-one-knows-why.

12. Brendan O'Neill, "Why Extinction Rebellion Seems So Nuts," *Spiked*, November 11, 2019, www.spiked-online.com/2019/11/07/why-extinction -rebellion-seems-so-nuts.

13. Prachi Patel, "New Projects Show Carbon Capture Is Not Dead," *IEEE Spectrum*, January 16, 2017, https://spectrum.ieee.org/energywise/green-tech /clean-coal/carbon-capture-is-not-dead-but-will-it-blossom.

14. Christa Marshall, "Clean Coal Power Plant Killed, Again," *Climatewire*, *E&E News*, February 4, 2015, reprinted by *Scientific American*, www.scientific american.com/article/clean-coal-power-plant-killed-again.

15. Dipka Bhambhani, "Everyone Wants Carbon Capture And Sequestration—Now How to Make It a Reality?," November 21, 2019, www.forbes

.com/sites/dipkabhambhani/2019/11/21/washington-to-wall-street-hears
-harmony-on-ccs-to-address-climate-change/#6d029ffe35da.

16. See Michael Barnard's answer on September 26, 2019, to "Are Industrial Carbon Capture Plants Carbon Neutral in Operation?," Quora, www.quora.com/Are-industrial-carbon-capture-plants-carbon-neutral-in-operation.

17. Brian Kahn, "More Than 600 Environmental Groups Just Backed Ocasio-Cortez's Green New Deal," *Gizmodo*, January 10, 2019, https://earther.gizmodo.com/more-than-600-environmental-groups-just-backed-ocasio-c-1831640541.

18. Robinson Meyer, "The Green New Deal Hits Its First Major Snag," *The Atlantic*, January 18, 2019, www.theatlantic.com/science/archive/2019/01/first-fight-about-democrats-climate-green-new-deal/580543.

19. Meyer, "The Green New Deal Hits Its First Major Snag."

20. James Temple, "Let's Keep the Green New Deal Grounded in Science," *MIT Technology Review*, January 19, 2019, www.technologyreview.com/s/612780/lets-keep-the-green-new-deal-grounded-in-science.

21. "Global Effects of Mount Pinatubo," NASA, Earth Observatory, https://earthobservatory.nasa.gov/images/1510/global-effects-of-mount-pinatubo.

22. Francisco Toro, "Climate Politics Is a Dead End. So the World Could Turn to This Desperate Final Gambit," *Washington Post*, December 18, 2019, www.washingtonpost.com/opinions/2019/12/18/climate-politics-is-dead-end-so-world-could-turn-this-desperate-final-gambit.

23. For a review of the potential pitfalls of sulfate aerosol geoengineering, see "Scientists to Stop Global Warming with 100,000 Square Mile Sun Shade," *The Telegraph*, February 26, 2009, www.telegraph.co.uk/news/earth/environment/globalwarming/4839985/Scientists-to-stop-global-warming-with-100000-square-mile-sun-shade.html.

24. Eli Kintisch, "Climate Hacking for Profit: A Good Way to Go Broke," *Fortune*, May 21, 2010, http://archive.fortune.com/2010/05/21/news/economy/geoengineering.climos.planktos.fortune/index.htm.

25. Gaia Vince, "Sucking CO2 from the Skies with Artificial Trees," BBC, October 4, 2012, www.bbc.com/future/story/20121004-fake-trees-to-clean-the-skies.

26. Johannes Lehmann and Angela Possinger, "Removal of Atmospheric CO_2 by Rock Weathering Holds Promise for Mitigating Climate Change," *Nature*, July 8, 2020, www.nature.com/articles/d41586-020-01965-7.

27. Daniel Hillel, *The Rivers of Eden: The Struggle for Water and the Quest for Peace in the Middle East* (Oxford: Oxford University Press, 1994).

28. Patrick Galey, "Industry Guidance Touts Untested Tech as Climate Fix," Phys.org, August 23, 2019, https://phys.org/news/2019-08-industry-guidance-touts-untested-tech.html.

29. "Fuel to the Fire: How Geoengineering Threatens to Entrench Fossil Fuels and Accelerate the Climate Crisis," Center for International Environmental Law, February 2019, www.ciel.org/wp-content/uploads/2019/02/CIEL_FUEL-TO-THE-FIRE_How-Geoengineering-Threatens-to-Entrench-Fossil-Fuels-and-Accelerate-the-Climate-Crisis_February-2019.pdf.

30. Kate Connolly, "Geoengineering Is Not a Quick Fix for Climate Change, Experts Warn Trump," *The Guardian*, October 14, 2017, www.theguardian.com/environment/2017/oct/14/geoengineering-is-not-a-quick-fix-for-climate-change-experts-warn-trump.

31. See Bjorn Lomborg, "Geoengineering: A Quick, Clean Fix?," *Time*, November 14, 2010, http://content.time.com/time/magazine/article/0,9171,2030804,00.html; Colin McInnes, "Time to Embrace Geoengineering," Breakthrough Institute, June 27, 2013, http://thebreakthrough.org/index.php/programs/energy-and-climate/time-to-embrace-geoengineering.

32. Marc Gunther, "The Business of Cooling the Planet," *Fortune*, October 7, 2011, https://fortune.com/2011/10/07/the-business-of-cooling-the-planet.

33. Benjamin Franta and Geoffrey Supran, "The Fossil Fuel Industry's Invisible Colonization of Academia," *The Guardian*, March 13, 2017, www.theguardian.com/environment/climate-consensus-97-per-cent/2017/mar/13/the-fossil-fuel-industrys-invisible-colonization-of-academia.

34. James Temple, "The Growing Case for Geoengineering," *Technology Review*, April 18, 2017, www.technologyreview.com/s/604081/the-growing-case-for-geoengineering.

35. "David Keith," Breakthrough Institute, https://thebreakthrough.org/people/david-keith; "An Ecomodernist Manifesto," www.ecomodernism.org; George Monbiot, "Meet the Ecomodernists: Ignorant of History and Paradoxically Old-Fashioned," *The Guardian*, February 24, 2015, www.theguardian.com/environment/georgemonbiot/2015/sep/24/meet-the-ecomodernists-ignorant-of-history-and-paradoxically-old-fashioned.

36. Gunther, "The Business of Cooling the Planet"; James Temple, "This Scientist Is Taking the Next Step in Geoengineering," *Technology Review*, July 26, 2017, www.technologyreview.com/s/608312/this-scientist-is-taking-the-next-step-in-geoengineering.

37. Peter Irvine, Kerry Emanuel, Jie He, Larry W. Horowitz, Gabriel Vecchi, and David Keith, "Halving Warming with Idealized Solar Geoengineering Moderates Key Climate Hazards," *Nature Climate Change* 9 (2019): 295–299, https://doi.org/10.1038/s41558-019-0398-8; Peter Irvine, the first author, is Keith's postdoctoral fellow. Keith, the principal investigator, signed his name at the end of the author list.

38. See this Twitter thread: Chris Colose (@CColose), Twitter, March 11, 2019, 3:03 p.m., https://twitter.com/CColose/status/1105227667689951234.

39. Ken Caldeira (@KenCaldeira), Twitter, March 23, 2020, 7:59 a.m., https://twitter.com/KenCaldeira/status/1242103749989949441; Ken Caldeira (@KenCaldeira), Twitter, August 24, 2019, 11:54 a.m., https://twitter.com/KenCaldeira/status/1165336530983874560.

40. Daniel Swain (@Weather_West), Twitter, August 24, 2019, 12:03 p.m., https://twitter.com/Weather_West/status/1165338821468123136.

41. Dr. Jonathan Foley (@GlobalEcoGuy), Twitter, August 24, 2019, 12:01 p.m., https://twitter.com/GlobalEcoGuy/status/1165338382655819776.

42. Matthew Huber (@climatedynamics), Twitter, August 24, 2019, 4:57 p.m., https://twitter.com/climatedynamics/status/1165412731379507200.

43. Michael E. Mann, "If You See Something, Say Something," *New York Times*, January 17, 2014, www.nytimes.com/2014/01/19/opinion/sunday/if-you-see-something-say-something.html.

44. Michael E. Mann (@MichaelEMann), Twitter, March 12, 2019, 6:23 a.m., https://twitter.com/MichaelEMann/status/1105459225852022785.

45. See Michael E. Mann (@MichaelEMann), Twitter, March 12, 2019, 6:53 a.m., https://twitter.com/MichaelEMann/status/1105466799657807872; Michael E. Mann (@MichaelEMann), Twitter, March 12, 2019, 12:14 p.m., https://twitter.com/MichaelEMann/status/1105547711569424385.

46. Toro, "Climate Politics Is a Dead End."

47. See Michael E. Mann (@MichaelEMann), Twitter, December 18, 2019, 1:44 p.m., https://twitter.com/MichaelEMann/status/1207416244460109824; Michael E. Mann (@MichaelEMann), Twitter, December 18, 2019, 1:50 p.m., https://twitter.com/MichaelEMann/status/1207417769119158272.

48. Temple, "The Growing Case for Geoengineering."

49. "Fuel to the Fire."

50. Umair Irfan, "Tree Planting Is Trump's Politically Safe New Climate Plan," *Vox*, February 4, 2020, www.vox.com/2020/2/4/21123456/sotu-trump-trillion-trees-climate-change.

51. Madeleine Gregory and Sarah Emerson, "Planting 'Billions of Trees' Isn't Going to Stop Climate Change: A Popular Study Claims That Reforestation Could Fix Climate Change, But Is That True?," *Vice*, July 16, 2019, www.vice.com/en_au/article/7xgymg/planting-billions-of-trees-isnt-going-to-stop-climate-change.

52. Mark Maslin and Simon Lewis, "Yes, We Can Reforest on a Massive Scale—but It's No Substitute for Slashing Emissions," *Climate Home News*, May 7, 2019, www.climatechangenews.com/2019/07/05/yes-can-reforest-massive-scale-no-substitute-slashing-emissions.

53. Emma Farge and Stephanie Nebehay, "Greenhouse Emissions Rise to More Than 55 Gigatonnes of CO2 Equivalent," *Business Day*, November 26, 2019, www.businesslive.co.za/bd/world/2019-11-26-greenhouse-emissions-rise-to-more-than-55-gigatonnes-of-co2-equivalent.

54. Gregory and Emerson, "Planting 'Billions of Trees' Isn't Going to Stop Climate Change."

55. Andrew Freedman, "Australia Fires: Yearly Greenhouse Gas Emissions Nearly Double Due to Historic Blazes," *The Independent*, January 25, 2020, www.independent.co.uk/news/world/australasia/australia-fires-greenhouse-gas-emissions-climate-crisis-fossil-fuel-a9301396.html.

56. Laura Millan Lombrana, Hayley Warren, and Akshat Rathi, "Measuring the Carbon-Dioxide Cost of Last Year's Worldwide Wildfires," Bloomberg Green, February 10, 2020, www.bloomberg.com/graphics/2020-fire-emissions.

57. Fiona Harvey, "Tropical Forests Losing Their Ability to Absorb Carbon, Study Finds," *The Guardian*, March 5, 2020, www.theguardian.com/environment/2020/mar/04/tropical-forests-losing-their-ability-to-absorb-carbon-study-finds.

58. Roger Harrabin, "Climate Change: UK Forests 'Could Do More Harm Than Good,'" BBC, April 7, 2020, www.bbc.com/news/science-environment -52200045.

59. Leo Hickman, "The History of BECCS," *Carbon Brief*, April 13, 2016, www.carbonbrief.org/beccs-the-story-of-climate-changes-saviour-technology.

60. See Robert Jay Lifton and Naomi Oreskes, "The False Promise of Nuclear Power," *Boston Globe*, July 29, 2019, www.bostonglobe.com/opinion /2019/07/29/the-false-promise-nuclear-power/kS8rzs8f7MAONgXL1fWOGK /story.html.

61. See Lifton and Oreskes, "The False Promise of Nuclear Power."

62. R. Singh, T. Wagener, R. Crane, M. E. Mann, and L. Ning, "A Stakeholder Driven Approach to Identify Critical Thresholds in Climate and Land Use for Selected Streamflow Indices—Application to a Pennsylvania Watershed," *Water Resources Research* 50 (2014): 3409–3427, https://doi.org /10.1002/2013WR014988.

63. M. V. Ramana and Ali Ahmad, "Wishful Thinking and Real Problems: Small Modular Reactors, Planning Constraints, and Nuclear Power in Jordan," *Energy Policy* 93 (2016): 236–245, https://doi.org/10.1016/j.enpol .2016.03.012.

64. James A. Lake, Ralph G. Bennett, and John F. Kotek, "Next Generation Nuclear Power: New, Safer and More Economical Nuclear Reactors Could Not Only Satisfy Many of Our Future Energy Needs but Could Combat Global Warming as Well," *Scientific American*, January 26, 2009, www .scientificamerican.com/article/next-generation-nuclear.

65. Nathanael Johnson, "Next-Gen Nukes: Scores of Nuclear Startups Are Aiming to Solve the Problems That Plague Nuclear Power," *Grist*, July 18, 2018, https://grist.org/article/next-gen-nuclear-is-coming-if-we-want-it.

66. See Lifton and Oreskes, "The False Promise of Nuclear Power."

67. See, for example, this op-ed by four leading climate science colleagues: Ken Caldeira, Kerry Emanuel, James Hansen, and Tom Wigley, "Top Climate Change Scientists' Letter to Policy Influencers," CNN, November 3, 2013, https://edition.cnn.com/2013/11/03/world/nuclear-energy-climate-change -scientists-letter/index.html.

68. "Bob Inglis—Acceptance Speech," John F. Kennedy Presidential Library and Museum, www.jfklibrary.org/node/4466.

69. See Lifton and Oreskes, "The False Promise of Nuclear Power."

70. David Roberts, "Hey, Look, a Republican Who Cares About Climate Change!," *Grist*, July 10, 2012, https://grist.org/article/hey-look-a-republican -who-cares-about-climate-change.

71. "How Fareed Zakaria Became the Most Conservative Liberal of All Time," *Deadline Detroit*, May 29, 2012, www.deadlinedetroit.com/articles /555/how_fareed_zakaria_became_the_most_conservative_liberal_of_all_time; Fareed Zakaria, "Bernie Sanders's Magical Thinking on Climate Change," *Washington Post*, February 13, 2020, www.washingtonpost.com/opinions/bernie -sanderss-magical-thinking-on-climate-change/2020/02/13/3944e472-4ea5 -11ea-9b5c-eac5b16dafaa_story.html.

72. See "Nuclear Economics: Critical Responses to Breakthrough Institute Propaganda," World Information Service on Energy (WISE), Nuclear Monitor #840, no. 4630, March 21, 2017, www.wiseinternational.org/nuclear -monitor/840/nuclear-economics-critical-responses-breakthrough-institute -propaganda; "An Ecomodernist Manifesto."

73. See "It's Worse Than You Think—Lower Emissions, Higher Ground," Yang 2020, August 28, 2019, www.yang2020.com/blog/climate-change; Ryan Broderick, "Andrew Yang Wants the Support of the Pro-Trump Internet. Now It Is Threatening to Devour Him," *BuzzFeed*, March 14, 2019, www .buzzfeednews.com/article/ryanhatesthis/4chan-vs-the-yang-gang.

74. Maya Earls, "Benefits of Adaptation Measures Outweigh the Costs, Report Says," *Climatewire, E&E News*, September 10, 2019, reprinted at *Scientific American*, www.scientificamerican.com/article/benefits-of-adaptation -measures-outweigh-the-costs-report-says.

75. Marco Rubio, "We Should Choose Adaptive Solutions," *USA Today*, August 19, 2019, www.usatoday.com/story/opinion/2019/08/19/rubio-on -climate-change-we-should-choose-adaptive-solutions-column/2019310001.

76. Andrea Dutton and Michael Mann, "A Dangerous New Form of Climate Denialism Is Making the Rounds," *Newsweek*, August 22, 2019, www .newsweek.com/dangerous-new-form-climate-denialism-making-rounds -opinion-1455736.

77. Francie Diep, "The House Science Committee Just Held a Helpful Hearing on Climate Science for the First Time in Years," *Pacific Standard*, February 13, 2019, https://psmag.com/news/the-house-science -committee-just-held-its-first-helpful-hearing-on-climate-science-in-years; Tiffany Stecker, "New Climate Panel's Republicans Seek Focus on Adaptation," Bloomberg Energy, March 8, 2019, https://news.bloombergenvironment .com/environment-and-energy/new-climate-panels-republicans-seek-focus-on -adaptation.

78. Steven Mufson, "Are Republicans Coming out of 'the Closet' on Climate Change?," *Washington Post*, February 4, 2020, www.washington post.com/climate-environment/can-republicans-turn-over-a-new-leaf-on -climate-change/2020/02/03/6a6a6bd8-4155-11ea-aa6a-083d01b3ed18 _story.html.

79. Greg Walden, Fred Upton, and John Shimkus, "Republicans Have Better Solutions to Climate Change," *Real Clear Policy*, February 13, 2019, www .realclearpolicy.com/articles/2019/02/13/republicans_have_better_solutions _to_climate_change_111045.html.

80. Michael Mann, "If There's a Silver Lining in the Clouds of Choking Smoke It's That This May Be a Tipping Point," *The Guardian*, February 3, 2020, www.theguardian.com/commentisfree/2020/feb/03/if-theres-a-silver -lining-in-the-clouds-of-smoke-its-that-this-could-be-a-tipping-point.

81. "Fire Fight: Tara Brown Finds Out What Australia Can Do to Prevent a Repeat of This Summer's Deadly Bushfires," Nine Network, Australia, February 9, 2020, www.9now.com.au/60-minutes/2020/episode-1.

82. Though, in what could pass for parody, Bolt argued that "it will be good for us." See Van Badham, "Now That Climate Change Is Irrefutable, Denialists Like Andrew Bolt Insist It Will Be Good for Us," *The Guardian*, January 30, 2020, www.theguardian.com/commentisfree/2020/jan/30/now-that-climate -change-is-irrefutable-denialists-like-andrew-bolt-insist-it-will-be-good-for-us.

83. Christopher Wright and Michael E. Mann, "From Denial to 'Resilience': The Slippery Discourse of Obfuscating Climate Action," Sydney Environment Institute of the University of Sydney, February 19, 2020, http://sydney .edu.au/environment-institute/opinion/from-denial-to-resilience.

84. Sarah Martin, "Scott Morrison to Focus on 'Resilience and Adaptation' to Address Climate Change," *The Guardian*, January 14, 2020, www .theguardian.com/environment/2020/jan/14/scott-morrison-to-focus-on -resilience-and-adaption-to-address-climate-change.

85. See "Honest Government Ad: After the Fires," The Juice Media, February 11, 2020, www.thejuicemedia.com/honest-government-ad-the-fires.

86. Graham Readfearn, "Australian PM Scott Morrison Agrees to Permanently Increase Aerial Firefighting Funding," *The Guardian*, January 4, 2020, www.theguardian.com/australia-news/2020/jan/04/australian-pm-scott -morrison-agrees-to-permanently-increase-aerial-firefighting-funding.

87. Sarah Martin, "Coalition Promises $2bn for Bushfire Recovery as It Walks Back from Budget Surplus Pledge," *The Guardian*, January 6, 2020, www.theguardian.com/australia-news/2020/jan/06/coalition-pledges-2bn -for-bushfire-recovery-as-it-walks-back-from-budget-surplus-pledge.

88. "Scott Morrison Announces $2 Billion Energy Deal"; Lucy Barbour and Jane Norman, "Rebel Nationals Wanting New Coal-Fired Power Stations Face Battle with Liberals and Markets," Australian Broadcasting Corporation, February 13, 2020, www.abc.net.au/news/2020-02-13/national-party-rebels -fighting-for-more-coal-power-stations/11959568; David Crowe, "New Resources Minister Calls for More Coal, Gas and Uranium Exports," *Sydney Morning Herald*, February 11, 2020, www.smh.com.au/politics/federal/new-resources -minister-calls-for-more-coal-gas-and-uranium-exports-20200211-p53zu5 .html.

89. M. C. Nisbet, "The Ecomodernists: A New Way of Thinking About Climate Change and Human Progress," *Skeptical Inquirer* 42, no. 6 (2018): 20–24, https://web.northeastern.edu/matthewnisbet/wp-content/uploads/2018/12 /Nisbet2018_TheEcomodernists_SkepticalInquirer_.pdf; "Matthew Nisbet," Breakthrough Institute, https://thebreakthrough.org/people/matthew-nisbet; Matt Nisbet, "Against Climate Change Tribalism: We Gamble with the Future by Dehumanizing Our Opponents," *Skeptical Inquirer* 44, no. 1 (2020), https:// skepticalinquirer.org/2020/01/against-climate-change-tribalism-we-gamble -with-the-future-by-dehumanizing-our-opponents.

90. See, for example, David Roberts, "Why I've Avoided Commenting on Nisbet's 'Climate Shift' Report," *Grist*, April 27, 2011, https://grist.org/climate -change/2011-04-26-why-ive-avoided-commenting-on-nisbets-climate-shift -report.

CHAPTER 8: THE TRUTH IS BAD ENOUGH

1. Justin Gillis, "Climate Model Predicts West Antarctic Ice Sheet Could Melt Rapidly," *New York Times*, March 30, 2016, www.nytimes.com/2016/03/31/science/global-warming-antarctica-ice-sheet-sea-level-rise.html.

2. Michael Mann, "It's Not Rocket Science: Climate Change Was Behind This Summer's Extreme Weather," *Washington Post*, November 2, 2018, www.washingtonpost.com/opinions/its-not-rocket-science-climate-change-was-behind-this-summers-extreme-weather/2018/11/02/b8852584-dea9-11e8-b3f0-62607289efee_story.html.

3. Nicholas Smith and Anthony Leiserowitz, "The Role of Emotion in Global Warming Policy Support and Opposition," *Risk Analysis* 34, no. 5 (2014): 937–948.

4. Clay Evans, "Ditching the Doomsaying for Better Climate Discourse," *University of Colorado Arts and Sciences Magazine*, December 18, 2019, www.colorado.edu/asmagazine/2019/12/18/ditching-doomsaying-better-climate-discourse.

5. Bjorn Lomborg, "Who's Afraid of Climate Change?" Project Syndicate, August 11, 2010, www.project-syndicate.org/commentary/who-s-afraid-of-climate-change.

6. Oliver Milman and Dominic Rushe, "New EPA Head Scott Pruitt's Emails Reveal Close Ties with Fossil Fuel Interests," *The Guardian*, February 23, 2017, www.theguardian.com/environment/2017/feb/22/scott-pruitt-emails-oklahoma-fossil-fuels-koch-brothers; Oliver Milman, "EPA Head Scott Pruitt Says Global Warming May Help 'Humans Flourish,'" *The Guardian*, February 8, 2018, www.theguardian.com/environment/2018/feb/07/epa-head-scott-pruitt-says-global-warming-may-help-humans-flourish.

7. Sam Langford, "'He's Cherry Picking with Intent': Here's What the Climate Scientist Andrew Bolt Keeps Quoting Would Like You to Know," *The Feed*, January 27, 2020, www.sbs.com.au/news/the-feed/he-s-cherry-picking-with-intent-here-s-what-the-climate-scientist-andrew-bolt-keeps-quoting-would-like-you-to-know.

8. See, for example, the op-ed I coauthored on this subject: Michael E. Mann, Susan Joy Hassol, and Tom Toles, "Doomsday Scenarios Are as Harmful as Climate Change Denial," *Washington Post*, July 12, 2017, www.washingtonpost.com/opinions/doomsday-scenarios-are-as-harmful-as-climate-change-denial/2017/07/12/880ed002-6714-11e7-a1d7-9a32c91c6f40_story.html.

9. Ketan Joshi (@KetanJ0), Twitter, January 11, 2020, 2:03 p.m., https://twitter.com/KetanJ0/status/1216118507500457985.

10. Max Hastings, *Winston's War: Churchill, 1940–1945* (New York: Vintage, 2011).

11. JC Cooper (@coopwrJ), Twitter, September 14, 2019, 1:25 p.m., https://twitter.com/CoopwrJ/status/1172969585097621504. Cooper is a materials scientist and zoologist.

12. Jennifer De Pinto, Fred Backus, and Anthony Salvanto, "Most Americans Say Climate Change Should Be Addressed Now—CBS News Poll,"

CBS News, September 15, 2019, www.cbsnews.com/news/cbs-news-poll
-most-americans-say-climate-change-should-be-addressed-now-2019-09
-15. See the cross-tabs for question #8 athttps://drive.google.com/file/d
/0ByVu4fDHYJgVdHFJWFRsbF90TDNSZFV3TklzMkVrRHh0TDNj/view.

13. See "Meet the Team," The Glacier Trust, http://theglaciertrust.org
/people; Joanne Moore, "Family Pay Tribute to Missing Hill Walker," *Gazette
and Herald*, March 8, 2016, www.gazetteandherald.co.uk/news/14328154.
family-pay-tribute-to-missing-hill-walker.

14. Michael E. Mann and Jonathan Brockopp, "You Can't Save the Climate by Going Vegan. Corporate Polluters Must Be Held Accountable,"
USA Today, June 3, 2019, www.usatoday.com/story/opinion/2019/06/03
/climate-change-requires-collective-action-more-than-single-acts
-column/1275965001; Michael E. Mann, June 3, 2019, Facebook, www
.facebook.com/MichaelMannScientist/posts/2327588820630640.

15. Zeke Hausfather and Glen P. Peters, "Emissions—the 'Business as
Usual' Story Is Misleading: Stop Using the Worst-Case Scenario for Climate
Warming as the Most Likely Outcome—More-Realistic Baselines Make for Better Policy," *Nature*, January 29, 2020, www.nature.com/articles/d41586-020
-00177-3.

16. Christopher H. Trisos, Cory Merow, and Alex L. Pigot, "The Projected
Timing of Abrupt Ecological Disruption from Climate Change," *Nature* 580
(2020): 496–501, https://doi.org/10.1038/s41586-020-2189-9.

17. Citizens for Climate Action (@CitFrClimACTION), Twitter, December
13, 2019, https://twitter.com/citfrclimaction/status/1205570515026501633.

18. Darlene "Rethink everything you thought you knew" (@DarleneLily1),
Twitter, https://twitter.com/DarleneLily1/https://twitter.com/citfrclimaction/
status/1205570515026501633. The tweet has since been deleted.

19. Mann and Brockopp, "You Can't Save the Climate by Going Vegan."

20. Raquel Baranow (@666isMONEY), Twitter, September 8, 2019, 12:46
p.m., https://twitter.com/666isMONEY/status/1170785503630614529.

21. Raquel Baranow (@666isMONEY), Twitter, September 13, 2019, 9:14
p.m., https://twitter.com/666isMONEY/status/1172725301576519680.

22. #ForALL CANCEL RENT NOW (@GarrettShorr), Twitter, December
12, 2019, 11:07 p.m., https://twitter.com/GarrettShorr/status/120538380877
9841536.

23. InsideClimate News (@insideclimate), Twitter, April 10, 2020, 1:20
p.m., https://twitter.com/insideclimate/status/1248707322899247104.

24. Michael E. Mann (@MichaelEMann), Twitter, April 10, 2020, 1:32
p.m., https://twitter.com/MichaelEMann/status/1248710415426748422.

25. Bruce Boyes (@BruceBoyes), Twitter, April 11, 2020, 2:36 a.m., https://
twitter.com/BruceBoyes/status/1248907679621251073. Boyes is editor and
lead writer of the award-winning *KM Magazine* in Australia.

26. Wild Talks Ireland (@TalksWild), Twitter, April 10, 2020, 1:36 p.m.,
https://twitter.com/TalksWild/status/1248711522953637896.

27. Jonathan Franzen, "What If We Stopped Pretending? The Climate
Apocalypse Is Coming. To Prepare for It, We Need to Admit That We Can't

Prevent It," *New Yorker*, September 8, 2019, www.newyorker.com/culture/cultural-comment/what-if-we-stopped-pretending.

28. Ula Chrobak, "Can We Still Prevent an Apocalypse? What Jonathan Franzen Gets Wrong About Climate Change: What If We Stopped Pretending the New Yorker's Essay Makes Sense?," *Popular Science*, September 11, 2019, www.popsci.com/climate-change-new-yorker-franzen-corrections.

29. Jeff Nesbit (@jeffnesbit), Twitter, September 8, 2019, 8:33 a.m., https://twitter.com/jeffnesbit/status/1170721760678797312.

30. John Upton (@johnupton), Twitter, September 8, 2019, 8:11 a.m., https://twitter.com/johnupton/status/1170716277977026560.

31. Dr. Jonathan Foley (@GlobalEcoGuy), Twitter, September 8, 2019, 10:45 a.m., https://twitter.com/GlobalEcoGuy/status/1170755004199657472.

32. Taylor Nicole Rogers, "Scientists Blast Jonathan Franzen's 'Climate Doomist' Opinion Column as 'the Worst Piece on Climate Change,'" *Business Insider*, September 8, 2019, www.businessinsider.com/scientists-blast-jonathan-franzens-climate-doomist-new-yorker-op-ed-2019-9.

33. Franzen, "What If We Stopped Pretending?"

34. Alison Flood, "Jonathan Franzen: Online Rage Is Stopping Us Tackling the Climate Crisis," *The Guardian*, October 9, 2019, www.theguardian.com/books/2019/oct/08/jonathan-franzen-online-rage-is-stopping-us-tackling-the-climate-crisis.

35. See Dr Tamsin Edwards (@flimsin), Twitter, October 26, 2019, 2:05 p.m., https://twitter.com/flimsin/status/1188199938284539904. For the lecture by Rupert Read, see "Rupert Read: How I Talk with Children About Climate Breakdown," YouTube, posted August 13, 2019, www.youtube.com/watch?v=6Lt0jCDtYSY&feature=youtu.be.

36. Roy Scranton, *We're Doomed. Now What? Essays on War and Climate Change* (New York: Penguin Random House, 2018).

37. The original tweet was https://twitter.com/royscranton/status/1073903831870857216.

38. Roy Scranton, "No Happy Ending: On Bill McKibben's 'Falter' and David Wallace-Wells's 'The Uninhabitable Earth,'" *Los Angeles Review of Books*, June 3, 2019, https://lareviewofbooks.org/article/no-happy-ending-on-bill-mckibbens-falter-and-david-wallace-wellss-the-uninhabitable-earth.

39. Alexandria Villaseñor (@AlexandriaV2005), Twitter, January 30, 2019, 3:16 a.m., https://twitter.com/AlexandriaV2005/status/1090569401345236997.

40. Scranton, "No Happy Ending."

41. David Roberts (@drvox), Twitter, https://twitter.com/drvox/status/1136321633499590656.

42. James Renwick, "Guy McPherson and the End of Humanity (Not)," *Hot Topic* (blog), December 11, 2016, http://hot-topic.co.nz/guy-mcpherson-and-the-end-of-humanity-not.

43. See Twitter exchange at Michael E. Mann (@MichaelEMann), March 21, 2020, 8:47 p.m., https://twitter.com/MichaelEMann/status/1241572174114304000, which concerns a video that McPherson posted in which he asserted that "by November 1st plus or minus a few months we would be out of

habitat for our species" (at roughly 2:10 into the video). The video is "Edge of Extinction: Coronavirus Update," YouTube, posted February 28, 2020, www .youtube.com/watch?v=vn4PoLOmCME&feature=youtu.be.

44. Scott Johnson, "How Guy McPherson Gets It Wrong," *Fractal Planet* (blog), February 17, 2014, https://fractalplanet.wordpress.com/2014/02/17 /how-guy-mcpherson-gets-it-wrong.

45. Catherine Ingram, "Are We Heading Toward Extinction? The Earth's Species—Plants, Animals and Humans, Alike—Are Facing Imminent Demise. How We Got Here, and How to Cope," *Huffington Post*, July 20, 2019, www.huffpost.com/entry/facing-extinction-humans-animals-plants-species_n _5d2ddc04e4b0a873f6420bd3.

46. "Rex Weyler," Greenpeace, www.greenpeace.org/international/author /rex-weyler; Rex Weyler, "Extinction and Rebellion," Greenpeace, May 17, 2019, www.greenpeace.org/international/story/22058/extinction-and-rebellion.

47. Aja Romano, "Twitter Released 9 Million Tweets from One Russian Troll Farm. Here's What We Learned," *Vox*, October 19, 2018, www.vox .com/2018/10/19/17990946/Twitter-russian-trolls-bots-election-tampering.

48. Craig Timberg and Tony Romm, "Russian Trolls Sought to Inflame Debate over Climate Change, Fracking, Dakota Pipeline," *Chicago Tribune*, March 1, 2018, www.chicagotribune.com/nation-world/ct-russian-trolls-climate-change -20180301-story.html.

49. Harry Enten, "Registered Voters Who Stayed Home Probably Cost Clinton the Election," *FiveThirtyEight*, January 5, 2017, https://fivethirtyeight .com/features/registered-voters-who-stayed-home-probably-cost-clinton-the -election.

50. See YouTube archive of McPherson's interviews for American Freedom Radio at www.youtube.com/results?search_query=American+Freedom +Radio+%22Guy+McPherson%22.

51. Guy McPherson, "Why I'm Voting for Donald Trump: McPherson's 6th Stage of Grief (Gallows Humor)," Nature Bats Last, March 11, 2016, https:// guymcpherson.com/2016/03/why-im-voting-for-donald-trump-mcphersons -6th-stage-of-grief-gallows-humor.

52. JC Cooper (@Coopwr), Twitter, September 14, 2019, 1:39 p.m., https://twitter.com/CoopwrJ/status/1172973057138315264.

53. Andy Caffrey (@Andy_Caffrey), Twitter, September 5, 2019, 12:50 p.m., https://twitter.com/Andy_Caffrey/status/1169699394574176256.

54. Johnson, "How Guy McPherson Gets It Wrong."

55. Eric Steig (@ericsteig), Twitter, November 11, 2019, 9:49 p.m., https:// twitter.com/ericsteig/status/1194130088784093185.

56. Jill (@sooverthis123), Twitter, July 30, 2019, 1:57 p.m., https://twitter .com/sooverthis123/status/1156307730224648193.

57. Dana Nuccitelli, "There Are Genuine Climate Alarmists, but They're Not in the Same League as Deniers," *The Guardian*, July 9, 2018, www .theguardian.com/environment/climate-consensus-97-per-cent/2018/jul /09/there-are-genuine-climate-alarmists-but-theyre-not-in-the-same-league -as-deniers.

58. Scott Johnson, "Once More: McPherson's Methane Catastrophe," *Fractal Planet* (blog), January 8, 2015, https://fractalplanet.wordpress.com /category/science-doing-it-wrong.

59. Ian Johnston, "Earth's Worst-Ever Mass Extinction of Life Holds 'Apocalyptic' Warning About Climate Change, Say Scientists," *The Independent*, March 24, 2017, www.independent.co.uk/environment/earth-permian-mass -extinction-apocalypse-warning-climate-change-frozen-methane-a7648006 .html; Howard Lee, "Sudden Ancient Global Warming Event Traced to Magma Flood," *Quanta Magazine*, March 19, 2020, www.quantamagazine.org/sudden -ancient-global-warming-event-traced-to-magma-flood-20200319.

60. Joshua F. Dean, Jack J. Middelburg, Thomas Röckmann, Rien Aerts, Luke G. Blauw, Matthias Egger, S. M. Jetten, et al, "Methane Feedbacks to the Global Climate System in a Warmer World," *Reviews of Geophysics* 56, no. 1 (2018): 207–250; Chris Colose, "Toward Improved Discussions of Methane and Climate," August 1, 2013, www.skepticalscience.com/toward-improved -discussions-methane.html. See also this older but still valid commentary by my colleague David Archer: "Arctic Methane on the Move," Real Climate, March 6, 2010, www.realclimate.org/index.php/archives/2010/03/arctic -methane-on-the-move.

61. See multipart Twitter thread at Michael E. Mann (@MichaelEMann), Twitter, September 14, 2019, 12:04 p.m., https://twitter.com/MichaelEMann /status/1172949203821219841.

62. Ben Heubl, "Arctic Methane Levels Reach New Heights," *Engineering and Technology Magazine*, September 16, 2019, https://eandt.theiet.org/content /articles/2019/09/arctic-methane-levels-reach-new-heights-data-shows.

63. Andrew Nikiforuk, "New Study Finds Far Greater Methane Threat from Fossil Fuel Industry," *The Tyee*, February 21, 2020, https://thetyee.ca/News /2020/02/21/Fossil-Fuel-Industry-Far-Greater-Methane-Threat-Study-Finds.

64. Ed King, "Should Climate Scientists Slash Air Miles to Set an Example?," *Climate Home News*, October 3, 2015, www.climatechangenews .com/2015/03/10/should-climate-scientists-slash-air-miles-to-set-an-example.

65. "About the Committee on Climate Change," Committee on Climate Change, www.theccc.org.uk/about.

66. Kevin Anderson (@KevinClimate), Twitter, January 28, 2020, 12:36 a.m., https://twitter.com/KevinClimate/status/1222076017008836609.

67. Dr Alexandra Jellicow (@alexjellicoe), Twitter, January 28, 2020, 12:42 a.m., https://twitter.com/alexjellicoe/status/1222077373337808897.

68. Kevin Anderson (@KevinClimate), Twitter, January 28, 2020, 12:53 a.m., https://twitter.com/KevinClimate/status/1222080140383080448.

69. Chris Stark (@ChiefExecCCC), Twitter, January 28, 2020, 12:58 a.m., https://twitter.com/ChiefExecCCC/status/1222081581944315904.

70. Dr Tamsin Edwards (@flimsin), Twitter, January 28, 2020, 1:03 a.m., https://twitter.com/flimsin/status/1222082804529364992.

71. Kevin Anderson (@KevinClimate), Twitter, January 28, 2020, 1:54 a.m., https://twitter.com/KevinClimate/status/1222095616140095489.

72. Zing Tsjeng, "The Climate Change Paper So Depressing It's Sending People to Therapy," *Vice*, February 27, 2019, www.vice.com/en_au/article/vbwpdb/the-climate-change-paper-so-depressing-its-sending-people-to-therapy.

73. Jem Bendell, "Deep Adaptation: A Map for Navigating Climate Tragedy," IFLAS Occasional Paper 2, July 27, 2018, available at www.lifeworth.com/deepadaptation.pdf.

74. Tsjeng, "The Climate Change Paper So Depressing It's Sending People to Therapy."

75. Ironically, one of the most thorough debunkings of Bendell's paper was provided by libertarian pundit Ron Bailey (more on that later) in "Good News! No Need to Have a Mental Breakdown over 'Climate Collapse,'" *Reason*, March 3, 2019, https://reason.com/2019/03/29/good-news-no-need-to-have-a-mental-break.

76. Jack Hunter, "The 'Climate Doomers' Preparing for Society to Fall Apart," BBC, March 16, 2020, www.bbc.com/news/stories-51857722.

77. Tsjeng, "The Climate Change Paper So Depressing It's Sending People to Therapy."

78. Hunter, "The 'Climate Doomers' Preparing for Society to Fall Apart."

79. David Wallace-Wells, "Time to Panic," *New York Times*, February 16, 2019, www.nytimes.com/2019/02/16/opinion/sunday/fear-panic-climate-change-warming.html.

80. Sheril Kirshenbaum, "No, Climate Change Will Not End the World in 12 Years: Stoking Panic and Fear Creates a False Narrative That Can Overwhelm Readers, Leading to Inaction and Hopelessness," *Scientific American*, August 13, 2019, https://blogs.scientificamerican.com/observations/no-climate-change-will-not-end-the-world-in-12-years.

81. A transcript of Thunberg's speech appears at *The Guardian*, January 25, 2019, www.theguardian.com/environment/2019/jan/25/our-house-is-on-fire-greta-thunberg16-urges-leaders-to-act-on-climate.

82. Francisco Toro, "Climate Politics Is a Dead End. So the World Could Turn to This Desperate Final Gambit," *Washington Post*, December 18, 2019, www.washingtonpost.com/opinions/2019/12/18/climate-politics-is-dead-end-so-world-could-turn-this-desperate-final-gambit.

83. Quoting from their official description at "The Truth," Extinction Rebellion, https://rebellion.earth/the-truth.

84. "Climate Fatalism," Freedom Lab, http://freedomlab.org/climate-fatalism.

85. "About," Freedom Lab, http://freedomlab.org/about-freedomlab.

86. David Roberts (@drvox), Twitter, https://twitter.com/drvox/status/1211713331603611648 (Roberts subsequently deleted the tweet).

87. Jonathan Koomey (@jgkoomey), Twitter, December 30, 2019, 10:48 a.m., https://twitter.com/jgkoomey/status/1211720645928611840.

88. Massimo Sandal (@massimosandal), Twitter, December 30, 2019, 11:47 p.m., https://twitter.com/massimosandal/status/1211916797554937858.

89. Will Steffen, Johan Rockström, Katherine Richardson, Timothy M. Lenton, Carl Folke, Diana Liverman, Colin P. Summerhayes, et al., "Trajectories of the Earth System in the Anthropocene," *Proceedings of the National Academy of Sciences* 115, no. 33 (2018): 8252–8259, https://doi.org/10.1073/pnas.1810141115.

90. Kate Aronoff, "'Hothouse Earth' Co-Author: The Problem Is Neoliberal Economics," *The Intercept*, August 14, 2018, https://theintercept.com/2018/08/14/hothouse-earth-climate-change-neoliberal-economics.

91. Richard Betts, "Hothouse Earth: Here's What the Science Actually Does—and Doesn't—Say," *The Conversation*, August 10, 2018, https://theconversation.com/hothouse-earth-heres-what-the-science-actually-does-and-doesnt-say-101341.

92. Timothy M. Lenton, Johan Rockström, Owen Gaffney, Stefan Rahmstorf, Katherine Richardson, Will Steffen, and Hans Joachim Schellnhuber, "Climate Tipping Points—Too Risky to Bet Against," *Nature*, November 27, 2019, www.nature.com/articles/d41586-019-03595-0.

93. Stephen Leahy, "Climate Change Driving Entire Planet to Dangerous 'Tipping Point,'" *National Geographic*, November 27, 2019, www.nationalgeographic.com/science/2019/11/earth-tipping-point; "Scientists Warn Earth at Dire Risk of Becoming Hellish 'Hothouse,'" *New York Post*, August 7, 2018, https://nypost.com/2018/08/07/scientists-warn-earth-at-dire-risk-of-becoming-hellish-hothouse.

94. David Wallace-Wells, "The Uninhabitable Earth: Famine, Economic Collapse, a Sun That Cooks Us: What Climate Change Could Wreak—Sooner Than You Think," *New York Magazine*, July 2017, https://nymag.com/intelligencer/2017/07/climate-change-earth-too-hot-for-humans.html.

95. See "The 'Doomed Earth' Controversy," Arthur L. Carter Journalism Institute, New York University, November 30, 2017, https://journalism.nyu.edu/about-us/event/2017-fall/the-doomed-earth-controversy.

96. Michael E. Mann, Facebook, July 10, 2017, www.facebook.com/MichaelMannScientist/posts/since-this-new-york-magazine-article-the-uninhabitable-earth-is-getting-so-much-/1470539096335621.

97. Mann et al., "Doomsday Scenarios Are as Harmful as Climate Change Denial."

98. Zeke Hausfather, "Major Correction to Satellite Data Shows 140% Faster Warming Since 1998," *Carbon Brief*, June 30, 2017, www.carbonbrief.org/major-correction-to-satellite-data-shows-140-faster-warming-since-1998.

99. Dana Nuccitelli, "Climate Scientists Just Debunked Deniers' Favorite Argument," *The Guardian*, June 28, 2017, www.theguardian.com/environment/climate-consensus-97-per-cent/2017/jun/28/climate-scientists-just-debunked-deniers-favorite-argue; Benjamin D. Santer, John C. Fyfe, Giuliana Pallotta, Gregory M. Flato, Gerald A. Meehl, Matthew H. England, Ed Hawkins, et al., "Causes of Differences in Model and Satellite Tropospheric Warming Rates," *Nature Geoscience* 10 (2017): 478–485.

100. The workshop was the 2018 Ny-Ålesund Symposium on Navigating Climate Risk. For details, see www.ny-aalesundsymposium.no/2018/Summary

_of_the_Ny-_lesund_symposium_2018.shtmlandwww.ny-aalesundsymposium
.no/artman/uploads/1/Ny-_lesund_Summary_and_Steps_Forward.pdf.

101. "Norwegian Seed Vault Guarantees Crops Won't Become Extinct," *Weekend Edition* with Lulu Garcia-Navarro, National Public Radio, May 21, 2017, www.npr.org/2017/05/21/529364527/norwegian-seed-vault-guarantees -crops-won-t-become-extinct.

102. For the transcript of my full interview with Wallace-Wells, see David Wallace-Wells, "Scientist Michael Mann on 'Low-Probability but Catastrophic' Climate Scenarios," *New York Magazine*, July 11, 2017, https://nymag .com/intelligencer/2017/07/scientist-michael-mann-on-climate-scenarios .html.

103. "Scientists Explain What *New York Magazine* Article on 'The Uninhabitable Earth' Gets Wrong: Analysis of 'The Uninhabitable Earth,' Published in New York Magazine, by David Wallace-Wells on 9 July 2017," Climate Feedback, July 12, 2017, https://climatefeedback.org/evaluation/scientists -explain-what-new-york-magazine-article-on-the-uninhabitable-earth-gets -wrong-david-wallace-wells.

104. "Scientists Explain What *New York Magazine* Article on 'The Uninhabitable Earth' Gets Wrong."

105. See Michael E. Mann (@MichaelEMann), Twitter, July 12, 2017, 10:21 p.m., https://twitter.com/MichaelEMann/status/885368503452262400; the tweet of Roberts to which it is replying is now reported as "not available."

106. "The 'Doomed Earth' Controversy," Arthur L. Carter Journalism Institute, New York University, November 30, 2017, https://journalism.nyu.edu /about-us/event/2017-fall/the-doomed-earth-controversy.

107. David Wallace-Wells, *Uninhabitable Earth: Life After Warming* (New York: Tim Duggan Books / Penguin Random House, 2019), 22.

108. Warren Cornwall, "Even 50-Year-Old Climate Models Correctly Predicted Global Warming," *Science*, December 4, 2019, www.sciencemag.org /news/2019/12/even-50-year-old-climate-models-correctly-predicted-global -warming.

109. "The Uninhabitable Earth," Penguin Random House, www.penguin randomhouse.com/books/586541/the-uninhabitable-earth-by-david-wallace -wells.

110. Yessenia Funes, "HBO Max Is Turning *The Uninhabitable Earth* Into a Fictional Series," *Gizmodo*, January 16, 2020, https://earther.gizmodo.com /hbo-max-is-turning-the-uninhabitable-earth-into-a-ficti-1841048114.

111. "'We Are Entering into an Unprecedented Climate,'" MSNBC, *Morning Joe*, February 20, 2019, www.msnbc.com/morning-joe/watch/-we-are -entering-into-an-unprecedented-climate-1445411907673.

112. Sean Illing, "It Is Absolutely Time to Panic About Climate Change: Author David Wallace-Wells on the Dystopian Hellscape That Awaits Us," *Vox*, February 24, 2019, www.vox.com/energy-and-environment/2019/2/22/18188562 /climate-change-david-wallace-wells-the-uninhabitable-earth.

113. David Wallace-Wells (@dwallacewells), Twitter, September 23, 2019, 9:32 a.m., https://twitter.com/dwallacewells/status/1176172433579159552.

114. Assaad Razzouk (@AssaadRazzouk), Twitter, September 22, 2019, 4:14 p.m., https://twitter.com/AssaadRazzouk/status/1175911365820764161.

115. Richard Betts (@richardabetts), Twitter, September 23, 2019, 12:56 p.m., https://twitter.com/richardabetts/status/1176223928785756161.

116. Eric Steig (@ericsteig), Twitter, September 23, 2019, 6:59 p.m., https://twitter.com/ericsteig/status/1176315272610758656.

117. David Wallace-Wells, "U.N. Climate Talks Collapsed in Madrid. What's the Way Forward?," *New York Magazine*, December 16, 2019, http://nymag.com /intelligencer/2019/12/cop25-ended-in-failure-whats-the-way-forward.html.

118. "Global CO2 Emissions in 2019," International Energy Agency, February 11, 2020, www.iea.org/articles/global-co2-emissions-in-2019.

119. Adam Vaughan, "China Is on Track to Meet Its Climate Change Goals Nine Years Early," *The Guardian*, July 26, 2019, www.newscientist.com/article /2211366-china-is-on-track-to-meet-its-climate-change-goals-nine-years-early.

120. Julia Rosen, "Cities, States and Companies Vow to Meet U.S. Climate Goals Without Trump. Can They?," *Los Angeles Times*, November 4, 2019, www.latimes.com/environment/story/2019-11-04/cities-states-companies -us-climate-goals-trump.

121. See the thread with Kalee Kreider (@kaleekreider), Twitter, December 17, 2019, 6:46 p.m., https://twitter.com/kaleekreider/status/1207129884 339949570.

122. See "UN Climate Pledge Analysis," Climate Interactive, www.climate interactive.org/programs/scoreboard.

123. David Wallace-Wells (@dwallacewells), Twitter, December 17, 2019, 6:08 p.m., https://twitter.com/dwallacewells/status/1207120372585381888.

124. Kalee Kreider (@kaleekreider), Twitter, December 17, 2019, 6:46 p.m., https://twitter.com/kaleekreider/status/1207129884339949570; Kalee Kreider (@kaleekreider), Twitter, December 17, 2019, 6:48 p.m., https://twitter .com/kaleekreider/status/1207130377946587136. See also "U.S.-China Joint Announcement on Climate Change," White House, Office of the Press Secretary, November 11, 2014, https://obamawhitehouse.archives.gov/the-press -office/2014/11/11/us-china-joint-announcement-climate-change.

125. Greta Thunberg (@GretaThunberg), Twitter, December 14, 2019, 12:52 p.m., https://twitter.com/gretathunberg/status/1205953722293145604.

126. Suyin Haynes, "Greta Thunberg Joins Youth Activists on TIME Panel at Davos to Say 'Pretty Much Nothing' Has Been Done on Climate Change," *Time*, January 21, 2020, https://time.com/5768561/greta-thunberg-davos -panel-time.

127. David Wallace-Wells, "We're Getting a Clearer Picture of the Climate Future—and It's Not as Bad as It Once Looked," *New York Magazine*, December 20, 2019, https://nymag.com/intelligencer/2019/12/climate-change -worst-case-scenario-now-looks-unrealistic.html.

128. Hausfather and Peters, "Emissions—the 'Business as Usual' Story Is Misleading."

129. Alastair McIntosh (@alastairmci), Twitter, March 16, 2020, 4:10 p.m., https://twitter.com/alastairmci/status/1239690611671916544.

130. Quoted in Christopher J. Bosso, *Pesticides and Politics: The Life Cycle of a Public Issue* (Pittsburgh: University of Pittsburgh Press, 1987), 116; Naomi Oreskes and Eric M. Conway, *Merchants of Doubt: How a Handful of Scientists Obscured the Truth on Issues from Tobacco Smoke to Global Warming* (New York: Bloomsbury Press, 2010).

131. "Dangerous Legacy," Competitive Enterprise Institute, 2016, www .rachelwaswrong.org.

132. Michael Mann, *The Hockey Stick and the Climate Wars: Dispatches from the Front Lines* (New York: Columbia University Press, 2013), 74–77.

133. Vijay Jayaraj, "Opportunistic Doomsayers Compare Climate Change to Coronavirus," CNS News, March 24, 2020, www.cnsnews.com/commentary /vijay-jayaraj/opportunistic-doomsayers-compare-climate-change-coronavi- rus. The Media Research Center received over $400,000 from ExxonMobil between 1998 and 2009. "Factsheet: Media Research Center, MRC," Exxon Secrets.org, www.exxon secrets.org/html/orgfactsheet.php?id=110. Accord- ing to Media Transparency, it received over $3 million from the Sarah Scaife Foundation between 1998 and 2009. Bridge Project, http://mediamattersaction .org/transparency/organization/Media_Research_Center/funders.

134. Mann, *The Hockey Stick and the Climate Wars*, 76.

135. Michael Mann and Lee R. Kump, *Dire Predictions: Understanding Climate Change*, 2nd ed. (New York: DK, 2015), 46–47.

136. Mann, *The Hockey Stick and the Climate Wars*, 160.

137. This is one of the leading climate denial myths documented at Skep- tical Science. See "Climate Scientists Would Make More Money in Other Careers," Skeptical Science, https://skepticalscience.com/climate-scientists-in -it-for-the-money.htm.

138. This is an accusation that was made by Paul Driessen, who has been vari- ously employed by the Center for a Constructive Tomorrow (CFACT), the Cen- ter for the Defense of Free Enterprise, the Frontiers of Freedom, and the Atlas Economic Research Foundation, among others—a virtual cornucopia of industry front groups. See Mann, *The Hockey Stick and the Climate Wars*, 202–203.

139. Alastair McIntosh (@alastairmci), Twitter, March 16, 2020, 4:10 p.m., https://twitter.com/alastairmci/status/1239690611671916544.

140. Ronald Bailey, *Global Warming and Other Eco Myths: How the Envi- ronmental Movement Uses False Science to Scare Us to Death* (Roseville, CA: Prima Lifestyles, 2002); Bailey, "Good News! No Need to Have a Mental Breakdown."

141. Michael E. Mann (@MichaelEMann), Twitter, May 5, 2017, 11:50 a.m., https://twitter.com/MichaelEMann/status/860567443059724288. The comment references Denise Robbins, "New Book Exposes Koch Brothers' Guide to Infiltrating the Media," Media Matters, February 17, 2016, www .mediamatters.org/koch-brothers/new-book-exposes-koch-brothers-guide -infiltrating-media. That discusses the Koch Brothers connection.

142. Michael Bastasch, "Scientists Issue 'Absurd' Doomsday Prediction, Warn of a 'Hothouse Earth,'" *Daily Caller*, August 7, 2018, https://dailycaller .com/2018/08/07/scientists-doomsday-hothouse-earth.

143. Roger A. Pielke Sr (@RogerAPielkeSr), Twitter, August 7, 2018, 10:50 a.m., https://twitter.com/RogerAPielkeSr/status/1026888246305775616.

144. Miranda Devine, "Celebrities, Activists Using Australia Bushfire Crisis to Push Dangerous Climate Change Myth," *New York Post*, January 8, 2020, https://nypost.com/2020/01/08/celebrities-activists-using-australia-bushfire -crisis-to-push-dangerous-climate-change-myth-devine.

145. Kerry Emanuel, "Sober Appraisals of Risk Are Ignored in Critique of Hyperbole," *Boston Globe*, June 5, 2011, http://archive.boston.com /bostonglobe/editorial_opinion/letters/articles/2011/06/05/sober_appraisals _of_risk_are_ignored_in_critique_of_hyperbole.

146. Jeff Jacoby, "I'm Skeptical About Climate Alarmism, but I Take Coronavirus Fears Seriously," *Boston Globe*, March 15, 2020, www.boston globe.com/2020/03/14/opinion/im-skeptical-about-climate-alarmism -i-take-coronavirus-fears-seriously.

147. Michael E. Mann, Facebook, July 10, 2017, www.facebook.com /MichaelMannScientist/posts/since-this-new-york-magazine-article-the -uninhabitable-earth-is-getting-so-much-/1470539096335621.

148. Michael E. Mann, "Climatologist Makes Clear: We're Still on Pandemic Path with Global Warming," *Boston Globe*, March 18, 2020, www.bostonglobe.com/2020/03/19/opinion/climatologist-makes-clear -were-still-pandemic-path-with-global-warming.

149. See, for example, Christiana Figueres, Hans Joachim Schellnhuber, Gail Whiteman, Johan Rockström, Anthony Hobley, and Stefan Rahmstorf, "Three Years to Safeguard Our Climate," *Nature*, June 28, 2017, www.nature .com/news/three-years-to-safeguard-our-climate-1.22201.

CHAPTER 9: MEETING THE CHALLENGE

1. See Michael Mann and Tom Toles, *The Madhouse Effect* (New York: Columbia University Press, 2016), 164–166.

2. The provenance of the quote is much-debated, but at least one authoritative source (*Miami Herald*) attributes the quote in this form to Groucho Marx.

3. Brendan Fitzgerald, "Q&A: Michael Mann on Coverage Since 'Climategate,'" *Columbia Journalism Review*, September 19, 2019, www.cjr.org /covering_climate_now/michael-mann-climategate-franzen.php, reprinted at State Impact Pennsylvania, National Public Radio, September 21, 2019, https:// stateimpact.npr.org/pennsylvania/2019/09/21/qa-penn-state-climate-scientist -michael-mann-on-news-coverage-since-climategate.

4. Scott Waldman, "Cato Closes Its Climate Shop; Pat Michaels Is Out," *Climatewire*, *E&E News*, May 29, 2019, www.eenews.net/stories/1060419123.

5. Richard Collett-White, "Climate Science Deniers Planning European Misinformation Campaign, Leaked Documents Reveal," September 6, 2019, www .desmog.co.uk/2019/09/06/climate-science-deniers-planning-coordinated -european-misinformation-campaign-leaked-documents-reveal; Nicholas Kusnetz,

"Heartland Launches Website of Contrarian Climate Science amid Struggles with Funding and Controversy Dogged by Layoffs, a Problematic Spokesperson and an Investigation by European Journalists, the Climate Skeptics' Institute Returns to Its Old Tactics," *Inside Climate News*, March 13, 2020, https://inside climatenews.org/news/12032020/heartland-instutute-climate-change-skeptic.

6. See Connor Gibson, "Heartland's Jay Lehr Calls EPA 'Fraudulent,' Despite Defrauding EPA and Going to Jail," *DeSmog* (blog), September 4, 2014, www.desmogblog.com/2014/09/04/heartland-science-director-jay-lehr-calls -epa-fraudulent-defrauded-epa-himself.

7. Waldman, "Cato Closes Its Climate Shop"; Alexander C. Kaufman, "Pro-Trump Climate Denial Group Lays Off Staff amid Financial Woes, Ex-Employees Say: The Heartland Institute Is the Think Tank Paying the Far-Right German Teen Known as the 'Anti-Greta,'" *Huffington Post*, March 9, 2020, www.huffpost.com/entry/heartland-institute-staff-layoffs-climate-change -denial_n_5e6302a6c5b6670e72f85fa5.

8. "Article by Michael Shellenberger Mixes Accurate and Inaccurate Claims in Support of a Misleading and Overly Simplistic Argumentation About Climate Change," Climate Feedback, https://climatefeedback.org /evaluation/article-by-michael-shellenberger-mixes-accurate-and-inaccurate -claims-in-support-of-a-misleading-and-overly-simplistic-argumentation -about-climate-change.

9. Graham Readfearn, "The Environmentalist's Apology: How Michael Shellenberger Unsettled Some of His Prominent Supporters," *The Guardian*, July 3, 2020, www.theguardian.com/environment/2020/jul/04/the -environmentalists-apology-how-michael-shellenberger-unsettled-some-of -his-prominent-supporters.

10. Kate Yoder, "Frank Luntz, the GOP's Message Master, Calls for Climate Action," *Grist*, July 25, 2019, https://grist.org/article/the-gops-most -famous-messaging-strategist-calls-for-climate-action.

11. Lissa Friedman, "Climate Could Be an Electoral Time Bomb, Republican Strategists Fear," *New York Times*, August 2, 2019, www.nytimes .com/2019/08/02/climate/climate-change-republicans.html.

12. Kusnetz, "Heartland Launches Website of Contrarian Climate Science."

13. Nathanael Johnson, "Fossil Fuels Are the Problem, Say Fossil Fuel Companies Being Sued," *Grist*, March 21, 2018, https://grist.org/article/fossil -fuels-are-the-problem-say-fossil-fuel-companies-being-sued.

14. Matthew Daily, "Dem Climate Plan Would End Greenhouse Gas Emissions by 2050," Associated Press, June 30, 2020, https://apnews.com /f72c5ae628bac72a7732d968a056878d

15. Justin Gillis, "The Republican Climate Closet: When Will Believers in Global Warming Come Out?," *New York Times*, August 12, 2019, www .nytimes.com/2019/08/12/opinion/republicans-environment.html.

16. George P. Shultz and Ted Halstead, "The Winning Conservative Climate Solution," *Washington Post*, January 16, 2020, www.washingtonpost.com /opinions/the-winning-republican-climate-solution-carbon-pricing/2020/01 /16/d6921dc0-387b-11ca-bf30-ad313c4cc754_story.html.

17. Damon Centola, Joshua Becker, Devon Brackbill, and Andrea Baronchelli, "Experimental Evidence for Tipping Points in Social Convention," *Science* 360, no. 6393 (2018): 1116–1119, https://doi.org/10.1126/science.aas8827.

18. "Attitudes on Same-Sex Marriage," Pew Research Center, May 14, 2019, www.pewforum.org/fact-sheet/changing-attitudes-on-gay-marriage.

19. Frank Luntz (@FrankLuntz), Twitter, June 8, 2020, 8:29 a.m., https://twitter.com/FrankLuntz/status/1270015144337141760.

20. "U.S. Public Views on Climate and Energy," Pew Research Center, November 25, 2019, www.pewresearch.org/science/2019/11/25/u-s-public-views-on-climate-and-energy.

21. Miranda Green, "Poll: Climate Change Is Top Issue for Registered Democrats," *The Hill*, April 30, 2019, https://thehill.com/policy/energy-environment/441344-climate-change-is-the-top-issue-for-registered-democratic-voters.

22. "Why Are Millions of Citizens Not Registered to Vote?," Pew Trusts, June 21, 2017, www.pewtrusts.org/en/research-and-analysis/issue-briefs/2017/06/why-are-millions-of-citizens-not-registered-to-vote; Aaron Blake, "For the First Time, There Are Fewer Registered Republicans Than Independents," *Washington Post*, February 28, 2020, www.washingtonpost.com/politics/2020/02/28/first-time-ever-there-are-fewer-registered-republicans-than-independents.

23. Ilona M. Otto, Jonathan F. Donges, Roger Cremades, Avit Bhowmik, Richard J. Hewitt, Wolfgang Lucht, Johan Rockström, et al., "Social Tipping Dynamics for Stabilizing Earth's Climate by 2050," *Proceedings of the National Academy of Sciences* 117, no. 5 (2020): 2354–2365, https://doi.org/10.1073/pnas.1900577117.

24. Mark Lewis, "Has Saudi Shifted Its Strategy in the Era of Decarbonisation?," *Financial Times*, March 15, 2020, www.ft.com/content/8c17582a-6547-11ea-a6cd-df28cc3c6a68.

25. Matt Egan, "The Market Has Spoken: Coal Is Dying," CNN Business, September 20, 2019, www.cnn.com/2019/09/20/business/coal-power-dying/index.html; Will Wade, "New York's Last Coal-Fired Power Plant to Retire Tuesday," Bloomberg Green, March 30, 2020, www.bloomberg.com/news/articles/2020-03-30/new-york-s-last-coal-fired-power-plant-will-shut-down-tuesday.

26. Leyland Cecco and agencies, "Canadian Mining Giant Withdraws Plans for C\$20bn Tar Sands Project: Teck Resources' Surprise Decision Drew Outrage from Politicians in Oil-Rich Alberta and Cheers from Environmental Groups," *The Guardian*, February 24, 2020, www.theguardian.com/world/2020/feb/24/canadian-mine-giant-teck-resources-withdraws-plans-tar-sands-project.

27. Peter Eavis, "Fracking Once Lifted Pennsylvania. Now It Could Be a Drag," *New York Times*, March 31, 2020, www.nytimes.com/2020/03/31/business/energy-environment/pennsylvania-shale-gas-fracking.html.

28. Fiona Harvey, "What Is the Carbon Bubble and What Will Happen if It Bursts?," *The Guardian*, June 4, 2018, www.theguardian.com/environment/2018/jun/04/what-is-the-carbon-bubble-and-what-will-happen-if-it-bursts.

29. Coryanne Hicks, "What Is a Fiduciary Financial Advisor? A Fiduciary Is Defined by the Legal and Ethical Requirement to Put Your Best Interest Before Their Own," *US News & World Report*, February 24, 2020, https://money.usnews.com/investing/investing-101/articles/what-is-a-fiduciary-financial-advisor-a-guide-to-the-fiduciary-duty.

30. Sarah Barker, Mark Baker-Jones, Emilie Barton, and Emma Fagan, "Climate Change and the Fiduciary Duties of Pension Fund Trustees—Lessons from the Australian Law," *Journal of Sustainable Finance and Investment* 6, no. 3 (2016): 211–214, https://doi.org/10.1080/20430795.2016.1204687.

31. Scott Murdoch and Paulina Duran, "Australian Pension Funds' $168 Billion 'Wall of Cash' May Lead Overseas," Reuters, September 9, 2019, www.reuters.com/article/us-australia-funds-pensions/australian-pension-funds-168-billion-wall-of-cash-may-lead-overseas-idUSKCN1VV07S.

32. Michael E. Mann (@MichaelEMann), Twitter, March 11, 2020, 12:54 a.m., https://twitter.com/MichaelEMann/status/1237647998575734785.

33. Gillian Tett, "The World Needs a Libor for Carbon Pricing," *Financial Times*, January 23, 2020, www.ft.com/content/20dd6b82-3dd1-11ea-a01a-bae547046735.

34. Huw Jones, "Bank of England Considers Bank Capital Charge on Polluting Assets," Reuters, March 10, 2020, https://uk.reuters.com/article/uk-climatechange-britain-banks/bank-of-england-considers-bank-capital-charge-on-polluting-assets-idUKKBN20X1NU.

35. Christopher Flavelle, "Global Financial Giants Swear Off Funding an Especially Dirty Fuel," *New York Times*, February 12, 2020, www.nytimes.com/2020/02/12/climate/blackrock-oil-sands-alberta-financing.html.

36. Steven Mufson and Rachel Siegel, "BlackRock Makes Climate Change Central to Its Investment Strategy," *Washington Post*, January 14, 2020, www.washingtonpost.com/business/2020/01/14/blackrock-letter-climate-change.

37. Bill McKibben, "Citing Climate Change, BlackRock Will Start Moving Away from Fossil Fuels," *New Yorker*, January 16, 2020, www.newyorker.com/news/daily-comment/citing-climate-change-blackrock-will-start-moving-away-from-fossil-fuels.

38. Juliet Eilperin, Steven Mufson and Brady Dennis, "Major Oil and Gas Pipeline Projects, Backed by Trump, Flounder as Opponents Prevail in Court," *Washington Post*, July 6, 2020, www.washingtonpost.com/climate-environment/2020/07/06/dakota-access-pipeline.

39. Nassim Khadem, "Mark McVeigh Is Taking on REST Super on Climate Change and Has the World Watching," Australian Broadcasting Corporation, January 17, 2020, www.abc.net.au/news/2020-01-18/mark-mcveigh-is-taking-on-rest-super-and-has-the-world-watching/11876360.

40. Richard Knight, "Sanctions, Disinvestment, and U.S. Corporations in South Africa," reprinted and updated from *Sanctioning Apartheid* (Lawrenceville, NJ: Africa World Press, 1990), http://richardknight.homestead.com/files/uscorporations.htm.

41. One Bold Idea, "How Students Helped End Apartheid: The UC Berkeley Protest That Changed the World," University of California, May 2, 2018, www.universityofcalifornia.edu/news/how-students-helped-end-apartheid.

42. See "A New Fossil Free Milestone: $11 Trillion Has Been Committed to Divest from Fossil Fuels," 350.org, https://350.org/11-trillion-divested.

43. Jagdeep Singh Bachher and Richard Sherman, "UC Investments Are Going Fossil Free. But Not Exactly for the Reasons You May Think," *Los Angeles Times*, September 17, 2019, www.latimes.com/opinion/story/2019-09-16/divestment-fossil-fuel-university-of-california-climate-change.

44. The provenance of this quote is murky. See Quote Investigator, https://quoteinvestigator.com/2018/01/07/stone-age.

45. "Global CO2 Emissions in 2019," International Energy Agency, February 11, 2020, www.iea.org/articles/global-co2-emissions-in-2019.

46. "Latest Data Book Shows U.S. Renewable Capacity Surpassed 20% for First Time in 2018. Growth Continues in U.S. Installed Wind and Solar Photovoltaic Capacity, Energy Storage, and Electric Vehicle Sales," National Renewable Energy Laboratory, February 18, 2020, www.nrel.gov/news/program/2020/latest-data-book-shows-us-renewable-capacity-surpassed-20-for-the-first-time-in-2018.html.

47. Seth Feaster and Dennis Wamsted, "Utility-Scale Renewables Top Coal for the First Quarter of 2020," Institute for Energy Economics and Financial Analysis, April 1, 2020, https://ieefa.org/ieefa-u-s-utility-scale-renewables-top-coal-for-the-first-quarter-of-2020.

48. Randell Suba, "Tesla 'Big Battery' in Australia Is Becoming a Bigger Nightmare for Fossil Fuel Power Generators," Teslarati, February 28, 2020, www.teslarati.com/tesla-big-battery-hornsdale-australia-cost-savings.

49. Sophie Vorrath, "South Australia on Track to 100 Pct Renewables, as Regulator Comes to Party," Renew Economy, January 24, 2020, https://reneweconomy.com.au/south-australia-on-track-to-100-pct-renewables-as-regulator-comes-to-party-96366.

50. I coauthored a similarly titled commentary in *Newsweek*: Lawrence Torcello and Michael E. Mann, "Seeing the COVID-19 Crisis Is Like Watching a Time Lapse of Climate Change. Will the Right Lessons Be Learned?," *Newsweek*, April 1, 2020, www.newsweek.com/fake-news-climate-change-coronavirus-time-lapse-1495603.

51. Debora Mackenzie, "We Were Warned—So Why Couldn't We Prevent the Coronavirus Outbreak?," *New Scientist*, March 4, 2020, www.newscientist.com/article/mg24532724-700-we-were-warned-so-why-couldnt-we-prevent-the-coronavirus-outbreak.

52. Harry Stevens, "Why Outbreaks Like Coronavirus Spread Exponentially, and How to 'Flatten the Curve,'" *Washington Post*, March 14, 2020, www.washingtonpost.com/graphics/2020/world/corona-simulator.

53. Ed Yong, "The U.K.'s Coronavirus 'Herd Immunity' Debacle," *The Atlantic*, March 16, 2020, www.theatlantic.com/health/archive/2020/03/coronavirus-pandemic-herd-immunity-uk-boris-johnson/608065.

54. Alex Wickham, "The UK Only Realised 'In the Last Few Days' That Its Coronavirus Strategy Would 'Likely Result in Hundreds of Thousands of Deaths,'" *BuzzFeed*, March 16, 2020, www.buzzfeed.com/alexwickham /coronavirus-uk-strategy-deaths.

55. Michelle Cottle, "Boris Johnson Should Have Taken His Own Medicine," *New York Times*, March 27, 2020, www.nytimes.com/2020/03/27 /opinion/boris-johnson-coronavirus.html.

56. John Burn-Murdoch (@jburnmurdoch), Twitter, April 3, 2020, 2:15 p.m., https://twitter.com/jburnmurdoch/status/1246184639540146178.

57. Patrick Wyman, "How Do You Know If You're Living Through the Death of an Empire? It's the Little Things," *Mother Jones*, March 19, 2020, www.motherjones.com/media/2020/03/how-do-you-know-if-youre-living -through-the-death-of-an-empire.

58. Jonathan Watts, "Delay Is Deadly: What Covid-19 Tells Us About Tackling the Climate Crisis," *The Guardian*, March 24, 2020, www.theguardian .com/commentisfree/2020/mar/24/covid-19-climate-crisis-governments -coronavirus.

59. Saijel Kishan, "Professor Sees Climate Mayhem Lurking Behind Covid-19 Outbreak," Bloomberg Green, March 28, 2020, www.bloomberg.com /news/articles/2020-03-28/professor-sees-climate-mayhem-lurking-behind -covid-19-outbreak.

60. William J. Broad, "Putin's Long War Against American Science," *New York Times*, April 13, 2020, www.nytimes.com/2020/04/13/science/putin -russia-disinformation-health-coronavirus.html.

61. Alex Kotch, "Right-Wing Megadonors Are Financing Media Operations to Promote Their Ideologies," PR Watch, January 27, 2020, www.prwatch .org/news/2020/01/13531/right-wing-megadonors-are-financing-media -operations-promote-their-ideologies; Julie Kelly, "Hockey Sticks, Changing Goal Posts, and Hysteria," American Greatness, March 31, 2020, https:// amgreatness.com/2020/03/31/hockey-sticks-changing-goal-posts-and-hysteria.

62. Benny Peiser and Andrew Montford, "Coronavirus Lessons from the Asteroid That Didn't Hit Earth: Scary Projections Based on Faulty Data Can Put Policy Makers Under Pressure to Adopt Draconian Measures," *Wall Street Journal*, April 1, 2020, www.wsj.com/articles/coronavirus-lessons-from-the -asteroid-that-didnt-hit-earth-11585780465. See "Benny Peiser," SourceWatch, www.sourcewatch.org/index.php/Benny_Peiser; "Andrew Montford," SourceWatch, www.sourcewatch.org/index.php/Andrew_Montford.

63. S. T. Karnick, "Watch Out for Long-Term Effects of Government's Coronavirus Remedies," Heartland Institute, April 2, 2020, www.heartland .org/news-opinion/news/watch-out-for-long-term-effects-of-governments -coronavirus-remedies-1.

64. Nic Lewis, "COVID-19: Updated Data Implies That UK Modelling Hugely Overestimates the Expected Death Rates from Infection," Climate Etc., March 25, 2020, https://judithcurry.com/2020/03/25/covid-19-updated -data-implies-that-uk-modelling-hugely-overestimates-the-expected-death

-rates-from-infection; Monkton, "Are Lockdowns Working?," *Watts Up with That*, April 4, 2020, https://wattsupwiththat.com/2020/04/04/are-lockdowns-working; Marcel Crok (@marcelcrok), Twitter, March 24, 2020, 4:59 a.m., https://twitter.com/marcelcrok/status/1242420742253432832; William M. Briggs, "Coronavirus Update VI: Calm Yourselves," March 24, 2020, https://wmbriggs.com/post/29886.

65. Katelyn Weisbrod, "6 Ways Trump's Denial of Science Has Delayed the Response to COVID-19 (and Climate Change): Misinformation, Blame, Wishful Thinking and Making Up Facts Are Favorite Techniques," *Inside Climate News*, March 19, 2020, https://insideclimatenews.org/news/19032020/denial-climate-change-coronavirus-donald-trump. A video comparison is available. See Michael E. Mann (@MichaelEMann), Twitter, March 25, 2020, 7:05 p.m., https://twitter.com/MichaelEMann/status/1242996165546848256.

66. Scott Waldman, "Obama Blasts Trump over Coronavirus, Climate Change," *Climatewire, E&E News*, April 1, 2020, www.eenews.net/stories/1062754487.

67. As pointed out by me on Twitter at Michael E. Mann (@MichaelEMann), Twitter, March 30, 2020, 9:32 a.m., https://twitter.com/MichaelEMann/status/1244663896893513729. Examples for both climate change and coronavirus are provided by these two articles, respectively: Scott Waldman, "Ex-Trump Adviser: 'Brainwashed' Aides Killed Climate Review," *ClimateWire, E&E News*, December 4, 2019, www.eenews.net/stories/1061717133; Isaac Chotiner, "The Contrarian Coronavirus Theory That Informed the Trump Administration," *New Yorker*, March 30, 2020, www.newyorker.com/news/q-and-a/the-contrarian-coronavirus-theory-that-informed-the-trump-administration.

68. Weisbrod, "6 Ways Trump's Denial of Science Has Delayed the Response to COVID-19 (and Climate Change)."

69. Jeff Mason, "Do Social Distancing Better, White House Doctor Tells Americans. Trump Objects," Reuters, April 2, 2020, www.reuters.com/article/us-health-coronavirus-trump-birx/do-social-distancing-better-white-house-doctor-tells-americans-trump-objects-idUSKBN21L08A.

70. Laurie McGinley and Carolyn Y. Johnson, "FDA Pulls Emergency Approval for Antimalarial Drugs Touted by Trump as Covid-19 Treatment," *Washington Post*, June 15, 2020, www.washingtonpost.com/health/2020/06/15/hydroxychloroquine-authorization-revoked-coronavirus.

71. Juliet Eilperin, Darryl Fears, and Josh Dawsey, "Trump Is Headlining Fireworks at Mount Rushmore. Experts Worry Two Things Could Spread: Virus and Wildfire," *Washington Post*, June 25, 2020, www.washingtonpost.com/climate-environment/2020/06/24/trump-mount-rushmore-fireworks.

72. The Daily Show (@TheDailyShow), Twitter, April 3, 2020, 11:45 a.m., https://twitter.com/TheDailyShow/status/1246146713523453957.

73. Bobby Lewis and Kayla Gogarty, "Pro-Trump Media Have Ramped Up Attacks Against Dr. Anthony Fauci," Media Matters, March 24, 2020, www.mediamatters.org/coronavirus-covid-19/pro-trump-media-have-ramped-attacks-against-dr-anthony-fauci.

74. Michael Gerson, "The Trump Administration Has Released a Lot of Shameful Documents. This One Might Be the Worst," *Washington Post*, July 13, 2020, www.washingtonpost.com/opinions/fauci-has-been-an-example -of-conscience-and-courage-trump-has-been-nothing-but-weak/2020/07/13 /7c9a7578-c52b-11ea-8ffe-372be8d82298_story.html.

75. See video clip and my comment at Michael E. Mann (@MichaelEMann), Twitter, March 23, 2020, 5:49 p.m., https://twitter.com/MichaelEMann/status /1242252283557093377.

76. Matthew Chapman, "Internet Explodes as Fox's Brit Hume Says It's 'Entirely Reasonable' to Let Grandparents Die for the Stock Market," *Rawstory*, March 24, 2020, www.rawstory.com/2020/03/internet-explodes-as -foxs-brit-hume-says-its-entirely-reasonable-to-let-grandparents-die-for-the -stock-market.

77. Bill Mitchell (@mitchellvii), Twitter, April 4, 2020, 7:21 p.m., https:// twitter.com/mitchellvii/status/1246623932767141890.

78. The remarkable parallels between the various stages of denial and inactivism with both climate change and coronavirus were explored in an exchange between me and *Sydney Morning Herald* environmental journalist Peter Hannam. See Michael E. Mann (@MichaelEMann), Twitter, April 5, 2020, 2:08 p.m., https://twitter.com/MichaelEMann/status/1246907494221451270; Peter Hannam (@p_hannam), Twitter, April 5, 2020, 2:02 p.m., https://twitter .com/p_hannam/status/1246906143932215297.

79. Mike MacFerrin (@IceSheetMike), Twitter, March 25, 2020, 6:40 a.m., https://twitter.com/IceSheetMike/status/1242808580350177287.

80. Dan Rather (@DanRather), Twitter, March 25, 2020, 9:10 a.m., https:// twitter.com/DanRather/status/1242846264963678209.

81. Michael E. Mann (@MichaelEMann), Twitter, March 25, 2020, 9:23 a.m., https://twitter.com/MichaelEMann/status/1242849532402114563.

82. Waldman, "Obama Blasts Trump over Coronavirus, Climate Change."

83. Steve Schmidt (@SteveSchmidtSES), Twitter, April 4, 2020, 3:05 p.m., https://twitter.com/SteveSchmidtSES/status/1246559631067021313.

84. Nicole Acevedo, "Democratic Lawmakers Want Answers to Trump Administration's Coronavirus Response in Puerto Rico," NBC News, April 3, 2020, www.nbcnews.com/news/latino/democratic-lawmakers-want-answers -trump-administration-s-coronavirus-response-puerto-n1175801.

85. Rebecca Hersher, "Climate Change Was the Engine That Powered Hurricane Maria's Devastating Rains," National Public Radio, April 17, 2019, www .npr.org/2019/04/17/714098828/climate-change-was-the-engine-that-powered -hurricane-marias-devastating-rains.

86. Torcello and Mann, "Seeing the COVID-19 Crisis Is Like Watching a Time Lapse of Climate Change."

87. Yasmeen Abutaleb, Josh Dawsey, Ellen Nakashima, and Greg Miller, "The U.S. Was Beset by Denial and Dysfunction as the Coronavirus Raged," *Washington Post*, April 4, 2020, www.washingtonpost.com/national -security/2020/04/04/coronavirus-government-dysfunction.

88. Ellen Knickmeyer and Tom Krisher, "Trump Rollback of Mileage Standards Guts Climate Change Push," Associated Press, March 31, 2020, https://apnews.com/98f311a6d4275334a9e4d3a804cd2e1a; Alexander C. Kaufman, "States Quietly Pass Laws Criminalizing Fossil Fuel Protests amid Coronavirus Chaos," *Huffington Post*, March 27, 2020, www.huffpost.com/entry/pipeline-protest-laws-coronavirus_n_5e7e7570c5b6256a7a2aab41.

89. Mark Kaufman, "Earth Scorched in the First 3 Months of 2020," *Mashable*, April 6, 2020, https://mashable.com/article/climate-change-2020-records.

90. Denise Chow, "Great Barrier Reef Hit by Third Major Bleaching Event in Five Years," NBC News, March 23, 2020, https://nbcnews.com/science/environment/great-barrier-reef-hit-third-major-bleaching-event-five-years-n1166676.

91. Noted environmental historian Naomi Oreskes, for example, declared that "coronavirus has killed neoliberalism." Naomi Oreskes (@NaomiOreskes), Twitter, April 5, 2020, 10:32 a.m., https://twitter.com/NaomiOreskes/status/1246853279507775488.

92. Michael E. Mann (@MichaelEMann), Twitter, April 5, 2020, 10:52 a.m., https://twitter.com/MichaelEMann/status/1246858265524342785.

93. John Vidal, "Destroyed Habitat Creates the Perfect Conditions for Coronavirus to Emerge," *Scientific American*, March 18, 2020, www.scientificamerican.com/article/destroyed-habitat-creates-the-perfect-conditions-for-coronavirus-to-emerge.

94. James E. Lovelock and Lynn Margulis, "Atmospheric Homeostasis by and for the Biosphere: The Gaia Hypothesis," *Tellus* 26, no. 1–2 (1974): 2–10.

95. Madeleine Stone, "Carbon Emissions Are Falling Sharply Due to Coronavirus. But Not for Long," *National Geographic*, April 6, 2020, www.nationalgeographic.co.uk/environment-and-conservation/2020/04/carbon-emissions-are-falling-sharply-due-coronavirus-not-long.

96. Michael E. Mann (@MichaelEMann), Twitter, March 18, 2020, 1:13 a.m., https://twitter.com/MichaelEMann/status/1240189600510799872.

97. Swati Thiyagarajan, "Covid-19: Planet Earth Fights Back," *Daily Maverick*, March 17, 2020, https://conservationaction.co.za/recent-news/covid-19-planet-earth-fights-back.

98. For examples, see Bill Black, "The El Paso Shooter's Manifesto Contains a Dangerous Message About Climate Change," *The Week*, August 6, 2019, https://theweek.com/articles/857100/el-paso-shooters-manifesto-contains-dangerous-message-about-climate-change; Charlotte Cross, "Extinction Rebellion Disowns 'Fake' East Midlands Group over Coronavirus Tweet," ITV News, www.itv.com/news/central/2020-03-25/extinction-rebellion-disowns-east-midlands-group-over-coronavirus-tweet.

99. I published a commentary expressing these thoughts: Michael E. Mann, "Climatologist Makes Clear: We're Still on Pandemic Path with Global Warming," *Boston Globe*, March 18, 2020, www.bostonglobe.com/2020/03/19/opinion/climatologist-makes-clear-were-still-pandemic-path-with-global-warming.

100. Jeremy Miller, "Trump Seizes on Pandemic to Speed Up Opening of Public Lands to Industry," *The Guardian*, April 30, 2020.

101. Nicholas Kusnetz, "BP and Shell Write Off Billions in Assets, Citing Covid-19 and Climate Change," *Inside Climate News*, July 2, 2020, https://insideclimatenews.org/news/01072020/bp-shell-coronavirus-climate-change.

102. David Iaconangelo, "100% Clean Energy Group Launches, with Eyes on Coronavirus," *Climatewire, E&E News*, April 2, 2020, www.eenews.net/energywire/2020/04/02/stories/1062762687.

103. Tina Casey, "And So It Begins: World's 11th-Biggest Economy Pitches Renewable Energy for COVID-19 Recovery," *Clean Technica*, April 5, 2020, https://cleantechnica.com/2020/04/05/and-so-it-begins-worlds-11th-biggest -economy-pitches-renewable-energy-for-covid-19-recovery.

104. Adam Morton, "Australia's Path to Net-Zero Emissions Lies in Rapid, Stimulus-Friendly Steps," *The Guardian*, April 3, 2020, www.theguardian .com/environment/2020/apr/04/australias-path-to-net-zero-emissions-lies-in -small-stimulus-friendly-steps.

105. Alison Rourke, "Greta Thunberg Responds to Asperger's Critics: 'It's a Superpower,'" The Guardian, September 2, 2019, www.theguardian .com/environment/2019/sep/02/greta-thunberg-responds-to-aspergers-critics -its-a-superpower.

106. Desmond Butler and Juliet Eilperin, "The Anti-Greta: A Conservative Think Tank Takes on the Global Phenomenon: How a Group Allied with the Trump Administration Is Paying a German Teen to Question Established Climate Science," *Washington Post*, February 23, 2020, www .washingtonpost.com/climate-environment/2020/02/23/meet-anti-greta -young-youtuber-campaigning-against-climate-alarmism.

107. "UK Parliament Declares Climate Change Emergency," BBC, May 1, 2019, www.bbc.com/news/uk-politics-48126677; "Climate Change: Ireland Declares Climate Emergency," BBC, May 9, 2019, www.bbc.com/news/world -europe-48221080.

108. Matthew Taylor, "Majority of UK Public Back 2030 Zero-Carbon Target—Poll," *The Guardian*, November 7, 2019, www.theguardian.com /environment/2019/nov/07/majority-of-uk-public-back-2030-zero-carbon -target-poll.

109. Christopher Walsh, "Teens Mobilize to 'Save the Planet,'" *East Hampton Star*, August 15, 2019, www.easthamptonstar.com/2019815/teens -mobilize-save-planet.

110. Walsh, "Teens Mobilize to 'Save the Planet'"; Jerome Foster II (@ JeromeFosterII), Twitter, August 18, 2019, 12:51 p.m., https://twitter.com /JeromeFosterII/status/1163176641016868865.

111. Gregor Hagedorn, Peter Kalmus, Michael Mann, Sara Vicca, Joke Van den Berge, Jean-Pascal van Ypersele, Dominique Bourg, et al., "Concerns of Young Protesters Are Justified," *Science* 364, no. 6436 (2019): 139–140, https://doi.org/10.1126/science.aax3807; Haley Ott, "Thousands of Scientists Back 'Young Protesters' Demanding Climate Change Action," CBS News, April 12, 2019, www.cbsnews.com/news/youth-climate-strike-protests -backed-by-scientists-letter-science-magazine.

112. Walsh, "Teens Mobilize to 'Save the Planet.'"

113. Luke Henriques-Gomes, "Andrew Bolt's Mocking of Greta Thunberg Leaves Autism Advocates 'Disgusted,'" *The Guardian*, August 2, 2019, www.theguardian.com/media/2019/aug/02/andrew-bolts-mocking-of-greta -thunberg-leaves-autism-advocates-disgusted.

114. See "Christopher Caldwell," Claremont Institute, Leadership and Staff, www.claremont.org/leadership-bio/christopher-caldwell, accessed April 7, 2020; "Claremont Institute for the Study of Statesmanship and Political Philosophy," SourceWatch, www.sourcewatch.org/index.php/Claremont_Institute _for_the_Study_of_Statesmanship_and_Political_Philosophy, accessed April 7, 2020; Christopher Caldwell, "The Problem with Greta Thunberg's Climate Activism: Her Radical Approach Is at Odds with Democracy," *New York Times*, August 2, 2019, www.nytimes.com/2019/08/02/opinion/climate-change-greta -thunberg.html.

115. "CO_2 Coalition," SourceWatch, www.sourcewatch.org/index.php? title=CO2_Coalition; Scott Waldman, "Climate Critics Escalate Personal Attacks on Teen Activist," *Climatewire*, *E&E News*, August 9, 2019, www.eenews .net/stories/1060889513.

116. Jonathan Watts, "'Biggest Compliment Yet': Greta Thunberg Welcomes Oil Chief's 'Greatest Threat' Label," *The Guardian*, July 5, 2019, www .theguardian.com/environment/2019/jul/05/biggest-compliment-yet-greta -thunberg-welcomes-oil-chiefs-greatest-threat-label.

117. Watts, "'Biggest Compliment Yet.'"

118. Max Boykoff, "The Kids Are All Right. Adults Are the Climate Change Problem," Center for Science and Technology Policy Research, reprinted from the *Daily Camera*, September 5, 2019, https://sciencepolicy.colorado .edu/ogmius/archives/issue_54/ogmius_exchange1.html.

119. Malcolm Harris, "Shell Is Looking Forward: The Fossil-Fuel Companies Expect to Profit from Climate Change. I Went to a Private Planning Meeting and Took Notes," *New York Magazine*, March 3, 2020, https://nymag.com /intelligencer/2020/03/shell-climate-change.html.

120. Michael E. Mann (@MichaelEMann), Twitter, April 10, 2020, 1:32 p.m., https://twitter.com/MichaelEMann/status/1248710415426748422.

121. "Wicked Problem," Wikipedia, https://en.wikipedia.org/wiki/Wicked _problem, accessed April 10, 2020.

122. Jonathan Gilligan (@jg_environ), Twitter, August 17, 2019, 11:01 a.m., https://twitter.com/jg_environ/status/1162786503208177664.

123. Paul Price (@swimsure), Twitter, December 24, 2017, 6:55 a.m., https://twitter.com/swimsure/status/944944603060424704.

124. Peter Jacobs (@past_is_future), Twitter, August 28, 2019, 8:54 a.m., https://twitter.com/past_is_future/status/1166740808810344450.

125. Michael E. Mann (@MichaelEMann), Twitter, August 17, 2019, 8:03 p.m., https://twitter.com/MichaelEMann/status/1162923050444165120.

126. Thomas (@djamesalicious), Twitter, April 9, 2020, 10:35 a.m., https:// twitter.com/djamesalicious/status/1248303643985674240.

127. Michael E. Mann (@MichaelEMann), Twitter, April 9, 2020, 3:55 p.m., https://twitter.com/MichaelEMann/status/1248384126572355586.

128. Thomas (@djamesalicious), Twitter, April 9, 2020, 10:35 a.m., https://twitter.com/djamesalicious/status/1248303643985674240.

129. John Kruzel, "Was Joe Biden a Climate Change Pioneer in Congress? History Says Yes," Politifact, May 8, 2019, www.politifact.com/factchecks/2019/may/08/joe-biden/was-joe-biden-climate-change-pioneer-congress-hist.

130. Shane Harris, Ellen Nakashima, Michael Scherer, and Sean Sullivan, "Bernie Sanders Briefed by U.S. Officials That Russia Is Trying to Help His Presidential Campaign," *Washington Post*, February 21, 2020, www.washingtonpost.com/national-security/bernie-sanders-briefed-by-us-officials-that-russia-is-trying-to-help-his-presidential-campaign/2020/02/21/5ad396a6-54bd-11ea-929a-64efa7482a77_story.html.

131. See "About This Book" on my website at https://michaelmann.net/content/tantrum-saved-world-carbon-neutral-kids-book. Available for purchase at https://world-saving-books.myshopify.com.

132. Graham Readfearn, "Great Barrier Reef's Third Mass Bleaching in Five Years the Most Widespread Yet," *The Guardian*, April 6, 2020, www.theguardian.com/environment/2020/apr/07/great-barrier-reefs-third-mass-bleaching-in-five-years-the-most-widespread-ever.

133. I said this on Twitter at Michael E. Mann (@MichaelEMann), May 7, 2019, 3:52 p.m., https://twitter.com/MichaelEMann/status/1125896127662960640.

134. Will Wade, "Going 100% Green Will Pay for Itself in Seven Years, Study Finds," Bloomberg News, December 20, 2019, www.bloomberg.com/news/articles/2019-12-20/going-100-green-will-pay-for-itself-in-seven-years-study-finds.

135. Lauri Myllyvirta, "Analysis: Coronavirus Temporarily Reduced China's CO2 Emissions by a Quarter," *Carbon Brief*, February 19, 2020, www.carbonbrief.org/analysis-coronavirus-has-temporarily-reduced-chinas-co2-emissions-by-a-quarter.

136. Glen Peters (@Peters_Glen), Twitter, April 10, 2020, 12:36 a.m., https://twitter.com/peters_glen/status/1248515055836160000.

137. See Anthony Leiserowitz, Edward Maibach, Seth Rosenthal, John Kotcher, Matthew Ballew, Matthew Goldberg, Abel Gustafson, and Parrish Bergquist, "Politics and Global Warming, April 2019," Yale Program on Climate Change Communication, May 16, 2019, https://climatecommunication.yale.edu/publications/politics-global-warming-april-2019/2.

138. Michael J. Coren, "Americans: 'We Need a Carbon Tax, but Keep the Change,'" *Quartz*, January 22, 2019, https://qz.com/1529997/survey-finds-americans-want-a-carbon-tax; Michael E. Mann (@MichaelEMann), Twitter, April 13, 2020, 10:31 a.m., https://twitter.com/MichaelEMann/status/1249751975824146432.

139. Michael E. Mann (@MichaelEMann), Twitter, April 11, 2020, 10:19 a.m., https://twitter.com/MichaelEMann/status/1249024208484601856; Michael E. Mann (@MichaelEMann), Twitter, April 11, 2020, 10:31 a.m., https://twitter.com/MichaelEMann/status/1249027242858090501.

140. David Roberts (@drvox), Twitter, April 12, 2020, 12:22 p.m., https://twitter.com/drvox/status/1249417607289036801.

141. Fred Hiatt, "How Donald Trump and Bernie Sanders Both Reject the Reality of Climate Change," *Washington Post*, February 23, 2020, www.washingtonpost.com/opinions/how-donald-trump-and-bernie-sanders-both-reject-the-reality-of-climate-change/2020/02/23/cc657dcc-54de-11ea-9e47-59804be1dcfb_story.html.

142. One user, for example, stated, at Laura Neish (@laurajneish), Twitter, April 12, 2020, 12:37 p.m., https://twitter.com/laurajneish/status/1249421480946892801:

Carbon pricing got hijacked by right wing extremists who want to:

-treat it as the *one* policy in place of any other regulatory action,

-tack on indemnity for ff companies

-make it an incredibly regressive tax one way or another

-use it to replace Corp and/or income tax

143. See "Beliefs and Principles," Unitarian Universalist Association, www.uua.org/beliefs/what-we-believe.

144. Sarah T. Fischell (@estee_nj), Twitter, April 12, 2020, 1:15 p.m., https://twitter.com/estee_nj/status/1249430997801873411.

145. Harris et al., "Bernie Sanders Briefed by U.S. Officials."

146. Jeff Goodell, "The Climate Crisis and the Case for Hope," *Rolling Stone*, September 16, 2019, www.rollingstone.com/politics/politics-news/climate-crisis-the-case-for-hope-884063.

Index

MICHAEL E. MANN is Distinguished Professor of Atmospheric Science at Penn State, with joint appointments in the Department of Geosciences and the Earth and Environmental Systems Institute. He has received many honors and awards, including the National Oceanic and Atmospheric Administration's outstanding publication award in 2002 and selection by *Scientific American* as one of the fifty leading visionaries in science and technology that same year. Additionally, he contributed, with other Intergovernmental Panel on Climate Change authors, to the award of the 2007 Nobel Peace Prize. In 2018, he received the Award for Public Engagement with Science from the American Association for the Advancement of Science as well as the Climate Communication Prize from the American Geophysical Union. He received the Tyler Prize for Environmental Achievement in 2019, and in 2020 he was elected to the National Academy of Sciences. He is the author of numerous books, including *Dire Predictions: Understanding Climate Change, The Hockey Stick and the Climate Wars: Dispatches from the Front Lines*, and *The Madhouse Effect: How Climate Change Denial Is Threatening Our Planet, Destroying Our Politics, and Driving Us Crazy*. He lives in State College, Pennsylvania.

PublicAffairs is a publishing house founded in 1997. It is a tribute to the standards, values, and flair of three persons who have served as mentors to countless reporters, writers, editors, and book people of all kinds, including me.

I. F. Stone, proprietor of *I. F. Stone's Weekly*, combined a commitment to the First Amendment with entrepreneurial zeal and reporting skill and became one of the great independent journalists in American history. At the age of eighty, Izzy published *The Trial of Socrates*, which was a national bestseller. He wrote the book after he taught himself ancient Greek.

Benjamin C. Bradlee was for nearly thirty years the charismatic editorial leader of *The Washington Post*. It was Ben who gave the *Post* the range and courage to pursue such historic issues as Watergate. He supported his reporters with a tenacity that made them fearless and it is no accident that so many became authors of influential, best-selling books.

Robert L. Bernstein, the chief executive of Random House for more than a quarter century, guided one of the nation's premier publishing houses. Bob was personally responsible for many books of political dissent and argument that challenged tyranny around the globe. He is also the founder and longtime chair of Human Rights Watch, one of the most respected human rights organizations in the world.

.   .   .

For fifty years, the banner of Public Affairs Press was carried by its owner Morris B. Schnapper, who published Gandhi, Nasser, Toynbee, Truman, and about 1,500 other authors. In 1983, Schnapper was described by *The Washington Post* as "a redoubtable gadfly." His legacy will endure in the books to come.

Peter Osnos, *Founder*